AMERICAN
MARKETING

WILLIAM J. SHULTZ

Bernard M. Baruch School
of Business and Public Administration
The City College of New York

AMERICAN MARKETING

WADSWORTH PUBLISHING COMPANY, INC.
BELMONT, CALIFORNIA

L.C. CAT. CARD NO.: 61-7377

PRINTED IN THE UNITED STATES OF AMERICA.

MANUFACTURED BY AMERICAN BOOK-STRATFORD PRESS, INC.

FIRST PRINTING, MARCH 1961
SECOND PRINTING, AUGUST 1961
THIRD PRINTING, JUNE 1962

To
my good friends
and
keen critics
MY STUDENTS

FOREWORD TO THE STUDENT

So you're going to study Marketing.

Why?

If you are planning on a career in any phase of Marketing—Advertising, Selling and Sales Management, Retailing, Wholesaling, Marketing Research, Foreign Trade—the answer is simple and positive. This basic Marketing course you are starting is the comprehensive foundation for the future specialized studies that will prepare you for your career. You will find this course doubly rewarding—because of the inherent interest of the subject itself, and because personal motivation will cause you to probe far deeper into many aspects of the subject than minimum course requirement.

But what if your career is to be in Accountancy, or Finance, or one of the Management fields, or Business Law, and you are taking this Marketing course primarily because it is a required element of the curriculum? Do you perhaps resent the requirement, feeling that a course on Marketing is unrelated to your career preparation and a waste of your college time? If this is your present view, I assure you it is a mistaken one. The business attorney, and the accountant if he is to be anything more than a slightly glorified bookkeeper, must have comprehensive knowledge in the three foundation business subjects—Management, Finance, and Marketing. Anyone who anticipates employment in the loan departments of commercial banks or in investment houses must have a penetrating understanding of many aspects of Marketing, for marketing considerations play a large role today in loan and investment appraisals. Management majors certainly should look upon Management and Marketing as Siamese twin subjects, mutually interpenetrating and inseparable. This course you are now starting will probably be your only opportunity for organized study of Marketing structures and techniques on which you must be informed for any business or professional career. Make the most of this opportunity.

A word of warning about your Marketing course. Many of you will find it one of the most difficult in your college curriculum—not because there is more information to remember, or because the subject is more difficult to understand, but because in this course you face a major task of *unlearning* before you can start learning. You have made purchases in all sorts of stores, you have seen advertisements and listened to radio and TV commercials, you have probably been witness to the efforts of salesmen to persuade members

vii

of your family or others to buy their products. As a result of these experiences you have undoubtedly arrived at firm personal convictions on many Marketing topics. Most of these convictions are not sound generalizations with respect to American marketing—if only because you as a college student are not typical of the American mass markets and your personal reactions are not representative of the reactions of the mass of American consumers. If you cling obstinately to your present preconceptions and close your mind to the presentations of your professor and of this textbook, you will be in trouble from the very outset. So be warned. Approach this course with an open mind, ready to revise many of your present ideas about the hows and whys of American marketing.

Finally, a few suggestions on how to use this textbook most effectively.

Immediately after reading an assigned chapter, go carefully through the "Review" at its conclusion. Be sure that you can answer specifically and in detail each of the questions there. If you discover that you are hazy about any of them, reread the relevant sections of the chapter and make sure this time that every important point is fixed firmly in your mind.

You should not be content with mere parrot-knowledge of the text material, however. The social, economic, and business implications of many Marketing topics extend far beyond what could possibly be covered in textbook presentation. What you read in this book should be a springboard for broad, creative thinking on your part. The "Discussion Topics" that follow the "Review" at the end of each chapter are intended to stimulate such thinking. Be careful in your approach to the quoted statements that are presented as bases for discussion. Some are correct summarizations on the subjects to which they relate. Some are categorically false. Most are exaggerations or understatements, or otherwise combine elements of truth and falsity. Your task is to think out and clarify your own ideas on the topic, then analyze the statement and appraise it in the light of your own ideas. Don't be surprised to discover that some of your classmates have arrived at conclusions contrary to yours. Maybe their thinking was at fault, maybe yours. Or the topic may involve controversial premises on which you and they have opposing convictions. In the latter case you won't convince them and they won't convince you, but there will be exciting and enlightening debate.

The "Problems" have been so constructed that for many there are not clearcut right or wrong answers. There may be several possible solutions. This is a realistic reflection of business actuality where we often see business concerns successfully applying diametrically opposed policies to some marketing procedure. In working with the "Problems" do what the business executive does when faced with similar issues. Think out all possible lines of action. Weigh carefully all the pros and cons of each. Then make your decision, and support it by a summary of the analysis that preceded it.

Above all, be practical in your "Problems" analyses. Think in dollars and cents terms, and take into account costs and relative returns that would be associated with alternative lines of action. Remember that Marketing is no ivory-tower subject, but a major basis of success or failure for most business enterprises.

And now—on with your study of Marketing. You have an exciting subject ahead of you.

W.J.S.

ACKNOWLEDGEMENTS

I have received assistance in the preparation of this book from executives in so many government divisions, trade and professional associations, trade magazines, and business service enterprises that it is impracticable to make individual acknowledgement to them. So herewith I offer a blanket expression of my gratitude for their courtesy and help.

Among my colleagues at the Bernard M. Baruch School of Business and Public Administration who read portions of the manuscript and generously gave me the benefit of expert knowledge in their special fields were: Professors Arthur E. Albrecht, Raymond R. Colton, Henry Eilbirt, Walter A. Gaw, I. Harold Kellar, Hedwig Reinhardt, David Valinsky, Robert Weintraub, John Wingate, and Dr. Leland Liang.

CONTENTS

ILLUSTRATIONS

PART ONE

INTRODUCTION

CHAPTER 1

THE SUBJECT AND FIELD OF MARKETING

Have you ever stopped to think how some wheat harvested by a farmer eventually reaches your table as a prepared breakfast food—of the complicated chain of business enterprises that share in this economic activity and what each of them does so that a few handfuls of wheat from a distant farm may appear on your breakfast table in an enticing form?

Most likely, the farmer trucks his wheat harvest to the nearest commercial town, and sells it there to a local grain dealer. The dealer and the farmer agree upon its grade according to official standards, and the dealer offers the farmer a price based upon the latest radio announcement of wheat prices currently quoted on the Chicago Board of Trade or some other grain exchange. The wheat is then stored in the dealer's elevator for some days or weeks, the dealer protecting himself against loss from a drop in wheat prices by hedging. To finance his operations during this period, he borrows from a bank on the security of the stored wheat.

Sooner or later the local dealer ships this lot of wheat, along with others, to Chicago or one of the other central market cities. There he may sell it to one of the huge central grain elevators, where it is stored until it is bought by the breakfast-food manufacturer. Or, through a broker or a commission house, the local elevator operator may sell the wheat directly to the manufacturer. In either case, the price is again determined by current quotations on the grain exchange.

The breakfast-food manufacturer processes the wheat in accordance with his prepared food formula—this is a "productive" rather than a "distributive" or "marketing" activity. The resulting breakfast food is now packaged in a sealed wax paper bag inside a cardboard box. Don't imagine for a moment that the size and shape of this box, and the printing on it, are matters of chance or indifferent decision. Marketing research has been employed to determine in what quantity consumers prefer to buy their prepared breakfast foods, what container shape packs best for transportation and is best accommodated on store shelves, and what combinations of color and design catch a consumer's eye on store shelves or show up most effectively on TV commercials. The registered brand name—"Wheaties," or "Pep," or "Wheat Chex"—is printed in eye-commanding type. An inexpensive premium may be included in the package, for these premium offers are powerful demand-stimulants to children who consume breakfast foods, and so to mothers who purchase them. And the manufacturer spends hundreds of thousands of dollars in advertising his product, so that you—and millions of others—will recognize and want it.

The manufacturer's salesmen call upon hundreds of grocery wholesalers to induce them to carry stocks of this breakfast food. Partly as a result of the salesmen's persuasions, and partly on their own judgment, the wholesalers order the food by carload lots. They do not pay in advance for these purchases, but buy on credit terms, so that the manufacturer has a never-ending task of checking upon their credit ratings and of delicately pressing slow payers.

Most wholesalers have salesmen calling upon the retail grocery stores in their market areas to persuade them to carry this particular brand of breakfast food, among the line of food items that the wholesalers offer. And because the manufacturer's advertising, and the premiums, and the quality of the food have created consumer demand for it, the grocers place their orders, to be delivered in the wholesalers' trucks. Grocers, too, must buy on credit terms, and the wholesalers must in their turn check the grocers' credit ratings and collect outstanding accounts.

The owner or manager of the grocery store from which your particular package of the breakfast food is purchased adds 12, or 15, or 20 percent to the wholesaler's price, and stamps a retail price on the package. A clerk places the package on a display shelf. And finally you, or some other member of your family, buy it.

Here is a case study—one among thousands—of the business concerns and activities involved in bringing a single item from its original producer to its ultimate consumer. Other examples might be simpler, involving fewer links in the chain of distribution, and fewer interrelated distributional activities. Others might be more complex.

These distributional or "marketing" institutions and operations are of major importance in the American economy. Farmers and manufacturers could not produce goods in significant quantities if our Marketing system did not create and mold demand for these goods and move them to consumers and industrial users. And what would be the plight of consumers if the goods they want were not made available to them by the Marketing system? One-quarter of our gainfully employed are occupied with Marketing activities. One-third of our national income is derived from Marketing.

Here is a worthy subject for our study—Marketing: the analysis of how production of goods is made to conform to the demand for them, of how goods are moved from producer to consumer, of the business institutions and techniques involved in this movement, of the relationship of these distributional institutions and techniques to other elements of our economy, of the effectiveness and weaknesses of these institutions and techniques, and of what may be done to improve them in the interest of better living for Americans.

MARKETING—THE SUBJECT

The most widely accepted definition of the term "Marketing" is: "the performance of business activities that direct the flow of goods and services from producer to consumer or user." * This compact definition specifically and by implication establishes a number of significant points about Marketing and the study we shall make of this subject:

1. Marketing consists of the performance of *business* activities. Personal buying motivations, the economic and social circumstances of individuals and groups influencing their buying, and governmental stimulation or control of various aspects of the distribution of goods and services, are not *business* activities, so they are not Marketing activities. They do influence profoundly many of the business activities that constitute Marketing, however, and we shall analyze them in some detail in our study of Marketing.

2. Marketing consists of the performance of business activities that direct *the flow of goods and services from producers to consumers and business users.* This consideration excludes all manufacturing activity, agricultural production, and extractive activity from the field of Marketing. However, we shall have occasion to inquire into various circumstances of manufacturing, agricultural, and extractive production, since knowledge of these is necessary for a full understanding of the Marketing activities relating to them. We shall also deal with the operations of farmers, manufacturers, and mining enterprises that relate to the *distribution* of their products, since these operations are truly Marketing activities. The *performance* of personal and business services is not a Marketing activity, but any means of establishing business relationships between the performer of a service and his customers, such as advertising or the use of agents, comes within our definition.

3. Marketing includes business activities relating to the flow of goods and services to *business users* as well as consumers. This considera-

---

* This is the definition recommended by the Definitions Committee of the American Marketing Association.

tion brings under Marketing all movements of raw materials from agricultural and extractive producers to manufacturers, and all movements of semi-processed materials and manufactured equipment and supplies among manufacturers.

It may occur to many students that our term "Marketing" is synonymous with "Distribution" as that term is often employed. Essentially it is. "Distribution," however, is sometimes given a narrower connotation than "Marketing." It may be applied primarily to the physical aspects of the movement of goods from producers to users and consumers—to the *mechanism* of the flow of goods. A number of principles and policies embraced by the term "Marketing" are sometimes excluded from the idea of "Distribution." In this volume, "Distribution" will be used as a substitute for "Marketing" only when no emphasis is being placed on policy issues. It should be noted, furthermore, that economists often use the term "Distribution" in a different sense—the sharing of the proceeds of our economy among the so-called factors of production, i.e., land, labor, capital, and management. Because of this double meaning of the term "Distribution," it should be used with care, and only when there can be no confusion as to its connotation.

Historical development of Marketing

Marketing activity predates recorded history. It developed, in rudimentary forms, soon after division of labor had evolved among family or communal units. Division of labor within the family unit, with the father and the older sons engaged in herding or the hunt, and the women and younger children undertaking agricultural and household tasks, would itself produce no flow of goods and services; that is, no marketing activity would appear *until an excess had been produced of goods over needs*. If a crippled clansman were restricted to making spearheads, and so had created an excess of them, and if a neighbor with many sons had killed extra quantities of game, a natural trade would suggest itself, a Marketing activity, in which the tools of the hunt could be bartered for the produce of the hunt. The spearhead-maker and the hunters would find mutual advantages in establishing a division of labor, and their continued relationship would then constitute a primitive Marketing procedure. Marketing thus came into existence when Production * was undertaken for exchange, instead of exclusively for personal use.

The scope and the social and economic importance of Marketing ex-

---

* The term "Production" is used in this chapter, not with any implication that Marketing activities or Marketing enterprises are in any way less "productive," in an economic sense, than agriculture, mining, manufacturing, or construction, but simply as a classification term that has common usage.

panded with every forward step in productive or distributive technology, in social and economic organization, in cultural achievement. Every advance in techniques of agriculture, of extractive industry, of manufacture, meant that an added surplus of goods became available for distribution through the agencies of Marketing. Every improvement in Marketing techniques— tangible as in the case of better transportation or storage, intangible as in the case of rising skill in the art of selling—meant wider distribution in ever-increasing volume, and enhancement of Marketing. Marketing, even more than Production, requires social order for its fullest flowering. Every step toward better organized societies, under governments that ensured greater domestic security if not international stability, broadened Marketing possibilities. Certain aspects of economic evolution, such as the creation of relatively stable monetary systems, and the development of a credit basis for many national economies, played vital parts in expanding Marketing activity. Finally, every improvement in the cultural levels of populations as a whole or of particular social classes, by enhancing demand for new kinds and qualities of material goods, adds to the scope and the significance of Marketing.

At first thought, Marketing and Production might seem to be economic twins, so that expansions and contractions of the one would be proportionately duplicated in the other, and expansion of either would be only a reflection of a general economic progress common to them both. There is some basis for this view. Growth in population enlarges demand for goods of all sorts, which must be both produced and moved through Marketing mechanisms to reach the larger number of consumers. Invention and development of any new product, provided it becomes an added element of consumption rather than merely a substitute for some prior item, expands the scope of both Production and Marketing in roughly equivalent proportion. An improvement in agricultural or industrial technology reducing the cost and price of an item, thereby increasing its consumption, tends to have approximately the same expansive influence on both Production and Marketing.

Many developments promoting both Production and Marketing, however, have a more marked influence on the latter. Anything which adds *more distant* customers or users for a commodity tends to expand Marketing activity more than Production activity, because of the additional transportation and handling that the new increments of the commodity must undergo. Improvements in transportation techniques, such as the introduction of refrigerated railroad cars and the advent of air freight, have this effect. So does the territorial expansion of a population, as happened in the United States during the Nineteenth Century. So do financial developments such as the establishing of nation-wide par collection of checks through the Federal Reserve System, or business developments such as the growth of nation-wide credit reporting by mercantile agencies like Dun & Bradstreet, or legal developments such as passage of uniform sales acts in large numbers of the states. So, too, do such incorporations into our standard of living as nation-wide consumption of citrus fruits grown only in California, Texas, and Florida, and Vitamin B_1 manufactured only in New Jersey. Improvements in storage techniques also tend to magnify the role of Marketing in the economy.

In consequence, Marketing tends to occupy a place of growing importance in any society as its economy progresses. In simpler phases of society, such as that of Europe during the Middle Ages, or of this country during the Colonial period, where most production was for immediate use rather than for exchange and where such exchange as existed was predominantly local, Marketing was likely to account for only a small percentage of the values embodied in whatever was consumed. With economic and social progress, the proportion of Marketing costs rises relative to the costs involved in agricultural and industrial activities. No long-trend data on the relative economic contribution of all Marketing operations and agencies in the United States or any other country are available to confirm this deductive generalization, but it is verified to some extent by a recent finding that the ratio of middleman costs to ultimate sales values in the United States increased from around 33 percent in 1869 to around 38 percent in 1948.*

A special impetus is given to Marketing expansion when the economy of a nation is transformed from one of scarcity to one of plenty, as occurred in the United States during the second quarter of the present century. So long as the disposable incomes of the masses of a country limit their purchases to the "necessities" of living, so long as these masses must spend on food, clothing, and shelter primarily with a view to getting the maximum "functional" return for their dollars, there can be little scope for the arts of Marketing. Business and public emphasis must be concentrated on Production, on technological improvement of agriculture, mining, and manufacturing, so that the disposable incomes of the masses provide them less grudgingly with the necessities of living. With the shift from an economy of scarcity to one of plenty, however, when a rising mass standard of living begins to superimpose an expanding margin of discretionary purchasing upon the necessities base, the arts of Marketing take on an enhanced significance. In planning products, the emphasis shifts more and more from mere functional utility to the incorporation of design elements that will appeal to motivations of pleasure, conscious and subconscious self-flattery, and status symbolism, which are now increasingly indulged. The roles of advertising and personal selling are expanded, for a growing proportion of consumers now have more and more purchasing power that

---

* See Illustration 29–2, p. 599.

does not have to be paid out for necessities, but which they may be induced to spend upon an expanding variety of conveniences and pleasures. Indeed, in an economy of plenty, the Marketing arts must take on the serious responsibility of creating an ever-increasing purchasing demand for the bursting output of field and factory, lest the economy collapse in a glut of "overproduction."

Marketing in the current American economy

We have two possible measures of the current importance of Marketing in the American economy: employment, and contribution to national income.

The numbers of people engaged and employed in various classes of occupations in 1959 are shown in Illustration 1–1. These employment figures understate the relative importance of Marketing in the economy. A substantial number of employees in the Production classification devote themselves exclusively to the Marketing operations of their enterprises. Furthermore, the work of many government, finance, and service employees is closely concerned with Marketing activity. A conservative generalization, taking into account the figures of Illustration 1–1 and their qualifications,

INDIVIDUALS ENGAGED AND EMPLOYED IN OCCUPATIONAL
CLASSIFICATIONS, 1959
(in millions)

PRODUCTION		MARKETING		OTHER	
CLASSIFICATION	NUMBER	CLASSIFICATION	NUMBER	CLASSIFICATION	NUMBER
Mining	.7	Wholesaling		Services	7.4
Agriculture	2.1	and Retailing	10.6	Finance	2.5
Manufacturing	16.2	Transportation	2.4	Government	10.1
Construction	2.9			Other	1.4
Total	21.9	Total	13.0	Total	21.4

Source: *Survey of Current Business,* February, 1960.

ILLUSTRATION 1–1

would be that one out of every four gainfully employed individuals is occupied full-time with Marketing activities, while practically all farmers and many others in other occupational classifications give some part of their time and attention to Marketing matters.

The derivation of national income in 1959, by an economic classification of enterprises, is shown in Illustration 1–2. According to this calculation,

DERIVATION OF NATIONAL INCOME, BY ECONOMIC
CLASSIFICATION OF ENTERPRISES, 1959
(in billions)

ECONOMIC CLASSIFICATION	TOTAL	ATTRIBUTED TO	
		PRODUCTION	MARKETING
Agriculture	$ 16.8	$ 13.4	$ 3.4
Mining	5.5	4.9	.6
Manufacturing	119.4	83.7	35.7
Construction	21.7	17.6	4.1
Total Production	$163.4	$119.6	$ 43.8
Wholesaling	$ 23.8		$ 23.8
Retailing	43.1		43.1
Transportation	17.5		15.7
Total Marketing	$ 84.4		$ 82.6
Government	$ 48.8		
Finance	40.5		
Services	45.1		$ 4.5
Miscellaneous	17.5		
Total Other	$151.9		$ 4.5
Grand Total	$399.7	$119.6	$130.9

Figures on national income from *Survey of Current Business,* July
1960, p. 13. Attribution of national income to Marketing activities for
agricultural, mining, manufacturing, and construction enterprises was made
as follows: agriculture, 9% of total value of farm output; manufacture,
10% of sales; construction, 7½% of new construction. An arbitrary 10%
of income produced by mining and service enterprises is attributed to such
Marketing operations as promotion, selling, and credit. 10% of income
produced by transportation enterprises is deducted from the Marketing attribution to cover transportation of persons.

ILLUSTRATION 1–2

Marketing *enterprises* accounted for 21% of the national income in 1959,
compared with 41% for Production *enterprises.* On an *activity* basis, however, the proportion for Marketing was 33%, and for Production 29%.

Our two measures of the importance of Marketing in our economy give
markedly differing proportions, according to the basis of the measure, and
according to whether we compare Marketing solely with Production or
whether we take into consideration other economic activities, such as
Finance and Government. Under the circumstances, we cannot claim that
Marketing accounts for any specific proportion of our over-all economic
activity. We can state, however, that by any measure Marketing plays a
very important role in the economy of the United States, at present only

slightly, if at all, below that of the country's combined total of Production enterprises and activities.

The probability for the near future is an increase, rather than any diminution, of the relative importance of Marketing in the American economy. In many areas of American living, a transfer is currently taking place from an economy of scarcity to one of plenty. This development will magnify the role of Marketing. As the scope of plentiful living continues to expand, the institutions and operations related to Marketing must further and further outpace those related to Production.

MARKETING—THE STUDY

Our study of Marketing must cover a territory considerably wider than the field of Marketing as defined earlier in this chapter—i.e., "the performance of business activities that direct the flow of goods and services from producer to consumer or user." Besides gaining an understanding of Marketing *activities,* we must learn about the business organizations that perform them. We must see these activities and business organizations not as isolated, unrelated phenomena but as closely integrated and interlocking elements of our national economy and business structure. We must discover the *whys* of Marketing as well as its *whats* and *hows.* The bare facts about a Marketing agency or procedure are only an incomplete part of the knowledge we seek. The reasons for the very existence of the agency or the procedure must also be understood. We must see Marketing institutions and practices not as static factors in our economy, but as among its most dynamic elements, for Marketing is constantly evolving, constantly changing its instruments and its methods.

We must survey several extraneous subjects that provide backgrounds for a broad range of Marketing topics. We must acquire an understanding of the American people as consumers—not merely quantitative data on their numbers and buying power, but some realization of the complex psychological motivations that determine what, where, and when they buy. We must likewise formulate a picture of the "industrial" market, which is the foundation of the buying done by business concerns. We must note the significant role that federal and state governments play in Marketing, not merely in limiting or controlling Marketing activities, but in facilitating and stimulating them.

To understand many of the agencies and activities involved in Marketing, we must probe far afield, and draw upon other fields of study. Psychology and Sociology contribute explanations of buying motivations, which must be taken into account in such Marketing operations as product planning, promotion, and selling, and upon which much of the art of successful retailing is based. From Law and Government are drawn basic arguments in support or condemnation of legislation and administrative procedures directed toward the stimulation or control of particular Marketing activities. Economics provides the foundation for a substantial part of Marketing theory.

Marketing and Economics

It is sometimes stated that Marketing should not be considered an independent field of study, but as a phase of "applied Economics." In support of this view it is argued that Economics concerns itself, among other topics, with "value"; that "value" results from creation of the four utilities of form, place, time, and possession; and that the utilities of place and time are largely created, and that of possession entirely, through operations and agencies of Marketing. Possession utility is achieved through Marketing when, by a series of sales and purchases, goods are transferred from their producers, for whom they have no use value, to their ultimate consumers or users, for whom the goods have maximum use value. Place utility develops when, incidental to the sales and purchases that produce possession utility, various Marketing agencies transport goods step by step from the place of production, where they cannot be used, to the retail stores where the ultimate consumers take possession, or even to the very residences of these consumers. Time utility results when, through public and private warehousing, goods are stored and so carried forward from a time when their use value is low to one when it is high.*

A further basis for claiming Marketing as essentially a subdivision of Economics is the extent to which various elements of economic theory are utilized as first premises for chains of reasoning about Marketing topics. Economic Theory of Exchange, and its derivative Theory of Trade Movements, provide the basic explanation of why many Marketing activities exist. Marginal theory, as developed by economists, has been taken over into many areas of Marketing practice—the assembling aspect of buying, determination of territorial market coverage, pricing, utilization of advertising media, devotion of salesmen's time to classes of customers and duties. Pricing policy, as studied in Marketing, must start with price theory as developed by Economics. The topic of market finance is essentially a segment of the broader Economics subject of banking and finance. Principles

---

* Production can also contribute to place utility; for example, when factories are purposely located close to the markets for their goods. It can also contribute to time utility through the scheduling of output to conform to fluctuating demand. Marketing can be considered to contribute to form utility when marketing executives concern themselves with product planning, and when retailers perform adjustment or installation services. But unquestionably, most form utility is created by Production, and most time, place, and possession utility by Marketing.

of consumer economics provide a springboard for much Marketing analysis on retailing and product planning.

All of these statements of the debt of Marketing to Economics are true. Economics was the mother study, Marketing the offspring. In the half-century of its lifetime, however, the study of Marketing has struck out in new directions, pressed toward new horizons, that were and are no part of the parent study. While drawing upon Economics for foundation elements of its own theory, Marketing study has done so in a critical spirit and with qualifications. Large areas of economic analysis deal primarily with problems of scarcity, with the allocation of limited resources to basic patterns of limited demand. Marketing study, more sensitive to current business issues, is more concerned with the problems of creating demand for the ballooning production of present-day industry.

By and large, until very recently, Marketing developed little original theoretical inquiry, except in the field of marketing research statistical procedures. Instead, it has tended to concentrate on coordinating an immense body of factual data on Marketing institutions and Marketing operations, and on developing an empirical body of doctrine on marketing policy—limited generalizations on the effectiveness or failure of various marketing procedures from the standpoint of business profit and loss. As Marketing is taught and studied today in most colleges, it is closer to being a major branch of the field of Business Administration than of Economics.

History of the study of Marketing

Marketing was not recognized as a field of study until the Twentieth Century. It has been developed predominantly by American writers.

This late development of Marketing scholarship is attributable in large measure to the ethical disrepute that was attached by classical Greek philosophy to marketing activities, and that clung to them well into the Nineteenth Century. Plato wrote in his *Laws* that trade corrupts the trader, so that mercantile activities should be forbidden to the citizens of Athens and be permitted only to outsiders. He argued that praising or "puffing" goods offered for sale should be a crime comparable to adulterating goods. Aristotle, too, held that trade was "unnatural" and "justly censured." Church philosophers of the Middle Ages continued this disapproval of trade; they condemned it for causing an increase of prices above the "just price" determined by the labor-cost of producing it.

Nineteenth Century economics removed the ethical stain from marketing activity by establishing that it created utilities—those of place, time, and possession—that are just as important to the economy as the form utility created by agriculture and manufacturing. The analysis of demand factors as a determinant of price was a foundation stone in the structure of Marketing theory. Still, this analysis was very one-sided by present standards, since it treated demand as something pre-existent and absolute instead of having the potential of being created and modified by promotion, selling, and other marketing activities. Hardly any empirical study was made of the business institutions that had been developed to carry on trade, or of their operations, and the assumptions made by Nineteenth Century economists on these matters, used as first premises for their deductive theorizing, were often wide of the mark.

True progress in Marketing study required fresh approaches. These came in the United States in the first quarter of the Twentieth Century. The organized study of Marketing in the United States may be said to have begun in 1902–1903, when the first courses in this field were offered by the Economics Departments of the Universities of Michigan, California, and Illinois. Not until the second decade of the century, however, did the subject gain substantial academic recognition. Two universities, Wisconsin and Harvard, were primarily responsible for this achievement. In the former, two groups of scholars and teachers made converging approaches to Marketing study. One, interested primarily in farm economics and the disparity between what the consumer paid and the farmer received for farm products, explored the distribution of agricultural products. The other, which included Paul Nystrom and Ralph Butler, authors of the first Marketing textbook, dealt with the subject primarily from the viewpoint of business administration. In the Harvard Graduate School of Business Administration there was also a two-fold approach to the study of Marketing. One group of scholar-teachers, among whom the best known were Paul Cherington, A. W. Shaw, and Melvin T. Copeland, developed institutional and "functional" treatments of the subject. The other group, including Harry Tosdal and Malcolm McNair, worked on the case study method of teaching the subject.

By the 1920's the study of Marketing had crystallized, with respect to scope of the subject and teaching approaches, into what is pretty much its present form. This crystallization process was accomplished by the publication of several excellent textbooks by the then outstanding academic authorities on the subject, which were in close agreement as to scope and contents. Evolution of the subject has continued, but largely within the framework established in the 1920's. Every topic and subtopic in the field has been probed by special studies. As more information accumulated, generalizations could be made in quantitative rather than qualitative form. With fuller information, many new Marketing principles—tested cause-and-effect generalizations—were formulated. There has been increasing emphasis on the business and policy aspects of Marketing, modifications of classifications, refinements of analysis, and incorporation of new subject matter as Marketing institutions and operations have themselves evolved.

One important element in the expansion of Marketing study during the 1920's and since has been an increase in available factual data on the subject. Statistical information collected and published by the U.S. Departments of Commerce and Agriculture to aid business men and farmers in their marketing problems has proven invaluable to students of Marketing. So also has the *Census of Business* series of the U.S. Bureau of the Census. Marketing research, itself a vigorous offspring of the growing study of Marketing, has provided the parent subject since 1930 with new tools of statistical methodology and a wealth of empirical knowledge on many Marketing issues which previously had been obscured by unproved and frequently false generalizations.

A major coordinating influence in the development of Marketing study has been the American Marketing Association. In 1915 a National Association of Teachers of Advertising was formed. During the 1920's it drew into its membership a number of teachers of Marketing, and then reorganized in 1926 as the National Association of Teachers of Marketing and Advertising. Five years later, an American Marketing Society was organized for teachers and practitioners of marketing research. The two organizations merged in 1937 as the American Marketing Association. From the outset, the AMA opened its doors to sales managers, advertising executives, marketing research analysts, and others in the *business* of Marketing. The resulting interpenetration of business and teaching approaches to Marketing has proved highly beneficial to both teaching and business members. The national organization has fathered thirty-three local associations, many of which in turn have sponsored local group organizations in specialized Marketing fields such as advertising, marketing research, industrial marketing, sales management, and the like. Student marketing clubs, also sponsored by the AMA, have been organized in some eighty colleges. Semiannual conventions of the national organization, and more frequent meetings of the local units and specialized groups, provide invaluable forums where professional and academic members exchange views and information. The Association publishes the quarterly *Journal of Marketing* as the organ of Marketing study and practice.

Approaches to the study of Marketing

Three approaches to the study of Marketing have proved fruitful: analysis of Marketing operations,* institutional analysis, and commodity or channel-of-distribution analysis.

---

* Professor Copeland and the other Harvard scholars who were among the founding fathers of the study of Marketing did pioneer work on analysis of Marketing operations, but because they sought to establish an analogy between Marketing institutions and biological organisms, they utilized the term "functions"—involving a concept of compulsion or inherent necessity—instead of the more obvious terms "operations" or "activities."

1. *Operational analysis.* One obvious way to study Marketing is to analyze *what is done,* and *why it is done,* in the course of moving goods from their producers to consumers or other users. Of course, some classification of all the varied business activities associated with Marketing is a prerequisite, otherwise we would face hopeless confusion. But most of these activities coalesce into a limited number of groups, each united by a specific distributional objective; each such activity group we can call an "operation." Thus there is a definite group of activities associated with efficient purchase of goods for resale or for business use; we can study these and their interrelations under the operational heading of "buying." Another group of activities, or "operation," which we may call "pricing," is associated with determining the prices charged for goods or services sold. Those associated with sound extension of credit at either mercantile or retail level constitute the "credit operation." And so on, through the entire list of activities involved in Marketing.

Given a comprehensive classification of Marketing operations, with every significant Marketing activity included under some operational heading, an overall Marketing course or textbook could be based on an operational approach. It would have the great advantage of exploring, *in unified fashion,* Marketing activities as engaged in by many different kinds of business enterprises. Such a unified approach would underline the parallel performance of most Marketing operations by widely differing classes of business enterprise. Also, it would provide an effective foundation for the study of Marketing policies, since most policy issues relate to operational problems. However, an exclusively operational approach in an elementary Marketing course or textbook would have two disadvantages. First, it might fail to draw attention to significant variations, within the basic parallel, in the performance of a Marketing operation by different types of business enterprise. For example, retail store selling, direct personal selling to consumers, mercantile selling to wholesalers and retailers, and selling of business materials and equipment have many common features which an operational study on Selling would indicate, but such a study might not emphasize sufficiently the contrasting methods, as among these several selling fields, of locating customers, appealing to their different buying motivations, and helping them to arrive at a buying decision.

Practically all Marketing writers since their day have followed the usage they established, though most have avoided giving any meaningful definition of the term "function" as they use it.

In its proper technical sense, the term "functions" is improperly applied to Marketing activities or operations, and may mislead some students. The present writer accordingly has chosen to break with the tradition and adhere to the more readily understood terms "operations" and "activities." The term "activity" will be used for any and all specific marketing actions; "operation" will be used for a group of interrelated activities with a common objective.

Second, a beginning student of Marketing might be left with a scattered and confused picture of the various classes of business enterprise undertaking the distributional activities being studied.

These two disadvantages do not apply to advanced or specialized study of Marketing subjects. Many special "how to do it" studies have been made on particular Marketing operations; we have literally hundreds of books on advertising, selling, traffic management, purchasing, and other Marketing activities. A collegiate school of business curriculum includes "operational" courses on such subjects. There are business professional associations for many of these Marketing operational fields, such as credit men's associations and sales executives "clubs," that publish technical and news journals for their members and otherwise promote operational Marketing study.

2. *Institutional analysis.* Broadly defined, a Marketing "institution" is any classification of business enterprise that engages in Marketing activities. Thus "grocery stores," or "supermarkets," or "chain stores," or "department stores" might each be considered an institutional classification, or all of these categories plus many others might be included in a broad institutional classification as "retailers." Manufacturers, farmers, certain governmental departments and bureaus, and collegiate bureaus of business research could also be treated as Marketing "institutions" under a broad definition of the term, since they also perform certain Marketing activities.* Textbooks and monographs have been published on various business groupings and their Marketing activities, under such titles as "Retail Store Management," "Chain Stores," "Commodity Exchanges," and the like. Trade associations have been established for these institutional lines, and many of these associations assist their members in various of their Marketing activities. Most college courses on Marketing incorporate some element of institutional approach.

There can be no question but that an institutional analysis gives a comprehensive picture of the different types of business organizations and other bodies that contribute to the movement of goods and services from producers to consumers and other users. If the Marketing activities of each institutional class are fully described, a comprehensive coverage of Marketing operations will be achieved, with due emphasis on the differing application of these operations by various institutional groups. In its presentation of the Marketing operations and policies, however, an exclusively institutional approach to the subject would be bound to suffer

---

* Note that the term "Marketing institution" is commonly given a narrower definition, limiting it to business enterprises and other organizations whose *major* activities relate to distribution of goods or services. Under this narrower connotation, manufacturers, farmers, and several other groups included under the broader definition are not deemed *Marketing* institutions, their major activity being something other than Marketing.

from an important weakness—because of the basic similarity of Marketing operations among different institutional groups, a comprehensive exposition of the Marketing activities of each institutional classification in turn would result in a great deal of repetition.

3. *Commodity or channel-of-distribution analysis.* Another way to study Marketing would be to deal with one product after another, or in some cases with groups of products with similar Marketing characteristics, and follow each from its producers to its ultimate consumers or users. In the course of such an analysis, the various Marketing institutions that constitute the chains or channels of distribution for each product would be studied, as would the Marketing operations performed by them. Various special Marketing studies using this approach have been published under such titles as "Food Marketing," "The Marketing of Textiles," and "Industrial Marketing." No important general studies of Marketing have been based primarily on this approach.

A commodity approach to Marketing study is a very practical one. Better than any other, it shows the actual interlocking of the different types of business units that share in the distribution of particular commodities. Better than any other, it shows how both Marketing institutions and Marketing operations derive from, or are adapted to, the physical and economic peculiarities of particular products. It permits examination of important issues of channel-of-distribution policy. It offers greatest opportunity for cost-of-distribution studies. As the basis for a general study of Marketing, however, it would involve repetition of institutional description, and even more repetition of operational exposition.

Organization of this volume

Our analysis of Marketing is a compromise one. It combines all three approaches above, in an endeavor to benefit from the special advantages of each while avoiding its disadvantages through the combined presentation. To provide background information and trace certain social and economic consequences of Marketing practices, several topics are developed that are not directly associated with any of the three basic approaches.

After a background survey in Chapters 2 and 3 of consumers as a foundation factor in Marketing, Part Two of this volume develops an institutional presentation of some of the subject matter of Marketing. In Chapters 4 through 11 the term "institutional" is used in its narrower sense— business organizations whose *major* activity is some phase of Marketing. The various categories of retailers and wholesalers, and some types of "facilitating" Marketing institutions, are studied. But there is no discussion here of the Marketing operations of manufacturers (which are developed in the operational discussion in Part Four), or of the relation of consumers to Marketing (covered in Chapters 2 and 3). Furthermore, several important categories of "facilitating" Marketing institutions whose activities are associated with some particular Marketing operation—as warehouses are with storage, or advertising agencies with advertising—are only mentioned in Part Two; fuller analysis of their structure and activities is postponed until Part Four where they can be studied in close association with the special operations they perform.

Part Three, consisting of Chapters 12 through 14, presents a commodity or channel-of-distribution analysis of Marketing, but a very limited one. Except for a few agricultural products representative marketwise of broad commodity classifications, no attempt is made to trace the detailed movement of individual products from their producers to their consumers or users. Instead, the analysis is generalized for broad commodity categories— agricultural products, manufactured consumer goods, industrial equipment, industrial materials and supplies, and services. Broad though it is, this commodity approach throws additional light on the specific place of various Marketing institutions in our actual distributional structure. It also opens the door to discussion of the important subject of Marketing policies associated with choice of channels of distribution.

Part Four, covering Chapters 15 through 27, is concerned with the Marketing operations and the Marketing policies deriving from them—the very heart and soul of Marketing study. From the viewpoint of subject matter relationship, it might well have preceded the other two analyses. Operational policy, however, is one of the most complex and difficult aspects of Marketing study, so it seems advisable to give as much background as possible in other Marketing topics before proceeding to a presentation of operations and operational policies.

Chapters 28 through 30, which constitute Part Five, deal with a small group of topics which, while properly or even necessarily a part of a survey course in Marketing, do not logically fall under the three basic approaches previously made.

REVIEW

1. Define "Marketing" and explain the significance of the elements of this definition.

2. Explain why manufacturing, and the purchasing activities of consumers, are generally not considered Marketing activities, although both of these topics must be analyzed to a considerable extent in any comprehensive study of Marketing.

3. Why should every forward step in production technology, in distribution technology, in social and economic organization, and in cultural achievement result in expanding the scope and the social and economic importance of Marketing?

4. How does Marketing currently compare with Production by the measures of contributions to employment and national income?

5. What are some of the contributions of Economics to Marketing? of Psychology and Sociology?

6. What are the possibilities and limitations of studying Marketing from: (a) an operational approach, (b) an institutional approach, or (c) a commodity or channel-of-distribution approach?

DISCUSSION TOPICS

1. "The relative place of Marketing in the economic structure of a country reflects that country's economic and social achievement."

2. "In an Economy of Scarcity, Production takes precedence over Marketing; in an Economy of Plenty, Marketing takes precedence."

3. "The economic importance of the salesman and advertising man in the present American economy equals, if it does not already surpass, that of the engineer."

4. Should Marketing be considered a separate subject, or primarily a branch of Economics?

5. Is Marketing an art or a science?

SUGGESTED READINGS

American Marketing Association, *Frontiers in Marketing Thought* (1955); *The Broadening Perspective of Marketing* (1956); *The Marketing Revolution* (1956); *Adaptive Behavior in Marketing* (1957); *Marketing's Role in Scientific Management* (1957); *The Frontiers of Marketing Thought and Science* (1958); *Successful Marketing at Home and Abroad* (1958).

Bakken, H. H., *Theory of Markets and Marketing,* Mimir Publishers, Madison, Wis., 1953.

Barger, H., *Distribution's Place in the American Economy since 1869,* National Bureau of Economic Research, Princeton University Press, N.J., 1955.

Converse, P. D., *The Beginning of Marketing Thought in the United States,* Bureau of Business Research, University of Texas, Austin, 1959.

Cox, R. (ed.), *Marketing: Current Problems and Theories,* Indiana University, Bloomington, 1952.

Selling the U.S. Market, Domestic Commerce Series No. 29, U.S. Department of Commerce, Washington, D.C., 1951.

Wales, H., *Changing Perspectives in Marketing,* University of Illinois Press, Urbana, 1951.

PERIODICALS: *Business Week, Dun's Review, Fortune, Harvard Business Review, Journal of Marketing, Nation's Business.*

CHAPTER 2

THE CONSUMER MARKET

In the American economy the Consumer is King—or rather, since most household buying is done by women, Mrs. Consumer is Queen.

The American economy is one of plenty, where most people buy what they *want,* not what they can get. Consumers' choice, not the preferences of manufacturers or of storekeepers, rules.

Because of this, every manufacturer, wholesaler and retailer of consumer goods must always ask himself two basic Marketing questions: (1) What is my market*—i.e., who are the actual and potential ultimate purchasers of my product or service, and where are they located? (2) Why do these people buy my product or how can they be induced to buy it? Most retailers have a third basic Marketing question to answer—Why do my customers buy from me, rather than from the competitor down the block, or in the next block, or in a neighboring town?

Correct answers to the first question give a manufacturer of consumer goods guidance on the quantities he should produce, where he should

---

* The term "market" has several common meanings: (1) It is most commonly used to designate the aggregate demand of potential consumers or other ultimate buyers of a product—for example, "There is a 2,000,000 market for hearing aids," meaning "There are 2,000,000 potential buyers of hearing aids." (2) Sometimes it designates a geographically concentrated group of middlemen in a particular business line together with their trading facilities and activities—for example, "the Chicago livestock market," or "the Boston fish market." (3) Sometimes it refers to the over-all trading activities of a key group of middlemen in some commodity field—for example, "the wool market was sluggish," or "the wheat market was active" (in both cases the reference would be to trading of these items on the appropriate commodity exchanges). (4) Sometimes it refers to a commodity's price tendencies, particularly when the commodity is traded on an exchange—thus, "The cotton market was weak today," meaning "Cotton prices on the cotton exchanges declined." (5) Sometimes it relates to a complex of conditions in which buyers and sellers make decisions which result in the transfer of some good or service—thus, "We shall now start our study of the livestock market."

In this chapter we are using the term "market" in the first of these five meanings.

locate factories and warehouses, what channels of distribution he should use to reach the ultimate buyers of his product, what advertising media and promotional techniques he should employ, and the type of sales organization he should establish. For a wholesaler or retailer, sound conclusions about his particular consumer market enable him to choose a good location for his warehouse or store, and to buy the right products in the right amounts.

An individual consumer-goods manufacturer, or a wholesaler or retailer, is interested in only one segment of the over-all consumer market—the circumstances of those individuals in his market area who can use his goods. Within the limited area, however, his analysis should be intense; he cannot know too much about *his* customers.

Our interest, as students, in the consumer market is much broader than that of the business man who has particular goods to sell to a particular group of consumers. We want to learn about the entire body of consumers and how they affect major aspects of American Marketing. A comprehensive objective analysis of the American population as consumers is obviously beyond the scope of a general Marketing text. We shall have to confine our survey to four major consumer market topics—population composition, consumer spending power, patterns of consumer expenditure, and the significance of women as purchasers of consumer goods. On each of these topics we shall explore trends as well as current status.

POPULATION

Popular writers sometimes cite an "American Market" of 180 million individuals (i.e., the population of the continental United States by 1960). This figure is meaningless to any consumer-goods industry, and to distributors who handle its products. The men's suit industry in 1960 did not produce for 180 million Americans, but for the 62 million males over the age of 14. Insulin is made for the 1 percent of the population suffering from diabetes. Home furnace manufacturers find little market for their product south of the 28th parallel. The market for yachts costing over $20,000 is limited to a few thousand high-income family units residing near oceans or large inland bodies of water.

For every product there exists a special potential market—a number of individuals with sex, age, health, hobby, and other particular personal characteristics which make them actively want the product, or which provide a foundation for their learning to want it, and with financial capacity to buy it. Furthermore, most consumer goods manufacturers, and practically all wholesalers and retailers, sell within limited market areas, so that their special potential markets are but fractions—in the case of retailers minute ones—of the over-all product markets. Competition further splits the special markets for particular businesses. It may happen that special local situations, which run counter to the circumstances and trends of the national population, are the all-important determinants of the Marketing operations and policies of a particular business. But national population considerations usually set a general pattern for most local market developments, and most manufacturers and many large wholesalers and retailers take these considerations into account in their market planning.

Increase

Although the total population of the country cannot be the market for any product or industry, the rate of increase of that total population, by influencing all special markets, is an important long-term consideration for most consumer-good industries. The average annual increase of the American population since 1946 has been 1.7 percent. An annual birth rate of 25 per thousand and a steady increase of life expectancy are the major factors; immigration makes only a minor contribution. Continuation of this rate of increase is anticipated, and a population between 231 million and 273 million is forecast for 1980. So a continuing substantial increase in the total number of consumers for all classes of products should be

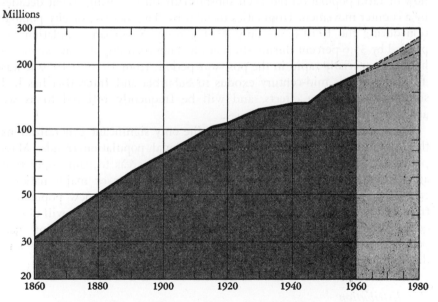

POPULATION   GROWTH   AND   PROJECTIONS   1860–1980
Source: *Statistical Abstract* and U.S. Bureau of the Census, Series P-25, No. 187

ILLUSTRATION 2–1

taken into account in prognosticating the long-term development of most special markets.

Regional and local distribution

The special markets for most individual producers and distributors of consumer goods are local and regional. To them, the important population trend is not that of the country as a whole, but their particular market area. National manufacturers also have a sharp interest in the geographic distribution of the American population, since its pattern influences the organization of their selling and advertising effort.

Consumers are distributed very unevenly over the territorial United States, with marked concentration in the Eastern and East Central regions, and thin scattering through the mountain and plateau areas of the West. Further contrasts in concentration and dispersion result from the location of major metropolitan centers and smaller cities. Over the past half-century the more thinly populated areas of the West have gained more rapidly than the older-settled sections of the East; the population expansion of the Pacific coastal area has been particularly marked.

All over the country there is a steady flow of young men and women from the farms and small towns to the cities. The cities' gain from this outflow of farm population has been substantially offset during recent decades by a counter movement from cities to suburbs. The increase of city population during the 1940's was only 13.9 percent. Suburban population expanded by 35.6 percent during this decade. Suburban population expansion has been especially rapid in the post-war period; from 1950 to 1959 it was 44 percent. This mid-century exodus to Suburbia and Interurbia has had significant marketing effects, and will be frequently referred to as we analyze particular Marketing topics.

These three developments constitute the only significant generalizations that can be made concerning local or regional population trends. Mass population shifts during the 1940's caused some areas to gain population at alarming rates, others to lose. Unless another war or major national emergency should occur, it is unlikely that there will be new population transfers on the scale of those of the 1940's, but some shifting will always occur. Where limited local areas are involved, the repercussion of such population drifts on the special markets of particular manufacturers and distributors may be substantial.

Age distribution

Still another market-determining factor for many producers and distributors is the age distribution of the population in a market area. Manufacturers and distributors of baby foods obviously have a special age market. So too have the makers and retailers of toys. So do the manufacturers of hearing aids, who sell a large proportion of their output to aged users.

The age distribution of the American population does not remain constant, for two reasons. The first is that the low birth rate of the 1930's, followed by the birthquake of the 1940's, produced a "population gap" that with the years moves steadily up the age scale. Manufacturers of children's items had to take this moving "population gap" into account during the 1940's. Its effects were felt by the producers of goods for teen-agers during the 1950's. Consumer durable goods manufacturers will be affected by it in the 1960's.

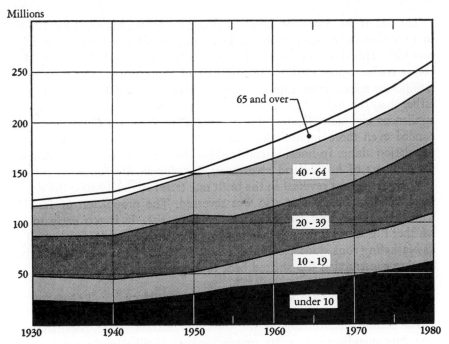

AGE DISTRIBUTION OF POPULATION, 1930–1975
Source: U.S. Bureau of the Census, Series P-25, No. 187
ILLUSTRATION 2–2

The second factor disturbing the balance of age groups is the increase in life expectancy. Advances in medical science and diffusion of health education are causing a constantly growing proportion of Americans to reach age ranges in the 60's, 70's, and 80's. In 1930, people over 65 constituted 5 percent of the population. In 1950, the proportion was over 8 percent. By 1960, it exceeded 9 percent, and will continue rising. This group of the "retired aged" is becoming a special market of growing importance to many manufacturers and distributors. They have special needs and special interests, and pensions and Social Security retirement payments provide them with an increasing income wherewith to satisfy these needs and interests.

Age distribution of the American population is not territorially uniform. The proportion of children is higher in suburban and rural areas than in urban centers. There is a heavy concentration of aged persons in southern California and certain other regions. Some of these variations from the national norm exercise considerable influence on the marketing policies of producers of items with major appeal to particular age groups.

Family size

The size of the American family declined fairly steadily until the 1940's. In 1890 there were 4.9 persons in the average family; in 1950 the number was 3.55. This downward trend in family size had several significant Marketing consequences during the first half of the century. The number of families increased more rapidly than the over-all population. The family, rather than the individual, is the purchasing unit for such items as home appliances and automobiles. Therefore the markets for these items expanded even more rapidly than would have been caused by the rise in population alone. In housing construction there was a stepped-up demand for numbers of houses and apartments, but for smaller units.

With the abrupt reversal in the birth rate trend in the 1940's, the downward trend in family size also was reversed. The proportion of families with three, four, and five children began to rise. It is too early to say whether this trend toward larger families will persist and to forecast all of its Marketing consequences. One effect, at least, has been noted—suburban housing construction has shifted back to larger units.

CONSUMER SPENDING POWER

The second determinant of the consumer market, after population, is consumer spending power. Its amount and its distribution in varying proportions among American families determine not only the over-all volume of consumer goods and services that can be sold each year, but also the kinds of such goods and services.

Disposable income, discretionary income, and consumer spending

The total of personal received income for any year is not available for consumption expenditure. One or more members in most families must pay federal income tax. In two-thirds of the states there are state taxes on

personal incomes. When these and other minor personal taxes are subtracted from the national total of personal received incomes, the remainder
is called by the economists "disposable income."

Consumers cannot freely apply all of this disposable income to spending
or saving, however. Some of it must be used for fixed commitments—repayment of home mortgage and installment debt, insurance and pension
payments, home tax and rental payments. It is the balance (with some
allowance for budgeted savings other than debt repayment) that constitutes
the financial measure of the potential American consumer goods market.
With the continuous expansion of the American economy, this "available"
personal income exhibits a long-term increase. From 1939 to 1959 the rise
was from $53 billion to $216 billion. With allowance for price inflation,
there was still a doubling of "available" personal income, as shown in
Illustration 2–3.

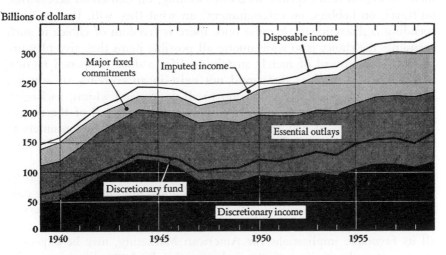

APPLICATION OF DISPOSABLE INCOME (IN "1959 DOL-
LARS"), 1939–1959

Derived from National Industrial Conference Board, Discretionary
Income (1958) and supplements

ILLUSTRATION 2–3

Much of the spending of "available" personal income is dictated by
necessity. Food must be bought to sustain life, with quality standards more
or less determined by the current American standards of living. Clothing
must be bought for decency and reasonable appearance, if not for high
fashion. Essential home furnishings must be bought, medical attention
must be paid for. These are counted as "essential outlays."

If all, or most, American families were limited in their spending to
"essential outlays," the Marketing picture would be far different from

what it is today. There would be little incentive to devise new products and designs to please individual indulgence, if the luxury of personal tastes and desires could not be afforded by most consumers. The arts of advertising and selling would be largely inapplicable if the masses could not afford what advertising and personal selling offer them. Our supreme Marketing problem, instead of being that of persuading families to apply discretionary purchasing power to buy the swelling output of our industry, would be that of moving a limited volume of basic necessities from field and factory to consumers' homes in the most economical way.

There are still millions of families in the United States whose available income just covers their essential outlays. More important from a Marketing standpoint, there is a large and growing proportion whose available incomes exceed the cost of a minimum American standard of living. These families have a margin of "discretionary" income.* This they can spend, at their choice, on better quality foods or clothing, on household accessories, on travel, on hobbies, on entertainment, on what they will. Because such spending *is* discretionary, because once there is freedom of choice in such spending, the choice is so wide among all possible items that give pleasure in some way instead of merely sustaining life, a door is opened to new Marketing opportunities that could not exist in an economy of scarcity. Product invention and design to cater to all desires and whims, packaging and display to stimulate impulse buying, advertising to tell of the real or imagined wonders of new products, and selling to persuade consumers to buy and what to buy—these come into their own only when discretionary spending by consumers reaches sizable proportions.

Illustration 2–3 shows that from 1939 to 1959, discretionary purchasing power, as indicated by the "Discretionary Fund" line, increased not only absolutely (in terms of "1959 dollars") but also more rapidly than essential consumer spending.** Expanded discretionary purchasing power, with all its favorable implications for American Marketing, may be expected; one recent authoritative estimate indicates that by 1970 discretionary income will be one-half of disposable income.

---

* Actually, since such families are acceptable risks for installment credit, their *discretionary purchasing power* is considerably greater than their *discretionary income*. This extra element of discretionary purchasing power, measured by actual installment purchases in each year, is shown in Illustration 2–3 in the "Discretionary Fund" line.

** It should not be overlooked that considerable elements of discretion inhere in the "essential outlay" spending of families whose "available" income allows them any margin over "essential outlay" requirements. In their purchases of food, clothing, and other "necessities," they are able to indulge in choice among brands and qualities. Discretionary *spending* constitutes a larger proportion of total consumer spending than is indicated by the relationship of "Discretionary Income" or "Discretionary Fund" to "Essential Outlays" in Illustration 2–3.

Family incomes and expenditure patterns

Most consumer spending is not done on an individual basis, but in family groups or with consideration for its effect on a family budget. From a Marketing standpoint, therefore, the significant figures are not those of per capita disposable income and per capita spending, but of family disposable income and spending.

Disposable family incomes are distributed unevenly. A few are in the six-figure range; some 13 million—about 23 percent of the total—are under $2,000. A seven-bracket distribution for 1957 (with all disposable incomes over $7,500 lumped together) is shown in Illustration 2–4. This average distribution is not uniform throughout the country. Average per-family income is much lower in the South and its distribution is weighted more heavily toward lower-bracket incomes, for example, than in the Northeast or West. These regional differentials are currently being reduced. There is considerable variation in average per-family income and its distribution even among neighboring market areas in a given region. It is

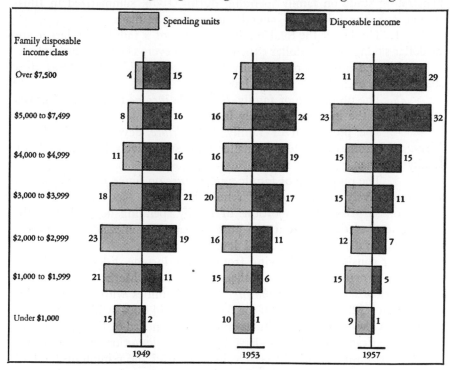

DISTRIBUTION OF FAMILY DISPOSABLE INCOMES, 1949, 1953, AND 1957

Source: *Federal Reserve Bulletin*, July 1954, p. 16, and University of Michigan Research Center

ILLUSTRATION 2–4

important for manufacturers and large wholesalers to determine just how territorial differences in family income and its distribution affect their special markets. They can then pin-point their promotional and selling efforts for maximum marketing efficiency. Accordingly, as described in Chapter 23, various marketing agencies go to considerable expense to collect and distribute up-to-date data that reflect these differences in the distribution of consumer purchasing power by local market areas.

The size of a particular family's disposable income influences not only the over-all volume of its spending, but also to some extent the pattern of that spending. The first conclusions on the relationship between family income and spending patterns were formulated during the third quarter of the Nineteenth Century by Ernst Engel, a German economist, and Carroll D. Wright, an American public administrator. These came to be known as "Engel's Laws of Consumption." Recent studies, while confirming some of the principles of Engel's Laws, indicate that not all of his original conclusions apply to the current American social economy. On the basis of a penetrating study on family spending during 1956, summarized in Illustration 2–5, the following generalizations may be made:

1. The larger the total received income of a family, the larger are its dollar savings and its dollar expenditures on every class of consumption.

2. The proportion of family *total income* paid out in *taxes* rises steadily with each higher income level.

3. The proportion of family *disposable income* that is *saved* grows rapidly with the increase of family income.

4. The proportion of family *expenditure* devoted to *food and beverages* becomes consistently smaller with successively higher levels of family income.

5. The proportion of family *expenditure* on *home furnishings* rises with successively higher levels of family income.

6. Surprisingly, proportions of family spending devoted to clothing, home operation, medical and personal care, automobiles, and recreation remain fairly constant for all levels of income.

Another consideration deriving from family income distribution that is important to manufacturers and others interested in Marketing is the distribution of *discretionary purchasing power*. Families with disposable incomes under $2,500, or $3,000, or $3,500, or $4,000—whichever is our particular view of what constitutes minimum-standard-of-living spending for an American family today—have little or no discretion in their spending. But all families with disposable incomes over the minimum-standard figure have some choice in their spending, and if their margin is much over this figure their choice is practically untrammelled. Even what they actually save may be considered at the outset as part of their discretionary purchasing power, since there is originally a choice between spending and

FAMILY SPENDING PATTERNS BY INCOME CLASSES, 1956

	ALL HOUSE-HOLDS	HOUSEHOLD INCOME BEFORE TAXES							
		Under $2,000	$2,000 to $2,999	$3,000 to $3,999	$4,000 to $4,999	$5,000 to $6,999	$7,000 to $9,999	Over $10,000
Total annual expenditure per household	$4,110	$1,933	$2,924	$3,839	$4,363	$5,016	$6,063	$7,946
Percent of total expenditure:								
Food, beverages, tobacco	29%	36%	33%	30%	29%	28%	26%	24%
Clothing, accessories	12	11	11	13	12	11	13	14
Home operation, improvement	19	17	20	18	19	19	18	18
Home furnishings, equipment, appliances	9	7	8	8	9	9	9	10
Medical, personal care	5	7	5	5	5	5	5	6
Automotive [1]	14	11	13	15	14	16	15	15
Recreation	5	5	5	5	6	5	5	6
Other [2]	7	6	5	6	7	7	9	7
Total	100%	100%	100%	100%	100%	100%	100%	100%

[1] Expenditures on automobiles in this category refer to net outlays after trade-in allowances.

[2] Includes life insurance premiums and nonmedical professional services.

Source: *The LIFE Study of Consumer Expenditures*, 1957, Vol. I, p. 20

ILLUSTRATION 2–5

saving it. If we take $2,500 as the minimum-standard family spending level, we had over 70 percent of American families in 1956 able to spend their disposable incomes entirely or in part on a discretionary basis. If we take a $4,000 minimum-spending figure, the proportion of families able to do discretionary spending was nearly half. By either basis of calculation, the target to which Marketing can apply its arts of enticement and persuasion is a generous one.

Trends in disposable family income

The increase in disposable family income over the past quarter-century has not been as rapid as the increase in the national total of disposable income, shown in Illustration 2–3, since the number of families was also increasing during this period. But it has been satisfyingly substantial. In "1959 dollars" average family disposable income was $6,600 in 1959, in contrast to $3,800 in 1929.*

Another significant trend is that, with respect to distribution of disposable family income among the various income groups, the rich have grown poorer and the poor richer during the past quarter-century. The levelling down from the top occurred during the 1930's and 1940's, as sharpened progression of the federal personal income tax left a much smaller proportion of large incomes "disposable"; this levelling-down effect has been inoperative during the past decade. Meanwhile, throughout this period, and still continuing as indicated in Illustration 2–4, there has been an "upgrading" of lower-income-bracket families through minimum wage legislation, substantial wage gains by organized labor, and improvement in farm earnings. The social distribution of disposable family income has definitely been equalized since the 1920's.

All prognostications indicate both a continued rise of average disposable family income, and a continued upgrading of families through the income levels, particularly among the lowest-bracket families. The broad consequence of these two trends has been, and should continue to be, a marked rise in the general American standard of living. Specifically, the following Marketing developments can be attributed to this increase and equalization of family disposable incomes:

1. There has been, and will continue to be, an upgrading of the quality of many staple necessities. Backed by rising and more equally distributed consumer purchasing power, mass demand has developed for better and more expensive grades of food items, wearing apparel, and hous-

---

* Part of the rise in consumer goods prices over the period we are considering represented added value in the form of upgraded quality of goods and improved distribution. Therefore our comparison of "real" disposable family income in 1929 and 1959 understates to some extent the true rise that has occurred.

ing facilities. Production, in response, has continually shifted its standards upward. In some cases this has resulted in reduced output of lower-quality staples that satisfy only the bare necessities of various aspects of living. Shoddy cloth (reworked wool) can hardly be sold any more, even at prices that make it a much better buy by technical standards than virgin wool cloth.

2. In the *distribution* of staple goods there has also been a quality improvement, which should continue. Small unit packaging of foodstuffs and various apparel items keeps them more sanitary and makes them more attractive than the old-style bulk packing. The dim, dusty neighborhood stores of yesteryear have been replaced by well-lit air-conditioned supermarkets and emporiums gleaming with plate glass and chromium. This "upgrading" of retail distribution involves costs incorporated into the prices that consumers pay, but they demand these marketing improvements and their enhanced "real" purchasing power enables them to pay for them.

3. The markets for "mass" luxuries, such as automobiles, TV sets, and household electrical appliances, have outstripped all others. The great bulk of American families have graduated from working primarily for a living; they now work for the pleasures of luxury spending. Shorter work weeks and longer vacations, and the increasing discretionary spending power of an expanding major proportion of American families, are creating a fabulous market for "leisure" goods. Americans own 35 million cameras and spend some $400 million a year on amateur photographic supplies and equipment. They own over six million pleasure boats and spend some $1.5 billion on this source of pleasure. Current "leisure market" spending is between $35 billion and $40 billion annually.

4. Markets for many "class" luxuries have thrived, but have had no expansion comparable to that for the more important "mass" luxuries. In some instances "class" luxury markets have dwindled; "million-dollar" mansions and yachts are not being built today, as they were forty or fifty years ago.

PATTERNS OF CONSUMER EXPENDITURE

No two individuals are likely to be impelled to buy a particular item by precisely the same qualitative and quantitative motivations. This does not mean, however, that a manufacturer takes into account a myriad individual tastes in designing a product, or that an advertiser can find no common denominators in his efforts to stimulate consumer demand for a product. Various economic and social considerations tend to mold the almost infinite variety of individual buying motivations into surprisingly consistent expenditure patterns. Many individuals fail to conform to the pattern that might be expected to apply to them; every large herd has its mavericks. Still, the general level of conformity is high enough to provide manufacturers, advertisers, and other sales planners with workable market guides.

Among the economic and social factors other than family income level that shape consumer spending patterns are: (1) regional preferences; (2) urban, suburban, and rural residence; (3) occupational and cultural considerations; (4) social stratification; and (5) the general economic outlook.

Regional preferences

Texans wear sombreros; Maine coastal dwellers in all occupations wear peaked lobstermen's caps. The South spends more heavily for carbonated beverages and cosmetics than the rest of the country. The West spends heavily for autos, cameras, and sporting goods. Boston housewives prefer brown eggs; New York women think white eggs are superior. Louisiana wants chicory in its coffee.

Some of these regional preferences relate to climatic differences. Many simply reflect custom. Regardless of basic causes, they are a Marketing factor of importance to many industries and marketing lines.

Urban, suburban, and rural residence

One of the market-determining factors in the United States to which major importance was formerly attached was the changing proportion of rural and urban dwellers. For one thing, most rural dwellers were farmers with special occupational needs who commonly owned their own homes. Their purchases differed in many respects from those of city dwellers, many of whom lived in rented apartments and worked in offices. Moreover, prior to the era of the automobile, the movies and the radio, the farm population lived in a marketing vacuum. The farmer and his family could not be reached by the major classes of advertising media. Rarely could they visit some metropolitan center and be influenced by the promotional window and counter display of department stores and specialty shops. The only two retailing agencies through which they could be sold were the village "general" store and the mail-order house, both of which were highly conservative with respect to carrying new products and style products.

There are still contrasts between some of the buying demands of the farmer and the city dweller, due to differences in their occupations and home characteristics. But the farmer is no longer beyond the reach of the various market influences that condition the city and suburban dweller's buying. The automobile has enabled the farmer's wife to desert the village general store, except for the purchase of convenience goods, and to patronize the department stores and specialty shops of distant shopping centers. Rural electrification has made farm families customers for electrical household equipment of all sorts. The radio, the movies, and now television, keep rural residents abreast of the latest styles and subject them to the promotional pressures that have long conditioned urban buying.

A special "farm market" for certain consumer products still exists. Preserve jars are sold by the millions to farmers' wives and only by thousands to urban and suburban housewives. Such items as well-pumps find most of their buyers in rural areas. The steady population flow from the farms to the cities, previously noted, affects the markets for such products. But by and large, the differences between rural and urban living, as a consumer market factor, are no longer of major significance.

Rapidly growing Suburbia and Interurbia have spending patterns that differ in many respects from those of city inhabitants and of rural dwellers. The suburbanite is a home-owner and of necessity a do-it-yourself practitioner. He must own one car, often two. His leisure life is largely out-of-doors. His spending on household and auto accessories is high. He is a dream market for tools, particularly power tools, and for gadgets of all sorts. He and his family are the foundation for the casual clothes market.

Occupational and cultural considerations

Various statistical computations are available which apparently show that the families of wage earners in manual occupations have different expenditure patterns from those of clerical and professional workers who receive salaries. One recent study, for example, indicated that wage-earner families in the $4,000 income range spent 3.7% of their incomes on insurance, 0.2% on education, and 17.5% on recreation, durable goods and savings, while the proportions for "white-collar" families in the same income range were 7.7%, 1.9% and 5.4%. Probably such differences in family expenditure patterns are attributable less to occupational than to cultural and social considerations. The difference between a high school or college background and a grammar school background affects not only how a family unit will distribute its purchases quantitatively among such classifications as insurance, educational outlays, and clothing, as indicated in Illustration 2–6, but also the character and quality of its purchases within each class. Rising educational levels are elevating the "sophistication level" of broad elements of the American market, with profound effects on consumer reactions to product design, advertising, and other forms of promotion.

Accordingly, certain educational and cultural trends are of major importance to the long-term development of the special markets for some products. At present 6 percent of our population over the age of twenty-five have college degrees, and another 20 percent have completed high school. The trend has long been and still is in the direction of more edu-

PATTERNS OF FAMILY SPENDING AS INFLUENCED BY EDUCATIONAL LEVEL OF FAMILY HEAD, 1956

FAMILY SPENDING CLASSIFICATION	ALL HOUSEHOLDS	LEVEL OF EDUCATION ATTAINED BY HOUSEHOLD HEAD				
		Some grade school or less	Finished grade school	Attended high school	Finished high school	Some college or beyond
Food, beverages & tobacco	29%	34%	32%	31%	29%	25%
Clothing & accessories	12	12	11	11	13	13
Medical & personal care	5	6	5	5	5	5
Home operation & improvement	19	16	18	18	18	21
Home furnishings & equipment	9	8	8	8	9	9
Recreation & recreation equipment	5	5	5	5	5	6
Automotive	14	13	14	15	14	14
Other goods and services	7	6	7	7	7	7
Total goods & services	100%	100%	100%	100%	100%	100%

Source: *LIFE Study of Consumer Expenditures*, 1957, p. 23

ILLUSTRATION 2–6

cation for a larger proportion of the population. Not only are special markets for textbooks and other school supplies influenced directly by this factor, but the resulting rising cultural level of the general population means larger markets for publications generally, and for higher-quality goods in all fields. Schooling is not the only cultural factor to change expenditure patterns. The movies, radio, and television have probably exercised a more profound cultural influence on consumer expenditure patterns during the past three decades than the rise in educational levels during the same period.

Social stratification

Sociology and everyday observation establish that we are a country of social classes. The cleavage is not sharp, but the structure is undeniable. Size of family income is a major determinant of social status, but not an exclusive one. The source as well as the amount of income is important. Educational background of the members of the family is also a consideration. One estimate of the distribution of American families among social classes puts 5% in an "upper" class, 12% in an "upper middle" class, 65% (the "common man" group) divided between a "lower-middle" and an "upper-lower" class, and 20% in a "lower-lower" class.

Purchasing behavior varies sharply from class to class, but consumption spending patterns within each class have strong elements of uniformity among different communities and widely separated regions. There is less difference between the family buying of a southern California citrus fruit grower and a New York business man, both belonging to the "upper middle" class, than between that of the New York business man and a New York "lower-lower" class laborer. Manufacturers take this social stratification into account in product design, choice of advertising media and appeals, choice of channels of distribution, and other elements of their marketing policy. If a product is to be purchased by more than one social class, separate marketing approaches with differences in product design, promotion, pricing, and channels of distribution may be necessary. Retailers often have to make definite decisions as to the social class from which they will draw their clientele, and direct their entire appeal to that one class.

General business conditions

It has long been recognized that broad business fluctuations, by increasing or decreasing consumers' incomes, affect the volume and patterns of consumption expenditure. When a recession shrinks the flow of purchasing power to consumers, naturally many of them must lower their spending levels. An expanding flow of purchasing power to consumers generally leads to increased buying, if only because of the consumers' added ability to pay. Recent "consumer attitude" researches have indicated, however, that discretionary buying of consumer durable goods depends as much upon *consumers' opinion* on whether general economic conditions *will* improve or decline, whether prices *will* rise or fall, whether there *will* be shortages or not, whether their own incomes *will* go up or down, as it does upon actual increases or decreases in consumers' income. Shifts in consumer expectations on these economic matters do not always correlate with actual economic trends; when they do, mass opinion-changes tend to precede related changes in consumers' actual purchasing power.

WOMEN AND MARKETING

Marketing has a Woman Problem—or rather, three of them.

In the first place, a substantial proportion of American women are income earners. Four out of five single women, one out of two newly-married wives, one out of five married women with families, and a higher fraction of older married women whose children have grown up, hold jobs. Part of the earnings of these women is merged with general family incomes. But a substantial part is theirs to spend, either because they are independent or because their earnings in many cases are viewed as personal "pin money." Here is a substantial special market eagerly wooed by particular manufacturers and retailers.

Secondly, since many married women work full or part time, they must find ways of reducing their household labors. This increases the markets for prepared foods and ready-made clothing. Home labor-saving appliances are especially appealing to working-wife families, and the earnings of the working wives make possible their purchase.

Finally, the wife-mother is the purchasing manager in most families. Women buy or choose not only the items that they personally use, but *most* of the items for joint consumption or use by family units. They buy or influence the choice of a considerable proportion of the items consumed by the male members of their families. A recent survey has indicated that, besides dominating selection in such product fields as women's and children's clothing, groceries, drugs, and jewelry, women buy or influence the selection in 27% of men's clothing purchases, 51% of house appliance purchases, and 27% of automobile purchases. Accordingly, product design in all but a few consumer goods fields is directed substantially to appeal to women's tastes. A major proportion of advertising is channeled through media that will reach women, and embodies appeals directed at women's psychological reactions. Most retail institutions and units are planned to cater primarily to women—excessively so, perhaps, since some men do find their way into supermarkets and other "women's stores."

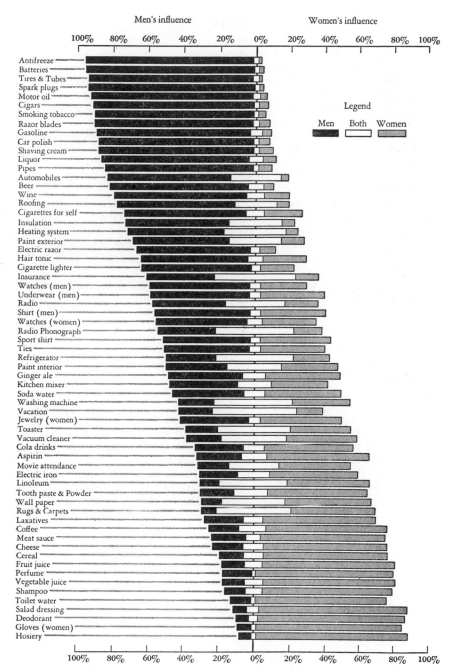

RELATIVE INFLUENCE OF MEN AND WOMEN ON RETAIL
PURCHASE SELECTION. *Courtesy of Fawcett Publications, Inc.*

ILLUSTRATION 2–7

REVIEW

1. State three general population trends, and indicate how they affect the markets for particular products such as breakfast cereals, prepared baby foods, hearing aids, toys, household refrigerators, automobiles.

2. How is the age distribution of our population changing? What is the Marketing significance of this change?

3. What are the trends in "real" received income, disposable income, and discretionary purchasing power, and what is their Marketing significance?

4. What were "Engel's Laws," and what is their Marketing significance today?

5. How is the distribution of family disposable income changing, and what is the Marketing significance of this trend?

6. What have been the Marketing consequences of the ending of rural isolation? of the expanding importance of the suburbs?

7. To what extent does social stratification influence consumer buying?

8. Why are women's preferences so important in American Marketing?

DISCUSSION TOPICS

1. "Mrs. Consumer is queen of American Marketing, and her wishes and whims are law to manufacturers and retailers."

2. "The continued trend of population from the farms to the cities is of declining Marketing importance, while the trend from the cities to the suburbs remains a vital factor in American Marketing."

3. "The emergence of a substantial and growing volume of discretionary purchasing power during the past quarter-century has had a revolutionary impact on American Marketing."

4. "The tendency toward greater equalization of disposable family incomes has had far reaching Marketing consequences."

5. The growing "teen-age market"; the growing "leisure market."

6. The differences between the "white collar" and "blue collar" markets are disappearing.

7. "The rising education level of the American population is changing the Marketing picture."

8. "Social status factors are coming to be as important, or even more important, than family income factors as determinants of American consumer buying."

9. "Manufacturers and retailers are catering excessively to women."

PROBLEM

Cranford Pharmaceutical Co.'s chemists have succeeded in isolating and synthesizing Vitamin Y, which reduces obesity and controls weight without any adverse side-effects. Cost studies indicate that the retail price of the dosage needed to reduce or prevent obesity in a person with a tendency to overweight will be around a dollar a week. The company plans to build a plant for the production of Vitamin Y. The equipment involved will have a ten-year life, so the company's management wants figures on the production capacity it should provide for on a ten-year projection of market demand. The company's research director calculates, from life insurance studies on the age groups affected by obesity, and the proportion of the population that could currently afford $50 a year for such a purpose, that the present national consumption potential is in the area of 150,000 kg. a year. Because of the antitrust laws, Cranford Co. will have to license the production of Vitamin Y to at least two other major producers. So 50,000 kg. is arbitrarily taken as Cranford Co.'s share of the *current* potential demand.

What statistical trends should be taken into account to arrive at a figure for the production capacity that the plant should have to satisfy Cranford Co.'s ⅓ share of the national potential demand ten years from now?

SUGGESTED READINGS

Canoyer, H., & R. Vaile, *Economics of Income and Consumption,* Ronald Press, New York, 1951.

Clark, L. H. (ed.), *Consumer Behavior:* Vol. I—*The Dynamics of Consumer Reaction* (1954); Vol. II—*The Life Cycle and Consumer Behavior* (1955); Vol. III—*Consumer Reaction to Innovation and Obsolescence* (1957), New York University Press, New York.

Cochrane, W. W., & C. S. Bell, *The Economics of Consumption,* McGraw-Hill Book Co., New York, 1956.

Dewhurst, J. F., & Associates, *America's Needs and Resources: A New Survey,* Twentieth Century Fund, New York, 1955.

Gilbert, E., *Advertising and Marketing to Young People,* Printers' Ink Books, Pleasantville, N.Y., 1957.

Hoyt, E. E., and others, *American Income and its Use,* Harper & Bros., New York, 1954.

Huntington, E., *Spending of Middle-Income Families,* University of California Press, Berkeley, 1957.

Katona, G., & E. Mueller, *Consumer Attitudes and Demand, 1950–52,* Institute for Social Research, University of Michigan, Ann Arbor, 1953.

Katona, G., *Consumer Expectations; 1953–56,* Institute for Social Research, University of Michigan, Ann Arbor, 1956.

Kelley, P. C., *Consumer Economics,* Richard D. Irwin, Homewood, Ill., 1953.

Kyrk, H., *The Family in the American Economy,* University of Chicago Press, Chicago, 1953.

LIFE Study of Consumer Expenditures—Vol. I, LIFE, New York, 1957.

Lippitt, V. G., *Determinants of Consumer Demand for House Furnishings and Equipment,* Harvard Economic Studies, Harvard University Press, Cambridge, 1959.

Markets of the Sixties, FORTUNE, Printed by Harper & Bros., New York, 1960.

Mazur, P. M., *The Standards we Raise: The Dynamics of Consumption,* Harper & Bros., New York, 1953.

Miller, H. P., *Income of the American People,* John Wiley & Sons, New York, 1955.

Morgan, J. N., *Consumer Economics,* Prentice-Hall, Englewood Cliffs, N.J., 1955.

National Industrial Conference Board, *A Graphic Guide to Consumer Markets,* New York, 1960.

Taeuber, C., & I. B. Taeuber, *The Changing Population of the United States,* John Wiley & Sons, New York, 1958.

Troelstrup, A. W., *Consumer Problems and Personal Finance,* 2d ed, McGraw-Hill Book Co., New York, 1957.

Wilhelms, F. T., *Consumer Economics,* McGraw-Hill Book Co., New York, 1959.

Zelomek, A. W., *A Changing America,* John Wiley & Sons, New York, 1959.

CHAPTER 3

CONSUMER PSYCHOLOGY

As we noted in the introductory paragraphs of Chapter 2, a basic question that every manufacturer and wholesaler must ask, if he is to design or offer the products consumers want and advertise them effectively is, "Why do people buy my products—and how can others be induced to buy them?" Retailers must ask themselves the additional question, "Why do my customers buy from me, rather than from my competitor?" The search for answers to these questions has led Marketing into the intriguing field of consumer psychology.

Classical Economics assumed, in its analysis of demand factors, that consumer purchasing was essentially rationally motivated. Each individual was presumed to have clearly defined schedules of marginal preferences for all the items he desired, and to be more or less consciously aware of them. One of the major divergences that the study of Marketing soon made from its parent body of economic doctrine was to discard the myth of "rational economic man" and realize that many nonrational motivations, usually not consciously recognized, exercise a substantial influence on consumer buying.

During the 1920's, when the ground-breaking Marketing studies on consumer purchasing were being written, Psychology could offer students of Marketing little guidance on this subject. The early Marketing writers had to devise their own empirical classifications of the psychological drives that prompt consumer purchasing. Still influenced by their backgrounds in Classical economic theory, they posited two classes of buying motivations —rational and emotional. The rational ones covered such considerations as the desire for *physical* satisfaction from purchased items and the economic urge to "get the best value for the best buy." A broad list of possible emotional motivations was suggested, including pride, the spirit of emulation, and the desire for personal distinctiveness. This rational-emotional classification unfortunately started the study of Marketing on a misleading track with respect to consumer buying motivations. When a housewife buys a "bargain" regardless of its nonsuitability to her needs, or regularly buys the most expensive among a choice of brands because she assumes it is therefore best, or patronizes a store because it gives trading stamps, her economic motivations have a substantial emotional foundation. When a junior executive lives "beyond his means" in an effort to "keep up with the Joneses," it may be with the rational objective of maintaining an appearance of successful achievement for business reasons. The rational-emotional classification of consumer buying motivations has largely been abandoned by present-day Marketing writers.

The past two decades have seen considerable but scattered light shed upon the subject of consumer buying motivations from three sources. First, advertising agencies have made many tests of consumer reactions to alternative advertising appeals, with the practical objective of making their ads more effective. The results of these tests should be analyzed and generalized by psychologists, but to date the scholars best equipped to interpret them have ignored them. The same is largely true of the second source of data for the study of consumer buying motivations—analyses, often based on the test of experience, by salesmen and writers on salesmanship, of how people may be persuaded to buy. The third, the most recent and best organized approach to the subject, is "motivation research," a newly developed branch of marketing research.

Currently, students of Marketing have a considerable body of tested but unco-ordinated information, mixed with a mass of misinformation, on consumer buying motivations. Little has been done yet to sort out and build these data into a body of *knowledge* on consumer psychology. In our own approach to the subject we shall employ the traditional effective three-fold classification of consumer buying motivations into those related to product selection, those related to buying intent or habits, and those related to store patronage. The findings of recent advertising, salesmanship, and motivation research fit well into this classification.

CONSUMER PRODUCT PURCHASE MOTIVATIONS

When a woman buys a particular dress, her action is the culmination of many motivations, for the most part not consciously recognized. She is buying some physical comfort, in the form of protection from the elements. She may be buying zippered convenience. She is buying the pleasure of her personal esthetic satisfaction. She is buying the approval, and possibly the envy, of other women. She is buying the appreciative regard, perhaps of her husband, certainly of other men. And, since this dress presumably satisfies all of these desires better than any other that she has seen in the same price range, she feels that she is "getting her money's worth."

Consider the motivations that induce a man to buy a particular house. He ministers to his physical comfort by providing himself with shelter. He satisfies his esthetic sense of home architecture. The garden and game room promise him recreation. Fireproof construction relieves him of fear of conflagration. A deep-seated satisfaction will be derived from the feeling of property ownership. He is providing a home for the family he loves. He is acquiring a residence that will give him social standing in the community. At the price agreed upon, he feels that he has made a good long-term investment.

Nearly all consumer products are bought because they appeal to a complex of motivations on the part of their purchasers. Repeat buying of particular products or brands may be done largely on the basis of habit, but this habit had to be initiated through some motivation complex. Accurate understanding of these product purchase motivations is prerequisite to successful designing of products by manufacturers, to successful buying by wholesalers and retailers, and to effective advertising and selling by manufacturers and retailers. These motivations may be studied under the fourfold classification * of: (1) physical-functional, (2) personal, (3) social, and (4) economic.

Desire for physical services of the product

Most of the things we buy are purchased because, among other considerations, they provide us with some physical service. A chair is something to sit on, as well as an item of interior decoration. Pencils and ball pens write, with varying degrees of eradicability and convenience. The automobile, currently significant in terms of status symbol and psychological image projection, is also bought as a transportation vehicle with variant offerings, in different makes and models, of comfort and speed. A detergent cleanses. These basic physical services or functions of various products satisfy desires of which we are consciously aware, or have been made aware, by advertising or salesmen.

Personal motivations

There are four personal product purchase motivations derived from what the psychologists call "drives." Some of these we consciously recognize. Others are based on urges whose roots are embedded deep in the subconscious psychology of the human animal.

---

* There are almost as many classifications of consumer buying motivations as there are writers on the subject. One marketing research organization uses a check list of 600 possible motivations in preparing its surveys. The classification presented in the text has been selected as being comprehensive, avoiding excessive complication, and encompassing the findings of recent motivation research.

Pleasure. Pleasure, whether in the form of direct physical sensations or esthetic appeal, or through the complex of sensations and emotional reactions that constitute recreational activity, is an important motivation in many of our purchases. We buy a cut of meat for its flavor and tenderness, as well as for its nourshiment. To possess the breathless beauty of a set of Swedish glass tumblers, a man may pay fifty times more than cast-glass items would cost. When a woman buys an expensive dress, she pays more for the beauty and distinction it will add to her appearance than for protection from the elements. The sports and hobbies markets are based almost exclusively on the recreation motivation.

Relief from fear. We buy automobiles with safety glass windows against the danger of glass cuts in the chance of an auto accident. We pay for medical examinations to free us from nagging fears of illness and death. We buy various forms of insurance because we fear the financial perils of certain unfavorable contingencies such as fire and accidents. If we are farmers, we buy tractors redesigned to *look* heavier in front, to free ourselves of the subconscious fear that the tractors will topple over backwards when going uphill.

Sense of possession. The feeling that "This will be *mine* if I buy it" plays a considerable part in many purchases of durable goods. Real estate salesmen develop this theme in displaying properties to prospects. The automobile salesman constantly refers to the car being shown to a prospect as "your car" to arouse this motivation. It is the very foundation of collectors' purchasing.

Self esteem. From highest to humblest, every human being constantly tries to reassure himself, in some way or another, that he is important; few of us are completely free of a haunting sense of inadequacy. One way to numb this sense of inferiority is to buy things that give us a feeling of immediate material achievement, or that promise us future achievement. We buy automobiles "a block long" not merely to impress our associates, but to confirm to ourselves that we have "arrived." We buy expensive suits because "we owe it to ourselves to be well-dressed." We buy technical books, pay for school registrations, and subscribe to correspondence courses because we are ambitious to raise our economic or cultural status. Motivation research discovered that many women were refusing to buy powdered coffee that was advertised as being "instant" and "time-saving" because such concepts conflicted with their pride in being good and painstaking cooks; when the promotional emphasis in powdered coffee advertising was changed to "millions of flavor buds," their resistance evaporated. Shrewd advertisers and salesmen have found appeals to pride and self-esteem among the most effective weapons in their armory; witness the "man of distinction" approach, of so many advertisements, implying that a man will mark himself as a superior individual if he buys the advertised product.

Social motivations

Human beings are social animals. We live as units of families, among neighbors, as members of country clubs and other social organizations, as citizens of communities. Many of our actions are conditioned by our regard for the others in these groups, and by the value we place on their esteem for us. Such social considerations frame two more consumer buying motivations.

Love of others, particularly members of the family. A man does not buy life insurance for himself, but for his dependents. Purchases of children's items are made primarily for the good of the children rather than of the parents who do the buying; indeed, general purchasing by parents is substantially based on an effort to provide a desirable environment for their children. This concern of most human beings for their families, and sometimes for others outside the family group, is a major motivation for much consumer buying. The advertiser or salesman who fails to make the most of it under appropriate circumstances, either directly or through implication, is bound to miss many marketing opportunities.

Social regard. Practically all of us deliberately or unconsciously adjust our manner of living and much of our purchasing to the standards of whatever social group, large or small, we belong to at the moment. We do so in three ways—by *conforming* to the spending pattern of our group, by *emulating* those in our group who are an economic or social step above us, or by seeking personal *distinctiveness* through setting ourselves apart from the group in some detail that we consider favorable. That everyone else in our neighborhood or in our social or economic group is buying some item is commonly a powerful reason for our purchase of it. A man may buy an expensive car, or join a country club because these are "status symbols"—it is a way of "keeping up with the Joneses," or in some cases of "getting ahead of the Joneses." An individual who seeks distinctiveness in his or her social group may endeavor always to be the first buyer of a new item, or may be attracted by "exclusive" models. The effect of our purchases on our standing in our neighborhood or social group is a major motivation in consumer buying. Many items we buy are purchased in part because of their social symbolism.

Economic motivation

Finally, but of major importance as a product purchase motivation, most consumers weigh the value of the services that a particular commodity will render to them in terms of its price, and in relation to alternative commodities. For all family units except those at the highest income levels, most purchases are conditioned by considerations of the over-all family budget. One purchase frequently means some other purchase cannot be made; if the house is to be painted this year, the new car must wait until next year. The appeals of various alternative items to all the various motivations are weighed—in a qualitative rather than a consciously quantitative manner—and the one with the strongest combination of appeals wins.

This economic analysis of values appears still more strongly as a product purchase motivation when a purchaser is faced with making a choice between different models or brands of the same item. This car has superior riding comfort, that car has more economical gas consumption; this one brakes better, that one has better body lines. Here are two vacuum cleaners, roughly equivalent in their cleaning effectiveness, but the more expensive one is the more durable; this utility has to be weighed against the higher cost. Here are two cans of peas, an expensive one, widely advertised, and a cheap one of unknown brand; the shopper weighs the virtues which advertising has led her to believe she will find in the first can, against her ignorance of the quality of the peas in the second can.

Utility and quality

Our analysis of consumer product purchase motivations provides a guide to the understanding of "utility" and "quality" in products.

The *utility* of a product is the sum total of the ways it satisfies all the physical, personal, and social buying motivations. The utility embodied in any product, in the first analysis, is essentially an individual matter. If a Mozart record gives pleasure to A, but not to B who is a rock-'n-roll fan, it has utility for A but not for B. An expensive car that has "snob appeal" for C, but not for D who is not interested in impressing his associates that way, possesses an extra element of utility for C absent in D's case. By cumulating all the varying appeals that a product has for all the people who might be interested in buying it, we can set up a generalized economic utility for each product.

Quality is the collective market judgment on the *comparative* degree to which different models, makes, or brands of a particular product satisfy possible combinations of consumer buying motivations other than price considerations. Sometimes quality involves the more efficient satisfaction of consumer comfort or convenience; a better quality fabric may give greater warmth. Or the quality factor may lie in greater esthetic appeal— the flavor of a particular brand of processed food may be preferred by a predominant group of consumers to that of other brands. Sometimes superior quality may consist of greater "snob" appeal—the extra chromium trimmings that distinguish the de luxe model of an automobile. In some cases, greater durability or higher efficiency in operation may be the determinant of quality.

When consumers are faced with a choice of qualities in various models or brands of a product, usually at different prices, the economic buying motivation of rational analysis of value comes into play. An article of superior quality offered at the same price as competing items of inferior quality will, given equivalent promotion and selling effort, outsell inferior items. Or it may be offered at a higher price and find a special market of buyers who are willing to pay more for superior quality. Because of price differences usually associated with quality differences, higher quality items do not necessarily or even usually drive lower quality competitors out of the market. The varying family expenditure patterns produced by income differences cause some purchasers to find their best values in lower-quality items at lower prices while others find theirs in higher-quality items at higher prices. The consequence is the existence of special markets for different quality grades of particular products.

Style and fashion

The product purchase motivations of esthetic pleasure and social regard require discretionary purchasing power for their exercise. Once discretionary purchasing power is present, these motivations come strongly into play in our buying of clothing, houses, home furnishings, automobiles, and other product lines. Our purchase of these items takes into account their "style," and whether or not they are "fashions." "Style" is a *characteristic* or *distinctive* mode or method of conception, expression, or presentation in any field involving esthetic aspects. It is some significant element of esthetic creation, be it in a pure art or in an applied one such as dress or furniture design, peculiar to an individual or a related creative group. If a style succeeds in appealing to immediate mass criteria of social acceptability and/or beauty, we call it a "fashion." * Within the scope of a basic "fashion," infinite variations in minor detail can be incorporated to cater to individual preferences, so long as these variations do not distort the basic mass-accepted elements of the design.

In product lines other than clothing and automobiles, the personal buying motivation of esthetic pleasure generally outweighs social motivations of conformity and emulation. But individual standards of beauty are rarely arrived at independently. They are dominated by the judgments of the herd. Our individual standards have usually been unconsciously conditioned by continuous exposure to popular tastes, so that our individuality tends to express itself only in relatively minor variances from these tastes. However, on esthetic matters the herd commonly does not have sharp convictions and single judgments. It may be split into two or more camps,

* Note that in popular usage, "style" is frequently but incorrectly used as synonymous with "fashion."

each of which has its own standards of what is beautiful in design but with tolerance for the view of the other camps. Thus, in product lines where esthetic considerations rule rather than concepts of what is socially correct, two or more broadly accepted styles can coexist for long periods. In suburban architecture the "modern," "colonial," and "ranch" styles all have their devotees, and suburban homes will be built in each of these styles for many years to come. In furniture there is quite a choice among the styles in which a home decorator may express herself.

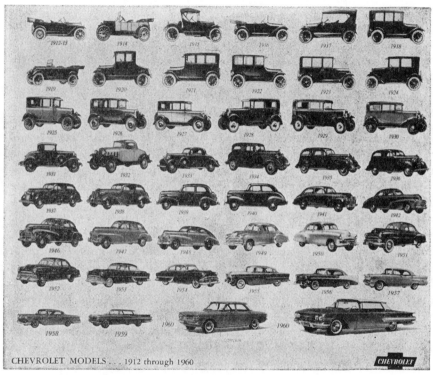

CHEVROLET MODELS . . . 1912 through 1960

EVOLUTION OF A PRODUCT STYLE: THE CHEVROLET AUTOMOBILE BODY. *Courtesy of the Chevrolet Division of General Motors Corp.*

ILLUSTRATION 3–1

Style acceptance based primarily on esthetic considerations evolves, but slowly. To some extent the change results from slow evolution of various elements in the cultural pattern of the nation. Change comes about, also, because technological innovations in production may make new materials available or certain features of design more practical. Change is produced, also, by deliberate effort on the part of manufacturers. If the design of a product, while conforming to an accepted basic style, can embody some variation from the norm that will have special appeal to a particular group of buyers, their demand for it will be intensified. This procedure of deliberate "diversification" of style products, with some variants gaining market acceptance and others failing to do so, is in effect a process of "market selection" that keeps styles evolving in conformity with changes in popular taste.

In product lines where considerations of social correctness rather than esthetics dominate consumer buying motivations, as in the case of women's wear, changes in basic design elements do not occur gradually, but so drastically and rapidly that we have short-term fashions rather than long-term style acceptance. Changes in popular taste in these lines do not develop through an unco-ordinated blind mass groping, but are deliberately organized through the efforts of two groups—the manufacturers and a small number of "fashion leaders." Design policy in the women's wear field, and to a lesser extent in the men's wear and automobile industries, is geared to the principle of "fashion obsolescence." Through concerted effort and agreement on design changes, the fashion of yesteryear is made the "out-of-fashion" of today, so that there may be a wider market for this year's production. This business policy is facilitated in the clothing lines by the existence of "fashion leaders," a small number of well-to-do women and men who seek personal prestige by being the first wearers of the manufacturers' new seasonal creations. These "leaders" are emulated by the social ranks below them. The buying motivation of conformity sweeps the mass of purchasers into line. The automobile industry has no "fashion leaders" to carry the ball for it in popularizing its design changes, and depends more upon advertising for its annual remolding of popular taste.

In women's wear, and to a lesser extent in men's and children's wear, there is a "fashion cycle." In each of these fields there are certain "innovating" manufacturers whose business is to make a limited number of high-priced "new creations"; in the case of women's dresses, French designers dominate the field. Some of the "new creations" win the favor of the "fashion leaders." Their selections are vigorously publicized by the fashion press, whose very existence depends on the broad interest in fashions produced by "fashion obsolescence." "Imitator" manufacturers quickly put out copies of the new fashions, in cheaper and ever cheaper models. Popularization of the new fashion progresses into mass acceptance, and the "imitator" manufacturers wage a furiously competitive struggle for shares of the mass market while it lasts. Meanwhile the "fashion leaders" have lost interest in these particular fashions, since mass acceptance ceases to give them distinctiveness. The "innovating" manufacturers are already producing the design modifications from which the "fashion leaders" will select the next fashions. By the following season, a new cycle will be under way.

Occasionally, some element of a short-term fashion will satisfy a previously unrecognized or newly developed basic consumer demand. Then it is likely to persist beyond its initial season and become a long-accepted style element. "Country casuals" in clothes, for example, were a new fashion in 1950. They proved so ideally suited to many aspects of suburban living and to expanding leisure-time out-of-doors living that they became a new style field, subject to its own fashion developments. The basic design modification of women's bathing suits from the bloomers-and-tent of the turn of the century to today's bikini-and-bra provides another example of style evolution underlying a sequence of yearly fashion changes.

CONSUMER PURCHASING INTENT

Writers on Marketing have long noted and analyzed four different degrees of consumer purchasing intent: (1) impulse buying; (2) convenience buying; (3) shopping; and (4) specific intent or "specialty" buying. This "purchasing intent" classification provides a basis for studying such retailing topics as the economic geography of retailing, retail store classification, store location, retail promotion, and retail selling.* It is also an important guide to manufacturers in determining the most effective channels of distribution for their goods, and in framing their packaging, advertising, and selling policies.

Impulse buying

A considerable proportion of consumer buying is done on impulse, without specific prior intent to purchase a particular item, or to purchase it at the particular time and place. A housewife doing her weekly food buying in a supermarket from a previously prepared list sees a display of a new sudsless detergent—something she had not thought of purchasing —and decides to give it a trial; or a conveniently placed display of a new brand of some item she has previously bought in another brand may prompt her to try the new one. A man walking along a street sees a tobacco store, remembers that he has only three cigarettes left in the package in his pocket, and drops in to buy another package; when he is in the store he sees a display of wallets, and is reminded that he has been thinking of replacing his present worn one.

---

* This classification has also been used as a basis for a four-fold classification of consumer goods—i.e., impulse goods, convenience goods, shopping goods, and specialties. The difficulty with this classification of *goods* is that any given item is likely to be bought by some consumers or under certain circumstances upon impulse, on a convenience basis, on a shopping basis, or on a specialty basis. A more useful approach is to avoid placing any product rigidly into any one of these four categories, but to analyze the marketing consequences resulting from the extent to which it is bought on an impulse basis, the extent to which it is bought on a convenience basis, etc.

With persons of moderate income, impulse in buying is largely with respect to the time and place of purchasing items which would have been purchased eventually in any case. If the impulse is directed at buying outside the scope of their regular purchasing, the object is usually an item of small price. A wealthy individual, however, may indulge a buying impulse regardless of the price tag. A dress costing hundreds of dollars or a piece of jewelry costing thousands may be bought on impulse if its display in a window or a show case catches the eye of the right person. The increase of discretionary purchasing power, noted in Chapter 2, has expanded the scope of impulse buying.

Some retailers, like costume jewelry and tobacco products stores, depend primarily upon impulse buying. For practically all stores it is a consideration of some importance. Some 70 percent of supermarket sales are items that housewives had no specific intention of buying when they entered the store. Impulse is the basis of many of the sales in department store cosmetics and notions departments. A shoe store may carry profitable "impulse" sidelines of stockings, handbags, and other accessories. Many beauty parlors find supplementary profit in a small display of novelty jewelry.

Stimulation of impulse buying should be an objective of practically every store. It should be a consideration in planning store layout, and a determinant of display and selling methods. The very location of a store depending largely on impulse buying is predetermined by this factor. As we shall see in later chapters of this volume, manufacturers of items bought to any substantial extent on impulse must also adapt their packaging, advertising, sales promotion, and channel-of-distribution policies to this circumstance.

Convenience buying

A large proportion of consumer purchases are of staple items bought intentionally and frequently. Groceries, toilet articles, nonprescription drugs, gasoline, and many hardware items are examples. When we go out to buy such items we know just what and how much we want. Generally we have particular brand preferences, where a number of brands of an item are on the market, but such brand preference is rarely so strong that we will not switch to another comparable brand if our preferred brand is not readily available. The major consideration in the buying of such items by most consumers is convenience—expenditure of a minimum of effort in comparison and buying. They are bought in the nearest store, or in one customarily patronized for some special reason. If the convenient or customary store does not have the preferred brand, an alternate brand will be accepted. If the prices of certain items are a few cents higher in the convenient or customary store than in one a few blocks away, or even a few doors away, these items may nontheless be bought in the convenient or customary store to avoid the time and trouble of going to the other store.

Almost all types of stores in small communities depend largely on the "convenience" factor for their patronage. In large cities, food stores, stationery stores, hardware stores, and drug stores draw and hold their customers through convenience. Department and variety stores owe their very existence to the convenience they offer of being able to buy many different lines of consumer goods "under one roof." It is the consideration of convenience buying that has induced supermarkets and many drug stores to add so many supplementary lines of merchandise that in some cases their "major" line accounts for only a minor proportion of their sales. As we shall see in the next chapter, this consideration of convenience buying is a major factor in the economic geography of retailing. For many manufacturers it is a key determinant of their channel-of-distribution and advertising policies.

Shopping

If a product is durable or semi-durable and so bought only at intervals, particularly if it comes in a variety of models or designs with a range of prices, or is sold at different prices in different stores, consumers are likely to make their purchases on a "shopping" basis. They start out with a clear intent, more or less, to buy some item in the general field, but first they want to compare a variety of offerings as to suitability, quality, style, and price. Possibly the entire comparison may be made in a single store that carries a wide assortment of the item. Possibly it is made by going from one store to another. Even in lines and stores where convenience buying dominates, some "shopping" comparison may occur. Some houeswives spread their regular household buying among three or four grocery stores to take advantage of price differences of a few cents per pound or per can for various items. One of the reasons for the popularity of supermarkets is the opportunity given housewives to "shop among" various brands of a particular item, weighing quality (according to label description) and price.

A significant retailing development of recent years is a decline of "shopping" by women. One reason is a reduction in their leisure time, either because more of them are now employed or because the declining supply and rising cost of domestic help confines them more to their homes. As a consequence, some lines of merchandise that were formerly bought primarily on a "shopping" basis are now purchased substantially on a "convenience" approach. Women's hose and undergarments have felt this influence. Another reason is that advertising has built up such strong brand preferences in some lines that what were formerly primarily shopping goods have become primarily "specific intent" goods. A number of house furnishings and household appliance lines have made this transition. This decline in "shopping" accounts for a number of important recent institutional changes in the retailing field which will be noted in subsequent chapters.

Specific intent buying

A manufacturer may include some special design or quality feature in his product or line of products, not found in the competing lines of other manufacturers, which gives it a special buying appeal to a sizable group of consumers, so that they insist on buying that particular product or line even at a higher price than competing ones. They will accept no substitute, but will go to a particular store to buy the product there, if that is the only place where it can be bought. Or, advertising may persuade a sizable group of consumers that a product is superior in some respect to competing items, and they will insist on purchasing it. When a product is thus bought with specific intent by a sizable consumer group, we call it a "specific intent" or "specialty" good.* Among the lines where speciality goods are most commonly found are expensive furniture, home appliances, automobiles, higher-priced clothing lines, expensive perfumes, and various "fancy" grocery items.

It should be an objective of every manufacturer to make his goods, as far as practicable, specialty goods. It should be an objective of every retailer to win a special-intent clientele. Thereby a manufacturer or retailer gains an element of quasi-monopoly and frees himself from some of the stringencies of competition. For a manufacturer, there are two means by which his products may achieve "specialty" status. He can diversify his goods by producing them in a variety of sizes and models not duplicated by his competitors, so that they conform more closely to special demands or desires of particular market elements. Or through advertising and other forms of promotion he may win a degree of "brand loyalty" that will hold some consumers more or less as a "captive market." A store wins "special intent" recognition by building up institutional goodwill. This may be accomplished in a number of ways—by achieving an outstanding low-price

---

* The term "specialty" has several meanings in retailing usage. As applied to goods, it has the meaning given above in the text. As applied to stores, particularly in the combination term "specialty shop," it most commonly means a women's wear store. It is also sometimes applied to stores that carry primarily "specific intent" goods or a restricted class of shopping goods. To minimize confusion, the terms "specialty store" or "specialty shop" will not be used in this text. A store carrying "specific intent" goods, or to which customers go with specific intent to patronize that particular store, will be called a "specific intent" store.

reputation, by achieving an outstanding quality reputation, by offering a selection of goods in its field that appeals especially to the taste of some special customer-group, by offering special customer services, by the winning personality of its proprietor, or by the superior courtesy of its sales clerks.

RETAIL PATRONAGE MOTIVATIONS AND APPEALS

Why do the customers of a particular store buy from it rather than from other stores offering identical or similar items?

The motivations for store patronage are the same as those for product purchase, except that sense of possession has no opportunity to operate. Personal motivations of *convenience* and *pleasure,* and the economic motivation of *getting the most for our money* play major roles in determining our selection of the stores in which we buy. The personal motivations of *relief from fear* and *self-esteem,* and the social motivations of *love of family* and *social regard* are less important generally in establishing store allegiance, but may be quite significant for particular individuals or under particular circumstances.

The major patronage appeals that stores can make, on the basis of these motivations, are the following:

1. *Price.* For some economy-minded individuals, price may be the all-important consideration in their retail buying. They are ready to forego customer services, sacrifice convenience, and ignore all other considerations to save a few cents or dollars on each purchase. Most consumers will favor a lower-pricing retailer, all other things being equal. But "all other things" include the remainder of the retail patronage appeals we are to consider, and they rarely are equal. So price becomes, for most retail buying, just one among a number of patronage appeals. A special aspect of price appeal is the lure for most women of a "sale," a store premium, or trading stamps. The prospect of a "bargain," of an apparent "something for nothing," will draw many into a store that they might not otherwise patronize, and give it an opportunity to win them as patrons.

2. *Location convenience.* When we make repeated purchases of food items, household supplies, toilet items and other staples of daily living, we give great weight to convenience of store location. Unless one of the other retail patronage appeals has considerable influence, we tend to patronize the nearest store—nearest to our residence if we live in a city, nearest to the other stores where we do our "convenience" buying if we live in a rural area or in a small community. This appeal has much less weight, of course, if we go out to purchase high-cost items with a shopping or special intent.

3. *Selection offered.* All of us have our personal preferences as to

quality range, esthetic taste, and fashion interest in the various items we buy. Naturally, where a choice of stores is available, we patronize those whose offerings most closely approximate our tastes. A wide selection of offerings within our personal taste range permits us to make shopping comparisons in one store, which is an added attraction. So a retailer who offers a wider selection in his line than competing stores has a double advantage; he can satisfy a wider range of personal tastes, and he can make a "shopping" appeal to many of his customers.

4. *Customer services.* When American consumers do their retail buying, they commonly want to purchase various "convenience" services as well as goods—delivery of their purchases to their homes, credit, "kiddie korners" where children are looked after while their mothers shop, the privilege of returning purchased goods upon subsequent change of mind, alterations on ready-made clothing, possibly the modelling of expensive dresses, pleasant rest rooms if extended shopping tours are involved. Provision of one or more such services by a store, particularly a store catering to "shopping" customers, is an important patronage inducement. Of course, such services add to a store's operating costs, and these may have to be reflected in higher prices, so that the price patronage appeal is reduced.

5. *Appearance.* A store can appeal to the pleasure motivation by its appearance—the architecture of its facade, its internal decor. A related pleasure appeal is the wooing of customers' ears by music.

6. *Store sales personnel.* Often we patronize a particular grocery store or drug store or other neighborhood shop, to the partial exclusion of price, convenience and other considerations, because the proprietor has an engaging personality and we like him. A large store that normally would depend upon shopping patronage may become a specific intent store and hold a faithful clientele because its sales clerks have been trained and inspired to exceptionally courteous and helpful service. Good store personnel can add pleasure to the other attractions of a store. The proper touch of deference in their attitude can flatter customer self-esteem.

7. *Other appeals.* Many minor considerations may influence the patronage or avoidance of particular stores by particular individuals. Some persons, especially the families of independent store owners, refuse to buy in chain outlets. Unkempt stores may lose patronage because they arouse health fears. "Snob appeal" unquestionably accounts for some of the patronage of metropolitan "exclusive" dress shops.

REVIEW

1. Name the eight consumer product purchase motivations. How might they influence the design, advertising and selling of some commodity other than a woman's dress or a home?

2. Explain "utility," "quality."

3. Explain "style" and "fashion." Explain the "fashion cycle."

4. Explain the significance to retailers and their operations of: (a) impulse buying; (b) convenience buying; (c) shopping; (d) specific intent buying. What significance does each of these types of consumer buying intent have for manufacturers' product planning and distribution policies?

5. List the major retail patronage appeals, and explain how each might influence your family's retail buying.

DISCUSSION TOPICS

1. Is it right to use our growing psychological knowledge to manipulate consumer purchasing through designing products, advertising, and selling in such a way as to appeal to subconscious and nonrational motivations?

2. What consumer purchase motivations are appealed to by the following advertising slogans?

a. "A thinking man's filter; a smoking man's taste" (cigarette).

b. "Good to the last drop" (coffee).

c. "79,000,000 jars sold last year" (medicament).

d. "Sales in millions; profits in pennies" (department store).

e. "Gentle as mother's hands" (baby talc).

f. "We won't be undersold" (department store).

3. To what extent are we likely to get better value for our money when we buy a higher-quality item at a higher price than a lower-quality one at a lower price?

4. Does fashion make sense?

5. Supermarkets started as food stores. Now they carry household items, tobacco products, toilet items, paper-back books, hosiery, and many other items. They are still increasing their non-food lines. How do you account for this trend?

6. How is it possible for so many small independent stores, with narrower selections and higher prices than nearby chain outlets, to remain in competition with them?

PROBLEM

A leading American automobile manufacturer that currently makes a high-priced "heavy" car two inches longer than any other American car is planning to bring out a new low-price "compact" car with high mileage to the gallon.

1. Apart from size, what differences in body design should be incorporated in the new car? Why?

2. What differences in motivational appeals would there be between the two cars?

3. How would these differences in motivational appeals be embodied in the advertising of the two cars?

SUGGESTED READINGS

American Management Association, *Changing Patterns in Distribution,* Marketing Series No. 83, 1952.

Bindra, D., *Motivation: A Systematic Reinterpretation,* Ronald Press, New York, 1959.

Cheskin, L., *Why People Buy,* Liveright Publishing Corp., New York, 1959.

Clark, L. H., & J. B. Carney (eds.), *Consumer Behavior: Research on Consumer Reactions,* Harper & Bros., New York, 1958.

Crawford, M. D. C., *One World of Fashion,* 2d ed, Fairchild Publishing Co., New York, 1955.

Davidson, W. R., & P. L. Brown, *Retailing Management,* 2d ed, Ronald Press, New York, 1960.

Dichter, E., *The Strategy of Desire,* Doubleday & Co., New York, 1960.

Ferber, R., & H. Wales (eds.), *Motivation and Market Behavior,* Richard D. Irwin, Homewood, Ill., 1958.

Katona, G., *The Powerful Consumer,* McGraw-Hill Book Co., New York, 1960.

Katona, G., *Psychological Analysis of Economic Behavior,* McGraw-Hill Book Co., New York, 1951.

Packard, V., *The Hidden Persuaders* (1957), *The Status Seekers* (1959), David McKay Co., New York.

Reisman, D., *The Lonely Crowd,* Yale University Press, New Haven, Conn., 1950.

Schreier, F. T., *Human Motivation: Probability and Meaning,* Free Press, Chicago, 1957.

Trends in Consumer Behavior: The Next Ten Years, Foundation for Research on Human Behavior, 1141 E. Catherine St., Ann Arbor, Mich., 1958.

Why Do People Buy?, FORTUNE, Printed by Mc-Graw-Hill Book Co., New York, 1953.

PART TWO

MARKETING
INSTITUTIONS

At the very outset of our institutional analysis of Marketing we are faced with a major issue—how broad shall our definition of "marketing institutions" be? As indicated in Chapter 1, a broad definition covering every classification of business enterprise that engages in marketing activities would have to include manufacturers, farmers, mining and forestry enterprises, and service enterprises, since individuals and companies in each of these categories unquestionably perform a wide range of marketing activities in beginning the distributive movement of the goods and services they produce. In many fields, indeed, manufacturers and service operators account for most of the marketing operations in their lines. Consumers as a class might also be considered a "marketing institution" under a broad definition of the term, since their buying activities influence all marketing operations right back to those of the initial manufacturers, farmers, and other producers.

For our institutional analysis in Part Two, we shall confine the meaning of "marketing institutions" to those business organizations whose *major* interest and activity is some group of marketing operations. This narrow definition excludes consumers on the one side, and manufacturers, farmers, service enterprises, and other "producers" on the other. This does not mean that we shall not consider the roles of these economic groups in Marketing. We have already noted some consumer marketing factors in Chapters 2 and 3, and will have frequent occasion in subsequent chapters to deal with other consumer marketing influences. Farmers' contributions to the distribution of their crops are studied in Part Three, where the general subject of agricultural marketing is considered. Manufacturers' marketing operations dominate several of the chapters in Part Four.

With our Part Two treatment of marketing institutions limited to those whose major purpose and activity is some group of marketing operations, we find three broad classes of such institutions—retailers, wholesaling middlemen, and "facilitating" marketing organizations which assist the marketing activities of other organizations but do not engage directly, either on their own behalf or as agents, in the purchase and sale of goods. The business organizations in each of these major classifications have specialized, with resulting increased efficiency, in certain categories of marketing operations—retailers in immediate distribution to consumers, wholesaling middlemen in middleman operations exclusive of direct distribution to consumers, facilitating agencies in a wide range of particular marketing operations other than actual buying and selling. Within each of these three classifications are many institutional subclasses—for example, supermarkets and mail order houses among types of retailers, full-service merchant wholesalers and manufacturers' agents among types of wholesalers, and advertising agencies and commodity exchanges among types of facilitating agencies. Each of these institutional subclasses represents still further specialization in retailing method or structure, in scope of wholesaling operations, or in some special set of marketing operations apart from actual buying and selling. Each has come into existence because it fulfills some marketing need of consumers, or of the business system, more efficiently than other pre-existing types of business. The list of business classifications that can be considered marketing institutions is long; it could not be otherwise because of the multiplicity of special consumer and business marketing needs.

The simplest and most understandable approach to the study of American marketing institutions, as we have defined them, is to begin with those which are most familiar to the majority of students. These are the retailers. Since the operations of important classes of wholesaling middlemen are substantially conditioned by the character of the retailers they supply, such an approach has logical as well as pedagogical advantages. Accordingly, the next five chapters are devoted to the study of retailing and retailers—the general economic geography of retailing, how retailers are organized, the services and operations they perform, and significant trends in store development and management. This analysis of retailers leads naturally to a survey of the organization and activities of wholesaling middlemen. Two chapters are devoted to this topic. The final chapter of Part Two covers certain classes of facilitating marketing organizations.

CHAPTER 4

RETAILING AND RETAILERS: GENERAL CONSIDERATIONS

A *retail sale* is a sale of goods to an *ultimate consumer* for *personal* consumption or use.

Retailing may be defined as the operations involved in selling directly to ultimate consumers. It is the final link in the chain of distribution of most products from initial producers to ultimate consumers.

Retailers are business units engaged *primarily* in retailing.* On the basis of legal structure, they may be individual enterprises, partnerships, business corporations, or mutual (cooperative) enterprises. They may operate as single establishments, or as chain or branch systems.

Retail sales may be made, and retailing activities may be performed, by business units that are not retailers. A manufacturer may sell his output direct to ultimate consumers by direct mail, by a sales force of house-to-house canvassers, or through his own retail outlets. A farmer may sell all or part of the vegetables and fruits he raises to consumers from a road-side stand. A wholesaler may do some incidental selling to consumers. But so long as such retail selling constitutes only a *minor* activity of these enterprises, we cannot classify them as retailers.

Note also that retailers may engage in nonretailing activities. Large mail order houses, department stores, or chain systems commonly buy and store their merchandise in ways more consonant with wholesaling than with retailing procedures. Occasionally retailers do some wholesaling as a sideline

---

* For reasons of tradition, the *Census of Business* classifies farm equipment and office supplies and equipment distributors who operate with selling premises as "retailers."

to their basic retailing business. Some local food stores sell to small restaurants, which subsequently serve these purchases to their customers. Hardware retailers often sell minor household installations and building supplies to small-scale building contractors, who in turn charge them to their clients. So long as these nonretailing activities remain a minor element, however, the concerns that engage in them are classified as retailers.

A *store* is a business establishment (in the physical sense), or a physically distinct section of a manufacturing or service establishment, used primarily for retail selling. Small stores are commonly called "shops," or "stands" if they are not enclosed. Most retailing is done through stores operated by retailers. As we shall see in Chapter 7, however, there are retailers who operate without stores, and there are retail outlets that might be called "stores" operated by businesses that are not retailers.

Our available business statistics relate generally to retailers rather than to retailing. But since retailers do all except a minute fraction of retailing and engage to only a minor extent in nonretailing activities, generalizations about retailers apply substantially to retailing. By the measures of number of business enterprises involved, number of people engaged or employed, and contribution to national income, retailers are definitely one of our nation's major business groups. As of 1958 there were some 1,900,000 retail establishments, which engaged or employed over 8,500,000 people—over 14 percent of the nation's gainfully employed. In 1959 retailers accounted for $43 billion of the national income, 11 percent of the total. They ranked behind manufacturers, but ahead of farmers, construction enterprises, service enterprises, and every other business grouping, in their relative contribution.

RETAILERS' OPERATIONS

What do retailers do to account for the important place they occupy in the national economy?

Economic functions

The retailer is the ultimate agent in accomplishing the three economic functions of Marketing that were stated in Chapter 1:

1. He makes a substantial contribution to Marketing's creation of *place utility*. Prior to purchase by the retailer, goods desired by consumers were located in wholesalers' warehouses and manufacturers' store rooms, their whereabouts generally unknown to consumers and difficult to reach. The retailer brings these goods into the shopping centers frequented by consumers, or even into the very neighborhoods of their residence. They are placed on shelves before the consumers' eyes, or on self-service counters where consumers' hands can reach them; and for those items that

cannot be made visible on shelves or counters, there is the old retailing slogan, "If you don't see it, ask for it." Finally, in many cases, after sales are made, the retailer delivers the purchased items to the consumers' homes —which for most consumer goods is the only place their use value can develop.

2. The retailer usually makes some contribution to the *time utility* of the goods he sells. He buys hours in advance of the time he resells (in the case of fresh fruits and vegetables), or days in advance, or weeks in advance, or months in advance (in the case of certain lines of jewelry), so consumers will be able to obtain the items they want *when they want them.* Storage, however, is not a major function for most retailers. Good retail management, as will be explained in Chapter 8, is directed at maintaining high rates of inventory turnover, which means that the average time that goods are in a retailer's store rooms or on his shelves should be held to a practical minimum. If protracted storing of a product is necessary to its efficient distribution, other marketing units are better equipped to perform this function than the retailer. But in maintaining his necessary operating inventories, the retailer creates some time utility.

3. Of the retailer's major contribution to the creation of *possession utility*—getting goods out of the hands of individuals or organizations for whom they have no use value, and into the hands of ultimate consumers who can use them and who therefore want them—there can be no question. Manufacturers and occasionally wholesalers by their advertising and sales promotion activities may have done much to make consumers want particular items which the manufacturers produce and the wholesalers handle. Nevertheless, it is the retailer who hands the items over to consumers. Often, moreover, by display and effective selling, the retailer reminds or actually persuades consumers that they want these particular items.

Marketing operations

To the consumer who patronizes a store, its principal operation appears to be selling—passive or active according to the nature of the items purchased, the extent to which the customer has already made up his mind as to what he will purchase, and the store policies. Actually, retailers as a class participate in all the Marketing operations—product planning, buying, storage, pricing, promotion, selling, utilization of market information, credit extension, market financing, and risk bearing—studied in Part Four of this book. For product planning and some other of these Marketing operations, retailer participation is relatively slight. Buying, pricing, promotion, selling, and credit, on the contrary, are major aspects of retailing activity. We shall analyze these operational aspects of retailing more fully in Part Four.

ECONOMIC GEOGRAPHY OF RETAILING

Some long-established large mail order houses, metropolitan department stores, and chain systems serve customers in broad areas or even all over the country. The characteristic retailer's market, however, is a local one. A typical retail merchant draws his customers primarily from his own community; not infrequently he serves only the residents of a small neighborhood area.

A retailer's general business ability influences to some extent the size of his trading area. Customers will frequently bypass a near, but inferior, store and patronize a distant one whose proprietor or manager has a more winning personality, or which has a more attractive appearance, or which offers lower prices, a wider selection of goods, or better service, or otherwise makes a superior appeal to some retail patronage motivation, even where the buying of convenience goods is involved. The main factors that determine the area from which a store can derive its patronage, however, are: (1) the character of the consumer buying intent to which the store primarily appeals—impulse, convenience, shopping, or specific intent buying; (2) the population size of the community in which the store is located, whether rural, suburban, urban, or metropolitan; and (3) a combination of transportation and communication factors, such as highways, motor bus routes, railway passenger routes and schedules, parcel post zone provisions, telephone rate zones, newspaper circulation, and spot radio and TV coverage. In the discussion that follows, these factors will provide the foundation for analyzing the retailing structure of rural communities, cities, metropolitan areas, and suburban areas. The principle of retail trade gravitation, which determines the demarcation between contiguous retail trading areas, is also derived from these three factors.

Rural retailing centers

The "retail trading area" centering on a village or small town * is quite different in its buying characteristics from that of a city and its environs, and the retailing business of such a rural retailing center has a distinctive character. The population of a rural retail trading area is usually too small to support a large department store, or an adequate assortment of stores carrying shopping and specific-intent goods in the village or town on which

---

* The Bureau of the Census and the Definitions Committee of the American Marketing Association define "trading area" only in terms of the individual selling establishment, not collectively for any contiguous group of retailers or wholesalers, on the ground that any common denominator in the individual trading areas of the individual members of such a group is rarely if ever possible to determine. If the concept of a collective trading area is not given a strict quantitative connotation, however, it can be a useful tool for elementary analysis, at least, of retailing geography.

it centers. Hence most of the purchasing of shopping goods for such an area is done either in some not-too-distant city or through mail order.

Village and town stores cater primarily to convenience buying, with scattered selections of impulse offerings. In some villages one store—a country "general store"—still offers all the retailing service locally available to the retail trading area. It carries broad lines of staple foodstuffs, basic hardware and household items, a limited selection of toilet articles and non-prescription drugs; outside is a gasoline pump. Few shopping or specialty goods are to be found, since the proprietor knows that his customers buy these items elsewhere. A town group of stores usually consists of several food stores (of which one may be a supermarket), an independent or chain variety store, a hardware store, a drug store, a stationery store, and several auto service stations.

Often these village and town stores enjoy a virtual location quasi-monopoly, since their nearest competitors may be miles distant. Their prices tend to run substantially higher than those of corresponding city stores. Usually this higher markup does not result in relative larger profit, since turnover on many items is necessarily slower than in city stores, and many country stores are inefficiently operated.

Small-city retailing centers

Communities with populations from 2,500 to 100,000 serve not only as over-all retailing centers for their own populations, but also as shopping and specialty-goods centers for a surrounding circle of rural territory usually including a number of rural retailing centers such as were described above. These small-city shopping centers support many different types of retail establishments, and are favored locations for units of chain store systems in variety lines, women's ready-to-wear and accessories, and general department stores. The casual traveler who visits a number of these small cities will be struck with the elements of similarity in their retail pattern. Although the communities may differ widely in their physical and industrial structure, their shopping centers are strikingly alike, supporting not only the same types of stores, but almost identical units of the same chain systems.

The choice of shopping goods in any line is not as wide, in any particular store or among competing stores, as in the metropolitan shopping centers, but it is usually enough to satisfy all but the most critical shoppers. Through their use of resident buying offices (explained in Chapter 10) located in the country's fashion centers, small-city department stores and women's wear stores are able to supply their customers with the latest and best current fashions.

For advertising media, small-city department and specialty-goods stores use the local daily or weekly newspaper, which is mailed throughout the city trading area, and "spot" radio and TV stations. Thus their promotional story reaches their rural customers as well as those actually resident in the city. Rural customers frequently order by mail, beside making occasional "shopping" trips into the city. Deliveries to rural customers are made by parcel post and by the package delivery services that now operate in many of these communities.

Metropolitan retailing centers

A city with a population of several hundred thousand, particularly one with a population over a million, has too wide a territorial expansion for its retailing to be concentrated on a single main street or in a single center. A process of partial retailing decentralization develops when a city grows into a metropolis. As a result, the retailing structure of a large city usually includes: (1) a central shopping district; (2) one or more secondary shopping districts; (3) neighborhood retailing centers; and (4) scattered retail sections.

The *central shopping district* of a metropolitan center is a grouping of large department stores and of shops offering particular lines of shopping goods—men's apparel, women's ready-to-wear and accessories, furniture, floor coverings, radio and television, photographic and home movie equipment, and innumerable others. Here, too, will be found many stores carrying specialty goods which may be comparison-shopped as to price. Also located here will be some large units of variety chains, novelty shops, and other stores catering to impulse buying, which thrive on the heavy shopping traffic.

The department stores and large limited-line stores of a metropolitan central shopping district draw their customers not only from the entire city, and from the suburban area around the city, but also from the country as a whole and even from abroad. Out-of-town visitors to a metropolis take advantage of their stay there to shop in its major stores for items which their home communities cannot provide. And no traveler from South America, the Antipodes, or Europe, who passes through New York City, misses the opportunity to patronize the wonder stores of that world shopping center.

Not infrequently, as a metropolitan community expands, one or more *secondary shopping districts* develop within it. These secondary centers may arise because physical barriers such as rivers, hills, parks, or railroads make it inconvenient for shoppers in one section of the city to reach the central "downtown" district. Where two or more such secondary centers are established, the combined volume of their shopping business may in time exceed that of the central district. Rarely, however, will two major shopping districts of equal importance exist in any large city; one tends to be primary or "central," the other "secondary." For example, in New York City the "downtown" shopping district located around 34th Street and along Fifth Avenue is the dominant shopping district of the city and the entire trading area. The secondary shopping district located in Brooklyn on Fulton Street serves as a center for the entire Brooklyn area but does not draw any substantial trade away from the central shopping district in Manhattan, as the Manhattan center does from Brooklyn. This type of central and secondary shopping district development has repeated itself in many other large communities: Chicago, Los Angeles, San Francisco, and Cleveland.

Large cities are likely to develop a number of *specialty* or *"category" centers*—a cluster of art galleries, another of interior decorator shops, a grouping of second-hand book shops, an "automobile row." The merchandise line featured in each of these specialty centers generally involves special intent buying, so that the customers of the stores that compose the center are willing to make deliberate trips to reach them. Consequently these centers may be located well away from the center of the city; the "auto row" of a large city may even be found at its outskirts. The grouping of the stores forming the center permits the customers to do comparison shopping within the line, to the mutual advantage of the stores in the group.

Neighborhood retailing centers, sometimes called "subcenters," characteristically develop at strategic points throughout a metropolis. They far outnumber the secondary shopping centers of the city, if any such exist. A neighborhood retailing center consists of a group of grocery stores, hardware stores, drug stores, stationery shops, and the like, commonly strung along a single street ("ribbon" development). These stores cater chiefly to convenience buying, with supplementary appeals to impulse buying. The market area of a neighborhood center is usually narrowly defined, the customers coming almost entirely from the immediate vicinity. These customers patronize their neighborhood stores primarily because of the convenience factor, and reserve their major shopping tours for visits to the downtown or secondary shopping districts.

Scattered *retail sections* are a rudimentary form of neighborhood retailing center. They occur in or near apartment buildings, in residential districts, on important traffic intersections, and in other locations where they can serve the convenience needs of nearby customers. The stores in these sections, characteristically small, have a small market. The majority of their customers are located within short walking distance. A retail section may be the beginning of a neighborhood retailing center. As the area develops, other stores may join the original group and a true retailing center may develop.

Suburban town shopping centers

During the past quarter-century, many suburban towns surrounding metropolitan cities have developed retailing centers that combine shopping and convenience purchasing facilities instead of limiting themselves essentially to convenience-goods stores, as most rural village and small-town retailing centers do. These suburban town shopping centers do not offer as wide a selection of shopping goods in any line as the neighboring metropolitan shopping centers, but they do offer their customers the advantages of being reached by relatively short automobile drives, and a fair provision of parking space. Since going any place by automobile is second nature to the suburban woman, these two conveniences take her to the nearest of these community shopping centers for a major part of her shopping buying —provided there is no integrated shopping center, as discussed below, within ten to fifteen miles of her residence.

These suburban town shopping centers have come into existence through two independent lines of development. Most were started when a metropolitan department store opened a branch, either in the pre-existing retailing center of a suburban community or on its outskirts where land cost was low and ample auto parking space could be provided cheaply. If this branch were successful, other branch department stores, women's wear shops, and home furnishings stores would take advantage of the already established shopping traffic and locate there. In space of time, a full-fledged shopping center would be in existence, serving not only the immediate suburban community but drawing customers from a wide radius.

Since World War II a considerable number of quite large suburban communities—"developments" of one to ten thousand homes—have been built as complete units by realty companies. In preplanning these communities, provision is made for a retailing center which will have not only all necessary convenience-line and impulse-line stores, but also a fair number of shopping goods stores. As in the case of suburban town centers that have developed without preplanning, these planned centers are favored locations for branches of metropolitan stores. The parent stores usually cooperate with the realty companies in designing the facilities that their branches will subsequently occupy. An advantage that these planned suburban town shopping centers have over the unplanned ones is better provision of parking areas.

Integrated suburban shopping centers *

While a few shopping centers of the type we may call "integrated" were constructed before 1945, the rapid and widespread expansion of this retailing institution is a post-War phenomenon. As of 1960, some 4,500 were in operation. Sales made through these centers in 1959 were around $40 billion, almost 20 percent of total retail sales.

A development company—usually a realty organization, but in some cases a subsidiary established by a department store or a supermarket chain to assure it favorable locations—acquires a substantial tract of land in a suburban territory, but outside of any settled communities, for the express purpose of erecting an integrated shopping center. Forty acres is considered the minimum requirement. Through market analysis the development company determines the present and prospective population of the suburban area to be served, its buying tastes and habits, and the retailing facilities currently serving the area. It contracts in advance of construction with at least two metropolitan department stores to locate branches in the proposed center, and erects the buildings for these branches according to the stores' specifications. Advance contracts are also made with other store organizations, chain and independent—a score or so in smaller centers, fifty or more in the larger ones. These other stores are primarily in shopping and specialty lines—women's ready-to-wear and accessories, men's wear, home furnishings, sporting goods, and others. A supermarket, a variety store, a drug store, a hardware store, and a few other convenience-goods stores are usually included; these are generally planned for customer self-service. The newer centers may also contain a civic auditorium, a movie theatre, a shoppers' restaurant, even a church or a chapel. Ground is always set aside for extensive parking facilities; a parking space three to four times the store area is the current formula. The site is landscaped with lawns, groves, pools, and fountains. Upon the well-advertised date of its "grand opening," such an integrated shopping center offers almost as broad a range of shopping facilities as any secondary metropolitan center.

While some of the first pioneer integrated centers experienced difficulties, most have been satisfyingly successful from the viewpoints both of their operators and of the stores that rent locations in them. Their appeals to their patrons are the convenience of "one-stop" shopping with a broad variety of selection in many lines, the certainty of auto parking space in an age when this is becoming desperately rare, and an attractive over-all atmosphere. The "pull" of these integrated centers spreads over a 15- to 20-

---

* There is no agreement among Marketing writers on the descriptive term to be used for this type of shopping center. They have been called "inter-city," "planned," and "controlled" shopping centers.

A MODERN INTEGRATED SUBURBAN SHOPPING CENTER.
Courtesy of Alexandre Georges, photographer.

ILLUSTRATION 4–1

mile radius through suburban territory, and even penetrates well into nearby metropolitan cities.

"Farmers' markets"

A curious byproduct of the success of the integrated suburban shopping centers has been the creation of a thousand or more cut-price integrated retailing centers which go by the misleading name of "farmers' markets." * Like the true integrated shopping centers, these "farmers' markets" are built by realty operators. In place of architectural masterpieces, however, the shops in these markets are housed in open-front booths and quonset huts. Food and soft-goods stores, dealers in second-hand and work clothes, retailers of irregulars in furniture, cut-price drug stores, auction establishments, and costume jewelry shops locate in them. Overhead is at an irreducible minimum, and the shops feature low prices. Most of these "farmers' markets" are located in the outskirts of Philadelphia and some other metropolitan cities; their annual sales exceed $1 billion.

* These should not be confused with the true farmers' markets, where truck farmers sell produce direct to retailers and to consumers, described in Chapter 12.

Retail trade gravitation

Our analysis of retailing geography to this point has indicated that rural, small-town, and suburban consumers do most of their convenience and impulse buying in their local communities, but may travel up to fifty miles or more to city and integrated suburban shopping centers to buy shopping and specialty goods. In these "shopping" trips, moreover, they commonly do a substantial amount of convenience goods buying, to take advantage of lower prices or wider selection, and also buy varying amounts of impulse goods. Where there are two or more city or integrated suburban shopping centers within practicable travel distance from a small community, how will the shopping, specialty, and related purchases of the small community be divided between the two cities? Where there are two or more city or integrated shopping centers whose practical retail trading areas overlap, how will custom from the overlapping territory be divided between them?

A number of studies on these two related questions have established the following empirical generalizations, commonly referred to as "Reilly's Law of Retail Trade Gravitation": *

1. The residents of a small town or rural area do not consistently patronize any one of two or more reachable shopping centers, but for all sorts of individual reasons divide their patronage between them.

2. Since a larger community generally offers a wider and better shopping and specialty-goods selection than a smaller one, there is a stronger tendency on the part of residents of an intermediate small town or rural area to patronize the stores of the larger city. Other factors equal, the custom of the intermediate town or rural area tends to be divided between the two cities roughly in proportion to their populations, provided that the population disparity is not too great. Thus, if Town X were located midway between cities A and B, and City A had a 70,000 population while City B had a 30,000 population, 70 percent of Town X's shopping trade would go to City A and 30 percent to City B. This rule does not apply, of course, where integrated suburban shopping centers are involved. An integrated center, located in "open" suburban territory, may offer shopping and special-intent buying facilities comparable to those of a medium-sized city. In such case, its "pull" upon the surrounding territory would be as great as that of a city center—possibly even greater because of superior organization, attractiveness, and better parking facilities.

---

* Dr. William J. Reilly, formulated these principles in 1928 for fashion goods shopping in areas with sizable cities, secondary towns, and rural villages, when he was a staff member of the University of Texas Bureau of Business Research. Later studies have qualified Reilly's original generalizations in many respects, but have also indicated that they apply, with qualifications, to other fields of retailing besides fashion goods, and to suburban areas as well as mixed areas.

3. Distance is a strong discouragement to shopping travel. When one integrated or city shopping center is further from a town than another, a disproportionate share of the shopping trade of the town goes to the nearer shopping center. According to Reilly's Law, the shopping trade of any intermediate town or area tends to be divided between the two unequally distant shopping centers inversely to the squares * of the highway distances involved. Thus, if Town X were 10 miles from City A and 20 miles from City B and both cities had the same populations, four-fifths of Town X's shopping trade would go to City A, and one-fifth to City B.

When we seek to determine how two rival cities divide the shopping trade of the area between them, the two formulas of retail trade gravitation can again be applied, in a combined form, as follows:

$$\text{Break-even point} = \frac{\text{Highway distance between City A and City B}}{1 + \sqrt{\dfrac{\text{population of City A}}{\text{population of City B}}}}$$

If an integrated suburban shopping center were involved, the relative shopping facilities of the two centers instead of their populations would enter the calculation. According to this formula, if City A and City B were 50 highway miles apart and if the population of City A were 80,000 and that of City B 20,000, the break-even point for the shopping trade of the intervening area would come at a distance of $33\frac{1}{3}$ miles from City A and $16\frac{2}{3}$ miles from City B. Of course, in practice there would be no point to divide the trade going to City A from that going to City B. For a short distance on either side of the $33\frac{1}{3}$–$16\frac{2}{3}$ mile point there would be a "margin of indifference," where trade would be divided approximately evenly between the two cities. On either side of this "margin of indifference" would be another wider area where shopping trade would still be divided between the two cities, but in uneven proportions, growing progressively more uneven as the one city or the other was approached. Where several roads connect the two cities, the "margins of indifference" on these roads connect to form a shopping "boundary margin" between the two cities. These relationships are shown in Illustration 4–2.**

Retail trading areas

Reilly's Law of Retail Gravitation indicates that every city and integrated shopping center exerts a "pull," *as far as shopping and special intent buy-*

---

* Some recent studies suggest that the cube of the highway distance may be a better empirical approximation than the square.

** These principles of retail trade gravitation apply also to the division of the convenience retail trade of an intervening area between nearby villages or towns, where the travel distance does not exceed ten miles.

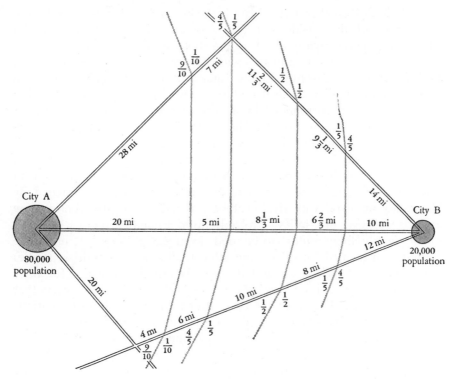

HYPOTHETICAL APPLICATION OF PRINCIPLES OF RETAIL TRADE GRAVITATION

The two cities A and B are 50 miles apart by the middle route, 60 miles by the lower route, and 70 miles by the upper route. The break-even line for retail trade gravitation in the territory between them occurs two-thirds of the distance from A to B by any route. At mid-distance between them by any route, four-fifths of the local retail trade will go to A and one-fifth to B. Other proportions for other relative distances are shown in the illustration.

ILLUSTRATION 4–2

ing is concerned, upon the territory surrounding it. If there is no rival center to establish a close-in "boundary margin," how far out does this pull extend to draw in significant numbers of "shoppers"? This question cannot be answered by any one- or two-factor formula. Quite a number of determinants are involved. One is the extent of the center's shopping facilities, which in the case of a city center is determined largely by the relative size of the city's own population; the greater the shopping facilities, the stronger and more far-reaching is the "pull" of the center. Another is the extent and character of the roads and highways surrounding the city or integrated center, from the viewpoint of providing easy and rapid auto access to it. Still another determinant is the bus and train system connecting the center with the outside area. Still another is the circulation area of a city's newspapers carrying the ads of the shopping stores of its centers. The "pull" of the center diminishes with the travel distance involved—in Reilly's formula, according to the square of the distance. Apart from "boundary margins" with rival centers, every city or integrated shopping center is therefore surrounded by a perimeter which marks the limit of its significant shopping "pull." The territory within its "boundary margins" and that perimeter is its "retail trading area" or "retail market area."

The radius of the retail trading areas surrounding city and integrated shopping centers has been steadily lengthening, with more widespread ownership of faster cars, and better roads. Except where shortened by "boundary margins" with rival centers, this radius for large centers now extends well over fifty miles—probably up to a hundred miles where fast motor superhighway routes can be used. Even though no single or simple formula can be used for calculating retail trading areas, empirical studies have established such areas, and the populations they contain, for most "shopping-center" cities and for the new suburban integrated centers that are being created. The results of these studies are available in tabulations and maps. This knowledge is valuable to the shopping stores of these centers. It helps them in their growth planning, in arranging parcel delivery schedules, in organizing their advertising. It is also valuable to manufacturers, who use it to plan their territorial coverage, distribution of their advertising coverage, and distribution of their selling effort.

TRENDS IN RETAILING

The retail institutional structure is dynamic, like all other phases of Marketing. Economic and social changes in the consumer market, such as we studied in Chapter 2, modify the demands that consumers make upon the retailing system. Development of new consumer product lines, like the automobile and its accessories, or radio and TV, may make possible the establishment of new retailing fields. A new retailing technology, like the automatic vending machine, may demand a new, special institutional set-up to make it operative. One thing is certain—whenever and for whatever reason a new retailing approach becomes profitable, the profit opportunity will be seized. Possibly existing types of retailers will adapt their operations to the changed circumstances, even to the extent of evolving into new institutional types—as Sears Roebuck and Montgomery Ward did by setting up department store chains when the automobile ended rural isolation and cut much of the ground out from under their mail order business. Completely new retailing types may come into existence to meet new circumstances as did the automotive supplies stores, or to satisfy a consumer demand ignored by the existing retailers as did the discount houses.

An institutional history of American Marketing would record many appearances, disappearances, and transformations of particular types of retailers. The Yankee peddler, with his saddlepacks of cutlery and knick-knacks, was a feature of Colonial times. The rural general store dominated Nineteenth Century retailing, but declined to relative unimportance in the Twentieth Century. Department stores, in the present sense of the term, entered the retailing scene in the 1860's and 1870's, and still flourish. The general mail order house had its start in the third quarter of the Nineteenth Century, reached its peak in the 1910–1920 decade by catering to farmers' shopping needs, then had to do an about-face and cultivate the suburban market when the automobile enabled the farmer and his family to do their shopping in neighboring cities. Chain retailing existed sporadically through the first three-quarters of the Nineteenth Century, developed at an accelerating pace during the next half-century, then levelled off to a balanced position in the retailing system. The first supermarkets, opened in the 1930's, now account for nearly 70 percent of total food store sales.

The retailing picture is still changing, both operationally and institutionally. We shall study many of these trends that relate to particular types of retailers in the next three chapters. Here we shall note three current operational developments—trend in store size, what is happening in the matter of customer services, and increasing efficiency in retailing—that affect all classes of retailers.

Store size

Average store size, in terms of physical volume of sales (or its equivalent, dollar volume of sales in fixed-purchasing-power dollars) is increasing. As indicated in Illustration 4–3, sales per store (in "1958" dollars) in 1929 were $54,688. In 1948 the figure was $92,746, in 1958 $105,045. In the thirty years between 1929 and 1958 the number of stores increased by only 29%, while per store sales (in "constant" dollars) expanded by 92%. The growth of American retailing in recent years is thus primarily attributable to expanding store size, rather than to increasing store numbers.

Three factors have contributed to the expansion of average store sales:

1. Successful stores—and these are the great majority—expand their operations year after year. Population increase in their market areas is a foundation for this expansion in many cases. So is rising family disposable income. But these are only passive elements in lifting a store's sales. The active element is the drive of most store owners and store managers to make each year's showing better than the last year's. This ambition to have one's store bigger and better operates all along the size range, up to and including the largest department stores. Perhaps some of the depart-

NUMBER AND SALES OF RETAIL ESTABLISHMENTS, 1929–1958

YEAR	NUMBER (in thousands)	TOTAL SALES (in billions)		SALES PER STORE ("1958" dollars)
		Actual dollars	"1958" dollars	
1929	1,472	$ 47.8	$ 80.5	$ 54,688
1939	1,761	41.4	86.1	48,893
1948	1,668	128.8	154.7	92,748
1958	1,903	199.9	199.9	105,045

Source: U.S. *Census of Business* series for the indicated years. The *Census* basis of tabulation for 1958 excluded retail milk distributors with bottling plants and some 100,000 stores with sales between $500 and $2,500 and no paid employees, which were included in the earlier tabulations. Also, some 25,000 leased departments, previously listed separately, were included in 1958 with the stores in which they were located. For trend analysis purposes, the 125,000 excluded small stores and leased departments, and their $150 million in sales, have been added back to the *Census* figure for 1958. The U.S. Department of Commerce Retail Price Index is used for calculating sales in "1958" dollars.

ILLUSTRATION 4–3

ment store giants are being pushed beyond optimum size. There is evidence that after a certain point in store size is reached, costs of co-ordination begin to rise faster than savings of large-scale operation. So far, however, this consideration has not checked the drive to build big stores into superbig ones.

2. Occasionally a large store, like the New York Wanamaker's, closes its doors. The overwhelming proportion of store closings, however, is of shops and small stores. Many have been operated for only a few years, or even a few months. They have failed because they were started with inadequate financial resources or because of the business inadequacy of their founders. But many have persisted for some time in a static or declining state. Thus there is a constant seepage out from the bottom of the small-store category.

3. Of the new stores constantly being started, many are small and may be considered to replace a part of the small stores that fall out. Some of these new small stores will be numbered among the failures that subsequently seep out of the category. Some will succeed and move up the size scale. A growing proportion of store openings, however, consists of large-scale units—supermarkets and branch department stores geared from the outset to sales in the millions; of the 197 supermarkets opened in 1957 by members of the Super Market Institute, over 70 started on a basis of annual sales over $2 million. Chain systems, aware that their stores have high break-even points, have been shutting down their small units and

replacing them with much larger ones. Thus there is a steady, heavy, external feed-in to the large-store category.

Small stores are decreasing in number and declining in their relative importance in the retailing system. The change in the value of the dollar precludes direct comparison of the number of stores in particular sales-volume categories in different years, but we can gain an indication of this trend by comparing 1958 *Census of Business* sales-volume categories with categories of double the size in 1939, when the value of the retail dollar was over double that of the 1958 retail dollar. In 1958, 79% of the stores * had sales under $100,000, compared with the 93% of stores that had sales under $50,000 in 1939; 32% of the stores in 1958 had sales under $20,000, compared with the 57% that had sales under $10,000 in 1939. Over 24% of retail establishments had more than four paid employees in 1958, as against 17% in 1939.

Customer services

With respect to customer services, there are currently two diametrically opposed trends. In certain sectors of retailing the tendency is to maintain high levels of customer service and even raise them. In other sectors there is a striking movement toward eliminating certain customer services and translating the resulting economies into lower prices.

Substantial customer service has always been part of the American retailing tradition. These services add to store costs and result in higher prices. Still, there has always been a goodly proportion of customers who desire these services and are able to pay for them through higher merchandise prices, so that stores offering these services can hold their clienteles against price competition from non-service or limited service stores. Charge account credit dates back to Colonial times. Practically all shopping goods and special intent stores, and a considerable proportion of neighborhood convenience goods stores, have always made free delivery available, one way or another, to those of their customers who want it. From their earliest years, department stores in particular have looked upon customer services as a basic element in their competitive appeal. Besides credit and free delivery, and liberal returned-goods privileges, large metropolitan department stores have long provided elevators and escalators for floor-to-floor movement, attractive customer lounges, restaurants, emergency medical attendance, appliance repair divisions, and other special service departments operated at cost or low profit.

The current retailing effort to seek out and provide new services that

---

* 100,000 has been added to the *Census of Business* 1958 figures on numbers of stores and small stores, to compensate for stores with sales under $2500, included in 1939 but excluded in 1954.

customers may appreciate is operating along three lines. *First,* there is a never-ending catering to customers' convenience and comfort. Suburban stores provide parking areas and delivery of purchases to the customers' cars in these areas. Children's playrooms, with attendant, are appearing in department stores and large supermarkets. Summer air-conditioning is being installed in even the smallest stores. In-and-out doors that open automatically are becoming common. All sorts of stores, from department stores to supermarkets, are remaining open one, two, three, or even more evenings a week to accommodate husband-wife shopping and working-woman customers whose employment precludes day-time purchasing; there is growing pressure for Sunday openings in many retailing lines. *Second,* stores are being increasingly designed and decorated for esthetic appeal. Not only "snob" and "quality" stores, but supermarkets and neighborhood drug and hardware stores win the eye with harmonious lighting and color, woo the ear with recorded music, and spray the air with scents. One recently-opened supermarket has a fountain splashing under colored lights. The new integrated suburban shopping centers are landscaped with planted groves and reflecting pools. *Third,* with the increasing complexity in choice of household furnishings and appliances, progressive stores that handle these lines are seizing the service opportunity of providing their customers with genuine assistance in selecting these items. Many of the larger department and home-furnishings stores offer their customers the help of an interior decorating consultant. Aided by the appliance manufacturers, store managers are giving the sales clerks in their appliance departments intensive instruction in the construction and functioning of the units they sell so that they can help their customers with semi-expert understanding.

In contrast to this enhancement of customer services in many areas of retailing is the trend, in other areas, to self-service and limited-service. Self-service is not new in American retailing. The earliest 5-and-10 variety stores, in the 1880's, were based on customer self-service, with all merchandise displayed on counter tops. While sales clerks were stationed about the store, their functions were limited largely to wrapping items selected by the customers and taking payment. Present-day variety stores are still operated primarily on this principle. A new impetus to self-service retailing came in the 1930's when the first supermarkets, applying this principle to food sales, were established. Not only were the supermarkets able to cut operating costs and pass the saving on to their customers in lower prices, but they found that they were able to capitalize on the desire of many women to do "comparison shopping" in their purchase of food items and food brands. Self-service operation, with checkout counters for payment, has spread from the supermarkets to smaller food stores, drug stores, hardware stores, and other retailing lines, and is currently expanding. The most recent major development in limited-service retailing is the discount house, where credit and free delivery are eliminated and clerk service in the selling of household appliances and other consumer durable goods is restricted essentially to order-taking. The operations and significance of this new type of store are examined in Chapter 7.

Several factors have contributed to the success of self-service in supermarkets and reduced clerk-service in discount houses. A generation or two ago all retailers had to be, in a way, purchasing agents for their customers. They performed, and through high markups were paid for, such services as providing product information, advising on selection of goods, dividing large quantities into smaller amounts, packaging, and delivery. During the past two decades consumers have become better educated as retail purchasers, as explained in Chapter 30. Manufacturers have helped this development, by more informative labelling and promotion. They have also taken over the former retailing functions of dividing and packaging. Thus, in certain areas of retailing, the consumer has become his own self-servicing purchasing agent. With the universality of automobile ownership, rural and suburban consumers can undertake their own delivery of purchases. In large cities the delivery of nonperishable merchandise has been transferred by the retailers to parcel delivery services; this paves the way for discount houses and some other stores to end "free" delivery by having the customer pay the charge of the delivery service. With substantial elements of the consumer market no longer needing or wanting these services, opportunity was created for some retailers to eliminate them, reduce their markups since their costs were thus lowered, and make a special effective price-economy bid.

Retailing efficiency

Department stores, general mail order houses, chain systems, and other large-scale retailers early developed outstanding efficiency in many of their operations; this is one reason they achieved large-scale status. Prior to the 1930's however, the mass of American retailers operated generally in ignorance of sound retailing principles. During the past quarter-century there has been a striking improvement.

One reason for this progress has been a broad upgrading in the educational background, if not the innate ability, of new entrants into the retailing field. A growing proportion of the men assuming the responsibilities of store management have high school, college, or even business college educations. They are more aware than their predecessors that there are technical problems in retailing, and they are more prepared to learn the solutions to these problems. For those who are prepared to accept guidance, there is a growing body of assistance—from extension courses on retailing, from their own trade associations and trade journals, from the federal Small Business Administration, from manufacturers who are eager to help retailers do a better job of selling their particular products. There is satisfying evidence that the present generation of retailers are eager and able to learn how to improve their operations, and to apply what they learn.

A second factor in improving the general level of small-scale retailing is the existence of the generally efficient large-scale retailers with whom, in many cases, the small merchants are in direct competition. An idea that a small independent grocer or druggist might dismiss as "impracticable" or "not applicable to my store" when presented in a Department of Commerce *Small Business Aid* or in a manufacturer's sales promotion pamphlet cannot be ignored when it is obviously working well in a competing chain store unit. During the 1920's and 1930's in particular, many small independents in retailing lines hard-pressed by chain-store competition studied the superior retailing techniques of their enemies, adapted them to their own operations, survived and prospered. Those who could not or would not learn did not survive. This process of pioneering towards ever-greater retailing efficiency by the large operators who have the resources for the research and experimentation necessary for such pioneering, and selective imitation by the more alert among the smaller operators, still continues.

CLASSIFICATIONS OF RETAILERS

For purposes of study, retailers have been classified on a variety of bases. Some of the more important of these bases, and the classifications that can be established upon them, are:

A. Method of customer contact
   1. Store
      a. Owned
      b. Leased department
   2. Nonstore
      a. Mail order
      b. Canvassing
      c. Vending machines

B. Merchandise sold
   1. Limited-line—subclassified by merchandise lines
   2. Multi-line
      a. Rural general stores
      b. Variety stores
      c. Department stores
      d. General mail order houses
      e. Others

C. Integration (combination with wholesaling units)
   1. Unintegrated
   2. Integrated

    D. Functions performed
       1. Full service
       2. Limited service (cash-carry)
       3. Self-service

    E. Ownership
       1. Independent
       2. Chain
       3. Consumer co-operatives
       4. Manufacturers' outlets
       5. Government and company stores

    F. Store location
       1. Rural
       2. Suburban
       3. Urban neighborhood
       4. Shopping center

    G. Size (by sales volume or number of employees)
       1. Large
       2. Small

    H. Management organization
       1. Undifferentiated
       2. Departmentalized

    I. Operational techniques

Each of these classifications, taken by itself, though opening one avenue to retailing knowledge, would close off a multitude of others. A comprehensive study of retailing and retailers would have to cover each and every possible classification in turn, explore the information available with respect to it, and analyze the issues connected with it. Exhaustive analysis along these lines would involve extensive repetition and duplication. Supermarkets, for example, would have to be studied under the headings of merchandise lines offered, location, services offered, whether independent or chain-owned, size, undifferentiated or departmentalized management, and others.

The following four chapters offer only an elementary survey of retailing institutions and their operation. Accordingly a consistent, exhaustive, classification-by-classification analysis is not necessary. Instead, various of the above-tabulated classifications are used, in a limited way, as frames for topical treatment of retailing institutions. The topics developed are those which appear to be of major practical importance in current retailing. Chapter 5 explores the classifications of small-scale and limited-line retailing, emphasizing the supermarket as the most interesting recent development in this field. Chapter 6 covers the classification of multi-line stores, with most of the chapter devoted to the department store and its problems. Chapter 7 makes use of the store-ownership classification to analyze the chain store issue and to survey some special ownership classes of retailers;

for space reasons, mail order houses and some other nonstore retailers are also studied here. Chapter 8 presents some general issues of retail store management.

REVIEW

1. What economic contributions do retailers make?
2. What Marketing operations do retailers perform?
3. What differences would you expect to find between the stores of a rural town with less than 2,500 population and those of a nearby city with a 75,000 population? Why?
4. What differences would you expect to find between the stores of a neighborhood retailing center and those of a secondary shopping center in a city with a population of 1,500,000? Why?
5. What is the general retailing picture in the suburbs of a large city?
6. Explain Reilly's Law of Retail Gravitation.
7. What are "retail trading areas"? Why calculate them?
8. Why can't we base a study of retailers on some single, simple classification?

DISCUSSION TOPICS

1. How has the "flight to Suburbia" during the past quarter-century changed the economic geography of Retailing?
2. "The integrated suburban shopping center has added a new dimension to Retailing."
3. "Retailing operations and institutions must be dynamic."
4. Why is it that retail expansion is being accomplished more through growth in store size than by increase in the number of stores?
5. "The success of the supermarket and the discount house indicate that customer service is on its way out of the American retailing picture."
6. Is Retailing more inefficient than other forms of business? Is there much possibility of it becoming more efficient?

PROBLEM

Over the past ten years you have built up a flourishing hardware store on Elm Street, the store street of the Millwood neighborhood of Metro City. The Millwood neighborhood developed about forty years ago with blocks of continuous frame and brick two-story dwellings to house the working force of the Steelton Foundries, whose mills line Metro River. The neighborhood is still populated largely by the families of Steelton employees, a low- to middle-income group. Your store has carried low-price lines of household hardware, minor household appliances, and household supplies. You have operated it with the assistance of one full-time and one part-time sales clerk. You have stayed open until 8 P.M. each evening, because much of the buying in your store is done by the men of the neighborhood after they come home from work. Because of the competition of a second hardware store three blocks away on Elm Street, you have been economical in the decoration and installations of your store, and have held your operating costs down wherever practicable, to maintain a low-price policy with reasonable mark-up. Your promotional activities have been limited to a well-kept display window, "complimentary" ads in local church programs, and periodic "bargain" sales. You and your full-time clerk know hundreds of your regular customers by name, and your store has always been a "friendly" one.

The Johnson Development Co. is building Home World, a large suburban shopping center, on U.S. Route 19, thirteen miles out of Metro City. It is expected to serve the extended and rapidly growing suburban area north of Metro City. You see in it an opportunity to build up a larger business in your field than will ever be possible in the Millwood neighborhood. You apply for the hardware and home appliances unit in the Home World center, and your application is accepted. You sell your Millwood store, and start planning your Home World store.

Will the Home World store have to differ from your Millwood store from the standpoints of merchandise lines carried, customer service policies, layout and installation, promotion, pricing? In analyzing your problems, take into account the difference in the market areas of the two stores, possible differences in customer income classes and cultural types, possible differences in the intent character of buying at the two stores, possible differences in customer patronage motivations.

SUGGESTED READINGS: I

Barker, C. W., and others, *Principles of Retailing,* 3rd ed, McGraw-Hill Book Co., New York, 1956.

Brown, P. L., & W. R. Davidson, *Retailing: Principles and Practices,* Ronald Press, New York, 1953.

Dolva, W. K., & D. K. Beckley, *The Retailer,* Prentice-Hall, Englewood Cliffs, N.J., 1950.

Duncan, D. J., & C. F. Phillips, *Retailing: Principles and Methods,* 5th ed, Richard D. Irwin, Homewood, Ill., 1959.

Hahn, L., *Stores, Merchants, and Customers,* Fairchild Publications, New York, 1952.

Hollander, S. C., *Explorations in Retailing,* Bureau of Business Research, Michigan State University, East Lansing, 1959.

Jones, F. M., *Retail Merchandising,* Richard D. Irwin, Homewood, Ill., 1957.

Kelley, P. C., & N. B. Brisco, *Retailing: Basic Principles,* 3rd ed, Prentice-Hall, Englewood Cliffs, N.J., 1957.

McNair, M. P., *Dynamic Retailing in the Modern Economy,* National Retail Dry Goods Association, New York, 1954.

Wingate, J. W., & J. D. Weiner, *Retail Merchandising,* 5th ed, South-Western Publishing Co., Cincinnati, 1957.

Wingate, J. W., & A. Corbin (eds.), *Changing Patterns in Retailing,* Richard D. Irwin, Homewood, Ill., 1956.

PERIODICAL: *Journal of Retailing.*

SUGGESTED READINGS: II

Baker, G., & B. Funaro, *Shopping Centers: Design and Operation,* Reinhold Publishing Corp., New York, 1951.

Fine, I. V., *Retail Trade Area Analysis,* School of Commerce, University of Wisconsin, Madison, 1954.

Gruen, V., *Shopping Towns U.S.A.: The Planning of Shopping Centers,* Reinhold Publishing Corp., New York, 1960.

Jonassen, C. T., *The Shopping Center Versus Downtown,* Bureau of Business Research, Ohio State University, Columbus, 1955.

Kelley, E. J., *Shopping Centers: Locating Controlled Regional Centers,* Eno Foundation for Highway Traffic Control, Saugatuck, Conn., 1956.

McKeever, J. R., *Shopping Centers Restudied,* Urban Land Institute, Washington, D.C., 1957.

Nelson, R. L., *The Selection of Retail Locations,* F. W. Dodge Corp., New York, 1959.

Reilly, W. J., *The Law of Retail Gravitation,* reprint, Pilsbury Publishers, New York, 1953.

Smith, P. E., *Shopping Centers: Planning and Management,* National Retail Dry Goods Association, New York, 1956.

CHAPTER 5

SMALL STORES: LIMITED-LINE STORES

Two bases for classifying retail stores suggested in the preceding chapter were size (as measured by relative sales volume), and whether a store limits itself more or less to a major merchandise line or carries a group of lines. These two approaches to the study of retail institutions uncover a number of important retailing issues—the place of the small store in the retailing structure, the extent of limited-line retailing, the trend toward adding supplementary merchandise lines, the striking emergence and evolution of the supermarket as a retailing institution, and other significant limited-line retailing trends.

SMALL STORES

Although, as indicated in the preceding chapter, the small store, generally independently owned, is declining in numbers and importance, it still dominates the retailing picture. Of the 1,900,000 stores that operated through 1958, 79% had annual sales volumes under $100,000. Even more striking, half had sales under $50,000, and one-third had sales under $20,000. If we measure store size by number of employees instead of by sales volume, the same relative picture emerges. Two-fifths of our retail enterprises in 1958 were operated by their owners with the unpaid help of members of their families. Less than one-quarter had more than four employees.

Stores of practically every merchandise line are found in the small-store classification. Small-scale operation is particularly common among restaurants, auto service stations, grocery stores, stationery stores, and rural general stores.

Small stores are most likely to be found in rural trading centers and neighborhood retailing centers. Many also find niches in urban shopping centers, in office buildings, in bus and railroad stations, and on residential side streets.

Disadvantages

When in competition with larger retail establishments, small stores suffer three disadvantages:

1. Buying all items in small quantities, they do not qualify for quantity discounts and other price advantages available to larger competitors.

2. A large proportion of them are operated by persons woefully ignorant of the basic principles of good store management. They do not know how to gauge local demand as a guide for their buying choice. "Display" is a meaningless term to them. Their only concept of selling is to hand customers what they ask for. The simplest system of retail bookkeeping is beyond their grasp.

3. Able operators of small stores and their employees cannot specialize and become expert in particular aspects of retailing, such as buying certain lines of goods, or advertising, or setting up window and counter displays.

Advantages

Offsetting these serious disadvantages of small-store operation are several definite advantages:

1. Often a rural village, or a neighborhood retailing center, can support only one store, a small one, in a particular retailing line. Such a small store does not have immediate competition, and can survive and provide a living for its owner even if its prices are high, its merchandise selection poor, and its general operation inefficient.

2. The paid-out expenses of operating many of these stores are very low. If poorly located, as many of them are, the rent is low. There is no overhead of high management salaries. There is little outlay for store equipment, and often nothing for display and advertising. These economies may cost the store sales volume that would more than cover such payments. Still, they tend to offset more or less the higher prices that the small store must pay for small-quantity purchases.

3. A small independent store does not have to pay a fair manager's wage, and still produce a profit. Whatever margin is obtained on the small sales volume, less the low operating expenses, is income for the store owner. This income may embody no profit in the economic sense, and only

a low rate of compensation for the time devoted to the store by the owner and members of his family, but there is no penalty for failing to make a better showing.

4. Many small retail establishments are operated only for supplementary income. A printer's employee operates a little job-printing business in the evenings. A housewife conducts a small-scale millinery or dress shop for "pin money." An aged couple, supported primarily by their children, run a tiny confectionery or grocery store. These sideline retail establishments usually are conducted from the owners' residences. They involve practically no operating expenses. Their entire gross profit of a few hundred dollars, or a thousand or two, is net income for their owners.

The small store in the retailing structure

The following five-fold classification of small stores provides a foundation for appraising their position in the retailing structure:

1. A considerable proportion of small stores, in some cases chain-owned, are small, and must remain so, because: (a) they are the sole stores of their kind in communities or neighborhoods that cannot support larger enterprises; or (b) able competition limits them to only a share of the business in their line from a larger community or neighborhood. Many of these stores whose expansion is thus limited are small-scale models of good retail management.

2. Some stores with annual sales in the $50,000 to $100,000 range could be successfully expanded, but their middle-aged or elderly proprietors are quite content with the comfortable incomes they derive and do not wish to undertake the exertions and risks that further expansion would entail. Many of these stores are excellently managed.

3. A fair number of small stores are enterprises recently started by men and women of high ability. Their beginning capital is limited, their initial scale of operations is small, a substantial part of their early small profits are ploughed back, and their "take-home" incomes at the outset are much less than they would receive in other forms of employment. In time, however, they will be owners of profitable good-sized retail establishments; some will expand into chain operation with the prospect of real riches.

4. Too large a proportion of small stores are opened by individuals with no special craft or other earning ability, with a desire for personal independence which renders a low-level office or manual job obnoxious to them, and with small capital. Utterly unaware of the extensive business knowledge and the business skills necessary to modern successful retailing, they invest their small capital in a little grocery store or shop of some kind. Grimly and despairingly they hang on to their small business, their store and living expenses exceeding the little margin on their low sales, until

their capital is exhausted. After a year or two, perhaps only a few months, the store is closed.

5. As noted above, quite a number of small stores are operated as supplementary-income enterprises.

Small stores of the first three classes are valid business enterprises, and contribute a healthy tone to retail competition. The same cannot be said of the "fringe" stores in the fourth and fifth classes. Usually their only resource for staying in existence for any period is to cut their prices below the level necessary for the profitable operation of competing stores that must cover normal costs of operation. Sometimes their scale of operations is so small, their clientele so limited, that competing stores can ignore their price-cutting. Often, however, it must be met. Thus these "fringe" stores tend to act as a drag upon the retailing lines in which they are found in any substantial numbers.

LIMITED-LINE RETAILING

A product line is defined as "a group of products that are closely related, either because they satisfy a class of needs, or are used together, or are sold to the same customer group, or are priced within a given range, or are marketed through the same class of outlets." This definition, properly broad to reflect the broad usage given to the term, in effect permits many overlapping and interpenetrating "line" classifications of goods, so that there can be no general agreement upon what the various retail "lines" are. Most commonly the term is applied to the broadest possible classifications of goods satisfying various classes of needs—e.g., foods, apparel, drugs, hardware, tobacco products, stationery. Quite often various subdivisions of these broad groups are also called "lines." Thus meats, fish, groceries, dairy products, baked products, fresh fruits and vegetables, and confectionery may each be considered a "line" by itself, instead of a subline in the food group. For our analysis of retailers on the basis of what they sell, we shall use "line" in its broader meaning. We shall employ the term "subline" for subdivisions of a "line."

A "limited-line" store is one that concentrates on one "line" or "subline" of merchandise. It may, or may not, carry partial offerings of one or more supplementary lines. In practice, most limited-line stores do go in for supplementary lines, and a growing proportion of their sales is in these supplementary lines. We shall explore this trend at length later in this chapter.

In some merchandise lines, retailing specialization has developed to a point where important classes of stores carry only one or a few sublines of a general merchandise line. In the food field we have not only general grocery-and-meat stores but also meat shops, fish stores, fresh fruit and vegetable stores, dairy shops, and frozen food stores. In the apparel field we have not only men's wear and women's wear stores, but such further specializations as men's hat stores, millinery stores, shoe stores, dress shops, and hosiery shops. These stores dealing in particular sublines are also included in the category of "limited-line stores."

Frequently, the sublines of a general merchandise line involve variant buying, promotional, and selling approaches. Large stores carrying the full line, or several of the sublines in a field, generally solve the problem of divergent retailing treatments of a group of sublines by "departmentalization"—a separate administrative organization and sales force is established for each subline. Thus a large men's wear store might have separate departments for suits, shoes, hats, and haberdashery. Supermarkets similarly departmentalize their meat, grocery, vegetable, dairy, and other divisions. Departmentalization of sublines does not of itself convert a store to multi-line retailing. Departmentalization is merely an administrative structure applicable to either limited-line or multi-line retailing.

Extent

Over 96 percent of the retail establishments reported by the 1958 *Census of Business* were limited-line stores. Since all the large department stores, with their tremendous sales volumes, are included in the multi-line category, the proportion of the 1958 retail sales volume accounted for by limited-line stores was somewhat lower—89 percent. Limited-line retailing has been gaining over the past quarter-century at the expense of multi-line retailing; the proportion of sales made by limited-line stores rose from 82 percent in 1929 to 89 percent in 1958.

Reasons for the dominance of the limited-line store in retail trade are not far to seek. We have already noted that most retail establishments are small-scale enterprises. The selection offered by many of these small stores in their single or major merchandise line is commonly all too narrow as is. If their working capital and shelf and counter space were to be divided among several lines, the offerings in each would be inadequate. Furthermore, even with limited-line retailing, the owners of these small stores must carry a burden of managerial responsibilities already too complex for many of them. To add additional major lines would multiply these responsibilities.

When an ably managed store faces the possibility of expanding to medium- or large-scale operation, its owner often has the choice of sticking to his original line or adding new major lines. In many such cases, the second alternative has been chosen, sometimes with outstanding success. The more common decision is to stick to the merchandise line that the store owner knows intimately, and for which the store has developed a

LINE	NUMBER (thousands)				SALES ($ billions)			
	1929	1939	1948	1958[3]	1929	1939	1948	1958[3]
Food	482	561	461	356	$10.8	$10.2	$ 29.2	$ 49.0
(Supermarkets) [1] ..	–	(5)	(12)	(30)	–	(1.5)	(7.8)	(32.9)
Automotive	68	60	85	94	7.0	5.5	20.1	31.8
Gasoline service								
stations	122	242	180	206	1.8	2.8	6.5	14.2
Hardware, lumber,								
& farm equipment .	90	79	97	108	3.8	2.7	11.1	14.3
Apparel	114	107	111	119	4.2	3.3	9.7	12.5
Furniture & appliances	59	53	80	103	2.8	1.7	6.6	10.1
Drug	58	58	55	56	1.7	1.6	4.0	6.8
Other	325	520	528	650	7.2	7.7	25.8	39.1
Total limited-line ..	1,318	1,680	1,597	1,692	$39.3	$35.5	$113.0	$177.8
General stores	104	40	21	9[a]	$ 2.6	$ .8	$ 1.2	$ .9[a]
Variety	12	17	19	21	.9	1.0	2.5	3.6
Department [2]	4	4	3	3	4.3	4.0	9.4	13.4
General merchandise [2]	38	29	29	25[a]	1.2	.7	2.7	3.3[a]
Total multi-line ...	158	90	71	87	$ 9.0	$ 6.5	$ 15.8	$ 21.9
GRAND TOTAL ..	1,476	1,770	1,668	1,778	$48.3	$42.0	$128.8	$199.7
PERCENTAGE DISTRIBUTION								
Food	32	32	28	20	22	24	23	25
(Supermarkets) ...	–	(b)	(1)	(2)	–	(4)	(6)	(17)
Automotive	5	4	5	5	15	13	16	16
Gasoline service								
stations	8	14	11	12	4	7	5	7
Hardware, lumber,								
& farm equipment .	7	4	6	6	8	6	9	7
Apparel	8	6	7	7	9	8	7	6
Furniture & appliances	4	3	5	6	6	4	5	5
Drug	4	3	3	3	3	4	3	3
Other	21	29	31	36	15	18	20	20
Total limited-line ..	89	95	96	95	82	84	88	89
General stores	7	2	1	–	5	2	1	–
Variety	1	1	1	1	2	2	2	2
Department	b	b	b	b	9	10	7	7
General merchandise .	3	2	2	–	2	2	2	–
Total multi-line ...	11	5	4	5	18	16	12	11
GRAND TOTAL ..	100	100	100	100	100	100	100	100

[a] Excludes stores without payrolls, and their sales; exclusions are counted in totals.

[b] Less than 0.5%.

[1] Self-service food stores with sales in excess of $150,000 in 1939, in excess of $375,000 in 1948 and 1958.

[2] Size factor distinction between department and general merchandise stores was $100,000 sales in 1929 and 1939, 25 employees in 1948 and 1958. This change resulted in a considerable number of stores that had been counted as department stores in the earlier years being classified as general merchandise stores in the later years.

[3] 1958 data are not strictly comparable with those of earlier years because of exclusion of stores with sales under $2500.

Sources: *Census of Business* for indicated years. Supermarket figures are from *Progressive Grocer*.

ILLUSTRATION 5–1

reputation. Expansion can be accomplished by adding to store space and offering a wider selection in the original line, attracting more customers and frequently increasing average sales. Alternatively, it may be achieved by maintaining the store at its existing capacity with its original line unchanged, but starting a chain of stores in the same line.

Multi-line retailing offers rich possibilities, as we shall see in the next chapter, but only to large stores and to exceptionally able small operators. For so long as small stores and ordinary abilities predominate in American retailing, limited-line retailing will also predominate.

Secondary lines in limited-line retailing

A store of any given size can offer its customers a wider selection in its line of merchandise if it limits itself strictly to that one line. Breadth of selection in a particular merchandise line definitely attracts patronage to a store, as we saw in our study of retail patronage motivations in Chapter 3. But housewives with a shopping list including both food items and household staples unquestionably find it more convenient if their entire list of purchases can be made in a single store, and many will tend to patronize the store which covers all their regular needs most comprehensively. Moreover, impulse buying of many items ordinarily purchased on a convenience basis, or even through shopping, is an important factor in present-day retail merchandising, and its importance is constantly growing. Every retailer constantly wonders whether he may not be losing substantial sales volume because he does not carry some popular side line with impulse appeal.

Of the conflicting patronage considerations prompting retailers to limit themselves closely to their major lines, and those prompting them to branch out into secondary lines, the latter seem to have greater current influence. The leanings of alert retailers, in this respect, are further stimulated by the sales policies of manufacturers of items bought substantially on convenience and impulse bases who endeavor to have their goods carried in every possible type of outlet, whether as part of a main line or as a side line. Every retailer is subject to pressure from salesmen eager to persuade him that their products, even though outside his regular line, are just what he needs to increase sales to his regular customers and to draw new customers.

Innumerable instances could be cited of retailers whose ventures into side-line merchandising failed, and who subsequently limited themselves to their major fields. But the successes in side-line retailing in recent times far outnumber the failures. There is a definite and prevailing retailing tendency for limited-line stores in most fields to develop secondary merchandise lines. Supermarkets are finding profit in offerings of children's books, records, and women's hose. Apparel stores carry side lines of jewelry and cosmetics. Home furnishings stores, jewelry stores, farm and feed supply stores, lumber and building supplies dealers, book stores, and other fields of what used to be limited-line retailing report growing proportions of sales from secondary lines. In the drug, automotive accessories, and hardware retailing fields, this tendency has progressed so far that it is doubtful if most of these stores should still remain in the limited-line classification.

SUPERMARKETS

One of the most important retailing developments of recent years has been the establishment and growth of supermarkets. This class of retailing institution is defined as "a large retail business unit, usually departmental-ized, selling mainly food and grocery items on the basis of low markup, wide variety of assortments, self-service, and the use of extensive mer-chandise appeal." Currently accepted measures of "largeness" are annual gross sales in excess of $375,000 or of $500,000.*

History

The supermarket is definitely a modern retailing institution. There were some cash-carry groceries before 1910. Clarence Saunders established his Piggly-Wiggly chains with self-service, checkout, and cash-carry in Memphis in 1916. Not until the early 1930's, however, when depression made large masses of housewives acutely economy-minded, was there eager response to retail grocery self-service associated with price-saving. The initial supermarkets of the 1930's were opened by independents. Their exclusive appeal was low prices. After a period of watchful waiting, the major grocery chains were persuaded that this new retailing technique was a sound innovation, and one well-suited to their methods. They embarked upon a nation-wide program of converting from service-store systems to supermarket operation. Many enterprising independents also converted their service stores to supermarkets.

As of 1959, 32,000 supermarkets, doing a total business of $35 billion, were reported. Although these supermarkets accounted for only 11 percent of the total number of food stores, they were responsible for 69 percent of food store sales. Many supermarkets are operated by independents, many by grocery chains which began large-scale conversion to supermarket oper-ation after 1935.

---

* The lower figure is set by *Progressive Grocer;* prior to 1946 it was $150,000. The higher figure is used by *Super Market Merchandising* and *Chain Store Age.*

Characteristics

Five characteristics distinguish supermarket operation: (1) location; (2) customer service policy; (3) large sales volume; (4) scope of merchandise offered; and (5) price policy.

Location. The earliest supermarkets were located, not in pre-existing retailing sections, but on the outskirts of large communities where land was cheap and available. This made possible provision for ample parking space, which was a key consideration to the initial supermarket operators who anticipated that the major part of their clientele would come from housewives who owned and drove cars—in the United States this means a substantial proportion of the housewife population outside of the metropolitan centers. Patronage by car-driving customers would not only extend the market area of a supermarket from a radius of a few blocks to one of several miles, but it would enable customers to make large-volume purchases on each visit to the store.

This original location idea has been modified considerably. It has been discovered that the main street parking facilities of small towns and cities and of suburban communities can accommodate, though often with considerable annoyance to shoppers, the cars of supermarket customers. Hence many supermarkets have been established in the very heart of the retailing centers of such communities. A limited parking space near the store is provided if possible, but many of these supermarkets depend solely on the street parking facilities within a block or two. Many supermarkets are also found in the neighborhood retailing centers of large cities, where car ownership is limited, and where parking provision for shoppers who do own cars is so restricted that food shopping by car is practically out of the question. These city supermarkets cannot offer their customers the convenience of auto shopping, and must depend on other advantages.

A new location opportunity for supermarkets is the integrated suburban shopping center. The heart of these centers is their shopping goods stores, but most of their patrons like to include a major "stocking-up" purchase of food items and other convenience goods with their other buying. Also, because of ample parking facilities of these new integrated centers, many inhabitants of the territory within a five-mile radius become regular patrons of the supermarket there in preference to the ones in their own communities. Hence most of the recently constructed centers provide for at least one supermarket site. Over two-fifths of the new supermarkets opened in recent years have been in these centers.

Customer service policy. The concept of self-service is fundamental to the supermarket. Originally it was thought practicable only for canned goods, packaged groceries, and supplementary lines. In recent years it has been established that dairy products, fresh fruits and vegetables, and even fresh meats, can be sold effectively on a self-service basis. The prerequisite of self-service for these lines is that a selection of suitable portions be made up in transparent packagings. The greatest misgiving was experienced in introducing self-service in the meat departments of supermarkets, but it was discovered that only an infinitesimal proportion of customers really wanted to see a fowl or piece of meat before it was cut. Most housewives were actually more satisfied when they could "shop" among the various cuts and servings available on the self-service counters.

Effectuating the self-service idea worked a revolution in food store layout. Gone are the wall shelves accessible only to the proprietor and sales clerks, and the sales counter on which purchases were grouped and wrapped. In their place are tiers of wall- and "island"-shelves, sizes and heights carefully planned so as to maximize merchandise display and yet allow for optimum customer vision and accessibility. Provision of aisle space is a careful compromise between allowance for easy customer traffic and sacrifice of selling shelf space. The location of departments, and of classes of goods within departments, is thoughtfully planned for shopping convenience and at the same time to promote impulse buying. Once established for any store, such locations must be maintained with some consistency, so that regular customers can always know just where to find the goods they want. Another key feature of supermarket layout is the checking counters, located at the store exits, where customers' purchases are rung up on the cash registers and bundled.

The shelf tiers and other self-service fixtures of the first supermarkets were jerry-built. The modern supermarket is a food palace of chrome, plate glass and enamel, well-lit, air-conditioned—a merchandise fairyland planned to produce hypnoidal trance in its patrons and to minimize their resistance to impulse buying. Many have replaced the shelf tiers of their canned and packaged goods departments with arrangements of chutes, down which slide lines of each canned or packaged item, the lowest can or package on each chute readily available to the customer's eye and hand. This arrangement multiplies the selling potential of a wall area, and permits restocking from behind the tiers without disturbing customer traffic. Instead of the second-hand baby carriages provided as carriers by some of the first supermarkets, today's customers in such food marts trundle gleaming metal carriages with rubber tires and a collapsible seat for the baby; they are so constructed that they nest within each other when not in use, thus saving valuable floor space.

The self-service aspect of the supermarket was originally deemed a necessary evil whose only virtue was to cut costs and thus permit lower prices. Students of retailing and store operators were almost unanimous in their belief that most women wanted the services of sales clerks, and the food shopping advice that such clerks and store proprietors could give. To everyone's surprise, self-service proved to be a major attraction. After a brief period of adjustment to the new method of buying their foodstuffs and household supplies, housewives became enthusiastic over the opportunity to "shop" among the various items and brands offered. Their impulse buying was substantially expanded with consequent increase of their food and household bills—and they liked it.

INTERIOR OF A MODERN SUPERMARKET. *Courtesy of Super-Market Merchandising.*

ILLUSTRATION 5–2

During its quarter-century of existence the supermarket has undergone a substantial "upgrading" in the matter of customer services. Self-service still remains basic policy. In the matter of external façade and interior decoration, however, there has been a revolutionary transition from the initial penny-pinching indifference to heavy investment in good architecture and eye-satisfying interiors. Purchases are conveyed to customers' autos by moving-belt systems. Air-conditioning has become almost universal. Check-cashing service is offered. The newest supermarkets provide customer lounges, "courtesy booths," and "kiddie korners."

Sales volume. The heavy investment supermarkets must make in store equipment, and the resulting fixed heavy depreciation cost that must be covered, causes the break-even point for supermarket sales volume to be much higher than for ordinary service food stores. Hence supermarkets must be planned for large-volume operation. At food price and operational cost levels of the 1930's, most self-service food stores had to do at least $100,000 business annually to be profitable. In 1946, the trade magazine *Super Market Merchandising* set $375,000 as the bottom sales limit for true supermarkets; * in 1958 it raised the figure to $500,000. Most of the new supermarkets opened during the 1950's were planned for annual sales volumes from one to five million dollars; several were aimed at $10 million volume.

Scope of merchandise offered. Supermarket merchandise policy has developed three distinguishing characteristics: (1) emphasis on well-known brands; (2) variety in food offerings; (3) side-line "impulse" and "convenience" offerings.

Most supermarkets, with the exception of some large chain system stores which feature their own private brands, carry a predominant proportion of their stock of staple food items in well-known national brands. Experience has taught supermarkets that they must offer their customers brands they are predisposed to buy. There are no sales clerks to explain the merits of unfamiliar brands. Furthermore, well-known brand items make excellent cut-price "loss leaders."

The large number of customers served by a typical supermarket, with their variant tastes, compel it to offer a much broader range of food items and brands than the ordinary service food store. The shelves of a supermarket usually carry not one brand line of a class of food products, but two, three, or more well-known brand lines. Furthermore, semi-specialty food items, such as grenadine syrup, bitters, and various food delicacies, which would have very slow turnover in the ordinary service food store, when bought by even a small proportion of a supermarket's large clientele sell sufficiently rapidly to warrant being stocked. The availability of these semi-specialty items is a factor in drawing custom to the supermarket. In consequence, a supermarket is likely to carry from 5,000 to 10,000 items— as against the 500 to 1,000 item lines of a typical small service food store.

Experience has taught the supermarkets that they can profitably carry almost any item that may be sold on a convenience or impulse basis, if there is established demand for it, and if it has display possibilities. More than three-quarters of the supermarkets now sell health and beauty aids. More

---

* Self-service food stores with smaller sales volumes are called "superettes." They are commonly found in small city and neighborhood retailing centers. They depend more on local "foot" patronage than on the "auto trade." Their floor space is less, their fixtures simpler, the range of their offerings narrower, than those of the true supermarkets.

than half carry stationery and school supplies, children's books, baby bottles, electric bulbs, and fuses. More than one-quarter offer magazines and pocket-size books, aluminum and glass ware, plastic items, films, and toys. Some carry such items as handkerchiefs, women's hose, electric clocks. A major cigar company has persuaded many supermarkets to stock its product. Sales of these nonfood lines constitute from 7 to 10 percent of supermarket sales, and the proportion is rising. For individual stores, the proportion is up to 20 percent. These nonfood departments are usually operated as leased departments (described in Chapter 7) or are serviced by "rack jobbers" (described in Chapter 9).

Price policy. The typical supermarket of today features lower prices than those of service food stores. It can do this because the total expenses of supermarkets tend to run somewhat lower, in relation to their large-volume sales, than those of service food stores, in spite of substantial building and equipment depreciation costs that modern supermarkets must carry. Also, the heavy volume purchases of supermarkets often enable them to take advantage of quantity discounts not available to smaller food stores. Furthermore, high turnover permits supermarkets to work with smaller unit profit in their mark-ups, and still maintain satisfactory profit-to-investment ratios. The time is past, however, when price saving was the sole appeal of a supermarket. Convenience for auto-owning customers, self-service, attractive store appearance, and a wide scope of offerings, are probably more responsible for the current popularity of supermarkets than the slight differential between their prices and those of the more efficient service food stores.

Management

Some supermarkets are independently owned, some are units in small local chains, some are units in large regional or national chains. This ownership consideration makes little difference in their management. The owner of an independent supermarket is still a manager, occupied almost exclusively with administrative responsibilities. His tasks are practically identical with those of the manager of a chain unit.

Supermarkets are commonly departmentalized—meat department, fresh vegetable and fruit department, dairy department, canned and packaged groceries department, and possibly others. Each is a separate unit, doing its own purchasing and with separate sales accounts. The meat department, and occasionally some of the others, may be "leased"—they are not operated by the owner of the supermarket, but by unrelated lessees paying the supermarket owner either a fixed rent or a proportion of their gross sales. Often these leased departments in supermarkets are chain-operated, even where the supermarkets themselves are independently owned.

Supermarket operation involves certain economies, and certain extra costs, as compared with service food stores. Among the economies are: (1) lower land or rental cost when a supermarket is located on the outskirts of a community (though this may be largely offset by the necessity of providing a large parking area); (2) employment of graded labor, including lower-calibre and hence lower-paid stock clerks in place of sales clerks, and girls as checkers; (3) possibility of quantity discounts on purchase volumes larger than can ordinarily be made by smaller service food stores; and (4) elimination of credit, delivery, and other customer service costs. Among the extra costs are: (1) the necessity of alloting a substantial part of the floor space to "aisles" for customer movement; (2) the heavy investment that must be made in building and equipment, which must be depreciated. With good management—and the average supermarket is probably better managed, if only because it must be, than the average service food store—the overall ratio of expenses to sales is lower for supermarkets than for comparable service food stores.

Competitive position

Wherever there is a sufficient car-owning clientele to support the sales volume necessary, a supermarket can be established and will undersell competing service food stores. This does not mean that supermarket retailing is certain, or even likely, to replace all the service food stores of the area. In the first place, there are many housewives who so prefer such services as delivery, credit, telephone ordering, and sales clerk help that they will continue to patronize the service food stores in spite of the price-savings of the supermarket. Second, efficient management and conversion from full service to semi-service may enable a competing food store to cut its costs, and with them its prices, to a point where the price advantage of the supermarket is so slight that it is not a vital competitive threat.

There are many rural market areas where the population is too small to provide the sales volume necessary to support a supermarket. In such areas, small food stores with full or partial service are safe from the competition of supermarkets. The same is true in many of the scattered retailing centers of large cities. Often there would be no opportunity for customers of a supermarket to park their cars within convenient distance of the store. Under such circumstances, a major advantage of supermarkets would be lacking. One might be established there, but it would be less likely to survive than the smaller food stores suited to such a center.*

---

* An interesting recent development in this connection is the establishing and rapid growth of several chains of bantam superettes, located in neighborhood centers and developments, carrying a more limited selection than supermarkets, planned for $250,000 to $300,000 annual sales, and appealing primarily to "convenience" patronage motivations.

The current rapid pace of supermarket expansion is expected to slacken off in the early 1960's as a saturation point is approached. It is likely, also, that supermarkets will continue to enlarge their handling of non-food lines, though hardly to an extent that would transform them to "junior department stores."

FOOD STORES OTHER THAN SUPERMARKETS

Food stores other than supermarkets comprise the most important group, measured by numbers, of limited-line stores, and rank next to automotive retailers in sales volume. There were over 326,000 such stores in 1958, and their $17-billion sales were nearly 10 percent of the limited-line store total.

Size and location

Most food stores other than supermarkets are small-sized. Nearly 40 percent * in 1958 had sales under $30,000; 10 percent * had sales under $10,000. Most of these were "papa-mama" stores operated by members of a family, or with one paid assistant.

Food stores, except for the specialty food shops noted below, are primarily convenience goods outlets, although a good deal of impulse buying occurs in them. Nearly all of them are found in rural trading centers and in neighborhood retailing centers and scattered retail sections of cities and suburban communities. In metropolitan centers, however, there are some stores noted for rare types of canned fish, special cheeses, unusual and hard-to-get fruits, imported delicacies, and the like. Such specialty food shops usually serve a broader trading area than regular food stores, and are often located in substantial neighborhood retailing centers or close to central or secondary shopping districts.

Services

On the basis of services offered to customers, food stores range from full-service establishments, with a proprietor or clerks serving behind the counters, telephone order service, credit and delivery, to no-service stores similar to supermarkets but without the comprehensive coverage of food and related lines offered by the supermarkets.

The full range of customer services is most commonly offered by general grocery-and-meat stores, and by specialty-food shops. Such stores characteristically enjoy a substantial telephone order business, and maintain a stabilized following of customers. Because of their services, they operate

---

* The 1958 *Census of Business* did not report stores with sales under $2,500. Allowing for these would make the small-store percentages still higher than indicated in the text.

at considerably higher costs than do less elaborate and more-limited-service food stores. Hence their prices average higher than those of more-limited-service stores; also, they are likely to carry the higher-quality higher-price lines of foods. They are most often found in the neighborhood retailing centers of well-to-do metropolitan areas and in suburban retailing centers.

The trend in modern grocery store retailing is rather definitely away from full-service stores. Few new food stores are established with full customer service definitely in mind, and many old full-service establishments in recent years have converted to a more-limited-service basis.

Semi- or limited-service food stores are of two kinds. One group might be designated as "cash-carry" stores—the proprietor or clerks serve the customers, but no credit accounts are allowed and no deliveries are made. The second group, influenced by the success of the supermarkets, operate on a "superette" or customer-self-service principle, but deliveries are made to customers' cars, and credit accounts are maintained. In both cases, telephone service may be offered to the extent of allowing customers to place orders in advance and preparing such orders so that they are ready to be taken away when the customers call. The second type of limited-service store is relatively common in the food field, and may either be in a transition stage from full-service to complete self-service, or may be reverting from self-service to a limited-service basis. This reversion to limited service in food retailing is common in communities where intense food store competition exists. When the limits of price competition among self-service food stores have been plumbed, some of the independently-owned competing stores are likely to try for better competitive position by offering limited customer service. With the flexibility possible through independent ownership, these stores can adapt their service policy to the peculiarities of consumer demand and competitive conditions in their areas.

One type of customer service offered by full-service food stores and many limited-service stores is charge-account credit. Such credit is sought by some customers for convenience reasons, by others because of necessity. In suburban and well-to-do neighborhoods, many women like the convenience of an account with their regularly-patronized food stores, so that a momentarily empty pocketbook need not limit a heavy weekly purchase of food supplies. Rural food stores, and those located in poorer urban neighborhoods, in contrast, often give credit to some of their customers because without it at times these customers and their families would starve —a farmer may be literally without funds for a period until a crop is harvested or sold, or a wage-earner's wife may have exhausted her household money before next payday. These convenience and necessity credit extensions by food stores are generally made on an informal, personal basis. No special inquiry based on outside sources of information is made into the financial circumstances of the applicant. The proprietor of the store makes his decision on his own knowledge and hearsay report—often with a resulting bad debt loss to be written off.

Sub-line specialization

There are many combination food stores which purvey a fairly complete line of foodstuffs—groceries, fresh meats, sea food, fresh fruits and vegetables, dairy products, and frozen foods. Specialization on one or more subdivisions of the food line, however, is common in this field of retailing. Many grocery stores do not carry fresh meats. There are meat markets which sell no groceries, or only a few lines of canned goods closely associated with the meat line. There are sea food stores, milk and dairy product stores, poultry and egg stores, candy stores, confectionery and nut stores, fresh fruit and vegetable stores, bakery-caterers, and delicatessens. During the 1940's there was an abortive development of stores specializing in frozen foods.

Few of these sub-line food stores limit themselves completely to their special fields. As indicated above, meat markets commonly carry a few canned goods in addition to their fresh meats. Delicatessens and dairy stores are often miniature grocery stores. Bake shops may also carry candies. The very variety of store designations in the food field, however, indicates both the broad scope and the long persistence of this form of retailing specialization.

DRUG STORES

Drug stores provide an interesting example of far-reaching retail institutional evolution. At the close of the Nineteenth Century most drug stores still conformed to their name; their proprietors compounded prescriptions and offered a line of patent medicines and medical supplies. Early in the Twentieth Century they began to turn to supplementary lines—first cosmetics and toilet items, then confectionery, tobacco products, stationery and writing supplies. The drug store soda fountain became almost universal and in time was transformed to a luncheonette, often operated as a leased department. Magazines and books, electrical appliances, and photographic equipment and supplies were taken on. Currently one of the most active departments of one large drug store chain is prepackaged fresh fruits and vegetables. By now the drug and prescription sales of many drug stores constitute only a minor fraction of their total sales volume. Instead of seeking "convenience store" locations in neighborhood retailing centers, many drug stores are now established in shopping and business centers, where they catch substantial traffic for the impulse offerings constituting the greater part of their sales.

This emphasis on supplementary lines appealing to impulse or convenience buying has led some drug stores recently to reorganize on self-service principles. Their price-marked merchandise is arranged on convenient counters and shelves, carefully sectionalized and displayed for maximum impulse appeal. Customers select their merchandise from these counters and shelves, place it in basket carriers, and take it to a cashier-checker for payment and wrapping. Except in fixed-price lines, these self-service drug stores offer substantial price savings. Current indications are that self-service in the drug store field is just the beginning of a long-term large-scale trend.

AUTOMOTIVE ACCESSORY AND HARDWARE STORES

Another interesting recent retailing development involves two closely related types of limited-line stores—automotive accessory stores and hardware stores.

Prior to the 1940's, most automotive accessory stores were true limited-line establishments, offering almost exclusively tires, batteries, fan belts, spark plugs, and the myriad other parts and accessories of the modern automobile. In the larger cities they were nearly all located in the automobile sales and servicing districts of their communities. In large towns and small cities they were likely to be found on the fringe of the retailing center.

During World War II, these automotive accessory retailers encountered serious difficulty in obtaining the automotive items which had previously been their exclusive merchandise line. Many were forced out of business. The others sought substitute lines and expanded into the field of general merchandising. With the return of ample supplies of automotive accessories after the war, these dealers retained the profitable secondary lines they had developed. Newcomers who poured into the field also turned to a wide variety of secondary lines. The more aggressive automotive accessory stores of today do approximately half their business in their basic line, and the other half in such diverse secondary lines as general hardware, electrical appliances, toys, household goods, sporting goods, radios, phonographs and records, and even in soft goods lines such as work clothes and sportswear. Many of the new automotive accessory stores have been opened in large neighborhood retailing centers, in integrated suburban shopping centers, and in the secondary shopping districts in large cities.

Even before the automotive accessory stores entered in a major way upon general hardware retailing in the 1940's, limited-line hardware stores had been suffering from the competition of other types of stores. The retailing of hardware had long been a minor departmental line for most department stores. Variety stores had captured a substantial part of the market for cheap tools and household items. Lumber and building materials retailers, and electrical appliance and household stores, were taking on supplemen-

A SELF-SERVICE DRUG STORE. *Courtesy of American Druggist.*

ILLUSTRATION 5–3

tary hardware lines. The entry of the automotive accessory stores into the field magnified a situation already becoming insupportable for the hardware stores. The cumulated competition proved fatal for many hardware dealers who did not have the flexibility to adapt themselves to changing circumstances. Those that survived and prospered have done so largely by taking on sidelines, such as paints and wallpapers, household goods, gardening equipment and supplies, electrical appliances, sporting goods, and often work clothes. Except for the lack of automotive accessory lines, many of these present-day hardware stores would be indistinguishable from the newer type of automotive accessory store.

REVIEW

1. What major changes in supermarket ownership and operation occurred between the early 1930's and the 1950's?

2. What are the best locations for supermarkets? Why?

3. Is self-service an advantage or drawback to the success of supermarkets? Why?

4. How do the merchandise offerings of supermarkets differ from those of service food stores? Why?

5. Compare the price and service policies of supermarkets with those of service food stores.

6. Are supermarkets likely to force small service food stores generally out of existence? Why?

7. What significant changes have been occurring in drug stores? In automotive accessory and hardware stores?

DISCUSSION TOPICS

1. "The small store with less than $50,000 annual sales is an economically unsound retailing unit, and will soon disappear from the American scene."

2. "The limited-line store is likely to remain the predominant type of American retailing institution, but with increasing attention given to supplementary lines."

3. "The trend is toward an ever-increasing expansion of supplementary lines in so-called limited-line stores. The end result of this can only be obliteration of all distinctions between limited-line stores and a return to 'general store' retailing."

4. "The rise of the supermarket may be considered the most revolutionary retailing development of the past quarter-century."

5. "The supermarket settled once and for all the myth that the American housewife prefers customer services to price-saving."

6. "The steady expansion of non-food lines in supermarkets during the past decade indicates that these stores will soon evolve into 'junior department stores.'"

7. What does the future hold for drug stores? for hardware stores?

PROBLEM

Mr. Brown operates a meat and grocery store, founded by his father forty years ago, in Hilldale, a well-to-do suburban community with about 10,000 population. His store occupies a 40′ x 60′ space in a row of stores facing on Station Plaza, a large square, now used for metered parking, before the Hilldale railroad station.

The Brown store offers high-quality, relatively-high-price lines of meats, groceries, and a limited selection of fresh fruits and vegetables. Clerk service is provided by Mr. Brown, two full-time clerks, and a part-time high-school senior. Telephone orders are taken. Deliveries are made in the afternoon by the part-time boy, using a station-wagon. About one-quarter of the store's customers maintain charge accounts, not because they need credit, but as a matter of convenience. The store's annual gross sales are around $80,000. Mr. Brown's competitors are two other independent stores located in the station area, both of which offer similar food lines and the same customer services as the Brown store and do about the same amount of business, and a chain supermarket located about a mile away, outside the heavily settled section of Hilldale, which does about $600,000 business annually in food and supplementary lines.

A variety store which occupied the 60′ x 60′ premises next to the Brown store is closing down. Mr. Brown is considering renting this space, knocking out the wall between the two stores so as to create a single 100′ x 60′ store area and converting to a superette. By liquidating some personal investments in stocks and bonds and borrowing upon a life insurance policy, Mr. Brown will be able to finance all the capital costs of equipping the enlarged store.

1. List and discuss the changes Mr. Brown will have to make in (a) lines carried, (b) store equipment and layout, (c) customer service policy, and (d) price policy.

2. Could Mr. Brown expect to take any business away from the competing supermarket? Why or why not?

3. Would he be likely to gain business from, or lose business to, the two competing service stores? Why?

4. Taking all considerations into account, do you think Mr. Brown should rent the adjoining space and convert to a supermarket? Why or why not?

SUGGESTED READINGS

Cahill, J., *Experiences of Smaller Stores,* Fairchild Publications, New York, 1955.

Cahill, J., (ed.), *Success on a Shoestring: 53 Smaller Women's Fashion Shops and How They Grew,* Fairchild Publications, New York, 1953.

Handler, J. H., *Fundamentals of Selling the Supermarkets,* Fairchild Publications, New York, 1955.

Kline, G. E., *Modern Super Markets and Superettes,* 2d ed, Progressive Grocer, New York, 1957.

Super Value Study, Progressive Grocer, New York, 1958.

Zimmerman, M. M., *The Super Market: A Revolution in Distribution,* McGraw-Hill Book Co., New York, 1955.

PERIODICALS: *American Druggist, Progressive Grocer, Super Market Merchandising.*

CHAPTER 6

DEPARTMENT AND OTHER MULTI-LINE STORES

Multi-line stores may be defined as retail establishments that offer several major lines of merchandise. Their merchandising and organization policies present a number of sharp contrasts to those of the limited-line stores studied in the preceding chapter.

There are three types of multi-line stores—rural general stores, variety stores, and department stores (including general merchandise stores organized on departmental lines but not of sufficient size to come within the technical definition of "department stores"). As of 1958, these multi-line stores accounted for only 5 percent of the total number of retail establishments, but 11 percent of retail sales. During the preceding quarter-century, rural general stores had declined substantially in importance in the overall retailing picture, but the other forms of multi-line stores maintained a relatively stable position.

GENERAL STORES

In the horse-and-buggy era the village general store was the dominant retailing institution of rural America. It carried a selection of convenience merchandise, of which the most important specific line was food; the more important subsidiary lines were notions, apparel, hardware, and farm supplies. It was the one and only consumer-goods outlet for thousands of villages. Except for the distant competition of the general mail order houses, each such store had virtually a monopoly on the purveying of everything bought by the inhabitants of its village and of the surrounding rural area. Frequently the local post office was located on its premises. Its wooden bench and cracker barrels, drawn around a cast-iron stove, constituted the social center for the local menfolk during winter evenings.

The heyday of the general store ended with World War I. As villages grew they became able to support grocery and other limited-line stores offering better selections of convenience goods than the general stores. The automobile, by ending rural isolation, enabled countryside and village residents to make their shopping purchases in neighboring cities and towns, thereby killing this side of the general stores' business. Many general store closed. Others were converted to limited-line stores. In 1929, when th˙ decline was already well advanced, 104,000 general stores were reported. By 1954, the last year in which a full count of these stores was made, the number was below 18,000.

VARIETY STORES

Variety stores are multi-line retail establishments carrying a broad selection of goods usually in a low or popular price segment of the price range, sold primarily by open display and semi-self-service. In 1958 there were 21,000 such stores, with sales volume of $3.6 billion. They constitute a distinctive detail of the American retailing picture: Woolworth, Green, Grant, Kress, and Kresge are familiar names in most parts of the country.

Location

Much of the custom of variety stores is of an impulse character. A woman notices a variety store that she passes while engaged in other shopping, thinks of certain items she might buy there, drops in, and purchases not only the items that originally occurred to her but a number of others that she sees while in the store. Because of this partial dependence on impulse customers, variety stores usually choose locations with heavy pedestrian traffic—on Main Street in towns and small cities, in the heart of neighborhood shopping centers, in central and secondary shopping districts where they catch the shopping traffic between department stores and other shopping goods stores.

Price and merchandise policies

Until the 1930's the traditional variety store was primarily a "5-and-10-cent" store. The big variety chains held strictly to "convenience" and "impulse" merchandise that could be sold at these two prices. They featured notions, stationery, toys and other children's items, hardware, and kitchenware items that could be priced at a nickel or a dime. Some independents offered a 5-10-25¢ range, and a very few carried items priced up to $1.00.

Periods of rising prices always presented a problem to the 5-and-10-cent stores. The buying prices of their traditional stocks would be pushed up to where no profit margin remained at the 5-cent or 10-cent sales prices. For a long time the stores felt that their very existence was inextricably bound with the customary nickel and dime prices. Their only solution, when the profit margin on an item disappeared, was to find a cheaper substitute. Fortunately, American industrial technology and low-cost novelty imports from Japan kept them well supplied through the earlier inflationary periods with a sufficiency of items.

Price increases of the late 1930's and 1940's, combined with the nonavailability of Japanese goods during this period, spelled the end of exclusive 5-and-10-cent variety merchandising. The variety chains as well as the independents had to price over ten cents. With the old tradition broken, the major chains followed the lead already established by the more flexible independents, and boldly adopted two new policies.

1. Not only did they raise the prices of many of their standard items over ten cents, but they took on new lines of higher-unit-price items that could be sold by counter display. Tools costing up to a dollar were added to the hardware departments. Twenty-five and fifty-cent items appeared on the cosmetics counters. Women's and children's apparel accessory lines priced up to a dollar were offered. Cheap costume jewelry was featured. These departures from the old tradition having proved successful, many variety stores—particularly those located in shopping centers—have recently ventured into lines of house dresses and other items of women's apparel, kitchen electrical appliances, and various household articles priced up to five dollars. A few are apparently having success with radio sets, cameras, power lawn mowers, luggage, and other consumer durables costing up to fifty dollars.

2. The old tradition of "round" prices (5, 10, 20, 25, or 50 cents), which minimized making change, was to some extent discarded, and "odd" prices (13, 17, 19, 23, 37, 47, 73, or 97 cents) were introduced for many items. As explained in Chapter 20, "odd" prices give the illusion of a bargain, and had long been a familiar merchandising device in practically all other types of stores except the variety stores.

These recent developments in price and merchandise policies might appear to have shifted many of the variety stores into the department store class. Fundamentally, however, these two classes of multi-line stores are still widely differing types of retailing institutions. The major part of a department store's merchandise is shopping goods; a neighborhood variety store's stock is usually entirely convenience and impulse goods, and such goods still predominate in the offerings of shopping center variety stores. A department store sells through clerk service, a variety store by counter display. Department stores offer charge account and installment credit, delivery, and other customer services; variety stores are almost exclusively customer-selection cash-carry institutions.

Organization

Most variety stores, chain units as well as independents, are unitary organizations—the store manager has full responsibility for all divisions. Only in very recent years have a few of the very largest stores, having taken on extensive lines of women's and children's apparel and accessories, and electrical appliances and radios, set up separate departmental structures for these divisions.

Purchasing for the large variety chains is done through the central office, and is generally departmentalized. There are separate buyers for the various lines carried by the chain. These buyers have considerable supervisory authority, with respect to the store divisions handling their lines, over the pricing, stock-keeping, and display functions of the individual stores in the chain.

DEPARTMENT STORES

Department stores are large multi-line stores handling a wide variety of shopping and specialty goods, including women's ready-to-wear and accessories, men's and boys' wear, piece goods, small wares, and home furnishings, which are organized into separate departments for purposes of promotion, service, and control. The *Census of Business* limits the term to stores with 25 or more employees, and calls smaller establishments of this type "general merchandise stores."

In no one of the elements of this definition are department stores unique. As we have seen, there are two other classes of multi-line retailers—general stores and variety stores. Many limited-line stores carry one or another of the department store merchandise lines as their major line. Departmental organization is common among supermarkets and large women's wear stores. It is the consistent combination of these three factors—multi-line retailing, emphasis on shopping- and specialty-goods lines, and departmental organization—that distinguishes the department store from other classes of retailing institutions.

The 1958 *Census of Business* reported 3,157 department stores. Their sales amounted to $13.4 billion—6.7 percent of total retail sales for the year. A large proportion of the 40,000 or more stores classified by the *Census of Business* as "dry goods and general merchandise stores," which did over $4 billion business in 1958, qualified in most respects as department stores except that they had fewer than 25 employees.

Origin and development

Prior to the Civil War there were a number of large multi-line retail stores with departmentalized structures in the major metropolitan cities—

among them the A. T. Stewart store in New York, John Wanamaker's in Philadelphia, and Zion's Cooperative Mercantile Institution in Salt Lake City. It is doubtful, however, whether any of these would have come fully under the present definition of a department store. By 1870 the true department store had developed. Some of the better known of these department stores, all in existence, were Lord & Taylor, Macy's, Hearn's, and Stern Brothers in New York, Namm-Loeser in Brooklyn, Marshall Field and Carson Pirie & Scott in Chicago, Hudson's in Detroit, White's in Boston, Bullock's in Los Angeles, and The Emporium in San Francisco.

There is considerable dispute as to how or out of which type of retail store the department store developed. Unquestionably some department stores evolved out of what had been general stores. Others started as specialty stores, and gradually added other lines until they became full-fledged department stores. Still others were established at the outset as department stores. Our best conclusion is that there was no single predominant prototype for the modern department store. It grew in this country as a need developed for a large retail establishment carrying a wide variety of goods, particularly shopping goods. Its primary appeal was not convenience of location, but the offering of a broad variety of lines of shopping goods under a single roof. This feature made possible the satisfaction of many classes of needs in a single "shopping" excursion; it also offered a wide selection of merchandise in each line so that peculiarities of individual taste could be satisfied and gratification of choice could be given.

Location

Department stores are commonly thought of as metropolitan institutions. It may surprise many, therefore, to learn that barely one tenth of the country's department stores are located in cities with populations over 500,000, and that over half are located in communities with populations under 50,-000. On a sales volume basis, however, the picture is quite different. The metropolitan stores account for nearly one half of total department store sales. Several individual stores in this group have annual sales exceeding $100 million.

The basic habitat of the department store is the urban shopping center, primary or secondary. Indeed, the heart of each such shopping center is usually one or more department stores. Recently there has been a spread of department stores, through branch openings, to suburban and integrated shopping centers. A neighborhood retailing center offers poor ground for locating a department store. The market area around such a center normally does not have sufficient buying population to support even a small general merchandise store. The inhabitants of the area would be inclined in any case to travel to a primary or secondary shopping center for their "shopping" expeditions, because these major centers would offer them a wider selection of shopping goods in any line than could a small neighborhood store.

One of the phenomena of department store location is the tendency of two or more stores to seek neighboring, even adjacent, locations. This is sound policy. When buying shopping goods, women want to compare styles, qualities, and prices. Starting with one store, they will move on to another, and yet another, if these other stores are not too distant—and commonly enough end up by making a larger volume of purchases in the group of stores visited than they would have bought in any one. Each department store thus stands to gain more from its proximity to others than it loses by the competition.

Merchandise lines

As indicated in Illustration 6–1, 55 percent of department store sales are in women's, men's and children's apparel and accessory lines. Another 22 percent are in furniture and household lines. Some sales in these fields are unquestionably the result of impulse buying—a customer, primarily interested in shopping for other items, sees a dress, or a hat, or a pair of gloves that strikes her fancy and buys it on the spur of the moment. Essentially, however, apparel and home furnishings are shopping goods. A considerable proportion of the items in other departments are also shopping goods. At a conservative estimate, shopping goods account for well over 80 percent of total department store sales; the proportion would be lower for metropolitan department stores, higher for those located in smaller communities.

Metropolitan department stores have found it profitable to operate impulse and specialty goods departments. Among the more common impulse goods departments are drugs, tobacco products, costume jewelry, and stationery. A common specialty goods line carried by some metropolitan department stores is imported food delicacies; another is antiques and art items. Among department store specialty goods offerings have been prefabricated houses, airplanes, and Chinese art treasures.

Most of the merchandise fields in which department stores are interested cover a broad range from top quality products at very high prices to cheap low-quality items. A department store could not possibly offer its customers the entire gamut in the quality-price range of any product. It must choose a limited range of "price lines" to offer its customers. Department stores in small communities, particularly where there is only one department store in the community, usually concentrate on intermediate price lines. Metropolitan stores tend toward differentiation. Some build up a reputation as "quality" stores, with price lines in each merchandise field ranging from top to high-intermediate. Others emphasize "economy" and "bargains," and carry price lines ranging from low to low-intermediate.

A metropolitan department store ordinarily must be consistent in the price line ranges of its various departments. Customers of a "quality" store would not be interested in a cheap furniture line, and purchasers for such furniture would not be likely to enter the "quality" store in the course of their shopping. Likewise, failure would attend a single high-quality line in a store that otherwise catered generally to a clientele seeking low-price

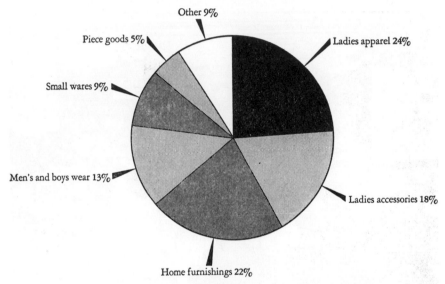

DISTRIBUTION OF DEPARTMENT STORE SALES BY MER-
CHANDISE LINES, 1959
Source: Board of Governors of the Federal Reserve System
ILLUSTRATION 6–1

goods. Some metropolitan department stores, however, have found two devices—the *bargain basement* or *basement store* on the one hand, and the *de luxe department* on the other, for straddling quality ranges in certain merchandise fields.

The "bargain basement" of a metropolitan department store is some-times operated through the administrative structure of the store's "up-stairs" merchandise departments. More often it is administratively semi-independent of the rest of the store, with separate planning, budgeting, and buying programs, its own buying staff, and sometimes even a separate receiving department. A "bargain basement" duplicates some, but not all, of the departments of the "upstairs" store. Top price lines generally begin at levels very slightly higher than the lowest price lines for the correspond-ing "upstairs" department, and range downward to whatever levels are competitively profitable. The bargain basement is frequently used as a clearance floor for odds and ends of merchandise which have not sold well in the "upstairs" store and have been reduced for quick movement. The majority of lines carried downstairs are bought specially for the basement, however, and consist of less expensive goods or broken lots and sizes which could not be sold strategically in the regular store program. In all, some 7 percent of department store sales are made through their "bargain basements."

A DEPARTMENT STORE BARGAIN BASEMENT. *Courtesy of Filene's, Boston.*

ILLUSTRATION 6–2

De luxe departments, called "boutiques" or "little shops," may be established as supplements to the regular house furnishings or women's wear departments. They represent a bid for a clientele which is a social and economic grade higher than that reached by the store's regular merchandise lines. As in the case of the "bargain basements," they are intended to attract a supplementary group of customers who, once they are in the store, will extend their buying to other departments.

Buying

One of the reasons for the rise of the department store, and its success in maintaining its position against the competition of other classes of retailing institutions, is its expert buying, which is often direct-from-manu-facturer. As indicated later in this chapter, departmental organization gives the store a group of department managers each of whom is an expert in purchasing his line of merchandise. So important is the purchasing function of these department managers that they are customarily called "buyers" rather than managers. Study and experience give them intimate knowledge of their product lines. Careful scrutiny of their departmental sales records informs them of what items and styles customers prefer and when they want them. They use the services of marketing research and style forecast-ing agencies.

The substantial volume of their purchases, even for minor items, makes it possible for department store buyers to purchase many of their require-ments, particularly in fashion lines, directly from manufacturers. This frequently gives them substantial economies in their purchase prices. Fur-thermore, direct buying gives department stores primary access to mer-chandise lines, thereby enabling them to be among the first in offering fashion merchandise and presenting new lines to the country. Independent nonmetropolitan department stores, whose buyers cannot be in direct daily touch with apparel manufacturers and other producers of fashion mer-chandise, are able to maintain indirect up-to-the-minute contact with fashion goods developments through resident buying offices (described in Chapter 10). Some department store chains maintain central buying of-fices in New York City with "resident buyers" who cooperate with the store buyers in purchasing fashion and home decoration goods.

Advertising, display, and other promotion

Established customers would probably visit a department store without any prodding from advertisement, display, or other forms of sales promo-tion, whenever an accumulation of buying needs warranted a "shopping trip." Absence of promotional effort, however, would deprive a department store of three major opportunities: (1) the goodwill and prestige built up by effective advertising and display bring new customers to a store and retain the loyalty of old ones; (2) advertisements of particular merchandise items attract new customers and bring in old ones on occasions when they might not otherwise have gone "shopping"; (3) advertised "sales" enable a store to make profitable disposal of special stock accumulations, bargain purchases, and end-of-season remainders. On the basis of these considera-tions, department stores have become the most prolific and expert of retail advertisers.

Most department store advertising takes the form of "notice-of-sale" advertising in local newspapers. Full-page displays are taken in the metro-politan dailies and in the weekly papers of smaller communities. These newspaper ads are usually devoted to illustrations of selected merchandise from different departments of the store, with brief "puffing" descriptions, and with prices prominently featured. Metropolitan department stores sometimes devote part of an ad space or entire advertisements to "institutional" promotion of the store, its prestige, and its services.

The window displays of metropolitan department stores have achieved the status of an art form. The merchandising objective—display of goods sold in the store to induce passers-by to enter and purchase the displayed items—is generally present, but is often subordinated, particularly in the case of the large metropolitan stores, to the objective of establishing institutional prestige.

Customer services

When women "shop," they want to compare merchandise as to relative utility, quality, style, and price. Prices can usually be readily compared. On the other features of the merchandise that interest her, a shopper often needs advice. Here is a double opportunity for the sales clerk—to win goodwill for the store by genuine customer service, and to crystallize sales out of the indecisions and conflicts of choice that beset shoppers. Sales-clerk service is one of the major keys to department store success. The larger department stores have recognized this, and their programs for selecting, training, and maintaining the quality of their sales forces are among the most advanced in the personnel field.

Credit, delivery, and phone order service have always been features of department store operation. Department stores were first to place retail credit and collection on an effective basis. For a long time department store credit extension was confined to charge accounts. Beginning in the 1930's they cautiously engaged in installment credit granting, under the name of "budget accounts." Furniture, kitchen and laundry appliances, radio sets, and musical instruments were the principal classes of merchandise sold on these accounts. Recently, many stores have instituted credit coupon booklets, paid for on an installment basis over three or six months, whose coupons may be used in all departments of the store.

Competing for customer goodwill, metropolitan department stores have sought every opportunity to create customer services. Well-appointed lounge rooms are provided for the relaxation of weary shoppers. Merchandise counsellors advise on interior decoration and the selection of gifts. Return privileges are so liberal that a considerable proportion of department store sales are, in effect, on an "on approval" basis. Free alterations are made on various classes of merchandise. Free instruction is given in sewing, cooking, interior decoration, and other fields of home economics. Some stores offer their customers theater ticket purchasing and vacation planning services. For the convenience of men and of the growing proportion of employed women, most metropolitan department stores instituted the policy during the 1940's of remaining open one evening a week; in the early 1950's many of them swung to a two-evenings-a-week policy. Recently-opened suburban branch stores not only provide parking space for customers' cars, but also kennels for their dogs while they shop, nurseries and attendants for their children, and "dens" to which husbands who have been dragged along on their wives' shopping expeditions are encouraged to retreat. Most of these customer services have come to be taken for granted. They form an important characteristic that distinguishes this type of store from most other classes of retail institutions, and that gives it both competitive advantages and cost disadvantages.

Price policy

Most department stores are highly price-conscious. They customarily exercise great care to keep their prices in line with those of competitors in their "quality" class. Many metropolitan stores operate under a "we will not be undersold" price policy, and employ professional "comparison shoppers" to check prices and assortments of competing stores.

Department store emphasis on customer service causes their operating expenses to run considerably higher, in relation to sales, than those of competing speciality shops and other limited-line stores. How, then, can the department stores hold their prices in line with the competition and still operate at a profit? To some extent buying economies offset higher expense. The major factor is their more rapid stock turnover, accomplished through buying efficiency and energetic promotion. This factor enables them to operate on narrower unit profit margins than competing types of stores but still realize satisfactory ratios of profit to investment.

Management organization

Careful planning is essential to department store success. A multiplicity of departments and merchandise lines raises problems that limited-line stores, even large departmentalized ones, do not face. Costs and expenses must be closely predetermined by budgeting and must be allocated among the departments. Inventories must be controlled, with various control techniques appropriate to different classes of merchandise. Buying and advertising, again with departmental allocations, must have advance scheduling. Such preplanning of complicated retailing operations requires a substantial behind-the-scenes management structure.

There are many different patterns of department store management organization. One of the most widely used management structures is the

Mazur Four-Functional Plan. This management system, first formally recommended for department stores in 1927, consists of four major divisions—Merchandising, Promotion, Finance and Control, and Store Management. The title of each of these divisions indicates its major function. The Mazur Plan has been widely criticized because it splits up some of the important retailing functions, and some critics consider that it overemphasizes the selling phase of department store activity. The test of a quarter-century's experience on the part of many stores, however, seems to support it. Macy's of New York, the largest department store in the country, is organized in accordance with the Mazur Plan with some minor modifications.

The operating units of a department store are the merchandise departments—one for each field of merchandise carried by the store. Under the Mazur Plan, these merchandise departments are all within the Merchandising Division. Each department is, in effect, a distinct retailing unit. It has its specified floor space in the store layout. Separate accounts are kept of its sales, costs, and operating expenses, and to the latter are added allocated shares of the store's promotional, administrative, and other overhead expenses. Each department must show an appropriate profit, taking into consideration its buying budget, allotted floor space, normal markup and turnover, competitive conditions, and special extraneous circumstances that might affect consumer buying—"or else."

The executive of a merchandise department is universally titled a "buyer." He—or in a large proportion of cases, she—is the purchasing head for the department.* He must hold purchases for the department within a budgetary allotment, and must conform with the store's general merchandise policy in quality and price selections, but otherwise he has substantial independence in departmental purchasing. A buyer is also the sales executive for his department. In many cases he is responsible for the entire training of his sales clerks; where a personnel department takes over the basic sales force training, each department buyer subsequently gives his clerks the special instruction they need in the department's merchandise and in any special selling techniques. Each buyer shares with the Store Management Division direction of the on-the-floor activities of his clerks.

Branch stores

In recent years, many of the large metropolitan department stores have established branches in rapidly-expanding suburban communities surrounding their cities or in newly constructed integrated shopping centers.

---

* Except in some department store chains where purchasing has been centralized for the chain. In such cases, the department managers in each store of the chain are primarily sales executives.

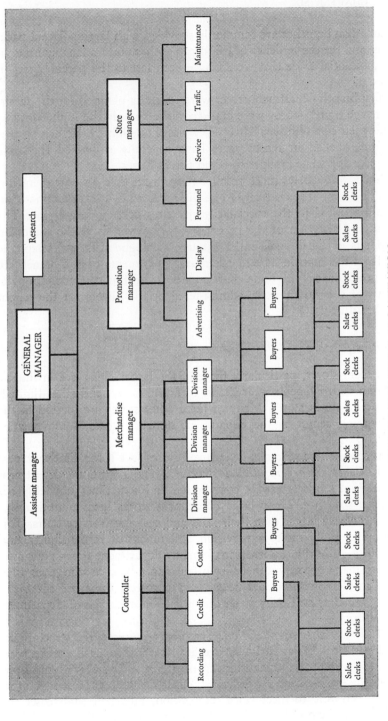

DEPARTMENT STORE ORGANIZATION

ILLUSTRATION 6–3

These suburban branches are commonly provided with large adjacent parking areas, and the convenience of car shopping has unquestionably brought them a substantial trade that would have been lost to the parent stores in the cities.

The first branch department stores were generally planned for the suburban "carriage trade"—they were expected to serve only the higher income classes of their communities. This policy was short-sighted. Branch department stores opened in recent years have generally embodied the same quality-price appeal as the metropolitan parent stores.

A branch store carries much smaller floor stocks than its parent institution. Its "pattern," too, is likely to be different, with greater emphasis on merchandise suited to the special circumstances of suburban living. The full stock and selection of the parent store, however, is at the command of customers of the branch outlet through catalogue lists and telephone service from the branch. The merchandise departments of the branch are usually not independent units, but extensions of the corresponding departments of the parent store, administered by the buyers for the parent store's departments.

Competitive position

Department stores, particularly those of the larger cities, are in intense competition with women's wear shops, furniture stores, and other limited-line shopping-goods stores. Many of these other stores are located in the same shopping center as the department store or stores; some may be adjacent.

In this competitive struggle, department stores face three disadvantages:

1. *Complex organizational structure.* The nature of department store operation tends toward a complicated and sometimes unwieldy administrative structure. Many large department stores have administrative staffs considerably larger than their sales and customer service staffs. This creates serious problems of supervision, assignment of responsibility, and delegation of authority. Salespersons in many department stores are supervised by so many executives that they often cannot be sure who gives what orders. Considerable effort has been made to correct these organizational problems, but they still exist as an important disadvantage of department store retailing.

2. *High costs of operation.* Complex administrative structure involves department stores in heavy overhead costs. Emphasis on customer services results in special operating expenses that other stores do not have, at least to the same extent. As indicated, department stores have heretofore generally been able to meet price competition, but their high costs and expenses leave them only a thin unit-profit margin. In their competition

with the discount houses, however, department stores have definitely lost heavily on home appliance sales, and they are feeling pressure from some other classes of limited-service retailers. Expense control and reduction is always a forefront issue with department stores, and some may soon have to turn a critical eye on particular high-cost elements of their liberal customer service policy.

3. *Range of offerings in any line.* Broad though its range of offerings in any particular merchandise line may be, a department store can rarely give as wide a choice as can a large women's wear shop or other large store that specializes in a single line. Department stores partially overcome this disadvantage by covering in their more restricted selection the established preferences of the classes of customers who are likely to patronize them. But this solution is at best a partial one. Many customers with particular tastes turn to the large limited-line stores, rather than to department stores, for the "perfect" satisfaction of their wants.

Five compensating advantages of department stores are:

1. *Expert, direct, large-volume buying.* As already indicated, department store buying, particularly that of the larger stores, is commonly of the most expert kind. These stores buy what carefully checked experience has indicated their customers want. Through their own departmental buyers, or through resident or central buying offices, they purchase fashion goods and many other lines directly from manufacturers. Departmental purchase volume often rivals that of large competing limited-line stores, and entitles them to substantial quantity discounts.

2. *General high efficiency of operation.* The complex administrative structure of many department stores, previously listed as a disadvantage, is a consequence of these stores' unrelenting efforts toward greater efficiency in operation. Their departmental organization, while it multiplies accounting labors and other administrative activity, unquestionably produces over-all buying and selling effectiveness. Their personnel programs, covering selective hiring, training, and skillful morale maintenance, while often costly, definitely raise the caliber of their staffs.

3. *Efficient promotion.* Department stores are generally more extensive and skillful advertisers than most limited-line stores. Their window displays are generally superior. They employ special "sales" and other promotional devices more intensively.

4. *Customer services.* The emphasis that department stores place upon customer services is the result of extensive experience which has established that such services bring customers into a store and retain them as regular patrons. Few if any women's wear shops or other limited-line stores are in a position to offer their patrons the wide range of services that have been developed by the large metropolitan department stores.

5. *Multiplicity of merchandise lines.* That a customer can buy a

dress, a cheese-grater, a television receiver, and a children's game within the one store has a double advantage. First, customers not interested in store-to-store comparison shopping can satisfy all shopping needs under one roof. Second, a customer who enters a department store with a definite product objective in mind often is made aware of other latent needs as she passes through various departments and decides to satisfy them while she is in the store. A limited-line store misses both of these sales possibilities.

There is no issue as to whether the advantages of the department store, in comparison with the limited-line shopping goods store, outweigh the disadvantages. Operational advantages and disadvantages balance sufficiently so that department stores can well hold their own with limited-line stores on a price basis. The relative appeal of the merchandise-line and customer-service policies of department stores as against those of competing limited-line stores varies for different customer groups. For some, the balance favors the department store. For others it favors the limited-line store. And for a very large proportion of customers the balance is so even that they divide their patronage, on various incidental considerations, between the two classes of retailing institutions.

The *Census of Business* figures, given in Table 5–1, show the proportion of department store sales to total retailers' sales declining from 9 percent in 1929 to under 7 percent in 1958. The explanation of this decline is not that department stores have been falling behind in their struggle with the various other types of stores that compete with them. It is the tremendous expansion of retail sales in the automobile and other fields outside the sphere of department store interest that has produced the lowered ratio of department store sales. In the group of merchandise lines to which department stores are primarily committed, their sales consistently accounted for 22 to 24 percent of total sales in these lines during the 1929–1954 period. Only in the recent substantial surrender of home appliance sales to discount houses have the department stores seriously lost ground to any competing type of retailer.

REVIEW

1. How do you account for the decline of the general store during the second quarter of the century? Is this decline likely to continue?
2. How do the pricing policies of variety stores influence their merchandise line offerings? Discuss recent changes in the price and merchandise line policies of variety stores.
3. From what type of store did the department store evolve?
4. Where are department stores generally located? Why?
5. What are the major merchandise lines in department stores?
6. Explain "bargain basements."

7. Explain: "One reason for department store success is expert buying, often direct-from-manufacturer."

8. Explain: "Department stores have become the most prolific and expert retail advertisers."

9. How can department stores, with cost-to-sales ratios generally higher than those of competing single-line stores, meet the price competition of these stores?

10. Explain the Mazur Four-Functional Plan of department store organization.

11. What are the responsibilities of a department store buyer?

12. How do the offerings of a branch department store differ from those of the parent store?

DISCUSSION TOPICS

1. "The variety store, based on low-quality low-price merchandise, was an appropriate retailing institution when this country was still in an Economy of Scarcity. Its foundations have been cut from under it by our transition to an Economy of Plenty."

2. "Variety stores had better start advertising—or else!"

3. Are department stores at an advantage or disadvantage with competing single-line stores? Which type is likely to force the other out of existence?

4. "The large metropolitan department store is likely to hold its key place in American retailing for a long time to come."

5. "The continued existence of the metropolitan department store represents the triumph of retailing efficiency over retailing economics."

6. "A 'must' for department store success is customer services."

7. "Those metropolitan department stores that survive over the next decade will owe such survival to their branch systems."

PROBLEM 1

Mr. Gleason has been for several years the manager of a Woolworth variety store in the shopping center of Metropolis City. He is considering resigning this position and starting an independent variety store of his own in the neighborhood retailing street of the residential area where he lives.

1. There are two locations that can be rented. One is a corner location with a 40′ frontage on the store street and 50′ frontage (with 20′ of display window) on the side residential street. The other is in the middle of the same block on the store street, with a 40′ frontage and a 60′ depth. The rent of the corner location is 25 percent higher than that of the other. Which would be preferable? Why?

2. How would the merchandise lines of a variety store in the neighborhood location differ from those of the Woolworth store that Mr. Gleason previously managed?

3. A stationery store close by carries an extensive toy line. Should Mr. Gleason include a toy line in his store? Why—or why not?

4. Should Mr. Gleason carry any of the following lines with prices in the 25¢ to $1 range—kitchen ware? tools? ornamental vases? aprons and house dresses? auto accessories? cosmetics? Why or why not?

PROBLEM 2

The Emporium, the leading department store of Metropolis City, is planning to establish a branch in Home World, a suburban shopping center under construction thirty miles from Metropolis City. Among the other stores in Home World will be a large women's wear shop, a home furnishings store with a limited line of furniture and an extended line of floor coverings, a large variety store, a gift shop, and Child Life—a store carrying children's wear, toys, and other children's lines.

1. Should the branch store's offerings differ in any respect from those of the parent store? Why?

2. How should buying for the branch store be handled? Why?

3. Should the customer services offered by the branch store differ from those of the parent store? Why?

4. Should the price policy of the branch store differ from that of the parent store? Why?

5. Should the branch store do any advertising or engage in other forms of promotion? Why? If so, what?

SUGGESTED READINGS

Baker, H. G., *Rich's of Atlanta,* School of Business Administration, University of Georgia, Atlanta, 1953.

Beil, P. J. (ed.), *Variety Store Merchandising,* Variety Store Merchandiser Publications, New York, 1956.

Carson, C., *The Old Country Store,* Oxford University Press, New York, 1954.

Edwards, R. H., *Tales of the Observer,* Jordan Marsh & Co., Boston, 1951.

Entenberg, R. D., *The Changing Competitive Position of Department Stores in the United States by Merchandise Lines,* University of Pittsburgh Press, Pittsburgh, 1957.

Gould, R. E., *Yankee Storekeeper,* Whittlesey House, New York, 1946.

Hahn, L., *Stores, Merchants, and Customers,* Fairchild Publications, New York, 1952.

Harriman, M. C., *And the Price is Right,* World Publishing Co., Cleveland, 1958.

Hower, R. M., *History of Macy's of New York, 1858–1919,* Harvard University Press, Cambridge, 1943.

Mahoney, T., *The Great Merchants,* Harper & Bros., New York, 1955.

Stanton, E. M., *Branch Stores: Planning, Merchandising, Operating, Promoting,* National Retail Dry Goods Association, New York, 1955.

Twymam, R. W., *History of Marshall Field & Co., 1852–1906,* University of Pennsylvania Press, Philadelphia, 1954.

Weiss, E. B., *Mass Marketing to the 400 Mass Retailers,* Funk & Wagnalls, New York, 1950.

Wendt, L., & H. Kogan, *Give the Lady What She Wants: the Story of Marshall Field and Company,* Rand McNally & Co., Chicago, 1952.

Winkler, J. K., *Five and Ten,* McBride, New York, 1940.

PERIODICALS: *Department Store Economist, Stores, Variety Store Merchandiser.*

CHAPTER 7

CHAIN STORES: MINOR TYPES OF RETAIL INSTITUTIONS

Two bases for classifying retailing institutions, as indicated in Chapter 4, are ownership and whether or not a store is utilized for retail selling. The ownership classification leads to the study of chain stores and of such minor retailing institutions as leased departments, consumer cooperatives, manufacturer-owned stores, and government stores. Nonstore retailing, also a minor element in our retailing structure, is performed by mail order houses, direct-selling retailers,* and automatic vending machines.

CHAIN STORES

Chain stores are certainly one of the most attention-demanding features of our retailing system. Yet only recently was agreement reached among marketing writers and governmental agencies upon definitions of "chain store" or "retail chain system." A "chain store system" is now defined as "a group of retail stores of essentially the same type, centrally owned and with some degree of centralized control of operation." A "chain store" is one belonging to such a system. Note that under these definitions a "retail chain" or "retail chain system" can consist of as few as two units. Note also that the legal form of common central ownership of a chain system—individual, partnership, or corporate **—is irrelevant. And note finally

---

* Direct-to-consumer selling by manufacturers through mail order and canvasser salesmen is dealt with in Chapter 13.

** Some writers use the term "corporate chain" in the same sense we are using "chain." Students meeting this term should not be misled into thinking that the possibility of individual or partnership ownership of chain systems is thereby excluded.

that voluntary associations of independent retailers for the mutual conduct of certain of their operations—which are sometimes called "voluntary
chains" but which we shall study later in this chapter under the heading of
retailer "groups"—are excluded from the "chain" concept.

Development

Chain stores date back to the early years of the Nineteenth Century.
Andrew Jackson was at one time the operator of a three-store chain in
Tennessee. By the middle of the century there were many local chains and
several regional ones. The Great Atlantic and Pacific Tea Co. (today's
familiar "A & P"), whose second store was opened in 1859, was merely
the first chain to develop to national proportions. The F. W. Woolworth
Company, which brought national chain retailing to the variety field, began
operation in 1879. The concept of chain retailing was obviously a sound
one, and increase of chain store systems until the World War I period was
steady though unspectacular.

During the 1920's the chain store movement mushroomed. By 1929,
7,083 retailing chains operated 158,029 stores and accounted for nearly 30
percent of retail sales. The A & P, largest of the grocery chains, had over
15,000 stores, Woolworth over 1,800, J. C. Penney over 1,400. During
this decade, chain retailing spread from the three fields of variety goods,
food, and drugs, where it had initially established itself, to practically all
other retailing fields—prominent among them women's and men's apparel,
furniture, department stores, and department store leased departments.

Between 1929 and 1948 the number of chain stores declined by one
quarter. Their proportion of total retail sales remained relatively constant,
however, around 30 percent. Three developments account for this check
to the expansion of chain retailing:

1. During the 1920's some of the retailing chains, particularly
those in the food field, had overexpanded and had opened stores in neighborhood centers and small communities where sufficient sales volume for
profitable chain operation could not develop. During the 1930's thousands
of these unprofitable units were closed. The A & P, for example, reduced
the number of its stores from over 15,000 in 1929 to 9,200 in 1939. In
many instances groups of small service grocery stores operated by chains
were replaced by supermarkets.

2. A powerful political anti-chain-store movement developed during the 1930's. Restrictive state and federal laws, discussed later in this
chapter were passed. These measures outlawed some of the chains' most
effective sales promotion tactics, and burdened them with special taxes.

3. The abler among the independent retailers, who found themselves in competition with the chains, learned from their rivals. As such

independents became more efficient, they were able not merely to hold their own against the competition of chain units, but in many cases to win the competitive struggle and force the withdrawal of the chain units.

The closing of small chain stores and the substitution of larger ones has continued during the post-war period, particularly in the food field. But since the war the new openings have outnumbered the closings, and the number of chain units increased moderately after 1948. During the 1950's the chains' proportion of total retail sales rose slightly over the 30 percent level that had persisted through the preceding two decades.

Chain system organization and control

Some two- and three-store chains are operated as individual enterprises or partnerships. The advantages of incorporation, if only to limit personal liability, are so definite, however, for a retail business expanding beyond the one-store stage, that the corporate form dominates this type of retailing. Among the incorporated chains there is no single pattern of system structure. Wide variations exist on such factors as chain size, corporate organization, management control, territorial coverage, and vertical integration.

Chain size. The public generally thinks of retail chains in terms of the A & P with its 5,000 food stores and Woolworth with its 2,000 variety stores. Actually, as indicated in Illustration 7–1, over one-third of the total number of chain stores, accounting for over one-fifth of chain sales, belong to two- and three-unit systems. These operate essentially as independents and are generally allied with the independent dealers in their lines in antagonism to the large chains. Large chains with over a hundred stores each operate over one-fourth of the chain stores and produce over two-fifths of chain store sales. It is these large chains that have given chain retailing its distinguishing characteristics of large-scale purchasing, assumption of warehousing and other wholesaling functions, mass-appeal merchandising policies, and efficient retailing operation.

Corporate organization. Many retailing chains, including some of the largest, are organized as unitary corporations. Many others are organized on a holding-company basis. Sometimes, as in the case of most of the department chain stores, each store is a separate subsidiary corporation. Sometimes, for tax reasons, a chain that operates in more than one state organizes a subsidiary for each state in which it has stores. Recently there have been a number of consolidations of local or regional food chains through holding-company arrangements.

Management control. Management control in retail chains ranges from nearly 100 percent centralization of authority to nearly 100 percent decentralization. There are chains, particularly in the tobacco products and newsstand lines, where the store managers are allowed no policy discretion and are merely senior sales clerks. There are intermediate types where the store managers have considerable merchandising freedom of action and are compensated in part by a share of store profits. In some holding-company chains in the department store field, like Federated Department Stores and Allied Department Stores, each individual store is a separate subsidiary corporation and its management has substantial independence on merchandise policy and operations. The only safe generalization on this subject is that the larger the store units in a chain system, the more likely there is substantial delegation of executive authority to the unit store managements; but there are many exceptions even to this principle.

SIZE DISTRIBUTION OF RETAIL CHAIN STORES, 1958

NUMBER OF STORES IN SYSTEM	STORES		SALES	
	Number	Percent	Amount (millions)	Percent
2– 3	68,565	37.5	$13,766	20.4
4– 5	13,310	7.3	4,176	6.4
6– 10	12,366	6.8	4,816	7.2
11– 25	14,670	8.0	5,115	7.6
26– 50	11,888	6.5	6,263	9.3
51–100	11,708	6.4	4,597	6.8
over 100	50,228	27.5	28,476	42.3
Total	182,735	100.0	$67,209	100.0

Source: *1958 Census of Business, Retail Trade.*

ILLUSTRATION 7–1

Territorial extent. Except in the department store and other shopping store fields, a retail chain with ten or fewer stores does not scatter its units widely over the country. It concentrates operations in and around a metropolitan city or in a group of nearby towns and small cities. Most of our retail chains operate locally in this fashion. Regional or sectional chains come into existence in some cases because local chains spread beyond their original territories, and in other instances by merger and consolidation of local chains. A regional chain is not necessarily an intermediate-size one. Some small-size department store and other "shopping" store chains operate regionally, as do several of the largest food chains. A few of the "national" chains, like the A & P, Woolworth, and Sears Roebuck systems, do have stores in all parts of the continental United States, though not necessarily in all states, but the term is usually applied to any large chain that operates in more than one region or section of the country.

Vertical integration. Most small chains limit themselves to strictly retailing operations, and depend upon wholesalers for assembling broad lines of merchandise from which the chain buyers can make their selections, for storage, and for other wholesaling services. Large chains generally discover that they can perform these wholesaling operations for themselves as efficiently and more economically than any wholesalers. They set up their own buying offices, warehouses, and truck delivery organizations. Some of the giant food chains have reached even further afield and operate or control canning establishments. One recently organized a subsidiary to establish integrated suburban shopping centers so that it can be assured of supermarket locations in such centers. In all these cases of "vertical integration," the retailing interests of the chain dominate their wholesaling and manufacturing activities. There are some cases, however, where wholesalers or manufacturers have established retail chains, or have bought controlling interests in pre-existing retail chains. At one time a substantial proportion of filling stations were owned by wholesale gasoline distributors; each distributor in effect operated its own retail chain. Manufacturer-dominated chains are found in shoes and men's clothing. The Robert Hall chain of clothing stores is part of a complex vertical integration, United Merchants and Manufacturers, which includes spinning and weaving mills, dyeing and printing plants, a converter, a factor, and a clothing manufacturer as well as the clothing store chain. In these cases of "forward" vertical integration, the wholesalers' or manufacturers' distribution policies dominate the chains' retailing policies; we shall study this situation again in Chapter 14 when we examine manufacturer-direct-to-consumer distribution.

Extent of chain operation

There is no uniformity among retailing fields as to the proportion of stores in each field belonging to chain systems and the proportion of sales accounted for by such stores. The following variations may be noted:

1. Chain retailing is considerably more prevalent in nondurable goods lines than in durable goods lines, as indicated in Illustration 7–2. One reason for this is that direct manufacturer-to-retailer distribution is more common in durable goods lines than in nondurables, so that in the former there is less opportunity for cost saving through bypassing wholesalers, which is one of the advantages of chain retailing.

2. The predominance of chains in the variety field—over two-fifths of stores, over four-fifths of sales in 1958—has a historical explanation. This field was initially developed by Woolworth and other chain systems. Independents subsequently entered the field, but on a minor scale.

3. The high place of chain retailing in women's apparel—over two-fifths of total sales for this field for 1958—has surprised many students

PERCENTAGES OF CHAIN RETAILING TO TOTAL FOR CLASS OF
STORES, MEASURED BY NUMBER OF STORES AND SALES
VOLUME, 1929, 1939, 1948, AND 1958

RETAILING FIELD	1929		1939		1948		1958	
	Stores	Sales	Stores	Sales	Stores	Sales	Stores	Sales
Food	19	43	12	39	8	38	9	49
Department stores	54	28	73	43	68	64	80	86
Variety stores	49	92	48	90	43	86	45	84
Apparel	a	a	24	44	21	39	25	44
Service stations	28	41	8	17	4	10	8	14
Drugs	14	28	14	34	11	28	13	29
Other nondurable	a	a	7	19	6	21	7	24
Total nondurable	a	a	11	34	9	35	10	41
Furnishings	12	30	11	26	13	26	12	25
Automotive	a	a	14	18	9	11	10	11
Hardware and lumber	5	37	17	26	13	22	12	19
Jewelry	7	21	9	23	10	22	10	26
Total durable	a	a	14	22	12	17	11	16
Grand Total	14	30	11	31	9	30	10	34

a Not available
Derived from U.S. Bureau of the Census, *Census of Business* series.

ILLUSTRATION 7–2

of Marketing. It was thought that the importance of the fashion factor in this field would preclude the standardized procedures characteristic of chain retailing. Through intelligent merchandising policies which recognize variations in demand in different communities, and through concentration on popular fashion items with price savings, however, many chains are operating with substantial success in this field.

Characteristics

Great care must be exercised in making generalizations about chain store policies, because of their wide variation in different retailing fields. A statement about location policy that might be accurate as applied to chain variety stores could be flatly false as applied to chain apparel stores. Customer service policies are radically different in chain grocery stores and chain department stores. Our analysis of the more significant characteristics of chain policies must therefore be constantly hedged with qualifications relating to the various retailing fields in which the chains operate.

1. *Store size.* The substantial central administrative structures of most large chains, which contribute so much to their merchandising efficiency, result in heavy allocations of central administrative costs to each unit of the chain. Except in the department store field, these extra overhead costs cause chain stores generally to have much higher break-even points with respect to sales volume than most independents in the same line. Hence chain units must usually be designed for large-volume operation, and tend to be opened only in locations where large-volume operation is possible.

2. *Location.* Chains in impulse and convenience goods fields are acutely conscious of the importance of proper location in the success of their businesses. Because of higher sales volume break-even points, they must avoid communities and neighborhoods with populations insufficient to provide the mass buying they need. The large chains employ marketing research techniques to determine which communities and neighborhood centers can support stores of their type and size, and also to ascertain the best locations within such communities and neighborhood centers for their stores. Their financial resources enable them to rent or, if need be, buy the superior locations. The superior locations of chain stores in impulse and convenience lines have always been one of their major competitive advantages.

3. *Merchandise policy.* Chain stores in most retailing fields seek a large-volume rapid-turnover sale of standard and popular items in the line. National brand merchandise, with definitely established demand, is generally favored over less-well-known brands. Many large national and regional chains in various retailing fields, however, have succeeded in establishing such customer goodwill for their own private brands that they are able to concentrate on their house brands with only incidental stocking of competing national brands. To a large extent, chain stores in most retailing fields have been willing to allow their independent competitors to assume the risks inherent in the handling of specialty items, high fashion goods, minor brand lines, and slow-selling types and sizes. Unquestionably this policy has given the chains the advantage of higher turnover than most of the independents they compete with, though they sacrifice the patronage of customers who desire the specialties which chain units do not carry and which are to be found on the shelves of neighboring independents.

Centralized determination of chain store merchandise policy tends to produce uniformity in merchandise offerings. This often runs foul of variations in special fashions and tastes of different neighborhods or communities. Herein lay one of the most serious earlier weaknesses of the chains. In recent years the more progressive chains have substantially overcome this flaw in their merchandise policy by heeding recommendations of their unit managers as to local modifications of the standard line. In the case of department store chains and some women's wear chains where buying selection, though not necessarily actual purchase, is more largely the responsibility of the unit managements, this weakness in merchandise policy has not developed.

4. *Standardized store-front, layout, and operational policies.* As retailing chains built up customer goodwill, they realized that easy visual identification of their units was a promotional advantage. Hence they early standardized their store fronts, and incorporated distinctive features of color, structure, or design. Thereby a patron of a chain unit in a particular field, shopping outside her regular neighborhood center or moving to a new community or neighborhood, would be able to spot immediately a store of her favorite chain.

Store layouts, like store fronts, also tend to be standardized in the retailing chains. Generally these layouts are the results of careful study, and their standardization represents uniform application of a highly efficient system. Likewise standardization of the operating methods of chain systems with respect to stock- and record-keeping results in more efficient retailing management than prevails with most of their independent competitors.

5. *Buying.* Most of the buying for large retailing chains, even some of the department store chains, is done through centralized buying divisions. These divisions are, in effect, wholesaling units for their systems, enabling the chains to bypass the regular wholesalers in their lines and buy direct from manufacturers. Buyers for the larger chains are specialists in their lines, and are more expert in their purchasing operations than most proprietors of independent stores in the same fields. Pooling of the buying for all the units in a chain results in large volume orders that give its buyers many advantages in the selection of suppliers, establishment of merchandise standards and specifications, and maintenance of secure sources of supply. Prior to the passage of the Robinson-Patman Act, the large retailing chains were able to force special low prices from their suppliers, sometimes below those paid by small wholesalers in their lines. The Robinson-Patman Act curbed this practice, but the large chains, buying directly from manufacturers and in quantities that entitle them to maximum quantity discounts, can still purchase at lower costs than most independents. Often they buy the entire output of particular manufacturers or packers, so that the Robinson-Patman Act cannot apply. Besides acting as their own wholesalers, some corporate food chains have pushed integration to the point of owning or controlling packing and canning establishments, and several apparel and furniture chains are closely associated with their supplying manufacturers.

6. *Warehousing.* Most large retailing chains maintain their own warehouses or other storage facilities. This aids their quantity buying and

enables them, within the operation of the Robinson-Patman Act, to obtain special allowances on their purchase prices.

7. *Policy on customer services.* Retailing chains in the impulse and convenience goods fields, and even in such shopping lines as shoes and cheaper grades of women's apparel, have consistently minimized customer service. They generally refuse to extend credit, and generally offer no free delivery service. Most large grocery chains converted from clerk-service to self-service wherever practicable as soon as the first supermarkets showed that self-service was a sound basis for this field of retailing. Department store chains, of course, have to meet the same standards of customer service that prevail among independent department stores.

8. *Price policy.* The major competitive weapon of most retailing chains has been low prices. The economies they effect on buying and through elimination of most customer services, their general high efficiency, their maintenance of rapid turnovers, and their large-volume selling, enable them to undersell many of their independent competitors on items not subject to resale price maintenance. Various studies of comparative pricing by chain stores and competing independents have indicated price differentials in the grocery field up to 10 percent, in the drug field up to 15 percent, and in some other lines up to 20 percent.

9. *Promotion.* Where a large chain system operates a considerable number of stores in a large community, it can profitably undertake joint advertising for all of these stores through newspapers and spot radio and TV stations. Such advertising is not practicable for most independents in convenience goods fields. The major grocery, auto accessory, and drug chains have been extensive advertisers.

The anti-chain-store movement

The rapid expansion of chain retailing during the 1920's was a sharp challenge to independent merchants. Some met it squarely by copying the efficiency and limited-service policy of the chains, and by achieving their own purchasing economies through joining voluntary and cooperative groups. To the majority of small independents, however, the threat of the chains seemed a lethal one, impossible to meet with purely business tactics. They turned to political action, joined with their wholesalers in organizing lobbies, and sought legislation that would constrain the chains.*

---

* There was a comparable campaign by small retailers against department stores during the 1890's. Restrictive state legislation was sought but not obtained. From 1910 to 1917 the small retailers instituted an anti-mail-order campaign, which resulted in the zoning of parcel post rates. The mail order houses met this by decentralizing their warehousing, which proved to be an advantageous development. During the 1920's the retailers' organizations sought political action against direct-to-consumer selling by house-to-house canvassers. Hundreds of local restrictive ordinances were passed. Until 1938 these anti-canvassing ordinances were held invalid by the courts whenever they affected interstate distribution of goods; more recently they have been upheld.

The independent merchants succeeded in having four classes of anti-chain-store legislation enacted. (1) "Fair trade" laws, validating intra-state resale price maintenance of well-known brand items, adopted in forty-five states, were intended to prevent underselling by the chains; the federal Miller-Tydings Act of 1937 and the McGuire Act of 1952 accomplished the same validation in interstate transactions. (2) "Unfair trade practice" laws, forbidding sales below "cost," were enacted in some thirty states to discourage the chains from employing "loss leader" promotions. (3) Chain store taxes were passed in twenty-nine states, are currently effective in fifteen. (4) The federal Robinson-Patman Act, forbidding price discrimination among classes of buyers, was expected to prevent the chains from obtaining special price allowances from their suppliers. In addition, the federal Department of Justice was induced to institute a series of harassing but inconclusive anti-trust actions against various national chains.

The repressive effects of the anti-chain-store legislation, while unquestionable, should not be exaggerated. With the trend toward larger-volume stores, the anti-chain-store taxes levied on a per store basis proved to be less onerous than had been expected. Development by large chains of their own private brands offset the restrictive effect of the fair trade laws, and the chains still remained entitled to substantial quantity discounts under the Robinson-Patman Act. From the anti-chain-store drive, moreover, the chain systems learned a valuable lesson, albeit a costly one—a retail store is not merely a profit-making enterprise, but an integral part of the economic, civic and social life of its community. Retailing chains are now keen to cultivate not only customer but community goodwill. They contribute to local community chests and civic enterprises. Their managers belong to local chambers of commerce and rotary clubs. As a consequence the anti-chain-store movement lost its cutting edge during the 1940's.

RETAILER "GROUPS"

One of the answers to the chain store challenge discovered by many independents, particularly in the grocery field, was to become members of retailer "group" organizations. While retaining their ownership independence, they could thereby enjoy the chain advantages of expert and low-cost mass buying, have well-promoted "private" brands, and obtain expert managerial and merchandising guidance. Three types of retailer "groups" have developed—voluntary groups,* retailer cooperatives,* and pooled selling and advertising groups.

---

* Some Marketing writers call these "voluntary chains" and "cooperative chains." If the term "chain" is utilized for these associations, some distinguishing adjective, such as the misleading term "corporate," must be applied to the centrally-owned chains. To avoid

Voluntary groups

. A voluntary group is a group of retailers, each of whom owns and operates his own store, which is associated with a wholesale organization or a manufacturer to carry on joint merchandising activities, and which may be characterized by some degree of group identity and uniformity of operation. The retailer members of a voluntary group contract to purchase all, or at least a "fair share," of their requirements from the sponsoring wholesaler or manufacturer. They place their orders by mail or telephone. This enables the sponsor to eliminate salesmen in its dealings with the retailer members. Savings on salesmen's commissions and expenses are passed along to the retailer members through lower prices. In the larger voluntary groups, the sponsors frequently provide a "private" or "house" brand of goods in their line which the retailer members can sell at a higher markup than the national brands. Since any betterment of the business of the retailer members of a voluntary group is reflected in larger purchases from the sponsor, sponsors of most voluntary groups provide their dealers with extensive management assistance. They employ management counsellors to help the dealers with their store appearance, layout, merchandising, inventory control, and display problems; the cost of this service is usually covered by a fee or service charge. Where several members of a voluntary group are located within an area covered by a newspaper or a spot radio program, the sponsor may arrange joint advertising for them.

In most instances the wholesaler or manufacturer sponsor has no ownership or financial interest in the retailer members of its voluntary group. Sometimes, as in the case of the Howard Johnson restaurant group and several service station groups, the sponsor makes substantial loans to the retailer members to enable them to purchase their equipment. Less frequently the sponsor holds preferred stock or minority blocks of common stock of incorporated member stores.

The earliest voluntary groups were sponsored by wholesalers, and most of them still are. A number, however, are manufacturer-sponsored. In these, the dealer members must buy their major line from the manufacturer sponsor, but are free to handle their other purchases as they will. Brown Shoe Stores is an example of such a manufacturer-sponsored voluntary group. More surprising, a number of large chain systems also sponsor voluntary groups. United Cigar Stores and Liggett-Rexall Drug Stores do this; in both cases recent growth has resulted primarily from expansion in the number of their voluntary group units.

The voluntary group movement started prior to World War I in the

---

this difficulty, the American Marketing Association Definitions Committee has recommended use of the terms "voluntary group" and "retailer cooperative" as they are employed above.

food field. The rapid expansion of the grocery chain systems during the 1920's was a strong incentive to independent food stores to enter voluntary group associations, and by 1930 some 35,000 belonged. Since 1930, while the number of chain stores in the food field has declined, the number of independents affiliated in voluntary groups has multiplied. The figure for 1959 was around 60,000, supplied by 425 sponsoring wholesalers; sales of these voluntary-group grocery stores was around $13.7 billion, compared with $7.2 billion for nonaffiliated independents, and $19.5 billion for chain grocery stores. Most of the group-sponsoring grocery wholesalers have affiliated themselves in a dozen or more organizations to gain further advantages of massed wholesale buying and broad private-brand promotion. One of these federations, the Independent Grocers' Alliance, includes over 70 wholesaler members who serve some 5,000 fully affiliated retailer members; retail sales of I.G.A. stores in 1957 were $3 billion.

Voluntary groups in other fields than groceries were also established during the 1920's. The movement has expanded but, except in the auto sales and auto service station fields, not to compare with the grocery field. Manufacturer-dealer franchise relationships in automobile distribution put the entire field of new-car retailing on a voluntary group basis. The relationships between most service stations and the gasoline distributors who supply them makes the service stations, in effect, members of voluntary groups under the sponsorship of the distributors. In the variety store line the outstanding voluntary group is the 2,300 Ben Franklin stores, sponsored by the wholesaling firm of Butler Brothers. As indicated earlier, the Liggett-Rexall system in the drug field, and the United Cigar Stores in the tobacco product field, are transforming from chain systems to voluntary group systems. The Howard Johnson system of roadside restaurants is a voluntary group.

Retailer cooperatives

The distinctive feature of a retailer cooperative is that it is initiated by a group of retailers who set up and own a cooperative wholesaling unit. Like a voluntary group, the member stores of a retailer cooperative may be characterized by some degree of group identity and uniformity of operation. Since the members do their major buying from their unit without the solicitation of salesmen, the unit saves the cost of salesmen's compensation and expenses, and can operate at a lower cost ratio than ordinary wholesalers in the line; the savings accrue to the retailer members of the cooperative either through lower prices or through patronage dividends. These cooperative wholesaling units also provide the retailer members with the same sort of management assistance as wholesaler sponsors of voluntary groups. Like these wholesaler sponsors, the wholesaling units of the retailer cooperatives in the food line have affiliated on a national basis; they have a single national organization—National Retailer-Owned Wholesale Grocers.

Retailer cooperatives have existed in the grocery field since the 1880's, thus long predating the voluntary groups. For a while, expansion of cooperative groups lagged behind that of voluntary groups. In recent years, however, large numbers of independent supermarkets have joined cooperative groups; in 1959, sales of the 35,000 retailer-cooperative grocers were $10.0 billion, compared with the $13.7 billion for voluntary-group grocers. The largest retailer cooperative system is Certified Grocers, whose members do $1.5 billion sales annually in California.

Pooled buying and advertising groups

A number of small retailers in some convenience goods line, all located within a limited area but sufficiently scattered so as not to be in immediate competition with each other—for example, three to ten meat store owners within a county, or in a small city, or in a section of a large metropolitan city—may form a "buying pool" or a "buying club," commission the most expert of their number to do joint buying for the group, and pay him a small percentage on such purchases. Thereby they obtain the benefit of the superior buying ability of the best one among them and become entitled to quantity discounts on the group purchases that none of them could obtain on his individual orders. Sometimes such groups do joint advertising.

These informal "pools," while definitely helpful to their participating members, are not of much continuing significance in the struggle between independent dealers and the chain systems. The more successful and durable among them tend to be taken over by alert voluntary-group-sponsoring wholesalers, or sometimes to expand into retailer cooperatives. The others come and go.

Retailer groups vs. chain systems

Voluntary groups and retailer cooperatives unquestionably give their independent retailer members added elements of strength in their competition with chain stores. They enable them to enjoy economies of large-scale buying. They stimulate and instruct their members to improve their operating efficiency. On an over-all basis, how does "group" retailing compare with chain retailing in the long-range struggle between the two systems?

Voluntary groups and retailer cooperatives have four weaknesses that do not afflict the chains:

    1. Members of retailer cooperatives are fairly firmly bound to their associations through mutual stock ownership of the wholesaling unit,

but the ties binding retailer members to voluntary groups are looser, and withdrawals are not uncommon. This is not an unmitigated weakness for voluntary groups, however, since the wholesaler and manufacturer sponsors are thereby kept alert to make membership in their groups of maximum advantage to the retailer members.

2. Retailer members do not always concentrate as much of their buying with their sponsoring or cooperative wholesaler as they should, and they are often indifferent to the managerial advice that the wholesaler gives.

3. The centralized purchasing of the voluntary groups and cooperatives, while producing substantial buying economies for their retailer members, may not give these members as low a cost for goods purchased as is enjoyed by large chains.

4. Fees paid for managerial service are an element of expense to the retailer members that offsets to some extent their buying economies.

The voluntary groups and retail cooperatives have three definite compensating advantages:

1. Ownership independence retained by the retailer members gives them elements of incentive, merchandising flexibility, and community goodwill that chain units usually lack. The importance of this factor cannot be exaggerated.

2. Charges for management assistance paid by retailer members are usually much less than the central overhead costs allocated to corresponding chain units. Not only is this an advantage *per se* for any store, but it enables members of voluntary groups and retailer cooperatives to operate with lower break-even points than corresponding chain units, and hence to establish themselves in communities and neighborhoods where chain units could not succeed.

3. Chain store taxes do not apply to members of voluntary or retailer-cooperative groups.

To judge by the substantial expansion of "group" retailing, particularly by the voluntary groups, during the past quarter-century, while chain systems have barely held their own in the retailing system, progressive retailers have found in "group" retailing an effective defense to the threat of the chains. The recent action of some large chains in several fields in shifting from further chain expansion to sponsoring voluntary group relationships with independent dealers in their lines may indicate that "group" retailing is more than merely a defensive strategy. It may well be that the factor of individual incentive and initiative that is preserved in "group" retailing outweighs all the advantages of chain operation, and that the long-range future of American retailing may belong to the "group" movement instead of to chain systems, as was once feared.

MINOR SPECIAL TYPES OF RETAIL STORE OWNERSHIP

Independent and chain stores account for over 97 percent of retail store sales. The small balance is divided among four other ownership classifications—consumer cooperatives, leased departments, industrial stores, and government stores.* We shall study the first three of these.

Consumer cooperatives

A consumer cooperative is a retail store owned and operated by ultimate consumers to purchase and distribute goods primarily to the membership. Its characteristic features are:

1. *Organization.* Each consumer cooperative is incorporated as a nonprofit organization under the membership corporation law, or a special incorporation law, of its state. Its shares, usually priced at $5 or $10, may be purchased by anyone regardless of race, creed, or occupation. A fixed, noncumulative, maximum dividend, ranging from 3 to 6 percent and usually called "interest," is established for these shares. A member can purchase as many shares as he wishes, with an investment objective, or to provide capital needed by the organization, but usually has only one vote regardless of the size of his shareholding.

2. *Patronage dividends.* Gross earnings of a consumer cooperative in excess of payment of the fixed dividend on its shares, and any ploughback for expansion (usually limited by state law), are distributed back annually to members and other patrons in relation to their purchases from the cooperative during the year. Patronage dividends of the more successful cooperatives are in the $2\frac{1}{2}$ to 5 percent range. In effect, they are a small rebate on the customers' purchases.

3. *Merchandise policy.* Consumer cooperatives generally avoid national brand lines, and endeavor to provide their patrons with high- and intermediate-quality merchandise for which there has been no brand promotion. Through their national organization, described below, they have established their own "CO-OP" brand, and merchandise many of their lines under it.

4. *Customer service.* Consumer cooperatives were originally intended to provide only store clerk service, with no delivery or credit. Nearly three-fifths of them currently allow member-patrons to buy on monthly accounts, however.

5. *Buying policy.* Consumer cooperative retail stores do most of their buying through some twenty or more cooperative wholesale establishments which the local stores have set up and own mutually. Thus in effect

---

* Some manufacturers sell direct-to-consumer through their own retail outlets. These are not separately classified by the *Census of Business.*

the entire consumer cooperative movement operates on a retailer-cooperative basis. The wholesale cooperatives have, in turn, established several "central" cooperative organizations which do mass buying for their wholesaler members, and arrange that many of the items purchased by the latter bear the "CO-OP" brand label.

6. *Price policy.* Consumer cooperatives generally make no attempt to undersell local competition. Indeed, their prices are likely to be above those of nearby chain stores. Any price benefit to their patrons comes through the patronage dividends instead of through initial low prices.

The consumer cooperative movement in the United States has fallen far short of the early hope of its champions, which was nothing less than to take over the major part of the distribution of most lines of nonluxury consumer goods, eliminating most other retailers and wholesalers in these lines, and turning back these retailers' and wholesalers' profits to consumer members. There were less than 2,500 true consumer cooperatives (exclusive of farm supply outlets) in 1954, with less than $300 million sales. Only among population groups of immigrant descent to whom European traditions of mutual action are familiar, and among farmers already familiar with cooperation in their marketing activities, has consumer cooperation struck abiding roots. Three reasons account for this failure of the consumer cooperative movement to secure a larger place in the American retailing structure: (1) the individualistic tendencies of most Americans do not provide a ready foundation for cooperative activity; (2) chain stores and large independent supermarkets can generally undersell consumer cooperatives, even taking the patronage dividends of the latter into account; and (3) until recently, when the cooperative wholesalers and "centrals" instituted correspondence training programs for retail cooperative store managers, the individuals who could be hired as managers for the local cooperatives were generally more marked by zeal for social crusading than by merchandising efficiency.

Leased departments

A leased department is operated, not by the store in which it is located, but by a lessee or concessionaire not connected with the store ownership. Thus a department store may contain, among others, leased millinery, shoe, or household appliance departments; a supermarket or other food store may have leased meat, fruit and vegetable, or baked goods departments; a variety store or a drug store may have a leased lunch counter; a women's apparel store may have leased millinery or shoe departments. In 1954 (the latest year for which such data are available) nearly 27,000 leased departments, with over $1 billion sales, were operating in some 19,000 stores.

LEASED DEPARTMENTS, 1954

FIELD	NUMBER OF STORES WITH LEASED DE- PARTMENTS	NUMBER OF LEASED DEPART- MENTS	SALES OF LEASED DE- PARTMENTS (in $ mil- lions)	PERCENT OF STORES WITH LEASED DE- PARTMENTS	PERCENT LEASED DE- PARTMENT SALES OF THEIR STORE SALES
Food	4,595	5,356	$ 206	1	16
Department store	1,320	5,289	377	48	5
Variety	659	1,394	32	3	7
Family clothing	439	771	49	*	13
Women's apparel and accessories	1,786	2,741	161	4	19
Drug	1,105	1,222	31	2	19
Other	8,902	10,139	233	*	15
Total	18,806	26,912	$1,089	1	9

* Not available
Derived from *1954 Census of Business,* Vol. I, pp. 6-11.

ILLUSTRATION 7–3

A store is most likely to lease one or more departments when: (1) they involve merchandise lines with which the management of a medium-sized store is not familiar; the owner of a grocery store may lease the meat department, or the owner of a meat market may lease a fresh fruits and vegetables department; (2) they involve special service or selling techniques that do not tie in conveniently with the store's general selling procedures; a department store may lease a shoe or optical goods department, or a variety or drug store may lease a lunch counter.

A leased department is operated in the name of the store in which it is located. In the quality-price range of its line, and in its display and appurtenances, it conforms to the general merchandise and promotion policies of the store. Its advertising, though paid for by the lessee, is incorporated with that of the store and is in the name of the store. To customers' eyes, nothing distinguishes it from the other store-operated departments. The lessee hires his sales staff, and trains them in the special techniques of his department. Rent for the department is paid on the basis either of a fixed periodic sum, or more commonly as a proportion of sales.

The advantages to a store of leasing one or more departments are: (1) experienced operators are acquired for departments involving special merchandise or special service procedures that the store itself might not be able to handle successfully; (2) the store is saved the finding and training of specialized sales and managerial personnel; (3) the store is saved an element of general managerial supervision; (4) the specialized department is acquired at no risk of loss to the store.

The operator of a leased department is in some cases an independent who manages just the one department in a single store. To an increasing extent leased departments are being developed by chain organizations that operate similar leased departments in two or more stores, which latter may be either independent or chain-operated. The advantages to these lessees of operating through leased departments instead of through their own stores are: (1) their specialties are often too limited to provide a basis for individual stores; (2) the clienteles of the stores in which they operate are ready-made for their departments; (3) in some cases the stores shed prestige on the leased departments they contain; and (4) all the customer services of the stores are available to patrons of the leased departments.

Leased department operation is apparently an expanding retailing development.

Industrial (company-owned) stores

As of 1948 (the latest year for which data are available) there were some 4,100 stores owned and operated by some 1,900 mining and industrial companies for the convenience of their employees. Two-thirds of these were maintained by coal mining companies, another 15 percent by lumber companies. They served an estimated 2,500,000 families, and their sales were around $1.5 billion.

Industrial stores developed an unsavory reputation during the nineteenth and early twentieth centuries. The transportation isolation of mining and lumbering areas gave the industrial stores of this period a location monopoly, of which they took advantage to charge exorbitant prices. Enforced repayment of excessive credit extensions of these stores through payroll deductions by the employer-operators, and payment of employees by scrip redeemable only through purchases at company stores, became instruments of employment peonage.

The automobile and construction of motor roads through mining and lumbering areas ended most of the location monopoly of the industrial stores. The scrip system and other abuses disappeared. Today most of these stores are operated with good merchandise policies, a definitely high level of management, and prices held to reasonable levels by the competition of independent and chain stores in accessible neighboring communities. They are able to extend reasonable charge account and installment credit since repayment is assured through payroll deductions if necessary. They meet a real convenience need in certain sections of the country. Half of their sales are food items; the other half, a wide variety of shopping and specialty lines including consumer durables. In effect they serve as a superior type of general store in their communities.

NONSTORE RETAILERS

Three classes of retailing institutions—mail order houses, direct-selling retailers, and vending machine companies—accomplish retail distribution without stores.

Mail order houses

A mail order house is a retail establishment that makes its sales primarily from a catalog or other printed material and receives most of its orders by mail or phone.* Some manufacturers sell direct-to-consumer by mail, but these are not considered retail institutions, and their mail-order system of distribution is studied in Chapter 13. Many department stores and other retail stores also do an incidental mail-order business, but on the basis of their primary activity these are considered stores and not mail order houses.

Mail order houses account for barely one percent of the total of retail sales. As of 1958 there were 33 general mail order houses (exclusive of Sears Roebuck and Montgomery Ward, the major part of whose sales are currently made through their stores), and over 2,500 special line mail order houses. The general houses were responsible for the major part of the $2 billions sales made by mail order houses in that year.

Development. General mail order houses, such as Sears Roebuck and Montgomery Ward were originally, had their start in the last quarter of the Nineteenth Century, and reached a peak in the decade 1910–1920. The reasons for their tremendous initial success were: (1) they offered many staple lines on a "convenience" basis to millions of farm families to whom the rural general stores gave inadequate service; (2) they made possible "catalog shopping" for these farm families isolated by the limitations of horse-and-buggy transport from city shopping centers; and (3) they won and retained the confidence of their customers by maintaining consistent quality standards in their merchandise and by adhering scrupulously to "money back" guarantees.

Ending of rural isolation in the 1920's by the automobile and the building of a nationwide web of good country roads cut away the main foundation of general mail order retailing as it had initially developed. There was

---

* This definition excludes Sears Roebuck and Montgomery Ward, the two organizations doing the largest general mail order business, since their department store sales currently outrank their mail order sales. In *Census of Business* tabulations they are included in the department store classification, not in the mail order classification. Hence *Census of Business* sales figures for mail order *retailers* fall far short of reflecting mail order *business*.

considerable mortality among general mail order houses during the 1920's. Those that survived and subsequently prospered did so by: (1) dropping many of their staple "convenience" lines which farmers now found no difficulty in obtaining in their rural trading centers; (2) shifting their merchandise lines to specialties and medium-styled shopping goods on which they could appeal to the growing suburban market, as well as to the rural market, on a comparative quality-price basis; (3) in the case of Montgomery Ward, Sears Roebuck, Spiegel, and a few others, establishing chains of department stores originally intended to supplement their mail order business, but which soon dominated their retailing activities.

Merchandise policy. General mail order houses currently make their best showing in specialty goods. They are successful, too, with many classes of shopping goods where style or fashion is not a major consideration, and where the principal comparison involved is the delivered price for a certain known or anticipated level of quality. Agricultural implements and other merchandise bought primarily by the farm market occupy a large space in general mail order catalogs, but no longer dominate them. The variety of style, model, and size offerings is a carefully calculated compromise between diversification and simplification, with a definite leaning toward simplification. The large general mail order houses refuse to offer low quality goods, which breed customer dissatisfaction no matter how cheaply they can be bought, and offer only intermediate- and high-quality grades in any line. National brand names are conspicuously missing from their catalogs. Instead they buy unbranded merchandise, often from manufacturers of well-known brand lines, and affix their own private brands which they have built up to be guarantees of consistent quality.

The offerings of special-line mail order houses are generally shopping goods or specialties in fields where brand name preferences do not control. The advantages of this method of retailing are marked in lines where potential consumer demand is too loosely scattered to sustain a store trade except in metropolitan centers—i.e., hobby items such as stamps or coins, or food specialties such as live lobsters and smoked turkeys. Price economies combined with assurance of quality, however, may provide a basis for mail order retailing of women's wear, men's wear, and other shopping-goods lines.

Promotion policy. The catalog is the basic promotion device of mail order houses. The large houses issue semi-annual catalogs of a thousand or more pages each, and supplementary between-season catalogs of several hundred pages each, many of the pages printed in color on gloss paper, listing scores of thousands of items. The cost of preparing, printing, and distributing its catalogs for one of the large general mail order houses is between 4 and 5 percent of its mail order sales. General mail order houses with department store chains have "order desks" in these stores where mail orders can be placed for items listed in the catalog but not carried by the stores. These large mail order houses have also established "order offices," where clerks give assistance in catalog ordering, in cities where they do not have stores.

EXCERPT FROM A MAIL ORDER CATALOG. *Courtesy of Sears Roebuck & Co.*

ILLUSTRATION 7–4

Newspaper and magazine ads, and direct-mail letters, have proven effective means of promotion for mail order specialty selling.

Price policy. Mail order houses save on many of the expenses incurred by the department stores and specialty-goods stores with which they compete—high-cost locations and store structures, store equipment, sales clerks, many customer services. The larger mail order houses, furthermore, enjoy superior buying economies on many of their lines. Allowing for the substantial cost of their catalogs, they have considerable advantage on costs and expenses. These are passed on to their customers in lower prices. After allowing for delivery charges paid by the customers, general mail order houses can usually undersell local department stores and other shopping-goods stores with respect to the quality-price lines offered by the mail order houses.

Direct-selling retailers

The door-to-door canvasser of books, tea and other food items, kitchen ware, and household supplies is a familiar personage. Also becoming increasingly common is the salesman of household furniture, furnishings, and appliances on installment terms. Sometimes these canvassing salesmen belong to a manufacturer's direct-to-consumer sales force. Sometimes they operate from stores, and bring their customers to these stores to consummate their sales. More often they constitute a distinct type of nonstore retailing—direct-selling retailing.

Some 64,000 direct-selling retailers were reported in 1958, with sales of $2.6 billion. Most of them operated as individuals, buying their merchandise from manufacturers and wholesalers and reselling it to consumers; the familiar "Fuller Brush men" work this way. About 10,000 were organizations, some of them quite large, that employed commission-paid salesmen.

Two recent developments in direct selling have contributed to the rapid expansion of this form of retailing. These are "party" and "club" selling. In "party" selling, the salesman obtains his customers by staging a small social party for a group of housewives. Under "club" plans, the salesman organizes a neighborhood "buying club" whose members make fixed weekly payments to accumulate credits entitling them to order from the company's catalog.

Vending-machine operators

The Tutti-Frutti Company installed the first chewing gum vending machines in elevated railroad stations during the 1880's. In time candy bars and peanuts also came to be sold through vending machines located in railroad stations and other public places. During the 1930's and 1940's, machines were devised for vending other classes of merchandise. In 1959 some $2 billion (retail value) of merchandise—mainly cigarettes, candy, gum, and beverages—were dispensed by 4,000,000 machines. Millions of dollars of machine sales were made of such products as hot foods, books, handkerchiefs, newspapers, soap, and perfumes. The number of vending machines and the types of merchandise sold through them are both rapidly expanding.

Most of these vending machines are owned and operated by some 8,000 companies that place them in desirable locations and pay rent (usually a percentage of each machine's sales) to the owners of the locations. A few stores own their vending machines. One supermarket chain is currently experimenting with automatic vending machines recessed into the fronts of some of its stores to make some 50 staple items, including bread, butter, milk, eggs, coffee, and meat cuts, available to customers at hours when the stores are closed; if this experiment is successful, it may point the way to wide store ownership of vending machines.

Machine vending has growing but limited possibilities. It is best suited to retail distribution of impulse goods in heavy traffic locations where stores are not practicable. It may sometimes be used with some success in clerk-

VENDING MACHINES INSTALLED IN A SUPERMARKET FOR
OFF-HOUR SERVICE. *Courtesy of the Grand Union Co.*

ILLUSTRATION 7–5

service stores to dispense various staple convenience items, thereby releasing some element of the clerk service. It may have possibilities for after-hours selling of heavy-demand items from store fronts. It is proving a useful basis for, or adjunct to, factory and office in-plant canteens. The development in 1959 of an automatic dollar-bill changer may have opened broad new markets for machine vending.

Machine-vended merchandise is preferably sold at even nickel, dime, or quarter prices, though change can be made by including pennies in the wrappings of the vended merchandise. Continuous refilling and servicing of the machines is necessary. Expenses of machine vending are relatively high, and it can rarely offer price economies. Location convenience is its fundamental advantage in its competition with store selling.

DISCOUNT HOUSES

A discount house is a retailing unit featuring consumer durable items, competing on a basis of price appeal, and operating on relatively low markup and with a minimum of customer services. The store architecture and decoration of discount houses are essentially functional. There are no charge accounts. If delivery is made, a special charge is added. No installation or maintenance service is customarily provided for mechanical equipment. Until recently there was little or no opportunity to examine or compare merchandise at the time of purchase; the customer was generally expected to know exactly what he wanted when he entered the store. The role of the store clerks was primarily to produce requested items, wrap them if necessary, and accept payment.

There is nothing new about "cut-price" limited-service retailing. This was the major appeal originally made by retailing chains in many lines. It was the foundation of the supermarkets. What distinguished the discount houses, which came into existence in the late 1940's, from other classes of "cut-price" retailers was their application of the policy to the consumer durables field. Four circumstances gave the discount houses their opportunity: (1) the department stores and others that carried consumer durable goods lines were generally geared to high-service, slow-turnover sales to a "class" market that was not sharply price-conscious, so that these stores had to and could operate with high markups; (2) resale price maintenance under fair trade laws (explained in Chapter 20) fixed retail prices for many major consumer durable goods lines at levels adjusted to the needs of the highest-markup retailers; (3) as the supermarkets had proved in the retailing of food and other convenience goods lines, there is a substantial proportion of customers willing to forego delivery, credit, and sales service in their retail buying if they can thereby save substantially on price; and (4) through means discussed in Chapter 30, a growing proportion of consumers was becoming intelligently informed on consumer durable goods in whose purchase they were interested, and needed little if any service in selecting among brands and models.

The initial discount houses sought to protect themselves against the prevailing fair trade laws by a legal subterfuge; they insisted that they were not "retailers" subject to these laws but "consumer buying clubs," and they issued "membership cards" to their customers. It soon became evident that most consumer durable goods manufacturers were so pleased to have discount houses as mass retailing outlets for their products that these manufacturers, upon whom rests the responsibility for resale price maintenance under the fair trade laws, would not enforce such price maintenance against the discount houses. The subterfuge was dropped, and the discount houses came out boldly as "cut-price" stores. They carried leading national brand lines of radios, TVs, home appliances, luggage, sporting goods, and other durables, which they sold at prices 10 to 25 percent lower than most other stores. Many of them have added lines of work clothes, tools, and household supplies. Their profits-on-investment—and these have so far been substantial—come from low unit profit on large-volume sales with fantastically high turnovers. The number, size, and sales volume of the discount houses have increased rapidly.

The discount house has made a permanent place for itself in the American retailing pattern. Fair trade laws, which fostered them in their first years, could be completely wiped out, and the present discount houses would hardly be affected. In the course of a decade, however, discount houses have evolved. Like the first supermarkets, the initial discount houses started as mere store shells, and offered only the irreducible minimum of customer service. Like the supermarkets, the discount houses have found it advisable to upgrade store appearance, and are establishing themselves in new quarters that are attractive if not sumptuous. They are steadily enlarging the range of their offerings. They are opening suburban branches. They still do not offer charge accounts, but they do aid customers to finance installment payments through finance companies. Their sales help is being trained to be not merely order takers and wrappers, but to give some assistance in merchandise selection. All of this "upgrading" adds to the expenses of discount house operation; overhead and operating expense for one of the largest discount houses rose from under 5 percent of sales in the 1940's to 14 percent in 1957. With rising overhead, their markups must be raised—and so their competitive price advantage is shrinking.

Meanwhile, in reaction to the inroads made by the discount houses, other sectors of the retailing system are reviewing their merchandise line, customer service, and markup policies in relation to durable goods. Some department and home furnishings stores have definitely abandoned certain appliance lines to the discount houses. Others are studying the possibility of shaving customer services, operating on smaller inventories, and otherwise cutting costs so that markups can be lowered to levels that will enable them to stay in competition with the discount houses, if not on a strict price basis, at least on a price-plus-moderate-service basis. Some department stores are experimenting with the possibility of operating their appliance departments on radical cost-cutting principles not applied in other departments so that their appliance prices can be in line with those of competing discount houses. Just as in the food line the original gap between the supermarkets and the service grocery stores was narrowed until a workable balance was struck between the two classes of stores, so a beginning is being made toward achieving a practicable equilibrium between discount houses and service durable-goods stores.

REVIEW

1. Why did chain systems stop expanding relative to other types of retailing institutions in the 1930's?
2. Name three retailing fields in which chain systems are important. Explain the reasons for chain development in each of these fields.
3. How do chain stores differ from competing independents on store size? location? merchandise policy? store-front, layout, and operational policies? purchasing? warehousing? customer service policy? pricing? promotion?
4. What was the anti-chain-store movement? How successful was it?
5. Explain voluntary groups and retailer cooperatives.
6. Explain the organization and operation of consumer cooperatives. Why have they had so little success in the United States?
7. Explain leased departments, and their advantages to the lessors and lessees.
8. Explain how the general mail order business has been able to survive after its original foundation of rural isolation disappeared in the 1920's.
9. What is a discount house? How has consumer durable goods retailing been affected by the advent of the discount house?

DISCUSSION TOPICS

1. "Chains are an un-American monopolistic attack upon the small independent business man."
2. "Consumers would benefit if chain systems generally superseded independents in our retailing system."
3. "Voluntary groups and retailer cooperatives will dominate the American retailing picture in ten years."
4. "Company stores should be prohibited."

5. "Mail order retailing is a wonderful opportunity for a man with a small capital to build up a profitable business."

6. "Twenty years will see the retail sales clerk completely replaced by the automatic vending machine."

7. "Unless something is done to check price cutting by discount houses, they will bring ruin to thousands of more ethical retailers."

PROBLEM 1

Great Valley Stores is a self-service grocery chain with some 200 stores in the Middle West. All its units have a distinctive blue-and-white store front. It has its own "Greval" brand of canned fruits, vegetables, coffee, and other items. Until four years ago all of its units were chain-owned. Studies made during the two preceding years indicated that its large supermarket units were all profitable, but that many of its smaller superettes were marginal or involved loss. It then decided not to establish any more corporate-owned units in communities where it could not anticipate sales volumes in excess of $500,000. Instead it would give Great Valley franchises on a voluntary-group basis to suitable independent superettes in such communities. A condition of such a franchise is that the independent superette have prospects of sales over $100,000, adopt the Great Valley store front, and buy all of its groceries line from Great Valley at the same prices as Great Valley charges its corporate-owned units. The Great Valley organization provides the members of its voluntary group with management advisory service on a cost-charge basis, and shares their local advertising costs. To date, 15 independent superettes have been given Great Valley voluntary franchises.

Great Valley is considering establishing a unit in Rivertown, a growing industrial community with a present 6,000 population which is the retailing center for a surrounding rural area. The town already has two large chain supermarkets at the south end of the town each of which does an annual business estimated at around $700,000, and four independent grocery stores. Three of these are clerk-service stores, one a superette owned by a Mr. Apgood. The superette does around $80,-000 business, and each of the clerk-service stores around $50,000. The Apgood superette shows evidence of fairly good management, but could be improved in a number of respects.

1. Would it be better for Great Valley to erect a supermarket on available land at the north end of the town, or to try and persuade Mr. Apgood to take a Great Valley franchise? List all the arguments for and against each alternative.

2. If the decision were to persuade Mr. Apgood to take a Great Valley franchise, what arguments could the Great Valley representative use to influence Mr. Apgood to take this step? From Mr. Apgood's standpoint, what would be the arguments against this step?

PROBLEM 2

Jim Wagner, 24, college graduate, with $2,500 capital, wants to start a mail order business. He has established contact with a manufacturer of beautiful metal candlesticks, wall sconces, and other art metal items, and with a manufacturer of attractive ceramic vases and lamp bases. Wagner plans to begin his mail order business with the lines of these two manufacturers, hopes to expand it to comprehensive coverage of home decoration items.

1. Is the home decoration line a suitable one for a mail order business? Why?

2. How can Wagner locate and inform potential customers at the start of his business? Will he use the same methods if he succeeds in building it to general coverage of home decoration?

3. Should he set his prices so that, with average delivery costs added, they will run a little over city department store and home furnishing store prices for comparable items? Why?

4. Should he offer a money-back guaranty on returns made for any reason (or lack of reason) within 10 days after receipt? Why?

SUGGESTED READINGS

Adelman, M. K., *A & P: a Study in Price-Cost Behavior and Public Policy,* Harvard Economic Studies, Harvard University Press, Cambridge, 1959.

Alexander, K., *How to Start Your Own Mail Order Business,* Stravon Publishers, New York, 1950.

Baker, R. H., *Help Yourself to Better Mail Order,* Printers' Ink Books, Pleasantville, N.Y., 1954.

Beasley, N., *Main Street Merchant: the Story of the J. C. Penney Company,* Whittlesey House, New York, 1949.

Emmet, B., & J. E. Jeuck, *Catalogues and Counters: a History of Sears, Roebuck and Company,* University of Chicago Press, Chicago, 1950.

Johnson, O. S., *The Industrial Store,* Division of Research, University of Georgia, Atlanta, 1952.

Kleid, L., *Mail Order Strategy,* The Reporter of Direct Mail Advertising, Garden City, New York, 1956.

Kossove, H. B., *Retailing in the Chain Store Era,* Exposition Press, New York, 1949.

Lebhar, G. M., *Chain Stores in America, 1859–1959,* 2nd ed, Chain Store Publishing Co., New York, 1959.

Marshall, M. V., *Automatic Merchandising,* Division of Research, Harvard Business School, Boston, 1954.

Schreiber, G. R., *Automatic Selling,* John Wiley & Sons, New York, 1954.

Woolworth's First 75 Years, F. W. Woolworth Co., New York, 1954.

PERIODICALS: *Chain Store Age* (administrative edition).

CHAPTER 8

RETAIL STORE MANAGEMENT

The proportion of failures is higher for retailing than for any other field of business activity. Nearly 60 percent of these retailer failures are stores established less than five years.

Several reasons account for this high rate of failure. Important among them is poor management. Too many individuals, with a small capital and a yearning for business independence, think that all that is needed for retailing success is to rent a store, have it stocked with goods by a wholesaler's salesman, and thereafter serve a horde of eager customers. Knowing little or nothing of the many facets of the retailing art, they bungle their task. Their anticipated horde of customers proves to be only a dwindling trickle, expenses outrun gross margins, and sooner or later they succumb to inevitable liquidation. Retailing, whether conducted on the scale of a major department store or chain system, or through a one-man neighborhood shop, is a business art that demands a high degree of knowledge, know-how, and creative imagination.

Several of the major elements of retail store management—buying, pricing, display and other promotional procedures, selling, and credit—are analyzed in considerable detail from operational and policy viewpoints in Part IV of this volume. Here we shall note some broad features of the retailing art: (1) merchandise line, (2) customer service policy, (3) store location, (4) physical features of the store, (5) stock management, (6) sales check and cash control system, (7) store organization, and (8) stock turn as a measure of retailing effectiveness.

MERCHANDISE LINE

The opening of any new store is obviously preceded by the owner's decision on its merchandise line—that his store will be a grocery store, or a variety store, or a drug store, or a dress shop. From prior employment experience in the field, from observation of existing stores, from advice offered by suppliers and others, he can derive a fairly clear advance picture of the items that will constitute his major line and possibly a supplementary line or two.

Many retailers fail to realize that an initial decision on merchandise policy should not be treated as a final one. To succeed, even to survive, a store's merchandise policy must evolve to meet changing circumstances. During the war economy of the 1940's when supplies of auto accessories dwindled, alert automotive accessory retailers took on lines of hardware, electrical appliances, and radios and phonographs. Supermarket operators have found profitable side lines in household supplies, cosmetics, and children's books and records. Sometimes merchandising adaptability dictates the dropping of a previously developed line. A drug store that carried a tobacco counter might wisely eliminate it, and use the freed space for other merchandise, if a stationery-and-tobacco store opened next door.

CUSTOMER SERVICE POLICY

Retailing tradition to a large extent determines the types of service customers expect of a particular store. A quality-line metropolitan department store is expected to provide credit and delivery service, returned-goods privileges, and customer conveniences such as drinking fountains and rest rooms. A "name" fashion store must offer not only salesperson attendance, credit, and delivery, but also modelling of the styles displayed in tastefully furnished modelling rooms, and custom adaptation of items purchased to the individual purchaser. In contrast, a customer in a variety store expects to make self-selection from items displayed on counters. Tradition is far from being an absolute determinant of store service, however. The success of the self-service approach of supermarkets during the 1930's and of discount houses in the 1940's is a potent witness to the possibility of revolution in service policies for a major retailing line.

Customer service policies, although they generally have more long-run consistency for the individual store than do the details of its merchandise policy, may sometimes have to be radically changed. Many small full-service grocery stores, hard-pressed during the 1930's by the competition of the supermarkets, found that they could cut costs by eliminating some of their service functions. In contrast, many supermarkets that had started on a strict no-service basis, found it advisable eventually to provide delivery-to-car and check-cashing services. During the early 1950's, many stores of many types—including the largest metropolitan department stores—found it advisable to extend their selling hours, and remain open one or more evenings in the week, to accommodate the substantial proportion of their clienteles who, because of employment, have to do a major part of their "shopping" after working hours. A limited-line store expanding to department store status may find that it must offer new services—customer conveniences within the store, and charge account credit—commonly associated with department stores.

Customer services mean added overhead or operating costs. In many cases, a store's prices can be raised to cover these costs in full, since its clientele is content to pay extra for the services. In other cases, with no increase in prices, so much additional custom may be attracted by the services that the increase in the store's sales volume may maintain or increase its total net profit, although net profit per dollar of sales is reduced. It is quite possible, however, for a store to exceed an optimum point in its performance of customer services, and involve itself in costs that cannot be recovered through higher prices or increased sales. Careful judgment is required on the issue of customer services. It must take into account what is expected in the way of service by the store's clientele, the relative attractions of service and price economy to the customers, and what services competitors are offering.

STORE LOCATION

Locating a store is commonly considered a problem that a retailer has to face only once—when he initially starts business. Four situations may compel established retail enterprises also to deal with issues of location: (1) the original location of the store may be a bad one; (2) the store may have evolved into a different type requiring a different location; (3) the surrounding market may have changed character; (4) a chain system may wish to open new units, or a department store may wish to establish branches.

There is no single set of principles for store location. What would be a good location for a large department store would probably be a bad one for a grocery store, and vice versa. A costume jewelry shop and a renowned quality jewelry store would need different locations. The merchandise line of a store is the major determinant of its location objectives. The two location considerations to which a retailer must give consideration are: (1) choice of a suitable community (or, in some cases, of a suitable shopping district or neighborhood retailing center within a large city); and (2) choice of a suitable store site within the community or retailing center.

Choice of community or retailing center

Among the factors that influence the desirability of a community or neighborhood as a location for a store of a particular type are: (1) its population and that of the surrounding trading area that it serves; (2)

whether the community is a growing or a stagnant one; (3) the purchasing power of this population, and whether or not there are wide extremes of wealth and poverty; (4) the buying habits of the population, from the viewpoints of merchandise line interests and customer services expected; (5) availability of suppliers and shipping facilities and distances involved; (6) availability and circulation of advertising media; and (7) nature and strength of competition in the particular merchandise line.

As was indicated in Chapter 4, a rural community or a neighborhood retailing center offers little opportunity to a store appealing primarily to shopping motivations but, given a satisfactory competitive situation, may promise profitable operation to a grocery store, hardware store, or variety store. A fair-sized city might be an excellent place to establish a third or fourth department store if the city was experiencing expansion, but not if its population was stable or declining. A wealthy suburban community might offer opportunity to a high-price antique shop, whereas a mill town of the same size would not. A drug store with supplementary lines that based its promotion on weekly advertising of "specials" would face difficulties in a community or neighborhood that had no local newspaper.

Location within a community

Within any given community, desirable locations for a store are determined primarily by its major merchandise line or lines.

A large department, apparel, or other store appealing primarily to shopping motivations must establish itself in one of the shopping centers of a city or in an integrated suburban shopping center, in spite of the high rents prevalent there, because most of the prospective customers for such goods go to the shopping center rather than to any particular store there, with a view to comparing styles and prices. A store which has achieved "specialty" status, by reason either of inherent character or the outstanding quality of its merchandise, has a somewhat wider choice of location. Many are found in shopping centers, but quite a few succeed admirably in "fringe" locations around a shopping center, and some maintain themselves at addresses totally unrelated to the retailing patterns of their communities.

In large cities, neighborhood retailing centers and scattered retail sections provide good locations for grocery, drug, hardware, and other convenience-goods stores. Stores that depend primarily upon impulse trade, such as variety, stationery, and tobacco products stores, may also find niches in neighborhood centers. Stores that draw their customers primarily on impulse appeal, however, may strike root wherever pedestrian traffic is heavy, and thrive in shopping centers, business centers, railway and bus terminals, and the arcades of major subway stations.

To a store that drew practically all of its customers on a special-intent, shopping, or convenience basis, it would matter little on which side of the street it was located, or whether it was in the center of a block or at a corner. Customers intent on comparing styles and prices, or heading for a favorite grocery or drug store, are not deterred by a street crossing or an extra hundred-foot walk. In marked contrast, stores depending largely upon impulse trade capture their customers primarily by the suggestion or reminder effects of their fronts and window displays. The number of customers who enter them is in direct proportion to the number of passers-by on whom the store front and display can operate. The heavy-traffic side of the street is obviously preferred for impulse-appeal stores. A corner store with windows facing on two pedestrian arteries can draw impulse customers from two flows of passers-by, and is an ideal location for a tobacco store, or for a drug store whose major business is in supplementary impulse lines. Even a store dependent largely on convenience or shopping trade may find that a heavy pedestrian traffic before its display windows brings in so many additional "impulse" customers that a good impulse location warrants the heavier rent.

Determining a store location

Most small independent retailers locate their stores where they do on the consideration of the availability of a store site at the time, the rental asked, and the existing competition in the immediate vicinity. A few make hit-or-miss inquiry into the potentialities of the community or neighborhood by personal observation, by attempting to probe the complexities of Census figures and other market data, and by questioning the local chamber of commerce or bank.

Chain systems planning to open new outlets, and department stores projecting suburban branches, generally base their location decisions on exhaustive market area studies of the communities or neighborhoods under consideration. If impulse trade is involved, traffic counts are made on possible store sites. Some large chain organizations have their own research departments for making such studies continually; in other cases, independent marketing research agencies are employed.

PHYSICAL FEATURES OF THE STORE

Another factor contributing to retailing success or failure is the physical features of the store—the suitability of the store building, the wisdom of the departmental layout, the appropriateness of the counters, display cases, and other merchandising fixtures.

The store building

Most small retailers occupy rented premises in store blocks. These are usually built in advance of any of their store units being leased, so that there is no preplanning for any particular retailer's special merchandising problems. The store units in a block usually have uniform frontage, and uniform depth. The only possibilities of adaptation to individual store requirements are the combining of two or more units by removal of intervening walls, variations in the partitioning off of rear storage space, and diversity in the choice of fixtures.

Department stores, large specialty-line stores, and large chain units often have their buildings constructed to special order. In such cases, management and architect collaborate to produce an edifice functionally adapted to the store's special mode of operation. Many recent store buildings are windowless except for ground-floor display windows on the street side. Natural light and ventilation are disadvantages in most types of retail mer-

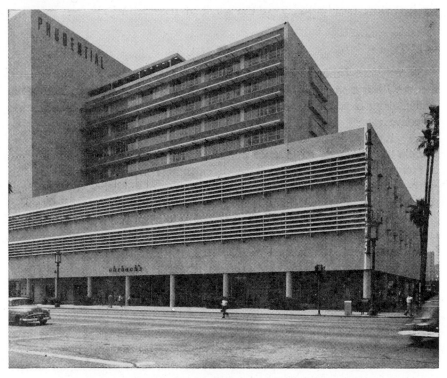

MODERN DEPARTMENT STORE ARCHITECTURE. *Courtesy of Ohrbach's.*

ILLUSTRATION 8–1

chandising. Indirect and fluorescent lighting systems that give shadowless balanced intensity, and mechanical ventilation including air conditioning, are infinitely superior. Well-planned provision is made for nonselling facilities—for stock rooms, receiving and delivery divisions, office sections, and personnel conveniences. Stairways, elevators, and escalators, with capacities determined by anticipated store traffic, are incorporated.

Striking ingenuity is displayed by modern store façades. The part of a store building that fronts on a shopping street—particularly the first two stories of such frontage—has important display possibilities. By employing materials and developing lines that contrast with surrounding structures, and by use of marquees and other structural incidentals, a store can capture the attention of shoppers and other passers-by. It can suggest quality or cheapness, according to the store's merchandising objective. In the case of chain units, the store front may embody elements of design that identify the chain and capitalize whatever special elements of goodwill it has developed. It should make provision for display windows. Effective façade design is not limited to new, specially constructed store buildings. Some of the best store façades today are the result of remodelling.

Layout

Store layout—the arrangement of service facilities and selling departments within a store building or upon a store floor—can be an important contributing factor to retailing success. Sound store layout has three major objectives:

1. Store layout should make the store *attractive, inviting,* and *convenient* to customers. Aisle space should be free of bottlenecks and planned to accommodate the differing flows of customers in different parts of the store—wider near entrances than at rear sections of the store, wider where self-service is involved than in clerk service departments, wider to the right of entrances (facing in) than to the left since more customers turn to the right upon entering a store. Stores that cater chiefly to women, but have departments that attract men, often segregate these departments so that the male customers can reach them without having to pass through the other departments.

2. Store layout should be *promotional.* The display potentialities of the various departments or counters should be taken into account. Related merchandise lines, such as the dress and millinery departments in a department store, or a bottled soda shelf and a stand of drink flavorings in a supermarket, may be grouped together so that each suggests the other. Counters for fast-moving items should be in the most convenient locations. Impulse goods departments or counters should be located near the entrances of a store, and "intent" goods further back, so that customers entering the

store to buy the latter are carried past and subjected to the display suggestion of the former.

3. Store layout should contribute to *operating facility*. Counters should be planned so that they can be efficiently served by sales personnel. They should provide shelf space to hold a day's supply of merchandise. Otherwise, facilities should be provided for restocking them during the selling day without inconvenience to customers, as by the side- and rear-wall slide-chutes for canned and packaged items found in some modern supermarkets.

1=Vestibule
2=Show Windows
3=Displays
4=Furnishings
5=Sportswear
6=Triplicate Mirrors
7=Reserve Stock
8=Fitting Rooms
9=Island Show Case
10=Hats
11=Cash and Wrap
12=Stairs
13=Low Hanging Units
14=Display Tables

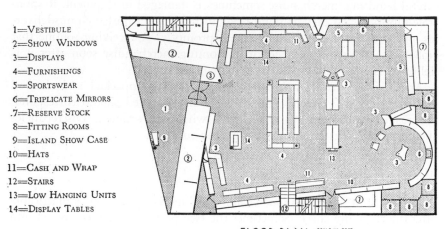

FLOOR PLAN   SCALE IN FEET

LAYOUT FOR A MEN'S WEAR SHOP. *Courtesy of Telchin & Campanella, architects.*

ILLUSTRATION 8–2

Fixtures

Store fixtures—counters, shelves, racks, and other appurtenances—have an important role in retailing. They should show as much of the stock as possible; hence the replacement of wooden counters by glass-topped and glass-fronted ones. They should display the merchandise attractively. Where self-service is the objective, the fixtures should facilitate such self-service. Where clerk service is available, the fixtures should be planned to maintain the displayed items in good order, and protect them from indiscriminate handling. All fixtures should be in themselves pleasing to the eye, but with the pre-eminent objective of displaying merchandise.

STOCK MANAGEMENT

Good stock management is a nonglamorous but contributory element in retailing success. It embraces receiving routine, marking system, and inventory control.

Receiving routine

The most reliable suppliers make occasional errors as to kinds or quantities of merchandise shipped to retailers. With the best packing and most careful handling, merchandise sometimes is damaged in shipment. Responsible suppliers and carriers stand ready to rectify or adjust such misdeliveries, provided the retailer notifies them promptly. A receiving routine that embodies some system of checking incoming merchandise soon after it is delivered is essential to effective store management.

Arriving merchandise should be expeditiously unpacked and checked with the supplier's invoice. The merchandise received should correspond, both as to items and quantities, with what was ordered. Discrepancies should be immediately taken up with the supplier.

Marking system

In most stores, incoming merchandise is "marked" as soon as practicable after the receiving check. Sometimes the two procedures are combined into a single routine.

What is "marked" on the merchandise depends on the store's customer and inventory policies. There may be information helpful to the customers and the selling force, such as sizes, styles, model names, colors, etc. There may be information intended solely for store operation purposes, such as the stock classification number or symbol, or the unit cost (in code). There may be information important to customers, to sales clerks, and to store operation, such as the retail price of each item.

The method of marking depends upon the nature of the merchandise. Prices may be crayoned on, or rubber-stamped. The "marked" information may be entered on string tags, button tags, pin tickets, or gummed labels.

Stock control

To guide buying policy, to provide financial information, and for other store management purposes, a retailer must, on occasion, know what merchandise he has on his counters and in his stock rooms. A small independent storekeeper may be able to keep constantly aware of all elements of his inventory simply by personal visual alertness. In a larger establishment,

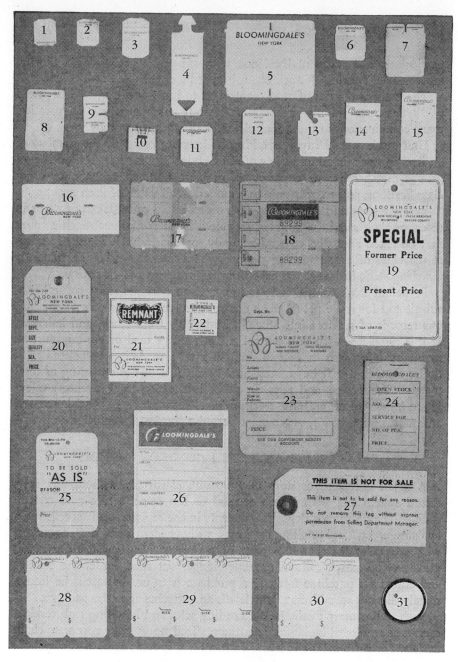

MERCHANDISE MARKERS USED BY A DEPARTMENT STORE.
Courtesy of Bloomingdale's, New York.

Nos. 6, 8, 16, 18, 19, 20, 23, 25, 27, 28, 29, 30, and 31 are string-attached. Nos. 11, 12, 14, 15, 21, 24, and 26 are wire-pinned. Nos. 7, 9, 13, and 17 are stubbed on. Nos. 1 and 2 are pasted on. Nos. 3 and 22 are sewn on. No. 4 encircles bow ties. No. 10 is a button tag. No. 5 is inserted.

ILLUSTRATION 8–3

particularly a departmentalized one with substantial delegated authority, more formal systems of stock control must be established.

There are two types of stock control as to basis—unit and dollar—and two types as to timing—periodic (physical) and perpetual. In practice, many combinations of these four elements of stock control are used.

Unit stock control involves taking or keeping count of the number of an item in stock, in all its variety of sizes, styles, and models. Dollar control groups merchandise by departments or store units in a chain, or other classifications, and records only the lumped retail value of such groups.

Periodic physical stock control rests on an actual count taken of items in stock, or their retail dollar value as shown by their markers. Such a count may be taken annually, or semi-annually, or quarterly. It is usually taken at the close of an accounting period, where intensive sales, substantially lowering stock in inventory, have been followed by a slack period.

Perpetual stock control is superimposed on periodic stock control, not substituted for it. Perpetual stock control involves maintenance of continuous records of receipts into stock, withdrawals from stock, and balances. If it is associated with unit control, a stock ledger card or bin tag must be maintained for each individual item in inventory. When associated with dollar control, it may be an incidental by-product of the recording of total merchandise receipts and sales. In either case, a perpetual inventory calculation must start off with the stock balances shown by a physical inventory, and must be checked by subsequent periodic physical inventories.

SALES CHECK AND CASH CONTROL SYSTEMS

A small independent store may operate effectively without any sales record system and with a cash register as the owner's sole cash control system. The proprietor deposits payments in the register, and records them by "ringing up" and totalling the items, without identifying dollar amounts with particular merchandise items or classes of merchandise. On credit purchases he merely takes a customer ledger out from under the counter and enters the purchase total. If a purchase is to be delivered, he immediately fills out an address tag or label, and attaches it to the package.

Such rudimentary methods of recording sales and handling cash receipts cannot be employed by larger departmentalized stores or by corporate chain outlets. For them sales check and cash control systems are a necessity.

Sales checks

The universal foundation of retail sales control systems is a multicopy customer sales slip or "check." Among the functions that a sales check system must perform are: (1) identify the type of sale—cash-take, cash-send, C.O.D. delivery, charge-take, charge-send, deposit or lay-away, installment, exchange—and thereby initiate the procedure for such sale; (2) provide the information needed for delivery, where that is involved; (3) provide the information needed for credit procedure, where that is involved, and for the bookkeeping associated with credit sales; (4) provide

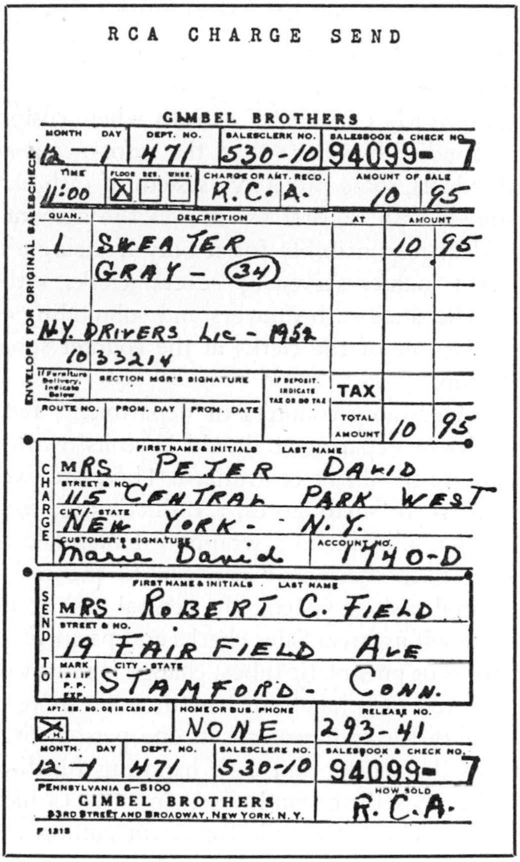
RCA CHARGE SEND

GIMBEL BROTHERS

MONTH DAY	DEPT. NO.	SALESCLERK NO.	SALESBOOK & CHECK NO.
12 – 1	471	530-10	94099- 7

TIME	FLOOR SEL. WHSE.	CHARGE OR ACCT. RECD.	AMOUNT OF SALE
11:00	☒ ☐ ☐	R.C.A.	10 95

QUAN.	DESCRIPTION	AT	AMOUNT
1	SWEATER	10	95
	GRAY – (34)		
	N.Y. DRIVERS Lic – 1952		
	1033214		
If Furniture Delivery, Indicate Below	SECTION MGR'S SIGNATURE	IF DEPOSIT, INDICATE TAX OR NO TAX	TAX
ROUTE NO.	PROM. DAY / PROM. DATE		TOTAL AMOUNT 10 95

ENVELOPE FOR ORIGINAL SALESCHECK

CHARGE
FIRST NAME & INITIALS / LAST NAME: MRS PETER DAVID
STREET & NO.: 115 CENTRAL PARK WEST
CITY, STATE: NEW YORK - N.Y.
CUSTOMER'S SIGNATURE: Marie David
ACCOUNT NO.: 1740-D

SEND TO
FIRST NAME & INITIALS / LAST NAME: MRS. ROBERT C. FIELD
STREET & NO.: 19 FAIRFIELD AVE
MARK IF P.P. EXP. / CITY, STATE: STAMFORD - CONN.

APT. RM. NO. OR IN CARE OF	HOME OR BUS. PHONE	RELEASE NO.
☒ H.	NONE	293-41

MONTH DAY	DEPT. NO.	SALESCLERK NO.	SALESBOOK & CHECK NO.
12 – 1	471	530-10	94099- 7

PENNSYLVANIA 6-5100
GIMBEL BROTHERS
33RD STREET AND BROADWAY, NEW YORK, N.Y.
HOW SOLD: R.C.A.
F 1318

A DEPARTMENT STORE SALES CHECK. *Courtesy of Gimbel Bros.*

ILLUSTRATION 8–4

the customer with a record of the sales transaction, which can be used as a basis for possible future complaints and adjustments; and (5) provide the information from which store, departmental, and individual sales records can be compiled, and from which other desired analytical and control data can be derived.

While accomplishing all these objectives, a sales check system should be simple, so that the ordinary sales clerk can master it readily and operate it rapidly. It must provide for one or more carbon copies of the original sales check, without complicated handling of the sales check book. It must be flexible, and be as adaptable to a credit sale charged to one party and delivered to another as to a cash-take transaction. Such a combination of requirements and attributes in a sales check system is sometimes difficult to achieve, but can be accomplished by the application of intelligence and ingenuity.

Handling of cash

As soon as a store reaches a stage of growth where customers' cash payments have to be handled by others than the store-owner and one or two other trusted individuals, some protective system of cash handling must be devised. The ordinary cash register establishes the amount of cash taken in, but sets individual responsibility for it only if a single individual uses the register. So at a counter served by several clerks, either the register should be one with separate cash drawers and subtotaling of sales for the several clerks, or else one of the clerks at the counter should operate the register for the group.

A store with two or more counters or departments faces the issue of whether each counter or department should have its own cash register, or whether cash handling should be centralized. There are two basic types of central cashier systems. In small stores, a cashier's cage may be placed on the selling floor, often adjacent to a wrapping table. The customer or the sales clerk presents sales check and payment to the cashier. Under the second type of central cashier system, the central cashier unit is removed completely from the selling area. Sales checks and payments are transmitted to it by basket carriers or pneumatic tubes; change is returned the same way.

Centralizing a store's cash handling has three advantages. First, it concentrates responsibility for cash receipts in one person, or a small group. Second, it separates the selling and cash handling functions, so that the latter does not distract selling employees, and the cashiers can become experts at their tasks. Third, the unit for credit authorization on charge-take orders can be located adjacent to the cashier division, and the basket or pneumatic tube carriers can serve both functions.

STORE ORGANIZATION

Small stores can be unitary organizations—all aspects of their operation are undertaken, or directly supervised, by the owner or two or three partners. After a certain stage of growth is reached, authority must be delegated. Two types of departmentalization may occur. Firstly, the merchandising activities—buying, pricing, and selling—may be separated from the other store functions, with a special administrative structure created for the latter. As was indicated in Chapter 6, many department stores set up a three-fold organization for these non-merchandising activities—Publicity and Sales Promotion, Finance and Control, and Store Management; other effective administrative patterns are possible. Secondly, the store's buying and selling activities may be subdivided by merchandise lines or sublines. It is this merchandise line break-down that gives the department store its name. It is not confined to department stores however, but is frequently encountered in large women's wear stores, supermarkets, and other nominally limited-line stores.

Chain systems have a special administrative organization problem—to what extent should operational responsibilities be left with the individual units of the chain, and to what extent should they be centralized? There is no one best formula. Substantially complete unit independence is found in voluntary and cooperative groups in the grocery field, and in some of the "holding company" department store chains. By contrast, in some chains, the local units have responsibility for little more than the selling function and some display activity. Buying has been separated from selling, and is centralized at the headquarters office. Within the headquarters organization also are advertising, finance and control, real estate and store maintenance, research, and other administrative divisions. From headquarters stems a line organization of district managers and supervisors with administrative authority over the store managers.

"STOCK TURN" AS A MEASURE OF RETAILING EFFICIENCY

To many retailers and students of Marketing, "stock turn" or "turnover" is the supreme measure of retailing efficiency. "Stock turn" is the ratio calculated by dividing average merchandise inventory valued at cost into cost of goods sold during the year, or by dividing average inventory valued at retail prices into actual annual net sales.*

A high stock turn is commonly taken as an indication that a satisfactory volume of sales is being maintained with a given inventory, or conversely,

---

* For example: A store's March 31, June 30, September 30, and December 31 inventories, valued at retail prices, are respectively $14,000, $16,000, $18,000, and $12,000; its sales for the year are $108,000. The sum of its four quarterly inventories is $60,000, their average is $15,000. Dividing the $108,000 annual sales figure by this $15,000 average inventory figure gives a stock turn ratio of 7.2.

Note that the stock turn ratio used by retailers for self-analysis differs from the inventory turnover ratio used by credit men in financial statement analysis of their customers. Credit men use as a divisor a single inventory figure, that given in the end-of-year balance sheet, which is usually calculated on the basis of "cost" or "market," whichever is lower. A credit man's inventory turnover ratio for a retailer customer would therefore in most cases be considerably higher than the retailer's own calculation of his stock turn. In the above illustration, if the "cost" value of the store's December 31 inventory is assumed to be $9,000, a supplier's credit manager would calculate the store's inventory turnover ratio as 12.

that for a given volume of sales an effective low inventory is being main-tained. Under either interpretation, high stock turn is assumed to reflect good buying policy, good inventory control, and good selling. This as-sumption may have to be qualified, however, by one or more of the fol-lowing considerations:

1. Average inventory for a store, or for a department within a store, should properly be the average of inventory calculated at monthly, or at least quarterly, intervals. This is possible if a store maintains a per-petual inventory system. Most small stores, however, are content with a single annual physical inventory for financial statement purposes. The average of the beginning-of-year and end-of-year inventories, which is the only averaging possible under such circumstances, may be widely divergent from a true through-the-year average.

2. Normal stock turn differs according to lines of merchandise and store merchandising policy. A stock turn of 40 to 50 would be normal for fresh meats, while one to one-and-a-half would be a normal stock turn for quality jewelry. Normal stock turn would be considerably lower for a store that carried a wide variety of sizes, styles, and models, than for a store that limited its line offering to sizes, styles, and models for which there was mass demand. "High" or "low" stock turn, therefore, is a rela-tive concept, and can be determined only by comparison with a store's own previous experience, or with that of other stores carrying the same lines and applying the same merchandise policy.

3. Various retailers' trade associations and some other organiza-tions are doing valuable work in collecting and tabulating the stock turn ratios of various types of stores. The comparative figures that they issue cannot, however, take into account variations in merchandise lines carried by stores of a given category, or differences in their merchandise policies, which may sharply affect the stock turn figures. Consequently, truly com-parative stock turn ratios may not be available for a particular store.

4. Stock turn figures provide no guidance as to whether a store is well located, whether its pricing policies are sound, whether its expenses are in line with its service policies and sales, or to other important elements of store management. A store might have an impressively high stock turn, yet be incurring a daily loss.

We must conclude that for many stores, stock turn calculation would be a meaningless mathematical exercise except for trend comparison with their own prior year records. For a store for which comparative stock turn analy-sis would be significant, such analysis should be only one of a group of control calculations. Exclusive dependence on a good stock turn showing can be dangerous through fostering a false sense of security.

VOCATIONAL CONSIDERATIONS

Not too long ago retailing was considered an unworthy vocational objective for a college man or woman. This attitude is waning rapidly. The complexities of modern retailing are a challenge to the best-equipped and best-trained minds that our colleges are graduating. The rewards of successful retailing, either through the development of one's own establishment, or through progress up the management hierarchy of a large department store or chain system, compare favorably with those of any of the business professions that draw college graduates. The field is as open to the college woman as to the college man.

For success in developing one's own store, one personality characteristic is essential. The proprietor of a store should be at least mildly extroverted, the sort of person who likes to be with and deal with people, who intuitively knows how to make friends and influence people. He should be liked by his customers, and respected by his employees. For the rest, he should have an alert and trained mind, rather than any special aptitude. He must learn a tremendous lot about a great many things—he must become a master of all the phases of the retailing art that we have noted in this chapter and of others that will be studied in Part Four of this volume.

A retailing curriculum in a collegiate school of business is helpful to this end, but not essential, nor is it in any sense a complete and final training. Experience—for an interval as an employee, but sooner or later as owner and operator of his own store—provides the only true definitive training for a retailer. From actual performance of all the various activities of a retailer, and from the wealth of guidance offered to receptive retailers by suppliers, governmental sources, and trade associations, comes the major part of the vocational education of any retailer, including the college-graduated ones.

The picture is slightly different for college students who anticipate that their retailing careers will be in the structure of some large department store or chain system. Each of these retailing organizations is a business microcosm, embracing a wide variety of marketing operations. Some of these call for specialized aptitudes and training—for accountants, for individuals with special verbal aptitude for their advertising departments, for individuals with special graphic aptitude for advertising and display work, for individuals with capacity for the dispassionate analysis needed to head retail credit departments. The selling, buying, and general management executives of large retailing organizations, however, must have a broad, balanced range of business capacities. There is opportunity for nearly every type of individual, and for nearly every special aptitude and capacity, in the modern large retailing establishment.

The large department stores and the large chains definitely want college graduates as recruits for their executive forces. They prefer men and women who have taken retailing specializations in collegiate schools of business, but consider such college training only background preparation. Most of the larger establishments have their own employee training programs, which cover preparation for executive advancement as well as instruction on the immediate jobs to which their employees are assigned.

REVIEW

1. What are some of the factors that influence the desirability of a community or neighborhood as a location for a store of a particular type?

2. How can a good location for a store be determined?

3. How may the architecture of a store, and particularly its front, contribute to its success?

4. What are the main objectives of store layout? Explain each.

5. What checking routine should a retailer establish for incoming merchandise?

6. Explain: "Incoming merchandise should be 'marked' by a store as soon as possible after being received."

7. Distinguish between unit and dollar inventory control, and between periodic and perpetual inventory control.

8. What services may a store sales check and its copies perform?

9. When and why should the handling of a store's cash receipts be centralized?

10. Explain store departmentalization.

11. Explain "stock turn." Is a high stock turn always a sign of retailing efficiency?

DISCUSSION TOPICS

1. "A retailer's merchandise line policy should be dynamic— ever changing to meet ever-changing conditions."

2. "For every store there is some optimum level of customer services. Exceeding this level, as well as falling short of it, reduces the store's profit."

3. "Within any community desirable locations for a store are determined primarily by its merchandise line."

4. "The trend in store facades and decor is from functional to esthetic considerations."

5. "Store fixtures have an important role in retail merchandising."

6. "The sales check is a versatile retail management tool."

7. To what extent may a high stock turn be taken as a measure of retailing efficiency?

PROBLEM 1

Refresco Corporation operates a chain of "RefrescoBars" which serve fruit drinks, coffee, sandwiches, and pastries. The company plans to extend its operations to Metro City.

1. What areas in Metro City would be good locations for these RefrescoBars? Why?

2. How could choices be made among alternative specific locations in such areas?

3. How should the fronts of any premises rented for RefrescoBars be redesigned? Why?

PROBLEM 2

You are planning to open a hardware store in the retailing center of Hilldale, a suburb of Metro City. Your premises will be a store with 40′ front and 50′ depth, an extra 15′ in the rear for storage, and a basement which can also be used for storage. You will hire two full-time clerks to help you sell. Yours will be the only hardware store in Hilldale which currently has, among others, an auto accessories store, a small department store with home accessories and sports departments, a variety store, and two supermarkets that carry household accessory lines.

1. What will be good merchandise lines for your store? Why?

2. Draw a floor layout that will accommodate the merchandise lines you will carry. Explain your layout.

3. What customer services, apart from clerk service, will you provide? Why?

4. One of your clerks will handle arriving shipments. Write a list of directions for him. Explain the purposes of your directions.

5. What inventory control system will you adopt? Why?

6. Describe and explain the sales check system you will use.

7. At the end of your first year of operation, how will you calculate stock turn for your various merchandise lines and for your store as a whole? After you have the figures, what use can you make of them?

SUGGESTED READINGS

Beckley, D. K., *Improving Human Relations in Retailing*, Prince School of Retailing, Boston, 1955.

Bunting, J. W., *Essentials of Retail Salesmanship*, Bookman Associates, New York, 1954.

Corbman, B. P., *Mathematics of Retail Merchandising*, Ronald Press, New York, 1952.

Davidson, W. R., & P. L. Brown, *Retailing Management*, 2d ed, Ronald Press, New York, 1960.

McGregor, C. H., *Retail Management Problems of Small and Medium-Size Stores,* rev ed, Richard D. Irwin, Homewood, Ill., 1957.

National Retail Dry Goods Association, *Display Manual,* rev ed (1955); *Employment Standards and Techniques* (1954); *Expense Savers are Boosters* (1957); *Improving Personnel Administration* (1954), NRDGA, New York.

Robinson, O. P., & K. B. Haas, *How to Establish and Operate a Retail Store,* 2d ed, Prentice-Hall, Englewood Cliffs, N.J., 1952.

Robinson, O. P., and others, *Store Organization and Operation,* 2d ed, Prentice-Hall, Englewood Cliffs, N.J., 1957.

Robinson, O. P., and others, *Successful Retail Salesmanship,* 3rd ed, Prentice-Hall, Englewood Cliffs, N.J., 1961.

Spriegel, W. R., & J. W. Towle, *Retail Personnel Management,* McGraw-Hill Book Co., New York, 1951.

Tremain, A., *Successful Retailing,* rev ed, Harper & Bros., New York, 1951.

Wingate, J. W., *Fundamentals of Selling,* South-Western Publishing Co., Cincinnati, 1959.

NOTE: All the Retailing textbooks listed in *Suggested Readings,* Chapter 4, have chapters on various aspects of store management.

CHAPTER 9

WHOLESALING MIDDLEMEN

In the preceding four chapters we studied the class of marketing institutions—the retailers—through whom merchandise reaches ultimate consumers. Now our interest shifts backward to the various middlemen through whose efforts goods are moved from their original producers, be they farmers or manufacturers, to either (1) the retailers already studied, or (2) manufacturers, other business units, and institutions which further process such goods or otherwise utilize them in their productive or service functions.

No topic in Marketing is more booby-trapped with misunderstandings and misleading generalizations, for the advanced scholar as well as for the beginning student, than that of wholesaling. In part this is due to the grievous lack, until very recent years, of comprehensive information on the organization and activities of the many varieties of wholesaling middlemen. Wholesaling has been, and still is, the Dark Continent of American Marketing study. In part this is due to confusion of business nomenclature in this field, in part to the conflicting bases of classification applied to such data as have been collected and published. Furthermore, the operations of wholesaling middlemen are characterized by extreme operational and organizational flexibility, so that most generalizations about them require complicating qualifications and may hold true only temporarily.

Our tasks in Chapters 9 and 10 will be: (1) to establish the basic working definitions that will serve as tools for elementary study of wholesaling activities and of the middlemen who participate in these activities; (2) to examine the *Census of Business* data on wholesaling for an over-all picture of the field and certain fundamental trends that they show; (3) to survey the possible classifications of wholesaling middlemen as a means of ascertaining the major issues pertaining to them and their activities; (4) to use two of these classification systems—those based on merchandise title and operations performed—to make a detailed exploration of various classes of wholesaling middlemen and what they do; and (5) to use some of the other classification systems for more cursory explorations of certain special wholesaling problems.

We shall get only a partial picture in these two chapters of the vital role that wholesaling middlemen play in our distributive economy, and of the great services they perform for the parties with whom they deal. For full understanding of this subject, we need some comprehension of channel-of-distribution structure for the various classes of products with which wholesaling middlemen deal—the output of farms, manufactured consumer goods, and industrial equipment and material. Accordingly, our study of these middlemen is divided between two parts of this book—analysis of their institutional structure in this and the next chapter, and the major analysis of their economic and distributional contribution in Chapters 12 through 15.

DEFINITIONS

Much of the confusion that has plagued the study of wholesaling stems from the failure of Marketing authorities and collectors of Marketing statistics to agree on exact definitions. Some of this disagreement has been cleared in recent years. Some still remains. The following definitions avoid the major ambiguities that still persist on this subject.

1. A *wholesale sale* is one where the purchaser is other than an ultimate consumer buying for personal use. Thus all product sales to (a) retailers, (b) other middlemen, (c) industrial, professional, and business users (including such service enterprises as restaurants and laundries), and (d) institutional users (such as hospitals, schools, and governmental bodies), are wholesale sales. The character of the seller is irrelevant. All sales by farmers and manufacturers (except those direct-to-consumer) are wholesale sales. So also are the sales of all types of wholesaling middlemen except when they sell direct-to-consumer. Retailers may also upon occasion make wholesale sales, as in the case of hardware stores selling items to building contractors or stationery stores selling office supplies to business concerns. The size of a sale has no bearing on whether or not it is a "wholesale" transaction. A fill-in sale involving only a couple of dollars by a notions jobber to a dress manufacturer is as much a "wholesale" transaction as is the sale of a boat-load shipment by a grain dealer.

2. The term "wholesaler," unfortunately, is used both popularly and in technical writing in two conflicting senses. In its broad denotation, covering any enterprise whose major business is making wholesale sales, it is synonymous with "wholesaling middleman," explained below. Narrower usage, which currently has some scholarly sanction but not consistent ac-

ceptance, limits it to those wholesaling middlemen who take title to the goods in whose transfer they participate—i.e., to the "merchant wholesalers" discussed later in this chapter. To reduce confusion, the term "wholesaler" will be avoided in this book wherever possible, and when used will always be accompanied by a limiting adjective—e.g., "merchant wholesaler," or "grocery wholesaler."

3. With "wholesaler" eliminated because of its ambiguity, some other term is needed to cover all the various classes of business establishments whose major activity is making wholesale sales, whether they buy and sell on their own account or act as agents for others. Neither trade custom nor scholarly usage * has established any other generally accepted term. We shall accordingly employ for this purpose the term *"wholesaling middleman"* (with "wholesale distributor" used occasionally as a synonym where the meaning is clear). Included in this "wholesaling middlemen" concept are not only merchant wholesalers and all forms of agent middlemen, but also agricultural marketing cooperatives and all other enterprises engaged in assembling farm products and moving them to market, petroleum bulk stations, and foreign trade houses of both merchant and agent types. Excluded from this definition are: (1) farmers, mines, manufacturers,** construction enterprises, and others whose primary activity is production; (2) service enterprises that do not deal in products; (3) retailers that sell primarily to ultimate consumers; and (4) facilitating marketing institutions such as commodity exchanges, advertising agencies, and finance companies which contribute to the distribution of goods but do not engage in buying and selling either on their own behalf or in an agency relationship.

In connection with the above definitions, it should be noted that "wholesale sales" and "wholesaling middlemen's sales" are not identical. Included in the former and excluded from the latter are: (1) all sales by manufacturers, mines, and farmers other than those made direct-to-consumer; and (2) wholesale sales by some retail establishments which carry on a secondary wholesale business. Included in "wholesaling middlemen's sales" and excluded from "wholesale sales" are the retail sales made by some "semi-jobbing" distributors.

---

* The Definitions Committee of the American Marketing Association has defined "wholesaler" in the narrow sense of "merchant wholesaler," and "middleman" in a broad sense including retailers.

** The *Census of Business* includes manufacturers' branch sales offices in its "wholesaling middlemen" category. The reasons are traditional rather than logical, and the inclusion distorts the wholesaling picture. Accordingly, in the statistical presentation of wholesaling later in this chapter, which is based on *Census of Business* data, manufacturers' sales branches and their sales have been excluded.

PLACE OF WHOLESALING MIDDLEMEN IN THE MARKETING SYSTEM

In 1958 there were 261,000 wholesaling middlemen, with sales of $196 billion.* In the same year there were 298,000 manufacturing establishments with $315 billion sales, and 1,778,000 retailers with $200 billion sales. It will amaze many beginning students of Marketing, and shed new light on the economic importance of wholesaling, to discover that the volume of wholesaling middlemen's sales approaches so closely that of retailers' sales.

At first thought it might seem impossible that wholesaling middlemen's sales could match retailers' sales, since some retailers buy direct from manufacturers and since those retailers who do buy from wholesale distributors add substantial mark-ups to the wholesale prices they pay for their merchandise. The explanations of this apparent discrepancy are: (1) over one-third of wholesaling middlemen's sales are of items sold to manufacturers, other business units, institutional users, and other non-personal users, which never enter the tabulation of retail sales; (2) over one-fifth are sales by wholesaling middlemen to other distributors; (3) a very small fraction represents export sales which do not enter domestic retail distribution; (4) another very small fraction represents incidental retail sales made by business units whose major activity is wholesaling. In all, only one-third of wholesale distributors' sales are to retailers.

Over the past quarter-century, despite many claims that "the wholesaler was disappearing from the American scene," wholesaling middlemen and wholesaling activities seem to have maintained their places in the marketing structure. Between 1929 and 1958 the number of wholesaling middlemen increased by 73 percent, in contrast with a 20 percent increase in the number of retailers and a 42 percent increase in the number of manufacturers. The expansion of wholesaling middlemen's sales during this period was almost identical with that of retailers' sales.

Economic functions

Like retailers, wholesaling middlemen contribute in varying degrees to the creation of place utility, time utility, and possession utility in the goods they handle. Through their ministrations, raw materials are transferred from the farm and the mine to the plants that process them, foods are moved from the farm to the retail food stores that accomplish the final sales to consumers, and manufactured items are carried from factory to retailers or nonpersonal users. The "movement" involved in these whole-

---

* These are the *Census of Business* figures, with manufacturers' sales branches and offices and their sales subtracted.

WHOLESALING MIDDLEMEN AND THEIR SALES, 1929, 1939, 1948, AND 1958

CLASSIFICATION	1929 NUMBER	1929 SALES ($ MILLIONS)	1939 NUMBER	1939 SALES ($ MILLIONS)	1948 a NUMBER	1948 a SALES ($ MILLIONS)	1958 a NUMBER	1958 a SALES ($ MILLIONS)
Wholesale merchants and jobbers	{ 70,485	$24,554 {	92,026	$19,442	117,105	$ 62,041		
Textile converters		791	631	425	1,091	1,736		
Industrial distributors	3,432		1,471	730	1,944	2,812		
Total full-service wholesalers	73,917	$25,345	94,128	$20,597	120,140	$ 66,589	173,434	$106,051
Cash-carry jobbers	756	$ 179	1,198	$ 109	978	$ 355		
Truck jobbers	817	90	2,398	80	1,065	147		
Drop shippers	583	242	937	475	1,615	2,604		
Retailer-cooperative warehouses	136	91	222	223	260	667		
Total limited-service wholesalers	2,292	$ 601	4,755	$ 887	3,918	$ 3,773	10,232	$ 4,792
Foreign trade	3,016	$ 3,316	2,744	$ 2,158	5,059	$ 6,171	6,062	$ 10,864
Total Merchant Wholesalers (other than "assemblers")	79,225	$29,262	101,627	$23,642	129,117	$ 76,533	189,728	$121,707
Petroleum Bulk Stations	19,611	$ 2,390	30,825	$ 3,808	28,351	$ 10,483	30,424	$ 20,131
Merchandise brokers	3,689	$ 4,038	4,710	$ 3,391	4,325	$ 9,236	4,359	$ 8,851
Commission houses	3,479	4,695	2,758	2,748	1,977	7,291	6,972	11,521
Selling agents	3,266	2,623	1,487	1,742	2,477	4,916	2,069	6,836
Manufacturers' agents	6,987	1,775	9,778	1,397	6,151	3,673	9,985	10,218
Purchasing agents	{ 151	296	473	575 {	185	1,729	302 }	1,189
Cooperative agencies					192	1,294		
Total domestic agent middlemen	17,582	$13,427	19,206	$10,751	15,307	$ 28,139	23,687	$ 38,614
Auction companies	461	$ 374	649	$ 434	1,671	$ 2,870	1,840	$ 4,534
Foreign trade	345	$ 456	1,048	$ 915	1,160	$ 1,831	1,040	$ 2,077
Total Agent Middlemen	18,388	$14,257	20,903	$11,201	18,138	$ 32,839	26,567	$ 45,225
Marketing cooperatives	4,208	$ 1,458	2,774	$ 1,190	994	$ 1,410		
Cooperative grain elevators	{ 8,134	987 {	1,843	196	2,473	1,695		
Other country grain elevators			7,241	498	5,688	2,362		
Merchant assemblers	{ 21,884	2,304 {	9,866	792	4,052	2,130		
Commission buyers			1,523	123	1,080	1,460		
Others			5,875	290	2,500	863		
Assemblers (mainly farm products)	34,226	$ 4,749	29,122	$ 3,089	16,787	$ 9,920	14,096	$ 8,999
TOTAL WHOLESALING MIDDLEMEN	151,450	$50,658	182,477	$41,740	192,393	$129,775	260,815	$196,061

a 1948 and 1958 figures exclude establishments without paid employees (numbering around 25,000 in 1948) and wholesale milk bottling plants.

b Not listed.

SOURCE: *Census of Business* series.

ILLUSTRATION 9–1

saling transfers is twofold—a physical displacement of the items from less useful to more useful locations, and a transfer of title and possession of the items from owners who have little use for them toward the final purchasers who develop their ultimate utility through consumption. In the course of these wholesaling transactions, many of the wholesaling middlemen involved make a very substantial contribution to the "time utility" of the products they handle by storing them for longer or shorter periods. Some wholesaling middlemen, indeed, such as grain elevators, make their primary contributions to the economy as storing agencies.

Marketing operations

Like retailers, wholesaling middlemen also perform all the marketing operations analyzed in Part Four of this book except that of product planning.* Among some classes of wholesaling middlemen, particularly the full-service merchant wholesalers, many establishments range the full gamut of wholesale operations. They buy (and in buying accomplish either quantity assembling or line assembling), sell (and in selling perform a dividing operation), do some advertising (though usually only a slight amount since market promotion is usually undertaken by manufacturers or retailers rather than by wholesale distributors), price, ship, store, grant credit, and assume substantial market risks. As will be subsequently indicated, however, operational specialization has developed among wholesaling middlemen to an extent not met with in the retailing field. There are wholesaling middlemen who eliminate one or two of the normal wholesaling operations, such as drop shippers who do not have even temporary storage facilities, or cash-carry wholesalers who make no deliveries and provide no credit. There are more extreme cases of purchasing agents who perform only a buying operation, or manufacturers' agents who perform only a selling operation, or grain elevators and other warehouses whose storage operations are the foundation of their other activities.

CLASSIFICATION OF WHOLESALING MIDDLEMEN

Wholesaling middlemen can be classified on seven bases that are useful in elementary Marketing study: (1) whether or not they take title to the goods they deal in, (2) operations performed, (3) product field or line, (4) size and scope of operations, (5) integration, (6) chain organization, and (7) location. The first three of these are studied immediately below. The other four enter into later analyses of this chapter and the following one.

---

* Converters, by assuming responsibility for the design and finish of their products, also undertake the operation of product planning.

Title ownership

The initial basis for classifying wholesaling middlemen is whether or not they take title to the merchandise with whose distribution they are concerned. Those who take title to the merchandise, who buy it and sell it and make profit or take loss on the sequence of transactions, are called *merchant wholesalers*. Those who do not take title to the goods involved, but merely act on behalf of other principals, and are compensated by fees, commissions, or other "charges," are called *agent middlemen*.

This distinction between taking title or not taking title to merchandise is not an empty legalistic one. The merchant wholesaler owning the goods in which he deals is likely to be involved in the whole range of wholesaling operations. If he foregoes one or another of the usual wholesaling operations because he sees an opportunity for cost-shaving which can be translated into competitive price-saving, he still remains engaged in multi-operational activities. Usually he must command some capital—he must maintain some equity in the inventories of his goods, he may have to maintain storage facilities, he may require delivery equipment. The agent middleman, in contrast, is likely to be an operational specialist. He commonly concentrates on one particular operation—buying or selling, or (in the case of the auction companies) providing premises and personnel for auction transactions—with his other activities supplementary to the major one. In many cases an agent middleman needs practically no capital; rented desk space, with the rent past-due, has provided the business start for many ultimately successful selling and purchasing agents.

The *Census of Business* employs this title-ownership basis of classifying wholesaling middlemen as the foundation of its statistics on wholesaling. We shall also use it as a basic step in our analysis of the various types of wholesale distributors and their marketing services.

Operations performed

We may classify wholesale distributors very profitably on the basis of the operations they perform. As already indicated, the range is wide, from the "full-service" of many merchant wholesalers to the "single-service" of various classes of specialist agent middlemen. To some extent, operational classification parallels title ownership classification, since practically all full-service distributors are merchant wholesalers, while most agent middlemen tend toward specialization. But many limited-service middlemen are found among merchant wholesalers; in some cases, like the drop shippers, their specialization is as extreme as that of any agent middlemen.

The *Census of Business* employs a very detailed operational classification of wholesaling middlemen in the presentation of its statistics on Whole-saling. We shall use this Census classification in our analysis.

Product fields and lines

We should be able to enlarge our knowledge of wholesaling consider-ably if we could classify our data on wholesaling middlemen and their sales comprehensively by the five major product fields: (1) farm products moving from the farms to the various processing industries; (2) farm products that move to consumers in natural form; (3) manufactured con-sumer goods; (4) non-agricultural industrial raw materials; and (5) in-dustrial and business equipment and supplies. For more than twenty years the *Census of Business* has collected data on wholesale distributors classi-fied by over two hundred individual product lines. This information could be readily grouped by the product-field classifications indicated above but, except for one grouping on "Assemblers (mainly farm products)," the *Census of Business* has not presented any product-field grouping. Individ-ual scholarship has also ignored this opportunity.

On the subject of wholesaling classification by individual product lines, there is no dearth of information. Census figures are explicit on this detail and a growing number of active distributors' trade associations based on product lines are issuing valuable reports. Our subsequent analysis will explore this subject.

MERCHANT WHOLESALERS

As previously indicated, "merchant wholesalers" * are wholesaling mid-dlemen who take title to the goods they deal in, and derive their profit from the margins between purchase and sale prices. They dominate the wholesaling picture, operating in all fields of wholesale distribution. They include country assemblers of grains and other farm produce, jobbers and other wholesale distributors of groceries and fresh foodstuffs in the con-suming centers, middlemen for the raw materials used by industry, petro-leum bulk stations, mill houses and other distributors of industrial and business equipment and supplies, and thousands of "wholesalers" and "jobbers" in various consumer-goods lines.

FULL-SERVICE MERCHANT WHOLESALERS

Most merchant wholesalers are "full-service" (or "full-function") middlemen. Besides their buying and selling operations, they store mer-

---

* Merchant wholesalers, particularly small ones, in some lines are called *jobbers*. There is little consistency in the use of this term, and the extent of its use varies from trade to trade, and in different regions of the country.

chandise for longer or shorter periods, in many cases undertake some promotional activity, establish selling prices, grant credit, make shipments and deliveries, and assume the various market risks inherent in these activities.

Because of the wide scope of the distributional services that full-service merchant wholesalers perform,* their operating expenses often run surprisingly high. The average expense-to-sales ratio for full-service merchant wholesalers is close to 15%. Average ratios in excess of 20% are reported for wholesalers in a number of lines. The average expense-to-sales ratio for limited-service wholesalers other than truck jobbers is around 8%; for agent middlemen it is 3%.

These high operating expenses influence the margins that full-service merchant wholesalers must establish between the prices they pay and the prices they charge for their merchandise. It might be thought that this necessity of imposing greater mark-ups would put full-service wholesalers at a serious competitive disadvantage in relation to limited-service wholesalers or agent middlemen. However, because of the extra distributional services they perform for manufacturers they buy from, which the latter would otherwise have to undertake themselves, they sometimes obtain lower prices than do limited-service wholesalers in the same line. Because of extra services they render to retailers and other nonpersonal buyers, these customers are willing to pay them higher prices than are asked by cash-carry and other limited-service wholesalers in the same line. This makes them well able to meet the competition of the limited-service wholesalers. Where full-service wholesalers are in direct competition with various classes of agent middlemen, the lower prices they can command from manufacturers and the higher prices they can obtain from their customers, likewise afford them the wider margins needed to cover their higher expenses. Full-service merchant wholesalers dominate all lines of consumer goods and industrial equipment wholesaling and most lines of industrial supplies wholesaling, and they feature significantly in the assembling of agricultural products and other raw materials. Since 1929 full-service wholesalers have increased, both in numbers and in sales volume, more rapidly than agent middlemen, and more rapidly than any class of limited-service wholesalers except drop shippers.

Product specialization

In the mid-1930's the *Census of Business* reported a considerable number of "general" wholesalers who carried a broad range of "hard goods" lines and served rural general stores, hardware stores, auto accessory stores,

---

* A detailed analysis of the distributional services that full-service merchant wholesalers in manufactured-goods lines perform for the manufacturers they buy from and for the retailers they sell to, is presented in Chapter 13.

and other retailers that offered a variety of merchandise lines. No such group has been separately reported since 1935, current *Census* practice being to classify each wholesaler by his major product line. This action of the Bureau of the Census was not arbitrary, but reflected a significant development in the institutional structure of American wholesaling. In the Nineteenth Century and the first two decades of the Twentieth, the general wholesale house had played an important distributive role. It was the major and often exclusive source of merchandise for rural general stores. In the pre-auto days of rural isolation, each general store could be most economically served by some one general wholesaler whose salesman would take a single consolidated order of substantial magnitude covering the small requirements of the general store in the many lines it carried. The decline of the rural general store, described in Chapter 6, struck at the very foundation of general wholesaling. The automobile made it practicable and profitable for more specialized wholesalers to send their salesmen to rural trading centers, and the wider selection they offered in their particular lines tended to win the remaining rural general stores from their previous exclusive dependence on the "general" wholesale houses. Many old general wholesalers disappeared from the distributive picture. The others met the changed situation by concentrating their efforts upon some one or another among their combination of lines, and became essentially "line" wholesalers with supplementary sidelines.

Merchant wholesaling is predominantly specialized, not merely by broad commodity lines, but by special subdivisions of commodity lines. In the groceries and food line, for example, there are wholesale houses specializing in confectionery, in fish and sea foods, in meat and meat products, in canned foods, in coffee, tea and spices, in dried fruits and nuts, in flour, in frozen foods, and in a multitude of other particular product groupings. "Full-line" wholesalers selling a more or less full range of items in their line maintain a strong place in several commodity fields, however. There are full-line hardware wholesalers who carry house and builders' hardware and tools, electrical appliances, cutlery, paint, sporting goods, plumbing supplies and materials, and even some staple house furnishings and house wares. There are full-line automotive supply wholesalers who handle parts, supplies, and equipment for all makes of automobiles, including tires, batteries, seat covers, accessories, body paint, and other lines normally carried by an automotive retailer. There are full-line grocery wholesalers who stock canned goods, cereals, teas, coffees, spices, flours and flour mixes, soaps, and a host of other nonperishable items found in typical grocery stores. In the food and drug fields, although the full-line wholesalers are outnumbered by the specialty wholesalers, their sales volume is greater.

Converters as extra-service wholesalers

The converter is an extra-service merchant wholesaler that has developed primarily in the textile field, and to a lesser extent in the leather, paper, and some other lines. A textile converter buys unbleached yardage—"greige" or "gray" cloth—from the weaving mills, and determines the color shades for dyeing or develops the designs to be printed on the cloth. The actual dyeing or printing is usually done in an outside plant, which charges the converter for this service on a yardage basis. Finally, the cloth is sold by the converter to clothing manufacturers, or to piece-goods jobbers who resell it to piece-goods retail outlets, or directly to such retail outlets. Since it is the dyeing or printing of cloth that primarily determines its market-ability, the textile converter relieves the mills of this major risk in textile production. There are over 1,000 textile converters making over $2 billion in sales.

Converters in other fields such as leather and paper similarly buy a semi-finished product from the manufacturers, assume the responsibility of determining the finishing process that establishes the product's market appearance, and resell the product to industrial users, or to other middle-men who undertake the final wholesaling step.

LIMITED-SERVICE MERCHANT WHOLESALERS

In a few lines of distribution, some of the merchant wholesalers have stripped themselves of one or more of their normal operations—storage, or credit, or delivery, or selling through a force of salesmen—with a view to lowering their operating expenses. They are consequently able to set lower mark-ups, and to bid for customers on a basis of price-saving.

There are four * types of "limited service" (or "limited-function") merchant wholesalers—drop shippers, cash-carry wholesalers, truck jobbers, and mail order wholesalers. Drop shippers, the first of these four groups, have increased in numbers and in relative sales volume far beyond the general wholesaling average since 1929. The other three are losing ground to their full-service competitors.

Drop shippers

Drop shippers, sometimes called "desk jobbers" or "drop mill shippers," are an anomaly in wholesaling—merchant wholesalers who, in most of their transactions, take title to goods but do not acquire possession or exercise physical control over them. They operate primarily in coal and coke

* The warehouses operated by retailer cooperative chains, classified by the Bureau of the Census as limited-service wholesalers, are excluded from our analysis of limited-service merchant wholesalers who serve the general market in their field.

(where they outnumber the full-service wholesalers with yards), and lumber. Customarily they make their sales in carload or truckload quantities before placing the purchase orders necessary to cover their commitments. Each balancing purchase order to mine or mill provides for shipment to be made from the mine or mill directly to the drop shipper's customer. Thus, without ever possessing inventory of a pound of coal or a foot of lumber, and without any facilities for storage or business equipment other than desk space,* these dealers transact between $2 and $3 billion of business a year.

Drop shippers must generally buy at higher prices from the mines and mills than their competitors who maintain storage yards. Only one shipment—from producer to user—is involved in drop shippers' transactions, however, instead of the two—from producer to middleman, and from middleman to user—in the case of wholesalers with storage yards. Thus drop shippers effect a major saving in freight charges and handling expenses. They also avoid all the expenses incident to maintaining storage facilities. Furthermore, they avoid all risks of price decline or destruction loss on their inventories. These expense economies may more than offset the higher prices that drop shippers have to pay on their purchases. All in all, they enjoy some very real advantages in their competition with full-service wholesalers in their lines. This circumstance, plus the consideration that an energetic individual with good trade connections but no capital can readily enter the business and prosper, have given a strong stimulus to this form of wholesaling.

There are definite limits to the relative expansion of drop shipping, however. This type of merchant wholesaler can establish himself only in the distribution of raw or semi-processed materials, sold by standard specification in carload or truckload lots, for which freight charges and handling expenses bulk large in the costs of distribution. Furthermore, since the drop shipper carries no inventory and provides no storage, the line must be one where the producers have the capital and facilities to maintain all the inventories required by the line. Not many fields of distribution conform to these specifications.

Cash-carry wholesalers

Cash-carry wholesalers are found primarily in the grocery line, with a few in other food product lines and in the tobacco field. As their name indicates, they offer no credit or delivery service. Furthermore, their retailer

---

* It should be borne in mind that, in this form of wholesaling, as in most others, the classification is not a clear-cut one. There are many full-service wholesalers who undertake drop-shipment transactions upon occasion. And there are some drop shippers with limited storage facilities who conduct part of their business upon an inventory basis.

customers must generally make their purchases in unbroken bulk packages. Their offerings are usually limited to fast-turnover staples. They rarely use salesmen for customer solicitation, and do little advertising or other promotion.

Such shaving of wholesaling service of course reduces these distributors' costs of operation. This cost reduction is passed on to the cash-carry wholesaler's retailer customers in the form of price reductions.

The cash-carry wholesaler had his start in the 1920's when independent grocery retailers, and the wholesale houses that served them, were seeking desperately for means of meeting the competition of the chain systems. The lower prices which the cash-carry wholesaler offered to retailers with light delivery trucks or station wagons with which they could pick up their purchases were a godsend to many independent retailers hard-pressed by chain competition. The pressure of the 1929–1933 depression expanded the opportunity of this form of limited-service wholesaling. There were sharp limits, however, to this substitution of cost-shaving for distributor service. Cash-carry wholesaling received retailer support only in the food, drugs, and tobacco products lines, where the competition of the chains was most severely felt. In those lines, the development of this form of wholesaling was checked in the middle 1930's when chain competition and the business atmosphere both eased. During the 1940's and 1950's the number and relative sales volume of cash-carry wholesalers declined.

Truck jobbers

Truck jobbers (sometimes called "wagon jobbers," or "store-door-service" distributors) are individuals who provide fast producer-to-retailer delivery in certain product fields where fast delivery is important. Each day they restock their trucks, which often constitute their only storage facilities, from local producers or even from other middlemen. They and their driver-salesmen have regular routes of retailer customers to whom they sell directly from their trucks, usually for cash. Most truck jobbers are small-scale enterprisers; frequently one or two light trucks constitute the major part of their capital investment.

The field wherein truck jobbers have found their greatest opportunity is perishable and semi-perishable food specialties and confectioneries, where they constitute a valuable marketing channel in moving the output of small producers of fresh-cooked and fresh-prepared food specialties rapidly to the dairy shops and other food stores that retail such items. Lack of storage facilities constitutes no drawback to the truck jobber in this distribution. A second truck jobbing field is that of fresh vegetables. In some cases these jobbers buy directly from farms located around metropolitan areas and resell within the day in the city. In other cases, they do their buying in city markets to which the farmers bring their crops. Two other fields where truck jobbers have established a small place for themselves, although perishability of product and speed of delivery are not involved, are petroleum products and tobacco products.

In spite of the fact that the only important expenses of most truck jobbers are the upkeep of their trucks, and the compensation of themselves and such driver-salesmen as they employ, the small scale of their operations causes their expense-to-sales ratio to be strikingly high. This puts truck jobbers in a disadvantageous competitive position. Between 1939 and 1948 they apparently lost ground in the wholesaling picture; their number decreased from 2,398 to 1,343. While the dollar volume of truck-jobber sales expanded over the nine-year period, the increase was proportionately much less than for most other phases of wholesaling.

During the 1950's two developments widened the opportunities for truck jobbing. The first was the introduction of many lines of frozen specialties, such as bake-and-serve biscuits, whose distribution can be handled effectively by truck jobbers. The second was the emergence of an advanced type of truck jobber, the "rack jobber." * This new type of wholesaler markets specialized kinds of merchandise to certain types of stores, and provides special services of selective brand and item merchandising and the arrangement, maintenance, and restocking of display racks. Stores that buy from rack jobbers are enabled to carry highly profitable supplementary lines that are outside their general merchandising experience and know-how. Many supermarkets and other food stores depend upon rack jobbers to maintain their toiletries, small house wares, and other nonfood departments. Other classes of stores are also turning to rack jobbers for help in building up supplementary lines. As a consequence of these two developments, the number of truck jobbers increased five-fold, and their sales nine-fold, between 1948 and 1958.

Mail order wholesalers

Many distributors conduct part of their business, sometimes a considerable part, upon a mail order basis. This is particularly true of the wholesaling units in wholesaler-voluntary groups, which employ salesmen to bring new retailers into the group and to make occasional calls upon the retailer members, but which make a substantial part of their sales to their established retailer members on the basis of catalogs and price lists. Many industrial distributors likewise depend substantially upon catalog ordering by the mills and factories that purchase from them.

Complete or major dependence on wholesale mail order distribution at one time seemed to offer as brilliant a marketing opportunity as mail order

---

* Currently classified by the *Census of Business* among full-service wholesalers.

retailing. Butler Brothers established a successful mail order wholesale business in the 1870's, and had a number of equally successful imitators. The automobile cut the ground from under mail order wholesaling. Salesmen, more effective than catalogs and price lists, could now visit retailers located in the smallest out-of-the-way villages. Most of the large mail order wholesalers shifted to salesman solicitation. Mail order operation as a primary wholesaling basis now is rare and is on the decline *—so much so that the *Census of Business* ignored it after 1939. Catalog selling on a small scale—and none of the present mail order wholesale houses operate on a large scale—often costs more than selling through salesmen, so the mail order wholesalers can rarely offer any substantial price bargains. In the sharp competition that marks most wholesaling lines, an impersonal catalog can rarely match the man-to-man persuasion of a salesman. Only the wholesaling units of retailer-cooperatives can hold the allegiance of their owner-customers exclusively through catalogs and price lists, and even they complain that their group members are often prevailed upon by the salesmen of competing wholesale houses.

REVIEW

1. Define: (a) a wholesale sale; (b) a wholesaling middleman.
2. Explain how "wholesale sales" and "wholesaling middlemen's sales" may differ.
3. What economic functions and marketing operations are performed by wholesaling middlemen?
4. What are converters?
5. Explain drop shippers. What are the possibilities and limitations of this form of wholesaling?
6. Explain cash-carry wholesalers. Why has their relative importance declined since the early 1930's.
7. Explain truck and rack jobbers.
8. Why is mail order wholesaling so unimportant?

DISCUSSION TOPICS

1. "The wholesaling middleman is a parasite in the American marketing system, adding to the cost of distribution but performing few or no services that could not be done as well or better by producers and retailers."
2. "The wholesaler is disappearing from the American scene."
3. "The relatively high operating costs of full-service merchant

---

* Recently there has developed a group of "catalog houses" that sell brand-name goods by mail order to door-to-door canvassers and consumer "buying clubs." The latter sell directly to consumers on the basis of the wholesalers' catalogs.

wholesalers put them at a serious disadvantage in their competition with other classes of wholesaling middlemen."

4. "Specialized full-service merchant wholesalers enjoy a growing advantage over their full-line competitors."

5. "Incidental drop shipping and cash-carry wholesaling holds possibilities for many full-service wholesalers."

PROBLEM

Metro Drugs, Inc., is a small but growing wholesale house located in Metro City, selling to independent drug stores in that city and the surrounding suburban territory. Heretofore it has specialized in brand-advertised "packaged" items. Its prices are slightly lower than those of two competing national general drug wholesale houses that also serve the Metro City territory, and on the average match those of another local "packaged" drug wholesaler. Its well-managed sales force of five turned in $1,500,000 total sales last year. Its "warehouse" is a small converted garage on the outskirts of Metro City. It has three delivery trucks.

Mr. Jones, owner of Metro Drugs, wants to expand the business, and a recent inheritance has provided him with funds to increase the capital investment of Metro Drugs if this is necessary. He is weighing the following possibilities of expansion:

(1) Keep the line of Metro Drugs the same, but hire additional salesmen to cover the territory around Metro City to a distance of roughly 100 miles. Included in this territory are three small cities and some fifty smaller communities.

(2) Cover the expanded territory on a mail order basis, with all prices to mail order customers lowered by the difference between the savings on the salesmen's commissions and the added costs attributable to mail order promotion and higher delivery costs.

(3) Keep the present territory. Register "Metro" as a drug brand name. Buy a number of standard "package" drug items—such as aspirin, cough drops, an antiseptic—in unbranded bulk and hence at lower price, package them with the "Metro" brand, and sell them to the drug stores at lower prices (but still with a higher markup for Metro Drugs than on its regular manufacturer-brand items). With lower purchase prices, the drug stores can apply larger markups than is possible with price-fixed manufacturer-brand items. Because of this greater unit profit, they will be encouraged to "push" them to their customers, and thereby sell them in spite of the fact that "Metro" has not heretofore existed as a drug brand name. Metro Drugs would offer its "Metro" brand line not as a substitute for its regular line of manufacturer-brand drugs but as a supplement to it.

(4) Keep the present line and the present territory, but build up a voluntary group of retail drug stores based on Metro Drugs as the wholesaling unit. Members of the group would order their "packaged" drug requirements from catalogs by mail or phone.

They would be given assistance in their store management and display problems. Prices to them would be lowered by the difference between the savings on salesmen's commissions and the added costs attributable to the store management assistance.

(5) Keep the present territory, but add broad lines of prescription pharmaceuticals, toilet items, sunglasses, and other common drug store items.

(6) Take on a limited line of popular-brand toilet items and cosmetics, and combine these with certain items of Metro Drugs' present "packaged" drug line to make up a "drug and cosmetic department" for supermarkets and other self-service food stores. The regular salesmen would do the initial selling of the proposition to the supermarkets and food stores. The drivers of Metro's delivery trucks would make weekly calls at which they would check on each store's drug and cosmetic inventory, deliver needed replacements from stock carried on the truck, and arrange selling and promotional displays on the store's drug and cosmetic shelves or counters.

Analyze each of these proposals from the standpoints of (a) how would they change Metro Drugs' present operating and cost set-up; and (b) taking such changes into account, what are the profit prospects?

SUGGESTED READINGS

Beckman, T. N., and others, *Wholesaling: Principles and Practice,* 3rd ed, Ronald Press, New York, 1959.

Bromell, J. R., *Dry Goods Wholesalers' Operations,* U.S. Department of Commerce, Washington, D.C., 1949.

Cassady, R., & W. R. Jones, *The Changing Competitive Structure in the Wholesale Grocery Trade,* University of California Press, Berkeley, 1949.

Revzan, D. A., *Wholesaling in Market Organization,* John Wiley & Sons, New York, 1961.

Weiss, E. B., and others, *How to Sell through Wholesalers,* Harper & Bros., New York, 1937.

PERIODICALS: *Modern Distribution.*

CHAPTER 10

WHOLESALING MIDDLEMEN
(Concluded)

AGENT MIDDLEMEN

Agent middlemen * negotiate purchases or sales or both, but do not take title to the goods in which they deal (though in some cases they take possession). They usually perform only some single marketing service, or a limited group of services.

The *Census of Business* classifies agent middlemen as follows: (1) merchandise brokers; (2) commission houses; (3) selling agents; (4) manufacturers' agents; (5) purchasing agents; (6) agricultural cooperatives operated on an agency basis; (7) export and import agents; and (8) auction companies. Our analysis in this section will cover only the first five of these types; the other three are studied in later chapters.

In practice, the operations of many agent middlemen overlap several of the above classifications. Particular firms may engage in brokerage operations for some of their clients, serve others as manufacturers' agents, and still others as selling agents. Furthermore, in many cases they may act as merchant wholesalers, buying and selling on their own account. Their classification by the *Census of Business* and in our analysis is determined by their *major* wholesaling activity.

Agent middlemen engaged in domestic distribution far outnumber the limited-service merchant wholesalers studied in the preceding chapter, and the volume of their transactions is many times greater. Compared to full-service merchant wholesalers, however, they constitute only a minor fraction of the middleman field.

---

* These were formerly called "functional middlemen," but the term is fortunately falling into disuse.

Merchandise brokers

A merchandise broker is a representative or agent for sellers or purchasers. He negotiates on their behalf the sale or purchase of specific physical lots of goods, without himself taking either title to, or physical control of, the goods or otherwise assuming control over them.* In theory there is no continuity of relationship between a merchandise broker and any of his principals. A seller or a buyer operating through brokers is usually under no contractual obligation to employ any particular broker for any series of transactions or over any period of time. In practice, however, principal-broker relationships may be close and long-lasting.

The services performed by a merchandise broker for his principals are extremely limited. When representing a producer or other seller he may sell, and when representing a purchaser he may buy. His undertaking of even these basic services is often very restricted, for his authority may extend merely to locating would-be purchasers or suppliers for his principal, who then negotiates the actual sale or purchase transaction. A merchandise broker may be given authority to set sale or purchase prices which will bind his principal, but often his service in this connection is only to ask or offer prices established by the principal. Rarely if ever does he advertise or engage in other forms of promotion. He does not store. He does not extend credit or engage in other financing activities. He assumes no market risks. Quite frequently, however, he serves his principals as a source of market information. For his limited services a merchandise broker receives a commission, ranging from a fraction of one percent to a few percent, of the dollar sales or purchase volume involved, or a fee related to the physical quantity of the transaction. Brokers in the women's apparel line charge a 5 percent commission, while brokers dealing in fresh vegetables generally charge a specific fee of so many dollars per carload.

From the standpoint of numbers and sales volume negotiated, merchandise brokers are an important category of agent middlemen.** They have a significant place in three marketing lines.

Merchandise brokers contribute to the distribution of cotton and some other agricultural raw materials. These raw material brokers frequently

---

* The merchandise broker is to be distinguished from the commodity-exchange broker. The former, as indicated, negotiates transactions in tangible goods. The latter, operating upon a commodity exchange, negotiates transfers of documents of title (negotiable warehouse receipts or bills of lading) to exchange-traded commodities, and contracts for future delivery or receipt of exchange-traded commodities, for speculators and hedgers as well as for spot sellers and purchasers of the commodities. Commodity-exchange brokers are considered facilitating marketing agents, and are studied in the next chapter.

** *Census of Business* statistics would seem to establish merchandise brokers as the most important class of agent middlemen. More than half of the Census "broker" classification, however, are "food brokers" who are more properly to be classified as manufacturers' agents.

represent purchasers. A textile mill, for example, may turn to a "mill" broker to locate a number of bales of a specified grade of cotton for it. In such case, the broker acts on behalf of the mill rather than the seller of the cotton, and may receive his commission from the mill. More commonly, however, these "mill" brokers serve the cotton merchants who seek mill customers for their holdings. A second class of cotton broker, the "F.O.B. man," sells the holdings of larger planters, ginners, and local cotton buyers to central market cotton merchants.

A second field in which merchandise brokers are of importance is the marketing of cotton piece goods. The unbleached—or "gray"—cotton cloth as it comes from the mills is usually highly standardized as to quality of yarn and texture of the weave. Brokers are therefore in a position to negotiate its sale on a description basis. They are utilized for this purpose by small mills which do not have their own sales forces and which do not need the broader and more expensive services of selling agents.

Merchandise brokers have an interesting place in the women's wear field. Some 250 such apparel brokers,* located in New York City, serve as middlemen between the manufacturers of women's ready-to-wear, millinery, furs, and men's wear, operating in and around New York City, and several thousand out-of-town small department stores and specialty shops. These apparel brokers receive a 3 percent commission from the manufacturers. Actually, however, they serve the out-of-town stores that buy through them. They keep these stores apprised of the style developments in the New York fashion market. When orders are received from the out-of-town stores, the apparel brokers place these orders with those manufacturers on their lists who, in the brokers' judgment, produce the merchandise best suited to the stores' needs.

Commission houses

By the measure of sales volume transacted by the various categories of agent middlemen, commission houses ** rank next to brokers.

The commission house, as a wholesaling middleman, has six distinctive characteristics. (1) It is an agent middleman that represents only sellers. Its compensation is a commission on the sales made for its principals. (2) Although as an agent middleman it does *not* take *title* to the products it handles, such products are shipped to it by its seller-clients on consignment,

---

* Apparel brokers are frequently called "resident buyers," but this term is better reserved for a different type of apparel agent middleman, described later in this chapter.

** The *Census of Business* term for this type of agent middleman is "commission merchant." The use of the word merchant here is unfortunate, since it might mislead the student into thinking that this class of wholesale distributors are merchant wholesalers. In the trade, these distributors are called "commission houses" more often than they are called "commission merchants." The less confusing trade term is used in our analysis.

so that it does exercise physical control over them. Such control is usually for very short periods, since the commission house generally endeavors to sell the consigned products at the earliest possible opportunity. (3) Consignments may be shipped to a commission house without advance contractual arrangement or notice. (4) It has complete authority to sell the products entrusted to it to any buyer at whatever the "spot" market price may be if there is such a market price for the products, or at whatever best price it can obtain for its principal. (5) Frequently its principals draw sight drafts on it covering their shipments, with the draft amount calculated at some margin under current "spot" prices for the product. The commission house thus often advances to its principals a substantial part of the value of their shipments before it has any opportunity to sell them, sometimes even before it receives them. (6) The principal field of commission house operation is in the marketing of grain, livestock, and other agricultural products in the raw state. Another field where the commission house has found some place is the marketing of textile piece goods.

The commission house provides a valuable marketing service to farmers and cattle-raisers, and to local dealers in agricultural products, who are in a position to make car-lot shipments. Such producers and dealers may have no direct contacts with central market buyers. Brokers might succeed in locating particular buyers who are willing to accept shipment, sight unseen, from the producers or local buyers, but this cannot always be counted on, and in any case, the producer or local buyer must store the products until the transaction is negotiated. Where the sale is handled through a commission house, however, the shipment can be made without delay, before ever an actual purchaser has been located, and in many cases the producer or local dealer can obtain an immediate advance on the shipment by means of a draft.

Commission houses handling agricultural products generally locate in the central market cities where major trading in their products occurs. Commission houses dealing in grains are found primarily in Chicago and other grain terminal centers; some of the larger firms have seats on the Chicago Board of Trade and other grain-trading exchanges, and are in a position to make direct spot sales of their car-lot consignments there. The major livestock commission houses are located in the stockyard cities. These distributors receive their consignments at the stockyards, display the animals there, and sell them to the packer buyers. Commission houses handling fresh vegetables and fruits are found in the metropolitan centers where they can dispose of their consignments to the wholesalers and chain buyers who cluster there.

The decline and ultimate disappearance of the commission house was frequently predicted during the 1930's and 1940's. The reasons given were: (1) the irresponsibility of many commission houses toward their principals in the matter of falsely reporting sales prices lower than those at which the principals' products were actually sold; (2) the taking over by agricultural marketing cooperatives of channels of distribution previously dominated by commission houses; and (3) increased direct buying by the large meat-packing houses. It is true that between 1929 and 1948 the number of commission houses declined by more than 30 percent, but their sales increased during this period in approximately the same ratio as that of other classes of agent middlemen. The significant tendencies in commission house marketing during the second quarter of the century were not any general decline of this type of agent middleman, but: (1) a competitive squeezing out of the smaller and more irresponsible firms in this field, with a resulting concentration of business among the larger and more responsible firms; (2) a steady improvement in operating efficiency of commission houses so that by 1948 the average expense-to-sales ratio was below 2 percent—the lowest for any major category of market middlemen except merchandise brokers; (3) a consequent steady competitive lowering of commission rates; and (4) a self-policing of this field of business through trade associations of the commission houses in the various product lines, which established and enforced codes of ethical practice and regulated commissions and other charges. In some half of the states, these trade association codes are backed by regulatory legislation. The 1927 Federal Produce Agency Act and the 1930 Perishable Agricultural Commodities Act required that brokers and commission houses handling certain commodities must be licensed, and established considerable control over their activities. The earlier criticisms of false-dealing and inefficiency that were with some reason directed against commission houses as a class had little justification by the mid-century. During the 1950's there has been a tremendous influx of small firms into this field. Whether this development has affected the performance standards previously achieved by commission houses remains to be seen.

Selling agents

Selling agents,* third in importance among classes of agent middlemen by the measure of sales volume, are active largely in manufactured goods lines, particularly in the textile field. They also play a substantial role in the distribution of coal and coke, where they vie with merchant wholesalers who have yards, though the sales of both combined fall below those of

---

* This is a textbook and *Census of Business* classification term. In trade terminology these agents are called sales agents, sales representatives, commission men, commission brokers, commission merchants, manufacturers' agents, manufacturers' representatives, and "old-line factors," according to the usage of particular business lines or the designations they give themselves.

drop shippers. They operate, on a much smaller scale, in the metal products, clothing and furnishings, and groceries fields.

The selling agent has seven distinctive characteristics. (1) His relationship with his principal or principals is usually a continuing and closely-knit one. (2) He usually has the complete responsibility of selling the entire output of his principal's mill or plant. In effect, he is his principal's sales organization. His selling territory is the entire marketing area served by the principal. (3) He usually has wide authority as to sales prices. (4) He commonly advises his principal on market, style, and merchandising trends as a guide to product design. (5) Occasionally he stores the output of his principal until it is sold. He holds such stored merchandise upon consignment terms. (6) Often he performs the credit and collection function for his principal; sometimes he assumes responsibility for any credit losses resulting from his decisions. (7) Occasionally he advances funds to his principal on the security of the latter's accounts receivable or even his inventory.*

Some selling agents serve only a single principal. More commonly they represent groups of mills or plants producing related but not directly competing products. By this latter arrangement, a selling agent accomplishes two objectives: (1) he augments his sales volume; and (2) he achieves a degree of line assembling that both reduces his unit selling costs and gives him the advantage of being able to offer buyers a broader line. So long as none of the principals in his group compete directly with each other, a selling agent can benefit himself through group representation without sacrificing the interests of any of his principals.

In size, selling agents range from one-man units to national organizations with scores of salesmen operating out of branch offices, and with advertising, traffic, and credit departments. Their commission rates likewise vary widely, depending upon the services they perform for their principals. Where a selling agent's services involve little more than handling the routine of a mill's orders from a group of established customers, the commission may be as low as 1 or 2%. Where pioneer selling over a broad territory is involved, and the agent further performs storage, promotional, traffic, credit, and collection services, the commission rate may be between 20 and 30%. The common range of selling agents' commissions is from 2 to 10%, with the average around 5%.

A selling agent can be an invaluable boon to a small mill or mine. The principal is relieved of all marketing responsibilities, and can devote its

---

* Selling agents in the textile field, performing this seventh function, were the progenitors of the present-day "factors," studied in Chapter 26. The recent tendency has been to separate the selling and financing functions of selling agents. The firms which evolved into factors generally allowed their selling functions to lapse. Those which have remained essentially *selling* agents have generally withdrawn from financing their principals.

limited financial resources and managerial personnel exclusively to production operations. If the selling agent is competent and conscientious, his commission is likely to be considerably less than the cost to the mill or mine of undertaking with equal effectiveness its own marketing activities.

Manufacturers' agents

Like selling agents, manufacturers' agents * are agent middlemen who undertake the selling function for their principals, most of whom are manufacturers. They differ from selling agents in seven respects. (1) A manufacturers' agent generally sells in a specific market area, where he may represent a considerable number of manufacturers, usually noncompeting, in his line. A selling agent, as we saw, customarily operates throughout the entire territorial market for his principal's goods. (2) A manufacturers' agent handles only such part of a principal's output as can be sold in the agent's market area, while a selling agent is customarily charged with selling the complete output of each principal. (3) A manufacturers' agent is bound by the principal's policy regarding prices and terms of sale. A selling agent, in contrast, frequently determines his principal's marketing policies, in any case usually has wide discretion in applying them. (4) Since manufacturers' agents operate within specific areas, many of them maintain warehouse or depot facilities for their principals' goods, from which local deliveries are made. They hold these goods on consignment. Storing by selling agents on behalf of their principals, while it occurs, is much rarer, and is not particularly related to local distribution. (5) While manufacturers' agents commonly advise their principals on local market conditions, they usually have little to say on product design and general merchandising policy. Selling agents, as we noted, are often very influential in this respect. (6) Manufacturers' agents may not perform credit and collection services for their principals, and practically never undertake to finance the latter in any way. (7) Because manufacturers' agents in general perform fewer services for their principals than do selling agents, the commission rates of the former, in any line where both types of agents operate, run substantially lower than those of the latter. For some fast-moving lines the commission rate of manufacturers' agents is only one percent.

Manufacturers' agents constitute a very useful link in the distributive chains of many commodities. A small manufacturer who does not produce a general line of goods can not usually sell successfully direct-to-retailers or direct-to-industrial-users with his own sales force because of the high unit cost of distribution. If there is no well-established demand for his items, the merchant wholesalers in his field may refuse to carry them, or if

---

* This term also is *Census of Business* and textbook nomenclature. Trade parlance gives these agents many and misleading names.

they do take them on may not give them the necessary promotional selling. The product may not be sufficiently staple or standardized for handling by merchandise brokers. A selling agent might solve the manufacturer's distribution problem, but the manufacturer may not need the broad scope of services which a selling agent would charge for. A judicious selection of manufacturers' agents in the market areas he wishes to exploit would provide such a manufacturer with energetic marketing of his output at minimum cost. Many large manufacturers cover nearby areas with their own sales forces, but use manufacturers' agents to develop more distant areas as an alternative to opening branch offices there. Often the use of manufacturers' agents in outlying market areas is a temporary expedient on the part of large manufacturers. When a market in an outlying area has been built up by manufacturers' agents, the manufacturer opens a branch office there and takes over the area from the agents.

There are nearly four times as many manufacturers' agents (exclusive of food brokers) as there are selling agents. The sales of the former, however, exceed those of the latter by less than 20 percent. In contrast to the selling agents, many of which are substantial enterprises with branch offices and large selling staffs, a considerable proportion of the manufacturers' agents are one-man enterprises. This is a field, like drop shipping, where an energetic salesman, without capital but with a good knowledge of his trade field, can readily establish himself. Many of the more successful manufacturers' agents in time venture into merchant wholesaling, buying merchandise directly from their former principals and reselling it on their own account and to their own profit, instead of merely serving as sales agents. A large proportion of the distributors classified as manufacturers' agents probably engage in some merchant wholesaling; and a not inconsiderable proportion of merchant wholesalers in lines where manufacturers' agents also operate started as such agents and evolved into merchant wholesalers, but still conduct part of their business on an agency basis.

The field in which marketing through manufacturers' agents is currently most common is that of industrial machinery, equipment, and supplies. They are also important in the metal products, dry goods, clothing, and furnishings lines. Food brokers, who should be classified as manufacturers' agents rather than as merchandise brokers, account for nearly one-third of food sales to retail grocers. The food broker is exclusively a selling agent middleman. He may be a one-man organization, but is more likely to employ a small sales force. He may serve canners, small packers, manufacturers of packaged specialty foods, and sugar refiners, located anywhere in the country. He sells on their behalf to distributors, chains and other large retail buyers, and sometimes medium-size independents, in the limited territory of his field of operation. He tries to serve producers of many different food items, so that he can offer customers fairly broad lines of food products. A food broker's principals generally specify the prices at which he may offer their products; in setting these prices, however, these principals are likely to be influenced strongly by the broker's recommendations, since he is in a better position to know market conditions than they are. Shipment of products sold through a food broker is usually made by the producer directly to the customers the broker has obtained.

Purchasing agencies and resident buying offices

Purchasing agencies * represent buyers instead of sellers, and are usually paid by the buyers they serve on a fee or commission basis. They are distinguished from merchandise brokers, who often act for buyers, in two respects: (1) they act for buyers only, never sellers; and (2) their relations with their purchasing principals are not limited to the individual transaction as in the case of merchandise brokers, but are continuing.

The most important class of purchasing agency is the *resident buying office*. This type of organization, found in New York City, Chicago, and Los Angeles, serves out-of-town department stores, women's wear and other fashion goods stores, and home furnishings stores, primarily in their purchases of apparel, but also in furnishings lines.** Some fashion goods and furnishings wholesalers also purchase through resident buying offices. Technically, most resident buying offices might be classified as facilitating marketing institutions, since their service operations generally outweigh their actual buying operations on behalf of their clients. For smaller clients they may actually undertake major seasonal purchases, but for their large ones their buying is often limited to fill-in orders. Among their important service operations are: (1) close follow-up of fashion changes with reports to their clients; (2) facilitating direct-from-manufacturer purchasing on the part of their clients; (3) working with store buyers to develop particular styles, with specifications given to the manufacturers; (4) expediting deliveries to their clients; (5) helping stores purchase supplies such as boxes, bags, and gift wrappings; (6) arranging seasonal meetings of store buyers and promoting interchange of purchasing information; (7) taking care of in-city arrangements for their clients' buyers, including appointments with salesmen; (8) in some cases developing private brands; (9) arranging joint promotions by their clients. All representative resident buying offices have sales promotion and advertising departments at the disposal of their clients.

Prior to the 1940's, purchasing agencies were also found in the hardware

---

* The middleman purchasing agency is to be distinguished from the purchasing manager of an industrial concern or purchasing clerk of a business concern, who is often, erroneously, called a "purchasing agent."

** In contrast to the group of New York City apparel brokers, previously noted, who operate only in apparel lines.

and some other lines where new products and new models were constantly coming upon the market. They represented merchant wholesalers and large industrial buyers of the items concerned. They maintained contact with hundreds of small manufacturers of the items received by their clients, and obtained price lists and catalogs from these manufacturers. The information so obtained was compiled and made conveniently available to the agencies' clients. Besides keeping their clients informed of new product developments in their fields, these purchasing agencies also did specialty purchasing for them. By consolidating specialty orders, they were often able to obtain quantity discounts for their clients. They commonly charged "brokers' fees" to manufacturers, which were passed on as price reductions to the clients. For their services they usually charged their clients fees related to these clients' purchases. In 1939 the passing on of discounts and "brokers' fees" to the clients, which constituted the major financial advantage of such agency purchasing, was held illegal under the Robinson-Patman Act. In consequence, the purchasing activities of these agencies were considerably reduced. They have since continued in the marketing picture primarily as facilitating marketing organizations, rather than as agent middlemen.

SIZE OF WHOLESALING ESTABLISHMENTS

Wholesaling is predominantly a field of small business. More than half of the country's full-service merchant wholesalers have net sales under $200,000. Brokers' and agents' sales volumes tend to be considerably higher than those of merchant wholesalers—their average net sales in 1958 were $1,700,000 compared with the $641,000 average for merchant wholesalers—but with them also there is a heavy preponderance of small establishments. Such sales volume figures, compared with the $112,000 average for retailing, may seem relatively large. But unit wholesaling transactions in any line are many, many times larger than unit retail sales, and a corresponding relationship in the aggregate transactions of establishments should be looked for. The true small scale of most wholesaling establishments is even more strikingly indicated by the figures on the numbers of their employees. Average number of employees for merchant wholesalers in 1954 was 10; for agents and brokers it was 5. In contrast, average employment for manufacturing enterprises was 59.

Individual successful merchant wholesaling houses and agent middlemen naturally grow with the years, increasing their sales volume, increasing their capital investment and number of employees. Combinations and integrations may also step up unit establishment size. On the other hand, new middleman enterprises generally start on a minimum scale, thus tending to offset the rising sales and employment figures of the more successful older firms. The combined effect of these opposing tendencies during the past thirty years has been to reduce slightly the average business volume (on a "constant dollar" basis) of merchant wholesalers, and to expand substantially that of agent middlemen.

Significantly, wholesaling is a field where unincorporated enterprises predominate. Half of the merchant wholesalers are proprietorships or partnerships, and more than three-fifths of the agents and brokers are unincorporated.

While wholesaling in general is predominantly a field of small-scale enterprise, and shows every indication of so remaining, there are several thousand merchant wholesalers with sales over $5,000,000, and a small sprinkling of giants. An electrical products wholesaler has sales over $500,000,000; a combined drug-liquor-chemicals wholesaler has sales of nearly $600,000,000.

INTEGRATION

As in manufacturing and retailing, integration in the wholesaling field has occurred both horizontally and vertically.

Chain and branch wholesaling

Wholesaling, like retailing, has experienced "horizontal" chain integration. Over a seventh of the wholesale establishments belong to chain systems. Most common are two-unit chains, but there are some 75 chain aggregations with a hundred or more units. One chain drug-liquor-chemicals wholesaler has over 140 units. Sales of wholesale chains represent nearly 30 percent of the total sales of domestic merchant wholesalers. Chain operation has apparently achieved the same relative position in wholesaling that it has in retailing. Chain organization among agents and brokers is less common, but some of the larger merchandise brokers and selling agents maintain branch offices in key market centers.

Wholesaling chains have come into existence and expanded through two different methods. Some, like the McKesson & Robbins drug house, were originally formed, and subsequently grew, through the combination of previously independent units. Others, upon achieving initial success as unit enterprises, opened branches.

Wholesaling expansion through chain development carries several advantages. (1) The massed purchasing of the chain enables it to take advantage of maximum quantity discounts. In many cases wholesaling chains contract for the entire output of various manufacturers, thereby reducing the distribution costs of these manufacturers. These cost reductions are passed on to the wholesaling chains through prices well below the best ordinary manufacturer-to-wholesaler levels. (2) Large-scale buying by the chains enables them to hire or develop expert purchasing managers, and generally to do their purchasing on a more scientific basis. (3) The larger wholesaling chains can establish and promote their own brands. Their margin on their own brands is greater than that on the handling of manufacturers' brands. (4) The large scale of their operations enables them to develop programs of dealer aids and other forms of sales promotion beyond the capacities of smaller single-unit distributors. Retailers who benefit from these programs naturally tend to give preference to such distributors. (5) The large chain distributors generally have more scientific procedures of salesman selection, salesman training, and sales force management than do their smaller competitors. (6) A chain wholesaler also retains the advantage that each unit sells and ships locally.

There is no anti-chain movement in the wholesaling field comparable to the one in retailing. The only two disadvantages to chain wholesaling are that much of the managerial responsibility rests on paid employees instead of business owners inspired by profit motivation, and that heavy management overhead costs result. This second disadvantage is more apparent than real since, if the chain operation is soundly conceived, the additional managerial effort should produce offsetting economies in purchasing and operating costs, and result in more effective selling.

One special possibility of branch wholesaling in the grocery field is that some of the branches can be operated as cash-carry depots, with lower price lists. An established full-service grocery wholesaler can thus reach out for a special market of cost-saving retailers.

Vertical integration

Vertical integration involving distributors takes three forms: (1) association of manufacturing and wholesaling operations; (2) association of retailing and wholesaling operations; and (3) association of manufacturing, wholesaling, and retailing operations.

Manufacturing-wholesaling integration. In some wholesaling lines, it is customary for distributors to assume responsibility for some of the manufacturing or conditioning processes associated with the products they handle. Converters, as we have seen, decide on the designs for the fabrics they buy from the mills, and have these fabrics dyed or printed. Coffee distributors and grocery wholesalers commonly roast their coffees. Drug wholesalers compound many standard pharmaceutical items. Commission houses in the grain trade may clean and otherwise condition grain consigned to them.

Large distributors in various lines frequently buy the entire output of particular mills, which may produce exclusively to the distributors' specifications; this is very common where selling agents are involved. In such cases, whether or not there is any corporate control of the mill by the distributor is immaterial; the distributor is likely to dominate the mill. Reverse forms of manufacturer-wholesaler integration, where a large manufacturer dominates a group of wholesale distributors, are not uncommon, particularly in the electric appliance field. In such cases the distributors operate in effect as branch sales offices of the manufacturer. Sometimes they are actually wholly-owned subsidiaries of the manufacturing corporation. Most of the petroleum bulk stations belong to the great oil companies which operate refineries as well as handle the distribution of petroleum products. Finally, there are instances, as in the case of the Beechnut line of products, where a wholesaling corporation and a group of manufacturing corporations are bound together by a common holding company.

Retailing-wholesaling integration. Many merchant wholesalers of consumer goods seek an extra incidental profit by selling directly to consumers who have established contact with them. Some distributors, who have developed such retailing activity to sizable proportions, are known as "semi-jobbers." For merchant wholesalers as a group such incidental retail sales amount to less than 2 percent of their total volume. For agents and brokers the proportion is well under 1 percent.

Close association of groups of retailers with a wholesaling unit are found in the grocery, automotive, and drug fields. As indicated in Chapter 7, there are nearly 600 wholesaler-voluntary grocery groups, each sponsored by a wholesaling unit. Usually there is no corporate control of the retailer members of a wholesaler-voluntary group by the distributor, but they are more or less obliged to make the greater part of their purchases through such distributor, and he provides them with managerial and merchandising services. There are also nearly 200 retailer-cooperative groups in the grocery field, and several in the drug field, in each of which a wholesaling unit is mutually owned by the group of retailers belonging to the chain.

Quite frequently in the past the large grocery chains and other large-scale retailers established dummy merchant wholesaling or brokerage units, through which they made their purchases. These dummy distributor units insisted on receiving the wholesalers' trade discounts or brokerage commissions common to the line which went, of course, to the retailing organizations which maintained the dummies. The Federal Trade Commission, in applying the Robinson-Patman Act, denied such discounts or commissions to these dummy organizations, and they have now largely disappeared from the Marketing picture.

Manufacturing-wholesaling-retailing integration. One of the largest textile converters is a member of a corporate integration, controlled by a holding company, which includes a group of textile mills, dyeing and printing plants, a men's-clothing manufacturer, and a chain of retail men's-clothing stores. Here is a case of complete vertical integration reaching from the spinner of the thread to the retailer who sells a man's suit. On the basis of marketing control, though not corporate control, a considerable degree of complete vertical integration is found in the automobile field, where manufacturers, controlled finance companies, exclusive distributors, and exclusive dealerships form closely bound channels of distribution.

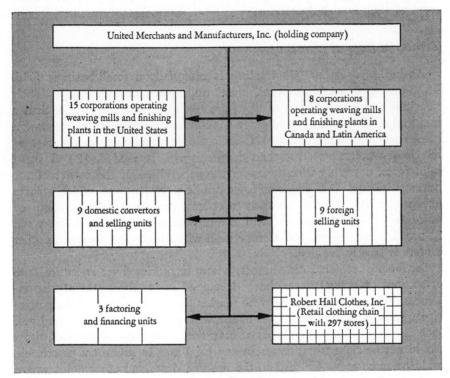

CORPORATE STRUCTURE OF UNITED MERCHANTS AND
MANUFACTURERS

ILLUSTRATION 10–1

LOCATION AND MARKET TERRITORIES

No meaningful generalization can be made about the locations of distributors as an over-all group. Each major category, each subgroup, is differently distributed about the country according to the special circumstances of the locations of its suppliers, the locations of its customers, and the requirements of its marketing practices and customs. Most assemblers of farm products are found in the local trading centers of the agricultural sections of the country, with a few of the larger ones in the central market cities for the various agricultural products. The 29,000 petroleum bulk stations and terminals are scattered throughout the country, their specific locations determined by relative land costs, consumption needs of various areas, and the existence of the pipe line, railroad, and port facilities through which petroleum products are transported. The locations of other merchant wholesalers and agent middlemen are determined by the special circumstances of the production of products they handle, and by the territorial scope of their market operations.

Territorial scope of market operations

As indicated earlier, wholesaling is essentially a small-business field. Most merchant wholesalers and agent middlemen operate locally. Their sales territories, in the East at least, are likely to radiate not more than a hundred miles around their office or warehouse city. Such limited operation carries several advantages. (1) Only a single warehouse, in the case of merchant wholesalers other than drop shippers, is needed. (2) A small sales force, operating directly under the supervision of the owner of the business, suffices. (3) The sales force can be a resident one, which reduces expense by enabling the salesmen to operate directly out of the company office. (4) Shipping costs are held to a minimum. (5) Quick delivery can be promised and given. (6) Competition with distributors located in other centers is largely avoided.

Sectional or regional distributors, whose territories cover an entire state or sections of several states, have developed under three sets of circumstances. Firstly, selling agents, who market the entire output of their principals, must often seek customers over a wide area. Secondly, in some lines, such as hardware or certain types of industrial equipment or supplies, there would not be enough customers in any local area to support a practicable middleman business. Thirdly, in the grocery, drug, and other fields where local distributors predominate, a larger-scale specialized-line distributor can balance the inherent advantages of local houses in a number of ways. It can: (a) purchase individual items in larger volume than local distributors do, and so profit by quantity discounts not available to them; (b) offer greater selection of items and brands in its specialized line; (c) establish market acceptance for its private brand lines, which many retailers take willingly because they can be sold with wider retailer margins yet at lower prices than national brands; (d) develop dealer aid programs which retailers appreciate but which smaller local distributors are not in position to formulate and apply; (e) select its sales force more carefully, train it better, and supervise it more effectively than local distributors; (f) partially overcome the big handicap of higher transportation costs because of longer shipping distances by establishing branch houses in suitable locations.

Wholesaling has its giants that operate on a national scale in several fields. Among others, there is McKesson & Robbins in the drug field, Cohn-Hall-Marx in converting, Graybar Electric in electrical equipment, Carson Pirie Scott & Co. in dry goods, Hibbard, Spencer, Bartlett & Co. in hardware, and Francis H. Leggett & Co. in groceries. Some of these national distributors are chains, some are unitary organizations. Generally, they solve the problem of long distance shipping costs by maintaining branch warehouses at strategic market centers. They limit their distributional efforts to the heavily populated areas surrounding such centers, and leave the more thinly populated in-between territories to local distributors. Many of their shipments are in carload lots, to local jobbers and large retailers who can take advantage of the economies of such quantity purchases. In nearly all cases, these national giants have their own private brands, and have developed market acceptance of them so effectively that they outrank all but the very top manufacturers' brands in their fields.

Location

The above analysis of the scope of the operations of distributors, other than farm product assemblers and petroleum bulk stations, provides a key to their location. (1) Local distributors for consumer goods lines, agent middlemen as well as merchant wholesalers, are scattered throughout the country, in small cities as well as large, roughly in proportion to the populations of these cities and their surrounding market areas. (2) Sectional and national merchant wholesalers of consumer goods lines have their main offices, if not all of their warehouses, in major metropolitan centers. New York and Chicago are headquarters for a large number of the national distributors. (3) Industrial distributors, and distributors of business and professional equipment, many of which operate on a national scale, also locate their offices in the major metropolitan centers. (4) There is also a heavy concentration of merchandise brokers, particularly those operating in basic commodity fields, and of drop shippers, in the metropolitan centers.

New York City is the great wholesaling center of the country for two reasons. Many thousand local distributors, who serve the metropolitan area and the heavily populated area within a one-hundred-mile radius, are located there. It is a preferred location for head offices of national consumer goods distributors, for many types of industrial distributors, for most business equipment and supply distributors, for most selling agents, and for many classes of merchandise brokers. With one lone exception—beer and ale, where Chicago takes primacy—it is the leading wholesaling center for every commodity line in which middlemen operate. For the textile field, it is the only major wholesaling center; over 90 percent of the textile converters and textile jobbers have their offices there.

REVIEW

1. Explain merchandise brokers. Describe the operations of food brokers.

2. Explain commission houses and their methods of operations. Is there any federal or state control over them?

3. Explain selling agents.

4. Explain manufacturers' agents.

5. How extensive is integration of (a) manufacturing and wholesaling, (b) wholesaling and retailing, (c) manufacturing, wholesaling, and retailing?

6. Contrast the advantages and disadvantages of national or regional wholesaling with those of local wholesaling.

7. Why is New York City so preeminent as a wholesaling center?

DISCUSSION TOPICS

1. "Without brokers, the cost of marketing raw materials would be doubled or tripled."

2. In what way is the taking of possession without title a key to the commission house's role in American marketing?

3. Why do some manufacturers prefer to use manufacturers' agents rather than open branch sales offices in the areas involved?

4. "The resident buying offices have closed the fashion gap between Fifth Avenue and Main Street."

5. "Wholesaling is large-scale business. The small company stands little chance."

6. "The same forces that produce chain retailing are operative in the wholesaling field."

7. "We are not ever likely to see the American economy organized substantially into a set of vertical integrations combining manufacturer, middleman units, and retail outlets."

PROBLEM

Weldon Mill, a small mill located in Patterson, N.J., produces a good quality of cotton sheeting which can be used, according to the finish given to it, for bed clothes, cheap handkerchiefs, dresses.

1. What types of wholesaling middlemen could handle its output?

2. From the viewpoint of Weldon Mill, what are the advantages and disadvantages of each type?

3. Are there possibilities that it might sell through more than one type, or should it limit itself to just one type of distributor? Why?

SUGGESTED READINGS

Beckman, T. N., and others, *Wholesaling,* 3rd ed, Ronald Press, New York, 1959.

Hill, R. M., *Improving the Competitive Position of the Independent Wholesaler,* Bureau of Business Management, University of Illinois, Urbana, 1958.

Leffler, M., *How to Become a Successful Manufacturers' Representative,* Prentice-Hall, Englewood Cliffs, N.J., 1952; *How to Increase Your Sales Volume as a Manufacturers' Agent,* Prentice-Hall, Englewood Cliffs, N. J., 1958.

Merchandising Service and the Food Broker, National Association of Food Brokers, Washington, D.C., no date.

Staudt, T. A., *The Manufacturers' Agent as a Marketing Institution,* U.S. Bureau of the Census, Washington, D.C., 1952.

Thayer, L., & G. E. Harris, *Sales and Engineering Representation,* McGraw-Hill Book Co., New York, 1958.

Wedding, N. (ed.), *Vertical Integration in Marketing,* Bureau of Economic and Business Research, University of Illinois, Urbana, 1952.

CHAPTER 11

FACILITATING MARKETING INSTITUTIONS

Besides retailers and wholesaling middlemen, our marketing structure includes thousands of facilitating marketing institutions—enterprises which perform specialized services that assist marketing activity but which do not participate, directly or in an agency relationship, in the movement of goods along the channels of distribution. Included in this category are commercial auctions, commodity exchanges, trade associations, stock yards, industrial designers, advertising agencies, marketing research agencies, sales or credit service organizations, public warehouses, freight carriers and transportation service organizations, finance companies, and other specialized service units.

The first three classes of these auxiliary marketing institutions—commercial auctions, commodity exchanges, and trade associations—are studied in this chapter. Consideration of the others is deferred to Part Four where each is examined in relation to its particular Marketing activity.

COMMERCIAL AUCTIONS

The 1958 *Census of Business* listed 1,840 commercial auction companies through which over $4.5 billion of sales were made.* These figures represent a tremendous expansion during the past quarter-century of number and activities of commercial auctions—far greater relatively than for any class of wholesaling middlemen previously discussed. The commercial auction is assuming an enhanced importance in the American marketing

---

* The *Census of Business* classifies auction companies as agent middlemen, since many of them actually participate in the sales transactions involved. Although there are excellent grounds for this treatment, it seems advisable for purposes of comparative study to group them with commodity exchanges as facilitating marketing institutions.

picture. Over 90 percent of tobacco is sold through auctions. The institution is important also in the marketing of livestock, poultry, fresh fruits and vegetables, and cotton, and has some place in other product lines.

Auction procedure

The following generalizations may be made about commercial auction procedure:

1. The sellers at commercial auctions are producers selling directly or through agents, and wholesaling middlemen who have purchased from producers. At the tobacco auctions the sellers are, with few exceptions, the planters. At fruit auctions most of them are fruit-growers' cooperatives and commission houses. At livestock auctions they are primarily cattle-raisers, with some local cattle dealers.

2. The commodities sold through auctions are usually "lots" of similar grade or quality. At a fruit auction the lot is a carload or a group of crates of a particular fruit, all of the same commercial grade. At a tobacco auction the lot is a pile of similar-quality tobacco leaves. The fur auction lot is a bale of comparable furs. The furniture auction lot is a number of identical chairs, or tables, or other items. Even at the livestock auctions, the cattle may be grouped in lots of similar animals.

3. Arriving shipments are usually delivered to the auction company premises, consigned to salaried representatives of large shippers, or to "auction receivers" who act as agents for small shippers. In some cases, the auction company itself may be the agent consignee. These representatives and receivers prepare the lots to be put up for sale, arrange with the auction company for their sale (perhaps also establishing a minimum "reservation" price), prepare samples (where inspection of samples by the buyers before the sale is practicable), provide the auction company with the information needed for its catalog, sometimes do advance promotion of their "lots" to individual buyers before the sale, and subsequently collect the sale proceeds from the auction company and remit them, less commissions, to their principals. At livestock auctions they even water and otherwise care for the animals until these are sold.

4. In many cases the auction company prints a catalog, or "buyers' sheet," with brief descriptions of the lots to be sold at each auction. Each lot is a "line" in the catalog. At fruit auctions, there are usually only a few hours between the arrival of final consignments and the sale itself during which the catalogs can be composed and printed. Nevertheless, through miracles of quick printing, they are in the buyers' hands before the sale begins.

5. Commercial auctions are open to the public. But the "public" that attends any commercial auction is a distinctive one, composed of busi-

10		
LINES	MARKS	DESCRIPTION

Monday, April 25, 1960

KRASS-JOSEPH, Inc.

Tasty Treat BRAND	PFE 200356 Orchard Siding, Wash. Std. Refrig. ALL ONE GROWER

DELICIOUS
Extra Fancy

LINES	MARKS	DESCRIPTION
4059	80	11 Friday Cartons Tray Pack
4060	88	29
4061	100	149
4062	113	122
4063	138-2,150-1	3
Extra Treat		
4064	80	6
4065	88	9
4066	100	27
4067	113	23
4068	125-6,138-3	9
4069	150	103
4070	163	60
		ALL APPLES WRAPPED

16		
LINES	MARKS	DESCRIPTION

Monday, April 25, 1960.

Sunkist Growers
W. J. McHALE, District Manager
Orange County Fruit Exchange
ORV LA 11966

ALPHABETICAL BRAND	PFE 62954 Villa Park, Calif.

LINES	Sunkist	VALENCIA ORANGES
129	56	19 Cartons
130	72	62
131	88	176
132	113	49
133	138	9 / 315
Bird Rocks Brand Sunkist		
134	56	88
135	72	185
136	88	355
137	113	88
138	138	25 / 741
Jester Brand		
139	88	30
140	113	20
141	138	10 / 60
ERIE		1116 Total

5		
LINES	MARKS	DESCRIPTION

Monday, April 25, 1960

SULLIVAN, WOOD & CO., Inc., Agents

PINNACLE PACKING CO., Inc.

Pinnacle BRAND	PFE 9503 Medford, Oregon Std. Refrig.

D'ANJOUS
US #1

LINES	MARKS	DESCRIPTION
4011	80	4 Boxes Poly Liners
4012	90	5
4013	100-1,110-4	5
4014	120	9
4015	135	21
4016	150	2
4017	195	7 / 53
Pic-O-Pac Brand Fancy		
4018	135	63
4019	150	155
4020	165	99
4021	195	94 / 411
ERIE		UNLOADING ½ OF CAR.

PAGES FROM A FRUIT AUCTION CATALOG. *Courtesy of New York Fruit Auction Corp.*

ILLUSTRATION 11–1

ness buyers. At the tobacco auctions, buyers are mostly salaried representatives of the large tobacco processing companies with a scattering of purchasing brokers. The dominant group of buyers at fruit and vegetable auctions are wholesalers buying on their own account, with some brokers representing out-of-town jobbers, and some buyers acting for retail chain systems, hotels, restaurant chains, and dining car companies. At the livestock auctions are found farmers buying for breeding and feeding purposes, salaried representatives of meat packing companies, livestock dealers, and various agent representatives. Whatever the field and whatever the status of these buyers, they are usually experts in judging their product by inspection. Customarily, they make a first-hand inspection of the lots that interest them before the sale begins.

6. The mechanics of the sale differ according to product fields. In the tobacco and livestock auctions, the auctioneer and his assistants move

from lot to lot, the buyers following him. In the fruit auctions the buyers gather in a large room, the auctioneer and his assistants stand at a pulpit, and the sale proceeds by catalog lines. If each lot is sold only as a single unit, the bidding starts with a low price and works up. If, as in fruit auctions, a carload lot of a particular uniform shipment is sold off by the crate, the auctioneer starts with a high price and works down, with more and more of the crates composing the lot taken up at successively lower prices, until the entire lot is cleared. In either case, the auctioneer calls out his prices rapidly, in condensed form. He uses a jargon incomprehensible to outsiders, but readily understood by the buyers present. Their bids are usually made silently, by the raising of fingers and other standardized gestures. Bids that close sales are instantly translated into memoranda that bind both seller and buyer. In a couple of hours, scores of thousands of dollars of merchandise may be thus sold.

A FRUIT AUCTION IN PROGRESS. *Courtesy of Penn Industries, Inc.*

ILLUSTRATION 11–2

7. Buyers at a commercial auction usually provide their own transport for removing merchandise they have purchased. At tobacco auctions this is not necessary, since the sale is made in the warehouse and the buyer may leave his purchased lots there for continued storage.

Auction companies and their services

Tobacco auctions, numbering close to a thousand, are generally operated by the tobacco warehouses on whose premises they are held. Auctions in other lines are made possible by corporations organized for this express purpose. Some of these corporations are private enterprises created and operated for profit. A growing proportion are mutual companies, established by the major sellers and buyers who utilize them. Country berry and vegetable auctions are operated by the growers' cooperatives.

Auction companies perform a number of important services for sellers and buyers who use their facilities. (1) Fruit auctions are held daily. Others are held weekly at certain seasons of the year, or at irregular intervals. In the latter case, the auction companies notify sellers of the date and time of each auction sale. (2) The companies generally provide temporary storage space to accommodate arriving consignments—shed space in the case of the fruit and vegetable auctions, pen space at the cattle auctions, floor space at most of the others. (3) In cases where the auction is not held directly over the actual lots, the companies provide special auction rooms. (4) In some cases they print special catalogs or "buyers' sheets." (5) They supply and pay auctioneers and their assistants. (6) They move sold goods from the auction floor to a delivery platform where the buyers can load it on their trucks. In some cases they provide delivery at a charge, to the buyers' place of business. (7) Where auction purchases are on credit terms, as in the fruit and some other types of auctions, the auction companies pass upon the acceptability of the buyers as credit risks and extend credit to them, while remitting the sales proceeds to the sellers within twenty-four or forty-eight hours. (8) These services to the sellers are rendered for a commission charge based on the realized sales receipts, and ranging from 1 to 5 percent, according to type of auction and scope of services rendered.

Location

No one rule governs the location of the commercial auctions.

The fruit auctions are all located in metropolitan centers. Each of these cities is a major concentrated consuming market, and the heart of a wide regional market, for the fruits sold through its auction.

Fur auctions have been established at St. Louis and New York, the two major centers of the women's clothing industries which use furs. Auctions of furniture, apparel, and other manufactured lines likewise are found in centers where the buyers of the product are concentrated.

In contrast, auctions for tobacco, livestock, dairy products, berries, and fresh vegetables are held at local centers in the *producing* regions. These classes of auctions are frequently called "local" auctions.

Effectiveness

As a marketing institution, the commercial auction has a number of drawbacks. (1) Prices are influenced directly by short-term—in some cases day-to-day—variations in supply and demand in narrow market areas, and accordingly are often widly erratic. (2) Collusion among important groups of buyers, or "puff bidding" by unrecognized agents of sellers, would seriously undermine the "open" character of auction prices; only unremitting vigilance on the part of the auction companies restrains these possible abuses. (3) An additional set of marketing activities, involving special facilities and individuals and additional marketing costs, is introduced between the producers of the goods sold and the distributors who buy at these auctions. (4) Auction procedure wastes the time of the buyers who must frequently wait through other transactions in order to participate in those which interest them.

Offsetting these drawbacks is the basic consideration that the commercial auction, as a marketing institution, quickly establishes prices that equate local supply and demand in product fields wherein supply is nonuniform and widely fluctuating and demand is sharply elastic. Within a minute or two, sometimes seconds, the rising bids of the buyers at an auction (or their falling bids, where there are a number of identical units in a lot) set a price which effects a sale. In a few hours' time, prices are reached which move the entire supply of the commodity on the local market, even though various lots may vary considerably as to quality and other details. Where highly perishable products are involved, as in fruit and vegetable auctions, quickness of price determination and effecting of mass sales are absolutely vital. Even in the case of less perishable items, certainty and speed of selling are substantial advantages.

The commercial auction does not necessarily represent an additional cost introduced into the distributional system, which either raises ultimate price of the auctioned items or reduces proceeds to the producers. An auction brings possible buyers together in a group. If a producer or his agent representatives had to contact and deal with them separately, the costs of individual negotiation might well equal or exceed those attached to auction selling. Individual negotiation, furthermore, might not inspire the buying competition present at the auction, which favors the seller.

Whether viewed as an actual agent middleman, or as a facilitating marketing institution, the commercial auction makes a pertinent contribution to marketing efficiency in a number of product fields. Developments of the 1940's and 1950's indicate that its role in the American distributive system may be an expanding one.

COMMODITY TRADING EXCHANGES *

A commodity trading exchange is a mutual organization which provides its members with facilities for trading on both "spot" and "futures" bases in a commodity either upon their own behalf or as agents for other parties. Unlike a commercial auction, a commodity exchange does not participate directly in the commodity purchases and sales transacted on its premises and through the facilities it provides. It is therefore rarely if ever classified as a wholesaling middleman but is deemed purely a facilitating marketing institution.

As indicated in Illustration 11–3, there are 14 commodity exchanges in the United States through which thirty-one commodities are traded. Approximately nine-tenths of commodity exchange trading involves grains.

Spot vs. futures trading

Two types of trading are usually possible on commodity exchanges— "spot" and "futures."

Spot trading consists of selling and buying quantities of a traded commodity actually available "on the spot"—i.e., in approved warehouses or elevators in or near the exchange city, or in cars on terminal sidings in the exchange city. Such spot selling and buying is commonly based on samples displayed by the seller or his broker on the exchange floor.** Delivery is effected by the transfer of negotiable warehouse receipts or bills of lading covering the spot lots of the commodity. Spot transactions on a commodity exchange are an incidental means of selling quantities of an exchange-traded commodity on hand at the exchange center.

Futures trading has little to do with the actual movement of commodities from their producers to their ultimate consumers or industrial users. It is a system developed with a market finance objective—to make possible the risk-minimizing technique of hedging, described in Chapter 27. A futures transaction in any exchange-traded commodity involves a contract whereby the "seller" obligates himself to deliver, during a specified future month, a specified quantity of a specified standard "basis" grade of the

---

* There are a number of associations among middlemen dealing in particular commodities which are called "exchanges" but whose only function is that of providing their members with information on supply, demand, and current price. No actual trading is transacted on these "exchanges." These associations are not included in the concept of "commodity trading exchanges" on which our analysis is based.

** In the case of eggs and other perishables, samples of which could not conveniently be displayed on the floor of an exchange, transactions are based on government grading certificates.

COMMODITY EXCHANGES AND THE COMMODITIES TRADED ON THEM, 1960

COMMODITY	New York Cocoa Exchange	New York Coffee & Sugar Exchange	New York Mercantile Exchange	New York Produce Exchange	New York Cotton Exchange	New York Commodity Exchange	New Orleans Cotton Exchange	Chicago Mercantile Exchange	Chicago Board of Trade	Kansas City Board of Trade	Minneapolis Grain Exchange	Milwaukee Grain Exchange	Seattle Grain Exchange	Memphis Board of Trade
Barley									X		X			
Burlap						X								
Butter								X						
Cocoa beans	X													
Coffee		X												
Copper						X								
Corn									X	X		X		
Cotton					X		X		X					
Cottonseed meal														X
Cottonseed oil				X			X		X					
Eggs								X						
Flaxseed											X			
Grain sorghums									X	X				
Hides						X								
Lard									X					
Lead						X								
Oats									X	X	X	X		
Onions			X					X						
Potatoes			X					X						
Rubber (crude)						X								
Rye									X		X	X		
Soy beans									X	X	X			
Soy bean oil				X					X					
Soy bean meal									X					X
Sugar		X												
Tallow				X										
Tin						X								
Turkeys								X						
Wheat									X	X	X	X	X	
Wool and wool tops					X									
Zinc						X								

ILLUSTRATION 11–3

commodity for a specified price. The "buyer" in such a transaction correspondingly obligates himself to accept such delivery during the agreed-upon month, and to pay the agreed price for it. We shall explore the subject of futures trading more thoroughly in a few pages.

Both spot and futures trading are possible for the more important exchange-traded commodities on the larger exchanges. Futures trading is many times greater than cash sales. Obviously, the major marketing contribution of commodity exchanges is not the physical distribution of the commodities traded on their floors. Rather, it is the amelioration, through the exchanges' provision for futures trading, of some of the marketing risks associated with this physical distribution. Also, as we shall note in Chapter 12, prices established on the exchanges for exchange-traded commodities immediately determine their prices all along their channels of distribution—backward to their origin, as well as forward to their ultimate purchase.

Commodities adaptable to exchange trading

Exchange trading is possible for any product with the following five qualifications:

1. The product should be of such nature that it can be marketed in a very limited number of standard grade classifications. The fewer the varieties of an exchange-traded commodity, the greater the efficiency of exchange trading. This consideration precludes exchange trading of most manufactured goods with their infinite size and design variations. Many agricultural products and most refined minerals, which tend to be homogeneous within the relatively broad designations of market grades, do meet this requirement. So also do first-stage manufactured products such as burlap, cotton-seed oil, and lard.

2. The volume of transactions in the commodity should be sufficient to provide for continuous or frequent exchange activity, and of sufficient magnitude to make it difficult for a single speculator, or a small group, to exercise any substantial influence on prices.

3. The commodity should have numerous competing producers with unhampered access to domestic markets. There should also be numerous independent buyers who can use the exchange. Control of either the supply of a commodity coming on an exchange, or of demand for it, by any small collusive group of sellers or buyers would lead to price manipulation that could be disastrous for traders not a part of the collusive group.

4. The price of an exchange-traded commodity must be free to fluctuate, at least within limits. Without that, there would be no need to hedge against price risks through futures transactions, and the major purpose of an exchange would be lacking. For this reason, there is no exchange

trading in gold or silver whose prices are fixed because of their relation to the monetary system. Grains, with prices affected by the federal parity price program, are exchange-traded because federal price control in this case merely sets annual "floors" to grain prices but leaves them complete freedom of fluctuation above and slightly below these "floors."

5. The commodity must not be quickly perishable. A certain proportion of futures contracts in any exchange-traded commodity is fulfilled by actual deliveries from stored stocks. An exchange-traded commodity must therefore be capable of being stored for periods of a month or more. In this connection it is interesting to note that the development of cold storage, by changing the character of butter, eggs and certain other commodities from relatively perishable to relatively nonperishable, made exchange-trading in these commodities possible.

Traders on commodity exchanges

There are four classes of sellers and buyers whose transactions are essential on commodity exchanges: (1) suppliers of spot-traded commodities, such as wholesaling dealers, elevators, and farm marketing cooperatives in the case of grains, or metal refiners and importers in other cases; (2) buyers of spot-traded commodities, such as millers, manufacturers and exporters; (3) hedgers in futures-traded commodities (described in Chapter 26); and (4) speculators.

Very few of these sellers and buyers are members of the commodity exchanges through which they trade, and cannot negotiate directly their sales or purchases on the exchanges. Most of the actual exchange transactions, particularly those in futures, are handled by a special type of agent middleman—the "commodity-exchange broker" *—who serves his principals on a commission basis.

Commodity exchange organization

The commodity exchanges are mutual institutions, in a few cases established by special state legislation, but usually organized under state membership corporation laws. The members who organize and maintain them are of three types: (1) commodity-exchange brokers who act for large numbers of small suppliers, buyers, hedgers, and speculators whose

---

* The term "commodity-exchange broker" is here used to distinguish the brokerage houses that serve their principals on the commodity exchanges from the merchandise brokers described in Chapter 10. Some of these exchange brokers, specifically licensed by the U.S. Secretary of Agriculture to handle and hold clients' funds, are called "futures commission merchants." Besides the exchange brokers who solicit and accept trading orders from outside parties, there are "floor brokers" who actually execute orders for the exchange brokers on the floor of a commodity exchange.

only access to the exchanges is through them; (2) a small number of large sellers and buyers of the exchange-traded commodities; and (3) a small number of large-scale speculators.

Trading on a commodity exchange is limited to members, and membership is not open to all applicants. Approval of the membership committee of the exchange must first be obtained. The number of "seats" on each exchange is specified by the by-laws of the organization, and an approved applicant can achieve his membership only by purchasing the "seat" of some present member.

Each commodity exchange has a "trading room" or "trading floor." In smaller exchanges, this may simply be a large room in an available building adapted to the requirements of exchange trading. Several of the larger exchanges have had their buildings constructed to their special needs, with "trading rooms" planned in various unique arrangements. A "trading room" must usually embody the following elements: (1) display tables or cases for the samples on which spot trading is based; (2) a "pit," "ring" or "post" for each traded commodity where the floor brokers do their actual trading; (3) a "board," visible from the entire trading room, on which the day's initial "calls" and subsequent prices can be written or flashed; (4) telephone facilities for frequent communications between the floor traders and their offices.

In addition to these physical trading appurtenances, a commodity exchange must establish the rules and procedures of its trading—the standard "basis" grades to which the trading will refer, the unit lots in which trading will occur, the terms of standard trading contracts, the margins to be required on futures contracts, the commissions to be charged by the commodity brokers belonging to its membership. A "clearing house" must be provided, to balance out and establish daily the net obligations of its members with respect to their "long" and "short" positions on their various futures transactions. All the commodity exchanges provide reporting services; information on trading volumes and prices is made continuously available to the national ticker services and to interested elements of the market.

Economics of futures trading

Under a futures contract, the "seller" agrees to deliver, and the "buyer" agrees to accept, during some specified future month, at a specified price, a specified quantity of one of the standard "basis" grades of the exchange traded commodity. Each party is required, by exchange rules, to deposit a specified "margin" as a guaranty of his good faith. These margins have to be maintained intact against adverse price movements. Assuming a futures contract has remained in force until the delivery month, the seller has the option to set the actual delivery date. Delivery upon a matured futures contract may be made by an actual lot of the commodity that is slightly superior or slightly inferior to the "basis" grade of the original contract; in such case the original price agreement is adjusted for a premium or a discount. In practice, however, less than 1 percent of commodity futures contracts are fulfilled by an actual delivery of the commodity. All the rest are cancelled out before maturity by counterbalancing futures transactions —i.e., the original "seller" at some time before delivery becomes a futures "buyer" for an identical quantity, and the original "buyer" becomes an equivalent futures "seller."

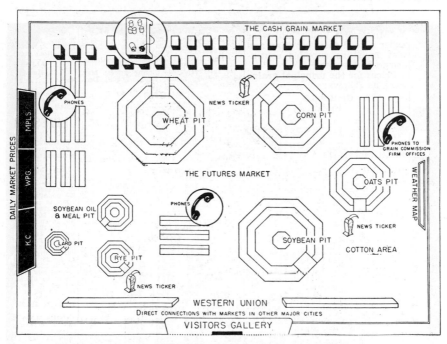

FLOOR PLAN OF THE CHICAGO BOARD OF TRADE. *Courtesy of Board of Trade, Chicago.*

ILLUSTRATION 11-4

Except in rare instances, there is a "spread" between the spot price of any commodity and its currently quoted futures price for any particular delivery month. If the national economy is stable, and supply of the commodity and demand for it are fairly well balanced, the spread of a futures-traded commodity tends to equal the average cost of carrying the commodity from the present time until the delivery month—the average of the handling charges, storage, shrinkage, insurance, interest on capital, and like costs. Thus, in "normal" times, if the spot price of cotton in September were 32 cents per pound, and the average monthly carrying cost of cotton were $\frac{1}{10}$ cent per pound, the spread to March delivery would be $\frac{3}{5}$ cent and the March futures price, as of September, would be 32$\frac{3}{5}$ cents. But, "normalcy" in the national economy and in supply and demand of many of the basic commodities has long been the exception rather than the rule. Rarely can any form of abnormalcy cause the spread of an exchange-traded commodity to exceed the average of its carrying costs, but many situations can cause it to fall under this average. If a commodity is in markedly short supply, its spread may be negative for long periods—i.e., the futures prices may be under the spot prices.

...dle Mississippi Valley still were under a good snow covering and that moisture supplies continued to be favorable.

Prices for the principal grains were as follows:

CHICAGO

WHEAT

	Open	High	Low	close	Prev. Close	Last Year
Mar.	2.04½	2.06¾	2.04½	2.06¾	2.04½	2.05⅞
May	2.05⅞	2.06	2.05¼	2.05⅞	2.05⅛	1.84¾
Jly	1.84½	1.84½	1.83⅞	1.84	1.83¾	1.86½
Sep.	1.86¼	1.86⅜	1.86¼	1.86⅜	1.86	1.86½
Dec.	1.91¼	1.91½	1.91¼	1.91½	1.91	1.91⅞

CORN

Mar.	1.14	1.14¼	1.13¾	1.14¼	1.13⅜	.....
May	1.16¼	1.16½	1.16¼	1.16⅜	1.16⅜	1.18¾
Jly	1.19	1.19½	1.18⅞	1.18⅞	1.19	1.19½
Sep.	1.15⅞	1.16	1.15¾	1.15¾	1.16	1.16½
Dec.	1.10½	1.10¾	1.10	1.10	1.10	1.13

OATS

Mar.	.75¼	.75¾	.74¼	.74¾	.75¼	.....
May	.74¾	.74¾	.74¼	.74¼	.74⅞	.66⅝
Jly	.71⅞	.71¼	.71¼	.71¼	.71¼	.64⅞
Sep.	.71	.71¼	.70¾	.71	.70¾	.65½
Dec.	.72¾	.73¼	.72¾	.72¾b	.72¾	.....

RYE

Mar.	1.20	1.20½	1.16½	1.16½	1.19⅜	.....
May	1.21	1.21½	1.19½	1.19⅞	1.21½	1.40¾
Jly	1.21	1.21½	1.19½	1.20	1.21	1.23¾
Sep.	1.23	1.23⅜	1.21¾	1.21¾	1.22⅞	1.20¾
Dec.	1.24¾	1.25⅜	1.24¼	1.24½	1.25¼	1.24

SOYBEANS

Mar.	2.12¾	2.13¼	2.11⅞	2.12	2.12⅜	.....
May	2.15¼	2.15½	2.14½	2.14⅜	2.14⅞	2.25½
Jly.	2.17⅛	2.17⅛	2.16½	2.16¼	2.16¼	2.27¼
Sep.	2.09¼	2.09⅜	2.08⅜	2.08⅞	2.09	2.15¼
Nov.	2.08	2.08⅜	2.07½	2.07¾	2.07¾	2.12¼

SOYBEAN MEAL

Mar.	56.35	57.00	56.05	56.45	56.35	
May	58.10	58.45	57.90	58.00	58.05	57.75
July	58.15	58.30	57.95	58.00	57.95	57.70
Aug.	58.00	58.20	57.95	57.95	57.80	56.70
Sept.	55.80	55.80	55.65	55.60b	55.60	53.50
Oct.	53.70	53.70	53.60	53.60	53.80	51.50

SOYBEAN OIL

Mar.	7.63	7.65	7.62	7.60b	7.58	....
May	7.74	7.77	7.73	7.77	7.70	9.21
Jly	7.87	7.89	7.85	7.88	7.80b	9.16
	7.87	7.92				8.83

May	1.80			44.31
July	44.40	44.35	44.31n	44.24
Sept.	44.25	44.20	44.25n	44.00
March (61)	42.00	42.00	42.00n	41.80

Closing: Dec., 42.65n. Sales, 41 contracts.

"R" CONTRACT

No sales reported. Closing prices: May, 25.90n; July, 25.05n; Sept., 24.80n; Dec., 24.15n.

SUGAR

CONTRACT No. 4

May	3.09	3.05	3.09t	3.08
July	3.16	3.13	3.16t	3.17
Sept.	3.22	3.18	3.21/.22	3.21
Oct.	3.23	3.21	3.23t	3.22
March (61)	3.28	3.27	3.27b	3.26
May	3.31	3.27	3.31n	3.28
July	3.33	3.33	3.31/.33	3.32

Closing: Jan. ('61), 3.26n. Sales, 230 contracts.

CONTRACT No. 6

May	5.81	5.80	5.80/.81t	5.80
July	5.89	5.88	5.88/.89t	5.89
Sept.	5.93	5.93	5.93t	5.94
Nov.	5.94	5.94	5.94n	5.95

Sales, 65 contracts.

CONTRACT No. 7

No sales reported. Closing prices: May, 6.22n; July, 6.37n; Sept., 6.42b.

COCOA

March	25.40	25.40	25.40n	25.40
May	26.25	25.83	25.92t	26.00
July	26.35	25.99	26.08n	26.13
Sept.	26.65	26.25	26.38n	26.43
Dec.	26.75	26.50	26.58n	26.60
Mar. ('61)	26.76	26.60	26.70n	26.70
May	26.90	26.70	26.78n	26.80

Closing: June, 25.99n. Sales, 249 contracts.

COPPER

March	31.75	31.45	31.45t	31.54
May	29.25	29.00	29.12t	29.02
July	28.37	28.20	28.28t	28.25
Sept.	28.04	27.94	28.01t	27.96
Oct.	27.97	27.97	26.95/.96	27.89
Dec.	27.95	27.82	27.92/.94	27.79
Jan. ('61)	27.93	27.80	27.90t	27.75
March	27.87	27.87	27.85/.88	27.69

Sales, 324 contracts.

COTTONSEED OIL

March	11.69	11.64	11.69	11.59
May	11.81	11.64	11...	11...
July				

Closing: 22.55n; 22.30n. Quotations in... ALE... Karn... Mar. ... May ... (Quotations in (5 tallaris eq equals 99.05 po...

LIVESTO...

CHICAGO, Mar... today's livestock... partment of Agr...

Hogs: 7,000;... later sales close... steady to 25 cen... on butchers, m... 230 pounds;... interests in trad... mixed grade No... 1 to 3, 200 to 2... 200 to 225 pou... lots No. 1s and... 220 pounds most... $16.25, eighty-f... lots mostly No. ... as $15.25; mixed... No. 3s 230 to 2... several lots most... $15.50 to $15.75... scarce; a few... and No. 3s up... mixed Nos. 2... $13.25 to $14.25,...

Cattle 4,500... supply increased... cattle, mainly... from Monday; s... a few sales 25c... mostly steady; ... a few loads hig... to 1,400 pound... choice steers $2... pounds included... good and choic... steers $24 to $2... holstein...

COMMODITY EXCHANGE QUOTATIONS IN THE *NEW YORK TIMES*

ILLUSTRATION 11-5

From day to day, indeed from minute to minute, the prices of traded commodities—both spot and futures prices—may fluctuate on the exchanges. The spot and related futures prices for each commodity tend to move together—not exactly parallel, but close enough so that *the propor-*

tionate changes in the spread are much less than the variations in the actual spot and futures prices. In this relative stability of futures *spreads* lies the major reason for the existence of futures markets. It enables raw materials dealers, manufacturers, exporters, and others, for whom price variations could constitute unendurable marketing risks, to avoid these risks by hedging, explained in Chapter 27.

The mass of traders on the commodity futures market are hedgers. They sell or buy futures to protect themselves against the risk of loss through price fluctuations. Often, through the machinery of a commodity exchange, futures sales by one group of hedgers may be matched directly with futures purchases by another group of hedgers. A substantial part of the hedging sales or purchases on the commodity exchanges, however, are taken up by the speculators.

The foundation of commodity market speculation is difference of opinion. At any exchange-established price for a commodity, even if it is but a momentary one, there will be one group of speculators convinced—through expert knowledge on the part of the professionals and hunch on the part of the amateurs—that it is going higher, and there will be a second group convinced that it will fall lower. The first group buys up the proffered futures sales of hedgers seeking protection against a fall in price, while the second group sells futures to hedgers who wish to buy as protection against a subsequent rise in prices. Thus the commodity exchange speculators perform the invaluable marketing service of maintaining a fluid market for the hedgers and relieving them of the risks of loss through price fluctuation.

Regulation

The Cotton Futures Act of 1916, the Grain Futures Act of 1922, and the Commodity Exchange Act of 1936 established federal regulation of the commodity exchanges on which there is futures trading in certain domestic agricultural products.

These laws specify records that the designated exchanges must keep and reports they must make to the Department of Agriculture. They provide for Department of Agriculture inspection of their records. They impose upon the exchanges obligations to prevent dissemination of misleading information, to prevent price manipulation through exchange trading, to permit farmers' marketing cooperatives to be members, and to provide enough delivery time—three to ten business days—after the close of trading in each delivery month to prevent development of "corners." Limitations are placed on the amount of speculative trading that may be done by any person during any business day and upon the amount of the net speculative position, long or short, that may be held by any person at any time.

All commodity-exchange brokers are required to register with the Department of Agriculture, protection of customers' margins deposited with these brokers is provided, and various frauds they might perpetrate upon their customers are listed and forbidden. Administration of these laws is placed with the Commodity Exchange Authority, consisting of the Secretary of Agriculture, the Secretary of Commerce, and the Attorney General.

MARKETING SERVICES OF TRADE AND MARKETING OPERATION ASSOCIATIONS

A trade association is a nonprofit voluntary organization of business enterprises in an industry or trade for their mutual business benefit. A few associations embrace entire economic fields, such as the National Association of Manufacturers, the National Association of Wholesalers, and the American Warehousemen's Association. Some 1,500 associations serve particular lines of manufacturers, distributors, or retailers, such as the National Association of Wool Manufacturers, the Wholesale Dry Goods Institute, and the National Retail Hardware Association. A few trade associations, such as the National Color Card Association, specialize in certain functional services and draw their members from various product lines.

Besides trade associations, there are several hundred "marketing operation" associations covering groups such as sales managers, salesmen, credit men, buyers, traffic managers, and other individuals associated with particular marketing operations.

Manufacturers' associations

Manufacturers' trade associations serve their members with respect to production, purchasing, personnel, and political problems as well as marketing matters. Generally, however, their marketing services predominate. Practically all of these manufacturers' associations serve their members as centers of information, commonly issuing bulletins on trade trends for their industries. Well over 70 percent of them undertake trade promotion for their industries—they search for new markets and new uses for their members' products, prepare exhibitions of industry productions, and carry on cooperative advertising campaigns; they are also active in developing trade practice codes. From 40 to 70 percent of these associations undertake nonparticularized marketing research for their members and make secondary-source statistical surveys. A similar proportion has also been active in sponsoring standardization and simplification of their members' products. From 25 to 40 percent make original statistical market studies for their members, sponsor trade shows, and issue "buyers' guides" or trade directories. Some provide their members with credit interchange and collection services, and make traffic and packaging surveys.

A TRADE EXHIBIT SPONSORED BY A MANUFACTURERS'
TRADE ASSOCIATION. *Courtesy of Gardner, Robinson, Stierheim
& Weis.*

ILLUSTRATION 11–6

Distributors' associations

Wholesale distributors' trade associations devote themselves more fully to marketing services than the manufacturers' associations do, but the scope of their marketing services tends to be somewhat narrower. Of course, they do not standardize, they do not simplify, and they are not much concerned with generalized advertising of products. On the other hand, many of these associations have delved profoundly into various aspects of their members' marketing management, and have produced invaluable studies on such topics as warehouse operation, inventory control, and marketing cost ratios. They help their members develop dealer aids and other sales promotion programs. They have been particularly active in the field of public relations, and have tirelessly promoted the virtues of dealing through wholesaling middlemen over direct-to-retailer selling or buying.

Retailers' associations

Some of the largest trade association memberships are found in the retailing fields. Many of these associations offer their members assistance in the basic function of store planning. Effective layout plans adaptable to member stores of various sizes are available on request. Guidance on store lighting and window display is provided. Help is given on purchasing policies and procedures. Model stock plans and inventory control systems are provided. Helpful suggestions on mark-up and other aspects of pricing policy, sales promotion aids, sales training programs and materials for the retailer himself as well as for his sales clerks, appropriately simple accounting systems—these are but a small part of the marketing assistance retailers' trade associations provide their members.

Retailers' trade associations have been active and effective lobbyists for state and federal marketing legislation to benefit their members. The anti-chain store tax laws were largely the accomplishment of retailers' associations. One such association, the National Association of Retail Druggists, was a major influence in the rapid spread of state resale price maintenance legislation during the 1930's and in the passage of the federal McGuire Act of 1952.

Marketing operation associations

There are more than a hundred salesmen's associations, some national in scope for salesmen in particular lines, others local or regional for salesmen of groups of related lines in an area. There are 179 local sales executives "clubs" in the United States and Canada with national affiliation through National Sales Executives. There are 141 local credit men's associations nationally federated through the National Association of Credit Management. There are buyers' and purchasing managers' associations, traffic managers' associations, and warehousemen's associations. There are associations for individuals or business units engaged in practically every special or specialized marketing operation.

These operational associations bring together individuals with like occupational interests at annual meetings and on other occasions, and so serve a pleasant social function. Some of them, like some of the trade associations, accomplish little more than this. But most make sincere and generally successful efforts to help their members educate themselves in their particular marketing fields. Most of these associations also strive to raise the ethical standards of their particular marketing operations, and to elevate the practice of these operations to professional level. Some—like the local credit men's associations and the National Association of Credit Management, which perform a ledger information interchange service, and some of the salesmen's associations that maintain "calling rooms" for visiting buyers or hold periodic trade "fairs"—undertake services which contribute directly to the greater effectiveness of their members' occupational activities.

REVIEW

1. Describe the sellers, buyers, and procedures at: (a) a fruit auction, (b) a tobacco auction, (c) a livestock auction.

2. What are the advantages and disadvantages of the commercial auction as a marketing institution in the product lines where it has established itself?

3. What is a commodity exchange? How is it organized and operated? Who buys and sells on a commodity exchange? What is a commodity-exchange broker?

4. What characteristics should a commodity have to be suitable for trading on an exchange?

5. Explain spot and futures trading on a commodity exchange.

6. Explain the usual relationships between spot and futures price movements of an exchange-traded commodity.

7. Explain the part played by speculators in hedging operations on a commodity exchange.

8. How are commodity exchanges regulated by the federal government? Is there any state regulation?

9. What marketing services could be performed for its members by: (a) a manufacturers' trade association; (b) a wholesale distributors' trade association; (c) a retailers' trade association; (d) a national association of sales executives; (e) a national association of industrial purchasing managers?

DISCUSSION TOPICS

1. Why don't we find commercial auctions in many more lines than the present few?

2. "A commodity trading exchange is a financial institution rather than a marketing institution."

3. "Commodity speculators are economic parasites."

4. "Commodity exchanges should be more strictly regulated."

5. "If trade associations didn't already exist, business would have to invent them if only for the sake of their Marketing services."

PROBLEM

The woolen trade is discussing the advisability of establishing a Wool Exchange in Boston, with fuller spot and futures trading facilities than are currently provided by the Wool Associates of the New York Cotton Exchange.

List the arguments for and against such action. In your opinion, on which side does the balance of argument lie?

SUGGESTED READINGS

Baer, J. M., & O. G. Saxon, *Commodity Exchanges and Futures Trading,* rev ed, Harper & Bros., New York, 1949.

Bakken, H. H., *Theory of Markets and Marketing,* Mimir Publishers, Madison, Wis., 1953.

How to Buy and Sell Commodities, Merrill Lynch, Pierce, Fenner, & Beane, New York, 1950.

Mitchell, W., *How to Use Your Trade Association,* Prentice-Hall, Englewood Cliffs, N.J., 1951.

PART THREE

CHANNEL-OF-DISTRIBUTION ANALYSIS

Our second approach to the study of Marketing is Channel-of-Distribution Analysis or, as it is frequently called, Commodity Analysis.

Chapter 12 describes how farm products—foods and industrial raw materials—move from the farms to their ultimate consumers and to the factories and mills that process them. The distribution of manufactured consumer goods from factories to consumers is studied in Chapter 13. Chapter 14 is devoted to marketing channels and procedures of industrial equipment and materials (other than agricultural raw materials) and of business and personal services.

In this approach to Marketing analysis, we review many elements of our previous institutional study of Marketing in the light of their actual application to specific classes of commodities and services. In particular, we see the many classes of wholesalers described in Chapters 9 and 10, in various combinations and patterns for different commodities; we view them as a strikingly vital element in the movement of commodities from original producers to ultimate consumers or users.

CHAPTER 12

AGRICULTURAL MARKETING

The first impression derived from a study of agricultural marketing is one of bewildering complexity. Except for the relatively small volume of fresh fruits and vegetables sold through rural roadside stands and urban "farmers' markets," every farm product passes through the hands of a chain of middlemen. For each product the chain is a different one, with differently-named middlemen, or with like-named middlemen whose operations differ. For some commodities there are several "central" markets; for others only one; for still others, none. National base prices for some commodities are "discovered" on commodity exchanges; for other commodities there are no national base prices but a wide series of local market prices apparently established independently, yet clearly interrelated.

In the face of this complexity, it would seem that few or no generalizations could be made about agricultural marketing, and that the only resort would be independent, unrelated study of the marketing of each separate farm product. Still, a number of economic and institutional factors are common to the marketing of broad classes of agricultural commodities. Our study of agricultural marketing will be limited to these common factors.

BASIC CONSUMPTION AND PRODUCTION CONSIDERATIONS

Marketing is an intermediary process, a linking together of the producers and consumers of each commodity. Its agencies and procedures must adapt themselves on the one hand to the special circumstances of the production of each commodity, and on the other to any special characteristics of its consumption. An initial and profitable approach to a generalized study of agricultural marketing is to note several broad, rather obvious factors in the consumption and production of farm commodities, and to trace their general influence on agricultural marketing. These are: (1) certain aspects

231

of consumption; (2) scattered, small-scale production of most crops; (3) localization in the production of most crops; (4) nonuniformity in farm products; (5) perishability; (6) seasonal production of practically all agricultural products; and (7) chance variation of crops.

Consumption considerations

An initial observation on the markets for several of the major American farm products is that they are two-fold—an export market as well as a domestic market. Over one-third of our wheat, nearly one-third of our cotton, over one-fifth of our tobacco, are exported. Two effects of such substantial exports on agricultural marketing are: (1) export distribution channels with special export agencies have developed for the commodities in question; and (2) until the federal export subsidy program described later in this chapter was developed, foreign market factors exercised substantial influence in the determination of domestic prices for these commodities.

Turning to the domestic market for American farm products, we find it to be primarily industrial. Most distribution chains that start at the farms and ranges end, not with individual consumers, but with factories, mills, slaughterhouses, and canneries that process the raw farm crops. Only a small fraction of farm output—part of the fruit and vegetable crops, part of the yield of the dairy farms—reaches consumers in the form it left the farm.

When studying the economics of farm pricing, we lump together all "food" crops, whether they reach the consumer in "raw" or processed form. A second grouping is made of the fibre crops—cotton, wool, and mohair—and tobacco. These are processed to nonfood uses and are commonly called the "industrial" crops. In general, the over-all demand for food is rather inelastic, although there is considerable short-term elasticity for individual food items that can be substituted for each other—as among the different kinds of meat, vegetables, and fruits. As a consequence, prices of the food crops are sharply sensitive to variations in supply, but display considerable resistance to fluctuations in consumer purchasing power. Demand for the end products of the industrial crops is relatively elastic. Hence substantial variations in the supplies of these crops can be absorbed with only moderate effect upon their prices, but these prices tend to be sensitive to the ups and downs of consumer purchasing power.

Small-scale production

As of the 1950's, there were some 4,500,000 "farms" in the United States. About 1,500,000 of these, however, were small "subsistence" homesteads and other units which made only an insignificant contribution to agricultural marketing. Our interest lies with the 3 million "commercial" farms whose crops went to market.

Some 100,000 of these "commercial" farms—less than 3 percent—have a gross production in excess of $20,000 annually. Gross production for the bulk of the "commercial" farms is within the $5,000–$10,000 range. Most of them divide this relatively small unit production among two or more crops. Production of most American crops is definitely the result of small-scale enterprise carried on by a large number of operators.

Two important consequences for agricultural marketing result from this multi-unit, small-scale character of American agriculture:

1. One major requirement for pure competitive pricing is thereby initially established for many crops. Until the mid-1930's, most farm products were so priced. Since then, as indicated later in this chapter, strong qualifications on this tendency toward pure competition have been introduced. Still, the tendency is there, and it remains a major factor in farm product pricing.

2. The initial stages in the marketing of nearly all agricultural products emphasize concentration and quantity assembling. Distributive agencies must exist to group the unit outputs of the thousands, or scores of thousands, or hundreds of thousands, of small producers of particular crops into larger and yet ever larger lots, for more efficient and economical handling.

Localization of crop production

The 3 million "commercial" farms are well scattered over the entire area of the United States, with occasional forest, desert, mountain and swamp areas showing up as blank spots on the agricultural map. Major production areas for each particular crop, however, tend to be considerably localized, as indicated in Illustration 12–1.

In some instances crop localization has resulted from market considerations. Many dairy farming and truck vegetable farming areas, for example, are accounted for primarily by their proximity to metropolitan markets. In most cases, however, territorial concentration of crops is attributable to production considerations—soil quality, temperature range, rainfall, land costs. Two marketing consequences of crop localization upon production are:

1. Long hauls may be necessary to move the crop from localized producers to ultimate markets. The necessity of long haulage for perishable crops has led to the creation of special transportation facilities—speedy freight trains that in some cases outdo the schedules of the fastest crack passenger "flyers," refrigerated cars, and serviced cattle transport. These

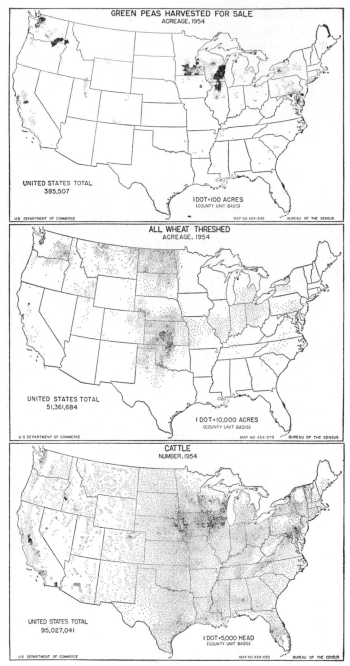

CONCENTRATION AND DISPERSION IN AGRICULTURAL
PRODUCTION

ILLUSTRATION 12–1

long hauls, and the special facilities they entail, add substantially to the distribution costs of these crops—offset, however, by the production cost advantages of the regions of specialized production.

2. Long hauls necessitated by crop localization are responsible for much of the complexity of the agricultural marketing structure. The vital necessity to reduce high long-haul freight costs by bulk shipment provides an opportunity for myriads of local middlemen who can undertake a quantity assembling function. Because these local middlemen are, in many cases, located far from the central markets to which their shipments must be made, there is further opportunity for many types of agent middlemen to facilitate their transactions with the central markets.

Nonuniformity of farm products

Men can and do set standards for agricultural commodities—uniform specifications that determine quality ranges in accordance with which these commodities are to be sold and bought. Nature, however, exhibits lordly indifference to man-made standards. Because of soil and climatic variations, wheat from different areas will differ as to grain size, moisture content, broken grains, and inclusion of foreign matter. Striking differences may develop in the crops of neighboring farms. Apples from a single orchard will vary as to size, color, skin imperfections, and other important marketing details. So if farm products are to be marketed in conformity to any sorts of standard quality ranges, provision must be made for their being graded in accordance with these standard ranges. In some cases grading may be done on the farm. More commonly, the grading operation has to be performed during the crop's movement to market, by some class of the middlemen who participate in its marketing.

Perishability of farm products

Some farm products, such as grains, cotton, or wool, are relatively nonperishable. Rough handling does not injure them. With reasonable protection from the weather, they will last unspoiled for years. In contrast, fresh fruits are fragile, the slightest bruise resulting in rapid deterioration. They have only a brief period of ripeness during which they can be marketed. For many fruits and fresh vegetables, unless special types of storage are devised, the maximum period that can intervene between the time they leave the farm and the time they are purchased by consumers is a week or less. For fresh milk, this period is a couple of days.

The marketing solution of the problem of the fragility of particular farm crops has been threefold: (1) Extreme care in handling each unit—when picking, when packing, when transporting—even when thousands upon thousands of units are involved, has become a matter of course in the marketing of these crops. (2) In some instances, special protective but inexpensive packing has been devised—paper maché egg cases are an example. (3) Speedy movement of crops from farm to consumer minimizes spoilage.

For the general perishability of fruits, vegetables and dairy products, the agricultural marketing structure has provided two solutions: (1) One is rapid distribution. Local assemblers of fresh fruits and vegetables are geared to within-the-day shipment to the wholesaling markets. There, through the agency of commission houses and fruit auctions, fruits and vegetables commonly move from railroad yards through agent middlemen and merchant wholesalers to retailers, and often from them to consumers, within a matter of hours. (2) Special "cold storage," at varying temperatures above freezing, has long been used to preserve eggs and other dairy products, meats, and root vegetables. The newer "quick-freeze" with subsequent storage at sub-freezing temperatures has made it possible to "fresh-store" a wide range of other farm products.

Seasonal production

All farm crops, except livestock * and dairy products, are highly seasonal. Within a few weeks, a crop in any area is harvested and moves into its marketing channels.

Were there no large-scale storage of farm crops, this seasonality of production would produce extreme swings in prices. During most of the year, the price for any agricultural item would be heaven-high, beyond the reach of most buyers no matter how pressing their needs. In the crop season, when the market was glutted, its price would fall to levels that would be ruinous to most producers and distributors. Storage, for nonperishable and perishable crops as well, has to be a major provision of the marketing structure for farm products.

Another result of the seasonality of farm production is the concentration of the work of the local "assembling" middlemen for some crops within a brief fraction of the year. Those who assemble the Delaware strawberry crop have only three weeks' business each year in connection with that crop. To maximize their over-all activity periods, these local assembling middlemen usually handle a considerable variety of crops, with harvesting periods spanning a good part of the year. Even so, winter and early spring brings a stretch of idleness to many. Their profits and commissions during the activity periods must provide them with their full-year incomes. Hence margins and commission rates for these local dealers must be relatively high—

---

* Even in the case of livestock, carloadings during September, October, and November average some 50 percent higher than during the rest of the year.

a consideration commonly misunderstood and bitterly resented by the farmers whose crops they market.

Because of the high margins and commissions obtained of necessity by resident local middlemen in many agricultural lines, two special types of middlemen have emerged in the agricultural marketing picture in recent years. One is the "travelling dealer," who moves with the seasons from harvest area to harvest area, buying local crops and forwarding them to central or wholesale market middlemen. He can pursue his business through most of the year; accordingly, he can operate on narrower margins and overbid resident local dealers. The second is the "trucking buyer" who, buying directly from the farmers of an area, transports his purchased lots to central and jobbing markets and sells them there, bypassing all intermediate middlemen. He is usually only a part-time operator in agricultural distribution; during the off-crop seasons he hauls other loads. Because of all-year-round activity, low overhead, and avoidance of transshipment costs, he too can overbid resident local dealers.

Chance variation of crops

Nature introduces chance factors, beyond the present power of man to control, into the quantitative aspects of agricultural production. Droughts, excessive rains, plant pests and blights, may reduce harvests far below original expectations. Perfect combinations of sun and rain can multiply yields. And so, for each crop, there are "lean" years and there are "fat" years. The agricultural marketing structure copes with this chance of under- and over-production of crops in two ways.

First, storage facilities far beyond maximum seasonal requirements are available for all nonperishable crops. The surpluses of "fat" years, sometimes more than a year's full crop, are carried over to be drawn upon in "lean" years.

Second, prices for farm products rise sharply, not only upon the actuality of a short crop, but even upon the mere anticipation of a poor harvest. The higher prices under such circumstances squeeze out various marginal uses of the crop, and thus leave a larger proportion available for more vital forms of consumption. Likewise, expectation of a bumper crop forces prices down, within the limits permitted by the federal farm price maintenance program. The lower prices encourage wider use of the product, thereby expanding the market for the bumper crop.

AGRICULTURAL MARKETING STRUCTURE

As was indicated earlier in this chapter, the distinctive feature of the initial marketing stages for every farm crop is a concentration movement.

The outputs of thousands, scores of thousands, or hundreds of thousands of independent farmers must be assembled to make possible the economies of large-lot storage, shipment, and trading. As indicated in the upper half of Illustration 12–2, there are three levels of concentration in agricultural product marketing—local assembly, district concentration, and the final funneling through central wholesale markets.

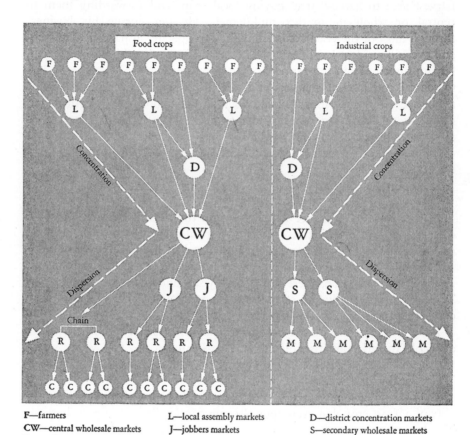

F—farmers	L—local assembly markets	D—district concentration markets
CW—central wholesale markets	J—jobbers markets	S—secondary wholesale markets
R—retailers	C—consumers	M—manufacturers

GENERALIZED STRUCTURE OF FARM PRODUCT MARKETING

ILLUSTRATION 12–2

For a considerable and growing proportion of farm production, distribution *as farm products* stops at some stage of this concentration movement. Packers, canners, millers, and other processors are found at each of these three levels of marketing concentration. They absorb part of the flow of farm commodities that reaches their level. After having been processed in one way or another, these commodities no longer move through the channels of agricultural distribution, but are marketed as manufactured consumer goods or as industrial materials.

Farm products that pass through the central wholesale markets enter upon various procedures of dispersion. In the case of fresh fruits and vegetables, central market wholesalers may sell direct to large retailers, chain and independent. In these lines, and in the meat and dairy products lines, another group of middlemen—jobbers *—commonly intervenes between the central market wholesalers and a major proportion of the independent food retailers. Agricultural raw materials used by industry, after passing through their central wholesale markets, spread out directly, or through secondary wholesale markets, to the processing factories. Finally, a minor fraction of some foodstuffs and industrial raw materials move from their central wholesale markets to export markets.

Local assembly markets

The first stage of market concentration for most agricultural products occurs at local assembly markets.

These local assembly markets are located at the county seats and other rural marketing centers. In the days of horse-drawn transport, practically every rural town on a railroad or navigable river was an assembly market for the farming area about it. Motor truck transport widened the rural radius that a local assembly market can serve. Consequently, during the last four decades the crop marketing activities of many small rural communities have been absorbed by larger neighboring centers, and the number of local assembly markets has declined.

Four classes of marketing agencies are found in local assembly markets:

1. *Processing establishments* of many sorts establish themselves in the local assembly markets. Among these are flour mills, feed mills, meat packers, canning plants, and quick freezing plants. A major part of some crops—peas and tomatoes, for example—is processed locally, so that they have little distribution as farm products beyond the stage of the local assembly markets. Frequently the local processors have contractual arrangements with the farmers who supply them, specifying acreage, details of cultivation, and price for the delivered crops.

2. *Merchant dealers* in wide variety and large numbers are found in the local assembly markets. In former days, local general storekeepers in many parts of the country carried on substantial merchant dealing operations. They purchased customers' crops, using the purchase price either to clear previous debt for retail purchases or to establish credits against which

---

* The student is reminded again, as in Chapter 9, that the term "jobber" has no definitely established meaning in trade usage. Most of the intermediary middlemen that we cover here by the term "jobbers" call themselves "wholesalers."

future retail purchases could be made. Cash payments played little part in this crop buying. But the storekeeper-dealer has practically disappeared in many parts of the country. The "country buyer" of today generally devotes himself full-time to this activity. Usually he is a permanent resident of the community; but, in the fresh vegetable lines, he may travel with the crop seasons, staying in each market community on his route only for the few weeks of the market season. These travelling dealers obviously must limit themselves to buying the local crops and immediately shipping them out without any other grading or packing than the farmers themselves have provided. The resident local dealers commonly perform additional marketing functions. In the grain lines, they frequently operate their own elevators and store the grain they buy. In other lines they may maintain grading and packing sheds. The travelling and resident buyers ship to central market commission merchants or to dealers in the central market, or to the nearest district concentration market.

3. Central market dealers and processors in the cattle and some other lines buy directly in local assembly markets through *agent buyers* or *salaried representatives.*

4. All *farmers' marketing cooperatives* conduct their initial collecting operations in local assembly markets. In the case of some of the small local cooperatives, their activity is limited to local assembling and shipping to central markets. Many of them, however, operate local grading and packing sheds. Most of the grain growers' cooperatives maintain local elevators.

In general, the role of the local assembly markets is declining in the over-all picture of farm marketing. They are being by-passed in three ways: (1) Many large-scale farmers, planters, and cattle raisers have established direct dealings with central market processors or dealers and ship to them without the intervention of any local market middlemen. (2) The district concentration markets, to be described, have in some cases absorbed the distributing activities formerly exercised by surrounding local markets. (3) The "trucking buyer," described earlier, who buys from farmers and transports his purchases directly to central markets and sometimes to still more distant links in the distribution chain, is becoming an important factor in the marketing of vegetables and some fruits.

District concentration markets

For some crops, particularly the grains, livestock, wool, dairy products, and fresh fruits and vegetables, an intermediate set of markets has developed between the local assembly markets and the central wholesale markets. These "district concentration markets," as they are commonly called, are currently expanding. To some extent they are absorbing and concentrating the marketing activities of groups of local assembly markets located within their extended operating areas. They are also absorbing marketing functions previously exercised by the central wholesale markets.

The predominant groups in these district concentration markets are various types of processors. Flour mills, livestock and poultry slaughterhouses, canneries, and egg drying and freezing plants are found in these centers. These processing establishments buy to some extent direct from large farms, but mostly from or through the middlemen of neighboring local assembly markets.

Besides these processors, the district concentration markets contain a wide variety of merchant and agent middlemen—dealers in the various farm commodities including grain elevators, cooperative units, salaried and agent representatives of central market organizations, cattle concentration yards, and livestock and dairy auctions. These middlemen deal directly with producers, and also buy from and through the middlemen of neighboring local assembly markets.

Central wholesale markets

The central wholesale markets for each agricultural commodity constitute the culmination of its concentration movement, and the beginning of its dispersal. For each major farm commodity, there are several central wholesale markets:

> Wheat—Chicago, Minneapolis, Kansas City, St. Joseph, Wichita, and others
> Livestock—Chicago, Kansas City, Omaha, St. Paul, Denver, and others
> Cotton—New Orleans, Memphis, Houston, Dallas, Atlanta, and others
> Dairy and poultry—Chicago, New York, San Francisco
> Fresh fruits and vegetables—all major metropolitan centers

No generalization can be made about the location of central wholesale markets. In the case of the relatively perishable products, the central markets developed in major consuming centers; this factor facilitated quick dispersal. Boston owes its position as the major central wool market of the country to the early localization of the wool textile industry in New England. Central markets for other relatively nonperishable commodities tended to develop within the producing areas for such commodities. This tendency is clearly evident in the case of the cotton and livestock markets. Chicago was originally centrally located with respect to cattle raising; it remained the major central livestock market, although the cattle-raising industry shifted far to the west.

A number of important marketing functions are exercised in the central wholesale markets for any farm commodity: (1) a final assembling through purchases from local assembly and district concentration markets; (2) large-scale storing for all commodities except fresh fruits and vegetables; (3) bulk purchasing by large-scale processors; (4) the major processing of grains and livestock; (5) sale and shipment to dispersal markets; (6) financing; (7) exchange trading and hedging for grains, cotton, and some other items.

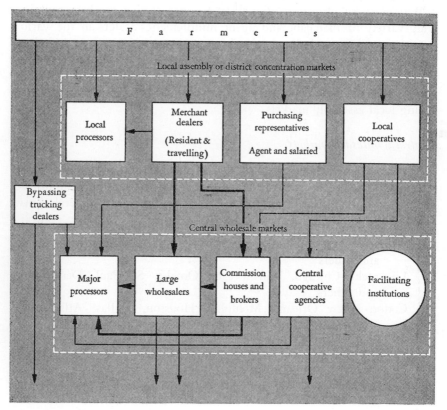

LOCAL ASSEMBLY AND CENTRAL WHOLESALE MARKET
INSTITUTIONS

ILLUSTRATION 12–3

The marketing agencies that perform these central market functions are:
    1. A wide variety of merchant dealers. Many of these are major enterprises with heavy investments in elevators and warehouses. Some, like the "yard traders" in the stockyards, operate practically "under the hat" with no fixed investment and a minimum of overhead.
    2. Public elevators and warehouses, where dealers and other traders

without storage facilities of their own may store their commodity holdings for a charge.

3. Agent middlemen, particularly commission houses and commodity brokers. The existence of commission houses is practically a corollary of central market operation for a number of agricultural commodity lines, since it is through shipment on consignment to commission houses that a substantial proportion of commodities reach their central markets.

4. Facilitating marketing institutions of various sorts, including stockyards, fruit and vegetable auctions, and commodity exchanges.* Existence of a commodity exchange in a central wholesale market means the presence there also of the exchange brokers and speculators who operate on the exchange.

5. In some lines, major processors of a commodity. The major meat packers have their establishments at the livestock central markets. Large flour mills are located in or close to the various wheat central markets.

Other markets

For certain classes of agricultural products, additional distributive focal points have developed beyond the central market stage. Fresh fruits and vegetables move from their central wholesale markets through *jobber markets* before reaching retailers. *Secondary wholesale markets* help mills to obtain their requirements of cotton and other agricultural raw materials more readily. The seaboard ports are *export markets* for cotton, tobacco, wheat, and other agricultural products exported in large volume.

Bypassing in agricultural marketing

One of the significant developments of recent years has been the growing tendency to "bypass" various steps in the pre-established structure of agricultural marketing. Agricultural cooperatives, after establishing themselves as substitutes for the local assembly market middlemen, in many cases set up central or federal organizations in central market cities and carried the distribution of their members' products through to final central market sale. The role of the trucking buyer in bypassing local, district concentration, and sometimes even the central wholesale markets, has already been described. We have seen how processing units formerly con-

---

* Not all central wholesale markets have commodity exchanges. There are none, for example, in the central wholesale markets for fruits and vegetables or for livestock. And not all exchanges are located in the central market cities for the products traded on the exchange: the New York Cotton Exchange, for example, is located in New York City, which is not a central wholesale market for cotton, and the Wool Associates of the New York Cotton Exchange operate in New York City, although the central wholesale market for wool is Boston.

centrated in the central markets have moved forward to district concentration markets, and even to local assembly markets, thereby reducing the transport and handling of the raw commodities they use. In addition, there is a definite tendency for large-scale farmers and cattlemen to contact district concentration agencies, or even central market agencies, to avoid the charges of the intervening middlemen. Finally, we should note that the larger food chains in many cases bypass the central markets, and buy directly from district concentration markets or even local assembly markets.

Of course, when any marketing middleman is bypassed, his operations of assembling, grading, storing, and market contacting usually have to be taken over by either the bypassing seller or the bypassing buyer. For example, fruits and vegetables purchased by a trucking buyer must be already graded and packed for the ultimate market by the farmer. When grocery chain systems purchase directly from local assembly or district concentration market agencies, they must make the supplier contacts at these market levels—ordinarily the responsibility of central market wholesalers. They must also undertake shipping and other activities that would otherwise be performed by the bypassed wholesalers.

The growing tendency toward agricultural market bypassing, though naturally deplored by the bypassed agencies, is in general a healthy development. It reduces agricultural distribution costs. In some instances this cost reduction occurs through an actual elimination of certain marketing operations. This is the case when processors of various agricultural products establish their plants at local assembly or district concentration markets. The marketing operations previously needed to move the products in bulk form through to the central markets, as well as the agencies that performed these operations, are no longer required. More often the bypassing eliminates a class of market middlemen, but not the operations they previously performed. These operations must now be performed either by the seller, by the buyer, or—as in the case of trucking buyers—by the newly substituted middlemen. The agencies now responsible for these marketing operations are likely to perform them at lower costs than the displaced middlemen.* This may occur because several previously successive marketing steps have been consolidated, as when grocery chain systems buy in local or district assembly markets and route shipments directly to their own wholesale units, or when a trucking buyer consolidates all the transaction and transportation steps between a group of farmers and a central wholesale or jobbers' market. Or, a single large integrated marketing agency may operate more efficiently, and hence more economically, than the chain of

---

* Though possibly not always as efficiently. Trucking buyers, for example, tend to deliver inflexibly to pre-established markets. Consequently, they do not accommodate the supply they deliver to the shifting demands of different market areas as do some of the middlemen they displace.

agencies it displaces—as has been true of many farm marketing coopera-tives. Whatever the reason, a lowering of agricultural distribution costs through market bypassing means greater profit for the producers, or lower prices for consumers, or some combination of both. In any event the national economy benefits.

FARMERS' MARKETING COOPERATIVES

Farmers' marketing cooperatives are one aspect of a broad effort by farmers to better their economic position through mutual action. Such organizations were established sporadically during the Nineteenth Century, particularly during the 1870's under the stimulus of the Granger Move-ment. Not until the 1890's, however, did the cooperative movement strike sound roots. The four decades from 1890 to 1930 witnessed rapid and widespread growth of farm cooperation, not only for crop marketing but also for purchasing of farm supplies, credit, insurance, rural electric and telephone systems, and other farm services. Congress aided the movement by relieving farmers' cooperatives of any taint of restraint of trade through the Capper-Volstead Act of 1922, by providing them with a fed-eral system of banks for cooperatives through the Agricultural Marketing Act of 1929, and by exempting them under certain conditions from the federal corporation income tax. During the 1930's the marketing coopera-tives lost some ground in membership, dollar volume of crops marketed, and proportion of total agricultural production marketed. Although the number of cooperatives continued to decline during the 1940's, this was due to consolidations rather than withdrawals; membership increased by more than 70 percent, and the share of total crops marketed increased from less than 20 percent to over 25 percent.

As of 1956 there were over 6,000 farmers' marketing cooperatives with over 4 million members. The agricultural lines in which their numbers and activities are greatest are dairy products, grains, and livestock. As far as can be determined, cooperatives market, at least in the initial stages, over half the farm output of dairy products and of grains.

Basic organization concept

Farmers' marketing cooperatives are established on a basis comparable to consumer cooperatives, already studied in Chapter 7. They are membership organizations, usually incorporated. They raise equity capital from their members by sale of common stock, preferred stock, and various forms of equity certificates paying limited dividends or "interest" from 4 to 8 per-cent. Capital growth is accomplished to some extent by paying patronage dividends in equity certificates instead of cash. Only "producers"—farmers raising the crop handled by the cooperative—can usually contribute equity capital. An individual "producer" can buy as many shares or other equity capital units as he wishes. Usually, however, the number of equity units bought by each member is loosely proportioned to the volume of distribution the cooperative performs for him. Generally, a member has only one vote, no matter how many equity units he owns. Gross "profits" of a marketing cooperative are distributed as patronage dividends pro rata to the dollar volume of marketing done for the various members.

Territorial and operational organization

Most cooperatives are small local units, serving crop-raisers of a limited area, with all their facilities in the local assembly market. Some are organized on a state or regional basis. Of the latter, some are federated organizations; some, centralized.

A centralized state or regional marketing cooperative in organizational respects closely resembles a local one. Its members are the crop-raisers of the state or region. It maintains local assembly or storage facilities in various local market centers of the state or region, but otherwise operates as a unit.

In contrast, a federated state or regional cooperative has no individual members. Its membership is composed of the local cooperatives of its crop field within the state or region. It serves these local organizations, not their individual farmer-members. Any patronage dividends resulting from its activities are distributed among the local cooperatives.

Independent local cooperatives generally confine their activities to local assembling of their members' crops, and ship their assembled lots to central market dealers or commission merchants. Some of the larger state and regional cooperatives maintain offices and facilities in the central markets for their crops, so that they are able to bypass the ordinary central market middlemen. Where there are a number of state and regional cooperatives for a crop, they may establish a mutual organization—a federated national cooperative—to handle their distributive activities in the central markets. The American Cotton Cooperative Association is the national federated cooperative for the cotton marketing cooperatives. For a while, the state and regional grain cooperatives also had a federated national unit.

The marketing cooperatives have established national organizations in a number of crop fields, not to handle central market distribution, but to serve as educational, promotional, or lobbying units. Such auxiliary national units are found in the milk, grain, and livestock fields.

Activities

The exclusive activity of many cooperatives is assembling their members' harvests at local market centers, and dispatching the accumulated lots to central markets. Some perform an even more limited distributive function; a few milk producers' cooperatives, for example, operate only as collective price bargaining agencies for their members, and some berry and vegetable cooperatives in the East merely provide auction sheds where their members' produce may be sold. In contrast, fruit cooperatives commonly grade and pack their members' crops for shipment. Most milk cooperatives standardize the butter-fat content of their members' deliveries; some pasteurize; at least one handles distribution through to retailers; quite a few make butter, cheese, dried milk, and other milk-derivatives. Grain cooperatives usually operate elevators, both local and terminal, and storage is a major aspect of their service. Some livestock cooperatives have ventured into packing their members' products, though with little success.

Finances

The financial arrangements between a farmers' marketing cooperative and its members * are somewhat complicated.

In the case of exchange-traded commodities, a cooperative can buy a member's delivery immediately at the exchange spot quotation, less transportation costs and a service charge, and protect itself against price decline by hedging. Or it can purchase from the member on the basis of a particular futures month quotation, and hedge itself by selling that month's futures.

Where a commodity is not exchange-traded and where there is no possibility of protective hedging, immediate outright purchase of a member's delivery is less common. The cooperative endeavors first to sell what it has received from its members, and then bases its payments on the proceeds of the sale. The cooperative does not sell each member's delivery separately, however. Deliveries of like grade from many members are lumped and shipped in carload lots. Payments to members must accordingly be made upon a "pooled" basis. Cooperatives use three "pooled" payment procedures:

> 1. *Seasonal pool.* Records are kept of members' deliveries by product grades. At the end of the marketing season, the total received for each grade, less transportation cost and a service charge, is divided among the members pro rata to their deliveries of such grade. Advances on this end-of-season payment are made at the time of delivery.

* A tax-exempt farmers' marketing cooperative may serve non-members as well as members. Except that they receive no dividends on their stock, non-members are paid by the cooperative on exactly the same basis as members, including sharing in the patronage dividend.

2. *Weekly pool.* This payment system is used primarily in the case of fresh fruits and vegetables, which are shipped out within very brief time from their delivery. Receipts from each week's shipments of each grade are paid, less service charge, to members pro rata to their deliveries of such grades during the week.

3. *Shipment pool.* Receipts from each shipment, less service charge, are applied to members' deliveries of the grade involved in such shipment in the order of those deliveries.

The service-charge deduction is usually liberally calculated. It must cover the cooperative's operating expenses and overhead, including payment of the prescribed dividend on its stock. Usually a substantial additional "margin" is allowed. At the end of the cooperative's accounting year, the extra "margin" ordinarily provides the cooperative with a gross "profit." All or most of this "profit" is distributed to the members as a patronage dividend pro rata to the value of their total deliveries during the season. Sometimes it is distributed in cash. Instead the members may vote to have the patronage dividend take the form of additional shares of the cooperative's equity units or interest-bearing scrip, thereby enabling the cooperative to retain the cash for expansion purposes.

Farmers' marketing cooperatives frequently make advances to their members at planting time and during the growing season. Funds for these advances, and those made on delivery, can be financed by the cooperative through loans from the federal banks for cooperatives.

Accomplishments

Farmers' marketing cooperatives have not proved to be the panacea for all agricultural marketing ills that many of their founders expected. Profits of local dealer operation, when this activity had been taken over by local cooperatives, proved disappointingly small when spread among all the farmers served by the cooperatives. Moreover, local cooperatives operated less efficiently in many cases than the independent middlemen they displaced; as a result, the members found their returns actually reduced.

Cooperatives proved to have several advantages, however: (1) When, by expansion or federation, state and regional cooperatives developed, and when these established central market facilities, substantial distributional economies began to emerge. (2) Not only could these state and regional cooperatives assume the functions and profits of central market middlemen, but some of them could also operate on a national basis through all the central markets for their crops, and could adjust supply to all the variations of local demand more effectively than the chains of independent middlemen they displaced. (3) Some cooperatives have undertaken broad programs of advertising and other forms of promotion for their crops, previously impossible where chains of independent middlemen were involved, and have markedly stimulated demand for such crops. (4) In a few cases, cooperatives have established virtual distributive monopolies in their crop fields and, through control of supply that has sometimes involved destruction of cull grades, have succeeded in holding prices for their crops above what would otherwise have been competitive levels. (5) Most of the larger cooperatives have undertaken programs of education for their members, teaching them how to improve their farming methods and to produce the varieties and grades of desirable crops.

The farmers' marketing cooperative movement is still at a stage of development and expansion. Many of its early weaknesses have been overcome, but broad areas of organizational and operational improvement still remain. There is no reason at present for anticipating that cooperatives will displace completely, or even to a major extent, the structure of independent agricultural middlemen in all crop and livestock fields. Further and substantial expansion of their activities in many fields may be expected, however.

AGRICULTURAL PRICE CONSIDERATIONS

Until the middle 1930's, agricultural pricing operated generally in accord with the principles of pure competition. All the elements necessary for pure competitive pricing, described in Chapter 19, were present. Modifying factors, if at all operative, influenced only incidental aspects of the marketing of particular crops.

This situation no longer obtains. As indicated above, agricultural cooperatives dominate the marketing of citrus fruits and are strongly influential in the marketing of many others. The federal government, through its parity price program (described in Chapter 30) and other farm aid measures, has limited the repressive effects of competition on farm prices.

The best approach to the study of agricultural pricing is still to view it as the outcome of pure competitive pricing. The quasi-monopolistic effects of the cooperatives in some crop fields, and the farm price program of the federal government, may then be treated as qualifications of an inherently competitive structure.

Demand and supply

Demand for any food crop is a composite of the needs and desires of multitudes of domestic consumers—hundreds of thousands for some less popular food specialties, over a hundred million for wheat—plus a varying export for certain crops. Over-all domestic demand for the total of the food crops is relatively inelastic. Furthermore, dietary custom establishes marked elements of rigidity in food preferences so that there is an undercurrent of long-term demand inelasticity for particular food crops as well. Because of the possibilities of substituting one form of food for another, however, short-term domestic demand for most crops is moderately elastic and for some it is highly so. Certain aspects of federal farm aid also create special elements of demand when particular crop prices are low.

Demand for agricultural raw materials, such as cotton, is a "derived" demand—derived from the consumption demand for the manufactured products made from the raw materials. There is a high degree of short-term elasticity in demand for most manufactured consumer goods, coupled with long-term inelasticity for staple items. These demand characteristics are reflected back to the agricultural raw materials from which the manufactured items are made.

It might seem, at first glance, that *short-term supply* of any farm product, except livestock, is bound to be rigidly inelastic. Planting is done long before harvest-time demand can be ascertained, and the chance of weather modifies planting-time expectations without regard to market demand. However, three factors of growing importance in recent years modify this basic short-term inelasticity of farm product supply. (1) Storage removes elements of a current harvest from the immediate market and reserves them for future times when current supply is not flowing onto the market. This may involve not merely a carry-over to later seasons of the year, but even to subsequent crop years. Formerly, only the "nonperishable" crops, such as the grains and cotton, could benefit substantially from this spreading of supply through storage. Fresh fruits and vegetables were essentially "glut" crops—the markets were flooded with them in the harvest seasons, and bare of them the rest of the year. Canning, cold storage, and quick-freeze storage now absorb excesses of current supply over current market demand at balanced prices for most important crops, and permit adjustment of current supply to current demand. (2) In a few cases where cooperatives dominate the distribution of particular crops, they have upon occasion deliberately destroyed some of the supply under their control so that the remainder would be better adjusted to current demand. (3) The federal parity price program (explained in Chapter 30) removes part of a crop from the market whenever there is an imbalance of current supply and demand, as reflected by low market prices.

As a consequence, there are now substantial elements of elasticity in short-term agricultural supply—the flow of a farm product to the markets of the country responds to fluctuations in its price, and so tends to moderate these fluctuations. Still, supply of farm products remains considerably less elastic than demand for them over the short term. Hence prices of these products fluctuate primarily on the basis of variations in their supply or, in the case of exchange-traded commodities, on the basis of anticipated changes in their supply.

Long-term supply of farm products is growing constantly more elastic. Through their cooperatives and through the federal Department of Agriculture, farmers are being educated to produce to long-range market demands. The planting-control features of the federal parity price program also operate to produce a long-range accommodation of supply to demand for the various crops. As a consequence, long-term farm supply is probably more elastic now than long-term demand for agricultural products. Over the years, price trends in particular farm commodities are probably more affected by such demand factors as changes in consumer purchasing power and dietary shifts than by blind operation of supply factors.

"Discovery" of agricultural prices

Between the tens or hundreds of thousands of farmers who produce a particular commodity and hence constitute its "supply," and the hundreds of thousands or millions of consumers who constitute its "demand," a multitude of middlemen of various kinds intervene. For orderly marketing to exist, a generally recognized "market price" of the moment must be established—or "discovered," in the economists' terminology—at some level in this distributive flow. Prices for transactions subsequent to the "discovery point" are the "market price" at that point, plus subsequent marketing costs and profit margins. Prices for transactions prior to this "discovery point" can be determined by reference forward to the "discovery point" price, with subtraction of marketing costs and profit margins to that point.

The "discovery point" for the pricing of any agricultural commodity—food item or industrial raw material—is its central wholesale market or some particular agency of that market.

In the case of "organized" central wholesale markets, where there is a commodity exchange, the exchange usually constitutes the "discovery point." There the entire flow of current supply of the traded commodity, and the entire pressure of demand for it, focus upon the flow of spot price quotations, even though the volume of spot transactions handled through the exchange may constitute only a fraction of total dealings in the commodity. Ticker tapes spread these quotations instantaneously throughout the country. Other central market buyers and sellers, and buyers and sellers at earlier and later levels in the distributive flow of the commodity, take these exchange prices as the starting point for their pricing calculations. Many differentials, sometimes positive, sometimes negative, must enter these calculations—differentials for variation between the actual lot of the commodity under consideration and the standard exchange grades, differentials to cover costs of transport, storage, financing, commissions and profit margins. All these differentials are built up or down from the exchange quotation. The circumstance that some commodities, such as wheat and cotton, are traded on more than one exchange does not introduce any pricing complexity; arbitrage * keeps the quotations on all of these exchanges in constant and close alignment.

When there is no single exchange or group of exchanges to serve as a central market pricing point, price "discovery" still occurs within the central wholesale market, but more circuitously and in a less sharply defined manner. In a metropolitan central wholesale market for fresh vegetables, for example, the leading wholesalers start a business day armed with a general background knowledge of how the season and the weather of the moment affect consumption of the items they are interested in, specific information on the preceding day's prices and sales in their own and other metropolitan centers, and specific information on the morning's commodity arrivals in their own city. Some of them telephone among themselves and exchange judgments. Even without such advance discussion, prices offered by the wholesalers soon come into close alignment through the wholesalers' competitive efforts to purchase their respective requirements at prices enabling them to resell their entire purchases at a profit. The day's sales and prices so established are reported daily by the Department of Agriculture throughout the length and breadth of the country. Dealers in every wholesaling center thus learn of volumes and prices in the other wholesaling markets, and their next day's price offers are influenced accordingly. Shippers take this information into account in routing their consignments to the various wholesaling centers, sometimes changing the destinations of their shipments while en route to temporarily more favorable markets. Thus a national consistency of central wholesale market prices for these products is effected.**

REVIEW

1. What is the Marketing significance of: (a) the fact that the major part of most American crops is raised on large numbers of small farms; (b) localization of much of the production of each important crop; (c) nonuniformity of agricultural production; (d) high perishability of some farm products; (e) seasonality of crop production; (f) year-to-year variations in crop yields?

2. What is a "trucking buyer"?

3. Describe the marketing agencies and activities of a typical local agricultural assembly market town.

---

* Sales of futures in the momentarily "high" market balanced by corresponding purchases of futures in the momentarily "low" market.

** Recent tendencies of retail food chains and some large wholesalers to deal directly, by telephone, with large local shippers of fresh fruits and vegetables may change this picture by pushing some of the price "discovery" in this field backward from the central wholesale markets to some of the local shipping centers.

4. What is a district concentration market?

5. What marketing agencies are found, and what marketing operations are performed, in the central wholesale markets for a major farm product?

6. Describe the organization of a farmers' marketing cooperative.

7. What marketing functions do farmers' marketing cooperatives perform for their members?

8. Explain the "pooled payment" procedures of farmers' marketing cooperatives.

9. Explain where and how agricultural prices are "discovered."

DISCUSSION TOPICS

1. "A major element of the present 'farm problem' is the economic burden imposed upon farmers by the overdeveloped structure of agricultural middlemen."

2. "Most crops undergo a concentration movement from the farms to the appropriate central markets."

3. Could the institution of "trucking buyers" be expanded to a point where the local assembly markets, and possibly the central markets, could be largely bypassed for most crops, thereby saving the tremendous middleman costs associated with these markets?

4. How significant is "bypassing" other than by "trucking buyers" in the marketing of farm products?

5. Appraise the role of central market commission houses in the marketing of farm products.

6. Appraise the accomplishments of farmers' marketing cooperatives.

PROBLEM 1

A bill has been introduced into your state legislature, with the backing of several national and state farm dealers' associations, to impose a rigid monthly sanitary inspection system for "trucking buyers' " trucks, financed by a special heavy license tax on such trucks. The purpose of the bill is to reduce or eliminate the activities of the "trucking buyers."

Prepare a summary of the arguments for and against this bill.

PROBLEM 2

The fruit growers of Webster County have heretofore marketed their apples and pears through two or three "travelling buyers" who come to the county seat for a few weeks during the harvest season. They are dissatisfied with the prices and services they are receiving, and are discussing the formation of a marketing cooperative.

Prepare a memorandum for them indicating: (a) what services the cooperative would perform for its members; (b) what owned or rented facilities it would need; (c) how it would be organized; (d) how its capital would be raised; and (e) what arrangements it would make for paying its members, and any others who used its facilities. Give the reasons for your proposals.

SUGGESTED READINGS

Benedict, M. R., & O. C. Stein, *The Agricultural Commodity Programs,* Twentieth Century Fund, New York, 1956.

Blankertz, D. F., *Marketing Cooperatives,* Ronald Press, New York, 1940.

Bowring, J. R., H. M. Southworth, & F. W. Waugh, *Marketing Policies for Agriculture,* Prentice-Hall, Englewood Cliffs, N. J., 1960.

Brunk, M. E., & L. B. Darrah, *Marketing of Agricultural Products,* Ronald Press, New York, 1955.

Johnson, D. G., *Trade and Agriculture,* John Wiley & Sons, New York, 1950.

Kohls, R. L., *Marketing of Agricultural Products,* Macmillan Co., New York, 1955.

Larson, A. L., *Agricultural Marketing,* Prentice-Hall, Englewood Cliffs, N.J., 1951.

Marketing: the Yearbook of Agriculture, U.S. Department of Agriculture, Washington, D.C., 1954.

Norton, L. J., *Markets for and Marketing of Farm Products,* University of Illinois, Urbana, 1954.

Sayres, P. (ed.), *Food Marketing,* McGraw-Hill Book Co., New York, 1950.

Schultz, T. W., *Economic Organization of Agriculture,* McGraw-Hill Book Co., New York, 1953.

Shepherd, G. S., *Marketing Farm Products—Economic Analysis,* 3rd ed (1955); *Agricultural Price Analysis,* 3rd ed (1950), Iowa State College Press, Ames.

Snowdon, O. L., & A. W. Donahoo, *Profitable Farm Marketing,* Prentice-Hall, Englewood Cliffs, N. J., 1960.

Stewart, J. J., *Foods: Production, Marketing, Consumption,* 2d ed, Prentice-Hall, Englewood Cliffs, N.J., 1948.

Thomsen, F. L., *Agricultural Marketing,* McGraw-Hill Book Co., New York, 1951.

Waite, W. C., & H. C. Trelogan, *Agricultural Market Prices,* 2d ed, John Wiley & Sons, New York, 1951.

Waugh, F. V. (ed.), *Readings on Agricultural Marketing,* Iowa State College Press, Ames, 1954.

CHAPTER 13

MARKETING MANUFACTURED CONSUMER GOODS

Most farmers, planters, and cattle raisers have little opportunity to select among alternative channels of distribution for their products except for the choice to sell to a local middleman or through a cooperative. They are powerless to do anything about the ultimate markets for their products. They do not establish prices, they accept them. Nor do farmers' cooperatives and agricultural middlemen, except for a few giants like The Sunkist Raisers Cooperative of the California citrus fruit growers, have much opportunity to exercise policy in reaching or developing the ultimate markets for their products. Agricultural producers and distributors alike usually conduct their distributive operations without being able to control them.

Most consumer goods manufacturers, by contrast, control to some extent, and often substantially, distribution of their products all the way to the retail sales to ultimate consumers. As we shall see in Part Four of this volume, they create special elements of demand for their products by promotion and selling, they establish the prices and terms of sale for their products, and sometimes they establish the prices at which their products are resold. Also, they can and commonly do make channel-of-distribution decisions on what classes of retail outlets should carry their products and through what intermediary channels, if any, these retail outlets should be reached.

Two circumstances give consumer goods manufacturers this distributive control. The first is that, by making their goods in distinctive models— "diversifying" them as described in Chapter 16 so that they are not identical with similar products of other manufacturers—and by attaching distinctive brand names to them, most consumer goods manufacturers *distinguish and identify* their products. This identification is maintained from the manufacturer's plant through middlemen and retailers to the consumers' homes. This *individualizing* of each manufacturer's output is the foundation of his distributional control over it.

The second factor contributing to this control is that the market movement of consumer goods is one of *dispersion*. In contrast to the concentration movement of agricultural products, a manufacturer's individualized product or line of products fans outward, possibly through wholesaling middlemen, to retailers and finally to consumers. Although other similar goods may join the particular manufacturer's product or line en route, its individualization is not lost; the manufacturer's control persists.

The degree of marketing control that manufacturers can exercise varies widely. At one extreme are the automobile and some photographic equipment manufacturers whose powers in this respect had to be limited by legislative action or the courts. At the other are many small producers, without marketing facilities or know-how, who delegate all their marketing responsibilities to selling agents.

Where there is marketing control, there must be *policies* on its exercise. Our study of channels of distribution for consumer goods is therefore best based on a *policy* approach. We must learn not only what the existing channels are, but also what considerations prompt a manufacturer's choice among alternative channels available to him.

MARKET AREA POLICY

It might be thought that shipping costs would set boundaries to manufacturers' market territories, by adding to buyers' cost or reducing sellers' profit with increasing distance of shipment. To a large manufacturer able to establish mills or assembly plants in different sections of the country this increase of shipping costs with shipping distance presents no problem; he locates a plant within each market territory he plans to cover. Even a one-plant manufacturer has possibilities of substantially reducing long-distance shipping costs so as to expand his market territory far beyond the limits set by short-distance freight charges. He can make carload shipments to distant storage depots or general merchandise warehouses at a fraction of the rates paid for small-lot shipments in his local territory, and then can serve the distant territories from these depots or warehouses. Shipping costs therefore impose only a mild handicap on expanding market territories for most consumer goods manufacturers.

Many consumer goods manufacturers market their products throughout the entire length and breadth of the United States. In some cases, their sales forces call directly upon the individual retailers who carry their products. More commonly, they depend upon hundreds of merchant wholesalers or manufacturers' agents, each serving a fairly well-defined local or regional area, to reach the thousands of potential retail outlets for their products.

Most manufacturers do not have enough capital to acquire the production capacity needed to meet the buying potential of a nation-wide market, or cannot finance nation-wide advertising, selling, and distribution. Such manufacturers should deliberately restrict their marketing efforts to local or regional areas, advertising to the consumers of these areas only, and selling only to the retailers or through the wholesalers there. To a point, the application of promotional and selling effort within territorial units operates on a principle of increasing returns. To spread limited resources thinly over too wide an area sacrifices distributional efficiency. With financial growth, some of these small manufacturers may in time expand their marketing areas and eventually achieve national distribution. Most, however, will continue as profitable small-scale or medium-size enterprises selling to limited market areas.

RETAIL OUTLET POLICY

Over 96 percent of manufactured consumer goods reaches consumers via retail stores. Hence, to all but a few direct-to-consumer-selling manufacturers, the two basic issues of distribution policy are: (1) Through what class or classes of retailers should we endeavor to sell our goods? (2) Should we endeavor to sell through a maximum number of stores in the selected class or classes, or instead limit our retail outlets?

Selection of retail outlet class

Should a new prepared baby food be sold through drug stores or food stores? Should an automobile polish be sold through hardware stores, variety stores, or service stations? Should a line of jellies be sold direct to the purchasing offices of food chains, or through wholesalers to independent grocery stores? Should an inexpensive home air conditioner be retailed through hardware stores, or home furnishings and department stores, or building supply stores, or drug stores?

Every consumer goods manufacturer must answer questions like these, whether he sells direct to retailers or through wholesaling middlemen. In the first case, he does not want his salesmen to miss calling on good outlets for his product or to waste selling time calling on impossible ones. In the second case, he must select middlemen who will sell to the classes of stores he wants to reach. It would be a misjudgment to seek a mass market for a prepared baby food by placing it with drug wholesalers, for example, if grocery stores have now become the accepted retail outlets for such foods.

As a general proposition, a product should be marketed through the class or classes of stores at which consumers currently buy similar items. In these days of dynamic changes in the retailing pattern, particularly in the carrying of supplementary lines by limited-line stores, some research may be needed to ferret out all practicable classes of retail outlets. One large biscuit maker sells its line not only through grocery stores but also through variety stores, department stores, drug stores, confectionery shops, service stations, frozen custard stands, and railroad- and bus-station newsstands.

Manufacturers of impulse and convenience goods should be alert for possible new classes of retail outlets where point-of-purchase buying impulse for their particular items may be aroused. The following recent examples illustrate strikingly the never-ending hunt for new but appropriate retail outlets for consumer products:

> A publisher of gardening and how-to-make-it handbooks induced hardware wholesalers to take on his line of books, who in turn persuaded hardware retailers to display them in their garden implement and tool departments. Sales soared immediately to figures far beyond the publisher's most optimistic estimates.
>
> A women's hose manufacturer persuaded a supermarket chain to display his line of stockings on self-service stands. In this case also, sales volume exceeded all expectations.
>
> Beauty shops have proven to be excellent outlets for low-price costume jewelry.
>
> Toiletry manufacturers have increased their supermarket outlets and supermarket sales volume by selling through a new type of wholesaler, the "rack jobber," who not only supplies supermarkets with this line but also services their display and self-service shelves.

Sometimes a manufacturer must choose between two classes of retail outlets. In the grocery field, for example, many small independent retailers want to be able to offer brands of canned goods, particularly quality lines, not carried by chains and large supermarkets, so that they will not have to meet price competition by the chains and supermarkets on these brands. The producer of such a brand line must definitely forego the possibility of whatever retail market the chains and supermarkets might provide in order to retain his retail market of small independents. In recent years a number of manufacturers of "fair-traded" home appliances and toys have chosen to sacrifice the sales volume that discount houses could give them in order to maintain the good will of other classes of retailers who want to sell at the listed retail prices.

Mass vs. selective retail distribution

Impulse and convenience goods, as was indicated in Chapter 3, should be marketed through as many retail outlets as a manufacturer, or his wholesalers, can arrange. They should have *mass* distribution. The potential consumers' latent desire for an item is stimulated, through impulse triggered by display, on a maximum of occasions. Consumer readiness to switch brands of convenience goods, when a mildly preferred brand is not immediately available, is minimized. Shopping and specialty goods, by contrast, are rather bought on intent. Consumers are generally willing to travel some distance to a known outlet for the product, or even search for a store carrying their brand. Accordingly, manufacturers of shopping and specialty goods are not constrained to press their products directly or through wholesale distributors upon every possible outlet. They can adopt a policy of *selective* distribution—selling only to particular stores of the categories that would be the natural retail outlets for their types of goods. Selective distribution involves, mostly, direct-to-retailer selling, since wholesale distributors' selling activities are not geared to picking and choosing among their retailer customers.

In applying selective distribution policy, a manufacturer sets store quality or minimum-purchase volume standards for the retailers to whom he will sell. Possibly many stores in a community will measure up to his standard and be potential customers. Perhaps no store in some particular retail market area will be acceptable. Territorial considerations ordinarily are not a determinant in selective distribution policy.

Selective distribution definitely limits the number of retail outlets that carry a manufacturer's line, and so sacrifices some potential sales volume. Since shopping or specialty goods are involved, however, the loss of sales volume is not the total of what the excluded stores might have sold. If one store in a shopping area carries the manufacturer's line, many consumers who might have bought his items in one of the excluded stores will visit the selected store in a comparative shopping tour among several stores or because they make a specific-intent trip to the selected store. Furthermore, several positive advantages may accrue from selective distribution: (1) The number of outlets to which the manufacturer's salesmen sell and endeavor to sell is reduced, with corresponding savings in distribution and bookkeeping costs. Quite frequently a manufacturer who undertakes a marketing cost analysis, as described in Chapter 29, discovers he is actually sustaining a loss on the small-quantity sales made to many of his customers. By setting a minimum order size, which automatically eliminates many of these customers, the manufacturer reduces his sales volume but, by reducing his marketing costs to a much greater extent, increases his profits. (2) A manufacturer of a well-known brand of quality merchandise may decide not to offer it to cut-price and other stores whose appearance or patronage would not reflect credit on his line. (3) Approach to any dealer under a selective policy by a manufacturer of well-known or quality merchandise is a compliment to the dealer, and this consideration may make it somewhat easier to obtain such preferred dealers as customers. (4) A closer relationship can be established between the manufacturer and a limited number of dealers, facilitating sales promotion work to them, resale price maintenance by them, and the performance by them of customer services associated with the manufacturer's products.

Exclusive outlet selling

"Exclusive outlet selling" is a special form of selective distribution policy. The basis of the limitation here is *territorial*. Only one retailer * is "franchised" to carry the manufacturer's line in small communities; two, three, or some other small number may be given the privilege in metropolitan centers. Automobile retailing, and the retailing of "name" lines in household appliances, furniture, and men's and women's wear, are done largely on exclusive franchise bases.

Giving an exclusive franchise to a retailer does not automatically bind him to reciprocal exclusive handling of the manufacturer's line. In many cases such reciprocal exclusive policy is the custom of the line, as in automobile and gasoline retailing. Often space and finance considerations preclude a small retailer from handling lines that compete with the one for which he has an exclusive franchise. It is often possible for a manufacturer with a well-known line to enforce reciprocal exclusiveness by withdrawing his franchise from a dealer that takes on a competing line. But specific contractual requirement of reciprocal dealer exclusiveness has been held "restraint of trade" and is forbidden under both state and federal law.

The advantages to a retailer of gaining the exclusive franchise for the good-selling line of a well-known manufacturer are obvious. A manufacturer may also have much to gain from exclusive outlet selling. (1) His marketing and bookkeeping costs are held down. (2) Freedom from competition in carrying the manufacturer's line is a powerful selling argument in obtaining the preferred retail outlet in each retailing center. (3) To obtain an exclusive franchise, a retailer may be required to carry the manufacturer's complete line. (4) Resale price maintenance is facilitated, not only because of the close relationship between manufacturer and retailers, but also because of the absence of immediate competition for the exclusive outlets. (5) The manufacturer can insist that the exclusive outlets perform substantial installation and maintenance services for the manufacturer's line in connection with selling it. (6) The manufacturer can assert a degree of control over the retailers with respect to sales quotas and sales promotion programs, including display and cooperative advertising. So extensive was the manufacturers' quota control in the automobile field,

---

* The term "exclusive outlet selling" is applied also to the giving of exclusive "franchises" to wholesalers' and manufacturers' agents for a manufacturer's line or brand.

and so galling to many of the dealers, that restrictive federal legislation—the Automobile Franchise Act—was passed in 1956.

CHANNELS OF DISTRIBUTION *

There are four basic channels of consumer goods distribution:

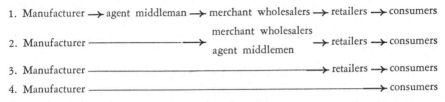

1. Manufacturer → agent middleman → merchant wholesalers → retailers → consumers

2. Manufacturer ⟶ merchant wholesalers / agent middlemen → retailers → consumers

3. Manufacturer ⟶ retailers → consumers

4. Manufacturer ⟶ consumers

Which channel or channels of distribution a consumer goods manufacturer should use depends upon a number of factors: (1) the manufacturer's own selling, advertising, and other marketing facilities; (2) whether he produces a single product or small group of related items, or whether he produces a large proportion of the items that are considered a "product line" in his field; (3) whether his financial position provides him with the working capital needed to cover distributive as well as production operations; (4) the extent to which his products are sold on impulse, convenience, shopping, or specific-intent bases; (5) whether the unit value of his goods is high or low; (6) whether retailers generally, or particular classes of them, buy his goods in large or small quantities; (7) whether provision of technical installation or maintenance service must be an element of the retail sale; (8) the availability and efficiency of the wholesaling middlemen in his line and in his market territories; (9) the character of the retailers who handle his product— whether they are independent limited-line stores, or chains, or department stores, or other special types of retailers; (10) whether the retailers for his line are territorially concentrated or widely scattered.

MERCHANT WHOLESALER CHANNELS

Manufacturer-to-merchant-wholesaler-to-retailer-to-consumer is generally believed to be the most common channel of distribution for manufactured consumer goods. One authoritative estimate gives 45 percent as the proportion of consumer goods that move through this channel. It is often referred to as the "normal" channel for consumer goods distribution.

Merchant wholesalers in any line add a markup to the prices of the goods they buy and resell—a markup that must cover their costs of opera-

---

* Note that the term "channel of distribution" covers intra-company organization units, as well as extra-company agencies, through which a product is marketing. We are concerned here only with the extra-company agencies.

tion and give them a profit. This markup may take the form of a trade discount given by the manufacturer, in which case his net price is that much lower than what he would receive if he sold directly to the retailers. In other cases the merchant wholesaler's markup is added to the manufacturer's net price, and the retailers must pay that much more than if they bought directly from the manufacturer. Either the manufacturer, or the retailer, or both on a split basis, are paying for the intervention of the merchant wholesaler between them.

Why should they? Why not eliminate the wholesaler and save this "wholesalers' spread"?

The reason why merchant wholesalers exist, and maintain their important place in the distribution of many lines of manufactured consumer goods, is that they perform services for the retailers who buy through them and for the manufacturers who sell through them. For most retailers and manufacturers these services are more valuable than the "wholesalers' spread."

Merchant wholesalers' services to retailers

Merchant wholesalers in any manufactured consumer goods line perform five services of great value to the small retailers who buy through them:

1. They perform a *buying operation,* including *line assembling,* for their retailer customers. A hardware wholesaler, for example, may buy hammers from one manufacturer, planes and chisels from another, saws from a third, and from still others nails and screws in all their many sizes, sandpaper, brackets, minor kitchen and household items, and all the hundreds or thousands of items that constitute the "line" of a hardware retailer. In the course of assembling his line, a wholesaler constantly surveys alternative products and manufacturers in the line, weighs the relative resale potentialities of alternative offerings in the light of his experience and market knowledge, and selects those items that appear to have the greatest retailing possibilities. Few small independent dealers, preoccupied with the problems of store operation, would have the time or the market knowhow to match the scope and selectivity of a wholesaler's buying. Moreover, they certainly could not do it as economically, because the buying activity of one wholesaler replaces that of scores or hundreds of retailers.

2. Merchant wholesalers enable their retailer customers to *buy small quantities at frequent intervals.* The manufacturer of an item may sell only in carload, truckload, or other large-unit lots. These quantities might be beyond the immediate resale capacity of a small retailer. Such large lot purchases and storages might tie up greater amounts of working capital and storage space than he could command. The merchant whole-

saler, however, resells the carload shipment by the case. For certain items he may maintain a "broken package" room, where cases are opened and their contents repacked in smaller lots for retailer purchases. His retailer customers can buy from him amounts adjusted to their rate of sale, storage capacity, and working capital—by the gram, dozen, gross, or case. They can reorder daily (where fresh fruits and vegetables or baked goods are involved), or weekly, or monthly, or at longer intervals, in accordance with the timing of their buying policy.

A WHOLESALER'S "BROKEN PACKAGE" ROOM. *Courtesy of McKesson & Robbins, Inc.*

ILLUSTRATION 13–1

3. A retailer without a light truck may be absolutely dependent on the *delivery* service of his merchant wholesaler. The manufacturers of some of the items he carries might be unwilling to arrange store-door delivery to a retailer. Moreover, he could not possibly obtain the efficient delivery service from a group of manufacturers scattered around the country that he can from his merchant wholesaler, located rarely more than fifty miles away.

4. Merchant wholesalers extend *credit* to their retailer customers who are acceptable credit risks. Of course, any manufacturer that sells direct to a retailer would also sell to him on credit terms, probably as favorable as those given by a wholesaler. A wholesaler in any line, however, has closer contact with his retailer customers than a large or medium-size manufacturer can ordinarily develop. If financial misfortune of any sort overtakes a retailer and he becomes unable to meet his trade obligations on their due date, the merchant wholesaler who supplies a major part of his requirements is more likely to take an over-all view of his situation, and to tailor his collection policy on the retailer's long-run capacity for recovery. If there is a good chance for eventual recovery, the merchant wholesaler will often "carry" the retailer for a period, supplying him the while, or arrange partial payment plans, while the manufacturer-supplier of a single item might be more rigid in his collection policy.

5. Efficient merchant wholesalers, and good wholesalers' salesmen, can be invaluable sources of *market and store management information* for their retailer customers. Many manufacturers, of course, help their dealers improve their selling, but their sales promotion efforts are usually directed to better selling of the manufacturers' particular products. A wholesaler, on the contrary, tries to step up all phases of his retailers' operations; any improvement of the retailers' business makes the retailers better customers for the merchant wholesaler. Voluntary groups, as was indicated in Chapter 7, exist primarily because of the store management aid given to the retailer members of the group by the merchant wholesaler. Wholesalers are currently enlarging the scope of these auxiliary services to their retailers.

Merchant wholesalers' services to manufacturers

For the consumer goods manufacturers whose goods they carry, merchant wholesalers perform six valuable services:

1. They relieve manufacturers of a substantial part of their *selling* operation and perform it more economically. A manufacturer selling direct to thousands, or in some cases to tens of thousands of retailers, would have to maintain a sales force commensurate with this task. Managerial effort and working capital would have to be diverted from production to this distribution activity. If the same manufacturer reaches his retailer market through merchant wholesalers, it is they who undertake the big task of reaching the individual retailers, and the manufacturer's selling efforts can be reduced to serving the much smaller number of wholesalers. Even if the manufacturer achieves national distribution, his immediate selling effort will not have to extend to more than a few hundred wholesalers. Moreover, the merchant wholesalers' salesmen carry not only the products

of the particular manufacturer, but a full retailers' *line* assembled from the outputs of other related-product manufacturers. Therefore the selling cost is distributed over the line instead of being borne by the products of the one manufacturer. Consequently, the merchant wholesalers' selling operation is generally performed at a much lower unit cost than could be achieved by the individual manufacturer.

Two qualifications should be made to the above statement of wholesalers' performance of selling services for consumer goods manufacturers: (a) Merchant wholesalers are not generally interested in doing missionary work to develop a market for new products or brands. They prefer to limit their lines to items for which retailer demand is already well established. Their doors are usually closed to new products and brands until the manufacturer can show that he has already, by other means, created both a consumer and a retailer market for them. (b) A merchant wholesaler serves a group of manufacturers in a field, not any particular one. His salesmen are not likely to undertake special promotional efforts, such as more persuasive sales presentations or arranging of special store-window or counter displays, for a particular manufacturer, even though he provides the wholesaler with special instructional materials and display items. Merchant wholesalers will cooperate with individual manufacturers on promotional programs, but only to the extent that these can be incorporated without special effort into the wholesalers' general distributional procedures. A manufacturer who wants his line to receive special promotional effort must supplement his wholesalers' activities by sending "missionary" salesmen to call on retailers.

2. Merchant wholesalers enable a manufacturer to handle his distribution in *large unit lots*—truckloads and carloads—instead of by case or package lots. Shipping costs, which would either reduce the manufacturer's profit or be added to the price of his goods as they reach the retailer, are thereby reduced. Moreover, the substitution of a few large-lot shipments for a multiplicity of small-lot shipments reduces substantially the manufacturer's bookkeeping labors and costs.

3. In some consumer goods lines—canned foods, for example— merchant wholesalers completely relieve the manufacturer of the *storage* function. His products move almost directly from the end of his production line to wholesalers' warehouses. In most consumer goods lines, storage is shared between manufacturers and merchant wholesalers.

4. Frequent *store-door delivery* to thousands, tens of thousands, or hundreds of thousands of retailers, many located hundreds of miles from manufacturers' warehouses, would in many cases be an impossible task. A net of merchant wholesalers, each serving a limited radius and possessing delivery equipment suited to the particular needs of his territory, can perform this service without undue complication. By combining delivery of an

individual manufacturer's goods with those of other related-products producers, consolidated deliveries can be made at a fraction of the unit cost that an individual manufacturer would sustain.

5. A manufacturer selling direct to retailers would have to set up a *credit* department capable of dealing with a large number of accounts, many of which would be borderline risks. Marketing through merchant wholesalers reduces the number of credit accounts to be handled, and holds them to a relatively good-risk category. Because retailers buy the products of many manufacturers through a single merchant wholesaler, he in effect consolidates the credit and collection activities that would otherwise have to be undertaken separately, and so performs the function on a lower unit-cost basis.

6. Merchant wholesalers are often a valuable source of *market information* to their manufacturers.

Conclusions on merchant wholesalers' services

Merchant wholesalers of manufactured consumer goods are of greatest value to small manufacturers and small retailers, particularly in convenience and impulse goods lines where mass distribution is sought. A large manufacturer may produce such a broad line in his product field that his goods do not have to be combined with related items from other manufacturers to provide retailers in his field with the line assembly that means so much to them. For such a manufacturer, merchant wholesalers can do little to cut unit selling, delivery, and credit costs through consolidated performance of these operations. They can relieve him of these operations, as well as some storage responsibility, of course, but not at a significant cost saving.

Likewise, a large retailer—a chain system, or a department store, or a mail order house—may be able to perform the buying operations as efficiently, or more efficiently, than any merchant wholesaler. It can handle its own storage; it does not need a merchant wholesaler as a source of market information. Large-scale deliveries to such retailers, and the handling of their credit relations, impose no special burden on manufacturers.

"Line" policy in selection of wholesalers

A consumer goods manufacturer who decides to sell through merchant wholesalers must often decide what "line" or "lines" of wholesalers he should approach. Should a prepared baby food be sold through drug wholesalers or grocery wholesalers or both? Should a low-price cosmetic be sold through variety goods wholesalers as well as toilette goods wholesalers?

The answer to these questions depends on the manufacturer's prior decisions as to the line classes of retailers he hopes will carry his products. He should endeavor to sell to the classes of wholesalers that serve the various retailing lines that will be his outlets—drug wholesalers if only drugstores are to carry the baby food, both drug wholesalers and grocery wholesalers if food stores will also sell this item.

MANUFACTURERS' AGENT-TO-RETAILER CHANNELS

A manufacturers' agent (or "broker" operating essentially as a manufacturers' agent) will locate retailer customers and sell to them on behalf of his manufacturer-principal, may maintain inventories of the manufacturers' line on a consignment basis and make deliveries from it, and may serve him to some extent as a source of market information. Ordinarily, however, a manufacturers' agent does not undertake for him any of the other marketing services that merchant wholesalers perform for their suppliers. For the retailers who buy from a manufacturers' agent, he commonly performs only the service of assembling a line of their products. He can do this because he endeavors to represent a group of manufacturers of related products.

Manufacturers' agents are not widely used as substitutes for full-service merchant wholesalers, but they are so used to a limited extent in some lines, particularly groceries. Why should any manufacturer, or any retailers, be satisfied with such limited middleman services? Manufacturers' agents are used to bridge the gap between manufacturer and retailers under two circumstances:

(1) A particular territory in which a manufacturer wishes to sell may lack a merchant wholesaler in his line, or the one who serves it may be inefficient, or he may not want to carry the manaufacturer's products. If there are one or more active manufacturers' agents available there, a manufacturer who elsewhere distributes through merchant wholesalers may in that territory avail himself of a manufacturers' agent. Of course, the manufacturer must assume credit operation, and may have to handle storage and delivery operations, normally undertaken by a merchant wholesaler. To offset this, the agent's commission is lower than the margin allowed a merchant wholesaler.

(2) A large manufacturer may be willing to undertake all the operations ordinarily performed by merchant wholesalers, except that of actually locating and selling to retailer customers. Or a large retailer, such as a chain system or a department store, may be willing to perform all the operations ordinarily performed by merchant wholesalers except that of locating suppliers of the merchandise it wants. Under either of these circumstances, an agent intermediary is more economical than a merchant

wholesaler, because his commission is lower than the merchant wholesaler's margin. For this reason, grocery chains buy much of their canned goods through food brokers.

AGENT-MIDDLEMAN-TO-WHOLESALER CHANNELS

Why should a manufacturer who reaches his retailers through merchant wholesalers ever use an agent middleman to reach his wholesalers? There are two circumstances which may make this procedure advisable:

1. As was noted in Chapter 10, many small textile mills market through selling agents, either because the mills prefer to maintain no sales departments of their own or because they need the financial assistance some of these selling agents provide their principals. These selling agents dispose of the mills' greige cloth to converters who, after it has been dyed or printed, resell some of it in piece goods form directly to retailers or indirectly through piece goods jobbers. Intervention of selling agents between manufacturers and wholesalers is found in some other manufactured consumer goods fields, but in no other field is this channel of distribution an important one.

2. In a line where output is highly seasonal and manufacturers many, small, and scattered, the selling capacities of the manufacturers and the buying capacities of the merchant wholesalers in the line may be inadequate to establish the needed multitude of buying-selling relationships in the brief time involved. Agent middlemen of various types, with the initiative and facilities for establishing wide contacts with both the manufacturers and the wholesalers, may provide a valued link between the two groups. In the canned and frozen foods lines, food brokers have long had an established place bridging the gap between the regionally concentrated food packers and the nationally scattered wholesale grocers.

DIRECT-TO-RETAILER DISTRIBUTION

The proportion of consumer goods sold by manufacturers directly to retailers is only slightly less than that sold through merchant wholesalers. There is much generalized argument that the proportion of direct-to-retailer distribution is increasing, but available statistical data do not permit proof or disproof of this claim.

The reasons for direct-to-retailer distribution fall into four categories: (1) nonavailability of suitable wholesalers; (2) nature of the product; (3) manufacturer initiative in bypassing wholesalers; and (4) retailer initiative in bypassing wholesalers.

Nonavailability of suitable wholesalers

Sometimes a manufacturer would prefer to market through wholesale distributors, but is compelled to undertake direct-to-retailer distribution because he cannot find merchant wholesalers or suitable agent middlemen to handle his products.

For many product fields, there are big territorial gaps in market coverage by wholesale distributors. In many territories, furthermore, there may be single merchant wholesalers or agent middlemen who are so ineffective in their distribution procedures that they are little if any better than no middleman coverage at all. A manufacturer interested in developing the true market potential for his products in such territories must undertake direct-to-retailer distribution, either through his own sales force or by mail order.

Furthermore, the existence of a good wholesale distributor in a territory does not necessarily mean that he is available to a particular manufacturer. As indicated earlier, merchant wholesalers are usually not enthusiastic about new products or new brands, and the producer of such a product or brand may be flatly turned down by distributors who serve territories which are good potential markets for the new product or brand. Even well-established items may find difficulty in obtaining merchant wholesaler sponsorship in certain territories. The one or two wholesalers who serve a particular territory may be satisfied with the sales they are getting from rival brands, and refuse to add another brand to their line, even though such brand is elsewhere an established seller, since to do so would not add to their total sales but merely shift sales among brands. In these cases, also, an initial period of direct-to-retailer selling is necessary to build up retailer demand for the new product or invading brand to a level where the merchant wholesalers of the territory are forced to carry it.

Nature of product

A highly perishable product is often sold direct-to-retailer by many of its producers to reduce the time element in its distribution. Furthermore, since storage can play no part in the distribution of these perishable goods, merchant wholesalers are not needed to perform this service for either the manufacturer or the retailers. Thus baked products, ice cream, and various delicatessen items are frequently delivered by their makers directly to the stores that sell them.

A large proportion of fashion goods in the apparel and accessories lines is also sold direct-to-retailer. Once a season's fashions have been established, speed in reaching the retail market with models conforming to these fashions is all-important. A few days' delay at the crucial beginning of a "season" can mean irreparable sales loss. Thus, both manufacturers and retailers are eager to maintain direct distribution and avoid the time loss that a middleman would involve.

Another reason for the popularity of direct-to-retailer distribution of fashion goods is the importance of personal selection of styles and models by each retailer, in accordance with the tastes of his particular clientele. Many retailers in these fields feel that they simply cannot allow middlemen to do their buying for them. Minute but all-important details in materials and design, which can spell the difference between success and failure of a fashion goods shop, must be sought in the offerings of various manufacturers. Merchant wholesalers cannot usually be counted on to exercise such discrimination in the selection of their inventories.

Manufacturer initiative in bypassing merchant wholesalers

Manufacturers of consumer goods tend to bypass the merchant wholesalers in their fields, and sell direct-to-retailer, under three circumstances:

1. A large manufacturer whose range of products constitutes practically *a full retailing line* for his field can perform certain of the operations ordinarily undertaken by merchant wholesalers as effectively and economically as the wholesalers. His salesmen can offer retailers the same major service that merchant wholesalers give—the convenience of a complete, or fairly complete, line of items in their field. Since the manufacturer's salesmen will be taking large-volume orders for a complete line at every sale to a retailer, unit selling costs will be as low as those of any merchant wholesaler. If, through branch depots or the use of general merchandise public warehouses, the manufacturer can solve the physical aspects of his delivery problem, the large volume of his "line" shipments will keep his delivery costs down to a merchant wholesaler's equivalent. Likewise his unit credit and bookkeeping costs should run no higher. In practically all respects, he can do a merchant wholesaler's job in any territory as efficiently and economically as a wholesaler. Under the circumstances, if he has the working capital to cover the added operations involved, and the managerial interest and capacity for these operations, he can take over the wholesaling of his "line" and absorb whatever wholesaling profit is involved. In addition, he is in a position to give his "line" more emphatic promotion than it would obtain from a merchant wholesaler.

2. As was indicated earlier in this chapter, merchant wholesalers rarely give intensive promotion to the products of any particular manufacturer among their suppliers. A manufacturer who wants to create or maintain the market for his products by *special promotion*—by having window and counter displays set up in retail outlets, or by stimulating or training retailers and their sales clerks to do better selling of his products—may find

himself thwarted by wholesaler indifference. Many manufacturers, faced with this problem, have solved it by abandoning wholesaler distribution and approaching retailers with their own sales force. The Big Three in soap —Lever Bros., Procter & Gamble, and Colgate-Palmolive Co.—have long used direct-to-retailer distribution for this reason. Unit costs of selling, delivering, and credit work are almost certain to be much higher, since there is no possibility of dealing with a complete "line" in taking or handling orders. These higher general marketing costs must be added to the costs directly attributable to the special promotional techniques used. In many cases, apparently, the results of the promotion justify the extra costs resulting from the direct-to-retailer marketing.

3. Manufacturers of shopping or specialty goods often adopt a *selective* or *exclusive outlet* policy, in preference to seeking to maximize the number of retailers carrying their products, as explained earlier in this chapter. Merchant wholesalers, who seek to place their lines in every possible outlet, are of no assistance to such manufacturers. Direct selling to their dealers is the only possible marketing program for them.

Retailer initiative in bypassing merchant wholesalers

Large retailers—chain systems, department stores, and general mail order houses—commonly bypass merchant wholesalers and make most of their purchases direct from manufacturers. They do this because the scope of their purchasing enables them to take over operations otherwise undertaken by merchant wholesalers, and to perform these operations at least as efficiently and economically as the wholesalers. The selections made by their skilled buyers are based on as wide market knowledge as those of any merchant wholesaler, and are likely to be better keyed to their particular needs. The quantities of their purchases from individual manufacturers match those of most merchant wholesalers, and so entitle them to maximum quantity discounts and minimum freight charges. They have their own storage facilities. They save the wholesaler's selling and delivery costs. They do not need any special treatment that merchant wholesalers might grant but manufacturers might refuse.

By such direct-from-manufacturer buying, these retailers save for themselves all of the merchant wholesaler's profit margin, and some of his costs of operation.

Merchant wholesalers' reaction to bypassing

Whether or not the bypassing of wholesalers has tended to increase during recent decades, the merchant wholesalers of the country have become aware that the practice constitutes, if not a threat to their very existence, at least a reduction of their potential business and profit. During the past quarter-century they have reacted sharply to the challenge in three ways:

1. With respect to bypassing initiated by large retailers, they have sought political protection. Merchant wholesalers' associations joined with associations of independent retailers to obtain passage of anti-chain-store-tax, fair trade, and unfair trade practice laws to hobble the direct-buying chains, and preserve various retailing fields for the independents, who purchase primarily through merchant wholesalers. They were instrumental in obtaining passage of the Robinson-Patman Act, which eliminates or reduces some of the purchase-price advantages that direct-buying retailers might obtain through such direct buying.

2. Merchant wholesalers' trade associations, on behalf of their members, have conducted extensive public relations campaigns to educate retailers on the services wholesalers perform for them, and to persuade the retailers to do their purchasing through merchant wholesalers.

3. Great numbers of merchant wholesalers, partly on their own initiative, partly at the urging and with the assistance of their trade associations, have revitalized their operations and made themselves more efficient distributors for manufacturers. They have stepped up the technical efficiency of their mechanical operations. In some cases, they have trimmed services to cut expenses, thereby making lower markups possible. They have improved the caliber of their sales forces through better selection, training, and supervision, and have developed better cooperation in the sales promotion programs of their manufacturers.

DIRECT-TO-CONSUMER DISTRIBUTION

Direct-to-consumer selling by consumer-goods manufacturers is a minor channel for consumer goods, totalling less than 4 percent of the total manufacturers' value of consumer goods.

Seven reasons account for direct-to-consumer distribution of consumer goods so marketed.

1. A new product may have so little market acceptance that retailers as well as merchant wholesalers are unwilling to carry it. By mail order or by canvassing the manufacturer must establish sufficient market acceptance to persuade retailers that the items will sell if they will carry them. Subsequently the manufacturer may use retailer acceptance as a basis for persuading merchant wholesalers to take on the items.

2. Consumers of an item may be so widely scattered outside metropolitan areas that they cannot be reached in sufficient numbers by ordinary retail outlets, and can be sold only through mail order. Publishers of special and deluxe editions of books face this problem.

3. Coupon advertisements in newspapers and magazines may de-

velop a wider mail-order market than ordinary retailer channels, or such retailer channels may be profitably supplemented by a coupon-advertisement mail order promotion. Many horticultural nurseries operate on one or the other of these bases.

4. A manufacturer of a high-quality or high-unit-value item may desire more intensive selling of his product than ordinary retailers would be inclined to give it. Establishing his own retail outlets, or creation of a force of direct-selling "canvassers," will give such intensified selling. Some apparel manufacturers have used the "retail outlet" techniques successfully. Book publishers, table silverware manufacturers, and Fuller Brush have sold direct-to-consumers through canvassers.

5. A few large manufacturers in various lines, who sell primarily through retailers, operate one or two retail outlets for market testing purposes. Through these they can obtain consumer reactions to product design, and can test display and other promotional techniques with a view to putting the successful ones into effect through their regular retail outlets.

6. Textile mills and some other factories sometimes operate small retailing units on the factory premises, primarily for their promotional value to passing tourists.

7. Producers of perishable products for local markets, such as bakeries and confectioners, commonly sell at retail on their production premises.

Methods

As indicated in the above discussion, there are three methods of direct-to-consumer distribution of manufactured consumer goods: (1) mail order, (2) manufacturer-owned retail outlets, and (3) canvassing.

Direct-to-consumer selling by *mail order* is most effective when it is based on coupon advertising in appropriate media. Use of consumer mailing lists from magazines and other sources as a basis for direct-mail solicitation is usually expensive in relation to results; this is so because of the unit cost of solicitation and the low proportion of a general consumer mailing list that may be prospects for a particular item. This generalization does not apply if the list is a specialized one, such as of doctors, golf players, or house-trailer owners, and the product to be sold has a particular appeal to the specialized group.

Manufacturer-owned retail stores have proved effective (other than for market-testing purposes) only when the manufacturer produces a line which normally constitutes a complete or major retail line for the type of retail outlet involved. Men's clothing stores for clothing manufacturers, and butcher shops for meat packers, are cases where direct-outlet selling has succeeded. Perishable-product outlets on the production premises, such as bakeries, also have an obvious possibility of success.

Commissions paid to *house-to-house* or *canvassing salesmen* generally range from 30 to 50 percent. With promotional and shipping costs taken into account, this method of direct-to-consumer marketing commonly results in higher costs of distribution than the normal channel through wholesalers and retailers, and this higher cost must be embodied in the prices charged to the consumer-buyers. Products that succeed best with this form of distribution are superior-quality items for which a higher price would not be unreasonable and whose higher-quality-at-higher-price needs the intensity of direct selling. Items whose utilization must be explained in detail before consumer desire for them can be established also benefit from canvassing distribution. One major drawback to developing large-scale distribution by canvassing salesmen is the difficulty of obtaining good salesmen for this work. With a large proportion of second- and third-rate people in this line, and with personal turnover up to 300 percent a year, this method of distribution is bound to be spotty at best.

REVIEW

1. In what ways do the circumstances of the production of manufactured consumer goods lay a foundation for a marketing structure differing substantially from that for agricultural products?

2. What considerations determine a manufacturer's market area?

3. What is "selective" distribution of consumer goods? When is it sound policy?

4. What is "exclusive" distribution of consumer goods? When is it sound policy?

5. List the ten factors that determine the channels of distribution used by manufacturers of consumer goods, and indicate how each may influence the choice of channels.

6. What services do merchant wholesalers perform for the retailers who buy from them?

7. What services do merchant wholesalers perform for the manufacturers of consumer goods who distribute through them? What disadvantages might they have for such manufacturers?

8. Under what circumstances may an agent middleman be profitably utilized as the link between manufacturer and retailer of consumer goods?

9. Under what circumstances do manufacturers of consumer goods use agent middlemen to reach merchant wholesalers?

10. What circumstances induce direct manufacturer-to-retailer distribution of consumer goods?

11. What have the merchant wholesalers of consumer goods done to minimized being "bypassed?"

12. When is direct manufacturer-to-consumer distribution sound policy? How can such distribution be accomplished?

DISCUSSION TOPICS

1. "Start local, spread later, is the only safe policy for marketing any new product or brand."

2. "A manufacturer cannot hope to sell a brand line both to chains and to the independents with whom the chains compete. He must choose one or the other class of outlets."

3. "Unless a manufacturer is prepared to fair-trade his line, he will not be able to find selective or exclusive retail outlets that will carry the line."

4. "The wholesaler is the independent retailers' best friend."

5. "Manufacturers' agents are a poor recourse for both manufacturers and dealers. They have all the disadvantages of merchant wholesalers as a channel of distribution, without any of the advantages."

6. A leading quality men's underwear manufacturer sells direct-to-retailer. Its leading competitor, with a line of the same quality and selling at the same retail price, markets through wholesalers. Which is right?

7. One leading brand of vacuum cleaners has been sold for thirty years by canvassers direct-to-consumers. All other brands are sold through stores. Which is the better method?

PROBLEM 1

Mrs. Brown's preserves have long been the delight of friends to whom she has presented them and of townspeople who have bought them at church fairs. She has been told that she could build up a wonderful business making and selling them commercially. Her friends and fellow-townsmen are ready to invest the capital needed for the enterprise.

1. What should be her market area policy? Why?

2. Should she seek mass, selective, or exclusive distribution? Why?

3. What will be the best channel of distribution for Mrs. Brown's preserves? Why?

4. Is she likely to have any initial difficulties in marketing her preserves this way? Why?

5. How will she probably have to start marketing her preserves? Be specific in your explanation.

PROBLEM 2

Procter & Gamble and other soap products manufacturers, selling their lines through wholesalers, were plagued by the wholesalers' tendency to buy inordinately large amounts of soap products on a speculative basis whenever a rise in raw tallow prices indicated that a manufacturers' increase in the prices of soap products might be in prospect. Until the speculative inventories so acquired by the wholesalers were worked off, they would stop buying soap products.

Because of the extremely wide swings of its soap products sales from this cause, Procter & Gamble's production schedule for its soap products was highly irregular, resulting in fluctuating employment, and there were broad variations in its inventories of finished products. Procter & Gamble felt that, if only its sales could be stabilized, it could regularize production with consequent economies in facilities, equipment, and operating costs, it could stabilize employment and introduce a guaranteed annual employment plan, it could effect economies in its purchases of materials and supplies, and it could minimize inventories with savings in both storage costs and financing.

Three proposals were advanced for stabilizing Procter & Gamble's soap products sales: (a) persuade or induce wholesalers to stabilize their purchases of the company's soap products; (b) disregard the speculative elements of wholesalers' soap products orders and put them on quotas based on the requirements of their market areas; (c) bypass the wholesalers and sell directly to retailers, who do buy on a fairly regular basis.

1. State the pros and cons of each of these proposals.
2. Which one, or what combination, would you choose? Why?

SUGGESTED READINGS

Clewett, R. M. (ed.), *Marketing Channels,* Richard D. Irwin, Homewood, Ill., 1954.

Davis, K. B., *Furniture Marketing,* University of North Carolina Press, Chapel Hill, 1957.

Davisson, C. N., *The Marketing of Automotive Parts,* Bureau of Business Research, University of Michigan, Ann Arbor, 1954.

Graham, I., *How to Sell through Mail Order,* McGraw-Hill Book Co., New York, 1949.

Hewitt, C. M., *Automobile Franchise Agreements,* Richard D. Irwin, Homewood, Ill., 1956.

Howell, L. D., *Marketing and Manufacturing Services and Margins for Textiles,* Technical Bulletin No. 1062, U.S. Department of Agriculture, Washington, D.C., 1952.

Olsen, P. C., *Marketing Drug Products,* Rutgers University Press, Rutgers, N.J., 1955.

Stewart, J., *The American Fashion Industry,* Simmons College, Boston, 1951.

CHAPTER 14

INDUSTRIAL AND SERVICE MARKETING

Industrial products are those destined primarily to be sold for use in producing other goods or rendering services, as contrasted with goods destined primarily to be sold to ultimate consumers. They are bought by manufacturers, other business enterprises, and institutions for use, not for resale. They may be classified, for purposes of marketing study, as follows:

1. Equipment
   a. Installations and other major equipment items, such as factory power plants, machine tools, and punch-card tabulators.
   b. Accessory or secondary equipment, such as gauges, hand or power trucks for internal movement of materials, and office equipment.
2. Materials
   a. Raw and refined materials.
   b. Fabricated materials and processed parts subsequently incorporated in finished products.
   c. Packaging materials.
3. Supplies—such as lubricating oils, typewriting paper, and factory or office maintenance items.

Some agricultural products, such as cotton and wool, are important industrial raw materials. Most industrial products, however, come from mines and factories.

Industrial marketing outweighs consumer goods marketing in volume and value. Over half the total of manufactured products is destined to industrial use. All the output of our mines and wells except for some oil and anthracite coal, most of the output of our forests, and a considerable fraction of our agricultural production—cotton, wool, flax, and byproducts of the meat packing industry, among other items—are industrial raw materials.

Industrial marketing resembles consumer goods marketing in one important respect. Practically all industrial equipment and some industrial materials and supplies are individualized and identified by their producers, and the distribution movement is one of dispersion, so that distributional control and policy on the part of the producers is possible. Otherwise, the differences in these two distributional fields are more significant than the similarities. The economic characteristics of the two markets, the purchasing motivations involved, and the channels of distribution are quite different.

THE INDUSTRIAL MARKET

All manufacturers, all wholesalers, all retailers, all public utilities, all companies in the extractive industries, all transportation companies, all construction organizations, all service enterprises, all institutions, and most governments—particularly the federal government—are purchasers of industrial goods.

Concentration

A few manufacturers of office supplies might consider all of the 3 million or more organizations included above as the potential market for their products. For some categories of office and store equipment, for various classes of factory supplies such as fuel oils and lubricants, for some basic standard tools like drill presses, there are perhaps hundreds of thousands of potential customers in many business fields scattered throughout the country. But most classes of industrial equipment and materials are produced for more specialized markets—for particular industries. The outstanding characteristic of each such specialized industrial market is *concentration,* which takes three forms:

1. Markets for equipment or materials adapted to the special needs of a single industry tend to be limited as to the *number* of potential customers. At most, there may be a few thousand possible purchasers, as in the case of a heavy-duty sewing machine produced for apparel manufacturers. More commonly, the total potential market for a single-industry material or equipment item is a few hundred or a few score manufacturers. Some manufacturers of highly specialized equipment produce for potential total markets of less than ten customers. Producers of military equipment may have only one customer—some branch of the national armed forces.

2. There is commonly great *disparity in size* among potential customers for an industrial product. Taking value added by manufacture as a measure of industrial purchasing demand, less than 10 percent of the

country's manufacturing units account for nearly 80 percent of manufacturers' purchases. In a great many industrial lines a small number of large-scale enterprises dominate the industry. Their purchases of materials and equipment outweigh those of hundreds of the small units in the line. Accordingly, distributional effort for many suppliers of industrial materials or equipment is heavily concentrated on a few "key" customers, with only incidental attention given to the remainder of the market. Often the few "key" customers are sold directly, while the much larger number of small plants in a line are reached through middlemen.

3. One important factor in shaping industrial marketing policy has been the high *territorial concentration* of American manufacturing activity into a few areas. Three city areas—New York (including adjacent New Jersey communities), Chicago, and Detroit—account for nearly one-fourth of the nation's total manufacturing production. Over one-half of our manufacturing output comes from another 129 city areas embracing only a few thousand square miles. For particular industries, this territorial concentration is even more marked. Often 90 percent or more of the prospective customers for some single-industry material or item of equipment are found in or around some three or four cities—for example, the concentration of the automobile industry around Detroit and of the men's hat industry in a few Connecticut cities. For reasons of national security an attempt is currently being made to disperse industrial establishments in certain lines, but this scattering effort has not yet significantly affected our industrial geography. Because of this concentration of many industrial markets, industrial promotional and selling efforts tend to be less diffuse, more pin-pointed, than is the general case in consumer goods marketing. This circumstance also favors short marketing channels—including direct producer-to-user distribution.

Purchasing organization and procedure

The purchasing operation in large industrial and institutional organizations is usually centralized (see Chapter 17 for a fuller discussion). However, buying decisions on major industrial purchases rest usually not with a single individual, but with a group. Specifications for materials and supplies are usually prepared by the heads of operating departments, with the responsibilities of the purchasing manager limited to the procedures of locating suppliers, placing orders, and obtaining delivery. Where factory equipment is concerned, the production superintendent, one or two experienced foremen, the head of the engineering division, the company's treasurer, its president, and possibly others, may all have a say before its purchase is authorized. Such multiple review of industrial purchasing propositions tends to screen out any subconscious emotional motivations that might influence the buying decision of any one of the individuals concerned. It certainly adds complications to industrial selling.

Salesmen of materials and supplies are always calling on industrial purchasing managers without being called first. Alert salesmen of equipment also call upon potential customers without waiting for inquiries from

HOW INDUSTRY BUYS MATERIALS

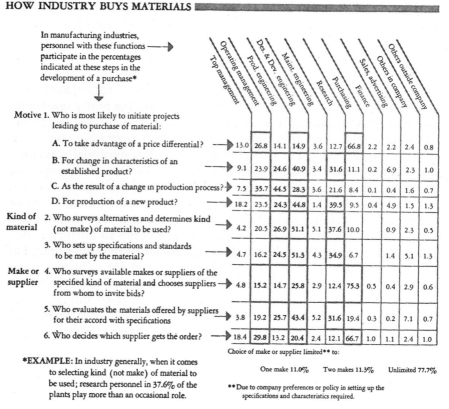

In manufacturing industries, personnel with these functions → participate in the percentages indicated at these steps in the development of a purchase*

	Top management	Operating management	Prod. management	Des. & Dev. engineering	Maint. engineering	Research	Purchasing	Finance	Sales, advertising	Others in company	Others outside company
Motive 1. Who is most likely to initiate projects leading to purchase of material:											
A. To take advantage of a price differential?	13.0	26.8	14.1	14.9	3.6	12.7	66.8	2.2	2.2	2.4	0.8
B. For change in characteristics of an established product?	9.1	23.9	24.6	40.9	3.4	31.6	11.1	0.2	6.9	2.3	1.0
C. As the result of a change in production process?	7.5	35.7	44.5	28.3	3.6	21.6	8.4	0.1	0.4	1.6	0.7
D. For production of a new product?	18.2	23.5	24.3	44.8	1.4	39.5	9.5	0.4	4.9	1.5	1.3
Kind of material 2. Who surveys alternatives and determines kind (not make) of material to be used?	4.2	20.5	26.9	51.1	5.1	37.6	10.0		0.9	2.3	0.5
3. Who sets up specifications and standards to be met by the material?	4.7	16.2	24.5	51.3	4.3	34.9	6.7		1.4	5.1	1.3
Make or supplier 4. Who surveys available makes or suppliers of the specified kind of material and chooses suppliers from whom to invite bids?	4.8	15.2	14.7	25.8	2.9	12.4	75.3	0.5	0.4	2.9	0.6
5. Who evaluates the materials offered by suppliers for their accord with specifications	3.8	19.2	25.7	43.4	5.2	31.6	19.4	0.3	0.2	7.1	0.7
6. Who decides which supplier gets the order?	18.4	29.8	13.2	20.4	2.4	12.1	66.7	1.0	1.1	2.4	1.0

Choice of make or supplier limited** to:

One make 11.0%   Two makes 11.3%   Unlimited 77.7%

*EXAMPLE: In industry generally, when it comes to selecting kind (not make) of material to be used; research personnel in 37.6% of the plants play more than an occasional role.

** Due to company preferences or policy in setting up the specifications and characteristics required.

INDUSTRIAL PURCHASING AUTHORITY IN PARTICULAR COMPANIES. *Reprinted from Industrial Marketing, October 1950, p. 38.*

ILLUSTRATION 14–1

them. With the extreme irregularity in the buying of equipment, however, it often happens that the management of a business considers buying particular equipment items in advance of any salesmen's calls. An industrial purchasing manager must then take the initiative of locating possible suppliers of the equipment and establishing contact with them. In preparation for such contingencies, industrial purchasing managers build up extensive files of the catalogs of relevant equipment suppliers. They are also helped in locating possible suppliers by the *Buyers' Guides* described in Chapter 17.

Product purchase motivations

Economic motivations, rather than personal or social ones, dominate industrial purchasing. Suitability of a material or supply for its purpose, the operating efficiency and economy of an equipment item, and cost, are usually the all-important considerations. The principals of small manufacturing businesses and the industrial purchasing managers who do this buying are usually well-informed, frequently experts, on what they are buying, and are keen judges of suitability, efficiency, economy, and cost factors. They buy on precise description and specification, not on hazy generalities. Hence industrial advertising and selling are essentially technical, with emphasis on the mathematics of operation and cost saving. The packaging of industrial goods has to be functional, with little opportunity for eye-appeal or other emotional stimulation.

Still, there is opportunity for personal and social appeal even in industrial selling, and good salesmen do not overlook it. The executives of an established business are often fiercely proud of it, and appeal can be made to this pride by a salesman who has quality equipment or material to sell. "Follow the leader" considerations also play a part in industrial purchasing, and a list of important customers is a persuasive point for a salesman to make when trying to sell a new prospect in the same field.

Patronage motivations

When two or more suppliers offer more or less the same equipment, materials, or supplies, how does an industrial purchasing manager choose among them? It might be thought that, with economic considerations dominating selection of equipment and materials, comparative price would be the all-controlling factor. It is important, more important than in the case of consumer buying. Sometimes it may seem to be the only factor, as when a large industrial or government purchasing department asks for sealed bids from would-be suppliers with the implication that the sale will go to the lowest bidder. But industrial purchasing managers set great store by the *reliability* of their suppliers—reliability as to producing consistently to specifications, reliability as to making deliveries, reliability as to maintenance and servicing of purchased equipment. Very often an industrial purchasing manager will pass over one or more would-be suppliers with lower prices or bids and give the order to one whose price or bid is higher but who is considered more reliable than the others.

Reciprocal buying—the principle of "you scratch my back and I'll scratch yours"—is unquestionably a factor in the purchasing policy of many industrial concerns. A steel mill will look with more favorable eyes on the offerings of equipment companies that purchase their steel requirements from it than upon equipment companies that purchase their steel elsewhere. Likewise, an equipment manufacturer will tend to favor a steel supplier that buys its equipment from him as against competing offers from mills that have closed their doors to his salesmen. An office-supplies manufacturer would certainly urge reciprocal purchasing upon the paper company from which it bought paper supplies—and *vice versa.* Reciprocity in industrial purchasing sometimes is carried to lengths distinctly unfavorable to one of the parties concerned. Normally it is limited to a buying policy of favoring a customer as a supplier, provided that his product and price are in line with competitors' offerings.

Economic considerations

All industrial demand for *materials* is *derived* demand. A woolen mill buys raw wool only because there is a consumer market for items made from woolen cloth. Any increase in consumer demand for a particular manufactured product, whatever the cause, increases the industrial market for the raw materials. A decline in consumer demand for a manufactured item causes industrial demand for the related raw materials to contract. These reactions may be almost simultaneous. More commonly, variations in the seasonal patterns of the production and consumption of various goods cause considerable time lag between consumer market changes and industrial market responses.

An industrial *installation* or a piece of industrial *equipment* is a durable capital item, with a life ranging from a few years to a score or more. Replacements are likely to be made only at long intervals, because the installation or equipment has worn out or because it has become obsolescent —i.e., although the original installation or equipment can still operate, more efficient or more economical substitutes have been developed. The demand for industrial installations and equipment is also a derived one. A factory does not buy a machine because it wants it for its own sake, but because there is consumer demand for commodities made by the machine. When general consumer demand declines substantially as a result of an economic recession, and factories are producing at less than capacity, they have no inducement to buy new installations or equipment, and they are generally able to postpone a major part of equipment replacements. Cutting of bids and prices by the producers of industrial items at such times does little to bring in orders. Contrariwise, in a boom period manufacturers in all lines rush to replace worn or obsolescent equipment and are amenable to suggestions about expanding their productive capacity. As a consequence, equipment industries reflect a feast-or-famine economy—operating over-time in good years, practically shut down in recessions.

An important exception to the above generalizations about the relation-ship of consumer and industrial demand should be noted. A considerable portion of current industrial production is for government—military and public works supplies for the federal government, highway and public buildings materials for state and local governments. Industrial production to government order is not dependent on the consumer economy. The vol-ume of federal military purchases is related to the actuality of or outlook for war. Federal public works expenditure, and state and local outlays for highways and buildings, have their special determinants; to the extent that current "fiscal policy" theories of government spending prevail, public works outlays are likely to vary in a cycle countering that of the private economy—rising when recession and unemployment threaten, declining when inflation is the menace.

INDUSTRIAL SUPPLIERS

There are many small-scale manufacturers of secondary industrial equip-ment, fabricated parts, and office equipment and supply items, as well as a few large ones. The picture is quite different for producers of major indus-trial equipment and materials (other than agricultural raw materials). For any line of major equipment or type of material, these are likely to be few in number and fairly large enterprises. Even where the factor of transpor-tation costs limits the market areas of certain producers of industrial mate-rials, as with steel mills, each individual plant serving a limited area is likely to be of substantial size.

Market area and producer size considerations

Transportation cost of a number of raw and semi-processed materials is high because of the relation of their bulk or weight to their price. Freight charges for long hauls add substantially to the gross cost of such materials. A plant producing such materials generally has a profitable market only within a limited surrounding area. How extensive or restricted this area may be is determined by the location of competing establishments. If such a plant tries to ship beyond this area with freight costs charged to the pur-chasers, the resulting gross purchase cost to them is likely to be higher than if they bought from a competing establishment; therefore, the plant is not likely to serve many customers outside its area. If it ships "F.O.B. destina-tion," thereby absorbing the freight costs in order to meet the prices of competitors more favorably located in relation to distant customers, the margin of profit on orders from distant customers is sharply reduced.

This limitation on industrial market areas does not necessarily mean scattered small producers in each industrial line. Many industrial producers are veritable giants. They meet the freight-cost problem by operating through large numbers of plants, located at strategic shipping points to give them maximum marketing area advantages.

Moreover, this factor of high relative transportation costs, though tending to restrict the market areas of plants producing certain industrial materials, also has its favorable aspect for many of the producers. Each plant, unless it has a close-by competitor, which is not common, enjoys somewhat of a location quasi-monopoly in its own market area. If the competing establishments ship F.O.B. mill or mine (freight costs charged to the purchaser), the local plant has a competition-free pricing margin equal to the shipping costs into its market area from its nearest competitor's shipping point. If its production capacity is roughly equivalent to the demand for its products in its own market area, it can incorporate in its prices a major proportion of the freight costs that would have to be paid on shipments from its nearest competitor, and still be able to undersell such competitor. Only a competitor with substantially lower production costs can seriously challenge the local plant in its home territory.

Until recently, the steel industry and a number of other industrial material industries chose to forego these individual-plant quasi-monopolies based on location and F.O.B.-mill pricing. In their place they developed systems of uniform industry-wide prices with transportation charges from different producers to any particular customer equalized by F.O.B.-basing-point or F.O.B.-destination provisions (these pricing provisions are studied in Chapter 20). Court decisions during the past few years have outlawed price uniformity and basing-point or destination treatment of freight charges whenever collusive industry agreements are involved. These decisions have tended to restore, for a time at least, the structure noted in the preceding paragraph of quasi-monopolistic local market areas for many industrial materials producers.

Industrial selling

Because industrial purchasing managers are highly skilled buyers, well informed on the technical aspects of the equipment and materials they purchase, the salesmen sent out by industrial producers must be of high caliber. They must be engineers primarily, able to analyze intricate issues of equipment installation and materials utilization, and salesmen only secondarily.* They must not only have a profound knowledge of the items

---

* Because of this consideration, until recently industrial salesmen were recruited almost exclusively from engineering colleges and from the ranks of science majors. Currently there is a growing tendency to employ Marketing-major graduates of business colleges and to provide these men with the requisite technical knowledge through company training programs.

they sell, they must be experts on the engineering and operational problems of their customers. Industrial engineer-salesmen require long periods of training, sometimes running into several years, before they are competent to represent their companies. If agent middlemen are used to sell industrial equipment, as described later in this chapter, they too have to be top-flight engineers as well as salesmen.

Service policy

An industrial sale is rarely completed with the writing of a purchase order. The purchaser's operating executives and foremen often have to be instructed in efficient utilization of unfamiliar equipment and material. Purchased equipment may require servicing that only the manufacturer can provide. Post-sale customer service plays a big part in industrial marketing. The sellers' engineer-salesmen, or the agent middlemen that some equipment manufacturers use, provide the advisory and instructional assistance. Maintenance service is usually the responsibility of special maintenance crews.

LEASING OF INDUSTRIAL EQUIPMENT

Leasing industrial equipment, instead of selling it, is gaining ground in industrial marketing. In a lease or rental of equipment, title remains with the lessor and never passes to the lessee. In practice, however, most equipment leases remain in effect for the operating lifetime of the equipment, so that the lessor disposes of the equipment almost as completely as if it had been sold and the lessee has as full use of the equipment as if he had bought it.

Industrial equipment leases are usually for terms of three to five years or longer with renewal provisions, but frequently contain clauses permitting the lessor to terminate the contract if the lessee breaches provisions related to maintenance of the equipment or use of the equipment to process materials not made by the lessor.

Rental arrangements for industrial equipment vary widely. Occasionally flat periodic rents, paid quarterly or annually, are charged. More commonly the rental is related to the lessee's use of the equipment, or is charged as a royalty on products made with the equipment. Sometimes the rental is embodied in the prices of materials and supplies sold by the lessor to be used in connection with the equipment.

An equipment manufacturer gains four advantages by leasing his equipment rather than selling it. (1) Some customers might not be able to afford the capital cost of expensive equipment, but can acquire it on a "pay-as-you-go" rental basis, even though ultimate rental cost may be higher than cash or installment cost. (2) By retaining responsibility for maintaining leased equipment, the lessor can be assured that it will be kept in proper working order, and will give maximum satisfaction. (3) Through "tying" clauses in the lease, the lessor may require the lessees to purchase materials and supplies sold by the lessor, thus assuring a market for these items. Such tying clauses have several times been held in restraint of trade, but there are still circumstances under which they are valid. (4) Rental income is less subject to cyclical fluctuation than that from sale of equipment.

A policy of leasing equipment compels the equipment manufacturer to have a much larger capital than would be required if the equipment were sold. There is no immediate sales income to cover the manufacturer's production and operating expenses. The rental income is usually utimately larger than sales income would have been, but its receipt is spread over years instead of being realized when the customer first acquires the equipment.

A recent institutional development has substantially expanded the scope of equipment leasing. Companies have been organized for the express purpose of such leasing. Representatives of these leasing companies call upon manufacturers and sell them upon the advantages of leasing new equipment. Upon closing a rental arrangement, a leasing company then purchases the equipment from its maker, frequently at a trade discount reduction, and has it delivered to the renting manufacturer. Through the operations of these leasing companies, many small equipment makers whose limited capital would not permit them to undertake leasing arrangements themselves can tap the extra market that leasing opens up. Rental is made possible for many manufacturers who might wish to rent equipment but cannot locate a maker willing to lease.

CHANNELS OF DISTRIBUTION FOR INDUSTRIAL EQUIPMENT

The outstanding characteristic of the marketing of industrial installations and equipment is the high proportion of direct-to-user selling. Middlemen —agent as well as merchant—have a place in the pattern of equipment marketing, but it is minor in contrast to their role in the distribution of manufactured consumer goods.

Direct-to-user distribution

Well over half * of the American output of industrial equipment is sold direct-to-user. The proportion is nearly three-quarters for machine tools and construction machinery, and over 90 percent for textile machinery. A

---

* These proportions are based on 1939 Census of Manufactures data. No more recent figures have been issued.

number of reasons account for this predominance of direct-to-user market-ing of industrial installations and equipment:

1. Many installations and large industrial equipment items are made to the buyer's special order. In such case, there is no standard item which can be stocked and resold by a merchant wholesaler. The seller's and the buyer's technical staffs have to get together and work out the de-tails of the planning and construction of the equipment. A specific price has to be calculated by the seller for each such custom-made item. Direct communication between seller and buyer is the most practical procedure for negotiating such transactions.

2. The market for most manufacturers of industrial installations and equipment is limited as to the number of potential customers, and is geographically concentrated. The task of determining and reaching every prospective customer is accordingly a relatively simple one for the sales departments of such manufacturers. They do not need middlemen to per-form this "prospecting" phase of the selling operation for them.

3. The number of suppliers of any specialized type of industrial equipment is even more limited. On the irregular occasions when a manu-facturer, even a small one, is thinking of purchasing a major item of equip-ment, it is no great task to ascertain all the producers of the item in question and contact them. No middleman is usually needed by the pur-chaser to perform this phase of the buying operation for him.

4. Unit value per sale of industrial equipment ranges from hun-dreds to tens of thousands of dollars. With such values involved, manufac-turers of equipment are disinclined to leave success or failure to middlemen whose selling effort might be inferior to their own.

5. A high proportion of the producers of industrial equipment are enterprises able to employ and train skilled engineer-salesmen. "Key" cus-tomers for industrial equipment in many lines are likewise large enterprises able to employ skilled purchasing managers. With highly compctent sell-ing or buying personnel at both ends of many industrial distribution chan-nels, the need for middlemen is reduced.

6. The technical sales presentations required to convince the executive group with purchasing responsibility for major equipment items can usually be made only by the seller's own engineer-salesman, who must be a competent engineer as well as a salesman, and an expert on his com-pany's line of equipment.

7. Because of the importance of the reliability of a maker of in-dustrial installations and equipment, for reasons indicated above, the purchasers of such equipment usually prefer to deal directly with them. Where servicing an installation or piece of equipment subsequent to pur-chase is involved, which is often the case, a buyer naturally wants to have

dealt with, and to have reached a complete understanding with, the seller who will fulfill any servicing obligations.

Industrial equipment and machinery middlemen

Although indirect marketing through middlemen accounts for less than half of the total sales of industrial equipment, the major part of *standardized* machines, secondary equipment, and industrial *tools* of all varieties is sold through distributors, both merchant wholesalers and agent middlemen.

Most of the industrial middlemen who handle equipment and machinery limit themselves to such items, leaving to other specialized middlemen the marketing of the materials and supplies used in association with the machines. This is particularly true of the middlemen who distribute office machines and furniture, trucks and road trailers, and construction equipment. A considerable proportion of standard factory machinery, however, is sold through "mill supply houses" and "industrial distributors" who carry broad lines of supplies and machine parts.

Merchant middlemen dominate the indirect distribution of industrial equipment and machinery. Where manufacturers' agents do operate, they generally represent, as in consumer goods lines, a group of manufacturers of related but noncompeting items.

Industrial equipment and machine middlemen are invaluable marketing collaborators to small manufacturers of industrial items. Since they handle *lines* of equipment, and may promote the items of several different manufacturers, costs per customer call are divided among the group of items instead of being borne fully by each individual one. When a mill supply house handles tools, materials and supplies as well as equipment items, its salesmen must make repeat calls on their customers. This builds up an element of customer good will which the one-call salesmen of a particular equipment manufacturer could never achieve. Industrial middlemen salesmen usually have engineering backgrounds, and are generally as competent to present the technicalities of standard equipment and tools as would the special sales representatives of manufacturers of such items.

CHANNELS OF DISTRIBUTION FOR INDUSTRIAL MATERIALS AND SUPPLIES

The distributive structure for industrial materials and supplies resembles that for industrial equipment, but differs from it in a number of important respects, so that separate analysis is desirable.

Direct-to-user distribution

Direct-to-user distribution does not bulk so large for industrial materials and supplies as it does for industrial equipment. There are some striking exceptions to this generalization. Over four-fifths of steel and rolling mill products, for example, are marketed direct-to-user. Agricultural raw materials, lumber, coal, industrial chemicals, and the major categories of industrial supply items, however, are distributed primarily through middlemen, sometimes through chains of middlemen.

The key consideration which determines the relative importance of direct-to-user distribution in any industrial material or supply line is whether the material or supply can be purchased and used in standardized form, or whether production tends to be to individual specification. Where an industrial material or supply item is marketed in accordance with well-established composition standards, as is the case with industrial chemicals, coal, and most agricultural raw materials, the purchaser has little interest in the particular producer of a purchased lot. He is therefore inclined to utilize middlemen, where the value of their services outweighs the cost margin involved. In contrast, a large proportion of steel production is made to specific order, both as to the chemistry of the steel and the physical dimensions of the units. Under such circumstances, there can be no alternative to direct purchase-and-sale negotiations between producer and user.

Very large industrial units, that can perform economically for themselves the services offered by a middleman, may profit by bypassing the middleman and purchasing particular materials or supplies in bulk lots directly from a producer. The bulk of small and medium-sized industrial units generally would derive no advantage from direct purchase of their materials and supplies.

From the viewpoint of many producers of industrial materials and supplies whose marketing policy is geared primarily to large-scale transactions, small-lot sales at their regular prices simply would not be profitable. While selling direct to large customers, they will refuse direct orders from small-scale buyers and refer these to their distributors, who sell in small lots but at higher prices.

Full-service distributors

Full-service merchant middlemen—frequently called "industrial distributors"—dominate the intermediate distribution of industrial materials and supplies, though not to as great an extent as in the marketing of industrial equipment and machines. Like merchant wholesalers in the distribution of consumer goods, industrial distributors relieve the manufacturers whose items they handle of most of their selling, credit, storage, and delivery operations. Industrial distributors serve their industrial and business customers by assembling lines of the materials and supplies in which the latter are interested, thereby simplifying their purchasing problems. Furthermore, industrial distributors enable their customers to purchase materials and supplies in small lots, for which the distributors supply factory-door delivery. Operating expenses, and therefore the margins, of industrial wholesalers are for the most part considerably higher than those of consumer goods wholesalers. Nonetheless, so essential are the services of industrial distributors to both producers and users of industrial materials and supplies that the high middleman margins are readily absorbed by the prices received by the producers and paid by the users.

There are a small number of "mill supply houses" which serve the requirements of a wide range of buying industries as to supplies, standard machines, secondary equipment, tools, and machine parts. These "houses" may carry inventories of as many as 40,000 to 50,000 different items in their efforts to stock the variant needs of their customers. Such generalized industrial wholesaling is the exception, however. Most industrial distributors are specialized in one of two ways. The more common type of specialization is by product line. Thus there are distributors who handle only standard steel items, or industrial chemicals, or electrical wiring supplies, or lumber, or coal, or particular metals. The second type of specialization is by customer line. There are hotel and restaurant supply houses, laundry supply houses, mortician supply houses, and mine supply houses. These customer-line distributors usually carry a wide assortment of supply items, covering many product lines, which their particular class of customers uses.

The cost of delivering small amounts of industrial materials and supplies over long distances is likely to be prohibitive. Moreover, industrial customers frequently want quick deliveries. These two circumstances tend to limit the geographical area that an industrial distributor can serve. A distributor of factory materials and supplies, whether he is product-specialized or customer-line-specialized, usually operates only in the industrial area immediately centered on the city of his location. Distributors of business and service enterprise supplies restrict their active sales efforts largely to the metropolitan centers in which they are located. Therefore a producer of materials or supplies who wishes national or regional coverage through industrial distributors must establish connections with a widely-scattered selection of product-line and customer-line distributors.

Drop shippers

As was indicated in Chapter 9, drop shippers have established themselves firmly in the distribution of lumber and coal. In the latter field they outnumber the distributors with yards, and handle more than double the sales of the latter. Both of these commodities are often ordered in carload lots even by small industrial users, so it is possible for the drop shippers to route deliveries direct from the sawmill or mine to the customer. The mills and mines are generally able to undertake storage, so the drop shipper's non-performance of this service presents no distribution problem. Even though the sawmills and mines charge higher prices to drop shippers than they do to distributors with yards, the lower pricing margins of the drop shippers enable the latter to undersell the yard distributors.

Agent distributors

Agent middlemen play considerable part in the distribution of several lines of industrial materials and supplies. They account for more than a third of the middleman sales of electrical wiring and construction supplies and of transport equipment and supplies (other than motor trucks). Agent sales of coal and coke exceed those of distributors with yards.

Brokers, employed by the seller or buyer, negotiate some of the sales of hides and leather, cotton gray cloth, and steel. Usually, the reason for employing a broker is that his commission amounts to less than a full-service middleman's margin because of his low operating expense. Brokers are also employed by buyers who wish to conceal their identity, or to hunt out "hidden" sources in a period of scarcity.

Selling agents are also found in the distribution of industrial materials and supplies, particularly in the marketing of textiles, coal and coke, and lumber. They take the place of sales departments for their clients. Hence their field of operations is not restricted to a limited territory, like that of most industrial middlemen, but covers whatever area the mill or mine might sell to with its own sales force. They may sell, on behalf of their clients, direct-to-user or through other middlemen. They commonly take entire charge of their clients' credit function, and may finance their clients by discounting their accounts receivable or lending on their inventories.

The most common type of agent middleman in the industrial materials and supplies field is the manufacturers' agent. He operates locally, representing a group of producers of related but noncompeting products. He may do limited storage by carrying some stocks of his principals' products on consignment, so that he can fill small orders immediately. The typical manufacturer's agent in an industrial materials and supplies field usually maintains a continuous and close personal connection with his customers. He is technically competent to give his customers genuine help in their purchasing problems, and may thereby hold their confidence.

MARKETING BUSINESS SERVICES

The 1958 *Census of Business* listed some 114,000 business service enterprises with a gross income close to $10 billions. Included in this tabulation were advertising agencies, mercantile agencies and retail credit bureaus, stenographic and duplicating services, employment agencies, window display services, and many others. These are only part of the business service picture, however. Specifically excluded from the Census concept of "business service" were transportation and all the auxiliary services related to it, the public utilities, all forms of warehousing, insurance, accountants, and lawyers.

Channels of distribution

Most business services are purchased on the basis of the buyer's confidence in the performer of the service. Certainly reliance on the known performance or reputation of an advertising agency, marketing research organization, stenographic service, window display service, accountant, or attorney is the persuasive consideration when contracting for the services of such organizations or individuals. Furthermore, many of these business services—those of the advertising agency, marketing research organization, attorney, and accountant, among others—involve closely confidential relationships between the performer of the service and the business client. Under the circumstances, purchasers of these business services are not likely to leave selection of the performers of these services to some third party or middleman. Direct negotiation between performer and user of the service is the marketing procedure for most.

There are a few business service fields where middlemen have proven of value and have established themselves. Among these are employment and the selling of the various forms of insurance used by business organizations. In the case of employment, many "sellers"—the individuals seeking employment—are not in a position to discover the potential employers who may be seeking the particular abilities and talents which the job applicants have to offer. They need a middleman—the employment agency—to perform this important function for them. The would-be employers, while they would not permit a middleman to choose particular employees for them, are not unwilling to have the employment agency provide them with a selection of applicants from which they may make their own choice. The employment agency acts as a broker, its service being limited to bringing the two parties together to work out mutually suitable terms of employment. The job applicant, as the "seller" in the negotiations, pays the employment agency a fee, usually based on the compensation to be received. Prizefighters' "managers" and "Hollywood agents" are employment agent middlemen of a special sort. Their relationship with their clients is continuous instead of incidental, and they frequently have substantial authority to contract on behalf of their clients. They are selling agents, rather than merely brokers. "Literary agents" or "authors' agents" occupy a similar middleman position between authors and the publishers and magazines that buy the authors' writings.

Promotion and selling

Attorneys and accountants are forbidden, by the ethics of their professions, to advertise, sell, or otherwise directly solicit clients. The initiative in establishing relationships is supposed to come always from the client. The attorney's or accountant's only promotional instruments are, presumably, his professional reputation and the knowledge of himself that he may spread through personal acquaintance, publication, and public appearance.

The marketing efforts of other business service lines are not limited by the professional ethical proscriptions that bind lawyers and accountants. They can advertise, and they do, primarily by direct mail. Trade magazines provide them an effective medium for published ads. They can sell, and literally thousands of full-time salesmen are employed by advertising media, credit services, freight forwarding agencies, and other large and medium-size business service organizations. More commonly, however, the "selling" of service organizations, particularly the "selling" done by the multitude of small ones, is undertaken by the principals of these organizations, who are also the individuals largely responsible for performance of the services, in their follow-up of inquiries resulting from reputation or from advertising.

MARKETING PERSONAL SERVICES

The 1958 *Census of Business* reported over 850,000 personal service establishments, among them 215,000 barber and beauty shops, 39,000 tailor shops, 28,000 shoe repair and hat cleaning shops, 104,000 auto repair shops and garages, 95,000 amusement and recreation enterprises, 29,000 hotels, and 41,000 tourist courts. To these should be added 275,000 physicians and dentists, and thousands of lawyers who serve primarily individuals rather than businesses.

In New York City some theatre tickets are sold through ticket brokers. There are employment agencies for domestic servants. Large dry cleaning and laundry establishments make their collections and distributions through agent representatives. Apart from these minor exceptions, the relationship between performers and users of personal services is, as with business services, essentially a direct one.

Doctors, dentists, and lawyers serving individuals are, like accountants and business lawyers, barred by professional ethics from soliciting, advertising, or otherwise directly promoting their services. All other personal service enterprises are free to sell and promote themselves as they will. Apart from laundries and photographic studios, many of which employ canvassers to establish first contacts with their customers, personal service enterprises undertake little direct selling. They rely primarily upon reputation and advertising.

A considerable variety of advertising media, most of them local, are used by personal service enterprises. Practically all, except theatres, find direct mail effective. In small cities and still smaller communities, such service enterprises as laundries, dry cleaning establishments, garages, and beauty parlors place classified ads in the local papers. In large cities some service establishments use car card advertising. Hotels advise approaching motorists and train travellers of their existence by billboards along traffic arteries leading into their communities.

Insurance companies have long utilized every resource of personal selling and advertising to market their policies. Investment houses also have had their "securities salesmen" call upon likely purchasers of newly issued bonds and stocks. By contrast, commercial banks, savings banks, and stock brokerage houses until recently felt that aggressive advertising and selling of their services would undermine public confidence in them. This reluctance to solicit personal financial patronage disappeared in the 1950's. Now banks offer premiums for the opening of new personal accounts and advertise these premium offers. Brokerage houses advertise on TV and radio as well as in financial journals, and their customer men ring doorbells to sell mutual funds and solicit trading accounts.

REVIEW

1. How is demand for industrial equipment and materials related to consumer demand?

2. In what ways does concentration of industrial purchasers affect industrial marketing?

3. How does industrial purchasing differ, with respect to organization and procedure, from mercantile purchasing of consumer goods? How do these differences affect the patterns and procedures of industrial marketing?

4. Evaluate the importance of seller reliability in the selection of industrial suppliers.

5. How do transportation costs affect the pattern of marketing of industrial materials?

6. Why is a major proportion of industrial equipment sold direct-to-user?

7. What is an "industrial distributor"? What is his place in industrial marketing?

8. What types of agent middlemen are found in industrial marketing?

9. For what classes of products and under what circumstances is the marketing of industrial materials and supplies done: (a) manufacturer-direct-to-user; (b) through full-service merchant distributors; (c) through drop shippers; (d) through agent middlemen?

10. Explain the growing popularity of leasing arrangements in the marketing of industrial equipment.

11. Describe and explain the marketing of business services.

12. Describe and explain the marketing of personal services.

DISCUSSION TOPICS

1. "Psychology has little to contribute to industrial advertising or selling."

2. "The structure of industrial marketing is much more efficient and cost-saving than that for the marketing of consumer goods."

3. "A company usually stands to lose rather than gain by allowing its purchasing of equipment, materials, or supplies to be influenced by considerations of reciprocity."

4. Should a manufacturer of industrial equipment or materials recruit its salesmen from engineering colleges or business colleges?

5. Contrast the place of middlemen in the marketing of industrial equipment with that of consumer goods middlemen. How do you account for the differences?

6. Contrast the place of middlemen in the marketing of industrial equipment and in the marketing of industrial materials and supplies. How do you account for the differences?

7. "The marketing problems of service enterprises are trifling beside those of manufacturers."

PROBLEM 1

Electro-Control, Inc., has been organized to manufacture and market a revolutionary new electronic control process for industrial production. A major Electro-Control system installed in a factory enables all of its "cycle" operations to be put on an automatic basis, and reports all these automatic operations, through gauges and dials, on a single central control board. A large number of individual machine attendants can thus be replaced by a small "flying squad" of mechanics, directed from the control board room, who make adjustments and repairs signalled by the control board. Such a major installation involves the use of special punch-cards and punch-tapes also made by

Electro-Control, Inc. These major installations cost from $10,000 to $100,000.

Electro-Control, Inc., also produces and sells smaller control units, costing from $50 to several hundred dollars, which may be attached to individual machines of various kinds to enable them to perform a cycle of operations automatically, stop them when anything in the cycle goes wrong, and signal the stoppage by a blinker light.

How should Electro-Control, Inc. market its systems and small units? Explain why.

PROBLEM 2

Winston Metal Foil Co. has developed a process for coating very thin metal foil with a carbon film. Tests show that it can be used as a typing "carbon paper" that will not wrinkle or curl; up to four copies at a time can be made, as sharp and clear as with regular good quality carbon paper. While more expensive on a per-sheet basis than a regular good quality carbon paper, it compares favorably costwise on a use-life basis.

The company is now studying the possibilities of marketing this item under the registered brand name "Metal-carb."

1. What are the possible channels of distribution, and which would be the best? Why?

2. Is this a product that should be advertised or otherwise promoted? If so, how?

PROBLEM 3

Alpha Steam Laundry faces hard times. More and more Center City residents are buying automatic washing machines or patronizing laundromats, and cutting down on the laundry they "send out." And Omega Laundry, Alpha's competitor in Center City, with approximately the same schedule of charges as Alpha, seems to be getting an increasing share of the dwindling amount of "sent-out" laundry.

Alpha has heretofore depended on its reputation for good, economical service, and has not used salesmen, agents, or any form of advertising. It uses five light trucks for collection and delivery.

What should Alpha do?

SUGGESTED READINGS

Alexander, R. S., and others, *Industrial Marketing,* Richard D. Irwin, Homewood, Ill., 1956.

Aries, R. S., & W. Copulsky, *The Marketing of Chemical Products,* R. S. Aries & Associates, Brooklyn, 1948.

Brown, N. C., *Lumber,* John Wiley & Sons, New York, 1948.

Corey, E. R., *The Development of Markets for New Materials,* Division of Research, Harvard Business School, Boston, 1956.

Friedman, W. F., & J. J. Kipness, *Industrial Packaging,* John Wiley & Sons, New York, 1960.

Lester, B., *Selling to Industry,* Industrial Press, New York, 1952.

Loberg, H. J., *Machine Tool Selling,* 2d ed, McGraw-Hill Book Co., New York, 1953.

Thayer, L. O., & G. E. Harris, *Sales and Engineering Representation,* McGraw-Hill Book Co., New York, 1958.

PERIODICALS: *Industrial Marketing, Industrial Distribution.*

PART FOUR

MARKETING OPERATIONS AND POLICIES

As indicated in Chapter 1, an infinity of marketing activities coalesces into a limited number of groups, each united by a specific distributional objective; we apply the term "operation" * to each such group of closely related marketing activities. A study of marketing operations is therefore an analysis of *what is done* in the course of distributing goods and services. This includes not only what is done by marketing institutions of the types studied in Part Two of this book, but also what is done by manufacturers, farmers, other producers, and other classes of business units whose major activity is not marketing, but which do participate in various ways in the movement of goods and services to their consumers and users.

The marketing operations of many small companies have developed in unplanned hit-or-miss fashion. Not so with large companies. At some stage in a company's growth it must subject its marketing op-

---

* Students should note that many Marketing writers use the term "marketing functions" to cover the concept of marketing operations and policies related to them.

erations to the discipline of *planning*. Thus *policy* enters the marketing picture. A study of marketing policy adds understanding of the *why* to the *what* of marketing operations.

When it comes to how to classify and subclassify marketing operations and policies, there is some diversity of opinion among Marketing writers. Some treat "assembling"—the grouping of small lots of fungible commodities into large lots and the grouping of related items into "lines" by certain classes of middlemen—as an independent set of marketing activities; others, present "assembling" as a special aspect of Buying. Likewise "dividing"—the splitting of large lots of a commodity into smaller lots for distribution by wholesalers to retailers and by retailers to consumers—is treated sometimes as a marketing operation in itself, sometimes as a subclassification of Selling. Some writers set apart the operations and policies involved in advertising and other forms of promotion as a separate activity grouping; others call them "indirect selling" and treat them as a phase of Selling. In some analyses Buying and Selling are combined in a classification called "activities of exchange," Transportation and Storage in a classification called "activities of physical supply," and Standardization, Marketing Research, Market Financing, and Market Risk Management in a classification of "auxiliary marketing activities."

We shall study *what is done* in Marketing and *why it is done* under the following topics:

1. Standardization and grading
2. Product planning
3. Buying (including assembling)
4. Storing
5. Pricing
6. Promotion, primarily through advertising
7. Selling
8. Procuring market information (including marketing research)
9. Credit extension
10. Transportation
11. Market financing
12. Market risk management
13. Manufacturers' marketing management

Standardization, which is not so much a marketing operation as a condition precedent for other marketing activities, and Grading, are dealt with at the very outset of our operations and policies analysis because an understanding of them is necessary to comprehend Product Planning, Buying, and many other marketing activities. After that, our study of marketing activities follows in a broad way the time sequence of these activities in a company as one of its products moves from the planning stage to ultimate customer delivery. Today, the initial marketing step for most manufactured commodities and for some farm crops is a "planning" of the product to maximize its market acceptability. Accordingly we move, with Product Planning, to this set of policies and activities. Next, for manufacturers, is the purchase of equipment, supplies, and materials needed for production of the planned commodities, whereas for most wholesalers and retailers the buying of the goods they intend to sell is the very start of their marketing effort; the policies and operations of Buying are therefore next on our list. An interval of storage usually follows purchase of materials and supplies, production of a commodity, or purchase of goods for resale. The sequence from Storage through Pricing, Promotion, Selling, Credit Extension, and Transportation is obvious. Procuring Market Information is an activity that overlaps Product Planning, Pricing, Promotion, and Selling; it is studied after Selling, not because this is its proper place in the time sequence of a company's marketing activities, but because a background of the other four operational and policy fields is needed for effective understanding of the uses of market information. Similarly, Market Financing and Market Risk Management have no particular place in a time sequence of marketing activities; their position in our list is arbitrary. A concluding summary survey of some aspects of manufacturers' Marketing Management shows how all the preceding market operation and policy activities are integrated in actual business practice.

Each of these operation and policy fields is studied from several viewpoints. Basic economic considerations that make the operation necessary, or that shape the policies associated with it, are analyzed. The relative place of the operation and associated policies in over-all distributional procedure, and for particular commodity classifications, is studied. Technical procedures associated with each operation are explored in some detail, for only through knowledge of these can any realistic understanding of a marketing operation be had. Policy analysis, in some cases, involves reference to federal or state law that limits or facilitates particular marketing policies. Where a special facilitating marketing institution is inextricably associated with the performance of a particular operation, as public warehouses are with Storage, or advertising agencies with Promotion, or various types of common carriers with Transportation, the institution is studied along with the operation.

CHAPTER 15

STANDARDIZATION AND GRADING

Standardization is the determination of basic limits or grade ranges in the form of uniform specifications to which particular manufactured goods may conform and uniform quality classes into which the products of agriculture and the extractive industries may be graded.* Many elements of manufactured consumer and industrial goods have been standardized, and the manufacturers of these goods embody the standardized features in their product designs. Standard quality grades have been established for most agricultural and extractive products, and the business world buys and sells these products on the basis of these standard grades. Shoe sizes, for example, have been standardized with uniform numbered length sizes increasing by one-third inch per size and uniform lettered width sizes increasing by one-sixth inch. Screw and bolt threads have been standardized by various width, depth, and angle dimensions. Standard grades for cotton are determined by fiber length, color, and imperfections.

Strictly speaking, standardization is not a Marketing *operation*. It is not a set of business activities regularly associated with the movement of goods from their producers to their ultimate consumers or users. It is an action taken once and once only, except for possible amendments, for any particular commodity, or element common to a number of commodities. This action is taken, not by the producers or distributors of a commodity acting

---

* This is the definition of *marketing* standardization. *Production* or *industrial* standardization, involving uniform specifications of product parts so that they can be interchangeable, is undertaken by the individual manufacturer and does not necessarily result in uniformity among products made by different manufacturers. Also to be distinguished from *marketing* standards for commodities are standards of *weight* and *measure,* established by the federal government.

individually but by outside agencies. It is an anticipatory or precedent one, and sets a pattern to which many of the Marketing operations and policies we shall study in subsequent chapters must conform. By contrast, grading is definitely a Marketing operation, performed regularly and consistently in the distribution of certain commodities.

STANDARDIZATION OF MANUFACTURED GOODS AND PROCESSED MATERIALS

In some consumer goods items, low-price novelty jewelry for example, there may be no standardized feature. An item of industrial equipment made to special order likewise may not embody any standardized element. Practically everything we eat, however, and most of what we wear, our household appliances, our automobiles and their equipment, our sporting goods, have one or more details for which their manufacturers had to take established Marketing standards into account.

Advantages

A number of important economic advantages, for producers and business buyers especially and sometimes for consumers, result from the establishing of standards for elements of manufactured goods and processed materials, and the production and marketing of such goods and materials in conformity with these standards:

1. Standardization makes it possible to have uniformity in similar items, and interchangeability of jointly used items produced by *different* manufacturers. Any standard electric light bulb produced by any manufacturer, for example, fits into any standard socket made by any manufacturer. Standardization may thus add to the utility of the items affected.

2. Because of this greater utility of standardized items, usually not associated with higher cost and higher price, the market for them is generally substantially wider than for corresponding unstandardized items.

3. Standardization often leads to simplification—reduction in the variety and models of an item produced by various manufacturers. The topic of simplification will be treated in Chapter 16.

4. Nonstandardized goods and materials must often be purchased on the basis of inspection, and sometimes detailed analysis, of samples. This is time-consuming, may be costly, and often requires expert knowledge on the part of the buyer. Standardized items can be referred to by the name, number, or symbol identifying the standard, and can be purchased by letter, telegraph, or telephone, without the buyer ever having to study a sample.

Bases

Of the many attributes that any manufactured commodity or processed material may have, only a few are ordinarily crucially pertinent to the reasons for its purchase. Only these pertinent market attributes are made the bases of marketing standardization. Standards for electric wire insulation are based on degree and consistency of nonconductivity, and upon durability under various conditions of indoor and outdoor use, because these factors measure the safety afforded by the insulation. In developing a set of standards for steel, the American Iron and Steel Institute first established a set of classifications by uses—as alloy steel, axles, carbon steel bars, cold-rolled strip steel—then proceeded to standardize chemical and alloy specifications for each class. Size standards for women's apparel, proposed by the U.S. Department of Commerce in 1954, were based upon body measurements of some 10,000 WACS.

The various factors or bases upon which several thousand materials and manufactured products have already been standardized are so multifarious as to defy any classification significant for analytical purposes. The following five-fold classification is submitted only to indicate to students of Marketing some of the complexities involved in establishing useful standards for manufactured items:

1. A readily comprehensible basis of standardization is physical dimensions. Random examples of this standardization factor are size specifications for paper bags, hypodermic needles, match boxes, bricks, steel joists, and wearing apparel, thread specifications for screw nuts and bolts, and thickness specifications for boxboard.

2. Physical quantitative elements other than dimensions are frequently employed as standardization bases. Cloths are standardized by thread count, bread by baked-loaf weight. The chemical or physical composition of many materials is standardized in this way.

3. Sometimes standardization is based on quantitative analysis of a commodity's performance. Coal grades are determined, among other factors, on the basis of thermal units—a measure of the heat produced upon burning. Standards developed by the Steel Joist Institute involve load capacities.

4. Sometimes standardization is effected on the basis of qualitative factors that can be given a quantitative expression. An excellent example is the accomplishment of the Textile Color Card Association in setting up specifications for over 200 staple colors and numerous seasonal fashion shades, so that descriptive terms for textile colors used by different manufacturers represent identical colors.

5. In the case of processed foods, drugs, and cosmetics, the stand-

ardization basis is a negative one. Such items must *not* contain specified harmful ingredients.

Agencies

Agencies that establish standards for processed materials and manufactured goods are the federal government and some state governments, trade associations, the American Society for Testing Materials, the American Standards Association, and the Commodity Standards Division of the federal Department of Commerce.

Very few standards for manufactured products are established by federal or state regulation. In nearly all cases, these legislation-authorized standards relate, directly or indirectly, to foods, drugs, or cosmetics. Two federal statutes, however—the Standard Barrel Act of 1915, and the Standard Container Act of 1916 and 1928—set specific size standards for barrels, baskets, and hampers intended for fresh fruits and vegetables. The Federal Security Administration, under the authority of the Food, Drug and Cosmetics Act of 1938, prohibits the sale of impure, harmful foods, drugs, and cosmetics, thereby establishing minimum quality standards in these fields.* A number of states have food and drug acts of their own, not always in conformity with federal law.

Trade associations are the most important agency in developing standards for processed materials and manufactured goods. Their work is rarely done independently, but in cooperation with the American Standards Association. This association, which has been a very potent force in promoting standardization of materials and manufactured products, was organized in 1918 by five national engineering societies to serve as a clearing house for coordinating their standardization activities. It was subsequently reorganized to expand its coverage into new industrial fields and to include consumer representation. As of 1959 the American Standards Association was composed of over a hundred trade associations, technical societies, government departments, and consumer organizations, and of over 2,000 corporations affiliated as company members.

The Commodity Standards Division of the U.S. Department of Commerce contributes to product standardization only through cooperative action. It establishes no product standards by itself. At the request of a trade association, the Division will gather information on a product, hold conferences, and make tests. In consultation with the association and the American Standards Association, it will devise suitable standards. These are submitted to the industry concerned. If 65 percent or more of the in-

---

* Standards for insecticides and naval stores are also controlled under federal legislation by the Federal Security Administration.

dustry approve, the Division publishes the approved specifications as a commercial standard.

With the exception of federal and state prohibitions on substandard foods, drugs and cosmetics, standards for materials and manufactured goods are permissive. Once formulated, however, they are closely adhered to and are generally self-enforcing. For one thing, standardization of a material or manufactured commodity is generally of great advantage to the producers, as we have already noted. Hence manufacturers' trade associations that have assumed the initiative in promoting standardization of their lines usually exercise pressure to have their members adopt and adhere to such standards. Also, because standardization specifications generally conform to the wishes and needs of major market elements in each field, the general market in any field adapts itself in a short time to the standards established for it. Consequently, any individual producer would find little or no market for a divergent product. Marketing substandard articles under misrepresentation that they conform to standard, besides constituting contractual breach of warranties that would be a foundation for damage suits, would be subject to action by the Federal Trade Commission, as explained in Chapter 30. Standard specifications, once they have been established, become a fundamental in product design.

STANDARDIZATION OF AGRICULTURAL PRODUCTS

Unlike standards for processed materials and manufactured goods, those for agricultural products are not categorical specifications to be embodied in product design, but are *quality classes* or grades to be assigned to individual units or lots of a commodity as they come into the market.

Advantages

Standardization of agricultural products, and grading in accordance with such standards, has five advantages:

1. Since buyers often desire only a particular grade, a mixed lot may contain many items with little or no utility to buyers. A mixed lot sorted into standard grades which can be sold separately accordingly has much greater over-all utility. Flour millers, for example, can order particular standard types and grades of grain producing particular qualities of flour, only because the grain elevators have previously consigned the grain brought to them by farmers or middlemen to standard grain class bins. Similarly, thanks to the grading of cotton according to the official standards, cotton mills can obtain the particular staple lengths and colors they desire for their spinning operations.

2. Cull (substandard) items in a mixed lot can be sorted out at the

production point, or close to it. There may be no general market for such culls, in which case the transportation costs which would be incurred by shipping them are saved. Or there may be a special-use market to which they can be routed, so that something is salvaged on them. Cull fruits, substandard as to size or external appearance, find a special market with fruit-juice producers.

3. As in the case of standardized manufactured products and materials, graded agricultural products can be bought and sold by standard grade reference, instead of sample and lot inspection. Marketing of such products is accordingly expedited, and marketing costs reduced.

4. Grade-identification buying makes possible hedging and financing on the security of warehouse receipts (both explained in Chapter 27). These two procedures are important facilitating elements in the marketing of several agricultural products.

5. Consumers are generally inexpert buyers, particularly when judging relative quality. Where standardized grades have been established for food products, and *if grade labelling is practiced* (as discussed in Chapter 30), consumers receive valuable guidance toward more effective purchasing.

Bases

As in the case of manufactured goods and materials, the bases for standardizing agricultural products are determined by market needs and wants. Factors that establish standard grades of cotton are length of fiber, color of the fiber, amount of foreign matter in the cotton, and fiber imperfections, because these factors determine the value of any lot of cotton to mills with particular textile objectives in mind. Based upon these factors, cotton is classified as American Upland, Egyptian, and Sea Island, with grade subdivisions for each of these. American Upland, for example, is subdivided into white and four other color classes, with 8 grades (Strict Good Middling, Good Middling, Strict Middling, Middling, Strict Low Middling, Low Middling, Strict Good Ordinary, Good Ordinary) specified for white and from 3 to 5 grades for each of the other classes. The specific determinants for each of these grades are samples maintained by the federal Department of Agriculture. Similarly, grain standards are based on the weight of the grain in relation to volume, its relative moisture content, the proportion of damaged to whole grains and particularly the proportion that may be heat-damaged, the proportion of foreign matter mixed in with the grain, and the relative intermixture of various grains; these factors establish the milling potentialities of a lot of grain.

OFFICIAL COTTON STANDARDS OF THE UNITED STATES FOR THE GRADE OF AMERICAN UPLAND COTTON

WHITE COTTON

Sec. 28.401 <u>Strict Good Middling</u>. Strict Good Middling shall be American upland cotton which in color, leaf, and preparation is better than Good Middling. This standard is effective on and after August 1, 1957.

Sec. 28.402 <u>Good Middling</u>. Good Middling shall be American upland cotton which in color, leaf, and preparation is within the range represented by a set of samples in the custody of the United States Department of Agriculture in the District of Columbia in a container marked "Original Official Cotton Standards of the United States, American Upland, Good Middling, effective August 1, 1954."

Sec. 28.403 <u>Strict Middling</u>. Strict Middling shall be American upland cotton which in color, leaf, and preparation is within the range represented by a set of samples in the custody of the United States Department of Agriculture in the District of Columbia in a container marked "Original Official Cotton Standards of the United States, American Upland, Strict Middling, effective August 15, 1953."

EXCERPT FROM U.S. DEPARTMENT OF AGRICULTURE'S COTTON STANDARDS SPECIFICATIONS

ILLUSTRATION 15–1

Agencies

The major agency for establishing agricultural product standards is the federal Department of Agriculture, under authority granted it by a series of laws, the first of which was passed in 1914. Nearly 200 farm products are now subject to Department of Agriculture standardization. The standards so established for cotton, grain, and tobacco are compulsory. The others are all permissive. However, grades according to federal standards must be shown on warehouse receipts for products stored under provisions of the federal Warehouse Act. A warehouse receipt that lacked such a statement of the grades of the stored products could not be accepted as collateral for a loan by a national bank and would not be so accepted by many state banks. So there is a strong compulsive element in these nominally permissive federal standards.

Several states have set standards for particular farm products, in some cases conflicting with the federal standards. Standards for coffee, sugar, rubber, cocoa, hides, tin butter, eggs, cottonseed oil, and other products traded on commodity exchanges were established by the exchanges; Department of Agriculture standards on these items are merely endorsements of the exchange standards.

GRADING OF AGRICULTURAL PRODUCTS

Farm crops cannot be produced to blueprint specifications, like manufactured goods. Chances of weather, and differences in seed, soil, and cultivation techniques, result in wide variations in the quality of harvested crops. For marketing purposes, these varying lots of farm produce must be *graded*—i.e., predetermined standard quality classifications must be assigned to individual units or lots of a commodity. Grading is accomplished in two ways—by sorting, and by sample inspection.

When the units of a product are of substantial size, as in the case of fruits, they are individually *sorted* into their standard grade classes. Sometimes this sorting is performed by the farmers themselves before they market their crops, sometimes by middlemen in the marketing chain. Farmers' cooperatives have assumed this sorting function to a substantial extent. Most sorting is still done by hand, but considerable mechanization of this operation is now taking place, particularly where the grading is done by cooperatives or large middlemen.

The second method of grading is to *inspect a sample* from a lot of a particular commodity and assign a standard grade to the lot on the basis of the sample. This is done when the units are not of a size or consistency to permit of individual handling. Tobacco, meat, grains, cotton, wool, other exchange-traded commodities, and certain classes of vegetables are graded in this fashion, as are certain processed foods such as cheese and canned fruits and vegetables. Sometimes this assignment of grades to lots is done on the basis of scientific testing of the samples, as in the grading of milk by the Babcock test for butter-fat content. Often it rests on the subjective basis of visual estimate, or tasting, or smelling, by experienced individuals. In some cases these experts are employees or principals of middleman firms whose judgment is accepted as authoritative throughout the market. Where such private expert opinion is not available or is not accepted, sellers or buyers may have produce graded by inspectors licensed by the federal Department of Agriculture. These licensed inspectors are in some cases employees of state agencies or of the commodity exchanges. In other cases they operate independently and charge prescribed fees for their services. The Department of Agriculture has established an organization for handling appeals from the findings of these licensed inspectors.

REVIEW

1. Explain standardization. What are its advantages in the case of manufactured goods? of agricultural products?
2. Who sets standards for manufactured products and materials?

3. How do standards for agricultural products differ from those for most manufactured goods?

4. Who sets standards for agricultural products? Are such standards compulsory or permissive?

5. Explain grading of agricultural products. How is it done? Who does it?

DISCUSSION TOPICS

1. Shouldn't there be federal legislation providing that, once the trade association of an industry has established marketing standards for that industry, all manufacturers of the products involved must conform to such standards or become subject to cease-and-desist orders by the Federal Trade Commission?

2. Shouldn't all agricultural standards be made mandatory?

3. "Government-established standards for agricultural products are one more example of the bad results of government interference in business matters. The 'standards' established by the Department of Agriculture are broad quality ranges. Sellers are legally free to mislead buyers by offering the minimum permissible quality within the range of each contract standard grade."

PROBLEM

Most manufacturers of briar pipes do not make the mouthpieces that are screwed or set into their pipes, but purchase them.

Several briar pipe manufacturers are wondering whether any action should be taken to standardize their product.

1. What elements or features of briar pipes might be standardized?

2. What, if any, would be the advantages of such standardization?

3. If such standardization is to be undertaken, how should the interested manufacturers go about accomplishing it?

SUGGESTED READINGS

Coles, J. V., *Standards and Labels for Consumers' Goods,* Ronald Press, New York, 1949.

Martino, R. A., *Standardization Activities of National Technical and Trade Organizations,* Miscellaneous Publication M-169, National Bureau of Standards, U.S. Department of Commerce, Washington, D.C., 1941.

CHAPTER 16

PRODUCT PLANNING

The first field of marketing policy and operations for every manufactured product and some agricultural products is planning what items will be made and their finished forms to the exact detail.

The product-planning decisions made by manufacturers, and by those farmers who specifically endeavor to conform their crops to market demands, have far-reaching effects, both for themselves, and upon the national economy. Success or failure for the particular manufacturer, and to some extent for the particular farmer, may turn substantially on the soundness of his judgment in product planning. The material richness of the American way of life for most classes of our population derives to a considerable extent from the constant effort of our manufacturers to develop products that meet the myriad special needs and tastes of particular market groups.

Our study of product planning will explore four aspects of this broad subject: (1) new product ventures, (2) broadening the scope of production, (3) product design, and (4) packaging.

NEW PRODUCTS

Except for fashion lines, most of the items manufactured in any year are identical with last year's market successes, or are close derivatives of them. There is a reasonable short-run probability, unless extraneous circumstances intervene, that what the market bought last year in sufficient volume and at high enough prices to yield a profit to the producers will continue to sell at a profitable level this year. But the profit on any well-established item, or a close imitation of it, is likely to be moderate, with a declining trend. The initial success that established it on the market breeds competition. Unless some fundamental feature of the product has patent protection, other companies reproduce it, or offer close imitations, often in improved form or at lower prices. Even when there is patent protection, new products may come upon the market which accomplish or surpass the purposes of the patented item and cut into its sales, as the electric shaver did to the safety razor. Against the short-run probability of continued success with an established product must be set the long-run probability that its successful market life will be a limited one.

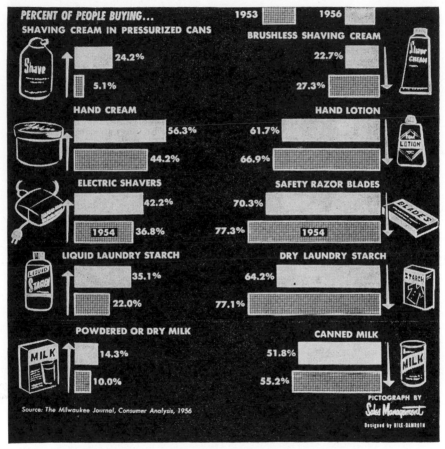

PERCENT OF PEOPLE BUYING... 1953 1956

SHAVING CREAM IN PRESSURIZED CANS
24.2%
5.1%

BRUSHLESS SHAVING CREAM
22.7%
27.3%

HAND CREAM
56.3%
44.2%

HAND LOTION
61.7%
66.9%

ELECTRIC SHAVERS
42.2%
1954 36.8%

SAFETY RAZOR BLADES
70.3%
77.3% 1954

LIQUID LAUNDRY STARCH
35.1%
22.0%

DRY LAUNDRY STARCH
64.2%
77.1%

POWDERED OR DRY MILK
14.3%
10.0%

CANNED MILK
51.8%
55.2%

PICTOGRAPH BY
Sales Management
Designed by HILE-BAMROTH

Source: The Milwaukee Journal, Consumer Analysis, 1956

COMPETITION BETWEEN NEW PRODUCTS AND OLD. *Courtesy of Sales Management.*

ILLUSTRATION 16–1

Almost every aggressive American manufacturer is constantly endeavoring to prolong the market life of the items he makes by improving them. More than that, forward-looking manufacturers and many individuals who seek to become manufacturers, are ever alert to the possibility of bringing new products upon the market; some companies provide for a "new products division" in their organizational structure. A successful new product can revivify a manufacturing business with a line whose market position is slipping. It can become the basis for expansion of a business already doing well. It can be the foundation upon which a new manufacturing business is started. And always there is the lure of the jackpot gains that reward the

A PRODUCT DEVELOPMENT LABORATORY. *Courtesy of E. I. DuPont de Nemours & Co.*

ILLUSTRATION 16–2

producer of a new "world-beating" item. The flow of new products onto the American market is simply fabulous. During the second half of the 1950's, in the food field alone, no less than 5,000 new items appeared each year. Over two-fifths of drug store sales in 1960 were of products introduced during the preceding five years.

Most new products are *adaptations*. An adaptation is a pre-existing item that has been substantially modified or added to, rather than merely improved in some detail. The electric refrigerator incorporating a deep-freeze unit, and light-weight ladders made of magnesium instead of wood, are examples of adaptations. An adaptation may improve upon the original, so that it can command a higher price. Or it may be of poorer quality, to be sold at an "economy" price. Adaptations coming upon the market have a fair probability of success, since the producer has the market experience of the original as a guide. Often a product that failed to win a market in its original form, succeeds in an adapted form because the adaptation eliminates certain weaknesses of the original.

A small proportion of each year's "new" products are true *innovations*— items intended to accomplish something not accomplished before, or to accomplish it in a radically different way. Thus radio, TV, each man-made fiber in turn, tranquilizer tablets, electric razors, the chain-saw, was each, in its initial market years, an innovation. Market success and profit returns on some innovations are staggering, and this is the lure that prompts many large corporations to appropriate millions of dollars every year to their research laboratories, and that entices individual inventors and their backers into starting businesses to produce and market the inventions. But most innovations prove to be market failures. Over 98 percent of all innovations introduced in the two years following World War II failed to win market acceptance; in general, less than one-fifth of new product ventures are profitable.

A large proportion of innovations and adaptations are manufactured and brought upon the market by small-scale manufacturers. In many cases, indeed, these new products are the basis of new business ventures. The inventor or adaptor and his backers start a business based exclusively on the new product, and its success or failure depends upon that of the product. These small-scale producers of new products generally build their expectation of success on two considerations: (1) their belief that their products are items which the market wants or can be induced, by promotion and selling, to want; and (2) a patent * that gives a new product protection from the competition of identical items manufactured by other producers, or in the absence of a patent the expectation that prior appearance of their new product will give them a profitable temporary quasi-monopoly before other manufacturers can market imitations. Too often these small manufacturers offer a new product before technical "bugs" have been completely eliminated. Too often they fail to check in advance whether their new product meets a pre-existing market need, or they neglect to create a demand for it by adequate advertising and other forms of promotion. It is these

---

* The nature of a patent is discussed in Chapter 30.

small-scale producers who are responsible for most of the innovations that fail.

Large-scale producers rarely base their new-product ventures on blind belief. They test technical performance of a new item exhaustively before committing themselves to its definitive design. They employ the procedures of marketing research, discussed in Chapter 23, to predetermine the market possibilities of any new products under consideration, and to guide them in adapting such products to market preferences. Favorable results from such "marketing presearch" are not a guaranty of the subsequent success of the new product, but do indicate reasonable probability of sucess. Unfavorable "presearch" returns may usually be taken as a warning that the new product, as it stands, will be a market failure, and that a stubborn attempt to force it upon an unwilling market will only pyramid losses.

Unsound pricing, inadequate promotion, and poor selling may rob a promising new product of success that it properly deserves. But the most brilliant promotion and selling can rarely establish profitable sales volume for an item whose basic service characteristics do not conform to some body of market demand. The only sound basis for decision to manufacture a new item is reasonable certainty that a substantial number of buyers will want the basic services yielded by the product at the price asked for it.

BROADENING THE SCOPE OF PRODUCTION

Few successful manufacturing enterprises remain long at the stage of manufacturing only one item in one single style or model. The impetus of business growth that comes with success soon forces them to face three issues of expansion: (1) Shall they "diversify" or "specialize" their product —i.e. develop it in variant styles and models—and how far should such product diversification be carried? (2) Shall they expand their production and marketing to embrace a "line" of related items in a particular product field, such as a "line" of packaged breakfast foods, or of canned vegetables or fruits, or of sporting goods, or of machine tools? (3) Shall they expand their production and marketing to embrace items, or lines of items, in unrelated product fields? The alternative decisions on each of these three issues present advantages and disadvantages. Where the balance of advantage and disadvantage lies in a particular case is usually hard to determine. Whether a compromise of maximum advantage and minimum disadvantage can be worked out, often involves difficult and crucial decisions on the part of management.

Product diversification

Manufacture and sale of an article in variant styles and models is commonly called "diversifying" or "specializing" the article.

Sometimes variations in the size or quality of an item are necessary to accommodate varying basic market needs. No one size of men's or women's shoes could fit more than a small fraction of the feet that must be shod. A 4-cubic-foot refrigerator would be almost as useless to a large family as no refrigerator. A family that could pay $50 for a table model radio might have to do without a radio altogether if only $500 console models were available.

Often the choice between different styles and models of an item satisfies only secondary market preferences. A family that wanted a 6½-cubic-foot refrigerator because such size was available would probably derive nearly the same satisfaction from a 6-foot size. Although sales of every one of ten different styles of a woman's shoe might be made if all ten styles were offered, most of the buyers would probably be equally satisfied if their choice were limited to two or three styles.

Regardless of whether the purchases of variant styles and models of a product are attributable to basic market needs or to secondary preferences, reasonable diversification by any manufacturer commonly enables him to tap elements of market demand that might not be won to a single or "staple" style of the product. Often a successful "specialty" model or design gives the producer a limited monopoly position in relation to the fraction of the market that prefers the specialty—the market "core" for the specialty—so that he can charge a higher price for it.

Product simplification

Product diversification is often overdone. So many diversified variants of a commodity may be produced for so many small fractions of the market that important economies of large-scale production and efficiencies of large-scale distribution are sacrificed. When a manufacturer, or a group of manufacturers, discovers that a product has been overdiversified, a reverse process of "simplification" *—i.e., reduction in the variety of sizes, styles, and models offered—must be introduced.

Simplification of a product may yield seven advantages: (1) manufacture of fewer models in larger quantities may be more economical, making

---

* Many writers on Marketing topics confuse "simplification" and "standardization," and use the latter term as including the former. Such practice wastes a valuable distinction between the two terms which is carefully preserved in this book (the subject of "standardization" was covered in the preceding chapter). In their general Marketing reading, students should analyze carefully any use of the term "standardization" to ascertain the meaning given to it by the writer.

possible greater profits, or lower prices, or a combination of both; (2) there is less likelihood of style obsolescence of individual models; (3) the same sales volume can be achieved with a smaller inventory, leading to economies resulting from more rapid turnover by manufacturers, distributors, and retailers; (4) advertising and selling, concentrated on fewer models, may become more efficient; (5) delivery may be improved, since fewer types of packing may be needed, and there is less likelihood of errors in shipment; (6) distributor and retailer goodwill is enhanced, since they also obtain the second, third, fourth, and fifth of the above advantages; and (7) there may be added consumer goodwill because of lower prices and improved dealer service.

Product simplification may be achieved in two ways—action by an individual manufacturer, or group action.

Individual manufacturer action. Occasionally an individual manufacturer who has overdiversified a product can simplify it merely by discontinuing production of the styles or models for which there is least demand, and concentrating production on those models for which demand is most intense. Such action usually lowers unit costs, and enables the manufacturer to offer the narrower range of styles at lower prices or at wider profit margins, with increased profit. Sometimes a manufacturer can accomplish simplification by making a single basic model, or a few basic models, with considerable diversification accomplished through variation in such superficial elements as color or decoration, or through association of the basic model with a variety of accessories. The automobile manufacturers have accomplished this happy compromise between diversification and simplification. Each of them makes one or two basic motor and chassis combinations, offers a limited choice of body styles, offers each body style in a fairly wide choice of colors, and finally presents a still wider choice of optional accessories. Individual tastes are catered to, with but little sacrifice in manufacturing economy.

Group action. In highly competitive lines of business, or in fields where there has been little development of market analysis, product diversification by many of the producers may be greater than is desirable both in the producers' and the consumers' interests. Yet no single manufacturer may dare to act alone in simplifying his style or model offerings, or perhaps none of the manufacturers realizes that he would derive an advantage from simplification. In such case, if desirable product simplification is to be achieved, it must be brought about by some outside agency. Trade associations often accomplish a great service for their members, and for consumers or users, by inducing a group of their competing members to act cooperatively on product simplification. The American Standards Association and the Commodity Standards Division of the federal Department of Commerce work closely with the country's trade associations in sponsoring and promoting product simplifications. Through these cooperative efforts, to take three examples, the types of steel poles for electric wires were reduced from 1,400 to 16, the sizes of steel heating boilers were reduced from 2,328 to 30, the sizes of a group of flat veneer products were reduced from 29 to 8.

Line expansion

Successful production and sale of some single article commonly leads a manufacturer to develop a "line" of related items, for three reasons. First, it is natural for a producer to assume that the success that attended his initial article will extend to ventures with similar articles. Second, within limits, the expansion of production resulting from line expansion may not be accompanied by a proportional increase of overhead, so that unit *production* costs on the larger volume may be somewhat lower. Third, substantial economies of *distribution* and other *distributive* advantages are almost certain. Among these distributive advantages are: (1) goodwill developed for a brand name by any one product in the line may be associated with that brand name when it is used for the other products of the line; (2) the company's advertising is likely to be more productive when it promotes a broad line than when it is limited to a single product; (3) unit costs of selling are likely to be reduced because orders obtained by salesmen for a group of products in the line should be larger than those for a single product; (4) if the line is expanded to a point where it covers the full scope of retailers' needs for such a field of goods, it may be possible and more profitable to sell direct to retailers instead of through wholesalers.

A manufacturing concern may expand its line by having its own research or engineering department develop the required new items. Often, however, a short cut is taken by acquiring, through outright purchase or by exchange of stock, smaller companies that are already manufacturing items that will serve to expand the larger company's line.

Expansion into unrelated product fields

Ordinarily the advantages noted above of developing a "line" of related products do *not* apply to expansion into unrelated product fields. Under certain circumstances, however, a manufacturer is warranted in making such expansion.

A manufacturing process may result in some by-product, quite unrelated in character to the basic objective of the manufacture, for which a profitable market exists. It would be folly to treat such a by-product as waste. The proper course of action is to perfect it and set up appropriate distributive machinery for it. Processing and marketing residue by-products of petroleum distillation has long been a profitable side line for oil companies. Packing houses are traditionally supposed to have found a profitable application of every part of the hogs they slaughter except the squeal.

A second circumstance that warrants producing unrelated products is that such manufacture may profitably employ equipment that cannot be used to full capacity on the producer's major activity. Many metal-working shops make wire nails when certain of their machines are otherwise unoccupied; indeed, during World War II there was a serious shortage of such nails because these shops were working at full capacity on war orders.

The manufacturer of a seasonal product may undertake production and sale of an altogether different type of product, involving perhaps completely different machines and equipment, with a contra-seasonal variation, to provide balanced year-round activity for his factory and selling forces. A manufacturer of farm and garden implements, that sold primarily in spring and summer, developed a line of sleds for winter sale. A metal toy manufacturer, whose sales were concentrated in the winter season, balanced his production and selling with a summer line of electric fans. Several breweries for this reason have expanded into candy manufacture, since the consumption peak of the latter in winter offsets the slump in beer consumption during that season.

Finally, entry into new product lines may be forced upon a manufacturer if technological innovation or style change wipes out the market for his basic line. What choice, other than failure, did a flypaper maker have when chemical flysprays were perfected, or a hairpin manufacturer when women ceased wearing their hair long, except to enter upon some new field of production?

PRODUCT DESIGN

Development of a product that satisfies some particular market need, or which the market can be educated to want, through advertising and other promotional techniques, is only the first step in making the product a marketing success. The second step—and it is a paramount one—is product design.

There are four objectives of product design: (1) to maximize the basic utility, or combination of utilities, of the product; (2) to incorporate in the product a maximum of supplementary utilities, thereby enhancing its quality; (3) to incorporate "selling design" in the product; and (4) to plan design so as to minimize product costs.

Maximizing basic utility

No manufacturer dare rest satisfied with the present level of effectiveness or efficiency of any of his products. He must improve, improve, improve each item. If he doesn't, his competitor will. His competitor does, anyway. And so, year by year the product designers add to the inherent utility of consumer and industrial goods. Automobiles are given more power, automatic gear-shift, and directional signals, because these add to their vehicular effectiveness; since automobiles are intended to be seen as well as heard, their body styling has evolved and they are currently produced, unlike the original Fords "in any color the customer wants so long as it is black," in all the colors of the spectrum. A rage for color has swept major product fields, and kitchen and bathroom installations and telephone sets have taken on pastel tints, for color is part of the basic utility of items that enter household decor. The typewriter is given tabulation stops, automatic margin stops, adjustable key tension, and finally is electrified, because these make it more efficient as a typewriter. Every manufactured product used by consumers or industry, from ant poisons to zinc plating electrodes, is being improved year after year by its makers.

And so we have the first injunction of marketing management to its product designers—by one means or another, add to the basic utility of the product as it now stands, and *keep on adding*. In competitive lines, the alternative to product improvement is usually cutting the price of the un-improved product. Price cutting can be answered by immediate counter-price-cutting. To product improvement, however, there is no immediate competitive reply.

Incorporating supplementary utilities

A fundamental point in manufacturing success, but one that many small producers fail to grasp, is that a product may be designed to embody more than one utility—i.e., service desired by some market group. The greater the number and importance of the supplementary utilities embodied in the product, the greater is its over-all utility. Market success for any commodity, disregarding for the moment the factors of promotion and selling, depends rather on its composite utility than on its basic utility alone. Where competing products offer approximately the same basic utility, the market success of one and failure of another may turn essentially on the presence of some supplementary utility in the first product and its absence in the second. Sales of one letter envelope manufacturer surged far ahead of the general trend when he added mint flavor to the gum used on the flap. A ball-point pen whose cap incorporated a small spring scale to weigh letters to determine postage enjoyed sweeping sales at nearly double the price of otherwise comparable pens.

Many of the supplementary utilities developed as elements of product design are ephemeral, here this season, gone the next. The test of the sales counter proves that they have no market value. Or their only market value is novelty, and when this wears off they must be replaced with other de-

BEAUTY ADDED TO FUNCTIONAL UTILITY IN KITCHEN-WARE DESIGN. *Courtesy of Raymond Loewy Associates.*

ILLUSTRATION 16–3

sign novelties. But some supplementary utilities eventually so merge with the basic utility of the product in which they are incorporated that they become an essential part of it. Today's automatic laundry, the automobile, the airplane, the typewriter, the oil furnace—each is a composite of many features added initially as supplementary improvements but which have since become inseparable basic utilities of these products.

Product improvement and price

By adding to the comparative acceptability of a product by enhancing its fundamental utility or incorporating additional supplementary utilities in it, a manufacturer widens and intensifies market demand for it. But added quality usually involves higher production costs—and higher price for the article. The higher price is likely to discourage some of the demand that might exist for a lower-quality item at a lower price. There may be sufficient market for a high-price high-quality item embodying more basic utility or several supplementary utilities to warrant a manufacturer's directing his entire design policy toward that objective. But it could also be sound design policy to sacrifice many of the improvements or supplements that might be incorporated in a product—to aim specifically at a lower-quality product—in order to be able to offer an item at a lower price to those elements of the market that prefer foregoing the added utilities to paying the higher price. Or, finally, many manufacturers find it possible to adopt the profitable compromise of designing a diversified *line* of models that incorporate successive increments of added utility and sell at successively higher prices.

Selling design

In many cases a product designer who limited his efforts to incorporating maximum functional efficiency and continuing emotional satisfaction in his product would miss an important marketing consideration—"selling design" or "point-of-purchase appeal."

The outward shape and design of an electric toaster, which not only toasts bread but adds to the decor of a well-set table, is part of the utility of the toaster. But the streamlined curves or architectonic planes of an electric iron generally yield no emotional pleasure to a housewife who owns such an iron. If she does her own ironing she is in no mood to appreciate the esthetics of style. Nor is an electric iron an item to be displayed to friends or acquaintances for "snob satisfaction." Nevertheless, streamlining an electric iron, or giving it a striking plane structure, helps to sell it because such design elements capture the eye of the buyer, when the iron is pictured in advertisements or is seen on a store shelf or counter. The esthetic appeal is only momentary, but in the crucial moment while the buyer is considering the purchase it accomplishes its objective—it *sells* the iron. The styling of the iron is directed at "point-of-purchase appeal."

The great field for "selling design" is packaging, discussed later in this chapter. There are two possibilities of incorporating "selling design" in products themselves. One is the "styling" of items whose uses, after the moment of purchase, preclude any possibility of esthetic satisfaction, as in the example above of an electric iron.* The other is the incorporation of supplementary utilities, often of a "gadget" character, whose actual contribution to the purchaser's satisfaction after purchase is insignificant, but which make good "talking points" for salesmen of the product. Few owners of console radios use the short-wave bands after the first week's fiddling for "distance," but the radio manufacturers have found that the curiosity appeal of foreign short-wave stations is such a strong selling point that hardly any console sets omit this feature.

Cost considerations

Cost of production can never be ignored in product design. If one design having a certain utility and point-of-purchase appeal can be produced at a lower cost than an alternative one with identical utility and appeal, the first will yield a larger unit profit, or permit sale at a lower price with corresponding increase in sales volume. Product designers must always take into consideration: (1) the relative costs of alternative materials; (2) the standard sizes in which materials are available, as they will affect wastage; (3) the equipment available to accomplish particular design results, or the relative cost of equipment that would have to be purchased to accomplish alternative design results; (4) the unit labor time necessary to produce particular design details; (5) the relative labor skills needed (and hence the relative labor costs involved) to produce alternative design effects; (6) relative breakage; and (7) other handling costs that might be associated with different designs.

While the product designer should, and generally does, have production cost factors in mind as he evolves a design, a comprehensive cost determination frequently cannot be made until the design has crystallized into tentative form. Then, quite often, it is discovered that production costs will run too high to allow a profit at the anticipated price, or in fact to break even on the venture. If the producer is in a quasi-monopoly position with respect to the new product, he may be able to change his pricing plans and set an ultimate price higher than the one originally anticipated. When the field is competitive and the new product or new design must meet an established market price, the designers are compelled to "shave the product"—they must alter their designs to allow substitution of cheaper, lower-

---

* Sight is not the only sense that may be appealed to in selling-design styling. Some brands of women's stockings and lingerie are delicately perfumed (after marketing research had determined the most effective scent) to make subconscious appeal to the shopper's nose. For the same reason, some brands of men's gloves—or the cases containing them—are sprayed with a transient artificial leather scent.

quality materials than were comprehended in the original plan, or eliminate features of the product that require special equipment, or high-cost production or assembly operations. Sometimes such "shaving" reduces the utility and appeal of the product hardly at all. Usually, however, the "shaving" results in some reduction of quality accompanied by a much greater relative reduction of cost, so that the new design is a market practicality where the original one was not.

PACKAGING

Packaging is a special aspect of product planning concerned with the designing of product containers. It has become the basis of a major indus-try; it is estimated that 600 billion packages a year—paper containers, cardboard boxes, paper and plastic bags, bottles, jars, cans, tubes—are currently produced at a cost of $10 billion. Demand creation for many consumer items actually owes more to packaging than to design elements of the products themselves.

Package design has four objectives: (1) to maximize container effec-tiveness, (2) to add selling design to articles whose inherent character precludes point-of-purchase appeal, (3) to serve other promotional pur-poses, and (4) to minimize transportation and storage costs.

Successful achievement of the first three of these objectives may add substantially to the market success of a product; sometimes it is a funda-mental element, as in the case of home fire extinguishers packaged in air-spray cans. Currently, packaging is one of the most dynamic fields of manufacturers' marketing effort.

Utility considerations

Goods sold by weight or measure instead of by units, such as liquids, salt, and many foodstuffs, require some sort of package-container for their ultimate delivery by retailers to consumers. Most packages, however, pro-vide other important service utilities besides that of mere containing. Modern packaging protects food items from contamination from the time of machine processing to the moment when the package is opened by the consumer. Air-tight packages preserve the contents from spoilage produced by air-borne bacteria. "Vacuum packing" of ground coffee in metal con-tainers enables it to retain its full flavor. Packages may be designed to facilitate dispensing their contents, as in the case of projectible pouring spouts on salt boxes, the familiar squeezable tube used for all sorts of slow-flowing substances from toothpastes to plastic wood, ball-bearing deodorant applicators, or aerosol cans used for a growing variety of products includ-ing foods. Because of the greater convenience to consumers, as well as

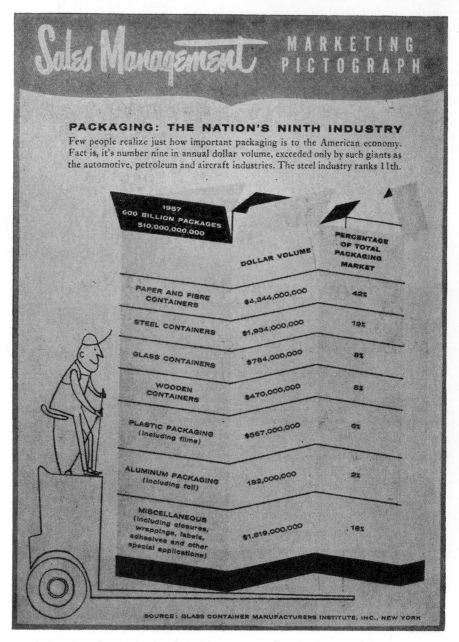

PACKAGING: THE NATION'S NINTH INDUSTRY. *Courtesy of Sales Management.*

ILLUSTRATION 16–4

elimination of handling costs and troubles for retailers and manufacturers, deposit containers have been almost completely supplanted by disposable containers.

In planning a package as a container, a decision must be made as to content volume. Many package sizes are custom-determined—the quarter or pint container for milk and other liquid items, for example, and the pound package for sugar, salt, soap powder, and thousands of other items. Recently, considerable marketing research has been applied to the subject of package size, and it has been discovered that many custom-established package sizes do not conform to the desires of important segments of the market for the packaged items. As a result, there is a current movement to diversify package sizes for many products—canned foods are offered in single-serving "minipacks," beer in "king-size" cans as well as the regular 12-fluid-ounce cans, detergents in "small," "regular," "large," "economy," and "giant" packages. It has also been discovered that "multiple" packaging—providing "carrier cartons" which hold two, three, four, or six regular size cans or bottles—substantially increases the sales of some items even though no price-saving is attached to the multiple purchase; in a test with cans of sardines, a four-can "pack" increased sales 34 percent, and a six-can "pack" 29 percent. "Multipacks" also prove to be effective media for introducing new products in an established line, for combining related products, for "gift combinations," and to give small items better shelf display impact.

A package may be planned to have a secondary noncontainer use. Some jellies and cheeses, for example, are packaged in decorative tumblers which are used for table purposes after their contents have been consumed. Breakfast cereal boxes have cut-out designs printed on them for children's play-pleasure when the boxes are empty.

Selling design

Style is rarely a true consumer utility in packages, yet infinite care and attention are given to package styling. The reason for this is the point-of-purchase appeal an effective package gives to a product which in itself cannot be made to embody selling design. Self-service retailing, firmly established in the food field by the development of the supermarket, and gradually being extended to other product fields, has magnified the importance of selling design in packaging. Pie-crust flour by itself has little point-of-purchase appeal, but the color and general design composition of its package may be planned to catch the eye of a housewife passing along the shelves of a self-service food store; the picture adorning it of a cut of pie may look so luscious that the housewife cannot resist giving it at least an initial trial. Dried peas make their purchase appeal in windowed boxes asparkle with dream-dust, and household ammonia in bottles modeled on the towers of the Taj Mahal. Package selling-appeal is not limited to goods sold by measure or weight. Hundreds of items of men's and women's wear have their sales-counter appeal magnified by packaging that catches the eye. Packaging is employed to add selling design to articles as humble as dish cloths, as well as to hunting rifles costing hundreds of dollars.

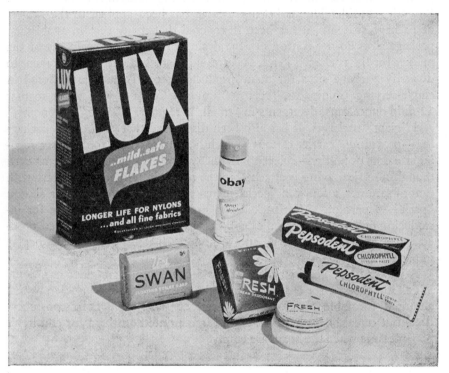

"POINT-OF-PURCHASE APPEAL" PACKAGING. *Courtesy of Raymond Loewy Associates.*

ILLUSTRATION 16–5

Promotional considerations

A counter or shelf display of a packaged item may make an immediate self-selling point-of-purchase appeal to some customers who thereupon buy. It may also act as a reminder advertisement to others who do not buy at the moment; at some later time subconscious recall of it may contribute to their decision to buy the item. In the case of packaged foods, as long as the package stays on a pantry shelf, and each time the item is dispensed, the package does a repeat job of reminder advertising. Package designers generally consider the advertising potentialities of a package as important as its point-of-purchase appeal. Brand names and trademarks—the very foundation of most forms of advertising, as explained in Chapter 21—are given prominent position on nearly all packages. In this connection, recent years have seen the redesigning of many packages so that their visual impact and trademark identification will be more effective in TV commercials. The labelling of packages is planned with as much of an eye to long-term promotional effect as to the immediate education of the purchaser on the contents of the package.

Transportation and storage considerations

Besides the three major considerations of utility, selling design, and promotional potentiality, a package designer must give thought to how the dimensions and shape of a package will affect its transportation and storage. Oblong rectangular packages with proper dimensions can be packed in standard shipping cartons without waste of space, and make effective "tower" displays on retail counters. Curved and odd-shaped packages with more selling design may involve high shipping and storage costs. Glass bottles with effective selling design for packaged liquids are more fragile and are likely to weigh more than metal cans, involving higher shipping costs. These conflicting considerations are usually not amenable to compromise, and the package designer must often choose between a selling design advantage and a transportation and storage advantage.

Cost considerations

Modern packaging definitely adds to manufacturers' costs, and therefore to prices. Even for such lines as hardware and automotive parts, where manufacturers are still backward on packaging policy, average packaging costs are from 4 to 5% of manufacturers' prices. A recent study indicated that packaging costs for 98 food manufacturers were 10% of sales. For drugs, cosmetics, and toiletries these costs exceed 35%. For inks and adhesives they are around 40%.

To the extent that the higher costs of modern packaging enhance container utility, consumers receive added value for the higher prices they pay. Where the higher costs are attributable to incorporation or intensification of selling design, consumers get nothing for the higher prices paid. To the extent that the selling design of the packages of a line of goods induces greater buying of the line as a whole, however, there is probably a general economic gain. But if the selling design of the packages merely switches or holds demand among the various competing brands in the line, much of the packaging cost may be clear economic waste.

ORGANIZATION FOR PRODUCT DESIGN

In a few instances, purchasers dictate to manufacturers the design elements that must be embodied in the items ordered. Much industrial equipment is produced to specifications prepared by the purchaser. Large mail-order houses, department stores, and chain store systems may specify to manufacturers the design particulars of consumer good items to be sold under the retailer's brand label.

Generally, however, product design is the manufacturer's responsibility. Large companies commonly have a "design division," usually part of the engineering or production department, whose sole function is to evolve new products and new product designs. Smaller organizations may have a principal who has design talent, or may employ a single designer. Increasing use is being made of the services of product design specialists, called "industrial designers," such as the Raymond Loewy Associates. These consultant organizations are prepared to add selling design to the specifications of an egg beater, a turret lathe, a pill box, or a package for spark plugs.

A product design project is barely started, however, when the designer submits his original drawings. The marketing research director and the sales manager must be consulted on the market potentialities of the proposed item. The advertising manager may have something to say about relative promotional possibilities of alternative designs. The traffic manager can advise on how product or package dimensions may affect shipping costs. The production engineer can contribute information on production practicability and production costs. The usual practice is to bring these various executives together in a "marketing committee" or a "merchandising committee" to analyze jointly a new product or design proposal.

A new product that needs packaging requires a new package, of course. Also, most packages require redesigning before many years have passed. Whenever the inventory of a company's packaging supplies runs low, or when new plates for the packages are needed, it is wise to review the old package and to consider revision. When sales fall off, packages should be checked to see whether they are outmoded. If a product is taken on by a new class of outlets, or if a new advertising medium such as color TV is being used, the old package should be checked to ascertain whether it is well adapted to the new outlets or medium. For a company to hang on to an old package through inertia after marketing changes have converted it from an asset to a liability, is to court disaster.

REVIEW

1. What actions should a manufacturer take before committing himself to the manufacture of a new product?

2. What would be the reasons for manufacturing a particular product in "diversified" styles, sizes, or models?

3. What are the advantages of product simplification? How is it usually accomplished?

4. What advantages might a manufacturer of a particular item gain by producing a "line" of related products?

5. What considerations might warrant a manufacturer to produce items belonging to different product "lines"?

6. Explain "selling design." Give examples.

7. What are the objectives of packaging? Give examples.

8. How do product and package designs come into existence?

DISCUSSION TOPICS

1. How might the extent of diversification of an individual company's product line be theoretically determined in terms of marginal doctrine?

2. Over 1,800 different wood screws are manufactured. The variant elements are composition (such as iron, galvanized, bronze), head (such as flat, oval, straight slot, Phillips slot), length and related head size, and diameter and related head size. Isn't this overdiversification? If some simplification were to be accomplished, how would this be done?

3. Can the production and sale of many widely different lines of products by such successful business giants as Du Pont, Westinghouse, and General Electric be justified on Marketing grounds?

4. To what extent has the evolution of the automobile resulted from increase of basic utilities and from incorporation of supplementary utilities?

5. Analyze current (a) typewriters, (b) electric kitchen mixers, and (c) ball point pens, from the viewpoint of their embodiment of basic and supplementary utilities.

6. What elements of selling design are or might be incorporated in (a) bed mattresses, (b) vacuum cleaners, (c) kitchen cleanser packages?

7. "Most of the cost of present-day packaging is economic waste, for which the consumer pays in higher prices."

PROBLEM

You have invented and patented (a) a detergent pellet which makes water flowing over it sudsy, and (b) an adjustable container for the pellet which may be attached to the hot water faucet of any kitchen sink, bathroom tub or basin, or laundry tub and which, by a switch, permits the water either to flow over the pellet or to avoid the pellet and flow clear. You are ready to begin commercial production and distribution.

1. In preparing production designs for the faucet attachment, what marketing considerations, other than producing something to hold the pellet at the mouth of a faucet and a switch that works efficiently and dependably, should you take into account? Explain.

2. Will you manufacture and sell your attachment in only one model or in several models? Explain.

3. How many pellets should your package contain?

4. What considerations would you take into account in designing the packages? Sketch your concept of a package for these pellets.

5. Would you package the container attachment? Why? If you think the container should be packaged, sketch your concept of the package.

SUGGESTED READINGS

American Management Association, *Developing a Product Strategy,* Management Report No. 39 (1960); *Establishing a New Product Program,* Management Series No. 8 (1958); *How to Plan Products that Sell,* Management Report No. 13 (1958); *Know Your Packaging Materials,* Management Report No. 5 (1958); *Packaging Research,* Research Study No. 37 (1959); *Packaging with Plastics,* Management Report No. 29 (1959); *Problems in Developing and Launching New Products,* Marketing Series No. 91 (1954); *The Integrated Approach to Product Planning,* Marketing Series No. 101 (1957).

American Marketing Association, Packaging series.

Barail, L. C., *Packaging Engineering,* Reinhold, New York, 1954.

Birren, F., *Selling Color to People,* University Books, New York, 1956.

Brown, K., *Package Design Engineering,* John Wiley & Sons, New York, 1959.

Chambers, B. C., *Color and Design,* Prentice-Hall, Englewood Cliffs, N.J., 1951.

Cheskin, L., *How to Predict What People Will Buy,* Liveright Publishing Corp., New York, 1957.

Design is Your Business, Small Business Administration, Washington, D.C., 1953.

Dreyfuss, H., *Designing for People,* Simon & Schuster, New York, 1955.

Fladager, V. L., *The Selling Power of Packaging,* McGraw-Hill Book Co., New York, 1956.

Ketcham, H., *Color Planning for Business and Industry,* Harper & Bros., New York, 1958.

Larson, G. E., *Developing and Selling New Products,* 2d ed, U.S. Department of Commerce, Washington, D.C., 1955.

Marvin, P. R., *Planning New Products,* Research Press, Dayton, Ohio, 1958.

Nash, B., *Developing Marketable Products,* McGraw-Hill Book Co., New York, 1945.

Phelps, D. M., *Planning the Product,* Richard D. Irwin, Homewood, Ill., 1947.

PERIODICALS: *Modern Packaging, Package Engineering.*

CHAPTER 17

BUYING

Purchase of goods for resale by retailers and wholesalers is generally viewed as a basic Marketing operation. On the buying of raw materials and supplies by manufacturers, and on the buying of industrial, store or office equipment, there is dispute. Some authorities consider such purchasing one aspect of the general Marketing operation of buying. Others hold that it should be treated exclusively as a Management operation.

Our analysis of the buying operation and of buying policy will cover both mercantile buying—i.e., buying for resale by wholesalers and retailers —and industrial and business purchasing. Its major emphasis, however, will be upon mercantile buying. Reference will be made to other categories of buying only where their policies or procedures differ from those of mercantile buying. The elements of buying activities and policy covered are: (1) "assembling" as an element of the buying operation; (2) choice of items to be purchased; (3) methods of selecting items for purchase; (4) determination of quantities to be purchased and timing of buying; (5) choice of suppliers; and (6) organization for buying.

ASSEMBLING

"Assembling" * may be defined as the concentration by wholesaling middlemen and retailers, from scattered sources, through acquisition of physical possession or title, of small lots of similar or related items into larger lots; ** it has the important Marketing consequence of facilitating

---

* Called "accumulation" by some Marketing writers.

** Marketing assembling must be distinguished from production assembly. In the latter, parts are *physically combined* to form new units, and subassemblies are *physically combined* to form larger unit assemblies. In Marketing assembling, the initial units retain their individual identities, such as they are, and are merely grouped or mixed together to constitute larger lots.

subsequent resale and purchasing. It is often treated as an independent Marketing function, but can be better comprehended as an aspect of the buying operation since it is accomplished only through buying procedures.

Marketing assembling takes two forms—quantity assembling, and line assembling.

Quantity assembling is the concentration, primarily through the buying of certain types of wholesaling middlemen, of small quantities of *homogeneous* items into larger lots. It occurs in the course of nearly all agricultural product marketing, as we saw in Chapter 12, and in the marketing of some lines of consumer goods. A local agricultural dealer performs quantity assembling when he buys grain or other produce from numbers of independent farmers. So does a central market wholesaler when he buys and concentrates under his control grain or other produce acquired by the local dealers. Such quantity assembling transforms small-lot dealing in a commodity to large-lot dealing, with subsequent economy in handling, transportation, and selling costs.

Line assembling is the bringing together, through buying by retailers and certain types of wholesaling middlemen, of quantities of *related* items obtained from different suppliers, which can then be resold in "lines" conforming to customers' needs. Such assembling occurs primarily in the fields of consumer goods and industrial supplies. A department store performs line assembling when it buys the products of many different manufacturers and wholesalers and brings them together under one roof, so that its customers do not have to shop widely for the variety of goods they want. A hardware wholesaler is a line assembler when he buys tools and other hardware items from many separate manufacturers, so that hardware retailers who buy from him can consolidate their purchasing of the manifold items they wish to stock into single orders. A mill house does line assembling when it buys thousands of supply and tool part items, so that factories can purchase a great part of their needs from a single source. Line assembling at any stage in a channel of distribution reduces the buying operation at the next distribution stage, where it would generally be less efficiently performed, and so makes distribution more effective and less costly.

CHOICE OF ITEMS TO BE PURCHASED

The purchasing manager of an industrial enterprise customarily has little discretion as to what items he may buy, and little choice as to the qualities he may select. He must buy in accordance with exact specifications prepared for him by the engineering or production department. A mercantile buyer, on the contrary, frequently has wide latitude of choice as to: (1) lines of goods he may purchase, (2) the price-quality range of his purchases, (3) choice between fast-turn and slow-turn items, (4) selection among brands, and (5) the degree of diversification or simplification of his buying. The scope of the buying done by any mercantile unit, therefore, raises a number of policy issues.

Line policy

The lines of goods a retailer or wholesaler buys are, with few exceptions, those he regularly sells. A variety store, a department store, or a general mail order house buys many lines because it is in the business of selling a broad combination of lines. Such a multi-line retailer can readily extend its buying to new lines because its customers are accustomed, and its selling organization is geared, to changes in its line offerings. A variety store, for example, that has not heretofore carried waste baskets, may safely take advantage of a special "good buy" in this item because its customers will readily extend their "impulse buying" to a bargain offer of such an item, and the store will find little difficulty in incorporating a display of the baskets in its lay-out. By contrast, a limited-line store in any field confines its buying essentially to its one line. Only if it sells related side lines may its buying extend afield. Even in those cases where an enterprising salesman persuades a retailer to take on a line of goods that he has never carried before, as when a large chain of supermarkets was induced to take on a line of illustrated children's books, the retailer's buying decision is still based on sales considerations—the salesman had to convince the chain's management that the stores could profitably sell the new line. Wholesalers, being more specialized in their selling lines than most retailers, are correspondingly more limited in their line buying policy.

Price-quality considerations

There is no merit *per se* in a store carrying the highest quality goods in its field, or the cheapest. There are customers for high-quality high-price goods, for cheap low-quality goods, and for intermediate quality and price grades. It is generally advisable for a store to cater to the price-quality demands of a particular economic or social class of customers, rather than attempt to accommodate all classes. Where a store does carry more than one line of items, it should be consistent in the price-quality offerings among its various lines.* A women's wear store would be ill-advised, for example, to concentrate on a quality line of dresses and a cheap line of coats, or vice versa. This element of selling policy limits the price-quality ranges of retailers' buying policy. They normally should buy only those price-quality

---

* Some "quality" department stores have developed an exception to this principle by offering lower-quality lower-price lines but segregating the selling area for these cheaper lines in a "bargain basement" (see Chapter 6).

offerings in any line falling within the scope of their original sales policy.

Within its established price-quality range, a store's buyers may often seize special price advantages that come their way. If a department store's women's dress buyer learns of a manufacturer's bankruptcy sale including goods within the store's established price-quality policy, he may be able to buy them substantially below the usual cost of such items, thereby enabling his store either to sell them on a wider margin or to offer them as a special promotional "bargain."

Most wholesalers, in their buying, are not limited to a particular quality-price range. They endeavor to carry the requirements of all retailers in their field, those who serve a quality trade as well as those whose appeal is cheapness. Thus the scope of wholesalers' purchasing customarily covers the quality-price gamut in their lines.

Turnover and margin considerations

Retailers' and wholesalers' relative gross profit on the carrying of any item is determined by two factors: (1) its sales volume compared with that of alternative items, and (2) the margin between the buying price of the item and the price at which they will be able to resell it, as compared with the margins of alternative items.

Store shelf and counter space given to fast-selling items generally produces a larger volume of sales than the same space given to slower selling items. A retailer can obtain greater over-all sales volume from his store by carrying faster-selling items. Furthermore, fast-selling items in any field are usually repurchased at more frequent intervals than slower-selling items. A retailer or wholesaler can therefore carry smaller average inventories, relative to his sales, of the faster-selling items. More rapid "turnover" of inventories of fast-selling items means that sales volume is obtained with a smaller investment of working capital in inventory, and with less storage space allocated to the inventories.

As will be indicated in Chapter 20, however, retailers' and wholesalers' margins on fast-selling items are usually lower than on slower-selling items. This generalization holds true whether the margin is set by the manufacturer through resale price maintenance contracts, or whether competitive considerations establish customary retailing or wholesaling markups. Therefore, a slow-selling item with a large margin may yield a greater gross profit over a given period than a faster-selling item with a smaller margin. Moreover, considerable customer goodwill may be developed by "accommodation" carrying of particular slow-moving items. Besides buying and appreciating the service of the "accommodation" items, customers also purchase quantities of fast-moving items that they might otherwise have bought in some other store or from some other distributor.

Obviously there is a real issue of buying policy involved in the choice of fast-moving and slow-moving items. Some wholesalers and retailers find profit in concentrating exclusively on fast-moving items, compensating for the loss of customer good-will resulting from the limited range of their offerings by cutting the prices of the fast-moving items they do offer. Most distributors and dealers seek to balance their purchases between fast-moving and slow-moving items in their fields, thereby providing "selection" without tying up too much of their working capital and shelf and storage space in slow-turnover items.

Brand policy

Brand names * play an important role in mercantile buying policy. The lines of two manufacturers may be closely comparable in quality and price. One may carry a brand name with wide market goodwill built up by heavy advertising or by long local familiarity, whereas the other may be relatively unknown. Despite their close correspondence in quality and price, the first will far outsell the second. A wholesaler or retailer offered the choice of these two lines would usually favor the first. The better-known brand would generally be favored even where its quality-equivalent competitor was offered at a lower price, unless the price differential was so substantial that the wholesaler or retailer could make a much larger margin on it or resell it at a markedly lower price than the better-known brand. Many large wholesalers and retailers, however, have established their own "private" brands for certain of the products they sell. In such cases they buy un-branded products at substantially lower prices and have their own "private" brand names placed on these products. By local advertising and by promotional over-the-counter selling, they develop local demand for their private brands.

Brand issues in mercantile buying are rarely so simple, however, as the choice between a single well-advertised manufacturer's brand and a non-branded line. Usually a wholesaler or retailer is faced with several established manufacturers' brands, as well as the possibility of buying un-branded products on which his own "private" brand may be placed. Each brand has some consumer devotees who are convinced of its superiority over all competing brands, and will accept no substitutes. Under these circumstances, mercantile buying policy with respect to brand choices must be a compromise between the disadvantages of overdiversification and those of oversimplification, as described below.

---

* Discussed more fully in Chapter 21.

Diversification vs. simplification in mercantile buying

Wholesalers and retailers, like manufacturers, are often faced with a difficult issue: whether to diversify their lines—i.e., buy and offer a wide range of models, designs, and brands—or limit themselves to narrow, simple lines confined to items and brands for which customer demand is constant and assured. Diversification holds the lure of attracting customers looking for unusual models, styles, or brands, who otherwise might be lost to the store. But the price of diversification is usually slow turnover of many inventory items, with consequent tie-up of working capital and storage and shelf space. An oversimplified stock, on the other hand, means not only missing a chance to sell specialty items, but also risks the loss of customers who will take their patronage to a competitor carrying such items. For every wholesaler and store there is some optimum compromise between diversification and simplification for each of its lines, with respect to brands, styles, sizes, colors, and prices.

Superior promotion and salesmanship can make fast movers of specialty items that normally would be sluggish. Therefore good retailers can profitably embrace a degree of diversification in their buying policy that would be disastrous for less effective stores in the same fields. In large cities an occasional limited-line store may build a wide specialty reputation for carrying a complete line in its field. All customers for unusual models and types come there, and it is able to maintain as rapid a turnover for many of its specialities as ordinary stores in the field with their more staple items. But for most small stores the optimum compromise between diversification and simplification in their buying policy usually lies closer to the latter than to the former.

Sources of information

Where can wholesalers and retailers obtain information about what items in their lines are available and what the buying public wants?

Every retailer and wholesaler has, in his past and current *sales records,* an invaluable source of information on the buying habits of his particular group of customers. Department stores, general mail order houses, and other large retailers maintain detailed records of sales of every single item they carry, broken down by models and sizes, to guide them in their selections for future purchases as well as quantities to be bought. Properly analyzed, these sales records reveal which are fast-moving profitable items, and which have such slow turnovers that the retailer's capital, storage space, and sales efforts are wasted on them.

Extensive marketing research projects costing thousands of dollars are not practicable for most retailers or wholesalers. But every wholesaler and

MERCHANDISE CALLED FOR — NOT IN STOCK AND LOW STOCK

WEEKLY REPORT

Dept._____

Week ending Sat._____

(Date)

Sales Clerk No.	BRIEF DESCRIPTION OF ITEM ASKED FOR	Price	Disposition By Buyer

Use as many sheets as needed and turn in every Monday with night Report.
If no items are recorded you must turn in the blank sheet marked —
"EVERYTHING ASKED FOR — IN STOCK"

A RETAILER'S "WANT SLIP." *Courtesy of the Gamble Co.*

ILLUSTRATION 17–1

retailer can establish a system of "customer want slips" on which salesmen or sales clerks note customer requests for items not in stock. Whenever there is a concentration of want slips for a particular item, serious thought should be given to including it in the line. Rival stores may provide guides to both item availability and consumer demand through their advertisements and window displays. Large department stores employ "comparison shoppers" who note the counter offerings of their rivals and try to learn how well various items are moving.

Suppliers' direct-mail advertising, catalogs, and salesmen are a major source of information on items available for purchase and to some extent on market demand. In some lines, such as women's wear, the manufacturers arrange individual seasonal style shows for their customers' buyers. The trade associations for many manufacturing lines mount annual exhibits or "shows" of their products, as shown in Illustration 11–6. All of these various supplier-sponsored sources of information are invaluable to industrial and mercantile buyers as indicators of what products are available. Suggestions or even flat statements by suppliers and their salesmen on the subject of consumer demand preferences, however, must be viewed with skepticism. Such information may be correct to the last detail, but there is always a strong probability that it is more or less colored by the suppliers' interest in making sales.

In most cases, the supplier takes the initiative in getting information about his products to his customers. Suppliers' salesmen constantly urge their wares on new prospects, and make periodic visits to their old customers. Trade advertising, published or direct-mail, is obviously a matter of supplier initiative. In certain lines, however, particularly those where style is a major factor, such as women's wear, men's suits, and jewelry, many or most of the buyers visit the suppliers—manufacturers or jobbers—examine the displays in the suppliers' show rooms, and make their selections there. The responsibility of mounting an annual trade show rests with the suppliers, of course, but the initiative of actually attending the show and studying the exhibits must be taken by the buyers.

Finally *market news*, published and unpublished, may be a very useful guide both to items available for purchase and customer demand for such items. Trade magazines and papers are published for many wholesaling fields. Retailers in particular lines often find it helpful to subscribe to trade publications intended primarily for the manufacturers or wholesalers in their field, or, in women's wear lines, to style magazines published for women as consumers. Although store buyers have their trade secrets which they guard jealously, they are generally quite cooperative in interchanging market news. Part of the service of resident buying offices to their out-of-town clients is to gather and disseminate information on product lines and fashions and on market acceptance of these lines and fashions.

METHODS OF SELECTING ITEMS FOR PURCHASE

Assuming a wholesaler or retailer, or an industrial purchasing manager, knows just what classes of items he wants to buy, the particular items purchased may be selected by one of four methods: (1) by grade or standard specification, (2) by catalog designation, (3) by sample, and (4) by inspection of the individual items.

Purchasing by *grade or standard specification* is possible only for commodities for which official marketing standards have been established by which all suppliers abide, and then only if the standard grade specifications conform to the buyer's quality needs. Industrial purchasing of metals and chemicals is commonly done on the basis of standard grade specification.

If a wholesaler, retailer, or purchasing manager is already familiar with a product and can rely on the supplier for consistent uniformity and maintenance of quality standards, purchasing can be done on the basis of a *catalog* or *price list* issued by the supplier. Most purchases of manufactured products by wholesalers and retailers are based on catalog designations.

When a buyer is not familiar with a product, or if the product is such that its quality cannot be maintained uniform over periods of time, or if the permissible quality range in a standard grade is wider than his buying specifications can allow, he commonly purchases on the basis of a *sample*. While a salesman may be able to sell his staple articles to established customers on a catalog or illustration basis, he usually has to carry a case of samples to win new customers and to persuade old customers to try new items in his line. The buyers at fruit auctions usually check a sample from each lot of fruit before making their bids. Although the cases may bear recognized brand names and established grade types of fruit, the condition of the fruit may vary from shipment to shipment. A buying agent for a woolen mill with strict specifications for the quality of wool it must obtain usually tests a sample from each bale before purchasing. Even though it conforms to specifications for a standard grade, the wool must also meet his client's particular requirements.

Finally, where there is no uniformity in the units of some line of goods, buying must be based upon *inspection* of each item. Dealers in antiques and works of art must purchase on this basis.

Purchase by standard grade specification, by catalog designation, or by sample, is always a sort of conditional purchase—the condition being that the product as delivered conform to the specification, description, or sample. To establish whether such conformity obtains, the purchaser must inspect the delivered items. Major industrial organizations and large dealers such as department stores may have testing bureaus able to make searching chemical, physical, and use analyses. Smaller dealers must usually be content with casual visual inspection.

QUANTITY AND TIMING OF BUYING

How frequently a wholesaler, or retailer, or industrial purchasing manager reorders a specific item, and the size of the reorder, are obviously closely interrelated. If a certain amount is to be bought over a period of a year, large-quantity buying will involve widely spaced purchases, whereas small-quantity buying will necessitate frequent reordering. Quantity considerations are usually the causative factor in this interrelation, and the timing of orders the effect. When retailers are dependent upon salesmen's calls for placing their orders, however, quantities ordered obviously depend upon the timing of the salesmen's visits.

Factors influencing quantity of purchase

The basic consideration in determining how much of a material or a supply item an industrial purchasing manager will order over any *long-term* period is obviously the *rate* of its *use* in his company's production processes. Likewise, the long-term quantities involved in a wholesaler's or retailer's purchase orders depend upon the item's *rate of resale*. A rapidly used or rapidly-moving item may be bought by the great gross or the gross, a slower one by the dozen.

Translation of volume of anticipated sales over a given period into quantity purchased must usually be modified by consideration of the inventory of the item already on hand. If there is already a substantial stock of the item on hand when the purchase order must be given, the quantity ordered will be lower than the anticipated use or resale of the item by the excess of inventory over minimum requirements. In this connection, the *model stock* *

---

* The following is an example of a model stock of lamp shades, by price line and material:

PRICE LINE	MATERIAL	PERCENT BY PRICE LINE	PERCENT BY MATERIAL	DOLLAR DISTRIBUTION	UNIT DISTRIBUTION
$3.95		50	100	$ 500	127
	Fabric		70	350	89
	Parchment		30	150	38
5.95		35	100	$ 350	59
	Fabric		70	245	41
	Parchment		30	105	18
6.95		10	100	$ 100	15
	Fabric		70	70	10
	Parchment		30	30	5
Higher		5	100	$ 50	5
	Fabric		70	35	3
	Parchment		30	15	2
Total		100		$1,000	200

With the above tabulation as a guide, particular styles may be selected from the manufacturers' offerings. While colors, too, may be selected as manufacturers' offerings are inspected, it would be desirable to prepare in advance an over-all color distribution and to check selections against the plan.

buying policy of many retailers should be noted. When an item is sold in a range of sizes, colors, or models, it is highly unlikely that each size, color, or model will sell at the same rate. The individual retailer's experience, or in some cases the researches of a product's manufacturer or of the retailer's trade association, may have established the relative rates of resale. These can be readily translated into the quantities of each size, color, or model that should be included in a balanced inventory of the item to cover various over-all sales volumes. This predetermined inventory relationship is called a "model stock" of the item. With a knowledge of the composition of his "model stock" of any item, and with an analysis at hand of his inventory at the time when a purchase order is to be placed, a retailer can determine the quantity of each size, color, or model that he should buy by subtracting his current inventory amounts from the figures of his "model stock."

When a retailer or industrial buyer has a choice between placing frequent small orders, or infrequent large orders for an item, an important consideration in many cases is the *quantity discount* offered by the seller (discussed in Chapter 20). A substantial quantity discount for buying by the gross, or some other large quantity, may enable a retailer to undersell competitors or make a larger unit profit on his sales. Ability to take fullest advantage of quantity discounts has been a significant advantage in the competition between chain stores and small independents. An appreciable saving on unit freight costs may also be an inducement to order in large quantities.

A dealer's *storage space* places a limitation on the quantities he can carry in stock and so on the size of the orders he can place. It would be folly for a small retailer seeking to gain a quantity discount to buy so large a stock of one item that he robbed himself of storage space needed for minimum stocks of other items. *Working capital* considerations also may place limitations on a dealer's ability to buy in large quantities.*

Finally, *price trends* influence the sizes of orders placed by dealers. Expectation of a price decline induces dealers to hold their inventories to practicable minima. Accordingly, they buy the smallest quantities consonant with the rate of sale, more or less on a hand-to-mouth basis, except where quantity discounts may be greater than the anticipated price decline. When

---

* When the buying operation is performed by departmental managers or buyers, as in department stores, chain store systems, and large wholesalers, the total buying potentiality of the store or business is allocated among the departments on a quarterly or some other time basis. At any date each department thus has an "open-to-buy" figure which limits its purchases for the balance of the given period. Part of mercantile buying skill lies in applying "open-to-buy" amounts in the most effective proportions among the various items, and their quantities, that the department carries. An "open-to-buy" is not a rigid limitation; if an exceptional buying opportunity occurs that can not be accommodated by the current "open-to-buy," the department buyer can usually seek special approval of the purchase by the merchandise manager or some other executive.

price rises are anticipated, on the contrary, future "inventory profits" may be realized by buying as heavily, with reasonable relation to future sales, as storage space and working capital permit.

The term "speculative buying" is applied to purchasing materials, supplies, or goods for resale, in anticipation of a shortage or price rise, substantially in excess of a season's or year's anticipated needs. The "speculating" purchasing manager, wholesaler, or retailer plans to make a special profit by carrying his overstock into a later season or year, or even to dispose of it at premium prices outside the ordinary channels of his trade. "Speculative" overbuying of this sort has on occasion yielded substantial profits to manufacturers and dealers who have indulged in it. Ordinary retailers, and even the heads of large wholesaling houses, however, while they may be experts on their product lines are usually not experts on the intricate economic and financial influences that determine general and particular commodity price trends. The probabilities are against their guessing consistently right on price developments over the long run, and over the long run heavy speculative buying generally results in inventory losses rather than inventory gains.

Timing of buying

There are five systems for timing buying in accordance with the quantity factors noted above: (1) "order" or "hand-to-mouth" buying, (2) timing ordering to salesmen's visits, (3) buying to minimum inventory, (4) quota buying, and (5) seasonal buying.

Order or *hand-to-mouth* buying in strict sense occurs when a dealer places an order for an item only when he has a specific immediate customer for it. Obviously, few wholesale or retail businesses could be conducted exclusively on this buying system. Customers would soon be repelled by the necessity of waiting for each purchase while the dealer obtained delivery. But for slow-moving specialty items, this "order" buying may be an excellent solution of the problem of diversification versus simplification of a retailer's line. He carries a proper stock of staple items and of heavier-demand specialties. When a customer asks for a rarely demanded specialty, he is unable to supply it immediately, but offers to have it within a short time—the time it takes him to get delivery from his supplier. Of course, on such "order" buying he sacrifices all possibility of quantity discount, and probably has to pay high delivery charges, so that his profit margin on the sale is reduced. But he saves storage space so that he can accommodate a larger inventory of fast-moving items, he ties up no working capital, and he does not have to fear style obsolescence or deterioration loss on a frozen inventory of specialties. Wholesalers and retailers are likely to shift to a modified sort of hand-to-mouth buying—in the sense that they do not build up normal inventories but place frequent small orders as current sales develop—when they anticipate slow demand and a downturn of prices. End-of-season fill-in orders for seasonal goods that are selling faster than expected are also put through on such modified hand-to-mouth basis.

Small independent stores that do not belong to voluntary or cooperative groups generally place most of their buying orders through the wholesalers' and manufacturers' route salesmen who call upon them; telephone or mail is used for the most part for emergency fill-in ordering between salesmen's visits. The timing of their major reorders is largely out of the retailers' control, for it is determined essentially by the *periodicity* of the *salesmen's visits*. Purchase quantities under these circumstances are also largely determined by the salesmen. The former tendency of wholesalers' salesmen to high-pressure retailers to buy more than they could reasonably be expected to resell is now rare. An experienced salesman who sells to a field of retailers becomes a shrewd judge of the volumes of his products which differently-circumstanced retailers can sell. He learns quick rule-of-thumb methods for helping his customers calculate their shelf and storage inventories. His long-run interest lies in persuading each retailer to buy just enough of each item to cover the retailer's maximum sale potentiality for that item until the salesman's next visit.

Buying to minimum inventory is a more scientific method of timing the buying of staple items. It is done by industrial purchasing managers, wholesalers, department store and chain buyers, and large independent dealers. It is possible only for items for which the purchaser has had some selling experience. It may be established with or without a constant or perpetual inventory system (which keeps a store or business continuously informed of the exact number of each item it has in its stock room). If a perpetual inventory system exists, each stock ledger page, or each bin tag, states the minimum inventory figure at which a reorder of the item must be placed. In the absence of a perpetual inventory system, each shelf or bin must have a minimum inventory line drawn upon it. When withdrawals from stock completely expose the line, a reorder must be made.

The minimum inventory quantity for any merchandise item is the maximum amount likely to be sold in the maximum time that may be necessary to obtain delivery.* For example, suppose that under a house-furnishings store's routine, after a stock boy noticed that the minimum inventory line on a shelf of a particular table lamp model was exposed, or after a stock clerk noted that the stock card for such item showed that the minimum

---

* In practice, department stores and other dealers apply many variants of this principle, according to the stock-keeping system used. For industrial purchasers, minimum inventory is the maximum amount likely to be *used* during the maximum time required for delivery.

inventory quantity had been reached, one day had to be allowed for the stock clerk to prepare and send a requisition to the buyer, and two days for purchase order routine in the buyer's office; also that up to eight business days might elapse from the time of mailing a purchase order to the lamp manufacturer before the shipment would arrive, be unpacked, and be placed on the stockroom shelves; and that up to 35 of this model of lamp were sold during eleven-day periods. Under these circumstances, 35 or 40 would be the proper minimum inventory number. Reordering to any higher minimum quantity would always leave a number of lamps on the store's stock shelves forever unsold. Reordering to any smaller figure might cause the store to run out of the lamp while it was awaiting delivery of a new shipment. The quantity of any item to be purchased on such reorder depends on the determinants of purchase quantities previously considered.

Quota buying, which accomplishes the same objectives as minimum inventory buying, but with less exigent stock supervision routine, is possible for staple items and large-volume specialties whose sales can be forecast with reasonable accuracy. An order quantity that will give the store the best quantity discount and freight charges, in relation to its storage space and working capital, is determined. This amount is divided into the anticipated annual sales volume. The result is a reorder period, in terms of weeks, or months, or fractions of a year, that may be utilized without a constant or minimum inventory check. Where there are seasonal variations in sales of the item, this variation can be taken into account, so the reorder period will be shorter in the active season and longer in the slack season. Periodic summaries of the store's sales records, and annual, semi-annual, or other periodic stock-takings, check the accuracy of the purchase quotas.

Seasonal fashion goods, such as women's dresses, present one of the most difficult problems of mercantile buying. Trade custom, and the objective of assuring that an adequate selection and stock of "good numbers" may be obtained, cause most stores to place the bulk of their orders well in advance of the selling season. A store buyer of seasonal fashion goods must therefore calculate, long before he can receive any guidance from actual sales figures, not only the over-all volume of his purchases, but also their break-down into specific style, size, color, material type, and price categories. To guide him in working out a "model stock" plan of purchase orders, he has his store's sales experience with this line of items in prior years, his "feel" for customer reaction to various types of fashion offerings, a steady flow of fashion news and fashion forecasts (frequently self-contradictory), and various forecasts of general and local economic conditions.

The best fashion goods buyers frequently admit that, for all the "science" they try to introduce into their purchase calculations, their orders in the last analysis are based on little more than "educated guesses"—with heavy penalties for guessing wrong. If they order any item too heavily, the unsold stock remaining at the close of the season must be moved by a "clearance" sale, often at substantial loss. If they underestimate on an item, they may be able to rectify their misjudgment as the season progresses with fill-in orders, but the prices charged for these will be high, and their store will make little profit on the resale. Worse yet, the manufacturers' stock may be exhausted by the time a fill-in order is placed, so that the store loses sales, and may lose customers to competing stores that still have the desired item in stock.

CHOICE OF SUPPLIERS

With the products to be purchased determined, and with quantity and timing settled, the final issue before an industrial purchasing agent or retail merchandise buyer is determining from whom he shall purchase his requirements. In many cases this issue involves three successive decisions: (1) Should he buy a particular product directly from the manufacturer or through a wholesaling middleman? (2) Where a particular product is made by several manufacturers, or an identical line is distributed by several wholesalers, should he buy his entire requirement from one, or should he split his orders among several? (3) Where he has a choice among manufacturers or distributors, which one or ones should he choose?

Buying direct-from-manufacturer or via a wholesaler

Often an industrial or retail buyer has no choice as to whether he should buy direct from a manufacturer or through a wholesaler. His order for a particular product may be so small that the manufacturer refuses to handle it directly. Or the manufacturer may have established a firm policy of dealing only through wholesalers. In such cases, the industrial or retail buyer must make his purchase through a wholesaler. Contrariwise, some manufacturers by-pass the wholesalers and send their salesmen direct to industrial users and retailers. Given this situation, direct-from-manufacturer buying is the only possibility. Where an item is produced to the particular specifications of the buyer, the order must likewise be placed directly with the manufacturer.

In many cases, however, an industrial or mercantile buyer can place his orders with either the manufacturer of a product or a wholesaler. The pros and cons of buying through wholesalers or bypassing them were analyzed in Chapter 13. As indicated there, the advantages of direct-from-manufacturer buying are generally available only to large-scale buyers. Small retailers usually find it to their advantage to buy through wholesalers. A considerable proportion of department store buying, even that of large department stores, is from wholesalers. This happens because many department store departments are, as regards their particular lines, in effect small-scale retailers.

Concentrated vs. dispersed buying

If an unbranded item, or one whose brands are of no market significance, is produced and competitively offered at the same price by several manufacturers of equal standing and repute, a manufacturer, wholesaler, or retailer buying direct-from-manufacturer has the choice of buying his entire requirement from one of these manufacturers, or of dividing his order among several of them. Likewise, a retailer in any field can usually find several wholesalers offering him approximately the same line at practically identical prices. Should he buy from one only, or should he split his purchases among several?

Concentrated buying—i.e., buying the entire requirement of an item, or a line, from one supplier—has two advantages. (1) Concentrated orders to one supplier may entitle the buyer to quantity discounts not available to him if his orders were split among several suppliers. (2) Because of the larger size of his orders, a sole supplier may accord him "favored customer" treatment, such as making special-design products for him, giving more attention to his "rush" orders, and keeping him supplied during periods of product shortages.

Dispersed buying—i.e., splitting orders for a product or line of products among several suppliers—has five advantages. (1) Because the buyer has the offerings of several competing suppliers constantly before him, he is likely to remain more alert in his purchasing. (2) Each supplier may offer certain items not carried by the others. (3) The competing suppliers are not likely to develop the complacency toward the buyer sometimes found when a sole supplier "feels sure" of a customer. (4) The buyer does not have "all his eggs in one basket" with respect to his sources; if any one of a group of competing suppliers fails him, he can turn immediately to the others to make up the shortage. (5) Many suppliers grant credit limits on the basis of arbitrary amounts or allow their customers credit limits equal to 10 percent of the customers' net worth; under these circumstances, a buyer may be able to obtain larger credit extensions by purchasing from several suppliers instead of one.

For small stores and small industrial purchasers the balance of advantage usually favors concentrated buying, because this may be the only way they can obtain quantity discounts, and because of the importance of "favored customer" standing. Wholesalers and large retailers lean more to dispersed buying. Their purchases may be so large that, even when split among several suppliers, they are still entitled to maximum quantity discounts and "favored customer" treatment from each. Their managements are likely to be more aware of the advantages of maintaining competitive eagerness among suppliers, and alertness in their buyers, than in the case of small retail stores. Their prestige, too, would suffer more if they were rendered unable to satisfy their customers because of the default of a sole supplier.

Considerations in selecting suppliers

Where choice among suppliers is possible, a number of considerations guide wholesalers, retailers, and industrial purchasing managers in selecting a sole supplier * or a group of suppliers for a product or line.

For small retailers, a major consideration is the *line range* carried by the various available wholesalers. Often having neither training nor experience to make them expert buyers of the hundreds of items that compose their stocks from the still larger number of manufacturers who make them, they must depend upon wholesalers to assemble a line for them. If one of several wholesalers carries a fuller line, or one more suited to the needs of a particular retailer, this would be a strong reason to favor this particular wholesaler. If a large manufacturer offers full line coverage under its brand name, retailers may buy direct from him while rejecting the salesmen of other manufacturers who can offer only fragments of the retailers' line. This consideration, of course, has little place in the purchasing by wholesalers and large retailers whose buyers are themselves experts in the assembling function.

For all buyers, the *price-quality* offers of competing suppliers are a major consideration in choosing a supplier. If one shirt manufacturer offers his line a few cents cheaper than competing lines of similar standard quality and no greater brand good-will, dealers can either take the few cents' difference as extra profit, or pass on the price differential to retail price with the expectation of greater sales volume. In either case they have strong reason for preferring this particular supplier over his competitors. The case for preference in mercantile buying is not quite so strong if one supplier offers a product or line whose quality is somewhat above standard for the general price attaching to the standard product. Unless the quality difference is great, there is little possibility of higher pricing it at retail, and there is little hope that the quality differential will lead to much added retail sales volume, since consumer buyers are notoriously inexpert in judging small quality differences. Still, even a small quality superiority in the offering of one of several competing suppliers constitutes a point,

---

* Department store and chain system buyers commonly refer to the supplier of an item they buy as a "resource."

albeit a minor one, in his favor. To industrial purchasing managers a quality differential is every bit as important as a price differential.

Price differentials enter mercantile buying not so much in actual quoted net prices as in discounts and other special terms of sale. The list prices of two competing suppliers might be identical, but significant differences in buyer's cost would develop if one supplier offered a larger quantity discount, related to quantities within the dealer's buying range, than the other; or if the one offered a larger cash discount or "anticipation" deduction for early payment than the other; or if one offered a longer credit term than the other and thus permitted longer postponement of payment; or if the list price of the one were "F.O.B. delivery" (so that the buyer did not have to pay shipping charges) while that of the other were "F.O.B. shipping point" (with the buyer paying shipping charges in addition to the price); or if both list prices were F.O.B. shipping point, but the shipping point of the first supplier were closer to the buyer than that of the second supplier, so that the shipping charges to be added to the first supplier's list price were lower. When factories, wholesalers, department stores, and chain stores buy, these terms-of-sale differentials are probably the deciding point in choice of supplier more often than differences in list prices.

Speed and frequency of delivery may sometimes be the deciding factor in the choice among suppliers. As should be evident from the principle of minimum inventory buying previously discussed, the shorter the delivery time that must be allowed for, the smaller can be the minimum inventory figure on which reorders are based. If buying to order is involved, a short delivery time means a shorter time to consummation of the sale.

Location of the supplier may sometimes be a supplier-choice factor. A close location usually means more speedy deliveries and lower freight costs when sales terms are F.O.B. shipping point. Personal contact with a supplier's executives and officers, often helpful in special-order buying, is facilitated.

One of the most important supplier-choice considerations is difference in the *reliability* of competing suppliers. Supplier reliability has a number of aspects, all important. Do deliveries always conform, in full detail, with salesmen's samples or with catalog descriptions? Does his product maintain consistent quality standards? Can he always be counted upon to make scheduled delivery? Can he be depended upon to make fair adjustments when, for reasons beyond his control, his deliveries fall short of his promises? So highly do mercantile and industrial buyers rate supplier reliability that in many cases they will forego a price-quality advantage offered by some supplier because they consider him less reliable than a competitor.

To be the *exclusive outlet* in their community for some well-known brand of products is a privilege eagerly sought by many retailers. Wholesalers similarly prize exclusive territorial jobbing contracts. Consequently, if a manufacturer offers a dealer an "exclusive" agency for his own brand-line of products, this may be a weighty consideration in the decision whether or not to carry his line.

A manufacturer's *distributive practices* may also influence wholesalers and retailers. If he does some direct selling to retailers, or maintains his own "manufacturer outlet stores" in some communities, wholesalers may be reluctant to buy his line. If he sells to chain stores, independent stores may be hostile to him. If he tries to develop a consumer mail-order business, retailers of all classes may shun him. On the other hand, if he maintains a force of "missionary" salesmen who introduce his line to retailers and turn the resulting orders over to the wholesalers servicing the area covered by the "missionary" sales force, these wholesalers will naturally be prejudiced strongly in his favor.

Finally, the *supplementary services* offered by manufacturers and wholesalers to their customers often influence choice of suppliers. Among the supplementary services which may turn a close supplier-choice decision are provision of retailers with point-of-sale promotional materials, window display assistance, cooperative advertising (whereby a manufacturer shares with a retailer the cost of advertising his line), and assistance by the manufacturer in training the dealer's sales clerks to sell the manufacturer's line more effectively.

Sources of information

In most mercantile transactions, contact initiative is taken by the supplier's salesman. Small independent retailers accomplish nearly all of their buying in response to visits by wholesalers' and manufacturers' salesmen. Their knowledge, not only of products available, but also of who are the suppliers in their lines and the pertinent characteristics of these suppliers, is derived from these salesmen. The more alert among the proprietors of small independent stores, however, and department and chain store buyers, wholesalers, and industrial purchasing managers, have a number of other valuable sources of information to guide them.

Experienced buyers find that one of their most valuable sources of information on suppliers is a set of *item and supplier record files,* sometimes called "resource" files. One file contains a card for every item purchased or which the buyer might subsequently consider purchasing. Listed on each card are all the suppliers of the item to which the buyer's attention has been drawn by visits of salesmen, or by any of the other sources of information indicated below. A second file contains a card for every supplier listed on the item cards. Each supplier card carries the name and address of the supplier, a list of products in his line, and such information as the buyer has assembled on the supplier's price and quality offerings, terms of sale, delivery time, reliability, and other pertinent matter. A third file, also arranged by suppliers' names, contains catalogs and price lists sent by suppliers. Often these second and third files are combined.

A second source of buyer information on suppliers is *direct visits by buyers* to suppliers. In a number of lines such as women's wear, men's suits, jewelry, furs, and furniture, a large proportion of buying and selling is accomplished by visits of buyers to the floor salesrooms of the manufacturers or wholesalers. This has been facilitated by a concentration of the suppliers in "market centers" of a few blocks in New York, Chicago, and other metropolitan centers. In some cases, a large group of major suppliers have sales offices in a single building, as the Jewelers' Exchange or the Furniture Exchange in New York. Buyers also derive considerable information about possible suppliers by direct correspondence with them, particularly on the matter of product specifications and price quotations.

TRIMMED HATS

$21.00 PER DOZEN

	Ad on Page
Albert, Artie,	
1040 Av. of Amer.........CHickering 4-8258	45
Album & Berman, 65 W. 39...CHickering 4-6611	43
Cohan & Schoen, 42 W. 39.....LOngacre 3-7068	32
Creiner & Brumberg, Inc.,	
49 W. 37.................Wisconsin 7-0066	42
Goldberger, Louis, Associates,	
42 W. 39.................Wisconsin 7-2468	13
Kahn, Leonard, 37 W. 39........BRyant 9-5077	41
Madcaps Co., 28 W. 39.....PEnnsylvania 6-8068	53
Paige Hat Co., Inc., 37 W. 37...Wisconsin 7-1349	46
Rittner, Abe, 63 W. 38.......WIsconsin 7-3033	55
Weinstein & Weil, 55 W. 39......OXford 5-3585	
	Front Cover

$19.50 PER DOZEN

	Ad on Page
Albert, Artie,	
1040 Av. of Amer.........CHickering 4-8258	45
Album & Berman, 65 W. 39...CHickering 4-6611	43
Bing, Inc., Gus, 1 W. 39.........BRyant 9-3510	34
Cohan & Schoen, 42 W. 39......LOngacre 3-7068	32
Creiner & Brumberg, Inc.,	
49 W. 37.................WIsconsin 7-0066	42
Goldberger, Louis, Associates,	
42 W. 39.................WIsconsin 7-2468	13
Kahn, Leonard, 37 W. 39........BRyant 9-5077	41
Mandell & Sachs, 55 W. 39.....LOngacre 5-4221	40
Paul Hat Sales Co.,	
55 W. 39.................WIsconsin 7-6779	3
Peters & Perry Hat Corp.,	
62 W. 39.................WIsconsin 7-4444	39
Weinstein & Weil, 55 W. 39......OXford 5-3585	
	Front Cover

For more information about lines see ads on pages indicated.

101

EXCERPT FROM A BUYERS' GUIDE. *Courtesy of Buyers' Index.*

ILLUSTRATION 17–2

Suppliers' *advertisements, catalogs, and price lists* are a third source of buyers' information on suppliers. Even if these items are not pertinent to a buyer's immediate purchasing plans, he will file them in his "resource" file for future reference.

"Buyers' Guides" and *trade directories,* containing listings of suppliers by product classes, are published by suppliers' trade associations and sometimes by private publishers. They are distributed free to interested buyers, their costs of publication and profit, if any, being covered by charges to the suppliers from their listings and advertisements.

Trade exhibits and *trade "fairs,"* previously mentioned as a buyers' source of information on products available, also give buyers a chance to make contacts with new suppliers and to derive information about them.

Finally, the buyers in any field frequently *exchange information* about their suppliers. Of course, a buyer who is getting exceptional values from some relatively unknown supplier will not advertise his source to competitors who have not discovered it on their own account. But buyers of even closely competing wholesalers or stores will often inform each other freely on the reliability of some supplier. Part of the service performed by resident buying offices is to keep their clients fully informed on sources of supply.

BUYING ORGANIZATION

The buying of an independent store or small wholesaler is generally performed by the owner or one of the principals. Department stores and chain stores, as was indicated in Chapters 6 and 7, and large wholesalers, have found it desirable to departmentalize their purchasing. It is done by the heads, or "buyers," of these departments. In department stores, these "buyers" are also the sales executives of their departments.

A similar distribution of purchasing authority is found in the manufacturing field. The owner or a partner in a small enterprise commonly assumes major purchasing responsibility for materials, supplies, and equipment. Sometimes a trusted foreman is allowed to buy supplies and incidental materials. In large industrial enterprises, purchasing of materials and supplies is generally centralized in a purchasing manager. Specifications on these items are likely to be prepared by an engineering or planning department, and quantities and timing of orders are commonly determined by requisitions from production and stock departments. Within these limitations, the purchasing manager locates and selects suppliers, and handles the actual purchase negotiations with them. Decisions on buying major equipment items involving relatively large investment generally raise so many important management and financing issues that they can not be left to the judgment of a single individual, even though he is a purchasing expert. Decisions on such purchases are usually joint matters, involving top management, the financial officials, and the production and planning executives of the enterprise, as well as the purchasing manager.

Under some circumstances, buying authority, both mercantile and industrial, may be delegated to outside agent middlemen. Many out-of-town department stores and specialty shops find it advisable to have selection and purchase of fashion goods done for them by "resident buying offices" located in the metropolitan centers where large numbers of suppliers in these fashion lines are found. The operations of these resident buying offices were described in Chapter 10. As was stated in Chapter 14, industrial purchasing managers sometimes use brokers to locate suppliers of special lots of raw materials needed by their companies.

BUYING PRACTICES

Most mercantile and industrial buying is done on the premises of the buying organizations. Salesmen of suppliers and would-be suppliers call in a never-ending stream upon business owners, upon store buyers, upon industrial purchasing managers. Partly through the salesmen's art, partly on the basis of the customers' independent judgment, most business buying decisions are made on the occasion or as a result of these visits.

Some reorders of goods and materials are made on the customer's initiative by phone or letter. A large proportion, possibly most, are the result of salesmen's return calls. A customer may feel that he could just as well take the initiative or reordering. The salesman, however, makes his repeat calls as a preventive measure against competing salesmen, and to sell additional items in his line.

Store buyers in fashion lines, unless they purchase through resident buying offices, make frequent visits to the manufacturers in their fields, to compare offerings, and to keep abreast of design trends. Many of their purchases are made in the manufacturers' offices. "Trade shows" staged by manufacturers also draw the purchasing people of the field. Few actual purchases are consummated at these trade shows, however. Their major purpose is to stimulate inquiries which will later be followed up by the manufacturers' salesmen.

REVIEW

1. Explain quantity assembling; line assembling.
2. How much freedom do retailers and wholesalers have in taking on new merchandise lines?
3. To what extent are retailers and wholesalers limited in their buying to certain quality-price ranges?

4. To what extent should a store buy relatively slow moving items? Why?

5. What issues are involved in the choice by a wholesaler or retailer as to the brands of merchandise he should buy?

6. To what sources of information may a store owner or department buyer turn for guidance as to what he should buy?

7. When is buying done on the basis of: (a) grade or standard specification; (b) catalog or price list; (c) sample inspection; (d) individual unit inspection?

8. What considerations determine the *size* of a buying order placed by a retailer or wholesaler?

9. What consideration determines *when* most retailers place their buying orders? Explain "buying to order," "buying to minimum inventory," and "quota buying." How are seasonal fashion goods bought?

10. What considerations should be taken into account in a retailer's decision to concentrate or disperse his buying?

11. What considerations should a retailer take into account in selecting the particular supplier, or suppliers, from whom he will buy?

12. From what sources can a retail buyer learn who are the suppliers of an item in which he is interested and derive information about them?

DISCUSSION TOPICS

1. "It is easy for a retailer to determine what items he should carry. The real problem is to decide upon the brands."

2. "For every wholesaler and store there is some optimum compromise between diversification and simplification in its buying."

3. "Too many small retailers buy according to the suggestions of their wholesalers' salesmen."

4. "Taking advantage of quantity discounts is an important factor in retailing success."

5. "A well-managed hardware store should be doing up to 5 percent of its buying on an 'order' basis."

6. "In both industrial and mercantile buying the initiative of making and sustaining the supplier-customer relatonship must rest primarily with the supplier."

7. "Pick your wholesaler for his reliability and the services he gives you, not because he sells a few cents cheaper on the case for this item or that."

PROBLEM

Centerville, population 35,000, is the shopping center for an extensive farming and grazing area. Until recently, Mr. Jones had the only home furnishings store in Centerville, with minor competition from two Centerville department stores.

The Jones Store, a two-story-and-basement building on Main Street, has a good layout. Mr. Jones has always had a flair for display, and the store's windows and interior are attractive. He has applied sound advertising and promotional policies, and the store sales personnel is efficient and courteous.

Mr. Jones' "blind spot" has heretofore been his buying. For the past fifteen years he has purchased a limited selection of traditional furniture through a single manufacturers' agent located in St. Louis, leaving the selection of items largely up to the agent. His carpeting is bought direct from one manufacturer, in a small number of designs and weaves. He carries five designs of linoleum, bought direct from one manufacturer. His lamps, ornaments, and other household accessories are supplied by a wholesaler; Mr. Jones has dealt with this wholesaler for fifteen years, and his selections of accessories have been made largely on the recommendation of the wholesaler's salesman. Except for the representatives of his regular suppliers, Mr. Jones has generally refused to see salesmen. Customers of the Jones Store often grumbled that it never had what they wanted, but since it was the only home furnishings store in Centerville, they had to take what the Jones Store offered or resort to the more limited selections of the department stores.

Recently another home furnishings store has opened in Centerville. The Jones Store is feeling the competition severely. Mr. Jones realizes that his buying policies must be revised if his store is to survive. What actions should he take on the following matters:

1. Should he add a line of household electric appliances, making room for it by rearranging and reducing his furniture floor display? State the arguments pro and con.

2. In each of his lines, how can he find out what items, styles, and designs are available from which he can make a selection for the Jones Store?

3. How can he determine which of the available items, styles, and designs will sell best in his store?

4. Should he adhere to a policy of a limited range of offerings in items, styles, and designs in each line, or should the Jones Store adopt a policy of "If it's for the home, we have it," or is there any third possibility? State the arguments for and against each of these policies.

5. Is buying "to order" practical for any aspects of the Jones Store's business? If so, how?

6. Are "minimum inventory" or "quota" buying possible and advisable for any items in a home furnishings store like the Jones Store? If so, name some, and indicate how these buying procedures would apply to them.

7. Heretofore Mr. Jones has done all of his buying for each line on a "concentrated" basis. Should the buying for any of his lines now be "dispersed"? State the arguments pro and con.

8. Should Mr. Jones drop his wholesaler of household accessories and buy the items in this line direct from the manufacturers? State the arguments pro and con.

9. If, as a result of his revised buying policies, Mr. Jones should want to contact some new suppliers, how can he locate them?

10. If, as a result of his revised buying policies, Mr. Jones should take on any new suppliers, on what basis should he select them?

SUGGESTED READINGS

Alijian, G. W. (ed.), *Purchasing Handbook,* McGraw-Hill Book Co., New York, 1960.

American Management Association, *Purchasing for Profits,* Management Report No. 20, 1958; *Purchasing Department Organization and Authority,* Research Study No. 45, 1960.

The Buyer's Manual: A Merchandising Handbook, Merchandising Division, National Retail Dry Goods Association, New York, 1957.

Heinritz, S. F., *Purchasing: Principles and Applications,* 2d ed, Prentice-Hall, Englewood Cliffs, N.J., 1951.

Lewis, H. T., & W. B. England, *Procurement: Principles and Cases,* 3rd ed, Richard D. Irwin, Homewood, Ill., 1957.

McMillan, A. L., *The Art of Purchasing,* Exposition Press, New York, 1959.

National Industrial Conference Board, *Purchasing for Industry,* Studies in Business Policy No. 33, New York, 1948.

Survey of Industrial Buying Practices, National Industrial Advertisers Association, New York, 1949.

Westing, J. H., & I. V. Fine (eds.), *Industrial Purchasing,* John Wiley & Sons, New York, 1955.

Wilson, I. H., *Merchandising Primer,* McGraw-Hill Book Co., New York, 1953.

Wingate, I. F., *Know Your Merchandise,* rev ed, Harper & Bros., New York, 1951.

Wingate, J. W., *Buying for Retail Stores,* 3rd ed, Prentice-Hall, Englewood Cliffs, N.J., 1953.

Wingate, J. W., & E. O. Schaller, *Techniques of Retail Merchandising,* 2d ed, Prentice-Hall, Englewood Cliffs, N.J., 1956.

CHAPTER 18

STORAGE AND WAREHOUSING

Storage management—holding and preserving tangible goods between the time of their production or purchase and that of their sale or use—was formerly considered a primary management responsibility. In recent years a strong trend has set in to treat it as a Marketing operation. Increasingly, storage policy and supervision of storage activities is seen as part of the sales manager's or marketing manager's job. Five aspects of storage are analyzed in this chapter: (1) storage purposes; (2) ownership of stored goods; (3) storage agencies; (4) public warehousing—services, receipts, charges, and control; and (5) selection of a warehouse.

STORAGE PURPOSES AND THEIR ECONOMIC SIGNIFICANCE

Except when the federal government acquires agricultural "surpluses" in connection with the federal farm aid program, or when it stockpiles supplies of strategic raw materials, storers have no broad economic purposes in view. Their objective is the narrower one of business profit. This profit may result from: (1) selling the stored goods at a higher price in the future, (2) buying at lower prices now than in the future, (3) obtaining quantity discounts and lower freight charges through bulk purchases larger than current needs, (4) improvement or "conditioning" goods during storage, or (5) maintaining inventories at effective operating levels.

Although the business units responsible for most of the nation's storing may give little or no thought to the economic consequences of their actions in the aggregate, these consequences are profound and generally beneficial. Storing usually adds a "time utility" to goods. Where "conditioning" of the stored goods occurs, "product utility" is enhanced. Inventory maintenance, if it be deemed a form of storage, contributes to effective marketing procedure.

Creation of "time utility"

Storage adds "time utility" to goods under three circumstances: (1) when it balances seasonal production and regular consumption, (2) when it balances regular production and seasonal consumption, and (3) when it relieves gluts and shortages.

Balancing of seasonal production and regular consumption. Over one-third of America's wheat crop is harvested in two months, July and August. Milling and other utilizations of this wheat are spread fairly evenly through the year. Production and consumption of most other crops is similarly un-synchronized. The necessary balance between the two processes is provided every year by storage. Each grain pours into a series of local and "termi-nal" elevators during the two or three months of its major harvest period, and is fed out during the balance of the year. Much of each vegetable and fruit crop is now canned or quick-frozen during the few weeks of its ripening period, and is moved into warehouses from which it is distributed evenly during the rest of the year. Coal and ores shipped on the Great Lakes are not produced seasonally, but there is a seasonal hiatus in their ship-ment each winter when the Lakes freeze; these items must also be stock-piled in summer and fall, to provide smelters and mills with a year-round supply.

Storage of seasonal crops prevents wastage of excesses over the possi-bility of current consumption in the harvest period, and makes these ex-cesses available in months when current production would be impossible. Price swings are ironed out—though not completely, for prices for stored commodities must rise during the seasons of their storage sufficiently to cover storage costs and yield some profit on the operation; otherwise the storage would not be undertaken. Over-all production is increased; the low "glut" price that would prevail if any crop had to be fully consumed in the period of its harvesting would discourage much production now profitably undertaken at harvest-time prices that reflect a year-round consumption.

Balancing regular production and seasonal consumption. Seasonal varia-tion, sometimes slight, often pronounced, marks the retail sale of most manufactured consumer items; examples of extreme variation in demand are garden tools, woolen blankets, straw hats, sporting goods, and holiday novelties. Sometimes manufacturers can maintain fairly level production schedules in the face of these seasonal swings in demand for their items by "rationalizing" their production—i.e., by producing several different com-modities with contra-seasonal demand schedules. In many cases such "rationalization" is not possible, or has not yet been achieved. For manufacturers in this plight, production for storage offers the only possibility of steady year-round operation.

The effect of storage in this case is not to relieve alternating periods of glut and shortage with corresponding alternation of low distress and high-stringency prices. Manufacturers can, after all, control their production timing and, by installing sufficient equipment and concentrating their production effort, they could make their output coincide with seasonal demand. But such concentration of seasonal goods production in a short period of each year would require much more equipment, and involve higher wages and personnel costs, than if it were spread evenly through the year. The higher equipment and production costs—much higher than the alternative costs of storage—would necessarily be reflected in higher prices for the seasonal goods. Storage, which permits economical equalization of production throughout the year, thus has the effect of generally reducing seasonal item costs.

Relief of gluts and shortages. Storage to relieve gluts and anticipated shortages has the Biblical precedent of Joseph's storing the surpluses of seven fat years against the leanness of seven years to come. The wisdom of Joseph is still sound policy in dealing with products of field and farm. In some years a favorable combination of planted acreage, agricultural technology, sun, and rain enables the farmers of the United States to plant and reap more grain than the American people can eat and the normal foreign market can buy. In other years, droughts may cause the country's grain harvest to fall below normal consumption and export demand. Or climate abroad, or the economic and social consequences of war, can cause foreign demand for American grains to soar to a level which, combined with normal domestic consumption, exceeds current harvests. Storage of grain harvest surpluses, sometimes on a turnover basis for an extended series of years, has provided reserves from which the demands of this country and other parts of the world can be met in years of deficiency.*

Industrial production, too, can experience gluts and stringencies. The momentum of planned production in many lines is such that production cutbacks cannot be made instantly upon a fall-off in demand. Inventories pile up. If rapid seasonal or style obsolescence is not involved, such surpluses may be held off a "soft" market by storage, to be fed out later when production has been cut back or when demand has recovered. Our steel plants and public utilities have learned to store mountainous reserves of coal against the contingency of a protracted miners' strike. The ultimate

---

* During the post-war period, as a consequence of improved agricultural technology and government price-support programs, there has been persistent overproduction of many crops, in contrast to a cyclical balance of over- and under-production. This has deprived agricultural storage of much of its glut-shortage-relief significance.

in storing against possible shortages is the Federal Government's current program of stock-piling various materials strategically necessary to national defense.

The economic benefits of this type of storage can be very great. Without the possibility of storage, occasional excess production of farm or factory might have to be treated as waste, an absolute loss to the producers and to the national economy. Or if such excess were "dumped" upon the market, the resulting price collapse could be disastrous not only to the individual producers, but also to the entire industry. Also, when a time of shortage arrives, the existence of stored surpluses from an earlier period of glut means availability of the item in question to many who would otherwise have to forego it. As stored goods flow onto the market, their addition to supply holds down the skyrocketing effect of scarcity on prices.

Quality improvement

Some products require a period of "aging" to acquire certain qualities that the market demands. Liquors, lumber, some cheeses, hides, and certain kinds of tobacco are examples. Hard and "cordial" candies generally require a three-to-four-months' "mellowing" period. Storage for these commodities does not necessarily create time utility, but adds a definite product utility. It may be considered a productive process required to achieve certain particular qualities which the market desires in such items.

Maintenance of operational inventories

The well-stocked larders or reserves of household linen maintained by many householders, the inventories of goods for resale which are the stock in trade of retailers and wholesalers, and the stock-room inventories of finished goods, raw materials, and work-in-process of manufacturers, may all be considered operational inventories and it is advisable to include them in any study of storage. Increasingly, manufacturers and wholesalers are maintaining these stocks in public merchandise warehouses instead of on their own premises. Furthermore, even where these stocks rest in consumers' pantries and closets, or on retailers' counters and shelves, or in the stockrooms of retailers, wholesalers, or manufacturers, they constitute commodity reserves whose increase or decrease, like that of warehoused items, helps adjust varying tempos of production and consumption to each other. Management of stockroom inventories of manufacturers, wholesalers, and large retailers is closely related to that of warehoused stocks.

Large manufacturers selling broad lines to a national market, have a special problem of inventory maintenance. The items that constitute their lines are often produced in widely scattered factories. These must be delivered, on orders covering many items in the line, to wholesalers and large dealers throughout the country. Such a manufacturer must set up stocks of his entire line in his own warehouses or in public warehouses, at judiciously selected distribution centers. Maintenance of these "territorial" inventories simplifies the filling of sales orders. It also produces shipping cost economies, since carload shipments of individual items can be made from factories to warehouses, and truckload or "mixed car" shipments from warehouses to customers.

America's operational inventories of manufactured goods have tended to increase, in volume and value, as the nation's business has expanded and price levels have risen. But the ratio of these inventories to sales has registered a long-term decline. Faster transportation, better delivery techniques, improved reliability of distributive agencies—all tending to lower the safety minimum of operational inventories—account for this falling inventory/sales ratio. Quantitatively, then, the storage operation for manufactured goods has lost some ground to the other marketing operations. But this very tendency of retailers, wholesalers, and manufacturers to operate with relatively smaller inventories has magnified the problems of storage policy and storage management.

OWNERSHIP OF STORED GOODS

Storage is commonly thought of as primarily a function of wholesalers and other middlemen. This assumption is correct with respect to agricultural products, incorrect as regards manufactured goods. Actually, ownership of stored goods is divided among farmers, manufacturers, wholesalers, retailers, and consumers. We shall note first the distribution of ownership of stored agricultural products, then that of manufactured goods prior to their acquisition by consumers, and finally the contribution of consumers to the storage function.

Agricultural products

Farmers store only a small part of the major agricultural crops. Their barns are usually constructed primarily to shelter their farm implements and contain fodder for the farm animals they maintain. Most farmers' barns can hold only a small fraction of their "pay" crops, and then only for limited periods. Furthermore, very few farmers store their crops after harvesting in public grain elevators or agricultural produce warehouses. They are not equipped, by interest or experience, to handle the speculative and financial problems of such storage, and for most of them the need for cash upon harvesting precludes postponing immediate sale of their crops.*

Most of the grain storage in "country" elevators is by dealers. Some own and operate the elevators they use as private storage units. Others utilize public elevators and warehouses in the country market centers. In recent years, farmers' marketing cooperatives have expanded their grain storage activities. Some large milling companies which buy their grain at the "country" markets also maintain country elevators and warehouses. Ownership of grain in the great "terminal" elevators is divided among large "terminal" dealers, milling houses, and speculators.

Some cotton stored in gin yards and local warehouses is owned by the raisers, but most belongs to dealers. Most of the cotton held in central market warehouses is owned by dealers; some belongs to mills. Warehoused tobacco is almost entirely owned by dealers.

Manufactured goods

Manufacturers' inventories, including raw materials as well as finished products, substantially exceed those of wholesalers and retailers combined. At the close of 1959 the figures were, respectively, $52 billion and $37 billion.

Manufacturers' stocks of raw materials are usually kept in their own private warehouses or stock rooms. In the case of finished goods inventories, however, manufacturers in some lines are turning to public merchandise warehouses as more efficient substitutes for private branch warehouses.

Wholesalers of manufactured goods also tend to maintain their stocks in their own private warehouses and lofts. Retailers' inventories are found primarily on their shelves and counters and in stock space on their store premises. General mail order houses, the large chains, and the larger department stores maintain private warehouses.

Consumers as storers

Consumers' "pantry" and "closet" stocks constitute a not unimportant element of the supply of canned foods and certain other classes of goods available for consumption. Occasional sudden expansions of consumers' "pantry" supplies through waves of "hoarding" and subsequent sagging of consumer purchases in certain lines when such "hoards" are consumed, can exercise temporarily disturbing effects on the national economy. A new and growing field of consumer storage has been opened by the development

---

* However, the federal farm parity price program, described in Chapter 30, induces large numbers of farmers to hold crops for short periods in public elevators and warehouses, and in some cases in their own barns, if adapted as field warehouses, whenever market prices for crops fall under a specified percentage of their parity prices.

of frozen food lockers and home deep-freeze units. In the over-all picture of storaging, however, the role of the consumer is minor.

CLASSES OF PUBLIC MERCANTILE WAREHOUSES

While store counters and shelves, and stock rooms, account for a substantial part of manufactured goods storage, the mercantile warehouse * is the distinctive storage institution. Warehouses may be private or public. The former are owned by large manufacturers, wholesalers, and retailers, and only their operators' goods are stored in them. The facilities and services of a *public* warehouse are available, as far as its facilities permit, to all storers of commodities for which the warehouse is maintained, subject to payment of listed charges.

Four classes of public mercantile warehouses are generally recognized: (1) special commodity warehouses, such as grain elevators, in which particular agricultural commodities are stored without refrigeration; (2) refrigerated (cold storage) warehouses; (3) general merchandise warehouses for manufactured goods; and (4) field warehouses. Storage in the first three of these classes of warehouses is both private and public. The fourth class involves exclusively public warehousing.

Special commodity warehouses

At latest report there were some 23,000 country grain elevators with a capacity of 1.6 billion bushels. A small proportion were "captive," belonging to private chain systems owned by dealer organizations and millers. Most were independent units, some operated by dealers on a private basis, others operated exclusively on a public basis, and still others combining private and public operation. The balance were owned by cooperatives, their services for the most part available only to the members. There are some 450 terminal market elevators with a capacity of about 9 billion bushels. From 50 to 60 percent of their capacity is available for public storage. The federal government also maintains elevators with a capacity of between 800–900 million bushels. The proportion of public to private warehousing for cotton, tobacco, and some other crops, is much higher than in the case of the grain elevators.

Public grain elevators perform little service other than storage for their clients. Private grain elevators, however, commonly perform various "conditioning" operations on the grain they receive. Facilities are available for cleaning grain, raising or lowering its moisture content, and making grade-mixtures. The private elevators can often deliver higher-grade, and so

---

* Household goods warehouses, which perform no *marketing* functions, are excluded from the classification of *mercantile* warehouses.

higher-priced, grain than they receive. This gives their owners a significant competitive advantage.

Refrigerated warehouses

A refrigerated (cold storage) warehouse is defined as one artificially cooled to a temperature of 45° F. or below, in which articles of food and certain other products may be held for thirty days or more. Various classes of foodstuffs require different temperatures for effective preservation. Most fresh fruits and vegetables have to be kept at approximately 35° F., eggs between 29° and 32°, butter at zero temperature, meat at 25°, and "frozen foods" at zero after an initial pre-storage freezing at a still lower temperature. Furs, rugs, silk, inks, and pastes are examples of non-food items which require cold storage. Most refrigerated warehouses are equipped to maintain a single temperature, or a limited temperature range, throughout their storage space, and hence can take only the particular food and other items for which that temperature or range is appropriate. A few are equipped to maintain different temperatures in separate sections.

Most packers operate their own private refrigerated warehouses. Cold storage warehouses for other commodities are generally public or combined public and private.

A recent striking expansion of refrigerated warehousing has occurred through the widespread establishment of *frozen food locker plants*. These plants rent individual refrigerated lockers, in which quick-frozen meats and other foods can be preserved, to consumers. Fresh cuts of meat, and fresh fruits and vegetables, are brought by the locker-tenants to the plant, are quick-frozen there, and are then kept in the lockers until withdrawn for consumption. These frozen food locker plants are not strictly public warehouses, since they do not control the entry or withdrawal of stored items, or issue warehouse receipts for them. Some responsibilities of the public warehouseman, such as maintaining proper preservative conditions and providing protection against theft, however, are involved. Some frozen food locker plants are operated by wholesale or retail butchers, others by ice manufacturing companies, others by consumer cooperative groups.

General merchandise warehouses

There are some 1,500 to 1,800 public general merchandise warehouses. These not only store occasional or seasonal surpluses, but also perform many distributive services for their clients, as described later in this chapter.

The *bonded warehouse* is a special type of general merchandise warehouse. These warehouses undertake a heavy surety bond to the U.S. Treasury and place their premises under the custody of an agent of the

Treasury. Given these arrangements, an importer who must pay customs duties, or a liquor distiller, tobacco products manufacturer, or producer of any other product subject to federal internal revenue excise, may store his goods in such a warehouse without having to pay the customs duty or excise for so long as his goods remain in the warehouse. In the case of liquors, which must undergo a protracted "aging" process in storage, this postponement of tax may be for several years. The customs duty or excise is paid upon withdrawal of the goods from the warehouse for sale.

Field warehousing

Field warehousing is an interesting arrangement combining private and public storage, whereby a manufacturer stores his product on his own premises, thereby saving the costs of renting public warehouse storage space and trucking his stocks to and from the warehouse, yet is enabled to enjoy certain financial advantages that ordinarily attach only to public warehousing.

Banks will not usually lend upon the security of a manufacturer's own inventory stored in his own stock rooms. There is no way that a bank can control such inventory and be certain that it remains unimpaired as collateral for a loan. The warehouse receipt of a reputable public warehouseman, however, is commonly acceptable security for a bank loan since possession of the receipt by the bank during the period of the loan ensures nonwithdrawal from the warehouse of any of the merchandise covered by the receipt.

Under field warehousing, a manufacturer walls off part of his storage space in such a way that there is no longer free communication between it and the rest of his premises. He then leases this space, for a nominal rental, to a public warehouseman. A custodian, who may be paid by the manufacturer but is an employee of the public warehouseman and subject to his control, is placed in charge. Now when any of the manufacturer's goods are placed in this storage area, they pass out of his possession and control into that of the public warehouseman. The warehouseman gives the manufacturer a regular warehouse receipt for the goods. Not until this receipt is subsequently presented to the custodian can the goods be removed from the storage area, even though it is on the manufacturer's premises. Under these circumstances, a "field warehouse" receipt is as acceptable for bank loan collateral as any regular public warehouse receipt.

Field warehousing is generally undertaken by organizations established for this exclusive purpose.

SERVICES OF PUBLIC WAREHOUSES

Public warehouses offer their clients three types of services: (1) basic "preservative" services inherent in the concept of storaging; (2) supplementary distributive services; and (3) certain financial services.

Preservative

Public warehouses of all classes perform three preservative services as a matter of course for their clients: (1) space accommodation for stored items; (2) protection from weather, fire, and other forces of deterioration and destruction; and (3) protection from theft and other human disturbance. Public cold storage warehouses offer controlled temperature, in addition.

In many cases the public warehouse can perform these bare preservative services for a client better or more cheaply than he could for himself. This is particularly true where storage volume requirements of the individual client are relatively small or highly seasonal. Still, with respect to the basic preservative functions, the advantages of public warehousing over private storage are usually slight. They only partly account for the growing place that the public warehouses, particularly the public merchandise warehouses, are establishing for themselves in the nation's marketing system. It is to their auxiliary distributive and financial services that the public warehouses owe much of their present position.

Distributive

Public warehouses enable a purchaser or seller to take advantage of the *in transit* privilege of railroad freight charge reduction (explained in Chapter 26). For example, a cotton goods manufacturer with plants in Chicago, Columbus, Detroit, Baltimore, New York, and Boston buys a large quantity of cotton linter bales in Jackson, Miss. At the time of purchase the company does not have adequate storage facilities, nor is its management certain just what quantities the different plants will eventually need. Accordingly, the entire purchase might be shipped from Jackson to a public warehouse in Memphis, under an *in transit* arrangement with the railroad. Months later the cotton would be shipped from Memphis to the various plants in the amounts then required. Instead of paying separate charges from Jackson to Memphis, and then from Memphis to each destination city, the lower through-rates from Jackson to each of the destination cities are paid. Freight savings per carload may be substantial.

Public merchandise warehouses may serve their clients as local shipping agents. A manufacturer can make CL shipments to a warehouse centered in one of his market areas. From these stocks the warehouse will make small-lot shipments, at the direction of the manufacturer's sales department, to individual customers in the area, using railroad LCL service, or freight forwarders, or motor freight carriers, or whatever other transport medium offers the best traffic advantages. Local deliveries may be made by the warehouse's own trucks. Packing and labeling of the individual shipments is done by the warehouse. In many cases, public warehouses will undertake forwarding service even where no storage is involved. A manufacturer can make up a pool car loaded with packages destined to various customers in a market area, and route it at a low freight charge to the warehouse, which handles the receipt of the car, its unloading, and the distribution of the individual shipments to the various consignees. By using several public merchandise warehouses in his market area, a manufacturer can obtain all the traffic benefits of a series of branch stock rooms without the costs of establishing them.

Tobacco warehouses provide auction facilities on their premises. Some public merchandise warehouses maintain conference and display rooms for their clients' salesmen, so that the warehouse buildings can be used to some extent as branch sales offices. Warehouses may make credit inquiries on local customers for their out-of-town clients, or even extend credit to approved customers on behalf of their clients. Because of these special selling services afforded by public merchandise warehouses, some manufacturers have found them effective substitutes in some areas for distribution through wholesalers.

Financial

As explained above in the discussion of field warehousing, if a client obtains a warehouse receipt from a reputable public warehouseman, he has an instrument that banks will accept as collateral for a secured loan. He can finance the carrying of his inventory while it is in the warehouse, even where he might not be an acceptable risk for an unsecured bank loan. This financial aspect of the warehouse receipt is sometimes advanced as the principal reason for the dominance of the public warehouse in the cotton storage field.

Sometimes public warehouses lend directly to their clients on the security of the goods stored with them.

PUBLIC WAREHOUSE RECEIPTS

The issuance, contents, and certain details of the form of public warehouse receipts are governed by the Uniform Warehouse Receipts Act which has been enacted by all states. Illustration 18–1 shows a standard form of negotiable warehouse receipt, embodying the requirements of the Uniform Act, which has been approved for public merchandise and refrigerated warehouses by the American Bankers Association, the American Warehousemen's Association, and the U.S. Department of Commerce.

A properly executed warehouse receipt, negotiable or nonnegotiable, constitutes an acknowledgement by the warehouse of receipt of the goods delivered into its charge. It is also the contract between the warehouse and

To be legal, it is not necessary that the Negotiable Warehouse Receipt be in this particular form, which has been devised solely for the purpose of attaining uniformity in warehousing forms and practices.

AMERICAN WAREHOUSE COMPANY
2121 AMERICAN AVENUE
AMERICA

Consecutive No.________
Date of Issue________

THIS IS TO CERTIFY that we have received in Storage Warehouse______situated at ________ for the account of________ in apparent good order, except as noted hereon (contents, condition and quality unknown) the following described property, subject to all the terms and conditions contained herein and on the reverse hereof, such property to be delivered to HIS / THEIR / ITS order, upon payment of all storage, handling and other charges and the surrender of this Warehouse Receipt properly endorsed.

LOT NO.	QUANTITY	SAID TO BE OR CONTAIN	EX CAR NO. INITIAL	STORAGE PER MONTH		HANDLING IN AND OUT	
				RATE	PER	RATE	PER
		NEGOTIABLE					

Advances have been made and liability incurred on such goods, as follows:

The property covered by this receipt has NOT been insured by this company for the benefit of the depositor against fire or any other casualty.

American Warehouse Company claims a lien for all lawful charges for storage and preservation of the goods; also for all lawful claims for money advanced, interest, insurance, transportation, labor, weighing, coopering and other charges and expenses in relation to such goods.

AMERICAN WAREHOUSE COMPANY

By________

This Receipt is Valid Only When Signed by an Officer of the Company.

NEGOTIABLE WAREHOUSE RECEIPT (Front)
(Printed on blue paper)

21

Devised by the Committee on Warehousing Documentation and Office Procedures of the American Warehousemen's Association, Merchandise Division, and approved by the Association at the 58th Annual Meeting of the American Warehousemen's Association at San Francisco, February, 1949.

MODEL NEGOTIABLE WAREHOUSE RECEIPT. *Courtesy of American Warehousemen's Association.*

ILLUSTRATION 18–1

the storer for the storing of the goods and performance of services connected with such storage. It must specify the warehousing company and the warehouse unit involved. It must explicitly indicate or describe the items stored and the quantities involved, and the services to be performed. It must also state the unit or total charges for the storage and services. Details of the general contractual interrelations of the warehouse and the storer are printed on the back of standard form warehouse receipts.

A *negotiable* warehouse receipt is a document of title, and establishes ownership of the stored items in the named storer or any other party to whom the receipt has been negotiated and delivered. In the specimen warehouse receipt shown in Illustration 18–1, negotiability is established by the stamped word "NEGOTIABLE" and by the statement in the "certification" paragraph that the stored items will be delivered to the "order" of the storer upon "the surrender of this Warehouse Receipt properly endorsed." A receipt without these provisions would also be negotiable if it were made out to "Bearer"; in such case delivery alone, without endorsement, would suffice to pass title. As the wording of a negotiable receipt indicates, the warehouseman's obligation under it is to deliver the goods covered by the receipt, upon its presentation, to any party whose title is established on the face of the receipt and any endorsements on its back. As a corollary, the warehouse will refuse delivery unless the receipt is presented, no matter what other proofs of ownership the claimant may offer.

A *nonnegotiable* warehouse receipt is identical in all respects with a negotiable receipt, except that it is stamped "NON-NEGOTIABLE" and does not contain the "order" and "surrender" provisions in its "certification" paragraph. Only the named storer can withdraw goods covered by a nonnegotiable receipt. He can do so without presenting the receipt to the warehouse; a written or identified telephone order suffices. If he wishes to transfer title to the goods without withdrawal, he can make a legal assignment; the assignee protects his title by notifying the warehouseman.

Nonnegotiable as well as negotiable warehouse receipts may be used as collateral for bank loans. For loan purposes a nonnegotiable receipt is either made out originally in the bank's name, or assigned to the bank. Banks generally prefer nonnegotiable receipts as loan security, because it is easier to authorize partial withdrawals by the borrower by merely directing the warehouse to permit the withdrawal, instead of having to present the actual receipt. For the same reason, manufacturers who do not need to borrow on their warehouse receipts usually also prefer nonnegotiable ones. About the only class of storers who really need negotiable warehouse receipts are middlemen in agricultural products and other raw material lines who expect to sell their stored products through spot transactions on commodity exchanges. Nonnegotiable warehouse receipts, accordingly, are far more widely used than negotiable receipts.

Warehouse receipts for agricultural commodities differ in minor details from the public merchandise warehouse form shown in Illustration 18–1, but their inherent content is essentially the same. There is provision on the face of the instrument for statement of the standard grade of the commodity as determined by official inspection at the time it is first brought within the warehouse.

PUBLIC WAREHOUSE CHARGES

Public warehouse charges are generally not controlled by public authority. Custom and competition, however, have made the quoting of warehouse charges fairly uniform, and the charged rates relate closely to the protection accorded the stored goods and the other services rendered.

Public merchandise warehouse charges are generally quoted in two parts: (1) a "handling" charge, quoted per unit or per cwt., which is fixed regardless of the period of storage; and (2) a "storage" charge, also per unit or per cwt., quoted by the month or fraction of a month. Grain elevators likewise set separate handling and storage charges on a per bushel basis, but their handling charges cover an initial storage period of five to twenty days, often spoken of as "free time."

Handling and storing charges vary according to the commodities stored. In determining the handling charges, the warehouses take into account the actual physical handling when receiving various classes of items, the labor and costs involved in their delivery to loading platforms and sometimes the costs of loading them on cars or trucks, and the bookkeeping costs involved. Storage rates vary according to the amount of floor space required for volume storage, physical characteristics of the merchandise and its packing as they affect stacking, requirements as to temperature and air humidity, capacity of the merchandise to absorb or give off odors, the value of the merchandise, and various liabilities that may be associated with its storage.

CONTROL OF PUBLIC WAREHOUSES

There is considerable uncertainty as to the status of public warehouses as instrumentalities of interstate commerce, and therefore as to the power of the federal government to control them. Federal regulation of certain phases of the activity of agricultural product warehouses, however, has been provided on a voluntary basis, so that the constitutional issue has been avoided.

Federal regulation of agricultural product warehouses

The U.S. Warehouse Act of 1916 provides for the *voluntary* licensing, inspection, bonding, and regulation of warehouse receipt issues, for public warehouses storing certain classes of agricultural products. Since federal licensing has come to be accepted as a guaranty of the proper conduct of warehouses in the fields covered by the Act, and the warehouse receipts of licensed warehouses are accepted more readily as financial security, most warehouses of the classes to which the Act is applicable have taken out licenses under the voluntary federal procedure.

State control of agricultural product warehouses

State control of agricultural product public warehouses is common. The usual features of state laws applying to these classes of warehouses are: (1) elevators and warehouses must be licensed by a specified state commission, and must be bonded to protect the storers; (2) they must not discriminate among storers as to services and charges, and their schedules of charges must be posted; (3) in a number of states, public grain elevator rates are specifically controlled, as to maximum rates that may be charged, by state commissions; (4) grading and weighing of grain and other products as received is done by state inspectors or is subject to their supervision; (5) issuance of warehouse receipts in accordance with the provisions of the state's enactment of the Uniform Warehouse Receipts Act is prescribed, sometimes with special provisions applicable to receipts for agricultural commodities, and issuance of fraudulent receipts is severely penalized; (6) the warehouses are given a lien on the stored products for unpaid charges.

Some twenty of the states have adopted, with rather wide variation in details, a Uniform Cold Storage Act regulating cold storage warehouses. These state laws provide for the licensing of such warehouses, forbid storage of tainted or contaminated items in them, specify the maximum periods during which different classes of foods can be stored, provide for the stamping or tagging of all foods stored in them as "cold storage" products, and require detailed records of stored items.

Terminal elevators and warehouses are often subject to further control by the commodity exchanges on which the stored products are traded by means of receipts issued by these warehouses. This control is particularly sharp where state control is lacking or lax.

Regulation of general merchandise warehouses

Except for the provisions of the State Warehouse Receipts Acts, mentioned previously, public merchandise warehouses are not subject to licensing or regulation by the federal government, or by more than half the states. In those states where there is licensing on a compulsory or voluntary basis, control usually takes the form of a bond requirement as security for the observance by the warehouse of its legal duties. Only four states assume jurisdiction over the rates and charges of public merchandise warehouses.

SELECTION OF A WAREHOUSE

Operation of a public or private warehouse involves highly technical managerial arts that can not be considered in a general Marketing textbook. The techniques of inventory control essential to sound storage management are also beyond our scope. But two phases of manufacturers' storage management—that of the choice between private storage and public warehouses and, if the latter alternative is chosen, the choice to be made among public warehouses—do deserve brief consideration here.

Private storage vs. public warehousing

Storage rates charged by a public warehouse cover not only operating and overhead costs, but also a profit element. If a manufacturer can operate his own storage facilities at no greater cost than a public warehouseman, there is no advantage in using public warehouse facilities. Large manufacturers making steady heavy-volume distribution throughout the year from central locations, or from large branches, can probably maintain and operate their private warehouses as efficiently and at as low a cost as any public warehouseman.

A small manufacturer, however, may not have a storage problem of sufficient magnitude to warrant establishing a fully equipped merchandise warehouse. Or a large manufacturer may want to establish a series of subsidiary distribution centers, none of which would be large enough for maximum warehouse efficiency. Or a manufacturer's storage requirements may be highly seasonal, so that storage facilities sufficient for his peak requirement would be largely wasted at other periods of the year. In these three cases, public warehousing may offer a manufacturer substantial economies over private storage.

Furthermore, as indicated earlier in this chapter, the warehouse receipts offered by public warehouses, including field warehousing companies, permit current financing through secured bank loans. This may not be possible with private storing. In other cases, the auxiliary distributive services of public warehouses may turn the scale in favor of public warehousing.

Choice among public warehousemen

The first determinant in selecting a public warehouse is its location. A small manufacturer with a seasonal market or supply problem would probably seek a warehouse in the same community as its factory. A large manufacturer planning to establish branch depots would look for public warehouses in cities that would be good distribution centers for its various sales territories. If *in transit* privilege shipping is a factor, the warehouse would have to be in a major rail center somewhere between shipping point and possible destinations.

If there is a choice among several public warehouses at a determined location, the factors that should determine selection among them are: (1) space availability in the light of the storer's needs; (2) special storage facilities that may be required or advisable in view of the nature of the commodities to be stored; (3) whether the warehouse is licensed and bonded, indicating that it conforms to minimum standards of security and reliability established by state law; (4) security from fire and other damage (the warehouse's insurance premium rate is an indication of this factor); (5) special distribution services that the warehouse may offer and the storer may find valuable; (6) storage rates, which may differ considerably among warehouses but will be closely related to the preceding factors; (7) the warehouseman's general reputation for responsibility and integrity.

REVIEW

1. Why do businesses store goods?
2. What are the economic values of storage?
3. Who or what classes of business are primarily responsible for the storage of agricultural products? of manufactured goods?
4. Explain the ownership and services of grain elevators.
5. Explain bonded warehouses.
6. Explain field warehousing.
7. What services do public warehouses perform for their clients?
8. What information is found on a public warehouse receipt? When is such a receipt negotiable? When would a negotiable receipt be preferred to a nonnegotiable one, and vice versa?
9. How are public warehouse rate charges determined?
10. In what respects are public agricultural product warehouses regulated by the federal government? by state governments? To what extent are public general merchandise warehouses subject to governmental regulation?
11. What considerations should a business weigh in (a) deciding whether to do its own storing or use a public warehouse; (b) selecting a public warehouse?

DISCUSSION TOPICS

1. "The development of quick-frozen storage had as profound social and economic consequences for the United States as did the development of TV."
2. Farmers' associations have long sought to have agricultural warehouses considered public utilities, subject to state regulation as to their operations and rates. Is there any justification for such treatment of these warehouses?
3. The American Warehousemen's Association claims that many manufacturers would benefit by closing branch sales offices and using the facilities of general merchandise warehouses in their place. Is there any foundation for this claim?

PROBLEM

Coverwell Co., a paint manufacturer, has its factory, warehouse, and sales office in Cleveland, Ohio. It sells to paint and hardware wholesalers. Starting with the area around Cleveland, it has spread its sales territory wider and wider. It now has salesmen covering the United States east of the Mississippi. The entire sales force is directed from the Cleveland office, and all shipments are made from the Cleveland warehouse.

The management now proposes to establish branch sales offices in Worcester (Mass.), New York City, Baltimore, Atlanta, and Chicago. It is proposed that a branch storage depot—rented if possible, bought if necessary—be associated with each branch sales office. Carload shipments would be made from Cleveland to the branch depots, and LCL and truck deliveries to customers would be made from the branch depots.

1. Could the Coverwell Co. use general merchandise warehouses instead of branch depots in its plan? What advantages, if any, would result? What disadvantages, if any, would there be? How would costs probably be affected? Why?

2. If the Coverwell Co. decided to use general merchandise warehouses for its branch organization, what considerations should it take into account in selecting the public warehouses it uses?

3. During the fall and winter of each year, exterior paint sales decline and the Coverwell Co.'s warehouse stocks increase. The same situation will occur in the branch depots or warehouses if their stocks are maintained in proportion to those in the Cleveland warehouse. Expansion is creating working capital problems for the Coverwell Co., and it will probably be necessary for it to obtain bank loans to carry the extra fall and winter stock of exterior paint. It can get unsecured loans at 6%, secured loans at 4%. How can it use the extra fall and winter stock of exterior paint in its Cleveland warehouse as security for a bank loan? How can it obtain loans secured by the extra fall and winter stock of exterior paint at the branches if it sets up its own branch depots? if it uses general merchandise warehouses?

SUGGESTED READINGS

Frederick, J. H., *Using Public Warehouses*, Chilton Co., Philadelphia, 1957.

The General Merchandise Warehouse, American Warehousemen's Association, Pittsburgh, no date.

Jacoby, N. H., & R. J. Saulnier, *Financing Inventory on Field Warehouse Receipts*, Studies in Business Financing, National Bureau of Economic Research, New York, 1944.

Schneider, W. J., *Field Warehousing as a Facility for Lending Against Commodities*, Macmillan, New York, 1941.

CHAPTER 19

PRICING PRINCIPLES

To set the prices at which goods are to be sold—that seems at first glance to be a childishly simple operation, compared to the complexities of product design or the difficulties of sound buying for resale, or the intricacies of advertising, selling, and the other marketing operations still to be analyzed. Yet let the output of a factory or stock of a store be priced a little too high, and it may be impossible to sell the goods. Let prices be set a little too low, and the goods will be sold without difficulty, but the factory-owner or store-owner may discover that his business is being conducted at no profit, or even at a loss. Avoidance of the pitfalls of "too high" or "too low" in pricing policy generally requires precise and delicate judgment, based upon an understanding of economic principles and a practical knowledge of current trade conditions.

The influence of pricing decisions extends far beyond the interests of the particular sellers who make these decisions. All sellers in any field are affected, as to the prices they may charge and the quantities they may hope to sell, by the pricing actions of every one of their number. The repercussions of individual pricing decisions on other producers or distributors in the field may be so slight as to be relatively imperceptible where the field is highly competitive and the sellers are many, but in some lines the pricing action of a dominant company may color the marketing picture for a whole field. Distributors' profit possibilities depend in part on the pricing decisions of the manufacturers whose goods they carry. Retailers' resale pricing freedom may be limited by manufacturers. Where they are free to set resale prices, their own pricing must start with the prices which their suppliers charged them. Consumers, of course, experience the cumulated effect of all the various chains of producers' and distributors' pricing decisions—which link up sometimes in augmenting fashion, other times in offsetting fashion.

Some business executives, with a hazy memory of college economics courses taken one or two generations ago, complain that economic theory provides little or no guidance to practical pricing policy. This is not a fair criticism of current economic doctrine. The theory of competitive, monopoly, quasi-monopoly, and imperfectly competitive price, as presented in recent economics textbooks, does constitute a comprehensive logical foundation for analysis of the present-day pricing policies of manufacturers and distributors. Our first step in the study of the pricing operation will be a brief review of economic doctrine on this subject.

PURE COMPETITIVE PRICE

The concept of "pure" * competition is not advanced by economists as closely reflecting market conditions in our actual business society. It is generally recognized that this concept is merely a working hypothesis, a useful tool based on a number of assumptions only partly realized in practice—what statisticians would call a "first approximation." Conclusions about pricing derived from the concept of pure competition should not be taken as the tenets of actual pricing policy for business in general. These conclusions do, however, establish a "boundary" or "ceiling" to the pricing policies of most American business enterprises.

The assumptions of the theory of "pure" competition are:

1. The units of the product sold are so homogeneous, similar, or standardized, that the offerings of all sellers are practically identical and can be readily substituted for each other. Terms of sale and services offered in connection with the sale of the commodity are practically the same for all sellers.

2. The number of sellers is so large, and the quantities of their offerings sufficiently comparable, that the actions of no single seller, or of no small associated group of sellers, can appreciably affect the total available supply of the commodity.

3. Within the practicable pricing range, all sellers produce or market the product over the long run upon an increasing unit cost basis.** Hence total supply of the commodity is elastic relative to price—it increases appreciably in response to higher prices, contracts with lower prices—since higher prices permit the inclusion, and lower prices induce the exclusion, of marginal high cost units by individual producers. This elasticity of supply may be accentuated by differences in the cost schedules of the individual sellers, leading to inclusion or exclusion of marginal high-cost suppliers in response to price variation.

---

* No distinction is drawn in this discussion between "pure" and "perfect" competition.
** Should any appreciable number of producers in an industry operate under circumstances of decreasing unit cost—as could occur temporarily if there were an excess of productive capacity in the industry relative to current demand—competition would be exaggerated, and price would be unstable. Such an unstable price would be still lower than "normal" competitive price.

4. The number of buyers is so large, and the quantities of their purchases sufficiently comparable, that the actions of no single buyer, or of no small associated group of buyers, can appreciably affect aggregate demand for the commodity.

5. Within the practicable pricing range, aggregate demand for the commodity is negatively elastic—shrinking in response to higher prices, expanding with lower prices—because of diminishing utility of successive units of the commodity to individual purchasers, differing intensities of demand for the commodity among indivduals, differing purchasing power among various market groups, and use competition of other commodities at various price levels.

6. There are no rigidities of supply, demand, or price. New capital can flow freely into or out of a business, enlarging or contracting its productive capacity. Demand is not frozen in the face of changing prices by long-term contracts, and is not bound to any particular supplier or group of suppliers by goodwill or other considerations. Price can vary cent by cent, free of extraneous control, and without any "stickiness," as supply or demand changes.

Determination

If all six of the assumptions noted above were fully realized in the marketing of any commodity, its price over the long run would tend to settle at that level where the aggregate amount produced at such price level just covered the aggregate buying demand at such price, with neither shortage nor surplus resulting. The price of any commodity produced under conditions of pure competition would act automatically as an equilibrator of its supply and of demand for it. Should effective demand for the commodity at any current price exceed its available supply, some of the would-be customers would bid up the price in an effort to satisfy their desire for it. At a higher price, some of the previous marginal demand for the commodity would evaporate, while existing producers would be induced to expand their output and new productive facilities might be created. Somewhere along the line of rising price the shrinkage of demand and the expansion of production and distribution would establish a new equilibrium. Similarly, an excess of supply over demand at any given price would lead to a price decline which, in turn, would induce quantitative expansion of demand and constriction of supply until renewed equilibrium was established.

A pure competitive price is not necessarily a territorially uniform one. Such a price for any commodity would ordinarily be established in the central market city or cities, where heavy volume transactions in the commodity occur. Elsewhere the price would be determined by central market transactions, but would be higher or lower by the amount of the normal freight charge and other shipping costs. An out-of-town seller whose produce must be shipped to the central market would receive the current competitive price less shipping and middleman costs. An out-of-town buyer purchasing from the central market would pay the competitive price plus shipping and middleman costs.

Competitive price, volume, and cost considerations for individual concerns

A pure competitive market price temporarily established for any commodity, as indicated above, by the marginal interaction of elastic demand for it and of an elastic cost-supply schedule for the industry, would be, for each individual producer or distributor of the commodity, an absolute figure to which he would have to conform. For each such producer or distributor, demand for his output would appear to be infinitely elastic with respect to the established market price. If he attempted to set his price ever so slightly higher than the established market price, he would not be able to sell any part of his output, since all of his customers would shift their patronage to his competitors. If he set his price ever so slightly lower, and his competitors maintained the previous market price, he would receive more orders than his capacity would permit him to fulfill, and would simply be sacrificing profit margin to no purpose. While an individual seller in a truly competitive market cannot have a pricing policy, he does have cost and volume problems. Whether he is a manufacturer, a wholesale distributor, or a retailer, he is likely to have a combination of fixed and variable costs such that the average unit cost of the products he sells tends to decline with increasing sales volume until the limits of his productive or handling capacity are approached; then it tends to rise. For most competitive sellers—the nonmarginal ones—there is a volume range for which average unit cost is below the current market price, allowing a profit margin. Each seller seeks to push his sales up to that profit range. Economic theory teaches that within that range there is a particular "optimum" volume, where *marginal* unit cost equals market price, which will give maximum profit (see Illustration 19–1). Few if any competitive sellers ever attempt to determine such an optimum volume. To achieve any volume within the profit range suffices.

It often happens that a competive seller's costs are such that, at the market price of the moment, his average unit cost remains above the market price for all possible volumes within his production capacity or sales possibility. The usual first approach to this problem is an examination of costs to ascertain if some may be "shaved." Frequently this is possible, and with the necessary sales volume the seller may break even or possibly squeeze some profit margin. Where shaving is not possible, or not sufficient to bring unit costs down to the current market price, or where sales volume

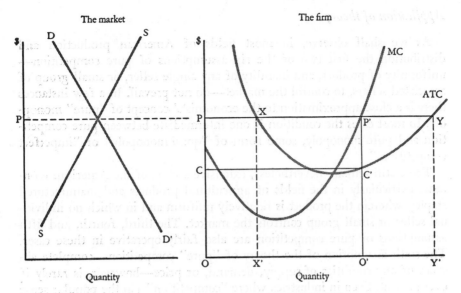

The market   The firm

THEORY OF PURE COMPETITIVE PRICE

Market interaction of rising supply cost and diminishing quantity demand establishes the price for a purely competitive commodity at P.

This market price becomes both the marginal and average unit revenue for every *firm* producing the commodity. In the illustrated case —an inframarginal firm—the firm would make some profit on any output between X' and Y'. Its optimum output, however, is O', at which quantity its marginal cost just equals its marginal revenue. At this quantity, its total revenue is the area in the rectangle PP'C'C. Because of the interrelation of the MC and ATC curves, any greater or lesser quantity would produce a total-revenue rectangle with an area less than that of PP'C'C.

This firm, or any other individual firm, could not sell at a higher price with a view to increasing total revenue, for there would be no buyers at such price. At a lower price it could sell any volume up to its ultimate capacity limits, but the crossing point of the MC curve and the lower price line would be at a still lower quantity figure than for the established market price, and it would only earn less total revenue or sustain a loss.

A firm that had higher costs would still find its optimum volume —maximizing its profit or minimizing its loss—to be the quantity at which marginal cost was identical with price, so long as there was any quantity range or point at which marginal cost was less than price.

ILLUSTRATION 19–1

can not be pushed up to the profit range, the unfortunate seller usually hangs on hoping for a price rise or an increase of his sales volume that will save him. If the hoped-for upturn comes before his finances are exhausted, he *is* saved; otherwise he becomes one more in the tabulation of business failures.

Application of theory

As we shall observe, in most fields of American production and distribution the first two of the six assumptions of pure competition—uniformity of product, and inability of any single seller, or small group of associated sellers, to control the market—do not prevail. In a few instances there is a close approximation to the economists' concept of "pure" monopoly. In most cases the condition is one intermediate between pure competition and pure monopoly, some form of "quasi-monopoly" or "imperfect competition."

There still remain, nevertheless, extensive sectors of the American economy, particularly in the fields of agricultural products and manufactured staples, wherein the product is relatively uniform and in which no individual seller or small group controls the market. The third, fourth, and fifth assumptions of pure competition are also fairly operative in these cases. The sixth assumption of the theory of "pure" competition—complete absence of any rigidities of supply, demand, or price—however, is rarely if ever present. Even in industries where "competition" (in the popular sense of the word) is most intense, supply is likely to be "sticky"—to employ the economists' very suggestive term—under certain circumstances. Furthermore, consumer irrationalities and governmental price controls produce many "sticky" price spots.

The theory of pure competitive price still has basic application in these cases of supply and price rigidity. Certain qualifications must be introduced into this basic price theory, however, to accommodate the effects of these rigidities, particularly with regard to their short-term effects.*

Supply rigidities

In spite of the availability of marketing research, many producers and distributors base their market plans on analytical procedures that are little better than blind guesses. But even where the fullest resources of marketing research are employed, the frequent need to forecast market conditions many months ahead, and the intervention of extraneous factors that the best research techniques cannot take into account, may result in commodity gluts or shortages. If ignorance, or mischance in forecasting, results in general overproduction of a competitive commodity, its current price is bound to sink, for a time, below its normal price according to pure competitive price theory. A shortage resulting from general misjudgment by the producers can cause a temporary market price considerably higher than the normal pure competitive one.

---

* Some Marketing authorities prefer to treat supply and price rigidities as aspects of the theory of "imperfect competition," rather than as empirical qualifications on the theory of "pure" competition.

An even more troublesome "stickiness" of supply may occur when the manufacturers' capacity for producing a competitive commodity becomes excessive, either because it was over-expanded through misjudgment of future demand, or because demand has contracted from a level that previously warranted the larger productive capacity. Excess productive capacity does not evaporate overnight, in accordance with pure competitive pricing assumptions. It continues. Price falls, and then a large proportion of the industry—instead of only a small marginal group of producers—must manufacture and sell at a loss. Eventually bankruptcy clears out part of the industry, not necessarily the least efficient, highest-cost producers, but rather the weakest producers financially. With capacity of the industry, and hence supply of the commodity, thus reduced, its price may eventually return to the level that pure competitive price theory assigns to it. Meanwhile a subnormal price—subnormal according to the theory of pure competition—may persist for months, or even for some years.

Price rigidities

Among the many manifestations of price "stickiness" or rigidity, four that significantly influence actual pricing practice are: (1) customary prices, (2) odd prices, (3) price lines, and (4) governmental price control.

1. Prices for certain items may become so well established during periods when retail price movements are moderate that they simply cannot be modified to accommodate subsequent small changes in demand, supply, or cost. Aggregate demand for such commodities becomes so elastic just above and below these *customary* retail price points that any rise in price would cause aggregate demand to decline so abruptly that the whole industry would be imperilled. The 5-cent candy bar and the 10-cent cigar are illustrations of *customary-price* commodities. When costs rose in the 1940's, normal price increases in these items could not be effected even though general demand was intensified because of increase in consumer purchasing power. Many candy manufacturers had to meet the situation by "shaving" their product to lower costs—among other economies they reduced the size of the 5-cent candy bar. In the case of the 10-cent cigar, the price held for a while in the face of rising costs, with consequent mounting loss to many of the producers. Then, not as a matter of concerted action by the producers, but as a result of general undirected market pressure, the price for these cigars rose generally to the next higher customary cigar price level—two for a quarter—and still later to the three-for-a-half-dollar level. Manufacturers and distributors of customary-price items occasionally felt that the best choice among the evils produced by rising costs was to maintain the original product at its customary price and accept reduced profit or even some loss for a time, hoping that, through improved pro-

duction technology or a change in general business conditions, costs would eventually be lowered and the customary price again yield profit.

Many customary prices resist downward pressure just as strongly as they do upward pressure. A particular section of the market comes, in time, to associate a particular price for a product with a specific quality level. Should the price be lowered, the market assumes a quality reduction. Loss of previous demand may be only partly compensated by new demand at the lower price. Cigar and cosmetic manufacturers have learned by some bitter experiences that price cuts do not necessarily open a door to wider markets.

2. Another element of price rigidity that often upsets pure competitive price theory is the phenomenon of *odd prices*. Because there is the illusion of a price reduction from the higher "round" price, such odd-amount prices as 23¢, 48¢, 97¢, $1.95, $4.73, $24.50, and $147 have an abnormal appeal to many consumers. Not only will demand at an "odd" price usually be very much greater than at the nearest higher "round" price, but demand may actually fall off below an "odd" price when the illusion of a bargain no longer holds.

3. Closely related to this phenomenon of "odd" prices is that of *price lines*. For women's dresses, for radio and television receiving sets, for refrigerators, ranges, and other kitchen equipment, and for many other medium- and high-unit-price fields, custom tends to establish at any time a sequence of "odd" prices which the buying public accepts as denoting successive quality classifications. For example, in 1960 the retail "price lines" for medium-to-high quality house dresses were $10.95, $11.95, $14.95, and $17.95. Each of these "line" prices operates as a rigid customary retail price to which most retailers in that particular quality division of the field must conform; producers who supply these retailers must sell to them at these "line" prices less the regular retailers' margin. If there is pressure from either the demand or the supply side of the market, the "line" price resists change until the pressure is sufficiently great to force a general shift by all competing sellers to the next higher or lower "line" price, with a general downgrading or upgrading of the quality standards for the entire series of "line" prices.

4. A final case of price rigidity qualifying true competitive pricing theory results from governmental price control. When a maximum price, lower than the true competitive price, is established for the benefit of consumers, demand for the controlled commodity expands beyond the equilibrium level, supply tends to contract, and a shortage results. Effective rationing may hold purchasing demand for the commodity down to the level of supply, so that an enforced equilibrium is established. If the rationing is not effective, a "black market" is established in which the true competitive price—or, more likely a higher one because of special costs and risks involved in the "black market" operation—illegally asserts itself.

The history of wartime control of consumer-goods prices in the United States and abroad provides innumerable illustrations of these generalizations.

When a minimum controlled price, higher than the true competitive price, is established for the benefit of producers, an opposite type of market disequilibrium is produced. The high control price discourages consumer demand, while stimulating production. The control is effective only if some means is currently employed to cut production back to a point where reduced output just balances reduced demand, or if the government purchases the excess production and disposes of it in ways that do not affect general purchasing demand for the commodity. The various efforts at federal farm price control from the 1930's on provide many examples of the possibilities and corollary requirements of governmental minimum price control.

PURE MONOPOLY PRICE

The theory of pure monopoly price, as formulated by the economists, assumes absolute control by a single producer of the supply of a commodity for which there is a substantial demand and no significant competition from possible substitute commodities within a substantial price range.

A monopolistic producer of a commodity, enjoying absolute control of its supply, could set any price without fear of losing part of his market to a competitor. But freedom from competition would not mean that the volume of his sales would not be affected by the price he set. Aggregate demand for the commodity would embody some element of elasticity—from the diminishing utility of successive units of the commodity to individual purchasers, from differing intensities of demand for the commodity among individuals, from differing purchasing power capacity among various market groups. Because of this partial elasticity of demand, larger quantities of the commodity would be sold if the monopolist fixed a lower price for it, and smaller quantities would be sold at higher prices.

The unit cost of a monopoly product, like that of the output of a competitive concern, tends to decline with increase of sales volume, because of the wider spreading of fixed costs, until the practicable limits of production capacity are approached. Then it starts rising, and continues to rise on an accelerating scale, with further expansion of production, because of reduced efficiency. For most monopoly products, there is a fairly wide range of volumes for which unit costs would be below the range of prices at which these volumes could be sold. At any price within this volume-price range, the monopolist would make a profit. The total profit he could achieve would not be uniform throughout this price range. There would be some "optimum" price within the range (associated with a volume at which the monopolist's marginal revenue would just equal his marginal cost, according to the economists' formula) which would give him a *maximum total profit*. At prices either higher or lower than the optimum level, total profit would taper off. These relationships of monopoly price, volume, cost, and profit are visualized in Illustration 19–2.

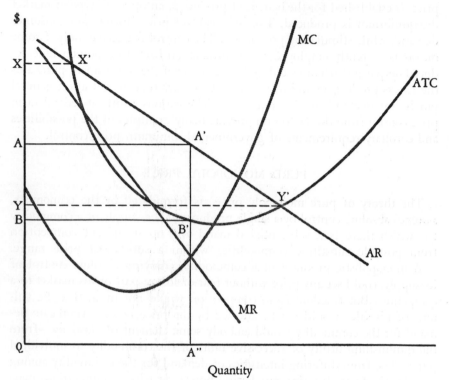

Quantity

THEORY OF MONOPOLY PRICE

A monopolistic firm would make some profit with its product priced at any figure lower than X or higher than Y. Its optimum price, however, would be A, since at the quantity A" it could sell at this price, marginal cost (MC) and marginal revenue (MR) would be identical. Its unit profit would be A'B'—the difference between average revenue (AR) and average total cost (ATC) for this quantity. Its total profit would be the area of the rectangle AA'B'B. Because of the interrelation of the AR, MR, ATC and MC curves, any other quantity related to any other price between X and Y would produce a rectangle with less area.

ILLUSTRATION 19–2

From a Marketing viewpoint, the significant feature of a production or distribution monopoly is not that there is theoretically an optimum price giving maximum total profit, but that the monopolist has freedom to price within a range that is usually fairly broad, and can derive a profit from all prices within that range. This freedom enables a monopolist to devise pricing *policies,* wisely or unsoundly conceived, and to act upon them without forcing himself out of business. These policies, as we shall see in Chapter 20, can be concerned with pricing objectives and with pricing techniques.

Extent of monopoly operation

Production and distribution monopolies can come into existence in the following ways: (1) through ownership of the sole source of supply of a raw material; (2) by achievement of exclusive position by a single producer, either through anterior establishment, or more rapid growth, or by merger of previously competing units, in the absence of government policy forbidding it; (3) as a result of the patent laws, which specifically award monopoly of a created product or product creation technique to the inventor for a limited period,* as a means of stimulating invention; (4) where there is only one retailer of a line of "convenience" goods in an isolated community; (5) by specific legislative action, as in the case of state liquor monopolies.

Through federal anti-trust action and the growth of competitive business units, true monopolies on a national scale, arising from the first and second of the above causes, such as existed in the old days, have disappeared. Still, there exist many true small-scale monopolies to which our analysis of monopoly pricing would squarely apply. Most common are patent monopolies. Many new products, so distinctive that they are truly different products rather than specialty variants of a pre-existing product, are manufactured by sole producers protected by patent rights. Even in these days of the almost omnipresent automobile, little retail monopolists are to be found in backwoods communities. Some one-third of the states, moreover, provide for the retail sale of liquor through monopolistic chains owned and operated by the states themselves.

QUASI-MONOPOLY PRICE

Probably a major proportion of American manufacturing and distributive enterprises operates under conditions of quasi-monopoly.** For one or another of the reasons analyzed below, these businesses are sheltered, *as individual units,* from the full impact of price competition in their lines. They are not completely removed from the competitive struggle, as in the

---

* Subject to the power of the Federal Trade Commission to compel licensing by the patent-holder of the right to make a patented item or use a patented technique to competing producers, where a serious economic monopoly is threatened.

** In this section and the following one we draw a distinction between "quasi-monopoly" and "imperfect competition" which is recognized in substance by most economists but which is not always framed in language. These two terms, and two others—"monopolistic competition" and "administered pricing"—are used loosely and sometimes interchangeably in economic writing.

case of true monopolies but their protection is limited—sometimes limited to a narrow price differential. Within the margin of that protection, however, they enjoy the all-important boon of comparative pricing freedom. Within that margin, like true monopolists, they can develop pricing *policy*.

Location advantages

Location advantages, under certain circumstances, may establish manufacturers or retailers as limited monopolists. In steel, cement, and other industries concerned with the manufacture of heavy-bulk products, freight costs for shipments to any considerable distance constitute a substantial fraction of delivered price. If a customary element of the industry's pricing policy is to quote "F.O.B. mill" (i.e., the buyer must pay all freight costs from the mill to destination), any buyer, other considerations being equal, will tend to patronize the nearest mill in order to minimize freight costs. Should a mill be the only one in an area large enough to absorb its entire output, the differential between the freight charges on its deliveries within its area and those of mills located outside the area relieves it of immediate price competition from the rest of the industry. It can, if it wishes, set its prices above the general competitive or "follow-the-leader" level by the amount of its freight cost advantage. Within this margin of freight cost advantage it is a quasi-monopolist.

A single retailer of any type in a rural community or urban neighborhood similarly enjoys a location advantage that may give him a quasi-monopoly position with respect to the convenience goods that he sells. The determining consideration here is not delivery costs, but the indisposition of consumers to travel any farther than necessary for their convenience purchases. A retailer thus fortunately situated can charge a mark-up substantially higher than those of more distant stores of the same type, and still retain his customers.

Product specialization

A *specialty product* is one that embodies some design variation that distinguishes it from the basic staple item in its field and other variants of this staple. If a sufficient number of consumers consider this particular variation superior, the manufacturer enjoys a monopoly with respect to this fraction of the market. His monopoly position is limited, however, by the existence of the staple commodity and other variants, which will be accepted as substitutes for the specialty product, even by the fraction of the over-all market that appreciate and desire the specialty variation, if the price differential becomes too great. This extreme elasticity of demand for a specialty product characterizes the lower as well as the upper part of its price range. As the price of a specialty is reduced and approaches the competitive price range of the staple, increasing numbers of the purchasers of the staple item find the variation of the specialty worth the lessened price differential, and so swing their purchases from the staple to the specialty.

The manufacturer of a specialty product may base his quasi-monopoly on a general patent covering some secondary features of the product, or on a design patent.* Such legal protection, of course, affords him no security against competition from the staple and other variants if the price spread is too great. In many cases, however, specialty product designs are not patented; the producer relies only on the priority—possibly quite temporary —of his specialty "product diversification" on the market.

Promotion

Advertising and other forms of promotion may make the market aware of the existence of a branded specialty product, and thus fortify its quasi-monopoly position. Often, however, advertising and other promotional techniques are employed to create the illusion of quality superiority, or some other form of product specialization, where it does not truly exist. That a particular heavily advertised brand is objectively indistinguishable from its less advertised competitors, or distinguishable only by irrelevant details, does not make it any less a specialty for the buyers influenced by the advertising. In these cases promotion creates market goodwill which establishes the branded product as a quasi-monopoly specialty.

Customer goodwill

Customer goodwill may establish a retailer or a manufacturer in a quasi-monopoly position so that he is not bound by strictly competitive considerations in his pricing. The personality of a retail proprietor, or a store's reputation for courtesy and service, may hold a clientele faithful in spite of an unfavorable markup differential. Customer services may be valued by a retailer's clientele above what they pay for these services through higher prices. Institutional goodwill advertising, as explained in Chapter 21, may also win favorable regard for a manufacturer or retailer, thereby easing him—though very slightly—from strictly competitive pricing pressure.

Superior selling

Finally, effective selling in direct-to-consumer distribution may create markets that otherwise would never have existed. The household appliance, vacuum cleaner, silverware, and encyclopedia companies that make

* General and design patents are explained in Chapter 30.

their sales through canvassers do not primarily obtain sales that otherwise would have gone to retail stores employing more passive selling techniques. In most cases their canvasser-salesmen persuade consumers to buy items they otherwise would never have purchased. During the period of the canvassing demonstration, the prospect is allowed little opportunity to exercise sound comparative judgment. If the canvasser-salesman makes an effective presentation, he can generally succeed in so sidetracking all competitive issues that the prospect makes the buying decision without considering possible alternatives. This limited monopoly situation at the crucial moment of the buying decision permits companies selling direct-to-consumer to price their offerings considerably above the retail price of comparable items and still make substantial sales.

Scope of quasi-monopoly pricing

In all these cases of limited product or seller monopoly, the seller has a true pricing monopoly with respect to the special fraction of the general market that he controls by reason of the actual or fictional specialty character of the product, or because of special customer goodwill, or because of direct-selling drive. Competitive price pressure is walled off by a psychological or economic curtain. This sheltering curtain is usually very thin, and holds only over a narrow price differential. Purchasing demand within the practicable pricing ranges of these quasi-monopolies tends to be considerably elastic, and shrinks appreciably with each slight increase in price over the general competitive level. Even this slight leeway in pricing, however, enables producers and distributors to apply the various pricing policies considered in Chapter 20, instead of being restricted to bare conformity with competitive market price.

IMPERFECT COMPETITION

Limited freedom from competitive pricing pressure may be achieved not only through an individual quasi-monopoly position, but also through certain forms of group action to which the term "imperfect competition" is frequently applied. Unlike quasi-monopolies, imperfect competition occurs rarely among small manufacturers. It exists largely in basic industries with large-scale producers. It takes three forms: (1) oligopoly, (2) tacit follow-the-leader pricing, and (3) collusion on pricing or market sharing.

Oligopoly

"Oligopoly" is a term applied by economists to a market situation where the supply of a product is controlled by a very small number of companies, each of which contributes an important share of the total supply, and all of which are intimately aware of each other's activities and can substantially anticipate each other's reactions. Such groups of companies, without any specific agreements, tend generally to quote identical or closely related prices. They pursue their competition along non-price lines. The common price quoted by such a group is likely to be well above what would be a pure competitive price for the product, but well below what would be the optimum price if the group were operated as a single monopolistic unit. This sustained group price may prevail over long periods, but is likely to collapse if a price war is inadvertently started. When such a price war develops in an oligopolistic group, prices may be forced to the loss point for all concerned. Upon occasion, such price wars have ended with the bankruptcy of the weaker members of the group and the crippling of the victors. More commonly these price struggles are brief, and a working understanding is soon tacitly restored among the group. Where price raising is involved, there is less likelihood of concerted action among the members of an oligopolistic group.

Follow-the-leader pricing

Follow-the-leader pricing may occur in industries where: (a) the product is highly standardized or widely advertised, and (b) production involves a high ratio of fixed to variable costs, so that pressure of excess capacity would be an inducement to serious price wars. These conditions have existed, in recent times, in the steel, cement, petroleum, and agricultural implement industries, among others. In such industries some one producer may take the initiative in making price changes. The price so established by the industry leader is usually well above what would be the "true competitive price" for the field. Without compulsion or any specific preagreement, the "followers" in the industry make corresponding modifications of their price schedules, thus maintaining such competition as exists in the industry upon other bases than price. Even the least efficient producers in the industry can survive under such an umbrella of price stabilization, and the more efficient companies prosper with limited business so long as they are "good" and do not upset the industry applecart by seeking more business through price-cutting. Follow-the-leader pricing is facilitated by the procedure provided in some trade association codes requiring each member to file notice of a price change, and a schedule of new prices, with the association in advance of such change. The other members of the association are then provided with copies of these "open" price lists, so that they may make simultaneous changes in their price lists.*

If the "leader" corporation in one of these fields could always count upon

---

* "Open price associations" were first condemned under the Sherman Anti-Trust Act, were later permitted by judicial construction.

being followed by the rest of the industry, it could establish its pricing policy upon pure monopoly principles, and aim at achieving optimum pricing for itself. In practice the "followers," with unit cost schedules varying from those of the "leader," can be counted on to follow the "leader" only within undefined but tacitly understood limits. Moreover, this sort of pricing "leadership" may shift from one corporation to another in the group. Under these circumstances, the optimum prices of pure monopoly theory are hardly ever achieved for "follow-the-leader" industries. Actual prices for these industries are established within a range whose lower limit is what would be the "true" competitive price level for the industry and whose upper limit is somewhat under the optimum price schedule of the industry "leader."

Collusion

A specific agreement among producers in any line to charge a common price higher than what would otherwise be the competitive price for their product was interpreted by the courts prior to 1900 as a "combination or conspiracy in restraint of trade" forbidden by common law and by the Sherman Anti-Trust Act. "Pool" and "cartel" arrangements whereby groups of producers bound themselves to limit individual production or sales to specified amounts, or to share markets in ways that gave them mutually exclusive market territories, were likewise outlawed in the 1890's. In one pricing detail, however, overt restrictive agreements were permitted until the 1940's; this was in the matter of *basing-point* pricing.

Under a basing-point agreement effected through a trade association code or otherwise, all the producers in a line agreed to quote their prices F.O.B. certain specified railroad transportation centers, without regard to location of the producing plants, or to transportation agency used. For example, the steel industry in 1948 quoted its prices F.O.B. 23 basing points, among which were Pittsburgh, Buffalo, Birmingham, Chicago, Cleveland, and San Francisco. Any steel mill located in the area using Buffalo as basing point would charge a customer in Rochester the freight from Buffalo to Rochester, regardless of the actual shipping cost. If the mill were located east of Buffalo, a "phantom freight" would be involved—i.e., the freight charged would be greater than actual shipping cost. If the mill were located west of Buffalo, it would have to absorb some of the actual shipping cost, which would be higher than the freight charged the customer.

Basing-point price policy had the effect of eliminating an important element of delivered-price differential. By itself, this would not have limited competition; indeed, it might have intensified F.O.B. price competition. But basing-point pricing developed primarily in lines where follow-the-leader pricing was already well established. Under these circumstances, it eliminated the last significant element of price differentiation between the selling organizations in any basing-point area, and intensified the quasi-monopoly effects of the follow-the-leader pricing policy.

The steel industry in the first decade of the Twentieth Century made the first major application of basing-point pricing, using a single basing point. The arrangement soon spread to the cement, cast iron, soil pipe, glucose, malt, maple flooring, welded chain, zinc, lead, and copper industries. Multiple basing-point pricing was subsequently adopted by the iron and steel, cement, hardwood, gasoline, sugar, chemical fertilizer, asphalt, roofing material, linseed oil, rigid steel conduit, fire brick, lubricating, and plate glass industries. In 1924 the Federal Trade Commission directed a cease-and-desist order against basing-point price by the steel industry. It was ignored, and the FTC did not press the issue. In two important cases involving the corn products industry, FTC cease-and-desist orders against basing-point pricing were upheld by the Supreme Court in 1945 on the ground that phantom freight and freight absorption involved in basing-point pricing resulted in price discrimination forbidden by the Clayton and Robinson-Patman Acts (explained in Chapter 30); the Supreme Court confirmed this position in a 1948 case involving the cement industry. In 1949 the Supreme Court further condemned basing-point pricing as constituting an unfair method of competition under Sec. V of the Federal Trade Commission Act.

REVIEW

1. What are the assumptions underlying the economic theory of "pure" competitive price?

2. In a situation of "pure" competition, how is price determined? In such a situation, what can an individual seller do about the prices for his items?

3. To what extent does "pure" competitive price determination operate in the American economy?

4. Explain "customary prices," "odd prices," and "price lines," and their significance in price theory.

5. Explain monopoly price theory. What is the Marketing significance of monopoly positions where they occur in the economic order?

6. Explain the various ways in which an individual company may achieve a quasi-monopoly position, and how this position can influence its pricing.

7. How may group action in an industry result in imperfectly competitive pricing practices?

8. What was "basing-point" pricing?

DISCUSSION TOPICS

1. Why, if there is so little "pure competitive" pricing, do we speak of the American economy as essentially a "competitive" one?

2. " 'Odd pricing' is logical nonsense but psychological sense."

3. Isn't "quasi-monopoly" or "monopolistic competition" a contradiction in economic theory as well as in terminology?

4. Several writers have argued that the ending of basing-point pricing, by discouraging competitive interpenetration of market areas, could produce local territorial monopolies in the industries affected, leading to higher prices. What is the reasoning behind this argument?

SUGGESTED READINGS

Read the chapters on Price Theory—as distinguished from those on Price Level Theory—in any good Economics textbook.

Bain, J. S., *Barriers to New Competition,* Harvard University Press, Cambridge, 1956.

Fellner, W. J., *Competition Among the Few,* Alfred A. Knopf, New York, 1949.

Galbraith, J. K., *A Theory of Price Control,* Harvard University Press, Cambridge, 1952.

Huegy, H. W. (ed.), *The Role and Nature of Competition in our Marketing Economy,* Bureau of Economic and Business Research, University of Illinois, Urbana, 1953.

Knauth, O., *Business Practices, Trade Position, and Competition,* Columbia University Press, New York, 1956.

Machlup, F., *The Economics of Sellers' Competition,* Johns Hopkins Press, Baltimore, 1952.

Machlup, F., *The Political Economy of Monopoly,* Johns Hopkins Press, Baltimore, 1952.

Mund, V. A., *Open Markets—an Essential of Free Enterprise,* Harper & Bros., New York, 1948.

National Bureau of Economic Research, *Business Concentration and Price Policy,* Princeton University Press, Princeton, 1955.

Shawver, D. A., *The Development of Theories of Retail Price Determination,* University of Illinois Press, Urbana, 1956.

CHAPTER 20

PRICING POLICY

In some respects, pricing by manufacturers, by wholesale distributors, and by retailers raises comparable issues. In many other respects, pricing policies of manufacturers and of those who resell goods follow dissimilar patterns. The differences are sufficiently marked to warrant separate consideration of the pricing policies of these two fields of business.

MANUFACTURERS' PRICING

As explained in the preceding chapter, a manufacturer in a field so highly competitive that it approximates the "true" competition of economic theory cannot exercise pricing policy. He must sell at the going market price, whatever it is. If there is a positive margin between this price and his total unit cost, he makes a profit. If there is a negative margin, he suffers loss. By adjusting his production volume he can sometimes improve his profit position or reduce loss, but he can do nothing about his pricing.

Most American manufacturers, however, operate under circumstances of quasi-monopoly or imperfect competition. And a few may enjoy true monopoly status. Such manufacturers have leeway in pricing—wide for true monopolists, relatively moderate for the others. Within these margins of pricing discretion, they can formulate and apply various pricing strategies as analyzed in this section.

An amazing number of small-scale manufacturers have no clear strategy in their pricing. In the past they have "made out well" by adding some arbitrary "margin" over their costs, and so they continue to use this margin. Or because some producers of related products use a particular margin over costs, others blindly follow their lead. The pricing leeway that a monopoly or quasi-monopoly position allows often provides a deep cushion for pricing misjudgments, so that these blundering rule-of-thumb approaches to pricing may be pursued by companies for years on end. Prices so established may be well above or below the optimums for the products. Manufacturers make less total profit than they could, but they do not know this. They are making profit, and they are satisfied.

Pricing objectives

Classical Economics assumed that the only pricing objective pursued by manufacturers not rigidly confined by competitive considerations would be maximum immediate profit. This assumption was false. A number of studies have established that maximum short-term profit is the goal of only a minority of the American manufacturers who have developed pricing strategy. Four other objectives play important roles in manufacturers' pricing policies.

Maximum immediate profit. Manufacturers setting maximum short-term profit as their pricing goal are generally young enterprises, frequently established on the basis of a new product. In trying to achieve this objective, their managements do not calculate carefully in accordance with the economists' formula the variations in demand that would result from particular prices, the marginal revenue that successive increments of production would produce, and the marginal costs of these increments, in order to determine the optimum price that would produce a sales and production volume at which marginal revenue and marginal cost would be equal. If they were aware of this formula—which many of them are not—they still would not be able to apply it, because business accounting and statistical techniques do not lend themselves to exact calculations along these lines. A monopolistic or quasi-monopolistic business which really aims at maximum short-run profit by charging "what the traffic will bear" can do so only by a trial-and-error approach. The common procedure is to start with some price arbitrarily determined—usually the highest remotely practicable —and work it down, noting the effects of the price changes on sales and profits, until the most favorable results seem to have been achieved.

"Ethical" pricing. There are a surprising number of business men who consider themselves entitled to only a "normal" percentage of profit on their sales or capital investment. Several surveys have indicated that "normal" profit is the predominant pricing objective of established manufacturing concerns. In some cases, management's concept of "normal" profit may result in setting a company's prices higher than the optimum resulting from its monopoly or quasi-monopoly position, so that the company actually makes less profit than it would at lower prices. In many cases, however, managements aiming at "normal" profit set prices well below optimum levels. "Ethical" pricing objectives are more likely to influence manage-

ments of small concerns dominated by individuals or small groups of "working" stockholders than of large publicly-owned corporations.

Promotional considerations. A monopolist or quasi-monopolist may anticipate increasing his capacity in such a way that his total unit cost and marginal cost schedules will eventually be lowered. With this change in cost schedules, his future optimum price—assuming maximized profit as a future objective—will be lower than at present, and he will be producing for a much larger market. Anticipating this development, the manufacturer may currently sell below his current short-term optimum price, with a view to building up the market for his product toward larger future volume. This factor plays a big role in the pricing policies of many manufacturers.

Avoiding encouraging competition. A high optimum price for a commodity, when the producer or distributor enjoys a temporary monopoly or quasi-monopoly, might be blatant invitation for competition to move into the field. The producer may content himself with the smaller profit that a lower price (and consequent large volume) yields, hoping to discourage competitive entry, so he can maintain his advantageous position.

Avoiding government prosecution. A high optimum price for a monopoly product might attract the unwelcome attention of the Federal Trade Commission or the Department of Justice. To escape such attention, a small-scale monopolist may forego the maximum profit that "charging all the traffic will bear" would yield, and set prices that result in a modest unit margin with greater sales volume.

Ultimate price vs. manufacturer's price

A consumer goods manufacturer may sell through wholesalers, and never have direct contact with the retailers who handle his product, let alone the consumers who ultimately buy it. A producer of industrial tools or supplies may similarly have no immediate contact with the factories that use these tools or supplies. The price these ultimate consumers or users pay for his product, however, is of vital concern to a manufacturer. The margin of pricing freedom that he may enjoy through quasi-monopoly is a margin of the price to the ultimate consumers or users, not of the intermediate prices to wholesalers or dealers.

A manufacturer's pricing calculation therefore does not stop with the price he will charge to middlemen or dealers who buy from him. If he starts with costs and works forward to price, he must take into account the markup that his wholesalers will add to the price he charges them, and the further markup that retailers will add to the price they pay the wholesalers. If he begins with price and works backward to design and costs, it is retail price that he starts with, and from which he subtracts retailers' and then wholesalers' markups to arrive at the price he receives. We shall see later in this section that some manufacturers specify and enforce the ultimate prices at which retailers sell their products to consumers. A much larger number of manufacturers recommend specific retail prices for their items, although they do not enforce these recommendations. Regardless of whether a manufacturer specifies compulsory or recommended retail prices, or leaves the subsequent resale pricing entirely to the wholesalers and retailers, he cannot ignore these ultimate prices in his own pricing calculations.

Techniques of price determination

There are three basic approaches to manufacturers' pricing: (1) cost plus margin; (2) cost and demand; and (3) working backward from price to design and cost. The first two may be employed when a manufacturer has some leeway of pricing freedom. The third occurs when customary price or competitive circumstances circumscribe pricing freedom.

Cost-plus-margin pricing. This is the commonest pricing procedure for manufacturers. It is the basis of all rule-of-thumb pricing and of all "ethical" pricing.

For some manufacturers, the "cost" that is the foundation for their pricing structure is *total* unit production and distribution cost calculated by cost accounting procedures at some arbitrary sales volume figure—usually the volume anticipated for the coming year. To this unit total cost figure is added a "normal" margin of 3%, or 5%, or 10%, or some higher percent, for net profit. Frequently, the "cost" figure on which manufacturers base their pricing calculations is unit *variable* productive cost—cost of materials purchased plus direct labor costs. With such a "cost" basis, the margin must cover distribution costs, overhead, and other fixed costs, as well as profit. In these cases the superimposed "normal" margin may be 25% of cost, or 50%, or 100%, or even higher. Various other formulas are reported, some highly complicated, but all deriving price from unit cost elements, with an arbitrary profit allowance. In many cases, it is interesting to note, the profit margin provided for in these pricing formulas is net profit *after* federal income tax.

Not infrequently, manufacturers find a cost-plus-"normal"-margin technique of pricing produces an obviously excessive retail price for an item, after wholesalers' and retailers' markups have been added on. The quasi-monopoly status of a specialty article is generally limited to a fairly narrow retail price differential, and if this differential is overreached in pricing, the specialty will suffer competition from comparable specialties or from the lower-priced nonspecialized field. Or even where immediate competition from other closely related items is not to be feared, a monopoly or quasi-monopoly item may be "priced out of the market"—its price set so high in the face of an elastic demand that its sales are a small fraction of what they would be at lower prices. When such over-pricing is recognized, the manufacturer must forego some of the add-on margin that he considers "normal," and content himself with some lower figure than his original "target" price.

The following calculation illustrates how a chemical company that developed a superior automobile polish applied the cost-plus-margin principle to establish the prices at which it sold this polish to wholesalers. Wisely or unwisely, this company had settled on a formula for calculating the initial "target" prices for its line of chemical products by multiplying the direct production cost of each product by 3. The resulting 200 percent margin covered its substantial product development costs, distribution costs, overhead costs of production as well as of distribution, and a profit which, in relation to its capital worth, had been eminently satisfactory over the years. In the case of the automobile polish, market presearch indicated an annual potential in the neighborhood of a million cans yearly, one-third in a higher-priced aerosol package, two-thirds in a lower-priced regular can. Cost analysis for this volume range gave a direct costs figure of 20¢ per regular-packaged pint; aerosol packaging would add another 5¢. The company decided a special promotional appropriation of $50,000 a year for advertising and sales promotion would be needed to launch the new product; this would amount to 5¢ per pint can. These figures provided the foundation for the following initial calculation:

	Regular can	Aerosol can
Labor and materials cost	20¢	20¢
Extra cost of aerosol packaging		5
Total direct cost	20¢	25¢
200% usual margin for product development, distribution, and overhead costs, plus profit	40	50
Special advertising allowance	5	5
Price to wholesalers	65¢	80¢

The question still remained whether these "target" prices to wholesalers would result in practical ultimate retail prices. The wholesalers who would handle the item generally operated with a 15 percent markup (calculated on their resale price). Automotive supply stores and hardware stores based their pricing of automobile polishes on a 30 to 35 percent markup (also calculated on their resale prices). Knowing this, the company made a further projection of their pricing calculation:

	Regular can	Aerosol can
Price to wholesalers	65¢	80¢
Wholesalers' 15% markup	11½	14
Wholesalers' resale price	76½¢	84¢
Retailers' average 33⅓% markup	38¼	47
Retail price area focus	$1.15	$1.41

These "target" retail prices were higher than those of other polishes currently on the market, but in view of the superiority of the company's product and the projected promotional drive, the difference did not appear competitively excessive. The company decided that no adjustments of its initial "target" prices of 65¢ and 80¢ to wholesalers were necessary. So priced, the product has made a place for itself on the market not too far off the company's original anticipations. Possibly a larger net profit might have been realized had the product been priced either higher or lower. The company will never know. Using its regular arbitrary cost-plus formula, however, it has succeeded in adding one more profitable item to its line.

Frequently a manufacturer of a "line" of products discovers that some of his prices determined by a uniform cost-plus-margin formula will result in competitive disadvantage, while others are still well within his area of quasi-monopolistic discretion. He must reduce the first set of prices below their original "target" levels, possibly to a no-profit point or even to loss figures, in order to maintain a market for the complete line. Customarily, this sacrifice of the originally projected profit margin for the competitive items is compensated by increasing the prices for the other products in the line over their original formula levels—which may bring them closer to optimum if they were previously lower, or may carry them further away from optimum if they were already above.

Cost-and-demand pricing. Exclusive preoccupation with cost considerations in most manufacturers' pricing techniques is definitely unsound, particularly if optimum price to produce maximum profit is the objective. Optimum price cannot be determined by cost factors alone. Elasticity of market demand for a product within its practicable monopoly or quasi-monopoly retail price range is just as important in establishing optimum price as cost considerations. Any manufacturer faced with a pricing issue should work with a retail price-demand schedule for his product as well as with his schedule of costs.

It is easy for an economist to make this recommendation. For a manufacturer to apply it may be supremely difficult. Information on retail price-demand schedules for individual products is hard and often costly to obtain. A market survey or a controlled experiment might yield the needed information, but the costs involved eliminate these methods for all but large-dollar-volume items. Sometimes a company can pick up clues—rarely more than clues—to retail price-demand relationships for its products by examining the past experience of the company and the line. Pooling "guesstimates" of experienced observers—the company's market managers and friendly distributors and dealers—is hardly a scientific technique, but it does provide conclusions with better than chance reliability, and is the most common approach to the problem.

Working backward from price to cost. A manufacturer planning to produce an item similar to others already on the market does not have much pricing leeway at the retail level. If his item must conform to a customary price or fit into a current price "line," he may have no leeway whatsoever. He must start with this retail price and work backward to his product design and costs. He subtracts the retailers' markup. If he reaches the retailers through wholesalers, he also subtracts the wholesalers' markup. This leaves him the price he can expect from the wholesalers. Next he subtracts his unit distribution and allocated overhead costs. The balance must cover his production costs and profit. Can he design the item at a unit cost less than this balance, so it will sell at the customary or "line" retail price? If so, one more profitable item is included in his production and sales program. If not, the project must be abandoned. This pricing approach dominates the women's wear industry, and at times enters the pricing of automobiles, consumer appliances, radio and TV sets, and other consumer durable goods.

Customer class pricing

A manufacturer who sells to two or more classes of business customers —i.e., to both full-service wholesalers and retailers, or to both full-service and limited-service wholesalers, or to both manufacturers and wholesalers —usually charges each class of customer different prices for his products. Thus a manufacturer selling directly to retailers as well as through wholesalers generally sets higher prices to the former than the latter; if he sells to both full-service and limited-service wholesalers, the latter may be charged higher prices. Variations in prices charged to different customer classes tend to reflect, though not exactly, differences in the costs of selling to customers in different categories and differences in the value to the manufacturer of the marketing services that customers in different categories ordinarily perform. To some extent, these price variations may also be related to differences in the distribution costs of various classes of middlemen. A manufacturer's schedule of prices to a customer class may be actual net prices or it may be achieved, as described below, by differential trade discounts from a listed retail price.

Prices to all customers within a class are usually uniform. Were this not so, every sale by a manufacturer would involve bargaining and haggling. This would magnify price considerations in selling, which is contrary to the interests and policies of specialty producers. It would result in disgruntled customers when those who had paid a higher price discovered the lower prices that others had obtained. With variations in prices paid by retailers for identical merchandise, there would be no possibility of compelling or inducing retailers to establish uniform resale prices to consumers.

While uniform customer class pricing is a normal element of manufacturers' pricing policy, there are exceptions. (1) In fashion lines the preferences and reactions of mercantile and industrial buyers differ widely, and one buyer will often pay far more than another for a particular item if he has to or can be persuaded to. Consequently the salesmen of textile converters and of dress manufacturers who do not produce to customary price "lines" find it necessary to bargain and "trade" on almost every order, shrewdly appraising each customer's desires, meeting customer bluffs with counter bluffs, and haggling the price on each transaction. (2) In "buyers' markets" during recession periods shrewd individual buyers can often wring special price concessions from distressed manufacturers desperate for sales at any margin of profit or even at no margin. (3) Until restraining legislation was passed, large-volume buyers such as retail chain systems, department stores, large specialty houses, and large manufacturers would use the volume importance of their orders to force price concessions not available to smaller competitors from their suppliers.

During the 1920's and 1930's independent retailers competing with chain systems suffered heavily from the discriminatory low prices which the chains were frequently able to obtain from suppliers selling both to the chains and to independents. One element of the anti-chain-store movement described in Chapter 7 was the passage of the 1936 Robinson-Patman Act and of special laws in 19 states which made uniform customer class pricing to business buyers a legal requirement. These laws are analyzed in Chapter 30. Here we shall note only that they provide that any discriminations in a manufacturer's pricing that would substantially lessen competition in his customers' fields are permissible only if the price variations reflect differences in his costs of distribution to different customers, or are necessary to meet a competitor's price, or are in response to changing conditions that affect the value of the goods. The provision allowing price differences that reflect cost differentials permits quantity discounts provided that they are uniformly available to all customers within a customer class.*

Discounts

A common manufacturer pricing practice is to quote a certain full or "list" price for an item, and then uniformly, under specified circumstances, allow certain deductions. These deductions are called "discounts." There

---

* A special Robinson-Patman Act proviso on quantity discounts authorizes the Federal Trade Commission to establish specific limits on maximum quantity discounts on a product, even though further cost savings may attach to larger purchases, when the Commission deems that further discounts on larger quantities would promote monopoly among the buyers. The Commission exercised this power with respect to automobile tires in 1952.

are five kinds of discounts: (1) quantity, (2) cash, (3) trade, (4) catalog, and (5) special.

1. *Quantity discounts* are given for large volume purchasing and delivery. Thus, if the manufacturer's list price for an item were $1.00 per dozen, a 2 percent quantity discount might be allowed on purchase of a gross, and an additional 2 percent on a purchase of twenty gross or more. Sometimes quantity discounts are fractional percents. They may rise, though rarely, to as high as 25 percent.

The theory of the quantity discount is that it passes on to the buyer all or some of the economies in selling, bookkeeping, packing, and other marketing operations that the seller develops from large-order handling. In competitive lines, the quantity discount operates in practice, within the limitations established by the Robinson-Patman Act, as a price cut to heavy-buying customers to attract their patronage.

Quantity discounts may be cumulative or noncumulative. If the latter, they are allowed on the basis of the customer's individual orders or—still more limited—on the basis of each specific delivery under an order. Cumulative quantity discounts are allowed on the basis of a customer's lumped purchases over a month, quarter, or year. Cumulative discounts usually do not reflect any distribution economies resulting from large-order shipping, but are essentially a price-cutting bait for heavy-buying customers, and a bid for exclusive customer patronage instead of dispersed purchasing. The Federal Trade Commission has disapproved several cases of cumulative discounting, on the ground that under the Robinson-Patman Act they constitute discriminatory pricing unsupported by differences in distribution costs.

In grocery specialty, drug, and other lines, quantity discounts sometimes take the form of "free deals." As an inducement to order in quantity, retailers are offered, not a reduction from the regular small-volume price, but a bonus of one or more of the item in question. The net result is the same as though a corresponding discount had been given, with the advantage to the manufacturer that the retailer receives a unit or two more than the discount quantity and pays the full price, instead of paying less for the discount quantity.

2. *Cash discounts,* discussed more fully in Chapter 24 as an aspect of mercantile credit terms, are commonly allowed to customers who pay within a specified period—usually ten days—from the invoice date instead of at the conclusion of the regular 30- or 60-day credit period. The deduction is usually 1 or 2 percent.

3. *Trade discounts,* sometimes called "functional discounts," are deductions from retail price given to classes of business buyers such as retailers, jobbers, wholesalers, and industrial users. For retailers, jobbers, and wholesalers, the trade discount is supposed to provide them with uniform

markups,* so that the product will reach consumers at a uniform retail "list" price, no matter what channels of distribution it has traversed. A recent survey indicates that a major proportion of consumer goods manufacturers price on a trade-discount basis with this consideration in mind, but that this pricing stratagem is declining. Unless a resale price maintenance clause is included in the manufacturer's sales contracts, however, there is no assurance that uniform trade discounts will result in uniform resale pricing by the distributors or dealers. Actually, trade discounts associated with many product lines are merely traditional, and bear no discernable relation to present wholesale or retail markups.

Several cumulated trade discounts may be deducted from the list price of a product which normally passes through several links of a distribution chain. By trade custom, the first of a set of such trade discounts is always the retailers' discount, and the subsequent ones apply to the middlemen who intervene between the manufacturer and the retailers. Thus a drug manufacturer's discounts of 33⅓–16⅔ would indicate a deduction of 33⅓ percent on sales direct to retailers, and a further 16⅔ percent deduction calculated on this retailers' price for sales to wholesalers (i.e., if the list price of an item were $1.00, it would be sold direct to retail druggists at $.66⅔ and to wholesalers at $.55⅝). Sometimes discounts of different amounts are allowed to various classes of wholesalers who perform different services. A full-service wholesaler may be allowed a discount of 10 percent, while a manufacturers' agent is given only 5 percent (actually this would be a commission disguised as a discount, a very common practice), and a drop shipper receives 2 percent.

One long-standing issue associated with trade discounts is whether the wholesalers' discount should be allowed to integrated retail chains and department stores which buy directly from manufacturers in large quantities —often larger than regular wholesalers. The Robinson-Patman Act was intended specifically to stop such practices. There is still some uncertainty, however, as to the application of this limitation to cooperative groups, various buying club organizations, and corporate integrations combining wholesaling and retailing units.

4. *Catalog discounts,* also frequently called "trade discounts," are commonly employed by manufacturers who must publish expensive catalogs, to allow them pricing flexibility in periods of changing prices without the necessity of frequently revising their catalogs. The catalog of such a manufacturer deliberately quotes prices slightly higher than are actually being charged. The manufacturer's salesmen are provided with "discount sheets"

---

* Although a trade discount must be uniform for all customers in a trade class under the Robinson-Patman Act, a manufacturer of a line of products does not have to give uniform trade discounts on all products in the line. It is quite common to give larger trade discounts on slow-moving items than on fast-moving ones.

enabling them to quote the actual current prices. Should these prices change, the original catalog can still be used, but the salesmen receive new discount sheets quoting larger or smaller discounts. This discount technique has the added psychological advantage that the customers generally appear to be receiving price cuts, regardless of whether prices are actually rising or falling. Producers of industrial equipment are most likely to use this discount pricing technique.

5. *Special discounts* or allowances were formerly common. They would be granted nominally as compensation for special services performed by distributors or dealers, such as cooperative advertising which featured the manufacturer's line, or using his window and counter display materials. Actually, in many cases the distributors or dealers made no effort to perform the services in question, and the special discounts operated as a concealed form of discriminatory price cutting. The Robinson-Patman Act has limited the use of these special discounts.

Treatment of freight charges

Who pays the freight—seller or buyer? How does any arrangement for paying freight charges affect contract prices? These questions may be of relatively minor importance where seller and buyer are neighbors, or in lines where transportation costs are a trifling proportion of the value of the products shipped. They may have decisive competitive significance, however, and influence substantially the pattern of industrial location, in many lines where the product is bulky and involves heavy shipping costs. Two systems of treating freight charges have developed: (1) F.O.B. shipping point, and (2) uniform delivered price.

1. When a seller prices his products *"F.O.B. mill,"* or *"F.O.B. warehouse,"* the buyer bears all transportation costs from the shipping point. True, the seller as shipper generally pays the shipping charges to the carrier, but he bills these charges to the buyer in the invoice for the goods.

Two advantages accrue to a seller through F.O.B. pricing. First, his quoted prices, since they do not have to include any freight charges, appear lower than if they had to cover an averaged transportation cost—and actually are lower as "delivered" prices for nearby customers. Second, he receives a uniform net for his products, which simplifies his pricing policy.

There are two disadvantages associated with this pricing procedure. First, uniform retail pricing to consumers on a national or regional scale is impossible, since the cost of an item to distributors or dealers varies with the distance from the shipping point, and uniform markups by these distributors or dealers result in a wide range of consumer prices. The second disadvantage affects manufacturers of bulky products (which involve heavy freight costs relative to their value) whose local markets do not absorb the full capacity of their plants. They are precluded from seeking customers in more distant markets served by local producers since the superimposition of a heavy freight charge on their regular prices places them at an insuperable competitive handicap in relation to the local producers.

Basing-point pricing—charging buyers the freight cost from some location other than the seller's actual shipping point—has been primarily an element of group pricing policy. As was indicated in the preceding chapter, in a number of cases such group basing-point pricing has been disallowed by the courts as constituting discriminatory pricing and unfair competition. It is uncertain at the time of writing whether these decisions also preclude any individual manufacturer from establishing some special basing-point for his pricing, provided that his action is *not* part of some group pricing policy. Such individual basing-point pricing is sometimes done by manufacturers who operate two or more plants or warehouses, but wish their delivered prices to relate only to the main plant or warehouse. Basing-point pricing has also been utilized by manufacturers who enjoy a quasi-monopolistic dominance in their local markets and who want to compete more effectively in a more distant market. They do this by establishing basing points close to the distant market. The freight charges to the basing point that they must absorb in the case of customers located in the distant market are counterbalanced by the "phantom freight" charged to local customers.

2. A seller may wish to quote a *uniform "delivered" price* to customers no matter where located, or to customers in a specified territory or region. He could do this by quoting his prices "F.O.B. destination," or "F.O.B. mill freight allowed." Obviously, to abide by such terms the seller must absorb all freight charges to the customers' various locations. The seller's actual net on particular sales differs according to the freight charges paid on the several deliveries. To achieve a desired over-all profit, the seller must add the average shipping cost to whatever his F.O.B. mill net price would have been.

Uniform delivered pricing enables a seller to provide and promote uniform customer prices within each "delivered price" territory. By making local markets, through the higher "territorial" price, bear part of the shipping costs to more distant areas, the seller achieves a more favorable competitive price position in those areas. The higher local price, of course, renders him more vulnerable to competitive invasion of his own local markets. Uniform delivered pricing has been developed essentially for products whose freight costs are low relative to their prices, such as arc-welding machines, household electric appliances, mechanics' hand tools, typewriters and other business machines, and cigarettes and tobacco products.

Resale price maintenance

Many manufacturers who, through consistent promotion, have developed wide customer acceptance of their products as brand-name specialties embodying superior quality and retailing at higher prices than similar unbranded or other-branded items, want to have all retailers sell their products at specified uniform prices. Advantages of this practice are: (1) limited-service retailers are prevented from cutting prices to levels that could not be met by regular-service retailers in the same market area, causing the latter to refuse to carry the products, to the ultimate disadvantage of a manufacturer's distributive policy; (2) cut-price loss-leader selling of these products by occasional retailers may undermine a "quality" emphasis which a manufacturer's promotion has attached to them; (3) a manufacturer can maintain an exceptionally high retailers' markup on his products, thereby inducing retailers to push them in preference to competing items with lower retailers' margins; (4) a manufacturer can undertake advertising featuring the specified uniform prices.

The majority of retailers would generally approve of resale price maintenance by the manufacturers of the branded goods they carry, if such price maintenance were consistently enforced. Effective resale price maintenance protects smaller, service-offering, high-cost stores from the price-cutting competition of chains, department stores, discount houses, and other lower-cost outlets, either because they are more efficient or because they offer fewer services or more limited selection to their customers, and so can operate profitably with lower markups. Such resale price maintenance also protects these stores from the competition of loss-leader price-cutting by business rivals large or small. Indeed, the only objectors among retailers to effective resale price maintenance are the minority of limited-service cash-carry stores, and the more efficient among the chains and department stores. These can profit on lower markup and would prefer the volume business produced by lower prices to the higher unit profit on smaller sales that selling at the manufacturer-specified price involves. Whether resale price maintenance involves a cost to consumers through higher prices cannot be decisively proved or disproved. There is a presumption that it does—one recent study indicates a differential of 4 percent—though proponents of fair trade argue strongly to the contrary.

Before 1930 there was some judicial uncertainty as to whether a manufacturer could legally include in any sales contract a clause compelling a retailer to resell his products at specified prices.* Certainly a retailer who had not agreed to price maintenance in his purchase contract could not be compelled to adhere to a manufacturer's price because other retailers were

---

* In a 1960 decision the Supreme Court ended this uncertainty. It held such compulsion a violation of the Sherman Antitrust Act.

so doing. As part of the anti-chain-store and general anti-big-store movement of the early 1930's, independent retailers' associations appealed to state legislatures for protection against price-cutting. They had the backing of many manufacturers who favored resale price maintenance. In 1931 California passed the first resale price maintenance or "fair trade" law. Forty-four other states enacted similar statutes. One-third of this number permitted manufacturers to set *specific* resale prices for their *branded* products; the other two-thirds permitted only *minimum* resale prices to be established for such products.

State fair-trade laws allow a manufacturer to bind not only retailers to whom he sells directly, but also wholesalers who must in turn bind their retailer customers to resale price maintenance. A striking feature of all but one of these acts was the "non-signer clause"—if a manufacturer binds a single retailer or distributor in the state by a resale price maintenance clause, every other distributor and dealer in the state who is informed of the provision is bound by it, even though it does not appear in his purchase contract. Only one state provides criminal penalties for violation of its fair-trade law; enforcement of the others is accomplished by making "knowing and wilful" violators subject to injunction or civil suits by the manufacturer, or to damage suits by other distributors or retailers who can show competitive injury.

These state fair-trade laws could apply only to intrastate transactions. In 1937 Congress enacted the federal Miller-Tydings Law. This statute exempted from the Sherman Antitrust and Federal Trade Comission laws all *interstate* resale price maintenance agreements which would be operative in the buyer's state. For fourteen years it was assumed that the Miller-Tydings Law covered all aspects of the state fair-trade laws. A 1951 Supreme Court decision held that the federal law provided no authorization for the "non-signer" provision of the state laws with respect to its application to transactions involving interstate commerce. This decision limited sharply the scope of resale price maintenance. A 1952 amendment, the McGuire Act, brought "non-signer" provisions again within the scope of the Miller-Tydings Law.

Like the state fair-trade laws establishing the right to resale price maintenance, the Miller-Tydings and McGuire Acts were purely permissive. They allowed resale price maintenance clauses to be included in interstate sale-and-purchase contracts, thereby giving manufacturers a contractual right to enforce such clauses. Efforts to enforce resale price maintenance against retailers who are cutting prices must be taken under the fair-trade laws of the retailers' states.

In the post-war period the tide has turned against resale price maintenance. As of 1960 the courts had voided either the fair-trade law as a whole or the non-signer clause in 15 states, leaving only 30 states with effective fair-trade laws. Even in these states resale price maintenance has lost ground, since it is enforceable only if manufacturers incorporate price maintenance clauses in their sales contracts and then are willing to enforce them through appropriate action. Many manufacturers who formerly actively supported fair trade have either openly abandoned it or, while still including price maintenance clauses in their sales contracts, are doing nothing about enforcing them. They find that a substantial proportion of their consumer markets are buying home appliances and other durable goods at "cut" prices through discount houses (described in Chapter 7) and "buying clubs" operated by employers and labor unions. Rather than lose sales made by such outlets, manufacturers allow their distributors to sell to the price-cutting outlets. In many cases the manufacturers themselves sell directly to large price-cutters. Some of the retailers' associations that originally fought most vigorously for resale price maintenance have become indifferent in their support since many of their members feel that with fair trade turning out to be largely unenforceable in a number of product fields, it is a losing proposition for those retailers who still try to abide by it. There still remains a strong core of fair-trade proponents, however. In recent years these have concentrated on obtaining passage of a federal fair-trade law which will take enforcement of resale price maintenance out of the unwilling hands of the manufacturers and make it the responsibility of the public authorities.

PRICING BY RETAILERS AND WHOLESALERS

It has been said that the entire subject of pricing by retailers and wholesalers is covered by the two words "markup" and "markdown." This is not too much of an exaggeration, if for "markdown" we substitute the broader term "price cutting." Our study of these two basic aspects of mercantile pricing is followed by brief examinations of the extent of uniform or "single" pricing at the retail level, and of the place of trade-ins in retail pricing.

Markup

No system of cost accounting would enable a retailer or wholesaler who handles hundreds, or even thousands, of items, and sells widely varying quantities of each item, to calculate a total unit cost schedule for each item. The only possible foundation figure that any distributor or dealer has for a pricing calculation is the unit cost of goods purchased. All his other costs, including sales force compensation, must usually be lumped together as "overhead" to be spread over the total sales of all the items carried

by the establishment.* Under these circumstances, most distributors and retailers are compelled to base their pricing on the adding of arbitrary proportional margins to the unit costs of goods purchased. These margins are
usually calculated as percentages, not of unit purchase costs of the items to
which they related, but of the *selling prices* of the items, and are called
"markup." **

Retail markups range from 5 or 6 percent for some supermarket items
such as sugar and cigarettes to 50, 60, and even higher percentages for
some household appliances, and to over 70 percent for prescription drugs.
Wholesalers' markups range from 1 or 2 percent on some staples to 10 or
15 percent. Relative markups are determined by: (1) manufacturers' list
price policies, (2) various product factors, (3) various distributor or
dealer factors, (4) the competitive situation, and (5) "odd price" considerations.

1. If the manufacturer of an advertised branded product sells on the
basis of a retail list price, with trade discounts for the retailers and wholesalers who distribute it, most wholesalers and distributors accept the discounts as their markups. Should the manufacturer enforce resale price
maintenance, retailers have no choice but to accept the list price as their
selling price, or at least as their minimum selling price.

2. Tradition plays a large rôle in the relative retail markups on various
product classes. Behind tradition, however, lie a number of rational considerations. One is product perishability. A considerable proportion of
fresh fruits and vegetables spoil and become unsaleable, or saleable only
at sharply cut prices, while they are in the retailers' hands. Markup on such
produce must therefore cover not only cost-of-purchase, overhead, and
profit on what has actually been sold, but also cost-of-purchase of the unsold spoiled items. Consequently, it must be considerably higher than the
markups on items like canned goods which have little likelihood of
spoilage.

---

* There are partial exceptions to this generalization. Where sales clerks are compensated in part by commissions on their sales volumes, the commission percentage could be
added, as a proportional variable cost, to the unit cost of goods sold. Departmentalized
stores can allocate sales force compensation and certain other costs directly to departments;
in some cases such departmental cost allocation can be extended into a cost allocation for
certain products which constitute the sole or major preoccupation of a department. Some
supermarket chains and department stores have recently been making careful studies on the
allocation of labor and shelf space costs to various categories of goods they carry, and on
relative turnover, movement costs, and markdown expectations, to guide them in their
markup as well as their buying policies. The term "merchandise management accounting"
has been coined for this type of study.

** Few details of Marketing cause such confusion, among small retailers and business
men as well as among students of elementary Marketing, as this customary calculation of
markup percentage on selling price. In a clarifying effort, which may or may not be helpful,
department store people have recently coined the term "mark-on" to denote the margin
percentage calculated on the basis of cost of purchase.

A related product consideration results in high markups for "high fashion" goods. Certain numbers in a purchased lot of women's dresses may miss the popular taste of the moment and require drastic markdowns to be moved. Or a bad season may leave the retailer with unsold items which must be offered at sacrifice prices since they will have no market whatsoever a year later. Markup on "high fashion" goods must cover the possibility of less-than-cost selling of some of them. Therefore it tends to be substantially higher than for nonfashion goods.

RETAIL MARKUP PERCENTAGES FOR VARIOUS SUPERMARKET ITEMS: AVERAGES FOR SIX STORES, 1957

PRODUCT CLASS	OVERALL AVERAGE MARKUP	LOW MARKUP ITEM	MARK-UP	HIGH MARKUP ITEM	MARK-UP
Meat	21%	Beef	16%	Variety meats	30%
Dairy	13	Milk	8	Noncarbonated beverages	36
Vegetables	33	Asparagus	19	Rutabagas	56
Citrus fruits	29	Grapefruit	26	Limes	41
Other fruits	33	Watermelon	8	Cocoanuts	47
Baked goods	18	Bread	16	Sweet goods	20
Frozen foods	20	Chinese food	15	Wax beans	28
Beverages	12	Instant coffee	6	Chocolate syrup	23
Tobacco products	6	Cigarettes	6	Cigars	15
Household supplies	28	Paint cleaner	15	Auto polish	47
Canned vegetables	21	Navy beans	19	Lima beans	25
Crackers and cookies	25	Crackers	20	Cookies	27
Paper products	23	Towels	20	Toothpicks	34
Detergents	11	Package soap	7	Synthetic fabric detergent	40
Toilet items	31	Bath crystals	23	Safety pins	53
Candy	26	Six-pack gum	15	Fancy candy	41
Canned fruit	22	Peaches	20	Boysenberries	25
Baking items	17	Flour	12	Cake decorations	36
Canned and dried soups	15	Tomato	8	Bouillon cubes	24
Spreads	24	Peanut butter	16	Honey	43
Sugar	8	Granulated sugar	7	Loaf sugar	16
Baby foods	14	Strained meats	12	Teething biscuits	22
Canned juices	19	Orange juice	15	Carrot juice	27
Housewares	25	Laundry items	18	Hardware	31

Source: *Progressive Grocer, "Super Valu Study,"* pp. 8-16.

ILLUSTRATION 20–1

Another product consideration leading to high markups is relatively slow turnover. An item with slow turnover ties up shelf and storage space and working capital. The markup on slow items should carry a proportionately larger overhead than the markup on fast-moving items. The grocery markup schedule shown in Illustration 20–1 reflects this factor of relative turnover as well as the consideration of possible spoilage.

A final product markup factor is the relative amount of retail service associated with selling the item. Packaged goods packed in cartons that are self-service dispensing units can carry a low markup. If the retailer has to weigh or measure out the item, its markup must be higher. Where installation service is necessary, as in the case of certain household appliances, markup may have to be in the 50–60 percent range to cover these retailer costs. Druggists set markups of 70 percent and higher on prescriptions to cover the compensation of the expert pharmacist who must be employed to fill them.

3. The higher a distributor's or retailer's overhead in relation to sales, the higher his markup must be to cover overhead and still leave some profit margin on a reasonable volume of business. A drop shipper can operate with profit on much lower markups than a full-service wholesaler in the same field. A full service retailer has higher relative costs than a self-service cash-carry store; therefore his general schedule of markup percentages must be higher.

Department stores customarily assign a particular over-all markup percentage to each department which takes into account the general characteristics of its merchandise, any special costs of services associated with the department, and its share of store overhead. Each departmental buyer must then work out markups for subclasses of goods in his department that will result in the assigned over-all markup.

4. A distributor or store basing its sales appeal on supplementary services, or on some quasi-monopoly position, can ignore the challenge of lower pricing by other sellers in the same field, provided the differential is not too great. But any wholesaler or retailer whose main appeal is price economy must pay close attention to the prices of competitors, and be ready to sacrifice normal markups on particular items to avoid being "undersold." Many an independent retailer has discovered that, after giving some item in his stock its normal markup, he was compelled to strike some amount off the price because a nearby chain store was offering the item at a lower price. Some department stores which have built their reputations on "economy pricing" maintain staffs of "comparison shoppers" who note prices charged by competing stores, so that the employer can meet or undercut them.

5. A retail price arrived at by the operation of the preceding principles of markup may be evidently unsound according to the odd-price principle

explained in Chapter 19. A 94¢ price for an article, for example, or a $1.00 price, would lack psychological "pull." In either case an adjustment to 97¢ or 98¢ would seem to be indicated.* In a recent study of retail newspaper advertisements, 64 percent of all advertised prices under $5.00 were "odd" prices. Most of these "odd" prices ended in -9, -8, -7, and -3. Prices ending in -1, -2, -4, and -6 were rarely used.

Retail price cutting

Price cutting is an important aspect of retail price policy. For some stores, it is a consistent basic element of their sales strategy. For most stores, it is a useful tactical manoeuver to gain promotional advantages.

The "cut-price store" is familiar in every city and large town. Its appeal is exclusively that of penny-saving. It offers the irreducible minimum of customer services. Its markups are shaved even beyond the savings effected through this service-paring. Therefore its break-even point on over-all volume is much higher than those of its full-service competitors. The price bargains that it offers are designed to attract an abnormal patronage— patronage drawn away from neighboring full-price stores. The higher break-even point is achieved and surpassed, and the "cut-price store" earns a profit on prices that would mean categorical loss to the full-price stores. The discount houses that sell standard brand consumer durable goods for cash only at reductions of 10 to 40 percent off list price, have a similar objective. Some automobile and household-appliance dealers effect an indirect cut-price policy by consistently giving excessive "allowances" on trade-ins.

Nearly all stores do occasional price-cutting on specific items for promotional reasons. A common promotional price-cutting technique is the "loss leader." A well-known brand-name item is offered at an obvious bargain price—often actually lower than the retailer's cost of purchase. Customers who enter the store to take advantage of the "loss leader" offer may be sold other items while they are there. Even if they make no other purchases at the moment, they are likely to think of the store as a happy hunting ground for real bargains and return to it in the future. From the additional sales and patronage thus obtained the store owner expects not only to recoup any loss suffered through the loss leader, but to make immediate extra profit or at least build long-term good-will. Another indirect retail price-cutting technique, closely related to that of the loss leader, is the offer of general premiums for patronizing the store, or cooperating with manufacturers in offering premiums for purchase of specific products.

---

* The first deliberate "odd" pricing was done by department stores, not for reasons of psychological appeal, but to force sales clerks to make change and thereby render it less easy for them to pocket customers' payments without recording sales, as they might have done with "round" prices.

A third form of retail price-cutting occurs when slow moving items are "marked down" to clear them. Retailers of fashion goods frequently have to make such markdowns at season-ends to disembarrass themselves of remaining stock before the new season begins, since carry-overs would have no market whatsoever next year. The principle is applicable to other than fashion goods. Any retailer with a sluggish item that pre-empts valuable shelf and stock-room space would be wise to cut the price sharply and push it as a "special."

Finally, retail price cutting may come about through competitive "price wars," such as the famous one in which Macy's, Gimbels', and other leading New York City department stores were involved in the summer of 1951. Normal rivalry between two or more stores sometimes gets out of hand. Instead of competitive considerations operating merely as a limiting factor on the markup policy of one or the other store, a violent competitive effort at "price slashing" erupts. Store managements become temporarily irrational, and the mutual price cuts are carried, beyond all dictates of business common sense, to the loss point and further. Sometimes a price war limited to a few items operates as a "loss leader" promotion for the competing stores and the losses on the "war" sales are more than compensated for by extra sales of items not affected by the war. More often both parties are net losers.

State legislation has imposed limitations on retail price cutting. The state *Fair Trade* laws which permit resale price maintenance by manufacturers have already been described. In addition, 32 states have *Unfair Trade Practice* laws which forbid the resale of goods, other than through liquidation sales and sales of damaged or deteriorated goods, below cost. Another 7 states have similar laws applying to cigarette sales. "Cost," under these laws, is interpreted as purchase or replacement cost of the goods sold, plus an arbitrary markup presumed to represent cost of doing business. The most common statutory markup provision for retailers is 6%, but 7% and 12% provisions are found in some of the laws. Several laws set 2% as the minimum markup requirement for wholesalers. These Unfair Trade Practice acts go beyond the Fair Trade laws in their enforcement methods; besides the authorization of civil suits for damages by injured competitors, the Unfair Trade Practice acts provide for criminal prosecution and penalties. To date, however, their enforcement has not been effective.

Trade-ins

The "trade-in" has long been a feature of automobile retailing. The dealer credits the allowance for the customer's old car against the price of a new one. So general is this practice that automobile dealers are provided with schedules of suggested trade-in allowances for cars of different makes and years. In recent years the trade-in practice has spread from the automobile field to other consumer durables—cameras, sewing machines, refrigerators, cleaners, carpets, electric shavers, power lawn mowers, and watches. These trade-in allowances have occasionally been manufacturers' subterfuges for temporary promotional price cutting, or retailers' subterfuges for cutting prices on fair-traded merchandise. To an increasing extent, however, true trade-in practice is entering a number of consumer durable goods fields. Where this has happened, the true price of the new items is reduced to a "net" basis, thus enlarging the market for them. At the same time a new market is created for the used items. This is complementary to, rather than competitive with, the market for the new items, so that total sales possibilities are increased.

Retail "single pricing"

A single price to all customers for all items has long generally characterized American retailing. In recent years this retail pricing policy has been given support by the growing practice of stating retail prices in manufacturers' advertisements, whether or not such retail prices are backed by resale price maintenance.

American retailing has gained much from this general elimination of haggling in retail transactions. So long as competing retailers adhere to a single price policy, and their actual prices are in line with differences in their service policies, they are relieved from an element of concealed cut-price competition which can only hurt all without benefitting any. The time of sales clerks and proprietors is not consumed by price bargaining. Customer good will is not lost by the discovery that others have "gotten away with" lower prices.

Breaches in consistent retail single pricing occur, however. To a greater extent in the near past than at present, dealers in the "foreign" sections of large cities would haggle with their customers. Single pricing was an incomprehensible concept to both. During "buyers' market" periods when sales are slow and dealers are overstocked, retail single-pricing policy tends to break under competitive pressure in such high-unit-price fields as autos, radios and TV, and household appliances. Insistent customers can often force prices for such items down to retailers' cost, plus sales clerk's commission, plus 5 or 10 percent. In lines where trade-ins are customary, allowances on trade-ins may constitute individual-customer price cuts of widely varying magnitude.

REVIEW

1. Describe manufacturers' pricing objectives.
2. Describe manufacturers' pricing procedures.
3. What is meant by manufacturers' "uniform-price" policy? What are its advantages? In what business lines is it impracticable? How does the Robinson-Patman Act affect "single-pricing"?
4. Explain "quantity discount," "cumulative quantity discount," and "free deal."
5. Explain "trade discount" and "cumulated trade discount."
6. Explain "catalog discount."
7. Explain "F.O.B. shipping point," "F.O.B. basing point," and "uniform delivered price" terms of sale.
8. Explain the state and federal Fair Trade laws.
9. Explain "markup," and the reasons for differing markup ratios.
10. Explain "loss leader," and "markdown."
11. Distinguish between state Fair Trade and Unfair Trade Practice laws.
12. Are there many exceptions to "single-pricing" by retail stores? Explain.

DISCUSSION TOPICS

1. "It is naïve to ascribe 'ethical' motivations to any aspects of manufacturers' pricing."
2. "If manufacturers would only utilize the services of economists, their pricing procedures could be much more scientific."
3. "Quantity discounts are a disguised form of price cutting to attract big orders or big customers."
4. "Trade discounts introduce an element of complexity into the business arithmetic of sellers and buyers that is not compensated by any benefits to either."
5. What are the pros and cons of fair trade? On which side does the balance of argument lie?
6. "Retail markups should be calculated on the basis of purchase price instead of selling price."
7. Shouldn't there be a much wider application of "trade-ins" in the retailing of consumer durable goods?

PROBLEM 1

Dart Co. manufactures a high-quality line of men's dress shirts, sport shirts, and underwear. It advertises heavily, and has created strong nation-wide market acceptance of the "Dart" brand name. It sells direct to dealers, on a "selective" basis.

For years it has priced its items by taking direct unit costs (labor and materials) at anticipated volume, multiplying these unit costs by 4 to reach a first approximation of retail sales prices, adjusting these figures up or down to reach good "odd" prices (e.g., $6.95 for a dress shirt, or 4-for-$4.87 for undershirts), then taking two-thirds of these retail "odd" prices as the prices of the items to dealers (thus allowing the retailers a 33 1/3 percent mark-up, if they chose to sell at the particular "odd" prices). No quantity or trade discounts are given. The company has made a fair profit over the years.

Now the management is seriously questioning Dart Co.'s pricing policy on the following points:

1. Is their basic pricing procedure the best one from the viewpoints of maximizing immediate profit and long-term development of the company's market? If not, how could they arrive at a better policy?

2. To win over stores that have previously refused to carry the Dart line, would it be advisable to offer them a special 10 percent reduction in price on their first six-months' orders?

3. Recently, in cities where two or more stores carry the Dart line, they have sometimes engaged in price-cutting "wars" on Dart items. The Dart management is worried that these price "wars" may lead consumers to mistrust Dart quality standards or the usual prices for the Dart items. Moreover, in several cases, one or more of the stores that have become involved in these price "wars" on Dart items have subsequently dropped the Dart line and shifted to competing fair-traded lines. Should Dart price-fix its line? What are the arguments pro and con? Is there any other pricing procedure short of fair-trading that would promote uniformity in the retail prices of the Dart line? Would this be preferable to price-fixing the line? Why or why not?

4. Should quantity discounts be offered? If so, what would be a reasonable allowance?

Advise the management of Dart Co. on each of these matters.

PROBLEM 2

Mr. Jones operates the one hardware store in suburban Greenville. Besides the usual lines of household hardware and paints, he carries lincs of household accessories, garden implements, and sports equipment. On seasonal lines such as the garden implements and sports equipment, Mr. Jones clears his end-of-season stocks by sales with markdowns up to 25 percent. He has a limited store display of General Electric appliances, and does considerable business selling this line from catalogs and buying to order when customers purchase. On the basis of suppliers' advice, Mr. Jones has established a wide range of markup percentages for his various lines—for example:

10%—the G.E. appliance line
20%—power implements and other "high ticket" items
33⅓%—paint, garden implements, grass seed

40%—"shelf" hardware, housewares
50%—household specialties (such as fireplace items)
60%—seasonal items, items requiring packaging

Recently Mr. Jones read an article about a hardware retailer who built up a successful business on the pricing policy of a uniform 33⅓ percent markup. He wonders if this policy would be superior to his present one.

Would it? Why or why not?

SUGGESTED READINGS

American Management Association, *Competitive Pricing,* Management Report No. 17, 1958.

American Marketing Association, *Pricing in Prosperity,* Marketing for Executives series No. 1, 1956.

Backman, J., *Price Practices and Price Policies,* Ronald Press, New York, 1953.

Bergfeld, A. J., *Pricing for Profit and Growth,* McGraw-Hill Book Co., New York, 1957.

Edwards, C. D., *The Price Discrimination Law,* Brookings Institute, Washington, D.C., 1959.

Kaplan, A. D. H., and others, *Pricing in Big Business,* Brookings Institute, Washington, D.C., 1958.

National Industrial Conference Board, *Administered Pricing, Economic and Legal Issues* (1958); *Dealer Margins,* Studies in Business Policy No. 42 (1950), NICB, New York.

National Wholesale Druggists' Association, *The Basis and Development of Fair Trade,* 3rd ed, NWDA, New York, 1955.

Nicholls, W. H., *Price Policies in the Cigarette Industry,* Vanderbilt University Press, Nashville, 1951.

Oxenfeldt, A. R., *Industrial Pricing and Marketing Practices,* Prentice-Hall, Englewood Cliffs, N.J., 1951.

Smith, G. R., & H. C. Smith, *An Economic Appraisal of Resale Price Maintenance,* Loyola University, New Orleans, 1957.

Taggert, H. F., *Cost Justification,* Bureau of Business Research, University of Michigan, Ann Arbor, 1958.

CHAPTER 21

ADVERTISING AND OTHER FORMS OF PROMOTION

Promotion * is nonpersonal stimulation of market demand for a product, service, or selling organization, directly to its potential ultimate purchasers or customers, or indirectly through middlemen and retailers. This task of stimulating market demand—even of actually creating it—is shared by promotion and personal selling, as we shall see in Chapter 22.

Promotional activities take seven forms: (1) advertising, (2) publicity, (3) price promotion, (4) sales promotion, (5) trade shows and exhibits, (6) display, and (7) trading stamps. Advertising, publicity, and price promotion are employed by all classes of sellers—manufacturers, wholesale distributors, and retailers. Sales promotion and trade shows are mainly methods of manufacturer promotion. Display and trading stamps are almost exclusively retailing techniques.

Advertising and many forms of sales promotion are practicable only because similar products are differentiated in buyers' minds by distinctive names and symbols. Some consideration of this topic of product identification must therefore precede our study of promotional principles and techniques.

---

* There is much confusion in the use of the word "promotion." It is frequently employed broadly to cover every form of customer education and reminder, including advertising and display. It is frequently used, also, in a narrower sense, to cover product education and reminder techniques, and manufacturer or distributor good-will techniques, *other than advertising and display.* We are using the term "promotion" in its broad connotation. The term "sales promotion" is used for the narrower concept.

PRODUCT IDENTIFICATION

Brand names * such as Heinz, Jello, Palmolive, Chevrolet, Kleenex, Frigidaire, General Electric, and R. C. A.-Victor, applying to individual products or to a company's line of products, are familiar to practically every man, woman and child in the United States. So are such brand symbols * as the child under an umbrella for Morton's Salt ("When it rains it pours"), the camel on the cigarette package, the script "Ford" signature, the face of King Gillette on razor blades. Advertising and other forms of promotion made these names and symbols familiar to the buying public. But it is also true that, had these names and symbols not been established for the products and product lines in question, no effective methods of promoting the products on a large scale could have been devised. Of what avail would it have been to the R. J. Reynolds Tobacco Company, for example, to spend millions of dollars promoting its cigarettes merely as *cigarettes,* if the only result of such advertising could be to induce people to ask for "cigarettes," and as likely as not get cigarettes made by some other manufacturer, instead of causing them to say "Give me a pack of Camels"?

Branded merchandise dominates most manufactured product lines today, and the trend is definitely toward wider developments in branding. In consumer product fields, even fresh fruits and vegetables, coal, and textile piece goods are now being marketed under brand designations. Brand names are appearing on semi-manufactured items and on industrial materials and supplies.

Purposes of branding

The primary purpose of a brand name is to focus market good-will created by advertising and other forms of promotion on a particular manufacturer's or distributor's products identified by it. A branded product or line can be advertised; an unbranded one cannot. Advertising builds sales volume for branded items. It creates consumer preference which, based on fact or fancy, establishes the branded product or line to some

---

* There is considerable confusion in popular use of the terms "brand" and "trade mark." The latter is frequently used as a synonym for "brand symbol," without regard to whether or not there is legal protection of the symbol. The following are the distinctions drawn by the Definitions Committee of the American Marketing Association. A brand is "a name, term, sign, symbol, or design, or a combination of them, which is intended to identify the goods or services of one seller or group of sellers and to differentiate them from those of competitors." A trade mark is "a brand that is given legal protection because it is capable of exclusive appropriation; because it is used in a manner sufficiently fanciful, distinctive, and arbitrary; because it is affixed to the product when sold; or because it otherwise satisfies the requirements set up by law."

extent as a specialty, lifts it from a purely competitive market status, and permits the charging of higher quasi-monopoly prices. Attaching a "family" or "line" brand name, for which established market good-will exists, to a new product frequently assures an immediate market for it.

As a secondary objective, some brand names are devised with an eye to their promotional suggestiveness—e.g., "Longwear" for a line of work clothes, "Lux" for a toilet soap, "Kleenex" for a cleansing tissue, "Frigidaire" and "Coldspot" originally for refrigerators.

The psychologists have established that visual patterns are more readily remembered as identification tags than word associations. Therefore many advertisers associate a brand symbol with their brand name. The symbol may be a simple formal pattern like Lucky Strike's target or Macy's Red Star. It may be a representation like Camel's camel or Quaker Oats'

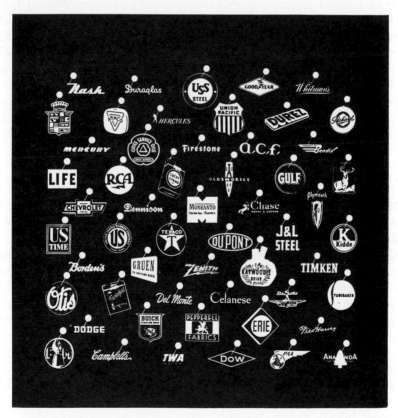

FAMILIAR BRAND NAMES AND SYMBOLS. *From the Remington-Rand brochure "You and Remington Rand."*

ILLUSTRATION 21–1

Quaker. It may be a particular way of printing the brand name like the Ford script signature, or a background shape for the brand name like the Chevrolet bar. Frequently, a brand symbol ties in with a slogan used in the product's advertising, as the day-old chick symbol of Bon Ami scouring powder that "Hasn't scratched yet." For advertising and display reasons, a brand symbol should be designed for effective visibility and recognition value.

Trade marks

The identification objective of brand names and symbols would be largely defeated if, as soon as advertising and other promotion had created substantial market good-will for a particular name or symbol, it could be copied and applied to competing products. Common law gave the originator of a brand name or symbol considerable protection. Federal trademark law, discussed more fully in Chapter 30, provides still greater protection by permitting brand names and symbols to be registered as *trade marks*. A trade mark, maintained in use, is protected for twenty years (with possibility of renewal) against any copying or imitation that might produce market confusion.

Practically all manufacturers and distributors who intend promotional development of a brand name or symbol have it registered as a protected trade mark; as of 1960, over half a million domestic trade marks had been registered.

Initiative in branding

Most brand names are established by manufacturers. These are commonly called "national" brands, even though distribution of the product and use of the brand name may be confined to a small territory.

Large wholesalers, particularly in the food lines, buy unbranded merchandise from packers, manufacturers, and other producers, and have their own brands affixed. "White Rose" is an example of a wholesaler's brand in the food field; "Graybar" is a wholesaler's brand in the electric appliance line. The major general mail order houses, large department stores, and chain systems also sell under brand names they have developed for themselves. Examples of these are the "Kenmore" and "All-State" brands of Sears Roebuck, the "SupreMacy" brand of the Macy department store, and "Ann Page" of the A & P chain. Wholesalers' and retailers' brands are commonly called "distributors'," "private," or "house" brands.

Private brands account for only a small fraction of merchandise sales. In the food products and household needs fields, where their position is relatively strong, they claim only one-quarter of the market. Retailers' private brands in some merchandise lines have been gaining at the expense of manufacturers' brands in recent years, however, although until recently most retailers did little or no direct advertising of their private brands. Three circumstances explain the growing importance of private brands. (1) Large retailers can commonly buy unbranded merchandise at much lower cost than comparable branded items whose prices must cover the manufacturers' promotional costs. Such merchandise, with the retailers' brands atttached, can be resold by the retailers with higher markups at prices well below those of the comparable manufacturer-brand items. The price saving attracts both bargain-hunting customers and knowing buyers able to judge the products on their merits. (2) Large general mail order houses, large department stores, and large chains, through advertising and by maintaining high standards of customer service over the years, have built up substantial institutional good-will. House brands have translated this institutional good-will into brand good-will, especially since these large retailers have been generally careful to attach their house brands only to articles and lines of good quality. (3) The state fair trade laws and the federal Miller-Tydings and McGuire laws for a while prevented many large retailers from offering fair-traded national-brand merchandise at reduced prices, as they would have liked to do and could have done profitably. But nothing stopped them from buying identical unbranded items, often from the very manufacturer of the fair-traded national-brand merchandise, affixing their house brands, and selling them at "bargain" prices to their customers. The fair-trading of many lines of national-brand merchandise is credited with being a major contributory cause of the rapid expansion of retailer-house-brand merchandising during the 1940's and early 1950's.

ADVERTISING

Advertising may be defined as "nonpersonal stimulation of demand for a product, service, or selling institution to prospective buyers by an identified sponsor through direct mail or a *paid* medium."

Advertising is by far the most important form of promotion. Some $11 billion was spent on American advertising during 1959, and the trend is toward still larger appropriations. Most advertising effort is directed at consumers on behalf of consumer goods, by the manufacturers,* whole-salers, and retailers ** of these goods. A smaller proportion is aimed by

---

* Manufacturers' advertising to consumers is commonly referred to as "national" advertising, though the special market to which it is directed may be very limited in numbers or restricted in territorial scope.

** Retailers' "notice of sale" advertising is commonly referred to as "local" advertising.

producers and distributors of industrial and business equipment, materials, supplies, and services at the users of such items. A minor share of the total is manufacturers' mercantile advertising, directed at wholesalers and retailers to persuade them to carry the advertisers' lines.

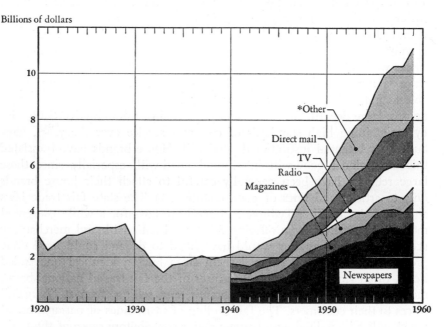

Billions of dollars

*Including premiums and other consumer promotions

ADVERTISING EXPENDITURES, 1920–1959

Source: *Printers' Ink*

ILLUSTRATION 21–2

Our survey of advertising as a promotional technique will cover: (1) purposes, (2) media, (3) psychology and techniques, (4) appropriations, (5) organization, and (6) control.

Purposes

The long-range objective of all commercial advertising is to stimulate sales. Sometimes this long-range objective is realized directly, as when the recipient of a direct mail advertisement is so impressed that he writes in an immediate order, or when a shopper enters a department store specifically to buy an item advertised in the daily paper or over a local radio station. More often the general objective of producing sales is accomplished indirectly by establishing and maintaining a favorable "brand image" of a product in consumers' minds, thereby making them more receptive to store display, the suggestions of store clerks, or the appeals of salesmen.

The immediate purposes, contributory to the long-range objective of sales stimulation, which advertisements may serve are many. These are the three major ones: (1) education about the product, (2) reminder of the product or the seller, and (3) notice of sale.

AN "EDUCATIONAL" AD. *Courtesy of Air Associates, Inc.*

ILLUSTRATION 21–3

Educational advertising. When a new product is fighting its way onto a market not fully familiar with its special qualities and virtues, or when a product brand is struggling for a due share of a generally expanding market, the primary advertising objective of the manufacturer is to educate the market on its chief selling points, and to point out superiorities over competing items. In the case of consumer items, the instructional process may take the form of merely reiterating one or two significant or imaginary virtues of a product brand with the hope that sheer repetition will produce drugged acceptance of the claim by a goodly proportion of those who have been the targets of the advertisements. Some industrial advertisers, in contrast, make their direct mail pieces and their trade journal ads miniature masterpieces of skilled technical exposition, to influence the engineers and experienced purchasing managers who make the buying decisions in their field.

Reminder advertising. Once a product brand has been established in a relatively stable market, there is little that its advertisers can do in the way of further instruction about it, except possibly to promote incidental news or special uses. The market knows, and knows thoroughly, all that advertising and experience can teach about it. Yet advertising must go on or, under the pressure of competitors' advertising, the brand image will be quickly forgotten and the market good-will so expensively built up will be lost. Under such circumstances, brand image advertising changes its purpose

A BILLBOARD "REMINDER" AD. *Courtesy of General Outdoor Advertising Co.*

ILLUSTRATION 21–4

from product education to simple reminders, if possible associated with a favorable emotional suggestion. A gasoline or automobile brand name is spread across highway billboards. The brand name of a soft drink is spelled out by an airplane against the sky. The brand name of a soap or a shoe is mentioned five times, and underlined with a jingle, in a radio commercial.

Sometimes reminder advertising is aimed at clinching the name of a seller, rather than the product sold. Department stores and large specialty stores sponsor radio programs so that their names will be mentioned frequently in the commercials. During the War years, when automobile manufacturers were making tanks and other military items instead of passenger cars, they took full-page advertisements in magazines to tell the public of their contributions to the war effort or full-page newspaper ads to urge the public to buy war bonds, so that their corporate images would be remembered in a favorable association. Such seller-reminder advertising is commonly called "institutional good-will advertising."

Notice-of-sale advertising. Such advertising informs the public that specified articles are to be sold on a given date, by a named seller (or group of sellers), at specified prices. The "local" advertising of department stores and other retailers usually is of this type. Manufacturers sometimes employ notice-of-sale advertising to launch a new product or model, naming their dealers or indicating the classes of outlets carrying the advertised item.

A "NOTICE-OF-SALE" AD

ILLUSTRATION 21–5

Media

Advertisers employ many channels of communication, or media, to reach their public. Among the more important are:

1. *Publications—magazines and newspapers.* Magazines are primarily media for manufacturers' "educational" advertising, and carry approximately one-third of such advertising. From an advertising viewpoint they may be classified as: (a) general reader interest periodicals (*Saturday Evening Post* or *Life*) for mass-market products; (b) class-reader interest periodicals (*Motor-Boating,* or *Popular Mechanics,* the important "women's

group" of magazines, or farm periodicals) for more selective audiences; and (c) trade journals (*Iron Age* or *Progressive Grocer*) for specific business markets. Newspapers are primarily media for retailers' notice-of-sale advertising, but nearly one-third of their advertising space goes to manufacturers' advertising.

2. *Radio and TV.* In network hook-ups these can serve mass-market manufacturers as media for nationwide or regional reminder advertising. The more costly TV has marked possibilities for certain types of product-education demonstrations. "Spot" broadcasts or telecasts over individual stations are commonly used by retailers for institutional good will or notice-of-sale advertising.

3. *Outdoor advertising—billboards and car cards.* These permit presentations of size and color in preferred positions, but are primarily of value for reminder advertising. Car cards have some possibilities as educational media.

4. *Direct mail.* Where product education on a consumer or business specialty product is important, and good selective mailing lists are available, this is a versatile medium for product-education advertising. Department stores and mail order houses also employ it for notice-of-sale advertising.

An advertiser's choice of the media he will employ involves four steps:

1. First, he must determine which media lend themselves most effectively to his advertising purposes. Newspapers, hastily read (except for special Sunday sections), are usually less effective for product-education advertising than magazines, but are excellent notice-of-sale media for large retailers. Highway billboards, practically useless for product-education advertising, are good low-cost reminder media for many classes of advertisers. Product education through visual demonstration is possible on TV, but not on radio.

2. The next consideration is the coverage of the advertiser's potential market given by each medium in a class. For example, a general-reader-interest magazine might have a circulation of one million, but only 10 percent of its readers might be home owners and hence prospects for an advertiser who manufactured home air conditioning installations. In contrast, a "home beautiful" magazine with one-quarter the circulation of the other might reach $2\frac{1}{2}$ times as many prospects for this particular advertiser. These 250,000 prospects might include a large proportion of the 100,000 prospect coverage of the first magazine, or the readerships of the two magazines might be largely mutually exclusive, so that quite different segments of the advertiser's total potential market could be reached through each medium.

An advertiser can readily discover the circulation of each published medium in a class through various advertisers' aids such as *Standard Rate and Data Service* and *Ayer's Directory of Newspapers and Periodicals.* Determination of the proportion of each medium's readers or audience that are prospects for the advertiser, and what part they represent of his general potential market, is more difficult. The advertisers' services noted above supply considerable information on the character and contents of each medium, from which an advertiser may "guesstimate" to what extent elements of his potential market will be included among the medium's readers or audience. Many magazines, newspapers, and radio stations have made research studies of their audiences, and have analyzed their market characteristics for the benefit of advertisers. Such information may enable an advertiser to calculate, instead of guessing at, the part of his potential market reached by a particular medium.

3. Next an advertiser must calculate the *per prospect* cost of each likely medium. His advertisers' service aids give him the rates charged by each medium. His previous "guesstimates" and calculations have given him the number of prospects reachable by each medium. Arithmetical division gives him per prospect cost for each medium.

4. With information before him on the suitability of various classes of advertising media to his advertising purposes, the market potential coverages of individual media within each class, and the per prospect cost of each medium, the advertiser then apportions his promotional budget among the various media. His objective is, within the scope of his available funds, to get the most effective presentation of his advertising to a maximum potential market. Other things being equal, he favors the lower-per-prospect-cost media. But other things are rarely equal. The issues presented are often intricate, and wise decisions require broad background knowledge and shrewd judgment.

Psychology and techniques

The first psychological objective of every advertisement is to capture attention. Unless an ad is noted by a fair proportion of the audience at which it is directed, everything else about it is wasted. Advertising art has devoted measureless ingenuity and skill to this end. Relative size, use of color, illustrations and their subject matter, layout, headlines—all are means to that all-important end of capturing attention.

For many types of reminder advertising, the drawing of attention to a familiar brand name is the be-all and end-all of the promotion. Product-education and notice-of-sale advertising, however, have further psychological objectives. Attention having been won, the ad must instantly arouse interest—otherwise attention is quickly forfeited and the ad fails of its purpose. The surest way to arouse interest is swift appeal, through illustration, headline, or opening sentence, to some buying motivation associated with the product. The eight classes of consumer buying motivations that advertisers may appeal to were analyzed in Chapter 3, and may be reviewed at this point.

Interest aroused, the way is clear for an advertisement to deliver its product-education or notice-of-sale message. This message must usually be terse, since the interest of most advertisement readers wanes rapidly. It must be so presented, moreover, that the initial interest is maintained or even intensified.

One of the most important psychological tools of advertising technique is *association*. Whether an advertisement is purely a brand-name reminder, or involves technical exposition of industrial materials, an advertiser should be ever alert to build up a favorable "image" for his brand and to avoid unfavorable emotional associations. The objective is not a logical cause-and-effect conclusion, but the establishing of pleasant subconscious emotional reactions to the brand name. A goodly proportion of advertisements for cigarettes, shaving creams, office equipment, and other items purchased by men use pretty girls, often quite irrelevantly, as part of the illustration —the picture of a pretty girl carries a pleasant emotional association for most men. Liquor, railroad, and men's wear ads feature dogs and other animals in their illustrations—another pleasant, sentimental association for most men. Personal pride, social distinction, good-housewifeliness, the imputation of culture, family affection—these are among the consumer buying motivations that advertising weaves by association into today's brand images.

Appropriations

Most advertising programs are planned for months, even a full year ahead. The allotted appropriation is commonly determined as a percentage of the company's prior-year sales, though this is far from being the soundest basis.

The range of advertising budgets, measured in relation to sales, is wide. For many manufacturers of unbranded goods and for most wholesalers and small retailers, whose only advertising is often merely a listing or a small ad in a classified telephone or trade directory, total advertising expenditures are only a fraction of a percent of their sales. The cost of department store advertising is generally between 2 and 3% of sales. Advertising budgets of manufacturers of brand-name consumer goods average around 5% of sales; for tobacco products manufacturers the proportion is from 10 to 12%. Manufacturers of cosmetics and proprietary medicines spend between 30 and 35% of their sales income in advertising.

Organization

A company's advertising could be handled internally, by an individual giving part or all of his time to this function, or by a sizable advertising department if the scope of the company's promotional activity warranted it. Most retail "local" advertising, including that of the large metropolitan department stores, is so handled. So is most direct mail advertising. But well over 90 percent of manufacturers' "national" advertising is created and directed by *advertising agencies*. A major part of regional advertising and considerable local advertising is also undertaken through these agencies.

According to the *Census of Business,* there are over 8,000 advertising agencies. They vary in size from one-man units to organizations with over 1,500 employees. Small or large, they function as service specialists—experts in planning, creating, and disseminating advertising for their clients. In addition, they frequently assist their clients in product design and undertake marketing research for them. The relationship between an advertising agency and a client is obviously a very confidential one. For this reason, an agency rarely if ever serves competing clients.

Agencies handling manufacturers' "national" advertising are compensated primarily, not by their clients, but by the media in which they placed the ads. They are paid a 15 percent commission on the media's space or time charge paid by the agencies' manufacturer-clients. The agencies charge their clients only for supplementary costs and special services. Consequently it costs manufacturers little if any extra to utilize the services of agencies in developing and placing their "national" advertising—a circumstance that accounts in considerable part for the entrenched place that agencies hold in this field. To an increasing extent, however, agencies are charging their clients directly for special services such as marketing research and assistance in product and package design.

Using the services of an advertising agency does not obviate a company's need for an advertising manager. Such an individual is still required to formulate or assist in formulating the company's general advertising policy, and to act as liaison between the agency and the company management. He may also be responsible for sales promotion and other forms of nonmedia promotion.

Control

A false advertisement works injury in three ways: (1) purchasers of the advertised goods are misled by it to their detriment; (2) competitors of the false advertiser may lose sales they would otherwise have made; (3) market faith in advertising generally is shaken, so that its efficacy is weakened. Public authority and the advertising profession have accordingly taken steps to prevent and punish false advertising.

Legislation against false advertising is described in detail in Chapter 30. Briefly summarized, the more important elements of this legislation are: (1) the Federal Trade Commission Act of 1914, which declared "unfair methods of competition in commerce" illegal and which was construed to apply to false or misleading advertising in any fields that gave the advertiser an unfair competitive advantage; (2) the Wheeler-Lea Act of 1938, which outlawed "deceptive" advertising generally and specifically mentioned "materially misleading" advertising of foods, drugs, and cosmetics; (3) the postal laws on fraudulent misuse of the mails; (4) "truth in advertising" laws in 43 states, which make untrue, deceptive, or misleading intrastate advertising a misdemeanor; (5) laws recently passed by New York and a number of other states prohibiting "bait" advertising (i.e., fake "bargain" offers).

Responsible advertisers, the advertising profession, and advertising media make substantial contributions to policing advertising. A number of trade associations have adopted trade practice codes which incorporate prohibitions of improper advertising practices. The three great national advertising associations—the American Association of Advertising Agencies (the 4As), the Association of National Advertisers, and the Advertising Federation of America—have jointly adopted a code which condemns specific elements of false or otherwise objectionable advertising. Many newspapers and magazines, and the radio and TV networks, do some screening of the ads they carry. The primary contribution of the advertising profession to the self-policing of advertising is the system of Better Business Bureaus. There are a National Better Business Bureau and 93 local bureaus. The national bureau is financed by large manufacturer-advertisers and advertising agencies. The local bureaus are supported primarily by retailers and other local advertisers. These Better Business Bureaus are the watchdogs of advertising. Through their own scrutiny of publications, and through complaints made to them, they spot cases of improper advertising. Their first action, and usually the only one needed, is to warn the offending advertiser. If he persists in the offense, they cooperate with the Federal Trade Commission or the appropriate state authority in taking action against the offender.

Despite this impressive structure for self-control and governmental control of advertising, a series of scandals and investigations in 1959 provided evidence that some areas of advertising were marred by implicit if not explicit misrepresentation and by bad taste. The advertising and governmental watch-dogs of advertising had grown slumbrous, and abuses had developed. The proportion of total advertising affected was small, but the public and the advertising profession were quite properly aroused. It may be anticipated that increased self-policing and more vigorous action by the Federal Trade Commission will be the beneficial results of this exposé.

Related to the issue of false and misleading advertising is that of meaningless advertising claims of product superiority. One brand of cigarette is stated to be the only one with "real menthol magic." A coffee is advertised as "the best coffee you've ever tasted." Fresh oranges "give your family 3 times more of the important protopectins and bio-flavonoids than frozen orange juice." Advertisments embodying such empty claims may, through frequent repetition, act as reminders of a brand name, but they certainly have little or no persuasive effect. The problem therefore is not one of control by the FTC or some other public agency for the protection of competitors or consumers. Rather it is a matter of advertising, through sheer ineffectiveness, failing to accomplish its avowed objective of stimulating consumer demand for the products so advertised. Such unsuccessful advertising is a form of economic waste which, through manufacturers' pricing methods which we studied in the preceding chapter, is passed on to consumers in the form of higher prices.

Vocational considerations

Advertising holds many career possibilities for college graduates. Copywriting and commercial art are but two of the vocational opportunities. Advertising agencies need salesmen, and they need administrators. Many of them employ marketing research staffs. There are positions in the advertising field for the introvert as well as the extrovert, for women as well as for men. But through all lines of advertising work two prime requisites stand out—keen imagination and a superior level of intelligence. For the higher levels of success in copy-writing and advertising art some degree of talent, if not a touch of genius, are needed.

The glamor attached to advertising in many young people's minds, and the striking pecuniary rewards of success in this field, have proven strong lures, and competition to get a start in advertising is severe. An exceptional gift with words or drawing may open the doors of an advertising agency or department to a college graduate without other preparation for an advertising career. Otherwise a comprehensive background of marketing knowledge, and a rigorous training in the procedures and techniques of advertising, such as most collegiate schools of business now offer in their advertising specializations, are generally needed for entry to this field.

PUBLICITY

Commercially significant news about a product, service, or selling organization in a published medium, or favorable presentation of it upon radio, TV, or the stage, is usually just as effective as advertising itself in reminding the market of a product or its seller, and in creating favorable associations. Often it is more effective, since many individuals discount advertised presentations but accept other mention at face value. Hence organizations and individuals with something to sell frequently find it an excellent promotional investment to go to substantial expense in order to obtain "free" publicity about themselves and their products.

Publicity has become organized. Experts in this art are employed as "public relations directors" or retained as independent "publicity agents." For the manufacturer or retailer of fashion goods they prepare "releases," with accompanying photographs, to appear in the fashion sections of the newspapers, and write illustrated articles for the fashion magazines; they arrange to have his items worn as costumes in plays, with appropriate mention in the program. The prizes offered in radio and television give-away programs, with brand names clearly enunciated, are publicity devices. The mile-long Thanksgiving Day parade, with bands, floats, clowns, and balloons, organized each year by the R. H. Macy department store, and written up in all the New York City papers, is publicity. So also, probably, is the brief article in a "home beautiful" magazine about a new type of floor covering—the chances are that the manufacturer's publicity director or agent labored hard to have it incorporated in the magazine.

PRICE PROMOTION

Market demand for an item is generally related to its price, of course, and any price reduction tends to stimulate purchasing, provided demand for the product is elastic within the range of the price change. *Promotional* use of price cutting, however, goes beyond this basic economic principle. A "promotional" price is deliberately set substantially below the normal long-run competitive or optimum price—low enough to be an obvious "bargain." During the limited time that a manufacturer's price promotion is in effect, he makes no profit or may actually sustain a net loss on every sale, but meanwhile the lure of the "bargain" introduces his product to many consumers whose attention might never otherwise have been drawn to it, and who will continue to purchase it after the price is raised to normal level. The retailer's "bargain prices" draw customers into his store, thereby enabling him to gain a new clientele and hold his old one against competition.

Manufacturers find promotional price cuts most effective when a new product or brand is being introduced, or when a marked improvement has been incorporated in an established product, or to counter sales promotion drives for competing products. To reduce the price charged to wholesalers and retailers, so that the latter could pass the price reduction on to consumers, would be unsound policy for three reasons: (1) many retailers might not pass on the price cut; (2) at lower prices the retailers and wholesalers would make smaller margins and so would be hostile to the promotion; (3) subsequent raising of the price would produce consumer ill-will that might more than offset all the good will produced by the price cut. Accordingly, manufacturers often put promotional price cuts into effect in two indirect ways. One is to invite purchasers to send in labels or tops from the purchased packages for a refund. The other is to distribute coupons, by direct mail or other means, that entitle the recipients to a stated price reduction on purchase of the item in question. The storekeepers who redeem these coupons must, of course, be compensated. Some 10 billion price-reduction coupons were issued during 1959; the resulting price savings to consumers averaged 15 percent on several billion dollars worth of goods.

Retailers' promotional price cutting takes two forms. One is "loss leader" reduction of the prices of particular items, described in Chapter 20. The other is "sale days" when prices are reduced on large numbers of items carried by the store. Either way, the store foregoes some or all of its normal profit on the cut-price items in order to attract customers into the store where, besides the cut-price items, they will probably buy other merchandise on which the store makes its full profit.

SALES PROMOTION

Many manufacturers have discovered two additional fields of sales stimulation which, while related to advertising and publicity, are definitely distinct from these. The two fields are: (1) consumer sales promotion, and (2) dealer sales promotion. For some classes of products, particularly those bought substantially on an impulse basis, consumer and dealer sales promotion are more important sales stimulators than medium advertising.

Consumer promotion

Consumer sales promotion may take four forms: (1) introduction of a new product to the market by distribution of free samples, (2) instruction of consumers on nonobvious uses of a product, (3) appeal to the "bargain" buying motivation by premium offers, and (4) stimulating special market interest in a product by a contest.

The *free sample* technique is not practicable for all types of merchandise. First, the item must be one which is consumed and repurchased with considerable frequency. Second, it must be a small- or moderate-priced item in its regular market package, or else capable of distribution in special miniature "sample" packages. Third, it must have inherent merits so that use of the sample will establish demand for it. The problems of distributing samples, moreover, are not always easy. Samples of an item with universal personal or household use may be effectively distributed by door-to-door give-away, or through suitable retailers. If the market is a special one, though, there may be serious problems in getting the samples to it.

Consumer instruction is helpful in promoting household appliances and other items involving intricacies of use. Where the use is not too complex, the instruction may be accomplished in retail stores by "demonstrators" paid by the manufacturer. For more complicated items, the instruction may have to take the form of "clinics" or classes provided by the manufacturer but held on the retailers' premises. Sewing machines have long been effectively promoted by sewing classes, and electric ranges by cooking classes. A number of cosmetics manufacturers provide occasional "beauty clinics" through their retailers.

A free *premium,* or one for which a nominal price is charged, can add "bargain" lure to a product purchase. It is usually more effective in revitalizing the sales of an established item than in introducing a new one. The two problems involved in premium promotion are: (1) to discover a low-cost premium item with genuine appeal to purchasers of the promoted product, and (2) to devise some method of distributing the premiums that will not tax the patience of the purchasers or irritate dealers who sell the product. Premium promotions are currently enjoying high favor; over $2 billion a year is being spent on this form of promotion.

A *contest* is an exciting and occasionally effective way of stimulating consumer interest in a product. The prizes may be offered for choosing a name for the product, or completing a sentence or jingle about it, or writing a brief statement of reasons for using it, or devising a special use. One soap company held a very successful national contest in which each purchase of the soap entitled the buyer to vote for a local "beauty queen," with the national selection receiving a movie "starlet" contract. A good contest may obtain widespread publicity, so that a double promotion is obtained. But an ill-considered one may easily backfire on the sponsor. Failure to advertise it, or a list of unattractive prizes, may result in a paucity of entrants. The ill-will engendered among the many losers may far more than offset the good will built up among the winners.

Dealer promotion

Most retailers, left to their own resources, would fall far short of selling effectively many of the items or lines that they carry. This is particularly true in the case of shopping goods and appliance specialties. Consequently a manufacturer who wishes to obtain good presentation of his products at the retail level must usually find ways of assisting his dealers in their handling of his line. Such assistance also wins dealer good-will, and aids the manufacturer in obtaining and holding retail outlets. Some common methods of such dealer promotion are: (1) assisting dealers to organize and manage their stores, by aiding them in planning store or department layout, providing them with special counters and other store equipment free or on a cost basis, and instructing them on simple stock control systems; (2) providing dealers with window and counter display materials and other point-of-purchase promotions; (3) aiding dealers in their local advertising, either by cooperatively sharing the cost with them, or by providing them with copy, mats, direct mail materials, and other items for their own advertising; (4) training dealers' sales forces in more effective selling of the manufacturer's line, and stimulating these sales forces to better selling of the line by "push money" and contests; (5) providing dealers with point-of-purchase premiums which stimulate both buying of the manufacturer's products and customer good-will for the store.

Interest in such dealer promotion is relatively new but is rapidly developing into a major phase of manufacturers' promotional activity.

TRADE SHOWS AND EXHIBITS

A trade show is a cooperative promotion, usually annual, held by manufacturers in a product field. A large hall or armory, or hotel suite, is rented for several days or a week. Each participating manufacturer subrents floor space and sets up his own exhibits. The opportunity thus provided for under-one-roof comparison of the offerings of many manufacturers is a magnet that draws potential customers to the show. Purchase orders may actually be placed at a trade show, but the primary purpose of the manufacturer exhibits is not to make immediate sales but to arouse interest and obtain inquiries which can subsequently be followed up by salesmen. Illustration 11–6 shows such a trade exhibit.

Most trade shows are industrial or mercantile, and many of the interested production executives and store buyers travel hundreds of miles to attend them. A few trade shows, such as the Auto Show, the Motor Boat Show, the Garden Show, and various home shows, are intended for consumers. New York City is the center for these consumer shows. Only the small fraction of the potential consumer market that resides in the New York area can attend these exhibits, but the nation-wide publicity that the show exhibitors receive carries the promotional influence of the show far beyond the direct impact upon the actual visitors.

Many manufacturers of industrial products rent space for exhibits at the trade association meetings of their customers' trades. Such exhibits reach ideally selected audiences under circumstances of unusual receptivity.

DISPLAY

Display is primarily a retail promotional technique although, as indicated above, manufacturers have a vital interest in assisting retailers in doing effective display work. Retail display takes two forms—window display and counter display.

Window display

A store's window display may serve four promotional purposes: (1) capture of attention, (2) suggestion of quality or cheapness, (3) promotion of particular articles or lines sold in the store, (4) general institutional reminder of the store.

A store window must capture the attention of passers-by if it is to accomplish any of its other promotional purposes. The techniques of winning attention are many—general composition of the display, use of eye-catching color effects, topical appositeness of the display subject matter, motion, even sound effects.

Inference of superior quality may be conveyed in a window display through subdued artistry of composition and color harmony, by focusing the display on a very limited selection of choice items, and by avoidance of price tags. Attention-attracting devices such as motion and color disharmony must be sacrificed, since any obvious attempt to draw attention to the window tends in itself to be a denial of quality. On the other hand, if a store bases its primary appeal on the economy of low prices, its display window is bound by none of these limitations, and liberal use of price tags can be an effective element of its promotion.

Display of specific items in a store window, particularly impulse and shopping goods, unquestionably stimulates their sale in the store. This purchase-suggestion effect of window display is strongest when the eye-appeal of the goods is one of their selling points. Obviously, only items in perfect condition, free of all defect or flaw, should be incorporated in a window display. Seasonal merchandise is particularly amenable to window display promotion. The purchase-suggestion influence of any window display wanes rapidly, so that if this is a primary objective of the display, it should be changed frequently—possibly as often as once a week. Store owners face a temptation to crowd as many different articles into their display windows as space permits. This policy is fallacious; a jumbled window usually fails to capture attention, and when it does so, the very multiplicity of items prevents buying interest from focusing on any one.

Finally, it is possible and often desirable to forego specific purchase-suggestion objectives altogether in a window display, and instead have it merely remind passers-by of the existence of the store in a favorable way.

Many leading department and specialty stores feature "holiday" windows with Christmas, Thanksgiving, Easter, and other holiday or seasonal tableaux. These are frequently works of high art, and leave the beholder with a pleasant memory to be associated with the store.

Creation of window displays is an art requiring inherent aesthetic taste, promotional comprehension, and some technical skills. The average store owner or store clerk is not likely to be endowed with this combination of aptitudes, and the displays of many small stores are miserable failures. The large metropolitan department stores employ highly-paid experts to produce their superb window displays. Many manufacturers, as an element of their dealer promotion, stand ready to provide their retail outlets with effective "packaged" displays—constructed, of course, around their particular product lines.

Counter display

Counter display is true point-of-purchase promotion. It draws attention to merchandise and serves as a purchase reminder at the crucial time when the customer is already engaged in buying. For impulse goods it is the supreme promotional opportunity.

In self-service stores, counter displays—and with them shelf and "island" displays—are the primary medium of self-service. The customer actually makes her buying selection by taking items from their display groupings.

TRADING STAMPS

"Trading stamps" are a form of retail promotion capitalizing on the "something extra for nothing" lure that appeals so strongly to so many consumers. The stamps are printed by some 225 companies that provide the premiums for which the stamps, pasted in books, are redeemed. They are sold to retailers at an average price of $2.25 per thousand. The retailers give them to their customers usually on the basis of one stamp for each 10 cents of purchase. The stamps are redeemed for premiums ranging from a metal wastebasket for 1,200 stamps to a combination washer dryer for 184,000 stamps; one stamp plan covers redemption for one-year life insurance policies.

This form of retail promotion dates back to the Nineteenth Century. Its peak of popularity came in the 1950's, however. By 1960 some 200,000 stores were giving their customers some 230 billion trading stamps. Food stores accounting for 41% of grocery sales, gasoline service stations making about 30% of service station sales, drug stores producing some 15% of drug store sales, and sizable proportions of other classes of stores, offered trading stamps. The first stores in any community that offer trading stamps gain substantially in patronage at the expense of their non-stamp competitors. Frequently their patronage gain is so great that the cost of the stamps to them is more than offset by the spreading of their overhead over larger sales volume; in such cases, in spite of the added expense of the stamps, they can increase their profits without raising their prices. With practically all stores of a particular retailing line giving stamps, as happens in many communities or neighborhoods, the promotional advantage cancels out. The $2\frac{1}{4}\%$ cost-on-sales of the stamps then simply becomes an additional general retail operating expense which cuts heavily into the retailers' profits or is partly incorporated in their markups and so passed on to consumers. Nonetheless trading stamp promotion continued to increase through 1960.

THE "PROMOTIONAL MIX"

With so many means of promotion available, what principles are there to guide a manufacturer or retailer in selecting from among them?

Different means of promotion have varying effectiveness with respect to particular promotional objectives. Promotional pricing and distribution of samples are exceptionally efficacious ways of inducing people to actually try new food items which can win acceptance on their merits. Advertising, according to the medium employed, excels in conveying information about a product and its uses or in inexpensively reminding consumers of an item with which they are already familiar. Manufacturers' provision of P.O.P. display materials is unmatched for sparking on-the-spot impulse buying. Thus what a manufacturer or a store seeks in the way of promotional accomplishment may dictate emphasis on one form of promotion rather than another.

Even where one particular form of promotion may be indicated as best for achieving some objective, however, other forms may serve useful supplementary or complementary purposes. A consumer contest or premium must usually be advertised to be effective; inclusion of notice of a contest or premium in an advertisement, moreover, often steps up the attention-attraction potential of the advertisement. The impact of a manufacturer's published advertisement is often cumulated by providing dealers with window or interior display materials that repeat the theme of the advertisement.

In many cases a manufacturer or store should aim at several promotional goals rather than a single dominating one. How should its promotion budget be apportioned in such circumstances? Here the principle of marginal utility offers some guidance. With each added increment of expenditure on any one form of promotion, after a certain minimum dictated by the nature of the promotion, the return in the form of immediate sales or long-run brand or institutional good-will declines. Initial incremental return for one form of promotion may be much higher than for another, but when expenditure on the first form is pushed beyond a certain point, its further marginal return may fall below the initial marginal return from the second form. Hence some element of further promotion expenditure should be upon the second form. With a still higher total promotion budget, the principle of maximizing marginal return might dictate bringing in a third form of promotion. To the extent that the marginal productivity of different forms of promotion for any company can be determined, utilization of each form within the limits established by the total promotion budget should be pushed to the point where the marginal return on each is equal.

Unfortunately quantitative determination of the marginal returns of different forms of promotion is impossible in most cases and can be only crudely ascertained in the rest. Establishing a company's "promotional mix"—the allocation of its total promotion budget among the various forms of promotion that may benefit it—is therefore not a scientific matter but at its best an intuitive art and in most cases rather blind happenstance. Probably most companies currently over-emphasize advertising in their "promotional mixes." But there are also many companies that devote disproportionate parts of their promotion budgets to price promotions, or premiums, or P.O.P. materials, or some other form of consumer or dealer sales promotion.

REVIEW

1. What is a brand name, a brand symbol, a trade mark? What is their marketing significance? What is the advantage of having a *registered* trade mark? Explain the difference between a "national" brand and a "private" brand.

2. What is the difference between "national" and "local" advertising?

3. What are the major immediate purposes of advertising? Give examples.

4. Name at least five advertising media. Indicate for what sort of advertising each would be suitable.

5. How does an advertiser, directly or through its agency, select the media for its advertising?

6. Discuss some applications of psychology to advertising.

7. What considerations determine the relative size of a company's advertising appropriation?

8. Discuss the services of advertising agencies and how they are compensated.

9. What controls are there to check false advertising?

10. Explain publicity.

11. Discuss promotional pricing.

12. Explain the methods of manufacturers' consumer promotion.

13. Explain the methods of manufacturers' dealer promotion.

14. Discuss the objectives of window display and how each may be accomplished.

15. Discuss counter display.

16. Discuss trading stamp promotion.

DISCUSSION TOPICS

1. Brand Names Foundation advertises: "Patronize national brands. You can depend on them." Do you agree with this ad? Why?

2. "American business spends too much on advertising."

3. "The ethical standards of advertising need improving."

4. "Like an iceberg the persuasion elements of advertising are one-eighth visible, seven-eighths below the surface. As with icebergs, it is the hidden seven-eighths that is dangerous."

5. "Advertising agencies should not be permitted to receive rebates from advertising media."

6. "Advertising must be seen and heard to be disbelieved."

7. "The powers of the F.T.C. to control advertising should be substantially expanded."

8. Would a contest be a good means of promotion for (a) baking flour, (b) a brand of aspirin, (c) a refrigerator, (d) a line of women's dresses, (e) a chewing gum? Why?

PROBLEM 1

Milady, Inc. is a manufacturer of high-quality ladies' pyjamas and negligees, marketed nationally, on a selective distribution basis, under the Milady label. Its sales are expanding—$3,000,000 a year ago, $3,500,000 this year, $3,750,000 anticipated for next year.

The advertising and promotion program for the coming year is being formulated.

1. What advertising and promotion appropriation should the management set for the coming year? Why?

2. Should the company employ an advertising agency? Why?

3. What class or classes of media should be used? Why? How should the specific media be selected?

4. Plan one ad for one of the media selected.

5. What are the publicity possibilities for Milady?

6. Can you suggest any effective consumer promotion?

7. Suggest two or more dealer promotions that should be undertaken.

PROBLEM 2

In the early 1950's, Procter & Gamble developed a new sudsing agent and bacteria fighter that would be very effective in a toothpaste. Deciding to base a new toothpaste on this ingredient, it undertook a long series of studies with consumers to determine preferences in color of the paste, color of the tube, flavor, aftertaste, and degree of foaming action. On the basis of these studies it produced the toothpaste which it named Gleem.

Its advertising department and advertising agency started planning an advertising and promotional campaign. Working on possible advertising "themes," they narrowed consideration to two. The first was directed against tobacco stains on teeth. The second carried the appeal, "For people who can't brush after every meal."

To accompany a comprehensive national advertising campaign, the department and agency gave consideration to three sales promotional approaches for introducing the product to the market: (a) mailing of samples to all households in cities of 25,000 population or more; (b) attaching a ball-point pen as a premium to the package of each economy-size tube; (c) having a consumer contest, with prizes including a trip to Paris, either for writing a 25-word essay on the subject "Why I like Gleem best of all toothpastes," or else for the photograph of the funniest drawing with Gleem toothpaste on a bathroom mirror.

1. Which advertising theme would you favor? Why?
2. Which consumer sales promotion would you favor? Why?

SUGGESTED READINGS

Agnew, C. M., & N. O'Brien, *Television Advertising*, McGraw-Hill Book Co., New York, 1958.

The Amazing Advertising Business, FORTUNE, Printed by Simon & Schuster, New York, 1957.

Aspley, J. C., *The Sales Promotion Handbook*, Dartnell Corp., Chicago, 1953.

Association of National Advertisers, *Advertising at the Point of Purchase* (1957), *Essentials of Outdoor Advertising* (2d ed, 1958), McGraw-Hill Book Co., New York.

Baker, S., *Advertising Layout and Art Direction*, McGraw-Hill Book Co., New York, 1959.

Bartel, F. W., *How to Manage Industrial Advertising*, Printers' Ink Books, Pleasantville, N.Y., 1955.

Bedell, C., *How to Write Advertising that Sells*, 2d ed, McGraw-Hill Book Co., New York, 1952.

Bellaire, A., *TV Advertising*, Harper & Bros., New York, 1959.

Borden, N. H., *Advertising in our Economy*, Richard D. Irwin, Homewood, Ill., 1945.

Borden, N. H., & M. V. Marshall, *Advertising Management*, rev ed, Richard D. Irwin, Homewood, Ill., 1959.

Brewster, A. J., and others, *Introduction to Advertising*, 6th ed, McGraw-Hill Book Co., New York, 1954.

Brown, L., *Advertising Media*, Ronald Press, New York, 1957.

Burton, P. W., *Principles of Advertising*, Prentice-Hall, Englewood Cliffs, N.J., 1955.

Caples, J., *Making Ads Pay*, Harper & Bros., New York, 1957.

Cole, R. H., and others, *Manufacturer and Distributor Brands,* University of Illinois, Urbana, 1955.

Crawford, J. W., *Advertising,* Allyn & Bacon, Boston, 1960.

Crisp, R. D., *How to Increase your Advertising Effectiveness,* McGraw-Hill Book Co., New York, 1958.

Davis, D. W., *Basic Text in Advertising,* Printers' Ink Books, Pleasantville, N.Y., 1955.

Dirkson, C. J., & A. Kroeger, *Advertising Principles and Problems,* Richard D. Irwin, Homewood, Ill., 1960.

Dix, W. R., *Industrial Advertising,* Printers' Ink Books, Pleasantville, N.Y., 1956.

Dunn, S. W., *Advertising Copy and Communication,* McGraw-Hill Book Co., New York, 1956.

Edwards, C. M., *Retail Advertising and Sales Promotion,* 3rd ed, Prentice-Hall, Englewood Cliffs, N.J., 1959.

Frey, A. W., *Advertising* (3rd ed, 1961), *How Many Dollars for Advertising?* (1957), Ronald Press, New York.

Frey, A. W., *The Advertising Industry,* Association of National Advertisers, New York, 1958.

Gaw, W., *Advertising Methods and Media,* Wadsworth Publishing Co., Belmont, Calif., 1961.

Geller, H., *Advertising at the Crossroads,* Ronald Press, New York, 1952.

Graham, I., *Advertising Campaigns,* Harper & Bros., New York, 1951.

Graham, I., *Encyclopedia of Advertising,* Fairchild Publications, New York, 1950.

Groesbeck, K., *Advertising Agency Success,* Harper & Bros., New York, 1958.

Gross, A., & D. Houghton, *Sales Promotion,* Ronald Press, New York, 2nd ed, 1961.

A Guide for Retail Advertising and Selling, 5th ed, Association of Better Business Bureaus, New York, 1956.

Haring, A., & W. O. Yoder, *Trading Stamp Practice and Pricing Policy,* Bureau of Business Research, Indiana University, Bloomington, 1958.

Hattwick, M. S., *How to Use Psychology for Better Advertising,* Prentice-Hall, Englewood Cliffs, N.J., 1950.

Hepner, H. W., *Modern Advertising and Principles,* 3rd ed, McGraw-Hill Book Co., New York, 1956.

Jones, E. R., *Those Were the Good Old Days,* Simon & Schuster, New York, 1959.

Kleppner, O., *Advertising Procedure,* 4th ed, Prentice-Hall, Englewood Cliffs, N.J., 1950.

Kroll, N., *Window Display,* Studio Publications, New York, 1954.

Manchee, F., *The Huckster's Revenge,* Thomas Nelson & Sons, New York, 1959.

Martineau, P., *Motivation in Advertising,* McGraw-Hill Book Co., New York, 1957.

Mayer, M., *Madison Avenue, U.S.A.,* Harper & Bros., New York, 1958.

Nelson, G. (ed.) *Display,* Whitney Publications, New York, 1953.

Pease, O., *The Responsibilities of American Advertising, 1920–1940,* Yale University Press, New Haven, 1958.

Retail Advertising and Sales Promotion Manual, 2 vols., National Research Bureau, Chicago, 1956, 1959.

Rowland, C. M., *Advertising in Modern Retailing,* Harper & Bros., New York, 1954.

Rowse, E., *Fundamentals of Advertising,* 6th ed, South-Western Publishing Co., Cincinnati, 1957.

Rowsome, F., *They Laughed When I Sat Down: an Informal History of Advertising,* McGraw-Hill Book Co., New York, 1959.

Sales Promotion Executives Reference Handbook, Sales Promotion Executives Association, New York, 1959.

Sandage, C. H., & V. Fryburger, *Advertising: Theory and Practice* (5th ed, 1958); *The Role of Advertising* (1960), Richard D. Irwin, Homewood, Ill.

Scott, J. D., *Advertising Principles and Problems,* Prentice-Hall, Englewood Cliffs, N.J., 1953.

Seehafer, G. F., & J. W. Laemmer, *Successful Television and Radio Advertising,* McGraw-Hill Book Co., New York, 1959.

Simmons, H., *Successful Sales Promotion,* Prentice-Hall, Englewood Cliffs, N.J., 1950.

Smith, R. B., *Advertising to Business,* Richard D. Irwin, Homewood, Ill., 1957.

Steinberg, C. S., *The Mass Communicators,* Harper & Bros., New York, 1958.

Sumner, G. L., *How I Learned the Secrets of Success in Advertising,* Prentice-Hall, Englewood Cliffs, N.J., 1952.

Swan, C. J., *Tested Advertising Copy,* Printers' Ink Books, Pleasantville, N.Y., 1955.

Turner, H. M., *Sales Promotion that Gets Results,* McGraw-Hill Book Co., New York, 1959.

Wales, H. G., and others, *Advertising Copy, Layout and Typography,* Ronald Press, New York, 1958.

Whittier, C. L., *Creative Advertising,* Henry Holt & Co., New York, 1955.

Wiseman, M., *The New Anatomy of Advertising,* Harper & Bros., New York, 1959.

Wood, J. P., *The Story of Advertising,* Ronald Press, New York, 1958.

PERIODICALS: *Advertisers' Digest, Advertising Age, Display World, Premium Practice and Business Promotion, Printers' Ink, Reporter of Direct Mail Advertising.*

CHAPTER 22

PERSONAL SELLING AND SALES MANAGEMENT

In the American economy the full market potentialities for a product can rarely be realized solely on the bases of its being designed with maximum primary and secondary utilities and selling design, being priced soundly in relation to competing products, and being made available to possible purchasers through appropriate stores or other channels of distribution. Left to themselves, many prospective users would never realize that they had a need, some lack which the product could satisfy. Or their awareness might be only latent, and require stimulation before it could become overt and lead to purchasing action. Or they might be fully aware of their need and of the capacity of the product to satisfy it, yet have a psychological block against committing themselves to the expenditure involved and require a helping hand around the inhibition. These obstacles between a product and its market exist not only when consumers are making personal purchases. They apply also, though less sharply, to purchasing done by retailers and wholesalers, who must be taught and constantly reminded of the profit possibilities lying in the resale of each particular product. Even industrial buyers, trained in purchasing techniques, must also be *shown* the advantages of a material or an equipment item before they will buy it.

Advertising and other forms of promotion, as we saw in the preceding chapter, can do much to stimulate market demand for a product or service. Promotional techniques are nonpersonal, however, and have their limitations. They can bring a product to the attention of a prospective purchaser, and frequently go far in rousing his interest in it. If he already has a latent desire for the product, promotion may stimulate that desire, make it active, and even prod some individuals into actually buying. But it is

446

usually difficult to create awareness of completely new needs through impersonal presentations, and promotional techniques are generally helpless
in overcoming our common inhibition against definite commitments to pay
out substantial sums of money. Personal selling *—direct oral presentation to prospective purchasers to assist and persuade them to buy—is a vital
element in the making of a major proportion of sales.

PERSONAL SELLING AND PROMOTION COMPARED

Personal selling on the one hand, and advertising and other forms of
promotion on the other, have many points in common, both as to objectives
and techniques. The individualized, personal, man-to-man aspect of the
former, however, in contrast to the nonpersonal mass approach of promotion, sharply distinguishes the two. They have complementary rather than
substitute rôles in Marketing.

Objectives

The ultimate purpose of personal selling and of promotion is the same
—to induce consumers and industrial buyers to buy particular products for
use, and to induce retailers and wholesaling middlemen to buy particular
products for resale. It is in their immediate objectives that promotion and
personal selling differ.

Educational advertising can bring recognition of latent needs forward
into consciousness, can sharpen our awareness of active needs, and can
direct our attention to particular products and brands that will satisfy those
needs. Reminder advertising, notice-of-sale advertising, display, and various forms of point-of-purchase sales promotion can maintain our awareness
of needs and of the capacity of particular products or brands to satisfy these
needs. Where impulse and convenience buying are involved, these promotional preparations sometimes create a brand good-will that crystallizes at
the point of purchase, so that consumers do buy the promoted items without the intervention of personal selling by store sales clerks. In the case of
shopping and specialty goods, coupon ads and direct mail advertising can
sometimes go beyond merely making us actively aware of a need and of
the capacity of some product or brand to satisfy it, and can actually crystallize buying action. But for some goods bought on the bases of impulse and
convenience, for most shopping and specialty goods, and for nearly all
mercantile and industrial marketing, advertising and other forms of promotion can create only product and brand interest. The groundwork is laid

---

* The term "selling" is commonly given a very broad connotation. It covers all activities that assist and/or persuade prospective purchasers to buy a commodity or service, or
patronize a store, including advertising and other forms of promotion. The term "personal
selling" is therefore used for the oral selling activities of salesmen and store clerks.

for buying action but personal selling, by store clerks or by salesmen who call upon the customer, is needed to convert interest to desire by further "educational" exposition, and to spark the customer's buying decision. The entire task of uncovering and stimulating a recognition of need, interesting the customer in a product or brand to satisfy that need, converting interest into desire, and crystallizing a buying decision, is sometimes left to personal salesmen.

Techniques

Promotion and personal selling both fulfill their tasks of stimulating buying demand by appealing to the complex of consumer and industrial buying motivations that we analyzed in Chapters 3 and 14. Sometimes the particular combination of motivations involved in the buying of a product or brand are self-evident. Sometimes marketing research is needed to uncover them. Where the customers' primary buying motivation is economic, and the primary selling points of a product are considerations of monetary gain or technical operating efficiency, as in most industrial and mercantile selling, both promotion and personal selling make their appeals in direct, rational terms. For most consumer goods, where emotional, personal, and social motivations are all-important, both advertising and selling must make their appeals through suggestion and other indirect methods.

While the appeals that promotion and selling must make are identical, their techniques differ in important respects. (1) Advertising and other forms of promotion must be directed at *groups;* personal selling is directed to *individuals.* Promotion determines the *greatest common denominators* among the buying motivations relating to a product or a brand, and frames its appeals to these common-denominator motivations. Personal selling determines the particular complex of motivations of each individual customer or prospect, and frames varying presentations hand-tailored to the individuals. (2) Personal selling techniques are more flexible than the procedures of advertising and other forms of promotion, since they can and must be adapted to each individual prospect, to his particular complex of buying motivations, and to his special questions and objections. (3) In personal selling, the salesman's or sales clerk's personality and manner of selling are commonly major factors in his selling success or failure.

The "marketing mix"

A minority of products or brands is sold entirely through coupon and direct mail advertising. Another minority is sold entirely through personal selling. Most products and brands are sold through varying combinations of advertising and other forms of promotion, and personal selling. The proportions in which these two selling elements are combined is commonly referred to as the "marketing mix." *

The composition of the "marketing mix" for any product or brand is not a matter of indifference. Experience and testing have established a number of generalizations on this subject.

1. In view of the longer channels of distribution that separate consumer goods manufacturers from the ultimate consumers of their products in contrast to makers and users of industrial products, and because of the average low level of store clerks' selling ability, advertising and other forms of promotion bulk larger in the "marketing mix" for consumer goods than they do in that for industrial products. Many producers of equipment and supplies rely exclusively on the personal selling of their salesmen or of middleman representatives. Where industrial advertising is employed, it is intended primarily to pave the way for salesmen.

2. Mercantile selling—persuading wholesalers and retailers to stock particular lines or brands of goods for resale—except for the relatively rare cases of cash-carry and mail-order wholesalers, is accomplished almost entirely by salesmen.

3. The proportion of advertising and other forms of promotion in the "marketing mix" for consumer goods bought on impulse and convenience bases is much higher than for shopping goods. Through promotion of impulse and convenience goods, the consumer's attention is captured on behalf of a product, her interest is aroused, her desire for it is stimulated, and her buying decision often crystallized to a point where she notes the item on her next "buying list" or takes it from a store counter or display rack. The sales clerk in the store where she makes her purchase has only to take her order and wrap up the merchandise. Where shopping items are concerned, advertising commonly has an important preparatory task, sometimes carried to the point of creating a definite desire for the specific advertised article. But usually the vital final selling step—crystallization of the customer's buying decision—and often one or more of the preceding steps, must be consummated by personal selling. The efforts of a sales clerk, or a salesman, are usually needed to commit the customer to the decisive act of exchanging the certain value of her money for the less certain value of the product, or to commit her to the choice of a particular model or brand.

4. High-quality high-price brands of consumer goods require relatively more personal selling, by sales clerks or canvasser salesmen, than their lower-quality lower-price competitors. Personal selling is needed to educate the customer to the superior quality elements that warrant the higher price.

5. New consumer articles commonly require a higher proportion of

* Note that the "promotional mix" discussed in Chapter 21, is a subdivision of the "marketing mix."

personal selling effort, by sales clerks or canvasser salesmen, during their introductory period than they do later on when advertising and other promotional techniques can take over the simpler task of maintaining an established demand.

ECONOMIC ROLE OF PROMOTION AND PERSONAL SELLING

A considerable part, though not a major proportion, of promotion and personal selling is competitive. It seeks to shift existing buying demand among various closely comparable brands or sellers, or protect brands or sellers from losing customers to competitive attack. Such competitive promotion and selling does not enlarge the scope of personal living or the effectiveness of business operations by uncovering previously unrecognized needs, pointing the way to their satisfaction by the purchase of products or services, and actually bringing about such purchase. While it may contribute to the success of some companies, and lack of it may lead to the failure of others, it does not add substantially to the national total of purchasing and contributes little to growth of the national economy. It must be considered largely economic waste, adding to the cost of the nation's goods and services. This is not in itself a condemnation of all competitive promotion and personal selling. This economic waste is a price that we pay for the maintenance of competition in American business, since brand-shifting and brand-retention promotion and selling are basic instrumentalities of business competition. For so long as it is our wish and intent to maintain competition in the American economic order, there is justification for competitive promotion and personal selling even though it be economic waste.

The greater part of promotion and personal selling effort, however, teaches us new wants, vitalizes latent wants, and induces us to satisfy those wants. It stimulates our propensity to consume as against our propensity to save. Such intensification of consumption steps up the tempo of our entire economic system. Production of all sorts that otherwise would not be practicable, because there would be no market for its output, is undertaken. Such added production creates added income that provides the wherewithal for the additional purchases induced by promotion and personal selling. In many cases, production expansion makes possible economies of larger-scale production which are translated into either greater profits or lower prices, thereby adding still further to the nation's purchasing capacity. Industrial activity, employment, and standards of living are raised and held to higher levels than would otherwise be possible. Credit for the high American standards of material living belongs not only to our engineers and production men but also to our advertising men and our salesmen, and to the marketing executives who authorize the advertising and are responsible for the salesmen's effectiveness.

As the American economy has transformed itself from one of scarcity to one of broadening plenty, as the margin of consumers' discretionary purchasing power has widened, a steadily increasing volume of promotional and selling accomplishment has been required to keep consumption demand level with the nation's productive capacity. Over the past quarter-century, this has been achieved by a striking increase in promotional and selling efficiency. In constant-dollar terms, an advertising dollar in 1957 bought $2\frac{1}{2}$ times the "prospect exposure to space and time" that it did in 1929, and the exposure was much more effective. As a consequence, the tremendous expansion of advertising impact during this period did not involve any diversion of gross national product to advertising services; on the contrary, the proportion of advertising expenditure to national income declined from 3.8 percent to 2.9 percent. There is no quantitative measure of the improvement in personal selling efficiency, but it probably was comparable. Coming years will demand still more advertising and selling accomplishment to keep the production and consumption aspects of the economy in balance. Whether this can be achieved through continued improvement in the technologies of promotion and selling, or whether it will require an increase in the share of the national income absorbed by promotional and selling effort, remains to be seen.

TYPES OF PERSONAL SELLING

Personal selling is commonly classified on a channel-of-distribution basis, because of the differing salesman qualifications and selling methods involved. Two of these classifications—store selling and consumer specialty selling—involve selling to consumers. One—mercantile selling—covers manufacturers' selling to wholesalers and retailers and wholesalers' selling to retailers. Two—business specialty selling and industrial selling—relate to industrial marketing.

Store selling

In many purchases made in stores, the customer requires and expects no assistance from the store personnel in making selections. In fact, insistent proffers of such assistance are commonly resented. There is no personal selling to be done under such circumstances. The only function of the store personnel is to take an order, wrap it, calculate and take payment, and possibly arrange delivery.

Opportunities for creative selling in the retail store are many, however. Often a customer enters a store with some interest in a product, which is far short of decisive desire for it. Whether a sale is made depends on the store proprietor's or store clerk's ability to build the customer's interest into compelling desire. Or sometimes a customer, having bought certain items upon a shopping or specific intent basis, is open to suggestion to make still other purchases, usually related to the original one. Again whether the customer makes these extra purchases or not turns on across-the-counter salesmanship.

Consumer specialty selling

When a radically new consumer product first comes upon the market, a sizable proportion of its prospective purchasers have to be actively taught, by personal selling, that they truly need and want it. An effective means of doing this is through consumer specialty salesmen who locate prospects, call personally upon them, and by presentation and demonstration persuade the prospects that they want the item. Aluminum kitchenware had to be sold this way when it first appeared, as were vacuum cleaners.

High-quality high-price brands of goods, whose superior merits would not be evident in casual store inspection, are also frequently sold by this method. High-unit-value items like automobiles and outdoor swimming pools are largely sold this way. To an increasing extent, furniture stores and household appliance stores are finding that an "outside" force of salesmen can locate prospects and make sales to prospects who otherwise might never have entered the stores.

Mercantile selling

Manfacturers' selling to wholesalers and retailers, and wholesalers' selling to retailers, are done almost exclusively by personal selling. This is "route" or "repeat" selling. A mercantile salesman calls on each of his customers every two weeks, or once a month, or at some other relatively fixed interval. To some extent a mercantile salesman's work is mere "order taking"—arranging shipment of quantities predetermined by the customer's inventory requirements. Broad opportunities for "creative" selling are present, however. It frequently takes supreme salesmanship to win over a customer from some other supplier to the salesman's firm. Often established customers have to be persuaded to take on additional or new items in the salesman's line. The "service" concept is important in mercantile selling; the salesman becomes a source of trade information to his customers, he gives them display assistance, he smooths out misunderstandings between his customers and the shipping or credit departments of his firm, thereby winning their good will for himself personally and for his firm.

Business specialty selling

Business concerns utilize many varieties of office equipment and supplies which must be sold to them. Likewise they use many forms of services— freight forwarding, credit reporting, space and time in advertising media, personnel testing, among them—which they must also be persuaded to buy. Here is a fourth great field of personal selling.

Like the consumer specialty salesman, the business specialty salesman is forever on the hunt for new prospects. His selling is not strictly the "one shot" variety, since he commonly must maintain contact with established customers so that they will, when the time comes, buy more of his company's office equipment or continue to subscribe to its service. Still, the greater part of his efforts are devoted to dealing with an endless parade of new prospects. He has little or no opportunity to settle down, like many mercantile salesmen, to a comfortable "route" of established customers. His prospects are alert business executives, able to appraise both advantages and disadvantages of the equipment or service that he offers. And the competition in these lines is keen.

Business specialty selling requires salesmanship of the highest order, continuously exercised. Salesmen of a superior caliber are need for this type of selling. Sales managers in this field must not only establish high qualifications for salesmen they hire, but must also provide intensive sales training.

Industrial selling

Not all industrial purchases of equipment and materials run to thousands of dollars per transaction, but a high proportion do; many involve tens of thousands, even hundreds of thousands, of dollars. Purchases of this sort are not decided upon through snap judgments. Usually a group of top management minds—engineer, production manager, purchasing manager, comptroller, the president of the company himself—analyze, calculate, compute, and debate a proposed purchase of major equipment or a change in the supplier of a basic material. Cold proof rather than emotional oratory is the key to industrial selling, but behind the cold proof must be the winning personality and the persuasiveness that are the foundations of all personal selling.

A man selling major items of industrial equipment or a basic raw material must obviously be an expert on the technical aspects of his company's equipment or material. He must also be an expert on competing items. He must also be pretty much of an expert on the technology of his prospects' businesses. Frequently his sales are made through working out changes in his customers' technologies that will permit use of his company's equipment or material. Industrial selling is usually beyond the capacities of a man who is only a *salesman,* even an exceptional one. This is the field for the *engineer-salesman*—a man with engineering training as well as the salesman's attributes of personality and persuasiveness.

SALESMANSHIP

Salesmanship—the art of personal selling—is not a uniform procedure, alike for all forms and fields of selling. There are wide differences between the personalities and methods of an engineer salesman who sells industrial equipment and a grocery store clerk, of a life insurance salesman and a hardware wholesaler's salesman, even between a textile converter's salesman and a salesman for a men's clothing manufacturer. One consistent element is inherent in all forms of personal salesmanship, however. Personal selling is not passive, a mere writing down of orders from customers who have made up their minds in advance. To fulfill its purpose, personal selling must be active, persuasive. This does not mean "pressure" selling— the overwhelming of an unwilling customer by aggressive persistence. It does mean educating customers to new needs, new desires, or stimulating latent ones, that can be satisfied only by purchase of what the salesman has to offer.

Let us briefly explore some major elements of personal salesmanship, of varying relative importance for different fields of selling.

Prospecting

Most store owners and store clerks do not have to go out and hunt down their customers. Advertising, or window display, or previously established store good will, brings customers into the store. But some retail dealers in recent years have found it profitable to send out salesmen to locate potential customers who might never have purchased in the particular store and induce them to visit the store. Automobile dealers, furniture stores, home appliance stores, radio and television stores, and other retailers of consumer specialty items now engage in this practice. For these retailers' salesmen, and for practically all consumer specialty salesmen, mercantile salesmen who sell to retailers and wholesalers, business specialty salesmen, and industrial salesmen, the first selling task is to locate their potential customers. The methods used by salesmen in searching for potential customers are commonly called "prospecting," and potential customers located by such search are called "prospects." Ingenuity and persistence in prospecting are often keys to selling success.

Analyzing prospects

A good salesman does not try to sell his company's automobile or book-keeping machine as simply a tangible item with certain mechanical attributes. What he presents to a prospect is the *services* that the automobile or bookkeeping machine will render to *that particular prospect*. To do this successfully, a salesman must, within practicable limits set by time and expense, acquire as much information as possible about each prospect, so that he will be able to adapt his presentation to the individual personality and buying motivations of that prospect. This collecting and analyzing of prospect information is sometimes called "qualifying" prospects. In some lines of selling, much of the analyzing of a prospect is accomplished in advance of the sales interview. In all forms of selling, including retail store selling, a good salesman can usually induce a new customer or prospect to reveal valuable information about himself without being aware that he is being skillfully probed.

Sales presentation

A good sales presentation by a master salesman is a creation of art, not chance. The opening, consisting perhaps of a question, perhaps of a few introductory sentences, is designed to capture the prospect's immediate favorable attention. The prospect's interest is won by arousing his recognition of various needs—buying motivations—which the salesman's product can satisfy. Sometimes these are needs of which the prospect had not heretofore been aware; the salesman must literally educate him to their existence. As the presentation progresses, the salesman develops one after another of the product's selling points. The conviction is borne upon the prospect that only this product, and no competing one, carries such a full measure of need satisfaction, and that the money spent for it will yield a greater total of satisfactions than any alternative expenditure. Interest in the product quickens into desire.

Good sales presentations are usually the results of careful planning. In some fields of selling it is possible for salesmen, or their managers, to develop standardized or "canned" sales talks which, with interchangeable and spare parts to fit special prospect situations, are effective with most prospects. For other types of selling, where the product or service offered must be more particularly tailored to each buyer's individual needs, no uniform presentation is possible, but each sales interview must be pre-planned in detail.

"Closing" sales

Most people hesitate to commit themselves to irrevocable decisions, even when they are fully persuaded that they have decided soundly, and often when postponement of the commitment may be obviously to their disadvantage. A customer may definitely want a particular item, and feel that it is a good bargain, yet be unable, of his own initiative, to say, "Yes, I'll buy that." The art of salesmanship includes several proven techniques of "closing"—psychological stratagems that *bypass* a customer's purchase inhibition instead of smashing squarely at it.

Salesman service activities

In many lines of selling the salesman must be a service man to his customers, as well as sell to them. The store sales clerk commonly wraps the customer's purchases after the sale is transacted. The mercantile salesman frequently checks the stock of his retailer customers, provides them with point-of-purchase display materials, and sets up their displays for them. The industrial salesman is often a technical consultant for his customers. In few lines of selling does a salesman's responsibility to his customers cease with the writing of their orders.

Control of personal selling

Personal selling, like advertising, if left untrammeled, would develop abuses which could be injurious to business generally as well as to the particular purchasers who were the victims. Under its power to act against "unfair trade practices" under the Federal Trade Commission Act, the FTC has issued cease and desist orders against many improper personal selling practices. Among these have been misrepresentation by a consumer specialty salesman that he was conducting marketing research, bribing store buyers or purchasing managers to obtain or hold their patronage, making false and disparaging statements about competitors' products and businesses, selling used items as new, and offering fake buying advantages.

Many lines of business have undertaken self-regulation of their selling and promotional practices through "voluntary fair trade practice codes" formulated and enforced by their trade associations. Several of them predate 1919. In that year the Federal Trade Commission undertook a program of stimulating the adoption of such voluntary codes. The first FTC-sponsored code was that of the creamery industry. Nearly two hundred such codes have since been adopted, and the marketing policies and practices of most major lines of American business are now governed by them.

A voluntary fair trade practice code is formulated at a conference of representatives of a line of business, usually meeting under the auspices of the trade association for the line. Representatives of the Federal Trade Commission sit with the conference. The code of practice formulated by such a conference usually embodies two sets of rules. The first set covers limitations already established by court decisions and Federal Trade Commission rulings. This part of any code must be referred to the Federal Trade Commission for approval. The second part of a code includes additional self-limitations that the conference may choose to apply. Once such a code is adopted by a trade association, it is as binding upon the members as any other by-law of the association.

SALES MANAGEMENT *

The art of salesmanship is only one aspect of the selling operation. Most of the men and women who practice this art are not entrepreneurs acting on their own behalf, but employees. How effectively they sell for their employers depends in substantial part on the effectiveness of the sales managment behind them.

All sales managers, including those of retail stores, must solve the problems of: (1) selecting the right men and women for their selling forces; (2) training them, (3) devising selling equipment for them to use, (4) planning a sound compensation system for them, (5) supervising their work, and (6) in the case of large sales forces, establishing effective sales force organization. In addition, all sales managers except those of retail stores must also: (7) assign proper territories to their salesmen, and (8) meet peculiar issues of maintaining their salesmen's morale. To gain some insight into the issues and procedures of sales management, we shall survey briefly three of these activities—training salesmen, planning their compensation, and maintaining their morale.

Training salesmen

Most sales managers would agree with the aphorism that "Good salesmen are made rather than born." A few "self-made" salesmen in various fields have, perhaps, taught themselves all about selling their lines that the best training course could possibly have given them. As a general rule, however, proper training will upgrade sales ability. For new recruits to the profession of selling, good training may make all the difference between morale-shattering failure at the outset and a fair start with clear promise of successful career development.

---

* This term formerly covered the planning, direction, and control of the entire marketing activity of a company or division of a company, including formulation of its marketing policy. During the 1950's a new term, "marketing management," was coined to denote this broad area of managerial responsibility. The meaning of the older term, "sales management," is now limited to the planning, direction, and control of a company's sales force.

There is no common denominator of the substance of salesmen's training courses. Every sales manager must devise a course fitted to the particular needs of his company's or his store's salesmen. They must be given a thorough knowledge of the products they will sell. They must learn about their company, its structure, its personnel, and its place in the general business scheme. They must gain an insight into the peculiarities of the company's or store's customers, and the most effective ways of selling to them. For certain types of consumer specialty selling, sales recruits must learn a "canned" sales talk as a basis for their subsequent sales presentations.

Methods of training salesmen also vary widely. Practically all salesman and sales clerk training programs involve a period of "field training," during which the sales recruit accompanies a trainer or experienced salesman to actual sales interviews, or joins an experienced sales clerk behind a store counter, observing the techniques of the experienced man and doing some practice selling under his eye. Some companies accomplish their entire sales training through this field work. More commonly, sales recruits are given a "vestibule" training course, either individually by the sales manager and his assistants, or in class groups. A number of companies have prepared costly motion pictures or sound-slide films for this "vestibule" training. Some manufacturers' sales training programs involve six months', or a year's, or even eighteen months' employment in various production and merchandising departments of the company, before the sales recruit is allowed to take his field training and finally represent the company to its customers.

Salesmen's training does not cease with their transformation from recruits to regular members of the company's sales force. If a new product is added to the company's line, all of its salesmen must learn about it, and be taught the most effective method of presenting it to prospects. If an experienced salesman experiences a "slump"—and this is not uncommon—he must be given "refresher" training. The entire sales force—"headliners" as well as laggards—can benefit from some review training at the company's annual salesmen's convention. Salesmen's training should be a never-ending process.

Establishing salesmen's compensation

Three objectives guide a sales manager in establishing the type and amounts of his salesmen's compensation: (1) the over-all compensation of each salesman should be commensurate with his abilities, as established by general or average compensation levels for such abiilties; (2) whenever possible, the system of compensation should give the salesmen strong incentive to achieve the maximum volume of sales possible for them; (3)

salesmen's week-to-week or month-to-month incomes should be stabilized as far as practicable.

To achieve these objectives a sales manager can choose between three basic types of salesmen's compensation, or various combinations of these types: (1) salary, (2) commission, (3) bonuses for various achievements.

Salesmen are usually paid salaries when various factors that determine the sales volume they turn in are beyond their control, or when they are called upon to perform promotional or delivery functions that do not directly produce sales. Store clerks are usually paid largely on a salary basis because they cannot control or influence the number of customers who enter the store and come to their counters. Sales engineers who represent industrial equipment companies are also paid primarily on a salary basis because much of their time must often be spent on promotional activity, and on advisory services to prospects, which in the long run lead to sales for their companies but which are not immediately reflected in the sales records of the individual salesmen.

Paying salesmen on a commission basis makes their incomes depend directly on their efforts and abilities, and is the favored method of compensation in many fields of selling. It is often combined with a salary system where the latter must be the basic method of compensation, for reasons noted above, in order to give the sales force some incentive stimulation. Store sales clerks are commonly paid a small commission on their sales, in addition to their salaries.

Straight commissions would produce very uneven compensation in lines of selling where sales volumes vary widely from period to period because of seasonal factors or other influences. To give salesmen some stability of income under these circumstances, they are usually allowed "drawing accounts"—they draw advances, somewhat below the average of the commissions they can be expected to earn, during periods when their sales are low, and repay these advances when their commissions subsequently rise.

Sales managers generally look with favor upon bonus systems to supplement their salesmen's regular salary or commission compensation. "Quotas"—sales volume goals—are often set for the individual salesmen, with the reward of a lump-sum or special commission bonus when the quota is exceeded. Or salesmen may be given bonuses for selling special quota amounts or proportions of hard-to-sell items in the company's line. Or they may be given bonuses for obtaining new customers. The lure of a bonus gives salesmen special incentive, over and above that of the regular salary or commission, to achieve particular objectives which otherwise might not interest them.

Maintaining sales force morale

Most field salesmen are susceptible to periodic or occasional emotional let-downs. This is natural in view of the nervous intensity that is essential to many types of selling, and the usual isolation of the field salesman, operating alone and without any comforting support from the immediate presence of fellow-workers or superiors. A sales manager, particularly one in charge of a force of field salesmen, has a special responsibility of maintaining the morale of his subordinates that is not matched by any other class of department manager.

The primary approach to salesmen's morale maintenance is to remove the sense of isolation that afflicts so many of them. A wise sales manager accomplishes this by making every salesman under him feel that he is taking a special, constant personal interest in the salesman's individual welfare. He deals personally with his salesmen whenever possible. If practicable, he has each field salesman telephone him at intervals. His letters to field salesmen are hearty, individualized, highly personal. Perhaps he uses form letters to cover situations that occur repeatedly for his sales force, but he disguises these with frequent second-person inserts of the salesman's name and with dictated paragraphs which are personal for the individual salesman.

A weekly, or semi-monthly, *bulletin* or *magazine* is one of the best sales force morale builders there is. It may incorporate sales training items, but primarily it is devoted to personal news of the salesmen—cheers for those who are turning in good sales records, anecdotes about curious or amusing experiences that various of the salesmen have reported, news about the men's family lives. Thus the individual field salesmen are given a feeling that, far from operating in a vacuum, they are part of a group, working together and sharing a mutual experience.

Salesmen respond to *contests*. A salesman will strive to achieve a sales record that will win a television set for his family, whereas he might be indifferent to the consideration, by itself, that making that same sales volume would increase his regular commission by several times the value of the set. There is quite an art to running a salesmen's contest. A graded series of prizes for many winners is more effective than a single big prize for one winner. Merchandise prizes are usually better morale stimulants than money prizes. The sales management must constitute itself a vociferous and impartial cheering section for the period of the contest, and be ready with enthusiastic congratulations for everybody—the bottom men as well as the winners—at its conclusion.

An annual *convention* for the salesmen of the company helps greatly in building esprit de corps in a sales force. The salesmen meet the management and their fellow-salesmen. They realize that they have a likable organization working with them and behind them. The company sees to it that they have a good time. They go back to their territories revitalized.

VOCATIONAL CONSIDERATIONS

Sales managers in industrial, consumer specialty, business specialty, and some mercantile lines are turning in ever-increasing numbers to the colleges as recruiting sources. A widening variety of career possibilities in selling is thus opening up for college graduates.

On the basis of average compensation, personal selling is the best remunerated of all the business professions and occupations. High five-figure incomes are more common in this business career than in any other. The rise to high-level compensation, whether on a salary or commission basis, is more rapid for successful salesmen than in any other form of employment. Selling success is the doorway to sales management positions which, in turn, are the most common road to top management.

Highly introverted and markedly submissive individuals are generally psychologically disqualified for personal selling careers. With the wide range of different qualifications requisite for the many fields of personal selling, however, some two-thirds to three-quarters of college men and a smaller proportion of college women could probably succeed at personal selling—provided they were interested, obtained employment with a company whose selling requirements matched their individual personality qualifications, and received good sales training.

Sales training should be the responsibility of the employing concerns. Many companies with large or medium-size sales forces have established excellent training programs for their sales recruits. Most small companies and some large ones, however, provide inadequate sales training or none. So a college man or woman who foresees the slightest possibility of a personal selling career should take the salesmanship course offered by his college, and back it up with vacation-time employment at some form of personal selling, if only canvassing. For the rest, a wide selection of Marketing courses should be taken. Extra-curricular student activities, where the future salesman can learn how to make friends and influence people, are also an invaluable preparation.

While selling is a rewarding career for many college graduates, most who enter upon this career look upon it as a stepping stone to the still broader opportunities of sales force management and eventually marketing management. Not all successful salesmen are equally capable of becoming good sales force managers. In addition to having been a good salesman, a sales manager should possess leadership, analytic capability, and a capacity for enduring long stretches of desk work. His student preparation for eventual sales management should include courses on sales force management, sales policy, advertising, and marketing research.

REVIEW

1. Compare and contrast the roles of advertising and personal selling in Marketing.
2. Describe the five types of personal selling.
3. Analyze the elements of the art of salesmanship.
4. List the responsibilities of a sales manager.
5. How may sales forces be trained?
6. What considerations should determine the method of compensating a company's salesmen?
7. Analyze the sales management problem of maintaining salesmen's morale.

DISCUSSION TOPICS

1. "Advertising and selling are parasitic activities that create no economic value, but add costs that are reflected in prices higher than they need be."
2. Salesmanship has been defined as "the engineering of purchasing consent." What do you think of this definition?
3. Wouldn't it be more ethical for life insurance salesmen, in "closing," to ask a prospect directly whether or not he wanted to take out the policy under discussion, instead of asking him what date he would prefer for the medical examination before he has specifically committed himself to the policy?
4. To what extent and by what agencies may personal selling abuses be constrained in the public interest? Does present control of these abuses go far enough?
5. Do you really think a man or woman can be taught how to sell in a college salesmanship course or in a company training program?
6. If you were a salesman, would you prefer to be compensated primarily by salary or by commission? Why?
7. "A sales manager should establish himself as a 'father image' to his men."

PROBLEM 1

Delta Co., with a factory in Yonkers, N.Y. and offices in New York City, has perfected and put into production a new home and office air conditioning unit. It can be plugged into any electric outlet to cool, control the humidity content, and freshen the air of an individual room. It is housed in a compact attractive console; the smaller home models are light enough to be moved easily by one person. It will retail from $87 up, according to the model size and console style.

Later the Delta air conditioners may be sold through stores and office equipment dealers. At the start, however, the Delta company plans to sell them direct to homeowners and offices.

1. How should Delta salesmen go about picking the "prospects" on whom they will call?

2. Select three selling points of the Delta air conditioner. How should a Delta salesman present each of these to a "prospect"?

3. How should a Delta salesman "close" a sale to a homeowner who seems to be persuaded by the sales presentation?

4. How should men hired as Delta salesmen be trained?

5. What compensation do you suggest for Delta salesmen? Why?

6. What "morale" program for its salesmen should Delta Co. put into effect?

PROBLEM 2

Mr. Bowen is a small costume jewelry wholesaler, located in Chicago. He himself sells to the Chicago department stores. He employs five salesmen who cover a territory with a radius approximately 300 miles around Chicago. They sell to some 1,300 stores of various kinds.

1. When Mr. Bowen needs to hire another salesman, he advertises in the daily papers for a man already experienced in the line. Is this a sound procedure? Can you suggest any better?

2. The only training he gives a new salesman is to talk over his line with the new man. Is this sound? What would you suggest?

3. Mr. Bowen pays his salesmen a 6 percent commission. They pay their own expenses. On this basis they earn from $6,000 to $8,000 a year. Would you suggest any change in the compensation basis? What? Why?

4. When a "morale" program is suggested, Mr. Bowen says, "My salesmen are men, not boys who have to be coddled." What do you think of his viewpoint? If you disagree, what sort of a "morale" program would you propose?

5. What should Mr. Bowen's salesmen do to maximize and maintain their customers' goodwill towards them?

SUGGESTED READINGS: I

Bell, H. S., *How to be a Winner in Selling,* Prentice-Hall, Englewood Cliffs, N.J., 1957.

Berman, E., *Successful Low Pressure Salesmanship,* Prentice-Hall, Englewood Cliffs, N.J., 1955.

Bettger, F., *How I Raised Myself from Failure to Success in Selling* (1949); *How I Multiplied My Income and Happiness in Selling* (1954), Prentice-Hall, Englewood Cliffs, N.J.

Breen, G. E., and others, *Effective Selling,* Harper & Bros., New York, 1950.

Canfield, B. R., Salesmanship: *Practices and Problems,* 3rd ed, McGraw-Hill Book Co., New York, 1958.

DeVoe, M., *Effective Self-Management in Selling* (1956); *Successful Telephone Selling* (1954), Prentice-Hall, Englewood Cliffs, N.J.

Englesman, R., *Keys to Modern Selling,* David McKay Co., New York, 1955.

Ernest, J. W., & G. M. DaVall, *Salesmanship Fundamentals,* McGraw-Hill Book Co., New York, 1959.

Frank, W. M., & C. Lapp, *How to Outsell the Born Salesman,* Macmillan Co., New York, 1959.

Gopel, R. A., *Sales Know-How,* Printers' Ink Books, Pleasantville, N.Y., 1954.

Greif, E. C., *Modern Salesmanship; Principles and Problems,* Prentice-Hall, Englewood Cliffs, N.J., 1958.

Gross, A., *Salesmanship,* 2d ed, Ronald Press, New York, 1959.

Hegarty, R. A., *Making Your Sales Presentation Sell More,* McGraw-Hill Book Co., New York, 1957.

Hobart, D. M., & J. P. Wood, *Selling Forces,* Ronald Press, New York, 1953.

Horvath, W. J., *How to Use Your Selling Power* (1951); *How to Overcome Objections in Selling* (1954), Prentice-Hall, Englewood Cliffs, N.J.

Husband, R. W., *The Psychology of Successful Selling,* Harper & Bros., New York, 1953.

Ivey, P. W., & W. Horvath, *Successful Salesmanship,* 3rd ed, Prentice-Hall, Englewood Cliffs, N.J., 1953.

Katz, J. H., *How to Make the Most of Your Sales Territory,* Prentice-Hall, Englewood Cliffs, N.J., 1957.

Kirkpatrick, C. A., *Salesmanship: Helping Prospects Buy,* 2d ed, South-Western Publishing Co., Cincinnati, 1956.

Kuesel, H., *How to Sell Against Tough Competition,* Prentice-Hall, Englewood Cliffs, N.J., 1956.

Laird, D. A., & E. C. Laird, *Practical Sales Psychology,* McGraw-Hill Book Co., New York, 1952.

Lapp, C., *Successful Selling Strategies,* McGraw-Hill Book Co., New York, 1957.

Lester, B., *Selling to Industry,* Industrial Press, New York, 1953.

Leterman, E. C., *The New Art of Selling,* Bantam Books, New York, 1958.

Lewis, C. W. (ed.), *Essentials of Selling,* Prentice-Hall, Englewood Cliffs, N.J., 1952.

Lohse, C. F., *Creative Selling,* Scribner's, New York, 1960.

MacDonald, J. A., *Strategies that Close Sales,* Prentice-Hall, Englewood Cliffs, N.J., 1959.

Mangan, J. T., *How to Win Self-Confidence for Selling,* Prentice-Hall, Englewood Cliffs, N.J., 1957.

Meloan, T., & J. M. Rathmell (eds.), *Selling: Its Broader Dimensions,* Macmillan Co., New York, 1960.

Murphy, J. D. (ed.), *Secrets of Successful Selling,* Prentice-Hall, Englewood Cliffs, N.J., 1956.

Pederson, C. A., & M. C. Wright, *Salesmanship: Principles and Methods,* Richard D. Irwin, Homewood, Ill., 1955.

Prentice-Hall Miracle Sales Guide, Prentice-Hall, Englewood Cliffs, N.J., 1959.

Prevette, E., *The Power of Creative Selling,* Prentice-Hall, Englewood Cliffs, N.J., 1954.

Revilo, N., *The Art of Selling,* Vantage Press, New York, 1958.

Roth, C. F., *Handbook of Big-Money Selling Techniques* (1959); *Handbook of Successful New Sales Ideas* (1957); *How to Find and Qualify Prospects and Get Interviews* (1954); *How to Hold and Develop Customers* (1952); *How to Make $25,000 a Year Selling* (1953), *How to Sell Your Way to Success* (1953); *My Lifetime Treasury of Selling Secrets* (1957); *Questions and Answers on Modern Selling Techniques* (1957); *Tested Methods of Successful Selling* (1958), Prentice-Hall, Englewood Cliffs, N.J.

Roth, C. F., *Professional Salesmanship,* McGraw-Hill Book Co., New York, 1949.

Russell, F. A., & F. H. Beach, *Textbook of Salesmanship,* 6th ed, McGraw-Hill Book Co., New York, 1957.

Seltz, D. D., *215 Successful Door Openers for Salesmen* (1956); *Successful Industrial Selling* (1958), Prentice-Hall, Englewood Cliffs, N.J.

Shaw, S. J., & J. W. Thompson (eds.), *Salesmanship: Modern Viewpoints on Personal Communication,* Henry Holt & Co., New York, 1960.

Simmons, H., *How to Develop Your Sales Ability,* Brown Book Co., New York, 1954.

Simmons, H., *How to Sell Like a Star Salesman,* Henry Holt & Co., New York, 1953.

Small, R. L., *Salesmanship,* Macmillan Co., New York, 1952.

Smith, A. F., *How to Get the Big Sales,* Prentice-Hall, Englewood Cliffs, N.J., 1959.

Sullivan, V. F., *How to Sell Your Way into the Big Money,* Citadel Press, New York, 1954.

Thorpe, M. H., *The Greatest Opportunity in the World: Selling,* Prentice-Hall, Englewood Cliffs, N.J., 1957.

Wheeler, E., *Selling Dangerously,* Prentice-Hall, Englewood Cliffs, N.J., 1956.

Whiteside, T., *The Relaxed Sell,* Oxford University Press, New York, 1954.

Whiting, P. H., *The Five Great Rules of Selling,* McGraw-Hill Book Co., New York, 1957.

PERIODICALS: *American Salesman, Specialty Salesman.*

SUGGESTED READINGS: II

American Management Association—Most of the *Marketing* series, and especially the following: *A Company Guide to the Selection of Salesmen,* Research Report No. 24 (1955); *The District Sales Manager,* Management Report No. 11 (1958); *Reporting Sales Data Effectively: the AMA Book of Sales Forms* (1958).

Aspley, J. C., *The Sales Manager's Handbook,* 7th ed, Dartnell Corp., Chicago, 1959.

Canfield, B. R., *Sales Administration—Principles and Problems,* 3rd ed, Prentice-Hall, Englewood Cliffs, N.J., 1954.

Corrigan, J. D., *How to Build Profit Value in Your Sales Dollars,* Ronald Press, New York, 1955.

Davis, R. T., *Performance and Development of Field Sales Managers,* Division of Research, Harvard Business School, Boston, 1957.

Gopel, R. A., *Managing Salesmen,* Printers' Ink Books, Pleasantville, N.Y., 1955.

Haas, K. B., *How to Develop Successful Salesmen,* McGraw-Hill Book Co., New York, 1957.

Haring, A., & R. H. Myers, *Survey of Special Incentives for Salesmen,* National Sales Executives, New York, 1953.

Hegarty, E. J., *Making Your Sales Meeting Sell,* McGraw-Hill Book Co., New York, 1955.

How to Stimulate Salesmen to Better Selling, National Industrial Conference Board, New York, 1958.

Kaufman, Z., *How to Run Better Sales Contests,* 2d ed, Harper & Bros., New York, 1954.

Lapp, C., *Personal Supervision of Outside Salesmen,* Bureau of Business Research, Ohio State University, Columbus, 1952.

Maynard, H. H., *Retirement Income Plans for the Outside Salesman,* National Sales Executives, New York, 1953.

Maynard, H. H., & J. H. Davis, *Sales Management,* 3rd ed, Ronald Press, New York, 1957.

National Society of Sales Training Executives, *Handbook of Sales Training,* 2d ed, Prentice-Hall, Englewood Cliffs, N.J., 1954.

Phelps, D. M., *Sales Management—Policies and Procedures,* Richard D. Irwin, Homewood, Ill., 1951.

Ruder, E. F., *Getting the Sales from Sales Training,* Sales Executives' Publications, St. Louis, 1958.

Sales Executives Club of New York, *Current Policies and Practices in Sales Management and Marketing Techniques,* 6 vols., Printers' Ink Books, Pleasantville, N.Y., 1956–1957.

Simmons, H., *Successful Sales Management,* Prentice-Hall, Englewood Cliffs, N.J., 1952.

Small Business Administration, *Sales Training for the Smaller Manufacturer,* Washington, D.C., 1954.

Stanton, W. J., & R. H. Buskirk, *Management of the Sales Force,* Richard D. Irwin, Homewood, Ill., 1959.

Still, R. R., & E. W. Cundiff, *Sales Management: Decisions, Policies and Cases,* Prentice-Hall, Englewood Cliffs, N.J., 1958.

Tosdal, H. R., *Introduction to Sales Management,* 4th ed, McGraw-Hill Book Co., New York, 1957.

Tosdal, H. R., *Selling in Our Economy,* Richard D. Irwin, Homewood, Ill., 1957.

PERIODICALS: *Sales Management, Sales Week.*

CHAPTER 23

MARKETING INFORMATION AND MARKETING RESEARCH

Our studies of product planning, buying for resale, pricing, promotion, and selling have indicated that continuing marketing success is possible only if a selling organization remains constantly and sensitively aware of the ever-changing conditions of its market and is flexible in its adaptations. A prerequisite to sound policy with respect to every one of the marketing operations so far studied and also, to a lesser extent, with respect to other marketing operations still to be studied, is continuous receipt and analysis of a substantial flow of pertinent market information. Without such information a business organization would be like a vessel that put to sea for a distant port without any means of determining its speed, and without benefit of charts, compass, chronometer, sextant, radar, and radio reception.

INTERNAL VS. EXTERNAL MARKET INFORMATION

Some important market information can be obtained by any company from within its own organization. Each of its executives, if he is properly expert in his field, has personal knowledge and information which he can contribute to the formulation of company marketing policy. Other internal sources of valuable marketing information can also be tapped. Proper classification and analysis of sales records will show market trends of various products in a company's line, and territorial differences in market potentials.* Salesmen's reports may indicate customer preferences, com-

---

* "Market potential," a term that will appear frequently in this chapter, is a key objective of much market information and marketing research. It is the sales volume that can be expected for a product, a group of products, or a service, when the market for such commodity or service is fully exploited.

petitive situations, variations in territorial business conditions, and other elements that affect sales. A good system for feedback of dealers' or distributors' suggestions and complaints can provide useful data for many aspects of marketing policy. The first approach of any established business to assembling market information should be comprehensive and ordered exploitation of its own internal records.

Though invaluable, with respect to what it covers, the internal market information available to a business unit is usually limited in scope. For many companies, the greater and most useful part of the information they need for framing marketing policy is obtained from external sources.

Five major types of market information are obtainable from external sources:

1. Demand information:
   a. Current and past sales of classes of commodities, and of some particular commodities.
   b. Number of potential consumers or customers.
   c. Potential purchasing power of consumers or customers.
   d. Competitive factors that may reduce the above potentials.
   e. Consumer or customer purchasing motivations and preferences.
2. Promotional information:
   a. Reactions of consumers and customers to different promotional techniques or appeals.
   b. Relative coverage and effectiveness of different promotional media.
3. Distributive information—availability and relative effectiveness of various distributive agencies.
4. Price information:
   a. Past, current, and prospective prices of particular commodities.
   b. Market reaction to variant prices for particular commodities.
   c. General price trends that may affect the prices of particular commodities.
5. Past and current production and supply information, to determine future prices and possible shortages.

External market information on these subjects is obtained in two forms: (1) published, and (2) developed through private marketing research.

PUBLISHED MARKET NEWS AND INFORMATION

In marketing, the past often throws much light on the present and on future prospects. Trend analysis, which may require data series that reach back over several years, is utilized in some phases of market forecasting. Some information that is utilized to frame market policy, therefore, may be of historical or semi-historical character.

Most market information, however, must be fairly current if it is to be of much use. A pharmaceutical manufacturer who wonders whether his vitamin preparations are forging ahead or slipping behind in the competitive race wants last month's figures on vitamin manufactures, not last year's figures. A dress manufacturer making his final decision on what quantity of a certain seasonal model he should produce, looks for guidance to last week's index of department store sales as well as to the index numbers for earlier weeks. By far the larger part of market information is collected and issued on a monthly basis, with a lag of only a few weeks between date of application and date of publication. A great many important statistical series are issued weekly with a lag of only a few days.

Finally, some market information must be immediate or "spot" if it is to be of practical guidance. A local dealer buying grain or livestock from farmers bases the prices he offers not on last month's quotations or last week's quotations, but on yesterday's quotations as published in many daily papers, or even on today's as given over the radio or on ticker tape. The monthly crop estimates of the U.S. Department of Agriculture's Division of Crop and Live Stock Estimates affect the buying and selling plans of dealers and speculators within minutes after they have been made public. Such "spot" elements of market information may be called market "news."

For convenience of study we shall divide market information into two fields—information on manufactured products, and information on agricultural products and raw materials. There is some overlapping between these two; information on some products in their initial processing stages might reasonably be assigned to either field. In general, however, the sources and to some extent the character of the two fields of market information differ to an appreciable extent.

Manufactured products

The five sources of market information on manufactured products are: (1) the Office of Business Economics of the U.S. Department of Commerce, (2) the federal Bureau of the Census, (3) certain other federal units, (4) business papers and trade magazines, and (5) various miscellaneous sources on special lines.

The Office of Business Economics of the U.S. Department of Commerce issues a monthly *Survey of Current Business,* and a biennial background compilation, *Business Statistics.* The *Survey* is a major source of current statistical information on many aspects of manufactured goods marketing. It contains statistical series on current production and prices of various commodities, on the sales of various classes of manufacturers, wholesalers, and retail institutions, and on general business conditions throughout the country.

Another important federal source of marketing information is the Bureau of the Census. The decennial population censuses are mines of information on consumer market potentials. Indeed, many of the annual market potential series are primarily adjusted projections of data from the last previous decennial population census. A *Census of Business* and a *Census of Manufactures* are published at intervals varying from two to eight years.* The Bureau also publishes a biennial *County Business Patterns* report and an occasional *County and City Data Book* compilation. The *Statistical Abstract,* an annual publication of the Bureau of the Census, provides a condensed summary of statistical data on many social, economic, and business subjects.

Several other federal units also publish valuable market information. The Tariff Commission releases monthly statistics on production and prices of certain commodities. The Bureau of Labor Statistics of the Department of Labor issues monthly wholesale and retail price indexes, and weekly indexes on prices of certain "sensitive" products. The *Federal Reserve Bulletin* and the monthly reviews of the twelve federal reserve banks contain invaluable guides to national and regional business conditions. The Board of Governors of the Federal Reserve System also releases monthly and weekly figures on department store sales and stocks.

Business papers and trade magazines are the most important nongovernmental sources of marketing news and information. For some companies and lines of business these publications are undoubtedly of more immediate importance than any of the federal agencies. They print market data applicable to their fields derived from various original sources. Often they collect and issue their own statistical series on production, sales, and prices for their fields. And, of course, they are vital sources for current news, if not spot news, in their fields. As representative of three classes of the hundreds of such publications we may cite the daily *New York Journal of Commerce* and *Daily News Record* (textiles), the weekly *Iron Age,* and the monthly *Rayon Organon.*

A number of miscellaneous sources of published market information on manufactured products should be noted. Some trade associations publish statistics derived from their membership. Many newspapers, magazines, radio stations, and other advertising media make statistical analyses of the market potentials represented by their audiences, and publish the results.

---

* A *Census of Business* was published in 1929, 1933, 1935, 1939, and 1941, and a *Census of Manufactures* biennially from 1919 through 1939. Both series were discontinued during World War II, but reinstituted afterwards. The first post-war *Census of Manufactures* was for 1947. The first post-war *Census of Business* covered 1948. The next census years for both were 1954 and 1958. It is presumed that successive censuses in these two fields will be made at five year intervals.

A special and exceptionally valuable source of data on market potentials is *Sales Management* magazine's annual volume on "Survey of Buying Power," which provides county-by-county and city-by-city measures of consumer buying power. A similar annual survey is issued by *Printers' Ink* magazine. The regular news columns and business sections of the large

ARKANSAS		*SM* POPULATION ESTIMATES, 1/1/					EFFECTIVE BUYING INCOME— *SM* ESTIMATES, 19							The sive
														Income Bre
COUNTIES CITIES (continued)	Met. Area Code	Total (thou-sands)	% of U.S.A.	House-holds (thou-sands)	Con-sumer Spend-ing Units (thous.)	Urban Pop. (thou-sands)	Net Dollars (000)	% of U.S.A.	Per Capita	Per Hsld.	In-come Per C.S.U.	Cash In-come Per Hsld.	$0-2,499 % % Hslds. Inc.	$2,500-3,999 % % Hslds. Inc.
Yell..................		11.3	.0063	3.1	3.1		11,308	.0034	1,001	3,648	3,554	2,974	50.5 26.1	29.7 32.7
Total Above Cities....		618.7	.3462	189.3	218.2		932,689	.2795	1,507	4,927	4,274	4,381	33.6 ·11.8	25.6 19.1
State Total..........		1,737.9	.9726	482.1	525.2	754.0	2,123,637	.6370	1,222	4,405	4,043	3,720	42.1 17.4	26.9 23.6	2

METRO. AREAS		*SM* POPULATION ESTIMATES, 1/1/					*SM* E. B. I. ESTIMATES, 19				METRO. AREAS		*SM* POPULATION ESTIMATES, 1/1			
		Total (thou-sands)	% of U.S.A.	House-hold (thou-sands)	Con-sumer Spend-ing Units (thous.)	Urban Pop. (thou-sands)	Net Dollars (000)	% of U.S.A.	Per Cap-ita	Per H'se-hold			Total (thou-sands)	% of U.S.A.	House-hold (thou-sands)	Con-sumer Spend-ing Units (thous.)
Fort Smith......		66.4	.0371	18.5	28.6	62.7	111,912	.0336	1,685	6,049	△Texarkana.....		102.4	.0574	30.0	30.9
Little Rock-North Little Rock.		260.0	.1455	78.1	86.7	208.4	420,622	.1262	1,618	5,386	Total Above Areas		428.8	.2400	126.6	146.2

CALIFORNIA— (Other Pacific States: Oregon, Washington)

COUNTIES CITIES	Met. Area Code	*SM* POPULATION ESTIMATES, 1/1/					EFFECTIVE BUYING INCOME— *SM* ESTIMATES, 19							Income Bre
		Total (thou-sands)	% of U.S.A.	House-holds (thou-sands)	Con-sumer Spend-ing Units (thous.)	Urban Pop. (thou-sands)	Net Dollars (000)	% of U.S.A.	Per Capita	Per Hsld.	In-come Per C.S.U.	Cash In-come Per Hsld.	$0-2,499 % % Hslds. Inc.	$2,500-3,999 % % Hslds. Inc.
Alameda.........143		890.2	.4982	293.6	335.1	878.8	2,124,375	.6372	2,386	7,236	6,338	6,667	13.7 3.1	15.3 7.4
Alameda..........		68.1	.0381	21.9	24.3		160,662	.0482	2,359	7,336	6,611	6,770	11.4 2.5	14.8 7.0
Albany............		19.1	.0107	6.1	6.2		43,464	.0130	2,276	7,125	7,010	6,774	11.6 2.6	14.4 6.8
Berkeley..........		122.2	.0684	40.1	54.7		332,951	.0999	2,725	8,303	6,078	7,155	13.0 2.7	12.9 5.8
Fremont..........		35.1	.0196	9.5	9.8		61,406	.0184	1,749	6,464	6,225	6,182	16.1 3.9	16.9 8.8
Hayward..........		68.6	.0384	20.9	22.4		143,492	.0430	2,092	6,866	6,380	6,425	13.8 3.2	15.8 7.9
Livermore.........		14.1	.0079	4.4	4.5		28,171	.0085	1,998	6,403	6,133	5,946	19.6 5.0	18.8 10.1
▲Oakland.........		408.0	.2283	140.6	159.6		1,020,809	.3062	2,502	7,260	6,395	6,649	13.0 2.9	15.2 7.4

For Retail Sales data, see Section 4 location on page 17. Before using
SM Standard (▲) and Potential (△) Metropolitan County Areas.

EXCERPT FROM *SALES MANAGEMENT* "SURVEY OF BUYING POWER." *Copyright 1960, Sales Management "Survey of Buying Power"; further reproduction not licensed.*

ILLUSTRATION 23–1

metropolitan dailies are "must" reading for all marketing executives. The Curtis Publishing Co., Hagstrom, and Rand McNally publish trading area maps used by sales managers in planning their salesmen's territories. Collegiate bureaus of business research frequently publish marketing studies of interest to particular lines of business or to business men in particular areas.

Agricultural products and raw materials

The Agricultural Marketing Administration of the U.S. Department of Agriculture is the most important source of farm product marketing information. It obtains daily reports on supplies, arrivals, sales, and prices, for over a hundred major products, from terminal markets and important producing area centers. Railroads make daily shipment reports to it; warehouses and elevators report receipts and deliveries. Information collected by the Administration's local agents that is of immediate local interest is released at intervals throughout each day to local newspapers, radios, and other news dissemination sources. All local figures are relayed to Washington, over thousands of miles of leased wires, where they are consolidated and reissued for national publication through ticker services, radio, and newspapers.

Besides its daily market news service, the Agricultural Marketing Administration publishes several monthly periodicals dealing with farm marketing matters. The monthly releases of the Agriculture Department's Division of Crop and Livestock Estimates, based on replies to questionnaires filled out regularly by hundreds of thousands of farmers and livestock raisers, exercise a key influence on futures and spot prices of the 150 or more commodities involved. The Agricultural Marketing Administration and the Bureau of Agricultural Economics publish many special reports every year on agricultural marketing topics. Finally, *Agricultural Statistics* and *Crops and Markets* published annually by the Department of Agriculture, are basic statistical reference books for agricultural marketing as well as agricultural production. The *Minerals Yearbook* issued by the Bureau of Mines of the Department of the Interior performs similar service to those interested in the marketing of mineral raw materials.

Some state departments of agriculture are valuable sources of crop and livestock marketing information for the farmers of their states. Commodity exchanges, through ticker services, issue minute-by-minute news on volume of trading and prices.

PRIVATE MARKETING RESEARCH *—FIELDS

Published marketing information is an excellent thing to have—as far as it goes. Usually it does not go far enough. Data on the specific line of

---

* The term "marketing research," defined as "the systematic gathering, recording, and analyzing of data about problems relating to the marketing of goods and services," covers not only research on specific marketing problems of individual companies, but also the gathering and publication of general market information by government agencies, trade associations, and others. The two types of marketing research differ in many respects, and should be distinguished in terminology. Accordingly the first type is called "private" marketing research, and the second type "public" marketing research.

business or on specific products that interest a particular company may be concealed in some broader classification. Or the statistics on a specific line of business or products, may be irrelevant to the issues on which the particular company wants guidance.

When the market information needed by a manufacturer or distributor is not available through regular publication in the form in which he requires it, his only recourse is to have it sought out or developed for him through private marketing research. The great possibilities of private marketing research were first generally realized, and its systematic development begun, in the early 1920's. Since then private marketing research application has expanded continuously and its techniques have been steadily improved. Actual projects have covered every imaginable phase of marketing policy. Most of the projects, however, deal with one or another of the following five subjects, or with some combination of them: (1) determination of market potentials; (2) determination of consumer reaction to variant possibilities of product design, pricing, or promotional appeals; (3) motivation research; (4) determination of the relative efficiency of alternative systems of distribution; and (5) forecasting various market factors that bear upon marketing policy.

Determining market potentials

A tool manufacturer put a new specialized tool into production without having made any check upon the size of the market for it. When sales fell sharply off after a year, a belated inquiry showed that the year's output constituted an eighteen-year supply for the country. To avoid such catastrophes of over-production or installation of excess production capacity, and also to avoid missing profit opportunities through under-production, a manufacturer may utilize marketing research to determine the market potential for each of his products—the maximum possible sales opportunities for all sellers of a product— and the market share of each potential that his company can expect.

In most cases, determination of the over-all market potential and individual company share for a product is not enough. Over-all potential and share must be broken down by territories, by states, even by counties and cities. Such breakdowns are needed to guide a manufacturer in his location of branch sales offices, distribution of sales and advertising effort, assignment of specific territories to salesmen, and sometimes the determination of salesmen's quotas. Most major companies selling on a national scale and advertising to a national market base their sales and advertising programs on more or less intensive analysis of the territorial distribution of their market shares. A recent survey of companies utilizing private marketing research indicated that analysis of market potentials and shares was ranked first in order of relative usefulness among the various research fields.

Determining consumer reactions

We saw, in Chapter 16, that a manufacturer should not proceed blindly to design his product or package. They should conform to the utility and taste demands of his market if he is to win out in the competitive race for sales. The surest way to determine these demands is to test for them—through marketing "presearch." By interviews or by mailed questionnaires, potential customers may be queried on their product design preferences. Trial runs of alternative packages may be prepared, and their respective appeals put to the crucial test of the sales counter under controlled selling conditions.

In view of the frequently irrational reaction of the market to prices, discussed in Chapter 19, a manufacturer or large retailer operating under circumstances of quasi-monopoly may deem it advisable to utilize private marketing research to determine the most favorable retail prices for certain of his products. There are interviewing techniques that may be used for this purpose, or test sales may be made at different prices.

One of the most active fields of private marketing research at the present time is testing advertising effectiveness—the relative influence of different buying appeals, the relative attention-attracting power of different sizes, positions, and formats of advertisements, the influence of repeated advertisements. Fantastically ingenious techniques have been developed for ascertaining reader and listener reactions to advertising. The marketing research division of one advertising agency publishes a complete magazine, with stories, feature articles, and advertisements, the only copies of which are used by its interviewers to obtain reader reactions. For testing purposes, magazines and newspapers often carry some coupon advertisements on a "split-run" basis—the advertisement to be tested appears in one form in half of the published copies and in another form in the other half, with a careful check kept on the coupon returns resulting from the two different forms of the advertisement. As yet no marketing research approach has succeeded in providing answers to the crucial question of the absolute or comparative effectiveness of particular advertisements or advertising campaigns in producing short-run or long-run returns. Considerable valuable subordinate or contributory information, however, has been derived.

Motivation research

Motivation research, which attained sudden prominence in the 1950's as the newest and most controversial field of private marketing research, is the analysis of the psychological and social motivations that influence market behavior, through a group of research techniques developed by behavioral scientists.

Consumers' subconscious motivations cannot be ascertained by simple direct questions contained in a questionnaire or put in routine form by an ordinary interviewer. The procedures used in motivation research are the individual "depth" interview, the Rohrshach blot test, group "free association," "projective analysis," and other psychological techniques. These

These two Rockwell Manufacturing Co. ads for power tools appeared in *Iron Age,* the first on August 20 (a poor date because some potential readers would be on vacation), the second on October 29. Both were full page two-color insertions. The technical advertising feature of the first was the illustration, small-scale, of nine power tools; that of the second was the illustration, large-scale, of a single power tool. *Which ad pulled best?*

The two ads were tested for potential customer reaction by an advertising research organization. The first scored substantially higher.

COMPARATIVE AD TESTING. *From Printers' Ink, May 20, 1960.*

ILLUSTRATION 23–2

interviews, tests, and discussions must be conducted by trained psychologists. Each interview, each test, each discussion is more likely to be a matter of hours than of minutes. Consequently, not many individuals can be studied in the course of an inquiry if prohibitive cost is to be avoided. Motivation research therefore has to proceed by the method of a small number of case studies instead of the survey technique employing substantial-sized samples.

So far, progress in motivation research has suffered from two serious faults, deriving from its inquiry technique. First, with regard to human motivations, personal and social psychology as sciences have not yet arrived at generally accepted bodies of basic principles. On this subject there are several schools of psychological and sociological thought bitterly at war with each other. A motivation research psychologist can hardly avoid conducting his interviews, tests, or discussions along lines dictated by his particular school of thought, and interpreting his findings according to the tenets of that school. This basic inquiry bias has led to cases of diametrically-opposed conclusions on product design and advertising appeal when the same problem was submitted to two different motivation research organizations. Second, case study analysis can yield only suggestions or indications, not statistically reliable conclusions. Some motivation researchers, however, better as psychologists or social analysts than as statisticians, have proffered the results of their case studies as absolute conclusions and sound bases for marketing action.

In spite of these shortcomings of motivation research at its present stage of development, it stands as a most promising area of private marketing research. Even if its findings can currently be taken only as suggestions, these suggestions have opened the eyes of marketing management to hitherto unsuspected factors of product design and promotional appeal that previous objective survey techniques had not discovered. In many cases, the suggestions produced by motivation research can be checked by suitably-devised large-sample surveys or by tests, to obtain conclusions with ascertainable reliability. Where this can not be done, a door still has been opened to trial-and-error experimentation along new and potentially productive lines.

Time and widening experience may be counted on to broaden the present overly-narrow scope and other major weaknesses of motivation research. Probing into the biological, psychological, and status drives that shape consumer reactions should be extended to cover esthetic, religious, and intellectual factors. Improved frameworks of theoretical concepts serving as effective first premises for reaching practical conclusions will be shaped. Research techniques that can transform present qualitative approaches to quantitative ones will be developed. Time will unquestionably bring higher professional standards of skill and ethical standards of usage to this newest of marketing arts, which is still in its infant stage.

Distribution efficiency analysis

Increasing attention is being paid to distribution efficiency analysis. It is a subject less developed than the three fields of private marketing research so far considered. It has three subdivisions: (1) distributor coverage and efficiency analysis, (2) sales force efficiency analysis, and (3) marketing cost analysis.

Manufacturers are often sorely perplexed as to the best agencies and

channels of distribution to employ. Should a particular manufacturer utilize wholesalers and jobbers? Do agent middlemen of a certain class—say,
food brokers—offer any distributional advantages? Should a manufacturer
give an exclusive contract to one wholesaler in each territory? Should he
sell direct to retailers? Should he work out some combination of wholesaler
distribution and direct-to-retailer selling? Should his products be retailed
primarily by chains, or primarily by independent stores, or should he try
to obtain full distribution by both? Should he employ selective or exclusive
policy in seeking retail outlets? Important distributive policy considerations,
discussed in Chapter 13, are involved here. Sound application of these
policy considerations, however, often involves knowledge of facts not immediately available to the manufacturer. Marketing research directed at
distributor coverage and efficiency analysis must supply them.

As was indicated in Chapter 22, efficient sales force management requires careful selection of men for the sales force, training them in the
most effective ways of selling the company's line, and ensuring that in their
routing and selling activities they make efficient use of their time. In a
small company, the knowledge needed to accomplish these results may all
be accumulated naturally by the sales manager in the normal course of
routine administrative duties—from his study of sales orders and salesmen's reports as these flow across his desk, and from his intimate first-hand
knowledge of the personality and procedures of each of his salesmen. The
sales manager of a large company, with hundreds of salesmen supervised
by assistant sales managers of varying abilities, needs an occasional *sales
force efficiency analysis* to enable him to devise effective systems of selecting, training, and controlling his sales force. Such an analysis involves organized research methods. It may be undertaken by the sales department's
own staff personnel, or by a research agency experienced in this special
branch of marketing research.

Marketing cost analysis *—research on the unit costs of a company's promotion, selling, shipping, and credit operations—is often viewed as a
special field of cost accounting rather than of marketing research. The
justification for considering such analyses a phase of marketing research is
that, for their maximum value to be realized, they must often involve comparative studies of the distribution costs for an entire business field. The
fairest interpretation would be to treat this type of analysis as a joint product of cost accounting and marketing research. The former provides the
unit breakdown of the company's marketing costs. The latter provides the
comparative data required for evaluation of the results of the "internal"
cost survey. Marketing cost analysis has helped companies to eliminate unprofitable product lines and unprofitable classes of customers, to develop

---

* This subject is explored more fully in Chapter 29.

more economical channels of distribution, and to develop sounder systems of salesman routing.

Forecasting

Plans for production facilities, production volume commitments, purchase commitments, pricing policy, promotion campaigns, and sales campaigns, must generally be based on *anticipation* of market conditions at some future time. Usually the future to which the plans apply is a near one —the next quarter, or the coming "season," or the coming half-year, or the coming year. Where plans for enlarging production facilities, or for developing a new sales territory, are under consideration, the "future" involved may run to several years. A comprehensive picture of present market circumstances is not sufficient for such planning. Forecasts must be made of the future to which the plans are to apply. Such forecasting of market factors is the fifth major field of private marketing research. Typical market factors for which forecasts must often be made are: (1) future market potentials for particular products; (2) style and market taste developments; (3) competitive product and brand developments; (4) price and cost developments; and (5) general economic conditions that may affect any or all of the four preceding factors in the future.

Market factor forecasting involves a combination of quantitative and qualitative techniques. Most of the quantitative forecasting techniques resolve themselves into variants of the statistical procedure of *trend projection.* This procedure is based on the assumption that most economic and social forces, once they are established as causative factors, even if only in a minor way, develop a persistence that preserves their influence over longer or shorter periods, subject of course to the effect of extraneous factors which frequently cannot be given statistical values. The qualitative side of forecasting involves the appraisal of these extraneous factors, with more or less arbitrary adjustment of the results of quantitative analysis for them. The reliability of market forecasting results primarily from the expertness of this qualitative analysis.

The most expert market forecasters cannot promise 100 percent certainty on their predictions, even when these apply to the relatively near future. The best they can offer is some degree of probability that their forecasts will be realized. In certain fields, this probability is amazingly high. Where forecasts for long futures are involved, the degree of probability may be only little better than the "educated guesses" that business management would have to make without the forecasters' help. Even where expert combination of quantitative and qualitative forecasting analysis results in predictions with only a slightly higher degree of probability than untutored management could achieve by itself, however, it enhances the chances of business profit, or it reduces the chances of business loss. This makes it a sound investment. With full realization that market forecasting is far from infallible, management is becoming increasingly dependent on it for both long-range and short-range planning.

PRIVATE MARKETING RESEARCH—TECHNIQUES

Private marketing research has developed four basic techniques: (1) statistical analysis of available quantitative data, (2) case studies, (3) surveys, and (4) tests.

Statistical analysis of available quantitative data

As indicated earlier in this chapter, market management has available for its guidance oceans of significant published quantitative data. Indeed, so great is the supply of some of this information that expert experience and knowledge is required merely to keep track of the information flow and to keep it properly classified and integrated. Moreover, there is wide variation in the reliability of various items of this information, and expert knowledge is required to evaluate it.

In their initial published form, these figures may not be directly pertinent to the problems and plans of a particular company. Correlations must be established between the published data and various aspects of the company's marketing problems. Such correlation analysis is the principal tool of private marketing research in many cases of market potential study. If forecasting is involved, correlation analysis is usually the foundation for the trend analysis that is the quantitative approach to forecasting.

Case studies

Case studies are intensive analyses of a small number of individual cases related to a marketing problem. For example, with dealer cooperation, a manufacturer might have detailed studies made of how their sales clerks go about selling his product. This would guide him in preparing a system of sales-clerk training for all his dealers. Or a motivation research psychologist might conduct "depth" interviews with a dozen or so subjects to determine the subconscious elements in consumer reactions to some element of a manufacturer's advertising appeal or product design.

Occasionally, as in a distribution efficiency analysis involving a limited number of wholesalers handling a manufacturer's line, case study research may offer a complete answer to the marketing problem posed. More often, the number of cases studied is too small in relation to the total market group involved to provide statistically reliable conclusions. Still, such case studies may be a proper preliminary phase of marketing research. They help define the problem. They indicate the factors involved. The quantitative importance of these factors, which is what marketing management wants to know, must be determined by one of the other marketing research techniques.

Surveys

A "market survey" is an analysis through questionnaires of a *sample* of the general market group, or "universe," about which information is desired. The analysis may cover some objective market factor, such as the proportion of the sample reached by telephone who are listening to a certain radio program at the moment, who say they buy a particular brand of coffee, who have the brand on their pantry shelves, or who read a certain magazine. Or the analysis may cover a subjective market factor—relative consumer preferences with respect to a choice of product styles or competing product brands, or the relative appeals of variant advertising approaches. Given a sample *representative* of its "universe," and *large enough* to be statistically "reliable," the conclusions derived from questionnaire analysis of the sample can be applied to the general market group. Most marketing research on consumer preferences is based on surveys. Some phases of market potential research and distribution efficiency research also employ the survey technique.

A major problem of survey research, on which many market survey projects have been wrecked, is to obtain a sample that is truly *representative* of the over-all group or "universe" with respect to all considerations that influence the subject of the survey. A group of school teachers would not provide a representative sample for a survey of general audience preference on radio programs, for example, since the school teachers as a group would probably have preferences on this subject widely different from those of other elements of the population. Statisticians have developed a number of ways of obtaining representative samples, two of which are widely used in marketing research. One is *random* sampling, based on the laws of chance. The other is the creation of *controlled* or *quota* samples, which are preplanned as to age, sex, income, and other compositional elements for the purposes of the survey.

A marketing research *panel* is a preselected, controlled sample used for a continuing series of surveys. The considerations of reliability and representativeness that apply to ordinary survey samples apply also to panels. They are expensive to create and sometimes troublesome to maintain, but they have the important advantage that they can be used for periodic re-surveys showing trends or changes in consumer preferences.

The instrument for analyzing a marketing research survey sample is the questionnaire. The questionnaire may be mailed to the individuals who constitute the sample, or it may be used for interviewing them personally or by phone. Each of these techniques has certain advantages, certain disadvantages; each is the preferred method for some classes of surveys, is inadvisable for others.

BENNETT – CHAIKIN, INC.   574 FIFTH AVENUE   NEW YORK 36, N. Y.   Job No. 124/2/36 July 19 ▪

DEALER LISTENING SURVEY

INTRODUCTION: I'm making a survey on the viewing and listening habits of food store owners (druggists) like yourself and I'd like
to ask you some questions. . .

1. Do you happen to own a TV set?   YES _____ 5-1   NO _____ -2

   a radio?   YES _____ -3   NO _____ -4

2a. I'd like to talk to you about radio first. . .
    Do you have a radio . . . . . . at home?   YES _____ 6-1   NO _____ -2

    (If "YES") How many? _____ 7-

    . . . . . in your car?   YES _____ 8-1   NO _____ -2   Don't own a car _____ x

    . . . . . in your store?   YES _____ -3   NO _____ -4

2b. (IF RADIO OWNED) Do you happen to have a battery portable?   YES _____ 9-1   NO _____ -2

3. How often do you listen to the radio at home: quite frequently, occasionally, rarely? (RECORD BELOW)
   While driving your car? (RECORD BELOW)
   On days off such as weekends and holidays (RECORD BELOW)

	At Home	Car	On Days Off
Quite Frequently	_____ 10-1	_____ 11-1	_____ 12-1
Occasionally.	_____ -2	_____ -2	_____ -2
Rarely	_____ -3	_____ -3	_____ -3
Never	_____ -4	_____ -4	_____ -4

EXCERPT FROM A MARKETING RESEARCH INTERVIEW
QUESTIONNAIRE. *Courtesy of Bennett-Chaikin, Inc.*

ILLUSTRATION 23–3

Tests

Some marketing problems can be solved better or less expensively by experimentation than by any form of survey. Customer reaction to various prices within a range is often determined by test sales at different prices in separate localities, or even in a single store, by giving fictitious brand names to lots of the same product and offering them at different prices. The "split-run" technique of testing alternative advertisements is another example of the experimental approach. Variant packaging designs are sometimes tested by local trial sales. Alternative package designs, advertising media, sales promotion ideas, and other marketing issues may be checked, prior to national usage, by preliminary trials in one or more of some 200 "test" cities.

PRIVATE MARKETING RESEARCH—AGENCIES

Private marketing research is undertaken by four classes of organizations: (1) marketing research departments or divisions of large business organizations, (2) independent marketing research "agencies," (3) the marketing research departments or divisions of advertising agencies, and (4) some advertising media.

Marketing research departments

Effective marketing research requires a blending of profound knowledge of the particular company's marketing problems and methods with equally profound knowledge of the techniques of obtaining the external market data needed for solutions. Consequently, the best arrangement, where practicable, is to have a company's marketing research undertaken by its own marketing research division or department. But only very large industrial organizations, and a few large mail order houses and retail chains, have sufficient continuing need for marketing research to keep a research director and his staff busy throughout the year.

When there is an internal marketing research division or department, its location in the company's organizational structure sometimes poses problems. There is an obvious strong case for making the marketing research unit part of the sales department organization. But the engineering department of a manufacturing company can claim a strong interest in the product design studies that it conducts. The advertising department, too, has a large stake in the company's marketing research activities. Accordingly, to avoid inter-departmental conflicts of interest, the marketing research unit of a company is usually made a staff division responsible directly to the president, the marketing manager, or some other top management official.

Independent marketing research agencies

Scores, possibly hundreds, of independent marketing research agencies have been established during the past twenty-five years. Some few were frauds. Most have performed a valuable marketing service, either making general marketing research possible for small and medium-sized business organizations, or else performing some highly specialized type of marketing research of value to large and small companies alike.

Some marketing research agencies offer general research service. They stand ready to pursue inquiries in any of the five fields of private marketing research previously described for any client in any line of business. The tendency, however, is toward specialization. Many agencies limit themselves to a particular research field—to consumer preference analysis, to market potential analysis, to distribution efficiency analysis, to motivation research, or to price and supply forecasting. Others restrict themselves to one line of business—the drug line, or a branch of the industrial equipment line, or the builders' supply line. Some offer expertness in a particular research technique, such as panel operation or psychological interviewing. Such specialization generally results in greater efficiency.

Advertising agencies

Advertising agencies were pioneers in developing certain fields of marketing research. In the beginning they undertook this activity to guide themselves in devising more effective advertisements and locating the best media for their clients. Soon they found it excellent promotional policy to place their skilled research departments at the disposal of their clients for inquiries not directly connected with the clients' advertising. Often this was done on a free service basis. In time, many of the larger advertising agencies established their marketing research work on a fee basis. Many of the leading names in private marketing research today are associated with advertising agencies.

Advertising media

Newspapers and national magazines discovered that they could sell their advertising space more effectively if they could inform advertisers of the specific market potentials that their readers represented. Many of them now conduct serious and valuable researches into the economic character and buying habits of their readers.

VOCATIONAL CONSIDERATIONS

As an expanding market function, the field of marketing research offers increasing career possibilities to the college graduate. Inherent qualifications are definitely high levels of general intelligence and mathematical aptitude. Preparatory training should include, beside a general course of marketing research, all the statistical courses that a student can take, and courses in general business economics, advertising, sales policy, and psychology. Adequate coverage of these subjects can rarely be accomplished in an undergraduate curriculum, even in collegiate schools of business, so that graduate work leading to a master's degree, or even a doctorate, is usually necessary.

As in any other marketing field career, these studies are only preliminary. Superimposed upon them must be the practical on-the-job experience of interviewing and statistical clerkship, and being an assistant to an experienced marketing research man.

The compensation of the marketing research directors of business organizations and advertising agencies, and the profits to be earned through operating an independent marketing research agency, are eminently satisfactory. Furthermore, for a man or woman with a keen, enquiring mind, a marketing research career offers a challenge of an endless series of new problems posed and solved.

REVIEW

1. List the major types of market information obtainable from external sources.

2. Describe the various classes of published market information on manufactured products and their sources.

3. Describe the various classes of published market information on agricultural products and their sources.

4. Describe each of the major fields of private marketing research.

5. What are the possibilities and limitations of private marketing research based primarily on analysis of available quantitative data?

6. What are the possibilities and limitations of private marketing research based primarily on case studies?

7. What is a marketing research survey? How may information be obtained from the individuals composing the sample? How reliable are the results of marketing research surveys?

8. What are marketing research "panels"? How are they used?

9. What are the possibilities of using tests in private marketing research?

10. What are the potentialities and limitations of motivation research?

11. What classes of business organizations do private marketing research?

DISCUSSION TOPICS

1. Shouldn't the Department of Commerce develop a system for daily collection and dissemination of news on prices and market situations for manufactured goods as the Department of Agriculture has done for agricultural products?

2. "Marketing research is a 'racket.' The basis for the expertness of most marketing research 'experts' is their claim that they are 'experts.' "

3. "The latin phrase *post hoc non est propter hoc* (because a thing has happened a certain way in the past is no basis for presuming it must continue to happen that way in the future) indicates the futility of statistical trend analysis as a basis for market forecasting."

4. How can survey analysis of a sample possibly give dependable information of the total group of which the sample is only a part?

5. Is motivation research ethical?

PROBLEM

National Bicycle Corp. has developed a compact efficient gasoline motor, to cost around $75 retail, which can be attachced to any standard bicycle. It is hardy, simple to operate, and gives speeds up to 30 miles per hour.

The company wants to plan a factory; management wants some idea of the potential American market for these motors. It needs to know how the national potential is distributed geographically, and as between urban, suburban, and rural areas. It would further like to know whether its present organization of National Bicycle dealers will be the best channel of distribution for the motors, or whether there are other channels that could be successfully used. Also, there is uncertainty as to whether the market would prefer a hand-throttle or a foot-pedal accelerator to control the speed.

A marketing research agency has been called into consultation. As director of this agency, prepare a preliminary report stating in detail and justifying:

1. the marketing research technique, or combination of techniques, you would use to solve each of the questions posed by the National Bicycle Corporation; and

2. the step-by-step procedure you would follow in carrying out the assignment.

SUGGESTED READINGS

Alevizos, J. P., *Marketing Research: Applications, Procedures and Cases,* Prentice-Hall, Englewood Cliffs, N.J., 1959.

American Management Association, *A Company Guide to Marketing Research,* Research Report No. 5 (1955); *Marketing Research Organization and Operation,* Research Study No. 35 (1959); *Materials and Methods of Sales Forecasting,* Special Report No. 27 (1957); *Sales Forecasting: Uses, Techniques and Trends,* Special Report No. 16 (1956).

Boyd, H. W., & R. Westfall, *Marketing Research,* Richard D. Irwin, Homewood, Ill., 1956.

Brown, L. O., *Marketing and Distribution Research,* rev ed, Ronald Press, New York, 1955.

Cheskin, L., *How to Predict What People Will Buy,* Liveright Publishing Corp., New York, 1957.

Coman, E. T., *Sources of Business Information,* Prentice-Hall, Englewood Cliffs, N.J., 1959.

Crisp, R. D., *Marketing Research,* McGraw-Hill Book Co., New York, 1957.

Ferber, R., & H. C. Wales, *Marketing Research: Selected Literature,* William C. Brown Co., Dubuque, Iowa, 1952.

Fox, W. M., *How to Use Marketing Research for Profit,* Prentice-Hall, Englewood Cliffs, N.J., 1951.

Frederick, J. G., *Introduction to Motivation Research,* Business Bourse, New York, 1957.

Hauser, P. M., & W. R. Leonard, *Government Statistics for Business Use,* 2d ed, John Wiley & Sons, New York, 1956.

Henry, H., *Motivation Research: its Practices and Uses for Advertising, Marketing and other Business Purposes,* F. Ungar Publishing Co., New York, 1958.

Hobart, D. H. (ed.), *Marketing Research Practice,* Ronald Press, New York, 1950.

Holmes, P., *Marketing Research: Principles and Readings,* South-Western Publishing Co., Cincinnati, 1960.

Kahn, R. F., & C. F. Cannel, *The Dynamics of Interviewing,* John Wiley & Sons, New York, 1957.

Lorie, J. H., & H. V. Roberts, *Basic Methods of Marketing Research,* McGraw-Hill Book Co., New York, 1951.

Luck, D. J., & H. G. Wales, *Marketing Research,* Prentice-Hall, Englewood Cliffs, N.J., 1952.

Marketing Research: a Guide for Capital Goods, Council for Technological Advancement, Chicago, 1959.

Nafziger, R. O. (ed.), *Introduction to Mass Communications Research,* Louisiana State University Press, Baton Rouge, 1958.

Newbury, F. D., *Business Forecasting,* McGraw-Hill Book Co., New York, 1952.

Newman, J. W., *Motivation Research and Marketing Management,* Division of Research, Harvard Business School, Boston, 1957.

Packard, V., *The Hidden Persuaders,* David McKay Co., New York, 1957.

Rewolt, S. H., *Economic Effects of Marketing Research,* Bureau of Business Research, University of Michigan, Ann Arbor, 1953.

Smith, C. W., *Targeting Sales Effort,* Columbia University Press, New York, 1958.

Smith, G. H., *Motivation Research in Advertising and Marketing,* McGraw-Hill Book Co., New York, 1954.

Stephan, F. F., & P. J. McCarthy, *Sampling Opinions: an Analysis of Survey Procedure,* John Wiley & Sons, New York, 1958.

Wold, H., & L. Jureen, *Demand Analysis,* John Wiley & Sons, New York, 1953.

CHAPTER 24

CREDIT

One-quarter of retail sales, and nearly nine-tenths of manufacturers' and wholesalers' sales, are made on credit—i.e., goods purchased are delivered to the customer on the basis of his promise to pay on some specified future date. Therefore, for a great many businesses, a sale is only a tentative transaction, subject to the condition that the purchaser is an acceptable credit risk. Final ratification of a sale made on credit terms must be preceded by an analysis of the customer's credit position. The group of activities involved in such analysis, together with those activities associated with collecting from customers who bought on credit terms but fail to pay their obligations when these fall due, constitute the *credit operation.*

MARKETING AND ECONOMIC SIGNIFICANCE

To assay the Marketing and Economic significance of retail and mercantile credit, the recipients should be divided into two groups. Individuals and businesses belonging to the first group have resources for immediate cash payment of their purchases. For them credit is merely a purchasing convenience, saving them the necessity of having currency always at hand for purchase payments or of having to write frequent and sometimes petty checks. Most individuals who maintain charge accounts at stores, and a small minority of business concerns, belong to this first group. For the second group, comprising most individuals who buy on installment account and most businesses, credit is a necessity. At the time of making a purchase they cannot pay, but expect to have the funds in a matter of weeks or months. Without credit, they could not make their purchases when they do.

Credit as a market convenience may have little economic significance, but it should not be dismissed lightly from a Marketing viewpoint. Charge accounts, as a customer service offered by department stores generally and by individual stores of other types, are a strong patronage inducement.

The credit investigations involved, and the billing and collection procedures, add to the operating costs of the stores that offer charge accounts, and are reflected in their markups. For a large proportion of customers, however, the service is worth the higher prices. In spite of the great expansion in recent years of cash-carry retailing, as evidenced by the supermarkets and discount houses, the service of charge account credit is still warmly appreciated by large sectors of the consumer market, and will unquestionably retain its place in the American retailing pattern.

Credit extensions through installment credit to consumers and through mercantile credit to businesses that must have the credit to buy when they do has more far-reaching consequences, both economically and marketwise.

Consumer installment credit

To the consumer who cannot pay cash for the new automobile he wants to buy, or the refrigerator, or the suit of clothes, paying for it "on time" carries two blessings. In the first place, he can get it *now,* and begin enjoying it immediately, instead of having to wait the months it would take him to accumulate the purchase price. Secondly, there is the consideration that he and his family might not have the will-power to hold back on their other purchases and save the required amount, so that he might never be able to have the car, or refrigerator, or suit of clothes. Of course, through interest and "finance charges" he pays, and pays heavily, for the privilege of postponing payment, but most installment purchasers ignore this cost or feel that it is a small price to pay for the advantages of immediate acquisition. The present generation takes buying "on time" for granted, and looks upon "living up to next years' income" as a desirable and proper system of personal finance.

The automobile dealer or store that sells "on time" unquestionably gains therefrom. People who otherwise would never buy his goods, or could not buy them so soon, do buy them—and from him. He need not even assume a risk of bad debt loss if he refinances his accounts with a finance company on a nonrecourse basis, as is frequently possible. The costs of refinancing, and of such credit investigation as he does make, and of such bad debt risk as he does assume, are passed on to the customer through higher markup or through a specific "finance charge"—often with some extra "loading."

At the close of 1959, $29 billion of consumer installment credit, $17 billion of it incurred for automobile purchases, was outstanding. The trend of consumer installment buying has been upward during the post-war years, as indicated in Illustration 24–1. A rising trend in installment buying, such as we have experienced since World War II, has three important economic effects. (1) It causes a larger proportion of consumer purchasing power to be expended for high-cost durable items purchased on installment terms, and a smaller proportion for current consumption items, than would otherwise be the case. (2) It results in a "pushing forward" of a substantial element of consumer purchasing power. If this occurs when employment is high and employee credit is good, further pressure is added to production and employment, with the possibility that balanced prosperity may be transformed into inflation, or that existing inflation may be exaggerated. (3) It makes the economy more vulnerable to sharp recession since, should the economy enter upon a downward swing, not only will the "forward push" of new installment buying fall off, but repayment of outstanding installment debt will absorb consumer purchasing power that otherwise would cushion the recession.

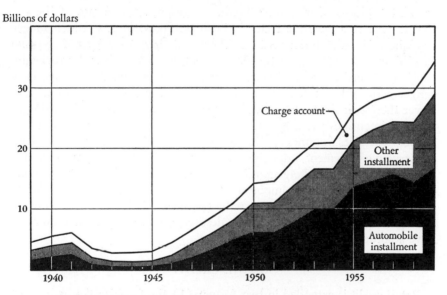

Billions of dollars

RETAIL INSTALLMENT CREDIT OUTSTANDING, 1939–1959
Source: *Survey of Current Business*
ILLUSTRATION 24–1

Mercantile credit

The American marketing system could not operate on its present scale without extensive utilization of mercantile credit. Most wholesalers and retailers, particularly small ones, do not have sufficient invested capital to cover in full the fixed and current assets needed for their scale of operations. The greater part of these business units would not be acceptable risks for bank credit. If they could not obtain a major part of their inventories on credit, some would have to go out of business altogether and the rest would have to curtail the scale of their operations.

Some marketing lines, moreover, experience wide seasonal fluctuations as to the inventories they must carry. A stationery store selling greeting cards, for example, must carry a stock several times larger than normal, prior to certain holidays. If such dealers could not buy from their suppliers on credit terms, the invested capital they would need for their peak periods would be much in excess of the requirements of the in-between months, and they would have idle bank balances for a large part of the year. This would be an inefficient use of capital, lowering the profit rate of the enterprises, and exercising a depressant effect on the national economy. Availability of mercantile credit in these seasonal marketing lines provides such business units with a valuable element of financial flexibility.

Most economists, unacquainted with credit managers and not instructed in the techniques of mercantile credit extension, are unaware of the part that it plays as a causative factor in business fluctuations. Credit managers are inherently of a cautious nature. They react sharply to signs of recession in business generally, or in their customers' particular lines, by reviewing their customers' credit positions. They cross off marginal accounts as no longer acceptable risks in view of the darkening business picture. They lower the credit limits they have been allowing to others. This cutting-off of sales intensifies the business difficulties of the customers affected, and reduces the sales volumes of the credit managers' own companies. Their conservative judgment undoubtedly saves their concerns some bad debt losses, but it also definitely aggravates whatever weakening of the economy may be developing. How important this intensification of the onset of recessions through the mercantile credit factor is, relative to other economic elements operating at such a time, deserves more study than economists have accorded it.

RETAIL CREDIT

Retail credit is extended in two forms: (1) the familiar charge account, usually involving monthly payment for purchases made during the preceding month; and (2) installment credit or "time payment," whereby weekly or monthly payment for a substantial purchase is spread over an extended period, often up to eighteen months or more. The dollar volume of charge account *sales* substantially exceeds that of installment sales. Because of the longer credit terms of installment sales, however, the volume of installment credit *outstanding* is usually much higher than that of charge account credit, as appears in Illustration 24–1.

Charge account credit

Most charge account credit is extended by stores. Recently, through a "credit card" system, travel spending—train and plane tickets, gasoline and auto service, and restaurant and hotel service—has been placed on a charge account basis by Diners' Club, American Express Co., and a number of other organizations. As of 1960 this "credit card" business had become a multi-million dollar one.

Until the 1940's, most retail charge account credit was extended on terms of "10 prox."—i.e., a customer's purchases during each month were lumped together, a statement covering them was submitted by the store shortly after the beginning of the next month, and payment was due on the tenth of that next month. Small stores still operate charge accounts on this basis. Most large department stores and public utility companies, however, have shifted to "cycle billing" of their charge account customers. Under this system, a store's charge account customers are usually divided into twenty groups, in the alphabetical sequence of their names. Each group has its monthly accounts rendered on a successive working day of the month. This procedure spreads the store's billing work evenly through the month, instead of concentrating it in the first two or three days. Payment by the customers in each group is due ten days from the date of their monthly statements.

Most charge account credit is requested, and extended, purely as a shopping convenience. The customer is well able to pay cash. With charge accounts at the various stores she patronizes, however, she does not have to go to the trouble of making out a series of checks or providing herself with sufficient cash to cover all the purchases she might make on a shopping trip. Starting out with only carfare, lunch money, and a few dollars for casual cash purchases, she can say "charge it" and return home the possessor of hundreds of dollars worth of new merchandise.

Some charge account credit, however, results from true financial need. A free-spending family dependent upon a monthly paycheck may count on charge accounts with local shopkeepers to provide it with food and other necessities during the last week or two of each month. Or a housewife may decide innocently to abuse the privilege of a charge account with a department store by buying a larger value of house furnishings than can be paid for in the following month, on the sound assumption that the store will not take a severe view of her spreading the payment over two or three months.

Installment credit

When an automobile, a radio or television set, a refrigerator, or a suit of clothes, is purchased on installment terms, the buyer is nearly always required to make a "down payment" of a fifth, or a quarter, or a third, or even a half, of the purchase price. The balance must be paid, weekly or monthly, over a specified period. For soft goods—clothes or house draperies, for example—the term of payment is likely to be limited to a few months. For consumer durable goods, such as an automobile or a furniture suite, payment may run to two years or longer. A "finance charge" is commonly added to the retail cash price of items sold under installment terms to cover the costs of credit investigation and refinancing by the seller. The purchaser generally signs a conditional sales contract or a chattel mortgage, which gives the seller the right to repossess the sold items in case of the buyer's failure to pay the full price.

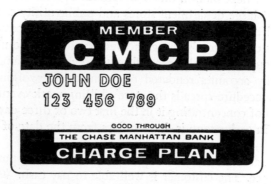

A CHASE MANHATTAN CREDIT CARD. *Courtesy of the Chase Manhattan Bank.*

ILLUSTRATION 24–2

A recent development of installment credit that is assuming large-scale importance for many department stores is "revolving credit." A customer is assigned a credit limit, say $150 or $250. When purchases have been made up to this figure, repayments (including an interest charge) are made in equal monthly amounts. But after any part has been repaid, further credit purchases can be made on the account up to the amount of the open balance. By a refinancing arrangement established in 1958 by the Chase Manhattan and some other banks, the "revolving credit" created by one of these banks for any customer can be used in any store subscribing to the plan. Originally intended to meet the needs of lower-income groups, these revolving credit accounts are currently being used increasingly by middle-income families as a method of "budgeting" their "shopping" purchases.

The credit decision

The credit manager of a department store or large women's wear store has a relatively simple task in deciding whether or not charge accounts should be opened for most applicants. His inquiry usually establishes that the applicants want their charge accounts only as a shopping convenience, and that they are well able to pay for any purchases they make immediately upon receipt of their monthly statements—even though, through oversight, they may often fail to make prompt payment. In such cases, the majority of those that come before him, he approves the applications "without limit" or with a generous limit.

Applications for installment credit, and the minority of charge account applications which reflect "necessity" cases, present a more difficult problem. The very circumstance that these customers are financially unable to pay cash for their purchases indicates a definite risk that some of them may be equally unable to pay the installment or charge account debt as it becomes due. The retail credit manager must make two decisions. First, is the applicant at all acceptable, on moral and financial considerations, as a credit risk? Second, how much installment or charge account debt may the applicant safely be allowed to incur? For example, a husband and wife with a $4000 income might be a sound risk with respect to payment of a $60 balance on a vacuum cleaner over six months, but be judged a dangerous risk for payment of a $1,200 balance on the purchase of a new automobile over eighteen months. Among the factors which the retail credit manager takes into consideration when passing upon installment and "necessity" charge account applications are: (1) the "moral risk" of the wage-earner in the applicant's family group—his previous record for paying debts; (2) the nature and permanence of his employment; (·3) his income in relation to the demands made upon it, including obligations to pay debts already outstanding and the repayment of the purchase-debt under consideration.

Sources of information

The proprietor of a local grocery store may know each and every one of his regular customers so well that he can safely base his decisions as to which ones may be allowed monthly charge accounts on his personal first-hand knowledge. A credit manager in a large department store or installment house could not possibly have such intimate knowledge about the thousands, or even tens of thousands, of customers who apply for charge accounts or installment credit. His information is derived primarily from two sources: (1) an application filled out by the customer seeking the charge or installment account, and (2) retail credit bureau reports.

Illustration 24–3 shows a standardized application form for charge account credit prepared by the National Retail Credit Association and used by many department stores. Application forms used by installment houses make provision for noting payments that the applicant is obligated to make on outstanding indebtedness.

In nearly all cases where a new charge or installment account is being opened, and whenever a customer becomes badly delinquent upon an exist-

APPLICATION FOR CREDIT

FOR EXCLUSIVE USE OF MEMBERS OF

NATIONAL RETAIL   CREDIT ASSOCIATION

GUARD YOUR CREDIT AS A SACRED TRUST

LAST NAME	FIRST NAME	INITIAL	AGE	HUSBAND'S FIRST NAME - WIFE'S MAIDEN NAME
RESIDENCE ADDRESS			TELEPHONE	
OCCUPATION	HOW LONG		TELEPHONE	
NAME OF EMPLOYER		BUSINESS ADDRESS		
FORMER BUSINESS OR OCCUPATION				
LOCATION OF REAL ESTATE OWNED			AMOUNT OF MORTGAGE	

	NUMBER OF CHILDREN	
	AT HOME	EMPLOYED

RENT HOME ☐   RENT APARTMENT ☐   BOARD ☐

NAME OF NEAREST RELATIVE AND RELATIONSHIP (OTHER THAN HUSBAND OR WIFE)   ADDRESS

PERSONAL REFERENCE

NAME OF BANK {   CHECKING ☐   BRANCH

SAVING ☐

LIFE INSURANCE   NAME OF INSURANCE CO.   APPROX. INCOME

$ $

TRADE REFERENCES

TYPE OF BUSINESS	KIND OF MDSE. BOUGHT	ACCOUNT IS NOW	
		OPEN	PAID IN FULL

LIST ON REVERSE SIDE OF THIS APPLICATION ANY UNPAID BALANCES ON INSTALLMENT ACCOUNTS AND MONTHLY PAYMENTS THEREON.

THE ABOVE INFORMATION IS FOR THE PURPOSE OF OBTAINING CREDIT AND IS WARRANTED TO BE TRUE. I AGREE TO PAY ALL BILLS UPON RECEIPT OF STATEMENT OR AS OTHERWISE EXPRESSLY AGREED.

DATE   SIGNATURE

CREDIT LIMIT	APPROVED
$	

PRINTED IN U.S.A.
FORM NA 1

A NRCA CHARGE ACCOUNT APPLICATION FORM. *Courtesy of National Retail Credit Association, 375 Jackson Avenue, St. Louis 5, Mo.*

ILLUSTRATION 24–3

ing account, a store credit manager obtains, by phone or mail, a report on the customer from the local retail credit bureau. There are some 1,700 local retail credit bureaus in the United States, supported by the stores and personal credit institutions of their localities. Every credit-granting retailer that is a member of one of these local bureaus supplies it with copies of all his charge account and installment credit applications. Bureau investigators check with employers, landlords, banks, and other references given in these applications. Local newspapers are clipped for news items that throw light on the personal history, employment, and finances of local residents whose names appear in the bureau files. Every month member-retailers send the bureau information on the purchases, payments, and delinquencies of their credit accounts. Thus each bureau builds up amazingly full files on all local credit-using residents.

When a customer applies for a charge account or seeks to make an installment purchase, the store's credit department can telephone the local retail credit bureau, or communicate with it by telescriber, and within a couple of minutes obtain a summary report that in most cases enables the credit manager to decide whether the customer should be allowed to make an immediate credit purchase and take the goods with her. For fuller information upon the customer, a comprehensive report, such as the one shown in Illustration 24–4, can be obtained by mail or messenger. If a store credit man wishes to check the seriousness of a customer's delinquency, the bureau will send him a "trade clearance" which summarizes the customer's recent credit dealings and payments.

Identification and authorization

Large stores with thousands of charge-account customers must establish some system of identifying customers who have approved accounts, so that sales clerks may readily know those who may make "charge-take" purchases. Such customers are provided with identification cards, or Charg-a-plates which both identify the customer and stamp her sales slip.*

An identified charge-account customer is usually allowed to make charge-take purchases up to $5 or $10 solely on her identification. If a charge-take purchase is for a larger amount, the store must check whether the account is in good standing at the time of purchase, and whether the credit balance is within whatever limit has been previously set. This is accomplished by an "authorization" system. A large store must have a "visible-index," or quick-reference, file covering all its charge-account customers, showing

---

* In New York City, and other metropolitan centers, where customers are likely to have charge accounts in several stores, a single Charg-a-plate, good for all the stores where a customer maintains accounts, is issued by a central bureau. This simplifies charge account shopping.

Factbilt REPORTS ARE BETTER

Associated Credit Bureaus of America
INCORPORATED
AN ASSOCIATION OF CREDIT BUREAUS SINCE 1906

CONFIDENTIAL

STANDARD CONSUMER REPORT
ACBofA No. 1
compiled by member bureau

1 REPORT ON:	PUBLIC,	MR.	JOHN Q.	(MARY A.)
	(Surname first)	(Mr. or Mrs.)	(Given Name)	(Spouse's name)
2 RESIDENCE ADDRESS:	7500 Parkway,	Forest Hills,	Queens,	New York
	(Street Number)	(City)	(County)	(State)

IDENTITY

3. Number of years covered: A. In file	A.	18
B. In investigation	B.	18
4. A. Age. (If near 21, confirm)	A.	45
B. Racial extraction (White, Black, Red, Yellow, Brown)	B.	White
5. A. Marital status	A.	Married
B. Number of dependents?	B.	2 children

HISTORY

6. A. Name of employer	A.	Never-Rip Shirt Corp.
B. Type of business	B.	Large Shirt Manufacturers
7. A. How long so employed	A.	1950
B. Position held	B.	Sales Manager
8. A. Does applicant have record of steady employment?	A.	Yes
B. Any recent employment change? (If yes, explain in remarks)	B.	None
9. Any suits, judgments or bankruptcies? (If yes, explain in remarks)		Record is clear

Character

10. Is applicant well regarded as to character, habits and morals?	Yes
11. Is applicant favorably regarded by employer?	Highly regarded
12. Any suspicion of illegal practice past or present?	None

RESOURCES

13. A. Estimate monthly income from present employment	A.	Est. $12,500. per annum
B. Estimate other income such as rentals, investments, etc.	B.	None known
C. Estimate income of others in household	C.	None
14. Own home, rent or board?		Rents apartment

CREDIT RECORD: (If feasible include whether subject has satisfactory bank checking account.)

Trade Line	How Long Selling	Date of Last Sale	Highest Credit	Terms of Sale	Amount Owing	Amount Past Due	Manner of Payment
Men's & Womens	Old	4/60	$114.	30 days	0	0	30-60 days
Dept. Store	1951	inact.	86.	30 days	0	0	30 days
Men's & Womens	1944	2/60	228.	30 days	0	0	30-60 days
Dept. Store	1946	4/60	99.	30 days	$41.	4/60	30-60 days
Gift Shop	1957	12/57	111.	30 days	0	0	30 days
Credit Card	1958	4/60	82.	30 days	26.	4/60	30-60 days
Auto Supply	1955	3/60	46.	30 days	11.	4/60	30 days
Finance	Several loans from 1951 to date, 1/60 financed Oldsmobile $4650., $1750. down, terms $150. month, owes $2300., not due, good a/c.						

REMARKS: A. Give brief word picture of subject's history, explaining any unusual condition.
B. Amplify any incomplete or adverse information in answers above. Use other side also for full details.
C. Include estimate of net worth if possible.

Local bank reports a joint account for subject and wife since June 1956. Balances average in medium 3-figure proportions; satisfactory, non-borrowing account. Came well introduced, impressions favorable.

Records show that prior to present residence address, subject and family lived for 6 years at 729 West 57th Street, New York City under good circumstances and had a satisfactory tenancy record. They also own a Summer cottage at Breezy Point, L.I. where they spend the summer months, valuation not disclosed.

Report for Member #99921

Date 4/15/- **Prepared by** J-1 (FF) Credit Bureau of Greater New York, N.Y. City, N.Y.
Name of member reporting bureau | City | State

A RETAIL CREDIT BUREAU SPECIAL REPORT. *Courtesy of the Credit Bureau of Greater New York, Inc.*

ILLUSTRATION 24-4

whether their accounts are open or suspended, and what their credit or order limits are. By carrier, telephone, or pneumatic tube the sales clerk sends a copy of the sales slip to the authorization department. In a few minutes, while the sales clerk wraps the customer's purchase, an efficient authorization department can check the customer's credit standing and send back an O.K. to the sales clerk or direct her to hold up the purchase. Small stores have a choice among several simple combination authorization-and-ledger systems which can be kept in a small file box or in a cash register cabinet.

Collection

Charge account customers whose accounts are mere shopping conveniences are often very careless about making prompt payment. They will miss a month's payment, or more, for no other reason than that their checkbooks aren't handy at the time when the stores' statements arrive. Subsequently the statements are mislaid. Sharp pressure for prompt payment cannot be put upon them, however, lest they be irritated and their patronage lost. Stores are very patient with them. A whole month passes, sometimes two, before the store even reminds them of their oversight. If nonpayment continues, the store's credit department commences a long series of patient, courteous appeals. Six to eight months usually elapse, a half dozen or more letters may be sent, and several telephone calls may be made, before the store takes the drastic step of placing a delinquent account in the hands of its attorneys for collection.

Delinquency on the part of a charge account customer with a low credit rating, or by an installment buyer, is not treated so leniently. Installment houses maintain visible index collection files which spot any customer who is a few days late in his payments. A series of collection letters and telephone calls, spaced at semi-weekly intervals, is immediately started. The first letter is only a reminder of the nonpayment, but the subsequent ones make courteous but firm demands for payment, with the threat of repossession of the purchased item soon introduced. Actually, installment houses try to avoid repossession wherever possible, since it is bad advertisement for the store, but it is done occasionally so that the threat exists.

MERCANTILE CREDIT

Any business that is an acceptable credit risk expects to buy on credit terms. Therefore all businesses selling to other business concerns must take it for granted that most of their sales will be on credit. In a small concern the credit-and-collection operation is likely to be handled, frequently inefficiently, by a partner of a bookkeeper-clerk. Large companies employ trained credit managers for this work, and sometimes have large credit departments.

Terms of sale

There is much more variety to "terms of sale"—i.e., credit terms—in mercantile transactions than in retail selling.

To begin with, there are four selling arrangements used with customers who are not deemed acceptable risks for "regular" credit terms:

1. C.O.D. terms—i.e., the familiar "cash on delivery"—are insisted upon when a customer is too poor a credit risk for regular terms. The seller runs the risk, of course, that the customer may be unable to pay upon delivery and that the goods will have to be returned with two-way charges.

2. SD-BL terms—i.e., "sight draft with bill of lading"—are used instead of C.O.D. terms when the carrier cannot be used as a collection agency. The goods are shipped on a negotiable bill of lading, so that the customer cannot obtain them from the carrier without presenting the bill of lading. A draft ordering the customer to pay the invoice amount is attached to the bill of lading. The two documents are sent to a bank or other agent in the customer's city with instructions that the bill of lading must not be surrendered to the customer until he has paid the sight draft. The payment, with a collection fee deducted, is remitted by the bank or other agent to the seller.

3. C.B.D. terms—i.e., "cash before delivery"—are insisted upon in some cases where no credit information can be obtained about a customer, or when goods are made to special order for a poor-risk customer, or when a customer's credit standing is so poor that the seller does not want to risk the cost of shipping to him C.O.D. or SD-BL and possibly having to pay return freight if the customer cannot pay on delivery.

4. In a *consignment* transaction, if legal requirements are properly observed, the "buyer" obtains possession but never acquires title to the consigned goods. He acts only as an agent of the original seller to resell the goods. Consequently, if a consignee becomes bankrupt, the original seller can regain possession of the goods. If a consignee fails to pay the seller for the goods after they have been resold, he can be criminally prosecuted for embezzlement.

When a customer is deemed an acceptable credit risk, he may be given "regular" single-order terms or lumped-order terms, according to the timing of his purchases and deliveries to him:

1. A single-order term of credit—e.g., "net 30"—gives the buyer the specified number of days *from the invoice date* in which to make payment. Such terms are ordinarily used when sales or deliveries are made less frequently than once a month.

2. Lumped-order terms—e.g., "E.O.M." (meaning "payment on all puchases or deliveries during the month due at the end of the month"), or "10 prox. net 30" (meaning "payment on all purchases or deliveries during the month due 30 days from the tenth of the following month")— are ordinarily used when sales or deliveries to a customer occur at frequent intervals.

A *cash discount* provision may be combined with either single-order or lumped-order terms. Terms of "2/10 net 30" would mean that the buyer could deduct 2 percent discount from the net price if he made payment within 10 days *of the invoice date;* otherwise the entire net amount would be due 30 days from the invoice date. The theory of the cash discount is that, when a customer pays within 10 days, the seller saves an interest cost on the amount of the payment for the remainder of the credit period, he saves possible overhead and direct expenses of collection, and he avoids all risk of bad debt loss. These savings are passed on to the customer through the discount. In practice, most cash discounts far exceed the savings of early payment to the seller. Under 2/10 net 30 terms, for example, a seller gives 2 percent to obtain his money 20 days before it is due. This is equivalent to giving the buyer 36 percent a year * on the purchase price—many times more than any possible saving to the seller. Accordingly there is considerable agitation among sellers for the abolition of the cash discount, but it is so advantageous to early-paying buyers, and so deeply engrained in American marketing custom, that there is little likelihood that it will soon be eliminated.

Instruments

Most mercantile credit is extended upon "open book account"—the seller merely charges the invoice amount to the customer's account on the receivables ledger. In certain cases, however, the customer may be required to sign instrumental evidence of his indebtedness to the seller.

A *trade acceptance* is a draft ordering the customer to pay the specified amount, on a specified date, to the "order of" seller, prepared and signed by the seller. It is sent to the customer for him to sign his "acceptance" and return to the seller. When completed by the buyer's acceptance, it is a negotiable instrument. Accordingly it can be transferred by endorsement, and may be discounted by the seller at his bank or used as collateral for a secured bank loan. Trade acceptances are regularly used, as a matter of long-established custom, in certain lines of business such as the fur trade. Quite commonly, in other lines, a customer who for special reasons is given

---

* The 20 days during which the discounting buyer foregoes his credit privilege is slightly less than one-eighteenth of a year. On an annual basis, the saving to the buyer is therefore the 2 percent discount multiplied by 18.

a credit term longer than the regular one, is asked to sign a trade acceptance covering his purchase indebtedness.

A *promissory note* is a promise, signed by the debtor, committing him to pay the specified amount on a certain date to the "order of" the creditor. It, too, is a negotiable instrument. Promissory notes are regularly used to cover credit sales in the jewelry line and some other lines. They are also used, in lines which customarily base their credit extension on open book accounts, when credit is extended to an inferior risk on consideration of guaranty of his obligation by an acceptable guarantor. The buyer signs the promissory note; accommodation endorsement of the note by the guarantor constitutes the guaranty. Promissory notes are also customarily used when an account who cannot pay on his due date is given a specific extension of time.

The credit decision

A mercantile credit manager's decision whether credit terms should be given to a particular customer depends on two considerations: (1) the degree of credit risk that his company can or wishes to assume; and (2) the degree of credit risk represented by the would-be customer.

The degree of credit risk that a seller can assume depends primarily on the gross profit margin on which it operates; the narrower the margin the higher must be its standard of credit risk acceptability. Other considerations may also influence a seller's standard of credit risk acceptability. If a manufacturing company is operating at capacity and unable to satisfy the demands of all who would buy from it, it can raise its credit standards and sell only to superior credit risks. Contrariwise, a seller with excess operating capacity might sell to substandard risks on the reasonable theory that the extra bad debt loss would be more than offset by spreading overhead costs over a larger volume of production and sales.

The degree of credit risk represented by each would-be customer, which establishes whether he falls into the category of a seller's acceptable or nonacceptable risks, is determined by the so-called three C's of credit analysis—Character, Capacity and Capital.

Character analysis of a customer is usually directed at learning whether there are any episodes in his business history that indicate he is financially untrustworthy—any intimations that he has ever defrauded business creditors. A record of several bankruptcies followed by the establishment of new businesses with unexplained new capital resources would be looked upon by credit men as indication of a questionable moral risk. So would a record of several fires with substantial insurance recoveries, or reports from other suppliers that a purchaser persistently tries to take unearned discounts or falsely claims allowances for damaged goods or insufficient deliveries.

Capacity analysis of a customer is directed at determining how efficiently and successfully the business is operated or, in the case of new businesses, what experience a man has had in the line of business he is entering.

"Capital" analysis—the third "C" of credit analysis—is a misnomer. A credit manager is not interested merely in the bare capital position of a customer. He wants a full picture of the over-all financial situation. He wants to know the customer's net worth, and the relation of liabilities to assets. But he is also vitally interested in whether a buying concern has been operating at a profit or loss, whether it may be expected to make profit or incur loss, and how successfully it is currently meeting its business debts.

A large corporation in good financial condition, buying moderate amounts from a small supplier, may well be an acceptable credit risk for orders of any size that it would be likely to place with that supplier. But a small retail store might be deemed by some of its suppliers an acceptable risk only for limited amounts—say, up to $500. Larger balances would indicate either that the store was buying more than it should, or was failing to pay its obligations when due, so that their cumulated total was mounting. A credit manager must therefore decide, for many of his company's customers, not only whether they are generally acceptable credit risks, but also for what amounts they are acceptable risks—i.e., what *credit limits* should be assigned to them. Most credit managers assign credit limits to their companies' customers by crude, rule-of-thumb methods. They may establish arbitrary uniform amounts, such as $100 or $500, to all new customers in some general class, without regard to variations among these customers as to buying needs or financial condition. Or they may adopt an equally arbitrary principle of giving all customers credit limits equal to 10 percent of their net worths. There are analytical techniques, however, whereby individual credit limits can be carefully tailored to the varying buying needs and financial circumstances of customers. Utilization of these more scientific methods of determining credit limits is slowly growing.

Decisions of credit managers as to whether customers, or would-be customers, are acceptable credit risks and what their credit limits should be, cannot be static. With the cyclical upswings and downswings of general business conditions, seller circumstances that determine the general borderline of customer credit risk acceptability often change. So do the circumstances of the individual customers that establish them as acceptable or nonacceptable risks according to the seller's standard. A credit manager must constantly review the business position of his own company and of its customers. He must constantly anticipate what the circumstances of his customers may be in the near future and how their credit standing may be changed.

Sources of information

Mercantile credit decisions, to be sound, must be based on detailed and intimate knowledge of each customer's history, operations, and financial position. Mercantile customers do not submit credit applications, as individuals do, when seeking charge accounts or making installment purchases. But mercantile credit managers have access to other sources of information enabling them, when the amounts and risk involved warrant, to build up comprehensive pictures of their customers' current credit positions.

The first source of customer credit information to which most credit managers turn is a *mercantile agency.* There are a number of mercantile agencies that serve particular lines of business. The furniture trade has one, there is one for jewelry manufacturers, and one for paper product manufacturers. But there is also one mercantile agency, Dun & Bradstreet, that serves all lines and branches of business other than retailers.

Every two months Dun & Bradstreet issues a new edition of its *Reference Book* containing names and credit ratings of over 3,000,000 business units in the United States and Canada. Part of a page from this *Reference Book* is shown in Illustration 24–5. Dun & Bradstreet also prepares detailed reports on most of the companies covered by the *Reference Book.* These reports give the credit rating of the company, a synopsis or summary of its current credit position, a business history of the company and of its principals, a detailed description of its method of operation, the company's financial statements for the past three years, if they have been made available to D & B, and a tabulation of the company's credit relations with a representative selection of its suppliers. A 1-page D & B report on a small business unit is shown in Illustration 24–6; reports on large corporations may run to five or six pages. Subscribers to the Dun & Bradstreet service obtain, in addition to the *Reference Book* and the reports, supplementary notices on customers in whom they are particularly interested whenever any development, favorable or unfavorable, changes the credit picture of those customers.

A second invaluable source of credit information is *interchange* of ledger data between the credit managers of companies selling to the same customer. Credit managers have long realized that close cooperation, even between competitors, is absolutely necessary to effective credit analysis. Whenever a credit manager must decide upon the standing of a new customer, or whenever he has doubts upon the continued soundness of an old customer, he will endeavor to find out how that customer is buying from and paying to other suppliers. Provided he is willing to give the same information, he can expect the credit managers of the other suppliers to tell him: (1) how long their companies have been selling to the particular

1670 ROP–Bec MICHIGAN

ROPER ▲ Deering 13
Bk town Fitch
55 11 Becton Motor Co.........Ats 7 D+ 2
52 21 Beetle John C NR....Plbgsup 4 G 3½
53 92 Biggs E Baldwin...........Dg C 1½
58 12 Bourke George...........Rst F 3
59x13 Eaton's Cut Rate.....DrgSstn 2 E 3
22 51 Grable Hosiery Mill.......... D+1½
52 11 Healey Frank A.........Lbr 5 E 3
57 12 Hummel Oscar F.........Frn 5 F 3
22x92 Kennedy Mfg & Sales Co...Laces ★★
(See Detroit)
A 55 41 Ritter Emil F...........Sstn 0 L 4
54 41 Thrum Mrs Alice C.......Cnf 7 H 3½

ROTTERDAM ▲ Ellis 197
Bk town Pryor
76 21 Alcott Henry S..........Elcrp E 2½
39 63 Blum Pearl Button Co*........ —
(Br of Des Moines Iowa)
24 21 Cleveland William J.....Sawmll 2
A 54 12 Coombs Wilfred L.........Gr 0 G 3½
56 12 Eldredge Lawrence W....MBcl 7 E 2½
17 21 Farmer Richard.....PtgPprhg 7 G 3½
53 31 Lathrop 5c-10c-$1 Store.....4 F 3
20 41 Rotterdam Flour Mills Inc....... D+1½
65 61 Rotterdam Gardens........Bldr D 1½
75x34 Scott Geo NR.......TrrpBsmith G 3½
A 57 12 Seaton Charles..........Frn 0 F 3½
59 BA Seaton Herman...........Flor K 3½
53 93 Shaver John & Margaret....Gs 2 G 3½
53 92 Smith Jonathan NR.......Dg 7 J 4
58 13 Wadsworth C T NR.......Tav 9 —
57 13 Waters Orland E........Flrcvg Inv
56 21 Zeller W F J..........Wnwr 7 G 3½

RUBY (See Hickman)

RUSH LAKE 1,214 Forest 2
Bk town Brushville
53 93 Anders Theodore...........Gs E 2½
43 21 Andrews Clifford.........Buses D+2½
55 41 Lyman Edgar.............Sstn 7 G 3½
59 13 McGuire William W........Drg C 2
C 50 42 Nielsen Christopher......W&RGr D 2
54 12
58 12 Noble Herbert W.........Rst 2 H 3½
53 93 Norris Winfield K.........Gs 7 D 1½
54x12 Palmer's Filling Station & Store Inv
GrSstn

RYANSBURG 1,022 Wright 13
Bk town Francis
57 23 Alling & Campbell Inc....Radios C 2
52 51 Bronzini Anthony..........Hwr F 3
56 21 Jones Mrs Evelyn M........Wnwr F 3
58 12 Mitchell Archie...........Rst H 3½

SACKVILLE ▲ Ontario 13
SACKVILLE BK............................$85M
E Z Phillips Pr Bryan Townsend Cas
59 62 Alberts Thaddeus NR....HayGrn E 2½
59 HA Ballman Ahab J..........Gifts H 4
39 11 Bartlett Mfg Jewelers........8 C 2
42 12 Bluman Frederick NR.....Trkg B 1
24 43 Callahan John.........CgBoxes G 3½
17 51 Daume Oscar V.........Carptr 6 J 3½
C 52x11 Fairlee Lumber Co*..LbrHwr 4 C 2
59 52 Harris & Harris NR.....Spgg 4 —
A 59 13 Heller's.................Drg 0 F 3
17 11 Hood Alan O & Son Inc...Plbg 7 G 3½
HtgCntr
54 13 Hunt Norman C........GrMt 2 H 3½
55 41 Kling Everett J............Sstn 3
C 76 52 Lachlan Bruce B.........Bcyrp 8 G 4
54 13 Larimer Rose (Mrs Chas) & Chas 7 F 3
GrMt
59 HA Le Blanc Charles A........Gifts H 3½
52 51 McNulty Michael...........Hwr F 3
20 11 Mavis-Costello.........MtPkr 4 2

55 11 Country Center Motor Co Inc...3 C 1½
Ats
15 11 Crowell Andrew B.......GCntr 9 3
57 12 Cutter Furniture Co*.......... F 3½
A 17x61 Danberg Roofing & Sand Co....0 J 3½
53 92 Dawley Bros..............Dg ★★
(See West Branch)
72 31 Delmonico Photo Service Inc..7 F 3½
59 69 Dobbin F G..............Frmsup —
72 21 Dolan Sinclair L.........Clg 8 G 3½
42 12 Early & Duggin...........Trkg 2
72 62 Easter R R...............Mort F 3
56x21 Edgehill Warren O......WnCwr G 3½
C 76 41 Ellery Upholstery Co..........6 F 3
54 22 Farber Bessie (Mrs A).......Mt C 1½
55 11 Fristoe Ray Motors Inc...Ats 5 F 3½
55 31 Freer Raymond T Co......Atsup D 2
52 51 Frost Ray...............Hwr 9 F 2½
52 11 Furby Lumber Co*............ D+1½
17 43 Furby Marble & Granite Co..Cntr 2
54 12 George Paul..............Gr 7 K 3½
53 93 Gerard Oliver.............Gs 6 3
14 29 Gerstein Crushed Stone Co..... AA A1
(Br of Wooster Ohio)
55 31 Gibbert Godfrey L..........Tr J 3½
58 12 Gilmore Buffet..............3 G 3½
16 11 Gilson Construction Co..RoadCntr C 1½
C 53 31 Girnsy Co Inc.............Vs 7 E 2½
55x11 Graham Hill Motors.....AtsRp 8 2x
14 41 Gray Horace G & Sons.....Sand C 2
Gravel
54 13 Gray Otto P...........GrMt 2 H 3
17 11 Gray Samuel G Inc........Plbg Inv
15 11 Griffith Homer M.......GCntr 2 E 2½
27 51 Grifton Bros & Co.........Prtg F 3½
59 EA Heather Margaret Smyth (Mrs L) K 3½
M's
59 21 Hight William S.............Lq F 3
57 12 Hinckey Horace C Jr NR...Frn 7 E 2½
24 91 Milner Raymond.........Wood 4 —
Preserving
22 51 Milner William A NR....Hsymll E 2
17 81 Nickerson P O..WaterWelldrlg 6 K 3½
01 41 Osterhout William...PltyFarm 7 C+ 2
50 52 Post John & Lucy.......Darpdt F 3
59x13 Rackham Arthur & Co.....DrgLq G 3
20 81 Redcliff Ginger Ale Co Inc...... 1
17 99 Redcliff Rockwool Co*....Cntr 2 F 3
55 41 Samson's Service Station NR..7 G 3½
54 12 Tobey Samuel & Son......Gr 9 3
76 21 Turton Elliott Q........Elcrp 8 J 3½
56 62 Voos Hans Joseph........MSh E 2½
65 61 Voos William O.........Bldr 7 Inv
52 21 Winslow Herbert....HtgPlbgeqp F 3
56 21 Wolfson Benjamin & Rose.......8 G 3½
Wnwr

SANBORN 1,819 Deering 13
Bk town Weehauken
53 92 Bigley George S Jr.........Dg C 1½
58 12 Boswell J & Son...........Rst E 3
54 41 De Laval Henry A.........Cnf 2 G 3½
55 41 Dodds Layton P...........Sstn G 3½
20 31 Doolittle Bros.......CannedSfd —
50 42 Dundee Co-operative Sales Assn
Inc ....Gr C 2
(Br of St Cloud Minn)
59x13 Eddington Cut Rate...DrgSstn 9 E 3
75 38 Foster Paynter B.........Atrp K 3½
52 41 Franklin David C.........Elcsup G 3½
22 51 Gruber Hosiery Mill......... D+1½
59 71 Hamilton Miss Amber........Jly E 3
52 11 Hannon George W..........Lbr 5 E 3
58 12 Harley Louis J............Rst 8 F 3
57 12 Hubbell A Orson..........Frn 5 E 2½
53 93 Loomis George M...........Gs G 4
55x41 Mosher Nelson D......SsstnGr 7 F 3½
59 12 Penny Cut Rate..........Drg 7 D+ 2
(Br of Chicago Ill)
16 21 Perry Elihu E........EngrCntr C 2½
20 81 Pettyjohn Bottling Co......... D 1½
54 12 Thomas Arthur C...........Gr H 3½
75 38 Thomson Auto Service

17 6
50 4
17 1
58 1
54 2
54 2
58 1
C 72 6
52 2
55x4
15 1
28 7
57 2
59 F
50 6
52 4
76 3
53 3
54x2
15 1
C 56 2
72 2
58 1
54 2
50 Z
42 1
55 4
17x3
56 1
72 3
56 6
35 2
52 3
16 1
17 1
54 2
A 53 9
55 1
53 9
75 3
55 4
59xJ
56 1
56 2
27 3
54x2
54 2
20 3
55 4
35 4
55x4
54 1
17 1
58 1
59 1
SHE
1st N
Curtis
WES
Oral
54 1
23 5
C 17 6
57 1
58 1
24x2
57 2
17 3
59 7
72 3
59 1
22 5
59 6
A 58 1
56 1
50 V

EXCERPT FROM THE DUN & BRADSTREET *REFERENCE BOOK.* *Courtesy of Dun & Bradstreet.*

ILLUSTRATION 24–5

Dun & Bradstreet Report

RATING
UNCHANGED

SIC	NAME & ADDRESS		STARTED	RATING

59 12   KENT STORE

CD 13 NOV 4 19- N
DRUGS

1949   E 2

124 KENT ROAD
ST BERNICE MICH
CARLTON COUNTY

TRADE   DISC.
SALES $89,232
WORTH $22,901
EMPLOYS   2 P.T.

MILES GROSS, PARTNER
HANNAH (MRS MILES) GROSS, PARTNER

SUMMARY   SALES ARE INCREASING AND FINANCIAL CONDITION IS SOUND.

TRADE

HC	OWE	P DUE	TERMS			SOLD
2431	2000		2-10-30	Oct 21 19-	Disc	Over 3 yrs
300			2-10-30		Disc	Over 2 yrs to 6-59
250			2-10-30		Disc	Over 3 yrs
136	136		2-10prox		Disc	Over 3 yrs
75			2-10-EOM		Disc	Last sale 10-59
15			30		Ppt	Over 2 yrs

FINANCE

Statement Sept 30 19-

Cash on hand	$ 304	Accts Pay		$ 3,724
Cash in bank	1,872			
Mdse	14,450			
Total Current	16,626	Total Current		3,724
Fixt & Equip	9,913			
Deposits	86	NET WORTH		22,901
Total Assets	26,626	Total		26,625

Net sales from Oct 1 1958 to Sept 30 1959 $89,232; gross profit $26,181;
salaries and drawings of partners $6,732; net profit over and above salaries
and drawings of partners $3,457. Monthly rent $150 on a five year lease.
Fire insurance: Mdse $10,000; Fixt $7,000.
Signed Oct 20 1959 KENT STORE by Miles Gross, Partner
Received by mail. No accountant indicated.

-----0-----

Residential construction has stepped up in this section with the result that both sales and profits of this business have mounted steadily.
Part of earnings have been re-invested in the business every year to finance
its steady growth.
On Nov 4, 1959 Miles Gross stated that sales are now picking up slightly,
as is usual in the Fall. Some thought has been given to opening a second
store, he said, but so far he has not been able to find the right location.

OPERATION   Operates a pharmacy and soda fountain. Drugs and prescriptions account
for 50% of sales, with the remainder equally divided among fountain, sundries
and confectionery. Fixtures and a twenty-foot soda fountain are new. Both
partners are active and there are two employed on a part-time basis. LOCA-
TION: Rents first floor of a two story building in good condition. Store
measures about 20 x 50 feet. It is located in a residential section developed during the past ten years.

HISTORY   The style, "Kent Store" was registered by the partners on April 30, 1949.
This firm was formed April 1949. Starting capital consisted of $10,500
savings, a $3,500 loan from Teachers Credit Union, and a $3,000 loan from the
partners' families, making a total of $17,000. Loans have since been repaid.
Miles Gross, 41, is native born. He was graduated from Columbia College
of Pharmacy. He then was employed as a pharmacist by Wark Pharmacy and by
Ray Drug Co. until this business was started.
Hannah (Mrs Miles) Gross is 36. She was a school teacher prior to formation of this firm.
11-4-   (158 85)

A DUN & BRADSTREET REPORT. *Courtesy of Dun & Bradstreet.*

ILLUSTRATION 24–6

customer; (2) the date of the last sale to him; (3) how much the customer owes their companies; (4) how much of this amount is past due; (5) the terms of sale given to the customer; (6) whether he takes cash discounts, pays promptly, or is slow in his payments; and (7) any general remarks on his credit position.

In many cases a credit manager will obtain such interchange information by telephoning or writing to the credit managers of other companies that he knows sell to the customer. Credit managers of a related line of business in a large city may hold monthly luncheons at which they exchange these items of information about particular accounts. Finally, through the Interchange Service of the National Association of Credit Management, a seller's credit department may obtain a report on a customer, containing the information indicated in the preceding paragraph, which has been contributed by credit managers all over the country. A sample NACM interchange report is shown in Illustration 24–7.

A third source of credit information which credit managers find very useful is the *financial statements* of their customers. Most American business enterprises today accept the view that their suppliers are entitled to copies of their financial statements, and these are readily sent at the request of the suppliers' credit managers, usually on standardized forms provided by the supplier. There are techniques of statistical analysis which, when applied to financial statement data, disclose valuable information on a customer's financial stability and on the probability that he will or will not continue to be an acceptable credit risk.

In certain lines of business, other sources of information have proved to be helpful in credit analysis—sometimes even more helpful than the three mentioned above. Wholesalers' credit managers find that salesmen's reports on their retail customers are valuable. In special circumstances, a local lawyer's or bank's report on a customer may contain the one crucial item of information needed for a sound credit decision.

Many small business units, where the credit work is handled incidentally by a bookkeeper or some other individual with other responsibilities, tend to rely blindly on the ratings of Dun & Bradstreet or some other mercantile agency. Sound credit decisions can be reached, however, only by exploiting all available sources of credit information and painstakingly collating the factors so obtained into a comprehensive picture of each customer's credit position.

Collection

Sound credit decisions alone will not save a seller from bad debt losses. Indeed, sound credit policy often involves selling to customer groups for which some bad debt loss is probable, provided the proportion of such

FORM 6

NATIONAL ASSOCIATION of CREDIT MANAGEMENT
Credit Interchange Report

OFFICES IN PRINCIPAL CITIES

------------------------GROCERY CO   ---------------, IOWA   MARCH 17,19-
                                     ----------- COUNTY

The accuracy of this Report is not guaranteed. Its contents are gathered in good faith from members and sent to you by this Bureau without liability for negligence in procuring, collecting, communicating or failing to communicate the information so gathered.

BUSINESS CLASSIFICATION	HOW LONG SOLD	DATE OF LAST SALE	HIGHEST RECENT CREDIT	NOW OWING INCLUDING NOTES	PAST DUE	TERMS OF SALE	DIS-COUNTS	PAYS WHEN DUE	DAYS SLOW	COMMENTS
IOWA 306-409										
Fdp	6-58	2-61	135	35		2-10-30	x	x		
GenM	yrs	2-61	150			2-10-30	x			
Fdp	yrs	2-61	1347	490		2-10-30	x			
LOUISVILLE 307-699										
Fdp	8-58	1-61	24			2-10-30		x		
Tob	1958	1-61	451	107	57	2-10-30		x	20	Improving
MINNESOTA 307-560										
Fdp	1957	2-61	162			2-10-30	x			
Fdp	6-58	3-61	2270	2270		2-10-30	x	x	15	Improving
Fdp	yrs	1-61	4000			2-10-30	x			
NEW ENGLAND 307-670										
Fdp	1957	2-61	1260			2-10-30	x	x		
Fdp	6-58	2-61	813	517		2-10-30		x	10	Getting slower
CLEVELAND 307-404										
Fdp	7-58	1-61	327			2-10-30	x			Takes U/D.
OMAHA & NEBRASKA 307-249										
Fdp	2yrs	3-61	650	237		1-10-30	x	x	10	No change
Fdp	7-58	2-61	227			S/D.				
CHICAGO 307-1301										
Fdp	yrs	3-61	945	537	50	2-10-30		x	x	
Fdp	yrs	2-61	1705	800		2-15-30	x	x		
Bu 36 MJ				4993	107					

A NACM INTERCHANGE REPORT. *Courtesy of National Association of Credit Management.*

ILLUSTRATION 24-7

anticipated loss to sales for the group is less than the seller's gross margin of profit. Only by effective collection policy combined with sound credit policy can a seller achieve a maximum of profitable sales with a minimum of bad debt loss.

The cardinal rule of mercantile collection policy is "Get your money if possible, but keep the goodwill of your delinquent customers while doing it." Business customers are usually not as sensitive as retail customers, so mercantile collection procedures are generally more firm-toned than those of retail collection. But in mercantile collection, as in retail collection, the iron fist of payment demand should always be clothed in the velvet glove of courtesy and compliment.

Letters and telephone calls are the prime collection tools of the mercantile credit manager. To customers whose payments have not arrived after a fews days' or a week's grace beyond the due date, a credit manager first sends a brief "reminder" note. If this does not produce the customer's check, a sequence of letters and phone calls is started, spaced at two-week intervals or on some other suitable timing. Finally the customer is warned that his account will be collected by draft, or that it will be turned over to a collection agency or an attorney. If, in the course of such collection procedure, a customer writes to the seller's credit manager and gives some fair and reasonable explanation for the delay in payment, the credit manager will usually cooperate with the customer, giving him an extension or arranging some part-payment plan, provided he is assured of the customer's good faith and believes that the customer will eventually be able to clear his debt.

Giving an account to a collection agency or an attorney is usually a last desperate measure taken by a credit manager only if he has made up his mind that the customer is not worth retaining by his company. Collection agencies and attorneys are experienced in writing "tough" dunning letters or making dunning calls on the customer. These methods often get results where the gentler persuasion of a credit manager has failed, but it is not likely that a customer subjected to such dunning will subsequently bear any goodwill toward the seller.

Most credit managers prefer to write off as a bad debt any account from which a collection agency or an attorney has not been able to collect, rather than bring suit. The seller will get a judgment, of course, if his claim is valid, but the judgment is likely to be worthless, and the cost of the suit wasted. If anything can be salvaged from such a customer, the better course is usually to join with other creditors in a receivership or a bankruptcy action.

INDUSTRIAL INSTALLMENT CREDIT

Installment purchase of industrial equipment is gaining ground in industrial marketing. In a number of equipment lines, installment sales currently exceed outright sales.

When a company buys equipment on installment terms, it pays some fraction of the price, usually a third, at the time of purchase. Payment of the balance is spread over a period ranging from one to five years. Interest on the unpaid balance and a financing charge are usually added to the net price. As part of the purchase-sale transaction, the purchaser gives a series of promissory notes, dated for monthly or quarterly intervals, covering the full series of payments on balance, interest, and finance charges. For further protection the seller nearly always provides for a reversion of title to the equipment, through a conditional sales clause or a chattel mortgage, if the purchaser fails to maintain the agreed schedule of payments. Such reversion of title provides a legal basis for repossessing the equipment upon the purchaser's default.

Installment selling of equipment makes it possible for many small or under-capitalized enterprises to purchase needed equipment at times when their resources would not permit on-the-spot payment of the full price. Equipment so purchased commonly pays itself off through the additional earnings attributable to its use during the period of payment. Thus the industrial equipment market is made substantially larger than would be possible under strict cash or ordinary credit terms, to the advantage of the industrial equipment manufacturers as well as to the equipment purchasers. Sellers need no additional working capital when their equipment is sold on an installment basis, since finance companies will refinance equipment installment credit as described in Chapter 26, enabling sellers to obtain the unpaid balances on such sales as soon as the sales are consummated.

VOCATIONAL CONSIDERATIONS

Credit management, retail and mercantile, has come to be one of the business professions for which college men and women are sought and trained. It does not hold forth the lure of the occasional high "jackpot" compensations to which exceptional sales managers and advertising men can aspire, but its members generally enjoy good middle-bracket incomes, and have exceptional security in their positions. To a growing extent the position of credit manager in large corporations is becoming a stepping stone to the office of treasurer.

Credit managers are usually a quiet, reserved type with strong will power. For mercantile work their training, in addition to thorough grounding in the techniques of credit analysis and collection, should include a good basic knowledge of accountancy and some study of commercial law and businesss finance. Training for retail credit positions should include comprehensive courses on retail store operation.

REVIEW

1. Distinguish between charge account and installment credit. How do they differ in their economic effects?

2. What considerations guide a retail credit manager in approving the opening of a charge or installment account?

3. What sources of credit information does a retail credit man use on charge account and installment customers?

4. What is charge account "identification" and "authorization"?

5. Explain retail collection procedures.

6. Explain the following terms of sale: C.O.D., SD/BL, C.B.D., consignment, net 30, 2/10 net 30, E.O.M.

7. Explain cash discounts. Why do many sellers disapprove of them yet continue to offer them?

8. What is a trade acceptance? a promissory note? How common is their use in mercantile credit?

9. How do a seller's operating and financial circumstances affect its credit policy?

10. Explain the "3 C's" of mercantile credit.

11. What is a "credit limit"? How is it commonly determined?

12. From what sources can a credit man obtain information about a business customer? What sort of information is obtainable from each source?

13. How does industrial installment credit operate?

DISCUSSION TOPICS

1. What contributions does retail credit make to American marketing and to the national economy?

2. "Installment selling should be made illegal. It encourages consumer extravagance. It involves many individuals in constant debt. It adds an element to the cost of consumer purchases for which the purchasers receive nothing. It makes our economy more vulnerable to recessions."

3. "The activities of retail credit bureaus in collecting personal information on individuals, and embodying this information in reports available to business concerns, are a violation of personal privacy."

4. What contributions does mercantile credit make to American marketing and to the national economy?

5. Is business credit a right or a privilege? Is it "commanded" or "granted"?

6. How much dependence can be placed on a customer's financial statement? Even if it is dependable, what information useful to a credit manager, other than whether the customer was solvent at the conclusion of its last accounting year, could be derived from it?

7. Would you trust any information about a customer that you obtained from the credit manager of a competitor?

8. "Only by effective collection policy combined with sound credit policy can a seller achieve a maximum of profitable sales with a minimum of bad debt loss."

9. Would you be interested in a career as a credit manager?

PROBLEM 1

Welter's Cash Store in Peoria has prospered, and Mr. Welter is enlarging it and converting it to a department store with a "cash basement." The "upstairs store" will offer charge accounts and sell furniture and appliances on installment credit.

1. Will selling on credit affect the prices of the "upstairs store"?

2. How will the credit manager of the Welter store be able to determine which applicants for charge and installment accounts are acceptable risks?

3. Will he apply the same standards of acceptability in judging charge account and installment credit applicants? Explain.

4. How will clerks in the store know which customers, who want to take their purchases with them, have charge accounts?

5. How should the Welter credit manager handle the case of an installment customer who has bought a furniture suite on a "time" plan and, with half the payments made, is temporarily unable to continue with his payments because of illness in the family?

PROBLEM 2

Mr. Cooke has just succeeded Mr. Jones as credit manager of Bell Co., manufacturer of auto batteries and accessories. Bell Co. sells to service stations and auto supply stores on 2/10 net 60 terms.

What should Mr. Cooke do about each of the following policies and situations which he has inherited from his predecessor?

1. Bell Co. subscribes to the Dun & Bradstreet service on a basis which entitles it to the *Reference Book* and 50 reports (without extra charge) a year. Mr. Jones looked up the ratings of all new accounts in the *Reference Book,* and also checked the ratings of all old accounts to see if there was any change of rating upon receipt of each new edition of the *Reference Book.* If a new customer was given a "high" or "good" rating in the *Reference Book,* Mr. Jones would approve the order without drawing a report. If the rating was "limited" he would refuse the order. If the rating was "fair" he would draw a report. He also drew reports on old customers if Dun & Bradstreet lowered their rating at any time. He usually drew between 60 and 70 reports a year.

2. Mr. Jones wrote to every new customer requesting a copy of their latest financial statement if one had been prepared. He did this so that they would feel that the credit department of Bell Co. was

"on its toes." He did not bother to look at any of the statements he received, but filed them in the customer account file.

3. Mr. Jones felt that every manufacturer's credit department should "stand on its own feet." He never asked other credit departments about any Bell Co. customers, and refused to give any information about Bell Co. customers to other credit managers who telephoned or wrote to him.

4. If a customer failed to pay a bill on time, Mr. Jones would wait a month, then send a form letter which called the customer's attention to the "oversight" of nonpayment. If the bill was not paid during the next four weeks, a second letter would be sent warning that Bell Co. "would be compelled to take action" if payment was not made immediately. After three months, past-due accounts were turned over to a collection agency.

5. One customer, the Pecksniff Service Station, always takes its 2 percent cash discount although it does not pay until the end of the 60-day period, and sometimes delays payment beyond that time.

6. One customer, the Dombey Auto Supply Store, which has heretofore always paid promptly, has written to ask an extension of 60 days on $670 due next week. The letter says that payments for an enlargement of the Dombey store have left Mr. Dombey temporarily short of cash.

SUGGESTED READINGS

American Management Association, *Credit Department Organization and Operation,* Research Study No. 34, 1958.

Beckman, T. N., & R. Bartels, *Credits and Collections in Theory and Practice,* 6th ed, McGraw-Hill Book Co., New York, 1956.

Board of Governors of the Federal Reserve System, *Consumer Installment Credit,* Washington, D.C., 1957.

Chapin, A. F., & G. E. Hassett, *Credits and Collection Principles and Practice,* 7th ed, McGraw-Hill Book Co., New York, 1960.

Cole, R. H., & R. S. Hancock, *Credits and Collections,* Richard D. Irwin, Homewood, Ill., 1960.

Consumer Credit Conference, *Consumer Credit Today,* University of Illinois Press, Urbana, 1951.

Credit Management Year Book, National Retail Dry Goods Association, New York.

Credit Research Foundation, *Credit Management Handbook,* Richard D. Irwin, Homewood, Ill., 1959.

Flanagan, G. A., *Secrets of Successful Collection by Mail,* New York Voices Publishing Co., New York, 1954.

Foulke, R. A., *Current Trends in Terms of Sales,* Dun & Bradstreet, New York, 1959.

Foulke, R. A., *Practical Financial Statement Analysis,* 4th ed, McGraw-Hill Book Co., New York, 1957.

Irons, W. H., *Commercial Credit and Collection Practice,* 2d ed, Ronald Press, New York, 1956.

Kisselgoff, A., *Factors Affecting the Demand for Consumer In-*

stallment Credit, National Bureau of Economic Research, New York, 1952.

Little, J. D., *Complete Credit and Collection Letter Book,* 2d ed, Prentice-Hall, Englewood Cliffs, N.J., 1953.

Neifeld, M. R., *Trends in Consumer Finance,* Mark Publishing Co., Easton, Pa., 1954.

Phelps, C. W., *Retail Credit Management,* Official Textbook of the National Retail Credit Association, McGraw-Hill Book Co., New York, 1949.

Schwartz, R. J., & A. M. Schiffer, *Credit and Collection Know-How,* Fairchild Publications, New York, 1953.

Shultz, W. J., & H. Reinhardt, *Credit and Collection Management,* 3rd ed, Prentice-Hall, Englewood Cliffs, N.J., 1961.

Wallace, H. A., *Starting and Managing a Small Credit Bureau and Collection Service,* Small Business Administration, Washington D.C., 1959.

Wood, J. L., *Better Sales Through Credit,* Vantage Press, New York, 1954.

PERIODICALS: *Consumer Finance News, Credit and Financial Management, Credit Currents, Credit Executive, Credit World, Time Sales Financing.*

CHAPTER 25

TRANSPORTATION AND THE TRAFFIC OPERATION

A bushel of wheat on a Kansas farm would have little value if it could not be moved to a Minneapolis miller, nor would the flour milled in Minneapolis have much value if it could not be moved to bakers in Philadelphia, New Orleans, and elsewhere through the country. Danbury (Conn.) is a hat manufacturing center because its hats can be shipped in every direction to hundreds of wholesalers and thousands of hat stores. The creation of *place utility*—the moving of goods from locations where they can not be used to other locations where there are users who want and will buy them—is one of the important contributions of Marketing to the national economy. The agencies of freight transportation that create this place utility are considered facilitating Marketing institutions, and analysis of their utilization by the sellers and buyers of goods is a phase of the study of Marketing.

FREIGHT TRANSPORTATION AGENCIES

There are five classes of freight transportation agencies providing basic shipping facilities: (1) railroads, (2) motor freight carriers, (3) waterway carriers, (4) pipe line companies, and (5) air carriers. Of the 1,278 billion ton-miles of freight carried in 1959, the railroads accounted for 46%, motor freight carriers for 22%, pipe lines for 17%, and waterways for 15%. Air freight is less than 1% of the total.

In addition, there are a number of freight transportation agencies which, while using some equipment of their own, depend primarily upon the shipping facilities of the agencies mentioned above. The more important of these supplementary freight transportation agencies are: (1) express companies, (2) the parcel post service of the U.S. postal organization, and (3) freight forwarding companies.

Railroads

The railroad web of the United States embraces 274,000 miles of "first-line" track, operated by more than a thousand carrier companies. Over its rails move multi-ton shipments of ores, grains, and metallurgical products, hundred-weight and pound shipments of manufactured products, and ounce shipments of high-value items.

The railroads cannot match the low costs of water-borne transport where time is not important, or of the pipe lines for free-flowing fluids. They cannot meet the speed of air freight, or the short-haul flexibility of motor freight. But, as traffic figures indicate, for the major part of America's internal commerce the railroads hold decisive advantages over all the other transportation agencies combined.

One reason for the continued dominant position of the railroads in the transportation field is the wide variation and adaptation of their services to meet individual shippers' needs. In the matter of speed, there is a range from the "drag" or "tonnage" trains—also called "slow" or "dead" freight—which are operated on indefinite schedule whenever sufficient tonnage accumulates to warrant movement, to scheduled freight "flyers" for particular perishable items which, on certain lines, have faster schedules than the crack passenger "flyers." Refrigerator cars are available for perishables, livestock cars for animal transport, tank cars for fluid cargoes. "Store-door delivery and pick-up" of small shipments was introduced in recent years. By paying demurrage charges, shippers can obtain temporary storage at terminals.

Waterway carriers

Waterway carriers offer a low-cost means of shipping bulky products that have low value in relation to weight, where slow movement does not matter. The eastward Great Lakes movement of grain and ores, and the return movement of coal, are an important and valuable contribution to our transportation economy. Buffalo is still an important milling center, for example, because of the availability of low-rate water transportation of wheat from Duluth to Buffalo. The Mississippi River system, including the Mississippi, Ohio, Monongahela, Tennessee, Illinois, Missouri and other tributaries, is a great natural highway for low-cost movement of such bulk products as coal and coke, sand and gravel, ore, iron and steel, grain, sugar, and petroleum products.

Shipments between coastal ports can move by coastal and intercoastal boat lines. Their charges are generally lower than competing railroad or motor freight transport.

Motor freight

Over 70 million trucks are operated on the nation's 3 million miles of highways and streets. Approximately seven-eighths of these trucks are engaged in intracity or local carrying. The other eighth are used for over-the-road transport.

On long hauls, and in the carriage of bulky low-value freight, the motor truck cannot compete with the railroads. But it can operate in three important fields closed to the railroads: (1) local deliveries, by wholesalers to retailers and by retailers to consumers, (2) "drive-in" delivery of animals to stockyards, and (3) the gathering of farm products and distribution of goods in rural areas. Furthermore, because of the flexibility of motor truck routing, motor freight transport has definitely established itself in several fields previously served exclusively by the railroads. Principal among them are: (1) the shipment of perishable farm commodities such as dairy products, truck crops, and fresh fruits and vegetables from areas surrounding cities into the city markets; and (2) small-load shipments of manufactured articles for distances up to 500 miles, where store door pick-up and delivery is wanted, or where overnight delivery is desirable.

The motor truck is commonly viewed as a competitor of the railroad, and the railroads can definitely point to valuable areas of short-haul traffic that they have lost to the motor freight companies. A large part of motor freight traffic, however, is complementary to railroad traffic, serving origins and destinations that the railroads do not reach, and much is directly contributory to railroad traffic. The major business of many local motor freight companies is collecting or distributing shipments that will move or have moved over the railroads. Indeed, so important is this contributory function of motor carriers that many railroads have acquired their own truck fleets for pick-up and delivery service. A recent development in the complementary relationship between railroads and motor trucking companies is "piggy-back" haulage, whereby loaded truck trailers are carried on railroad flat-cars for the long-haul stretches of their runs.

Air freight

Air freight is a newcomer in the field of transportation agencies. As yet, in terms of ton-miles, it is of minor importance in the economy. Rates are high, and weather conditions may cause flights to be postponed. Air freight is expanding rapidly, however, and is already an important factor in the distribution of certain products that have high value in relation to weight, or where speed of delivery is vital.

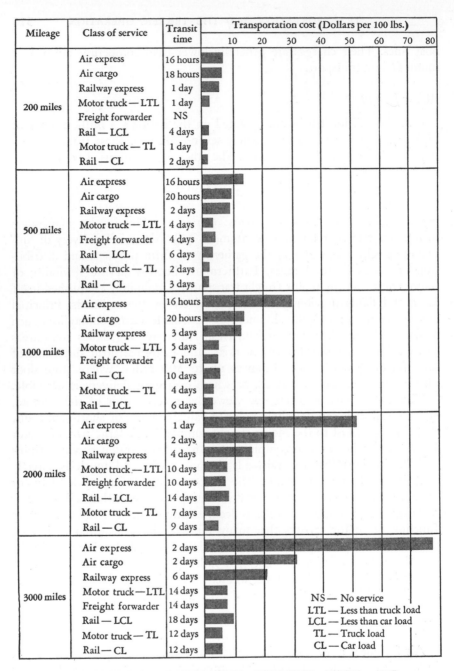

APPROXIMATE COMPARATIVE SHIPMENT TIMES AND RATES FOR VARIOUS CLASSES OF CARRIERS. *From R. C. Colton & E. S. Ward, Practical Handbook of Industrial Traffic Management (The Traffic Service Corporation, Washington D.C., 1959), p. 4.*

ILLUSTRATION 25–1

Parcel Post

The parcel post service of the U.S. postal system provides a convenient intermediate-cost method of shipping small packages. Store door delivery, but not pick-up, is provided; the delivery service includes rural free delivery. Shipments may be made C.O.D. Rates are based on a combination of weight and distance considerations; for weights under 70 lbs. they are generally lower than those of other transportation agencies. Air parcel post delivery is available at substantially higher rates. One drawback of the system is that the government will insure a package, upon payment of a moderate fee, only up to $200, and additional insurance through other agencies is difficult to arrange.

The postal system has its own light trucks for local parcel post deliveries, but uses railroad and airline facilities for nonlocal shipments.

Express

Express freight shipments are handled by Railway Express Agency, a nationwide organization owned and operated by the railroads. Its shipments are carried in cars handled on passenger train schedules and usually attached to passenger trains. For distances over 300 miles express shipments usually move faster than railroad or motor freight. Free pickup and delivery service is provided within specified zones. Packages may be sent C.O.D. and may be insured up to full value. Express rates on heavy shipments are generally higher than railroad and motor freight rates. They may, however, run lower on packages under 70 pounds, since the rates of these carriers are generally calculated on hundred-pound units.

Railway Express Agency, like parcel post, offers an air express service at higher rates.

Freight forwarders

Freight forwarding companies operate on the difference between carload and less-than-carload railroad freight rates (explained later in this chapter). They receive LCL consignments from shippers, and charge them the railroad LCL rates—or slightly lower or slightly higher rates. They combine these consignments into carload shipments, on which they pay the railroads the lower carload rates. Because of carload grouping of LCL shipments to a single destination, packages shipped through a freight forwarder often move faster than if handled on an LCL basis by the railroad. Moreover, the freight forwarder gives store-door pick-up and delivery and other service. These two considerations make the freight forwarder an important transportation agency for the many shippers whose deliveries must be on a less-than-carload basis.

Legal classification of transportation agencies

The law makes a three-fold classification of transportation agencies— (1) common, (2) contract, and (3) private—which cuts across the institutional classification presented above.

A *common carrier* is one that holds itself out to the general public as prepared to transport property, in accordance with stated conditions, for stated rates of compensation. Nearly all railroads, most domestic water carriers, all interstate and most intercity motor freight carriers, some air freight lines, the Railway Express Agency, and all freight forwarding companies, are common carriers.

A common carrier has four responsibilities: (1) to provide the necessary facilities for performing its type of transport service, and to perform such service for all who ask for and are prepared to pay for it; (2) to make safe delivery of goods entrusted to its charge, subject to the limitation of inability arising from acts of God and certain other circumstances recognized by the law; (3) to treat all customers without discrimination; and (4) to charge a reasonable price, and only a reasonable price, for its services. These responsibilities are enforced by federal and state administrative agencies—in the case of the railroads, motor freight carriers, express service, and freight forwarders, by the federal Interstate Commerce Commission and the state railroad and public utility commissions; in the case of air freight, by the federal Civil Aviation Board; in the case of waterway carriers other than those operating on inland waterways, by the Maritime Commission in the U. S. Department of Commerce.

A *contract carrier* is one offering transportation service only on the basis of individual contracts or agreements. Many motor truckers and some air freight carriers belong to this category. United Parcel Service, which in many cities delivers goods purchased from department stores and other retailers to their customers, is an outstanding example of a contract carrier. Such contract carriers operate subject to restrictive federal and state law, but are not bound by the four responsibilities and the governmental control indicated above for common carriers.

A *private carrier* is one that transports its own goods. The thousands of manufacturers, wholesalers, and retailers that make deliveries in their own trucks are private carriers with respect to such transport activity. They are subject only to ordinary state and local police control.

FREIGHT RATES

The heart of the American transportation problem, from the viewpoints both of economic significance and of business traffic management, is the level and structure of the freight rate schedules—particularly those of the railroads, since they have become the standards by which the rates of the other transportation agencies are measured.

Economic significance

The mere existence of transportation facilities is not enough to assure distribution of a product, or to assure a manufacturer that he can reach wide profitable markets, or to assure a region that it can develop a sound economy based on its agricultural, mineral, or manufacturing output. In all three cases the transportation costs—the freight rates—which are included in the prices charged to the purchasers of the goods, or which must be added to the prices paid by them, may be the crucial determinant of success or failure.

California citrus fruits, and apples from Washington, for example, find a major market in eastern seaboard cities because the charges for shipping them across the continent are low enough that, when subtracted from the prices these fruits command in season in the eastern markets, a fair profit remains for the growers. Manufacturers considering the location of a new factory must take into account, among other factors, the relative shipping costs from alternative locations to their anticipated markets, and sometimes the relation of alternative locations to *in-transit* privileges.

The long-term trend of railroad freight rates was downward until 1916. The average carload ton-mile charge for 1891–95 was .886 cents; in 1916 it was down to .719 cents. Railroad freight rates rose rapidly during World War I, declined again during the 1920's, 1930's, and early 1940's to an average of .932 cents per ton-mile in 1942. The rising costs of the 1940's and early 1950's led to another series of freight rate increases; during the 1950's the average ton-mile charge varied around 1.45 cents. However, even though railroad freight rates have doubled during the past half-century, so has the general wholesale price index. In effect, on a constant purchasing power basis, railroad freight rates have remained fairly stable. If allowance is made for the tremendous improvements in railroad freight service through this period, there has been a significant decline in "real" freight costs.

This long-term decline in "real" railway freight costs has had many favorable effects upon the American economy. In some cases it has helped to hold down retail prices. In other instances it has widened practicable markets for local or regional products, adding to the choice of goods available to consumers and increasing markets and profits for producers. It has widened the areas of direct price competition between distant manufacturers, to the advantage of buyers in the areas affected.

Railroad freight rate determination and control

Railroad freight rates are proposed originally by the railroads and submitted to the Interstate Commerce Commission (or, in the case of intrastate rates, to the appropriate state commissions) for approval.

A basic factor influencing railroad freight rate making is the atmosphere of mixed monopoly and competition in which the railroads currently operate. Under authorization of the Transportation Act of 1920, and with the fostering approval of the ICC, the railroad lines of the country are tending to integrate into a score or so of large "systems." While two or more of these railroad systems may have certain terminal points in common, and compete for traffic between such terminal points, within most of the territory served by a system it is likely to be free of immediate competition from other railroads. But while competition among the railroads themselves may exercise only slight influence on their freight rate policy, some railroads face sharp competition from waterway carriers for important categories of bulk freight. And all railroads must meet the competition of motor carriers for the profitable carriage of many classes of high-value manufactured goods.

This mixture of monopolistic and competitive factors would result, were it not for rate control, in a very confused and arbitrary rate structure. Most railroad managements of today take an enlightened view on rate issues. For a short-sighted monopolistic policy of charging "what the traffic will bear," they have substituted long-range principles of fostering the economic development of the territories they serve. They are inclined toward moderate rates and rate reductions that will build up traffic to the maximum their facilities can handle, and look for their over-all profit to a low margin on large traffic volume rather than to high margins on low volume. To meet unrestrained competition, however, they might have to cut some classes of rates to levels that would barely cover direct operating costs, and they would necessarily seek compensation by raising other classes of rates not affected by competition. Such a mixed pattern of freight rates would discriminate violently among classes of goods, and among particular localities. It would certainly be detrimental to the best economic interests of the country. Freight rate control by the ICC and by the state railroad and public utility commissions provides an ordered pattern of rates that substantially (1) protects shippers from extortionate and discriminating rate charges, (2) protects the railroads and other carriers from throat-cutting competition, and (3) balances with some degree of equity the relative freight burdens on different classes of commodities and among various sections of the country.

Railroad freight rates for any sort of shipment between any two points

are always quoted at so many cents or dollars *per 100 lbs.* Four factors *
enter the determination of the charge per 100 lbs that a shipper has to pay
for any particular shipment: (1) distance and terminal factors, (2) the
"classification" to which a shipment belongs, (3) whether carload or less-
than-carload shipment is involved, and (4) special services.

Distance and terminal factors

The actual costs to a railroad of *moving* any shipment tend to be proportional to the distance involved. In addition, there are *terminal* costs of
loading and unloading which remain more or less the same regardless of

FREIGHT TARIFF NO. 60-A   FROM NEW YORK

FROM Stations shown on pages 9 to 82 taking Rate Basis

TO Stations shown on pages 83 to 147 taking Rate Basis:	Albany . . . . .N.Y.	Batavia (G1 to G17) . . .N.Y.	Binghamton . . . .N.Y.	Croghan. . . . .N.Y.	Elmira (G1 to G55) . . .N.Y.	Geneva (G1 to G27) . . .N.Y.	Glens Falls. . . .N.Y.	Gloversville . . . .N.Y.	Hudson . . . . .N.Y.	Malone . . . . .N.Y.	Middletown . . . .N.Y.	Mineola. . . . .N.Y.	Montauk. . . . .N.Y.
	APPLY RATE	BASIS	NUMBERS(For	rates	see	pages	594	to 613)					
WISCONSIN													
Appleton	167	139	156	174	152	147	176	176	173	169	176	187	202
Clyman Jct	164	135	155	171	149	144	172	173	168	166	175	184	199
Dodgeville	169	140	158	175	153	149	178	178	175	169	179	191	207
Fond du Lac.	167	139	156	174	152	147	176	176	173	169	176	187	202
Green Bay.	160	132	147	167	145	142	168	167	165	163	168	179	195
Janesville	162	132	152	168	147	142	171	172	167	163	172	184	199.
Madison.	163	133	152	169	147	142	172	172	168	163	173	185	200
Marinette.	153	124	142	160	138	133	162	162	158	155	164	175	190
Milwaukee.	153	124	142	160	138	133	162	162	158	155	164	175	19C
Monroe	166	138	156	173	152	146	175	176	172	167	176	188	204
Oconto	160	132	147	167	145	142	168	167	165	163	168	179	195
Plymouth	160	132	147	167	145	142	168	167	165	163	168	179	195
Shoboygan.	153	124	142	160	138	133	162	162	158	155	164	175	190
Watertown.	158	129	147	165	143	138	167	167	164	160	168	180	196

EXCERPT FROM "FREIGHT TARIFF NO. 60–A." *Courtesy of
Trunk Line Association.*

ILLUSTRATION 25–2

the shipment distance. An equitable freight rate system should take both
of these costs into account. The basis rate schedule authorized by the ICC
for each freight rate territory does so; it is calculated as a per-mile rate to
which fixed terminal rates are added. So while railroad freight rates increase with the distance of the shipment they do not increase proportionately. Because of the factor of a fixed terminal rate, the rate *per mile* for
railroad freight shipments declines as the distance increases.

Railroad freight rates are not quoted to shippers in terms of per-mile

* A possible fifth factor is *demurrage.* This is a charge for leaving carload shipments
in a freight car longer than the two "free" days allowed for unloading.

distance rates plus fixed terminal rates. Instead, each railroad calculates a "basis rate" (per 100 lbs) between every two stations on its lines. Regional groups of linking lines consolidate these individual-line calculations into cross-reference tables, published in books called *Tariffs,* that enable a shipper to ascertain quickly the basis rate for shipment from any station to any station. An excerpt from a *Tariff* volume is shown in Illustration 25–2.

It is obvious that if a shipment moves a long distance from its origin to its ultimate destination, but with one or more stop-overs for various purposes en route, the freight charges will be considerably lower if the trip can be considered a single movement instead of two or more separate movements. In three cases the railroads permit a series of interlocking freight movements to be treated as a single, unbroken movement in determining their freight charges:

1. Fruits, vegetables, cotton, and certain other commodities may be shipped in carload lots from their original loading places to specified "diversion" points. At these points they may be inspected and diverted to other consignees, or to different destinations, or by other routes, than those originally specified. In spite of these changes, the shipments are charged only the "through" rates from loading place to new destination, plus a small extra charge. Such an arrangement is called a *diversion privilege.*

2. A similar *reconsignment privilege* allows low "through" rates to be applied to carload shipments which are billed to an original destination and then, without unloading, are ordered on to a new destination.

3. Under the *in transit privilege,* low "through" rates (plus a small extra charge) are applied to various categories of goods which, in carload shipments, have their through trips broken at intermediate points for storage or processing. One key requirement for allowance of the *in transit* privilege is that the continued movement for the freight after its stoppage at any intermediate point must be in the same general direction as the movement to the stoppage point. For example, a company collects dried meat scraps from New York City butchers, ships them in carload lots (36,000 lbs) to its plant at Trenton (N.J.) where they are stored and processed into poultry feed, some of which is shipped to a distributor in Wilmington (Del.). If there were no *in transit* privilege, the company would have to pay a $.40 rate (per 100 lbs) from New York City to Trenton, and a $.32 rate from Trenton to Wilmington—a total freight cost of $259.20 per carload. On an *in transit* arrangement, the company pays the $.41 New-York-to-Wilmington rate plus a $.09 *in transit* charge —a total freight cost of $180.00 per carload.

Classification

Railroad men, shippers, and regulatory bodies all agree that there should be differentiation among commodities as to freight rates, in relation to bulk and other considerations, charged for their transport. At least seven major factors are generally recognized as having a bearing upon this rate differentiation: (1) weight of the commodity per cubic foot, with special attention to cases of extraordinary size, shape, or weight; (2) value of the commodity in relation to its weight; (3) liability of the commodity to loss or damage from pilferage, breakage, leakage, spontaneous damage, or decay; (4) likelihood that the commodity may damage other freight; (5) competition and commercial necessity; (6) the volume of traffic produced by the commodity; and (7) provision of special services such as refrigeration or care of live animals.

UNIFORM FREIGHT CLASSIFICATION 5   5860–6345

Item	ARTICLES	Less Carload Ratings	Carload Minimum (Pounds)	Carload Ratings
5860	ALUMINUM—Concluded: Turpentine or latex cups, with or without aprons or hangers: Not nested nor flat, LCL, in barrels or boxes; CL, in packages, or loose, braced in car.......	100	14,000R	77½
	Nested or flat, LCL, in barrels, boxes or crates; CL, in packages, or loose, braced in car...	85	30,000	55
6770	Ashes or cinders, coal, LCL, in bags, barrels or boxes; CL, in bulk or in packages.............	50	50,000	17½
6775	Ashes or cinders, coal, mixed with crushed or ground brick, in bulk in open top cars.............		50,000	17½
6780 6790	ASPHALT, PITCH OR TAR: Asphalt (asphaltum), natural, by-product or petroleum, liquid, other than paint, stain or varnish, in containers in barrels or boxes, or in metal cans in crates, in pails, or in bulk in barrels; also CL, in Package 593 or in tank cars, Rule 35..	55	40,000	20
6800	Asphalt (asphaltum), natural, by-product or petroleum, solid, see Note 1, Item 6801, loose or in packages; also CL, in tank cars, Rule 35..	55	40,000	20
6801	Note 1.—Asphalt or pitch, the melting point of which is 140° or less, Fahrenheit, as determined by the Ball and Ring test in water or by the ½-inch Cube test in water, when shipped LCL, must be in metal cans in boxes or crates, or in steel pails not exceeding 3½ gallon capacity, or in steel barrels, or in tight wooden barrels, or in No. 1 wooden barrels, or in No. 2 wooden slack barrels with tongued and grooved staves. Such barrels must have heads at both ends.			
6810	Pitch, brewers', pine or rosin, in barrels, boxes, double bags or 4-ply paper bags, or in solid mass in Package 591; also CL, in tank cars, Rule 35...	55	40,000	22½
6820	Pitch, lignin, dry (dehydrated or powdered lignin liquor), in cloth or paper bags, or in barrels..	55	40,000	22½
6830	Pitch, montan, in bags...	55	40,000	22½

For explanation of abbreviations, numbers and reference marks, see page 196 and last page of this Classification; for packages, see pages 480 to 564.

208

EXCERPT FROM UNIFORM FREIGHT CLASSIFICATION NO. 5.
Courtesy of J. P. Hackler, Chairman, The Western Classification Committee.

ILLUSTRATION 25–3

Rate differentiation on the basis of the above seven factors has been accomplished by the ICC by classifying all commodities that may be shipped by railroad into over a hundred categories. The rate (per 100 lbs) for each category reflects a percentage of the basis rate stated in the *Tariff*. The percentage range is from 400 percent to 13 percent. Higher percentages apply to high-value manufactured items, packed in less-secure containers, and shipped in less-than-carload lots. Lower percentages apply to low-value raw materials and agricultural products shipped in carload lots. As indicated in Illustration 25–3, the freight rate for small shipments of antenna enclosures is four times the basis rate while for carload shipments of aplite rock it is $17\frac{1}{2}$ percent of the basis rate. ICC classifications for all commodities that might be shipped by railroad are published in a 500-page volume titled *Uniform Freight Classification,* which is kept up to date by frequent supplements; Illustration 25–3 is an excerpt from this volume.

Frequently a railroad wishes to charge less than the standard classification rate for a particular commodity. The reason may be that with respect to that commodity the railroad must meet low-rate or special-service competition from some other type of carrier. Or a freight-saving may be necessary for production of a particular commodity to develop in a certain area, and the railroad will realize a long-run gain from such development. If the ICC or other regulatory body concerned approves, such lower commodity rate may be put into effect.

CL and LCL rates

If commodities are shipped in carload (CL) lots (interpreted as a specified minimum weight for each commodity), they are classified in lower-rate categories than when they are shipped in less-than-carload (LCL) lots. The saving may amount to as much as three-quarters of the freight charge. As shown in Illustration 25–3, if anti-freeze compound is shipped in partially jacketed metal cans, the rate is 125 percent of the basis rate for LCL lots, but only 35 percent for CL shipments. This differential is so substantial that, as noted earlier in this chapter, the whole business of freight forwarding operates on it.

The railroads offer several intermediate-type shipping arrangements that enable large shippers to take advantage of the economy of CL shipping, even though their actual consignments are in LCL lots. A group of shipments of a particular commodity to a single consignee at a single destination, if they can be consolidated into a carload lot, moves at the CL rate for the commodity. The single consignee may be an agent of the shipper, and undertake delivery of the separate items in the carlot to the various customers for whom they were destined. A *mixed car* arrangement permits a shipper to make up a carload of different commodities for a given destination, and pay on the basis of the highest CL rate applicable to any commodity included in the shipment. Large appliance manufacturers such as General Electric make extensive use of mixed-car shipments to their dealers. It is this mixed-car provision that gives freight forwarding companies, previously mentioned, the primary reason for their existence. Under *pool car* arrangements, a shipper can make up a carload of shipments to two or more consignees along a route and obtain CL rates on the entire shipment to the first consignee's destination.

Special services

Special services provided by a railroad, such as provision of special cars or "flyer" service, are either taken into account in the official classification, or are compensated by special charges.

Other carrier classifications and rates

Motor freight common carriers, domestic water carriers, and air freight common carriers have established freight classifications similar to the railroad freight classifications. Their charges, within the framework of these classifications, are likewise based on weight and distance. The classifications of motor freight carriers and their charges have been subject to control by the ICC since 1935. Classifications and rates of interstate coastwise and Great Lakes common carriers have been subject to control by the Maritime Commission since 1936. Rates of internal waterway common carriers are not subject to federal control. Air freight charges are controlled by the Civil Aeronautics Board.

THE BILL OF LADING

The bill of lading is the key document of most transportation operations. In all cases it performs two vital functions: (1) it constitutes a receipt by the carrier for the goods delivered by the shipper to it; (2) it constitutes a contract between the shipper and the carrier for the transportation of the shipper's goods, fixing the obligations and rights of the two parties, and establishing the factual basis for the carrier charge. If the bill of lading is a negotiable or "order" bill, in addition to the above two functions it performs the third one of acting as an instrument of title and transferring title in the shipped goods from the shipper to the consignee or such parties as he transfers the bill to by endorsement.

The form and content of bills of lading were standardized by the federal Bills of Lading Act of 1917. An example of a "straight" or nonnegotiable railroad bill of lading is shown in Illustration 25–4. The wording of a negotiable railroad bill of lading is identical with that of the straight bill except that the word "ORDER" replaces "STRAIGHT" in the title, there is a sentence requiring surrender of the original copy of the bill before the carrier delivers the property, a line is provided for the name of parties to be notified of the shipment, and the consignment line reads "Consigned to order of . . . ." The fine print on the reverse side of both forms of bills of lading is the statement of the contractual law of the liabilities and rights of shipper and carrier. Modifications of, additions to, or waivers of, these provisions are invalid.

Bills of lading are usually made out by the shipper in triplicate. The second of the three copies goes to the carrier as its record of the shipping

---

(Form T. D. 6)

(Uniform Domestic Straight Bill of Lading, adopted by Carriers in Official, Southern, Western and Illinois Classification Territories, March 15, 1922, as amended August 1, 1930 and June 15, 1941.)   1st SHEET

UNIFORM STRAIGHT BILL OF LADING   Shipper's No._____

ORIGINAL—NOT NEGOTIABLE   Agent's No._____

Western Maryland Railway Company

RECEIVED, subject to the classifications and tariffs in effect on the date of the issue of this Bill of Lading,

at _____, 19 ____

from_____

the property described below, in apparent good order, except as noted (contents and condition of contents of packages unknown), marked, consigned, and destined as indicated below, which said company (the word company being understood throughout this contract as meaning any person or corporation in possession of the property under the contract) agrees to carry to its usual place of delivery at said destination, if on its own road or its own water line, otherwise to deliver to another carrier on the route to said destination. It is mutually agreed, as to each carrier of all or any of said property over all or any portion of said route to destination, and as to each party at any time interested in all or any of said property, that every service to be performed hereunder shall be subject to all the conditions not prohibited by law, whether printed or written, herein contained, including the conditions on back hereof, which are hereby agreed to by the shipper and accepted for himself and his assigns.

(Mail or street address of consignee—For purposes of notification only.)

Consigned to _____

Destination _____ State of _____ County of_____

Route _____

Delivering Carrier_____ Car Initial _____ Car No. _____

No. Packages	DESCRIPTION OF ARTICLES, SPECIAL MARKS, AND EXCEPTIONS	*WEIGHT (Subject to Correction)	CLASS OR RATE	CHECK COLUMN	
					Subject to Section 7 of conditions, if this shipment is to be delivered to the consignee without recourse on the consignor, the consignor shall sign the following statement:
					The carrier shall not make delivery of this shipment without payment of freight and all other lawful charges.
					(Signature of Consignor.)
					If charges are to be prepaid, write or stamp here, "To be Prepaid."
					Received $_____ to apply in prepayment of the charges on the property described hereon.
					Agent or Cashier.
					Per_____
					(The signature here acknowledges only the amount prepaid.)

*If the shipment moves between two ports by a carrier by water, the law requires that the bill of lading shall state whether it is "carrier's or shipper's weight."
NOTE—Where the rate is dependent on value, shippers are required to state specifically in writing the agreed or declared value of the property.
The agreed or declared value of the property is hereby specifically stated by the shipper to be not exceeding

_____ per_____

Charges Advanced:

$_____

_____ Shipper.   _____ Agent

© · Per_____   Per _____

Permanent postoffice address of Shipper_____   1

A NONNEGOTIABLE RAILROAD BILL OF LADING. *Courtesy of Western Maryland Railway Company.*

ILLUSTRATION 25–4

contract. The third copy is kept by the shipper as his record. In the case of straight bills, the original copy may also be kept by the shipper, for any purpose to which he may put it. But, in the case of order bills of lading, the original copy, which legally transfers title in the goods from the shipper to the consignee, must be sent to the consignee, or to someone who will deliver it to the consignee, since it must be presented to the carrier at desination to obtain release of the shipment.

Most freight is shipped on straight bills of lading. Negotiable bills are used in three cases:

1. Carload lots of fruits, vegetables, cotton, and other items may be shipped to brokers or agents, who seek customers for the shipments while the goods are en route. These brokers or agents utilize the privilege of diversion or reconsignment to have the shipment forwarded to the customers they locate. The bills of lading provide for original consignment to the "order of" the shipper, with the brokers or agents named as the "notify parties." When endorsed to the ultimate customers by these agents or brokers, the bills of lading effect the necessary transfer of title to the customers.

2. A consignee of slow freight, particuarly of grains moving by waterway carrier, may wish to borrow upon the security of the shipment while it is en route to him. A negotiable bill of lading provides him with an instrument of title which banks will accept as security for a short-term loan until arrival of the shipment. Hence shipments of this sort commonly move on negotiable bills of lading.

3. A negotiable bill of lading enables a seller to make C.O.D. shipments by carriers which do not perform collection service. The bill of lading, together with a sight draft for the amount involved, is sent to a bank or agent of the seller in the consignee's city. The consignee is notified that he may obtain the bill of lading, without which the carrier will not release the shipment to him, by paying the bank or agent the amount involved. This is called SD/BL shipment.

TRAFFIC MANAGEMENT

Every seller of merchandise, except a cash-and-carry retailer, must somehow or other arrange for delivery of the items sold to the purchasers. This making provision for delivery constitutes the "traffic" operation—an essential element of marketing management for most companies.

Where common or contract carriers are utilized for deliveries, traffic management involves: (1) selecting the best carrier for each delivery, and sometimes for incoming shipments; (2) freight charge calculation; (3) packing, marking, weighing, and otherwise preparing merchandise for shipment; (4) cooperating with the sales and production departments so that deliveries may be made in carload, pool car, or mixed car-lots, in order to take advantage of freight charge savings involved in such shipment; (5) preparing shipping papers; (6) arranging insurance on shipments; (7) expediting "rush" shipments; (8) tracing delayed or lost shipments; (9) arranging car supply; (10) in the case of companies with their own sidings, supervising loadings and unloadings on such sidings; and (11) handling claims. Where companies operate their own truck fleets for receiving local shipments and making local deliveries, traffic management also involves maintenance and operation of these truck fleets.

Selecting a carrier

A seller frequently has a choice of carriers in planning a shipment. For small shipments there is always parcel post, nearly always express, and often one or more freight forwarders. For certain combinations of points of origin and destination, there may be a choice between two or more railroads. There is often a choice among several motor freight carriers. Air freight or water freight may be a possibility.

The first step in selecting a carrier is to determine what choice there is among railroads, motor freight carriers, water carriers, air freight carriers, and freight forwarding companies. This step is facilitated by the existence of a series of "guides"—books that list carriers and their routes, with key-number and cross reference systems that permit quick identification of carriers serving a particular community. There is a "guide" covering all the railroads of the country, another for motor freight carriers, another for water carriers, one for air carriers, and a consolidated *Leonard's Guide* that covers all classes under a single cover.

Having determined all the carriers that could be used for shipping to a particular destination, the traffic manager must then select the one that offers the best combination of services and charges in relation to the shipment involved. Among the factors he must take into consideration are:

1. *Speed and special services.* Where speedy delivery or a special service is essential, cost must often be a secondary consideration. Speed is the basis for the very existence of air freight. Motor freight may save a day in comparison with railroad shipment. One railroad may offer "package car" service for LCL freight, or run a "fast" freight to a certain destination, while a competing line does not. Provision by a railroad or motor freight carrier of car or truck refrigeration may be the crucial consideration for a shipper selecting a carrier for perishable food items.

2. *Freight charges.* The charge for making a certain shipment to a specified destination differs according to the class of carrier employed. And as between several railroads or several motor freight carriers serving a given destination there may also be some variation in charge in conse-

quence of special commodity rates or because, although they all have a uniform distance rate basis for their charges, their routes may result in an appreciable distance difference. If speed or some special service is not an important consideration, freight shipments are likely to go to the carrier making the lowest charge.

3. *Carrier reliability.* Some carriers build up reputations for high dependability with respect to train or truck schedules, or care in handling fragile freight, or reasonableness in settling claims. A traffic manager will often ship by such a carrier, in preference to competing ones, even where its freight charge is slightly higher. Contrariwise, if a carrier has acquired a bad reputation, it will often be passed over in favor of a competitor with a slightly higher charge.

Freight charge calculation

A traffic manager is constantly calculating freight charges for two purposes: (1) to guide him in choice of carriers for his shipments, or for shipments to his company; (2) to enable the sales department to set F.O.B. destination prices and quote delivery costs to customers and prospects.

The first step in freight charge calculation is to establish the possible carriers that may be used by means of the *Guides,* as explained above.

The second step is to determine the basis rates (per 100 lbs) between shipping point and destination for the possible carriers. This is done by using the *Tariffs* published by individual carriers or by groups of carriers. The *Tariffs* generally present basis rates in cross-reference "to-and-from" tables.

The third step is to establish the classification to which the shipped commodity belongs. This is done by reference to the *Uniform Freight Classification* for railroads, and the *National Motor Freight Classification.* These publications list the freight classifications for all commodities, according to the manner of their shipment, as percentages of the basis rate, as shown in Illustration 25–3.

The fourth step is to multiply the basis rates for the particular shipment, as determined for the various possible carriers, by the classification percentage determined in the third step, to obtain the actual rates (per 100 lbs) for the particular shipment by the various possible carriers. This can be done by actual multiplication, or a traffic manager can use cross reference tables usually included in the *Tariff* volume.

The final step is to multiply the carrier rates for the specific shipment by the weight (in hundreds of pounds) of such shipment.

> *Example:* A manufacturer of anti-freeze compounds located in Batavia, N.Y., wishes to determine the freight charge for shipping

1,000 one-pound cans of the compound by rail to a customer in Madison, Wis. The cans are packed "jacketed."

The railroad *Guide* indicates several combinations of lines he could use to reach the destination. Next, he refers to the *Tariff* published by the Trunk Line Tariff Bureau, a tariff association to which all these lines belong. As indicated in Illustration 25–2, for all these lines there is the same basis rate for shipments to Madison—$1.33 per 100 lbs.

The *Uniform Freight Classification* volume indicates that his shipment falls into Class 85 (see Illustration 25–3)—i.e., the rate on the anti-freeze compound shipped as he intends to ship it is 85 percent of the basis rate.

He could calculate his freight rate by multiplying $1.33 per 100 lbs by 85 percent. By referring to the cross-reference table at the back of the *Tariff* volume, he finds his calculation already performed for him. The freight rate for his shipment to Madison is $1.13 per 100 lbs. The charge for his 1,000 lb. shipment will be $11.30.

Traffic departments and agencies

Large business organizations find that the savings that result from expert traffic management warrant large traffic departments with skilled "rate clerks." When such a department is established to handle all the traffic functions associated with deliveries, it usually also does traffic analysis for incoming shipments, and directs deliveries by the company's suppliers.

Many small businesses place their deliveries blindly with parcel post, express, some freight forwarding company, or one or two motor freight companies with which they have long-established relations. The result is often excessively costly or inefficient delivery service. A number of "traffic agencies" have been established which, for a service charge, advise small and medium-size businesses on the best carriers and routes for their deliveries.

REVIEW

1. What are the major classes of freight transportation agencies? What services or advantages does each offer?

2. What is a common carrier? What are its responsibilities? To what control is it subject?

3. What control is there over freight rates? What agencies exercise this control?

4. What is a "basis" railroad freight rate? How do distance and terminal factors affect basis freight rates? What is a carrier "tariff"?

5. What is the "diversion" privilege? the "reconsignment" privilege? the "in transit" privilege?

6. What are the freight rate classifications?

7. Explain CL, LCL, mixed car, pool car.

8. Explain the legal character, provisions, and procedures of bills of lading.

9. What functions does a manufacturer's traffic department usually perform?

10. When several carriers are available to deliver at a particular destination, how does a traffic manager go about selecting the specific one to be used?

11. How can a traffic manager calculate in advance the cost of shipping to a particular destination by each of several carriers serving such destination?

DISCUSSION TOPICS

1. "Highway construction and maintenance has been a major governmental subsidy to the motor freight industry. Fairness requires that the federal and state governments similarly subsidize the railroads. The lowering of freight rates resulting would so stimulate American business that the subsidizing governments would find their grants returned to them through increased collections from business and personal income taxes."

2. In what ways may the pattern of freight rates be important to individual manufacturers? to regions of the country? to consumers?

3. Is there any justification for the tremendous differentials between CL and LCL rates for most commodities?

4. Could there be any circumstances under which a packaged flour manufacturer located in Cincinnati, and selling in the Middle Atlantic area through food brokers without storage facilities, might improve his deliveries or save on freight costs through: (a) CL shipments, (b) reconsignment privilege, (c) *in transit* privilege, (d) pool car shipment, (e) mixed car shipment?

5. What means of freight transportation would the traffic manager of a large clock manufacturer located in Buffalo, N.Y. specify for the following incoming and outgoing shipments: (a) coal for power fuel, (b) sheet metal for the clock parts, (c) replacement of a broken part of a key machine made by a manufacturer in California, (d) return of a clock sent in for repair under the manufacturer's guarantee, (e) regular shipments to dealers in towns up to 100 miles distant, (f) shipments to a general merchandise warehouse near New Orleans from which deliveries are made to dealers in the Far South?

6. Would you be interested in a career as a traffic manager?

PROBLEM

L & V Co., a manufacturer of industrial chemicals located in Cleveland, has customers throughout the eastern United States. It prices F.O.B. destination. It sells to over a hundred customers around Chicago through several brokers in that city. It sells to several hundred customers in the Detroit, New York, and Boston areas through manufacturers' agents who maintain stocks taken on consignment. Contact with customers in other areas is maintained by the company's own salesmen.

Up to now L & V's liquid chemicals have all been shipped in cask-shaped carboys of various sizes and made of metals and other materials suitable to the chemical nature of the contents. Solid chemicals have been packed in cylindrical cans.

Shipping has heretofore been handled by the stock room. Most shipments have been made by railroad, the routes established on the advice of the freight clerks in the Cleveland New York Central R.R. station. These shipments have been all LCL, since no individual order up to now has amounted to a full carload. A few short-haul shipments are made through a motor freight company, which arranges any transfer shipments to territories which its routes do not serve.

L & V Co. has just hired a traffic manager.

1. What responsibilities should be given to him?

2. What can he do to cut freight costs on the company's shipments (with the possibility that some of these freight cost savings may be passed on as special discounts to customers) along the following lines:

    a. packing of the company's products;

    b. special shipping arrangements to customers in the Chicago area, provided the brokers there persuade these customers to collaborate;

    c. special shipping arrangements to the Detroit, New York, and Boston agents, provided they collaborate;

    d. special shipping arrangements to other customers, if the L & V salesmen persuade their customers to collaborate;

    e. possibly more economical or more satisfactory shipping routes.

SUGGESTED READINGS

Bigham, T. C., & M. J. Roberts, *Transportation,* 2d ed, McGraw-Hill Book Co., New York, 1952.

Bryan, L. A., & G. A. Wilson, *Air Transportation,* Prentice-Hall, Englewood Cliffs, N.J., 1949.

Bryan, L. A., *Traffic Management in Industry,* Dryden Press, New York, 1953.

Colquitt, J. C., *The Art and Development of Freight Classification,* National Motor Freight Traffic Association, Washington, D.C., 1956.

Colton, R. C., & E. S. Ward, *Practical Handbook of Industrial Traffic Management,* 3rd ed, Traffic Service Corp., Washington, D.C., 1959.

Daggett, S., *Principles of Inland Transportation,* 4th ed, Harper & Bros., New York, 1955.

Fair, M. L., & E. W. Williams, *Economics of Transportation,* rev ed, Harper & Bros., New York, 1959.

Frederick, J. H., *Commercial Air Transportation*, Richard D. Irwin, Homewood, Ill., 1954.

Grossman, W. L., *Fundamentals of Transportation*, Simmons-Boardman Publishing Corp., New York, 1959.

Hudson, W. J., & J. A. Constantin, *Motor Transportation—Principles and Practices*, Ronald Press, New York, 1958.

Ingraham, J. C., *Modern Traffic Control*, Funk & Wagnalls, New York, 1954.

Lewis, H. T., and others, *The Role of Air Freight in Physical Distribution*, Graduate School of Business Administration, Harvard University, Cambridge, 1956.

Locklin, D. P., *Economics of Transportation*, 4th ed, Richard D. Irwin, Homewood, Ill., 1954.

Morton, N., & F. H. Mossman, *Industrial Traffic Management*, Ronald Press, New York, 1954.

Mossman, F. H., & N. Morton, *Principles of Transportation*, Ronald Press, New York, 1957.

Nicholson, J. L., *Air Transportation Management*, John Wiley & Sons, New York, 1951.

Polakoff, A. A., *Basic Study in Traffic Management*, Kenmore Press, Baltimore, 1952.

Taff, C. A., *Commercial Motor Transportation* (1955); *Traffic Management: Principles and Practices*, 2d ed, (1959), Richard D. Irwin, Homewood, Ill.

Van Meter, T. W., *Industrial Traffic Management*, McGraw-Hill Book Co., New York, 1953.

Wilson, G. L., *Marketing and Traffic Management* (1950); *The Principles of Freight Traffic* (1956), Traffic Service Corp., Washington, D.C.

Wilson, G. L., *Transportation and Communications*, Appleton-Century-Crofts, New York, 1954.

Wolfe, T., *Air Transportation—Traffic and Management*, McGraw-Hill Book Co., New York, 1950.

PERIODICALS: *Traffic World.*

CHAPTER 26

MARKET FINANCE AND RISK MANAGEMENT

Marketing is only one of the phases of business that requires financing. Risk management, too, is involved in other aspects of business besides Marketing. But a very substantial proportion of the financing and risk management with which business must concern itself is attributable to its Marketing activities—to such an extent, indeed, that the over-all subjects of current financing and risk control are often discussed as though they were exclusively Marketing operations. In the analysis that follows, only those elements of finance practice and risk control that relate specifically to Marketing activities will be covered.

MARKET FINANCE MANAGEMENT

If the goods that a manufacturer produces, or that a distributor buys, could be sold for cash simultaneously with their production or purchase, there would be no problem of market finance. But for nearly all business enterprises there is a time lag, often a considerable one, between production or purchase of goods and their sale. And, since most mercantile sales and a large proportion of retail sales are made on credit terms, there is commonly a further time lag between sale and receipt of payment. Funds have to be paid out for the production or purchase of goods long before funds are received from their sale. From what sources may these funds to cover the carrying of inventories and accounts receivable be obtained? Of the available sources for such funds, which are the most economical? These two questions frame the problem of market financing.

Few business units supply the working capital needed to finance their marketing operations entirely from equity capital provided by the investment of their owners. In most lines of business, an enterprise is considered soundly and conservatively financed—by the so-called "acid test" and "current" ratios of credit analysis—if in its period of minimum seasonal activity it has current debt outstanding no greater than its cash plus outstanding accounts receivable, and no greater than one-half of its total current assets. At the peak of its marketing activity, where wide seasonal variation is involved, a solvent enterprise may conduct most of its current operations with funds derived from outside sources. A retailer selling on long-term installment credit may "refinance" all of the credit it extends to its customers.

The six external sources of funds for current market financing are: (1) sellers' mercantile credit extensions; (2) commercial bank loans; (3) "discounting" of accounts receivable by factors, finance companies, and commercial banks; (4) "refinancing" of consumer installment credit by finance companies and commercial banks; (5) financing of manufacturers' inventories by factors and of automobile dealers' inventories by finance companies; and (6) domestic bankers' acceptances.

Sellers' mercantile credit extensions

Extension of mercantile credit by sellers to buyers, as one of the regular Marketing operations, was analyzed in Chapter 24. From the viewpoint of the buyer such sellers' credit is a form of outside financing that enables a company to purchase an inventory of raw materials, or of goods for resale, at times when its own equity capital is insufficient to finance such purchase.

Mercantile credit is definitely not expected to finance a buyer's credit extensions to its customers. If a buyer needs external financing of its accounts receivable, some other source than the mercantile credit extended by its suppliers should provide it.

Commercial bank loans and discounts

Commercial bank loans are made for many purposes other than market financing, but a major proportion of them are attributable, directly or indirectly, to this reason.

Bank loans to finance marketing operations are made for the following four reasons: (1) some manufacturers must produce inventories of seasonal goods long in advance of the period of their sale, and require external funds to bridge the time gap between cost payments and eventual sales receipts; (2) some businesses must make heavy seasonal credit extensions to their customers, and require external funds to bridge the time gap between sale and receipt of payment; (3) some businesses that buy on mercantile credit terms involving generous cash discounts can profit by arranging bank loans to enable them to take advantage of the cash discounts, thereby in effect substituting bank credit for the mercantile credit they could otherwise obtain to help carry their inventories; (4) in some distributive fields—e.g., the grain trade—it is customary to pay sellers on cash or very short credit terms, so that the buyers must depend altogether on bank credit, rather than on mercantile credit, to carry their inventories.

Bank loans to finance marketing operations may be unsecured or secured. No calculation of the total of *unsecured* loans for marketing purposes is available, but the volume is substantial. A bank makes an unsecured marketing loan to a manufacturer or distributor on the same basis that a supplier extends mercantile credit—the credit risk of the applicant as represented by the character and business capacity of the principals of the company, and its financial position. The credit standards of commercial banks are usually much stricter, however, than those of mercantile suppliers, so that many a buying firm that would be an acceptable credit risk to its suppliers may not be able to qualify for an unsecured bank loan.

Secured bank loans for market financing are made upon the basis of four kinds of collateral: (1) liquid investment securities, (2) commodity paper, (3) customer paper, and (4) third party guaranties or endorsements.

A manufacturer or distributor whose current assets include *liquid investment securities,* such as government bonds, listed corporate stocks and bonds, or readily marketable over-the-counter issues, can pledge these with its bank as security for a mercantile loan. The bank always insists on some "margin" between the current market value of the stocks or bonds and the amount of the loan granted. Minimum requirements for such "margins" on certain classes of securities are established by the Board of Governors of the Federal Reserve System. Should the borrower be unable to repay the loan at maturity, or after one or more renewals, the bank can sell the pledged securities without difficulty and reimburse itself for the amount of the loan from the proceeds of the sale.

Commodity paper—i.e., negotiable warehouse receipts and negotiable bills of lading for goods moving by marine transport or slow freight—are a common form of bank loan security in the distribution of many basic raw materials. The commodities most frequently covered by such warehouse receipts and bills of lading are staples such as cotton, grain, hides, and sugar. There has been some development of bank lending on the security of receipts for warehoused manufactured goods. Should a bank loan secured by commodity paper be defaulted, the bank can sell the warehouse receipt or bill of lading carrying title to the goods through the appropriate commodity exchange or to some dealer, and thus cover itself. As in the case of loans based on liquid investment securities, banks insist on "margins" between the market value of the goods represented by warehouse receipts and bills of lading, and the amount of loan extended on the security of such commodity paper.

Customer paper—i.e., promissory notes and trade acceptances given by customers on credit purchases—have always been a recognized type of security for bank marketing loans. A bank may *discount* such paper, when it has been endorsed by the seller, by advancing the face value of the note or trade acceptance less prepaid interest, or some fraction of the face value, and subsequently reimbursing itself upon collection of the note or trade acceptance. More commonly, banks have their borrowers negotiate regular loans on the basis of the borrowers' own promissory notes, with the customer paper pledged as security.

If a bank client is not an acceptable risk for an unsecured loan and has no other acceptable collateral to offer as security, it may still be able to negotiate a loan for marketing purposes if it can find some third party, approved by the bank as an acceptable credit risk, to guaranty its loan or to make an "accommodation endorsement" on the borrower's note to the bank. Such *third party guarantees and accommodation endorsements* are quite common when a financially weak borrower is a subsidiary, parent company, or affiliate in a corporate integration that includes one or more strong members.

The *borrower's promissory note* is the *basic instrument* of both unsecured and secured bank loans. A note for a secured loan usually embodies an extensive pledge agreement.

Practically all unsecured bank loans for marketing purposes, and many secured marketing loans, are for specific time periods—30, 60, 90 or 120 days—with the possibility of renewals. Interest on these time loans is deducted in advance, on the discount principle. Some secured marketing loans are arranged on a demand basis, and the borrower can repay them within a few days, or keep the loan outstanding for months, according to his convenience and requirements. Interest on these demand loans is usually charged to the borrower on a monthly basis.

The procedure for securing a bank loan for marketing purposes usually embodies six steps. (1) A principal or officer of the borrowing firm confers with a loan officer at his bank. He states the amount of loan or line of credit * he desires. (2) He submits his company's latest financial statement, trial balance, and possibly its budget to the loan officer. (3) The loan officer questions him about the purposes of the loan and matters perti-

---

* A "line" of credit is requested when a borrower anticipates that he will have to borrow at intervals over a period. Neither he nor the bank wants the trouble of a separate application and credit inquiry on the occasion of each borrowing. Therefore he requests authorization to borrow, at his discretion and timing, up to a specified maximum amount or "line." Once a "line" is authorized, the borrower negotiates each successive loan up to the cumulated maximum of the "line" by simply presenting his note for the amount to the bank cashier.

nent to the credit position of the company, and makes notes for the client's loan file. (4) Later, the loan officer makes inquiries through regular credit channels as to the company's credit standing, and analyzes any collateral security that has been offered. (5) The loan officer submits the application and his findings and conclusions to the bank's loan committee, which approves or rejects the loan.* (6) If the loan is approved, the borrower is notified that, upon signing the requisite promissory note and depositing the agreed collateral, the amount of the loan will be credited to his account.

Discounting accounts receivable

As was indicated in Chapter 24, promissory notes and trade acceptances are employed as the regular instruments of mercantile credit in very few lines of business. Most sellers receive such notes and acceptances only from inferior credit risks. Their good credit risks are usually represented by open book accounts. If a bank or other financial institution is to lend upon the security of a client's receivables, a selection from these open book accounts would usually constitute better collateral than any notes or trade acceptances that the client might have received from poorer risks. Paradoxically, until the 1930's the commercial banks refused to make this kind of secured loan and, except for a few lines of business regularly served by factors, any company that borrowed on the security of its accounts receivable from any other source was presumed to have displayed bad faith toward its trade creditors. During the 1930's, however, the commercial banks changed their views on this issue, after the way had been paved by factors, and devised procedures for discounting (i.e., lending on the security of) clients' accounts receivable. Currently commercial banks account for over a third of accounts receivable discounting.

Factors ** are specialized financial institutions engaged in buying or discounting accounts receivable and lending on the security of inventories. Some of the present factoring houses are over a century old. They started as selling agents in the textile field, with financing of their principals as an incidental service. In time the minor activity became major, and they dropped their selling activities. They also extended their financing services from the textile trade to the paper, chemicals, furniture, and some other trades. With the expansion of accounts receivable discounting since the 1920's, many new factoring houses have been established.

To "discount" an account receivable is to lend to a seller on the security

---

* In many large banking units, the loan officers are empowered to approve, on their own authority, loans under specified amounts.

** The factoring concerns now under consideration should be distinguished from "cotton factors," who are primarily commission houses for cotton planters and dealers, and only secondarily financing agents. Note also that many of the recently established factoring concerns call themselves "finance companies" instead of "factors."

of an amount owed by his customer, carried as an account receivable in the seller's books. Since there is no written instrument signed by the customer involved in an open book account receivable, as there is in the case of a promissory note or a trade acceptance, factors and banks had to establish special security procedures. One is "notification" discounting, whereby the customer whose account has been discounted by the seller is notified of the transaction and ordered to make his payments directly to the discounting institution. Where the customer is not so notified, and will at the due date pay the seller, the seller (or an officer of the selling company) is made a trustee of the factor or bank with respect to the discounted account. His failure to turn the customer's payment over to the factor or bank in repayment of the loan would constitute embezzlement with a jail sentence as penalty.

The factor's or bank's discount of an account receivable may be made "with recourse" or "without recourse." In the former case, if the seller's customer fails to pay the account which is the security for the discount, the bank or factor requires the seller to make good the deficiency. If the discount is "without recourse," the discounting institution bears the loss. Because of the greater risk to the discounting institution, the charge for "nonrecourse" discounting is higher than for "recourse" discounting. Factors do considerable "nonrecourse" financing, banks hardly any.

Even where accounts receivable are discounted on a "recourse" basis, the discounting institution should make a very thorough credit analysis of its clients' customers and lend only on the accounts of good credit risks. For "nonrecourse" discounting this is vital. It is not surprising, therefore, that the credit work of the factoring houses is the most expert in the mercantile field. Many of their clients, as a consequence, operate without any credit departments whatsoever, and sell only to customers approved by their factors.

Refinancing consumer installment credit

An automobile dealer or store selling on the installment plan that "carried" all of its customers' notes until they were fully paid would need much more capital, relative to its sales, than a cash dealer. The alternative preferred by most installment sellers is to "refinance" their sales—i.e., to obtain loans secured by the promissory notes and chattel mortgages or conditional sales liens signed by their customers. Over 95 percent of automobile installment sales and nearly half of other retail installment sales are so refinanced.

As in the case of accounts receivable discounting, the commercial banks were originally chary of undertaking installment sale refinancing. This type of financial operation was developed during the second decade of the

Twentieth Century by a number of *finance companies* * that had previously been active in commercial accounts receivable factoring.

By the close of 1959 there were some 6,000 finance company offices, with over $10 billion in credit extensions outstanding. Three giants— General Motors Acceptance Corp., Universal C.I.T. Credit Corp., and Commercial Credit Corp.—dominated the field, accounting for over half

Billions of dollars

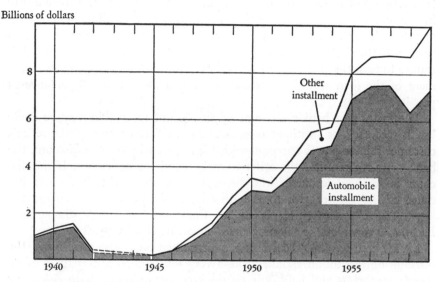

CLASSES OF FINANCE COMPANY CREDIT OUTSTANDING,
1939–1959
Source: *Survey of Current Business*
ILLUSTRATION 26–1

the refinancing credit advanced by finance companies at the close of 1959. While the primary business of finance companies is refinancing retail installment sales, particularly automobile sales, they also do some refinancing of installment purchases of industrial equipment, and some compete with commercial banks and factors in discounting mercantile accounts receivable.

With the feasibility of consumer installment credit refinancing established by the pioneering work of the first finance companies, commercial banks also undertook this service. They currently account for two-fifths of automobile refinancing credit and for two-thirds of other installment refinancing credit.

Refinancing of installment sales is very similar to discounting of mercantile accounts receivable, except that in the former the refinancing or-

* These "sales" finance companies should be distinguished from personal finance companies which lend to *individuals* on the basis of third party guarantees and other forms of security. It should not be forgotten that many of the newer factors call themselves "finance companies."

ganization obtains as security for the loan both a written instrument signed by the customer and a right to repossession (through the chattel mortgage or the conditional sale lien) of the sold item, and that the credit inquiry which must be made is into personal credit instead of mercantile credit. Practically all of the refinancing of automobile dealers' installment sales by finance companies is done on a notification basis. Indeed, it is customary for the notes and chattel mortgage signed by the car buyer to be made out directly to the finance company. Many stores now put installment selling of home appliances also on a notification basis, with payments made to the finance company instead of to the store. Some part of the refinancing of consumer installment purchases other than automobiles, however, is non-notification, with the sellers acting as trustees of the finance companies with respect to the customers' payments. The finance companies take over the chattel mortgages signed by the purchasers, or the sellers' liens under conditional sales contracts, so that in case of noncompletion of payments they can repossess. Automobile purchase refinancing and some other consumer installment refinancing is done "without recourse"—the finance company assumes all the credit risk. Otherwise this refinancing is usually "with recourse."

Borrowing upon inventory

As indicated previously, a bank may accept as loan security receipts for goods stored in a public or field warehouse. This does not help a would-be borrower whose inventory is not warehoused. There are two cases, however, where a business can borrow upon nonwarehoused inventories. Factors will make advances to manufacturer clients on their inventories, to enable them to make favorable purchases of raw materials or produce heavy advance seasonal inventories of finished products. Finance companies lend to automobile dealers on the security of their floor stocks of new cars. In both cases, the lending organization protects itself by establishing the borrower in a trustee relationship.

Domestic bankers' acceptances

Domestic bankers' acceptances are an indirect method of utilizing bank credit to obtain current market financing, available to certain lines of business. A grain merchant, for example, may wish to finance the storage of wheat in a grain elevator. He pledges his negotiable warehouse receipts for this grain to a bank. The bank, for a small charge, authorizes him to draw drafts against it up to an agreed total (less than the current market value of the stored wheat by the amount of the current "margin" for loans on such commodity paper). The dealer draws a series of drafts, usually in round figure amounts, for this total, and presents them to the bank for its acceptance—the bank's signed promise, on the face of the drafts, to pay them when due. So accepted, these drafts find a ready market on a discount basis (i.e., they are bought at prices less than their face values by the amount of the interest charge at the current market rate), as gilt-edge short-term investments. The accepting bank itself may buy them, or it may sell them for the borrower's account to other banks or financial institutions. At the due dates of the acceptances, when the bank must pay them, the wheat dealer makes balancing payments to the bank. Since the current discount rate on bankers' acceptances is usually substantially lower than the interest rate on bank loans, the wheat dealer may effect considerable saving on his financing costs.

MARKET RISK MANAGEMENT

Risk of loss is not peculiar to the marketing aspects of business. It is inherent in every phase and function of every business. Not only may stored goods deteriorate or be destroyed by fire, or a price decline produce an inventory loss, but a fire or explosion may destroy a factory, or machine troubles or a strike may interfere with production, or a corporation's investment in the shares of other corporations may shrink in value.

Certain classes of business risk arise primarily from Marketing operations, however. Some of these risks can be avoided by some of the business units subject to them. In many cases complete avoidance of a market risk is not possible; at best it may only be *reduced* by one means or another. Minimizing various market risks is considered one of the Marketing operations.

The generally recognized market risks are those pertaining to: (1) market volume, (2) the physical aspects of inventories and goods in transit, (3) prices of stocks of goods, and (4) payment for goods sold on credit. The avoidance and minimization of these risks constitute Market Risk Management.

Market volume risk

Because practically all businesses involve overhead costs not related proportionately to production or sale, they are subject to the rule of the "break-even point." For every product turned out by a manufacturer and given a specific price, there is a certain sales volume that must be achieved, or else its production and sale will involve the manufacturer in loss. Every wholesaler and retailer must achieve some particular total sales volume before his business can begin to earn a profit.

Here then is the first and most fundamental of marketing risks—that sales volume may never reach the break-even point for a product or for a distributive business, or that after an initial period of profit sales volume may fall below the break-even point. Failure to achieve the break-even level of sales for a product or for total sales means definite loss. Furthermore, where such failure is not anticipated—and it rarely is—excessive inventories are likely to accumulate. Such inventory accumulation increases the vulnerability of the enterprise to market risks of the second and third categories.

There are many possible reasons—most of them weaknesses of marketing policy—why market volume for a manufacturer's product or for a distributor's total sales may fall short of the break-even point. (1) Product design may be poor, either absolutely or relative to other competing items. (2) The buying judgment of a distributor may be faulty, so that he offers what the market does not want, and fails to offer what it does want. (3) Pricing policy may be at fault; prices may be set so low that no reasonable physical volume of sales could cover costs, or they may be set so high that the product or distributor is "priced out of the market." (4) Because of inefficiency, unit production costs or overhead costs may be so high that they compel the setting of prices too high for a competitive market. (5) Excessive advertising, selling, transportation, and other distribution costs, like excessive production and overhead costs, may make a profit-yielding price impossible. (6) Advertising and other promotional effort may be inadequate or inept, so that a potential market that could be reasonably anticipated is not achieved. (7) Poor customer relations because of carelessness in filling orders, lack of diplomacy in handling complaints, and brusque credit and collection procedure, may lose sales. (8) Poor selling or ineffective sales management may be the cause of failure to achieve an available market. (9) Competition of similar products, or of other manufacturers or dealers offering the same product, may cut sales volume below the break-even point in spite of sound marketing policies. (10) An unpredictable shift in fashion may wipe out demand for a product. (11) National or regional recessions may shrink purchasing demand or reduce the general sales volume of a distributor.

No business enterprise can completely avoid market volume risks, particularly those attributable to competition and extraneous economic factors. But nearly all enterprises can substantially minimize their market volume risks by: (1) improving their product design, buying, pricing, promotion, and sales policies, with or without the assistance of marketing research to provide them with the factual basis for such policy improvement; (2) in the case of manufacturers, diversifying their lines, so that an unavoidable loss of market volume for one product will not spell disaster for the enterprise; (3) anticipating national or regional economic developments, or maintaining keen current awareness of such developments, so that production or purchasing can be geared as closely as possible to them, to reduce inventory accumulation when recessions occur.

Large manufacturing and distributing enterprises are usually more successful in minimizing their market volume risks through these means than are small ones. Large units can afford to hire high-caliber management personnel with the experience and business intelligence to formulate effective market policies. Furthermore, these large units can afford extensive marketing research to provide themselves with factual guidance for devising effective market policies. They are also in a more favorable position to undertake diversification of production and distribution. Small manufacturers, wholesalers, and retailers can often be little more than the passive victims or beneficiaries of market chance.

Physical factor risks

Goods in inventory and transit are subject to three physical risks—deterioration, destruction, and theft.

Time alone causes certain goods to deteriorate. Many fresh fruits and vegetables lose quality rapidly. The natural impairment of more durable products is much slower but, given sufficient time, it may reduce their marketability or value.

Often the deterioration of inventory goods is attributable not so much to the bare time factor as to inadequate provision for their preservation while in storage. Dampness may encourage mold and rot. Too high or too low temperatures may cause spoilage of one sort or another. Dust may settle irremovably on surfaces. Careless handling by stockroom or warehouse personnel may result in damage.

Goods in transit, as well as those in inventory, may suffer deterioration. Delays in the transit movement or lack of proper packing or other special care, can produce various forms of spoilage. Carelessness in handling, or wreckage of the instrument of transportation, may result in damage.

Outright destruction of goods in inventory occurs most often through fire. Wrecks and other accidents may destroy goods in transit.

The law provides manufacturers and distributors some protection against these physical risks of marketing. If the deterioration, destruction, or theft of goods stored in a public warehouse is attributable to the negligence of the warehouse or its employees, the warehouse is liable for the resulting loss. Common carriers bear a similar responsibility for goods entrusted to them for transport.

Individual manufacturers and distributors can often eliminate or greatly reduce this form of market risk by avoiding the function of storage and through shipping their goods with title in the consignee. A hardware manufacturer who ships his products as rapidly as they come off his production lines to his wholesalers on F.O.B. factory terms has shifted all risks of deterioration, destruction, and theft of his goods to the wholesalers. Women's dress manufacturers who persuade some of their outlets to take early delivery of their orders on season dating terms transfer a part of their inventory risks from themselves to the outlets.

Another way of transferring inventory risks, which is open to practically all businesses, is *insurance.* Any risk of loss of goods in inventory or transit through deterioration, destruction, or theft, which would be crippling to a business if it occurred, but whose probability of occurrence is sufficiently slight in any individual case so that the premium cost is low enough to be absorbed as a regular cost of business operation, should be covered by insurance as a matter of sound business policy. The types of insurance against loss of goods in inventory and transit most commonly carried by business units are:

Fire. Fire insurance of a manufacturer's or distributor's inventories in stockrooms or on counters is usually incidental to a general fire policy on the premises. Goods in a warehouse may be covered by the warehouseman's insurance, or the storer may have them covered by a special policy.

Explosion. Grain elevators and certain other types of warehouses subject to explosion risk because of the nature of the commodities stored frequently carry explosion insurance.

Theft. This may be covered by a mercantile open-stock theft endorsement to a mercantile open-stock burglary policy.

Marine cargoes.

Domestic shipments. These may be covered by inland transit policies. Insurance may be had not only for risks not covered by the carriers' liability, but also for failure of a carrier to reimburse for loss on which it is liable.

Inventory risks should be minimized as far as possible by provision of proper safeguards in storage facilities, even where these risks are covered by insurance. Where public warehousing is involved, such provision is the responsibility of the warehouseman. But most of the country's inventories are in storerooms and private warehouses of manufacturers and distributors, and on the shelves and counters of retailers. The risks of deterioration, destruction, and theft to which these inventories are exposed are directly related to the type of storage facilities provided. A small additional investment in moisture-proofing, dust-proofing, air-conditioning, fire-proofing, fire sprinkler systems, and guarding against unlawful entry into storage areas would, in many cases, safeguard against sizable subsequent losses.

A good stock control system, combined with careful adjustment of production and buying to sales, as far as seasonal variations of production or selling permit such adjustment, also helps to minimize physical inventory losses. Obviously, if the inventories of a business are consistently held to minima that provide practical operating stocks, the opportunity for physical loss in connection with such inventories is less than where heavy excess stocks are carried for long periods. A rigid minimum inventory policy, however, might result in sacrificing the savings on quantity purchases and incoming quantity shipments. A compromise between these two interests is often necessary.

Price risks

Every time the market price of any product declines, all manufacturers and dealers who have it in their inventories experience an immediate inventory loss. Such price decline of a particular commodity may occur as an incident of a general price recession, or it may be the result of a special competitive situation.

Theoretically, insurance against price declines within a specified period would be possible. Practically, the premium cost would be so high that most businesses could not absorb it. Such insurance has not developed on any general scale.

Inventory price risks can be avoided in two ways—by hedging, and by transfer of risk. Hedging is discussed later in this chapter. The transfer of inventory price risks can be accomplished, like the transfer of physical inventory risks, by a few enterprises which more or less eliminate the storage function by selling their output immediately when produced, or by buying on a "to order" basis. But most businesses must carry the risk of inventory loss through price declines as an inescapable aspect of their marketing activities.

The risk of inventory loss from price decline, like that of physical inventory loss, can be minimized through development of good stock control systems and close adjustment of production or buying to sales.

Risk of nonpayment

Bad debt losses arise usually from unsound credit policies and weak collection policies. The obvious method of minimizing such losses is to tighten credit and collection management.

Sometimes an account that by all usual credit standards was a sound risk at the time credit was extended becomes insolvent, for reasons that defied detection at the time of the credit inquiry, or because of the intervention of some extraneous circumstance such as a strike or a fire. Or a recession may sweep a whole group of previously solvent customers into liquidation. Most businesses accept this risk as unavoidable. There is available, however, a form of business insurance—credit insurance—which permits avoidance of the risk of an excess of bad debt loss over what should be the "normal" for any enterprise.

HEDGING

Hedging is a special procedure for minimizing inventory price risks which is available to companies in certain manufacturing and distributive lines.

General principles

Hedging against price changes is possible under two circumstances:

1. A company is involved with an inventory of a commodity *for which there is futures trading on a commodity exchange,* * or it is compelled to carry stocks of an item whose price bears a consistent relationship to that of some exchange-traded commodity, and it wishes protection against a *decline* in the price of such commodity or item. Dealers in grains and other basic commodities, who may hold title to their purchases for only a few days or, if they own elevators or warehouses, for many months, are constantly in this position. A flour miller with a warehouse may buy grain months ahead of actually milling it, and desire such protection. So may a cotton or woolen mill that buys its raw material well ahead of its production schedule.

2. A company has made commitments which will necessitate future purchase of a commodity for which there is futures trading on a commodity exchange, and it wishes protection against a *rise* in price. A flour milling company which has made a commitment for future deliveries of flour based on current grain prices but which does not make "forward" purchases of wheat would seek hedging protection against a rise in the price of wheat prior to its actual spot purchases. Grain exporters frequently undertake exporting contracts based on current prices but involving future loading of the grain. They may postpone purchasing the actual grain until loading time and then have it transferred directly from the elevators to the ship's hold. Hedging guards them also against the risk of a price rise.

As was explained in Chapter 11, trading on the commodity exchanges includes dealings in futures as well as spot transactions. In a "normal" relationship, the futures prices for any commodity would exceed its spot price at any moment by the average of storage costs for the commodity from the present to the futures delivery months. For example, if the market for corn were "normal" and the spot price on the Chicago Board of Trade for a particular November day were $1.50 per bushel, the December futures price would be close to $1.51½ per bushel and the May futures price would be around $1.59 per bushel. "Normalcy" is the exception in commodity trading, however, and the "spread" between spot and futures prices more often than not is less than this average of storage costs. In

* Commodity exchanges and futures trading were studied in Chapter 11.

many cases, indeed, it is negative—futures prices are lower than the spot price. Over short periods the "spread" for any commodity is likely to remain constant, even though the spot and futures prices may fluctuate widely during such period; *futures and spot prices for any commodity, whatever their difference, over short periods tend to move up or down together by more or less the same amount.* Over periods of weeks or months, the "spread" of a commodity may change—the movement in its futures prices may exceed that of its spot price, or vice versa.* *Whatever variation occurs in the "spread," however, is usually proportionately less than the shifts in the spot and futures prices themselves.* A study of cotton trading indicated that changes in the cotton "spread" over a year were only 15 percent of changes in the spot and futures prices during that year.

It is this relative stability of "spreads" between the spot and futures prices of exchange-traded commodities that makes hedging possible. A manufacturer or dealer who *buys* a quantity of an exchange-traded commodity—or of some product whose price varies in harmony with that of an exchange-traded commodity—and who wishes to guard against a *fall* in the price of the commodity during the period it is in his inventory, can obtain protection by simultaneously *selling* a *futures* contract for an equivalent amount of the commodity. Thereby he substitutes for the risk that the price of the commodity may fall, the lesser risk that the "spread" between the futures and spot prices may widen. If the spot price has declined by the time he sells his holding of the commodity and the "spread" has remained constant (i.e., the futures price has declined by an identical amount), whatever loss he sustains on the purchase and resale of his holding of the commodity is offset by his profit on covering the futures contract. Should the spot price have risen with the "spread" remaining constant, the hedger makes a gain on his actual holding of the commodity, but this is offset by a corresponding loss on the futures transactions. However, the hedger was content at the outset to forego possible speculative gain in order to protect himself against loss, so this loss on the futures transaction is not a matter of regret. In the more likely case, for long-term hedges, that the "spread" itself has changed, the hedger will suffer some loss or enjoy some gain on the combined transactions in the actual commodity and his dealing in futures, but any loss so suffered will probably be far less than he would have risked if he had not hedged. Long-term hedges *do not eliminate* the risk of price decline; they *minimize* it.

Exporters and manufacturers who must hedge against the price *rises*

---

* One element of variation in "spread" can be foreseen and taken into account in planning a hedge. As each futures delivery month approaches, the "spread" between the spot price and the futures price for that month shrinks, and finally disappears when the delivery month actually arrives. In the case of hedging by grain elevator operators and other middlemen primarily interested in storage, this shrinkage of "spread" provides the very profit they seek to protect through hedging. This is illustrated in Example 2 below.

do so by *buying* futures in their commodity whenever they obligate themselves to make future deliveries based on present prices. Whatever loss they
might suffer through having subsequently to buy the commodity at a price
higher than that on which their commitments were based, will be entirely
or largely offset by the profit on the sale of their futures.

Examples

1. *Short-term dealer transaction in grains*

Late in November a country grain dealer buys 5,000 bushels
of corn from a farmer, which he intends to ship immediately on consignment to a commission house in Chicago, which will sell it to one
of the terminal elevators at the arrival date price. The spot price for
corn on the Chicago Board of Trade that day, as reported by radio and
ticker service, is $1.50. A spread of 11 cents per bushel will cover the
freight charge to Chicago and the terminal handling charges, and will
leave the dealer 2 cents per bushel—$100 on the transaction—to cover
his overhead and profit. He offers the farmer $1.39 per bushel, and
obtains the corn at this price.

Shipment to Chicago will take several days. During that period
the spot price of corn could rise or fall as much as 15 to 20 cents.
A rise of any magnitude would give the dealer a speculative profit. A
price break, however, could involve him in a loss far exceeding his
middleman's thin margin as a grain dealer. He is in the business of
grain dealing, not speculation. Accordingly he is willing to forego all
chance of speculative profit to safeguard himself against loss that, taking all his current grain operations into account, could not only wipe
out his middleman's margin but absorb his entire operating capital and
leave him insolvent. Therefore, immediately upon purchasing the
5,000 bushels from the farmer, he telegraphs an order to his Chicago
broker to sell 5,000 bushels of December corn futures on the Chicago
Board of Trade. With the spot late November price at $1.50 per
bushel, December futures are selling at $1.51½.

During the next few days while the grain is en route to Chicago, spot corn prices fall five cents. In this short-term price movement, futures prices for corn also move down five cents. The terminal
elevator buys the dealer's 5,000 bushels at $1.45. Without the hedge,
the dealer would have been in the position of having to sell his corn
at a price lower by $150 than his out-of-pocket expenses on the trans-
action. As it is, he covers (i.e., buys back) his futures contract at
$1.46½ a bushel, making a profit of $250 on the two futures transactions. This covers his $150 out-of-pocket loss on the spot transaction
and leaves him the $100 gross profit margin that was his business ob-
jective.

2. *Seasonal elevator storage of grain*

On November 28, a Chicago terminal grain elevator buys
600,000 bushels of corn from various local dealers at the spot price
of $1.50. It intends to sell off this grain to cereal manufacturers dur-
ing the next six months at prices that will cover a normal storage

charge of 1½ cents per bushel per month. (To simplify the analysis, we will assume that these sales are actually made in six equal amounts of 100,000 bushels each on the 15th day of each of the next six months. On this assumption, the total storage earnings on the 600,000 bushels sought by the elevator would be in the neighborhood of $31,500.)

Immediately after purchasing the 600,000 bushels of corn at $1.50, the elevator sells 100,000 bushels of December futures on the Chicago Board of Trade at the current price of $1.51¼ and 500,000 bushels of May futures at the current price of $1.58½. (Futures are generally sold for a delivery month in which actual spot sales are to be made, or for the next delivery month after such spot sales. The elevator anticipates selling 100,000 bushels on December 15. Hence the sale of a corresponding volume of December futures. The May futures cover the balance of the expected sales.)

On December 15, the elevator sells 100,000 bushels at the spot price of $1.54, which has also become the December futures price. To cover its previous sale of December futures, it may either buy in 100,000 bushels of December futures at the $1.54 price, or it may make delivery under the previous futures sale contract of 100,000 bushels from grain in its bins. (To facilitate calculation of gain and loss on the elevator's hedging operations, we will assume that it buys in 100,000 bushels of December futures at $1.54.)

On January 15, it sells another 100,000 bushels at the spot price of $1.51. Simultaneously it covers this transaction by buying back 100,000 bushels of its previous May futures sale at the current $1.56½ price for such futures. These balancing transactions, and subsequent spot sales and balancing repurchases of May futures on February 15, March 15, April 15, and May 15, are shown in the tabulation below. (Note that on May 15 the elevator again has a choice of covering its hedge by buying back 100,000 bushels of May futures, or by making delivery on its previous sale of this amount of futures from its own grain stock.)

Because of spot price developments between November and May, the elevator's purchase and subsequent sales of the 600,000 bushels of corn resulted in a loss of $3,500 on the purchase price, and no coverage of storage costs and profit. But since the "spread" between futures and spot prices narrowed fairly consistently as the delivery months approached (a consideration the elevator manager had in mind when he made the hedge), the trend of futures prices enabled the elevator to realize a $34,250 profit on its futures transactions. After deduction of the $3,500 spot loss, the elevator is left with a net gain of $30,750 on the two sets of transactions. This is $750 less than the gross profit it sought. It is far better, however, than the $35,000 it would have been out if it had not hedged. Furthermore, the loss could have been much greater than $35,000. Hedging changed the elevator's risk from a big one based on a possible fall in corn prices to a small one based on variations in the "spreads" between spot and futures prices.

TRANSACTIONS INVOLVED IN EXAMPLE 2.

| | SPOT | | | | | | FUTURES | | | | | |
| | BOUGHT | | | SOLD | | | SOLD | | | COVERED | | |
DATE	Bushels	@	Price	Bushels	@	Price	Bushels	@	Price	Bushels	@	Price
11/28	600,000	1.50	$900,000				100,000 (D) 500,000 (M)	1.51¼ 1.58½	$151,250 $792,500			
12/15				100,000	1.54	$154,000				100,000 (D)	1.53½	$153,500
1/15				100,000	1.51	151,000				100,000 (M)	1.56½	156,500
2/15				100,000	1.50	150,000				100,000 (M)	1.54	154,000
3/15				100,000	1.48	148,000				100,000 (M)	1.50¾	150,750
4/15				100,000	1.48½	148,500				100,000 (M)	1.49¾	149,750
5/15				100,000	1.45	145,000				100,000 (M)	1.45	145,000
Total			$900,000			$896,500			$943,750			$909,500

Spot loss $ 3,500

Futures gain $ 34,250

Net Gain $ 30,750

3. Forward sale of cotton

On September 15 a cotton merchant receives an order from a regular mill customer for 200 bales (100,000 lbs.) of cotton of premium Strict Midling inch grade, to be shipped F.O.B. warehouse on October 8. The merchant has no cotton of that premium grade in storage at the time, and does not anticipate having any by October 8. He plans to buy the premium cotton on the shipping date from some other cotton dealer in the area who has it in stock and have it shipped directly to his customer. He quotes a price, which is accepted, of 32.86¢ per lb. He arrives at this figure by taking the 31.25 current New York Cotton Exchange spot quotation and adding (a) 100 points (one point = .01¢) per lb. for the premium differential, (b) .60¢ per lb. for normal storage charge differential for the period involved, and (c) .01¢ per lb. for the costs of the hedging he will have to undertake.

Because of the necessity of buying to order and drop shipping, at the 32.86¢ price the merchant is handling the order essentially as an accommodation for his regular customer. Should cotton prices remain stable (i.e., advance by the normal storage charge differential for the period), he will make little or no profit on it. But he could suffer hundreds of dollars loss if cotton prices should rise substantially between the order and the delivery dates. Accordingly, immediately upon closing the order he directs his broker to buy two "units" (50,000 lb. is the Cotton Exchange trading "unit") of October cotton futures on the New York Cotton Exchange; the price of the October futures on September 15 is 32.50.

Cotton prices do rise, as the merchant had feared. New York spot cotton is up 1.15 to 32.40 on October 8, and the merchant has to pay 33.40 for the premium cotton to be delivered to his customer. But October cotton futures have risen .53 to 33.03 on this date. (Remember that a rise in futures over any period tends to be less than the rise of the spot price by the amount of average storage charge costs for the period. Had the tendency operated exactly for the September 15 to October 8 period, the change in the spot-futures spread between the two dates would have been the .60 the merchant had allowed for. In practice the tendency rarely operates exactly, and in this case the reduction of spread turned out to be .58). The merchant directs his broker to sell his two October futures units at the 33.03 price.

Brokers' charges on the two hedging operations were $10.00.

The net results of the cotton merchant's transactions work out as follows:

	Actual Cotton			October Futures	
Sept. 15	Sell	$32,860		Buy	$32,500
Oct. 8	Buy	33,400		Sell	33,030
	Loss	$ 540		Gain	$ 530
			Brokers' charges		10
			Net gain		$ 520

On the transactions in the actual premium cotton, the merchant lost $540. On his futures transactions he had a net gain of $520. Overall he has taken only a $20 loss on this accommodation deal in the

$32,000–$34,000 range. This might just as readily have been a correspondingly small profit had the movement in the spot-futures spread been different. So, through his hedging, the merchant was able to undertake the accommodation deal at only a trifling risk.

REVIEW

1. To what extent can a business ordinarily cover its working capital needs through the credit extended by its suppliers?

2. Under what circumstances would a business seek a bank loan to finance its working capital needs? Would a bank make an unsecured mercantile loan? What types of security might a bank accept on a mercantile loan?

3. Describe a promissory note given for a bank mercantile loan. Describe the procedure of arranging a mercantile loan from a bank.

4. Explain domestic bankers' acceptances.

5. Explain discounting accounts receivable. What is "notification" discounting? "recourse" discounting?

6. Under what circumstances, and from what sources, may manufacturers obtain advances secured by their inventories?

7. Explain "market volume risks." How can they be minimized? Are large businesses or small businesses more vulnerable to them? Why?

8. What physical factor risks are involved in Marketing? How can a business minimize them?

9. What can a business do to minimize the risk of a decline in the prices of its inventory items?

10. Explain hedging. Give a hypothetical illustration other than the ones given in the text.

DISCUSSION TOPICS

1. "If banks did not already exist, the mercantile world would have to invent them."

2. "A company's accounts receivable are part of its assets that its suppliers rely upon when extending it mercantile credit. If it discounts those accounts receivable and thereby gives a bank or finance company a prior lien upon them, it is in effect working a fraud on its business creditors."

3. "Non-notification discounting of accounts receivable deceives a company's customers who, while willing to be in its debt, might be unwilling to have a factor for creditor."

4. "Marketing risks may be minimized, but never eliminated."

5. What are the possibilities of making hedging, as a means of minimizing price risks, more widespread than it is today?

PROBLEM

Sheepscot Woolen Co. is an integrated woolen mill. It buys the raw wool, spins, weaves, and sells finished cloth, primarily to men's clothing manufacturers.

90 percent of its raw wool purchases for men's fall and winter suit cloths are made in December and January. Its sales of finished cloth for fall and winter suits are also concentrated, with 75 percent of the deliveries made in May, June, and July.

The excess of its wool purchases over immediate operating needs is stored in public warehouses. Its inventory of finished cloth is stored on the mill premises.

1. Advance purchase of wool, and the accumulation of finished cloth prior to May deliveries, cause Sheepscot Woolen Co. to have fluctuating inventories of both raw material and finished product, which become very heavy in certain periods of the year. Its net worth just suffices to carry its minimum inventory loads. How can it obtain funds to carry inventory excesses over these minima? Would any of these methods be more economical than others?

2. How can Sheepscot Woolen Co. minimize the following risks: (a) spoilage or destruction of the raw wool stored in the public warehouses; (b) deterioration of finished cloth in its store rooms from moths, mildew, and handling stains; (c) destruction or spoilage of the stock of finished cloth from fire; (d) damage to its cloth bolts while they are en route to purchasers; (e) a decline in the price of raw wool after a season's supply has been purchased; (f) a decline in the price of woolen cloth as a part of a general price recession; (g) bad debt losses on its accounts receivable?

SUGGESTED READINGS

Angell, F. J., *Insurance: Principles and Practices,* Ronald Press, New York, 1959.

Dauton, C. A., *The Consumer Finance Industry in a Dynamic Economy,* American Investment Co. of Illinois, St. Louis, 1959.

Donaldson, E. F., *Corporate Finance,* Ronald Press, New York, 1957.

Guthman, H. G., & H. E. Dougall, *Corporate Finance Policy,* 3rd ed, Prentice-Hall, Englewood Cliffs, N.J., 1955.

Hedging: an Insurance Medium in Marketing Agricultural Commodities, Chicago Board of Trade, Chicago, 1948.

Howard, B. B., & M. Upton, *Introduction to Business Finance,* McGraw-Hill Book Co., New York, 1953.

Husband, W. H., & J. C. Dockeray, *Modern Corporation Finance,* 4th ed, Richard D. Irwin, Homewood, Ill., 1957.

Irwin, H. S., *Evolution of Futures Trading,* Mimir Press, Madison, Wis., 1954.

Jacoby, N. H., *Business Finance and Banking,* National Bureau of Economic Research, New York, 1947.

Mowbray, A. H., & R. H. Blanchard, *Insurance,* 4th ed, McGraw-Hill Book Co., New York, 1955.

Phelps, C. W., *Accounts Receivable Financing as a Method of Business Finance* (1957); *Financing the Installment Purchases of the American Family* (1954), Commercial Credit Co., Baltimore.

Prather, C. L., *Financing Business Firms,* Richard D. Irwin, Homewood, Ill., 1955.

Prochnow, H. V., & R. A. Foulke, *Practical Bank Credit,* Prentice-Hall, Englewood Cliffs, N.J., 1950.

Rodda, W. H., *Fire and Property Insurance* (1956); *Inland Marine and Transportation Insurance* (1958), Prentice-Hall, Englewood Cliffs, N.J.

Schultz, R. E., & E. C. Bardwell, *Property Insurance,* Rinehart, New York, 1959.

Tungate, L., *Financial Management for the Small Businessman,* Chapman & Grimes, Boston, 1952.

CHAPTER 27

MARKETING MANAGEMENT*

Successful marketing requires generalship. This marketing generalship is a major responsibility of the top management of any manufacturing enterprise.

Marketing generalship has four fields: (1) strategic planning (i.e., planning marketing policy); (2) tactical planning (i.e., planning marketing operations based on predetermined policies); (3) tactical administration (i.e., the day-to-day administration of predetermined marketing operations); and (4) provision of an organizational structure for the policy planning, operations planning, and operations administration.

Progress in comprehensive and effective marketing management by manufacturers has lagged far behind progress in production management. There are still many small manufacturers who avoid most of the issues of marketing management by placing all responsibility for the distribution of their output with selling agents. Planned marketing policy is still conspicuously absent, and marketing operations are still conducted largely on a "seat-of-the-pants" basis, by a large proportion of companies, even by some that have developed fortuitously to substantial size. During the past quarter-century, however, recognition has been growing among alert manufacturers that careful planning of marketing policies, and careful planning and supervision of the marketing operations based on these policies, is as important to the success of a business as is good production management. The concept of a closely integrated overall marketing management, instead of loosely correlated product planning, purchasing management, promo-

---

* Until recently the term "sales management" was used to denote the planning, direction, and control of the entire marketing activity of a company or division of a company. This term was unsatisfactory because of its implication that "marketing" and "selling" were synonymous, that the "marketing" interests of a business were confined to its *selling* activities. The current general tendency is to use the broader term "marketing management."

tion, sales management, credit management, and traffic management, is largely a development of the 1950's.

In the preceding chapters of Part Four we surveyed one by one the various fields of policy and operations that enter marketing management for manufacturers. Here we shall look first at what is involved in the planning or policy phases, then survey three aspects of marketing management that manufacturers must frequently deal with, and finally note some recent developments in business structure or organization that contribute to better marketing management.

THE PLANNING ASPECT OF MARKETING MANAGEMENT

Market planning is frequently compared with planning for military policy and operations. The terms "strategic" and "tactical" are often applied respectively to marketing policy and operations planning, and the term "campaign" to the planned procedure for introducing a new product, or for entering a new market area. The military analogy is not far-fetched. Competition, active or latent, is always present in marketing. It need not be the "pure" competition of the economists. Competition is sharp even among companies in quasi-monopolistic situations based on brand names, design differentials, service policies, and other marketing elements. Competition has many of the aspects of warfare, "hot" or "cold," though the conflict is less likely to be a two-sided struggle than a form of the old battle royal—each fighter contending against all the others. There are aggressive marketing actions and defensive ones. There are surprise actions in marketing, and feints. Secrecy is employed to hide many marketing matters from competitors, and there is often mercantile spying to penetrate the secrecy curtain drawn up by competitors.

But the military analogy should not be applied too closely to market planning. A substantial part of market planning is devoted to creating and distributing *new* products to satisfy human wants, even to creating new *wants* that can be satisfied by new products, rather than merely to capturing competitors' markets or defending against their inroads. Federal and state legislation, the Federal Trade Commission, and American business itself through voluntary fair trade practice codes, bar many practices that might put marketing on a basis of true mercantile "war." Through trade associations, competitors frequently undertake cooperative activities for their mutual benefit. The penalty for failure in the competitive marketing struggle is not usually destruction or unconditional surrender of the loser. It is not necessarily the conversion of profit into loss, though that occurs, but rather some reduction of the higher profits that the loser might otherwise have gained. Description of market planning as "warfare" should therefore be considered a help in dramatizing the subject rather than a basis for understanding it.

Marketing problems

Market planning is problem solving. The very first problem facing marketing management is to determine what problems have to be solved. Failure to recognize an immediate problem as such, or to anticipate a problem, can be every bit as disastrous as a wrong solution for a recognized problem. It would be poor market planning, for example, for a kitchen equipment manufacturer not to realize the current vogue for color in stoves, refrigerators, and kitchen cabinets. It would be poor market planning for a manufacturer working on a campaign of market expansion not to anticipate that this will increase the credit work that must be done by his organization and to fail to provide for expansion of his credit department.

Market planning in the sense of problem recognition and solving applies to both marketing policy and marketing operations. Policy planning usually precedes operational planning. The latter in effect is concerned with implementing policy decisions. In a going enterprise, however, policy planning has to take into account the concern's existing marketing operations. A major factor in the market policy planning of a business is to base the policy on the concern's present operational structure and procedures, or to devise policies involving minimal modification of present market operations. For example, an industrial supplies manufacturer, whose research department produced an improved form of friction tape that had both industrial and household possibilities, decided not to develop household forms of the tape since the marketing of these could not be handled through its existing sales structure and channels of distribution, and the limited household market for the household tape would not warrant setting up a separate marketing organization alien to the rest of the company's operations.

What circumstances produce the problems that marketing management must solve? (1) Every aggressive expanding business is constantly creating new marketing policy problems for itself. Every idea for a new product, every effort to improve or diversify an existing product, every drive for broader market territory, every modification of channels of distribution, every proposal to change promotional or selling approaches, poses new policy problems that management must solve. Furthermore, as indicated above, every decision that management makes upon marketing policy usually raises a host of operational problems as to how the determined policy shall be implemented. (2) External factors may pose marketing policy problems to the management of a business. A shift in the national economic trend, toward regression or toward recovery, may force reevaluation of previously determined policy. So also may an unforeseen change in the competitive picture. So also may market institutional changes, such as the evolution of supermarkets as retail outlets for many nonfood items, or the sudden rise of discount houses as major retail outlets for many appliance lines. So also may federal and state legislation, or a significant policy change in Federal Trade Commission rulings.

As was emphasized in Chapter 1, the American marketing scene is dynamic. Marketing management must count on being faced not only with policy and operational problems created by self-growth, but ever more pressingly by those posed by external factors. There can be no surcease to the planning aspect of marketing management.

Marketing decisions

The end and aim of market planning is decisions—on whether or not to produce and market a product, on its design and packaging, on the channels of its distribution, on its pricing, on all the other policy and operational elements involved in its distribution. Marketing management reaches these decisions in three ways.

1. In some cases systematic calculation—"Systems Analysis" or "Operations Analysis" are the terms used for the more scientific approaches—or some other form of marketing research produces such overwhelming evidence in support of a line of action that management must accept this procedure as the best solution of the problem. Unfortunately, while scientific analysis and marketing research can usually throw valuable light on a marketing problem, the instances where they provide a clear-cut basis for a decision are rare.

2. By far the greater part of marketing decisions are made by management through the application of "insight" sharpened and reinforced by experience and the findings of research. "Insight," in the sense of managerial personal judgment that cannot be checked by mechanical computation, may seem a perilous basis for marketing decisions upon which are staked millions of dollars and the success or failure of enterprises. However, the human mind trained to decision making, as managerial minds are trained, can reason soundly along analogue lines and deal with fractional information and multiple variables beyond the capacities of any present cybernetic calculators. In marketing management, as in other management fields, no decision is usually the worst decision. Decisions must be made, no matter how inadequate or how complex their informational bases. Where systematic calculation cannot provide a firm foundation for a marketing decision, managerial "insight" may be the only other alternative to reliance on blind chance. In individual cases, this managerial "insight"

achieves the order of genius. In general, in the American marketing area, it operates well.

3. Sometimes, in the absence of an absolute calculated basis for a marketing decision, management can hedge upon its decisions through trial-and-error. This is possible when a marketing decision does not involve irrevocable commitments. Such is often the case in the pricing of new products where competition is not pressing. A price so high that it proves to be excessive may be tried first, with repeated lowerings until an approximation of optimum price is reached. If national marketing of a product is being approached by a series of regional steps, particular decisions that prove to be misjudgments when applied in the initial market areas can be corrected as the territorial expansion proceeds.

It should be emphasized that rarely is there only one single "right" policy for any given marketing situation. The diversity of market circumstances usually makes it possible for several differing but well-considered policies to have equal chance of success. The task of Marketing Management, therefore, is to arrive at any one of the several "good" decisions in a particular case, and to avoid all the "bad" ones. Moreover, market conditions change, so that this year's "good" policy may become a "bad" one next year, and vice versa. Marketing Management must maintain a flexible outlook and be ready to change policies when change is indicated. "Good" marketing policies should embody elements of flexibility that permit of their modification when needed.

INTRODUCING A NEW PRODUCT

As was indicated in Chapter 16, American business is now largely based on constantly introducing new products, either true innovations or adaptations of the successful innovations. Today the fortuitous inspiration of the individual inventor plays little part in creating market innovations, and practically no part in producing adaptations.

Product planning

Product research must be a regular operation of every manufacturing enterprise that hopes to survive, let alone expand. This research is conducted simultaneously along two lines—technological inquiry into how to produce a product that will do something, and marketing inquiry into human needs and buying motivations that the product will satisfy and the quantitative extent of the market that will want to buy the product, or can be induced to buy it, and can afford to buy it. The marketing and the technological inquiries must dovetail, for the findings upon wants and buying motivations are a determinant of product design, packaging, and the erection of production facilities, while the cost considerations associated with technological conclusions, by affecting prices, influence the markets that can be sold.

Market area and channels of distribution

With the design of a new product or product line and some idea of its general market potential determined, a decision must be made upon market area policy. Shall the new product be launched initially upon a national basis? Or shall the start be a territorial one, followed by area-by-area expansion on a predetermined schedule? A decision for immediate national distribution presumes adequate productive capacity, and substantial investment in preliminary promotional and selling operations. A decision to limit distribution territorially involves foregoing promotion through national media such as magazines and radio or TV networks, and may result in losing the uncovered areas by default to more venturesome competition.

With the ultimate purchasers known, and the market area issues decided, decisions must be made as to the best classes of retail outlets to be used, and the best channels of distribution to be employed. Some of the considerations that enter retail outlet and channel-of-distribution selection were studied in Chapter 13. A manufacturer's usual first choice is to distribute a new product through the classes of outlets and the channels of distribution that are normal for other products in the same general category, particularly if the manufacturer is already using these "normal' outlets and channels of distribution for other products that he is making. Still, as was emphasized in Chapter 13, an alert manufacturer is always on the lookout for new classes of retailers that might prove to be successful outlets for a particular product. If new classes of outlets are developed for a product, new channels of distribution may have to be tapped to reach them. If more than one ultimate market can be developed for a product— say, an industrial use as well as a consumer use—independent channels of distribution will probably have to be utilized to reach these differing ultimate markets.

Promotion and personal selling

Now, with markets and channels of distribution known, comes the task of planning promotion and personal selling. What type or combination of types of promotion is best suited to the new product and its market—shall it be advertising, and if so through what media? or shall it be some form of consumer or trade sales promotion? or are there publicity possibilities? or should there be a "mix" of promotional procedures? If the channel of distribution is to be direct-to-retailer or direct-to-industrial-user, what sort of sales force should be set up for this purpose? If wholesaling middlemen are to be used, how shall the selling to them be handled? All of these crucial decisions on promotion and selling must be made in the light of cost considerations—either how much are they going to add to unit costs of the product, or how much of a given promotional or selling activity can be undertaken with a given cost allowance allocated to it?

Pricing

Somewhere along the line of policy planning for a new product a decision must be made upon pricing. Actually, preliminary guesstimates of price must be utilized at the very outset in judging market acceptance. The final decision on price is often the last step of planning, since some idea of promotional and selling costs is needed for pricing calculations. If the product is to be sold upon a trade discount basis, the ultimate retail price must be determined, and allowances made for proper retailers' and middlemen's discounts. Even when manufacturers sell upon a net rather than a discount basis, they tend these days to calculate prices through to the retail level, making allowances for middlemen's and retailers' markups.

The "campaign"

An important timing factor enters the planning for the marketing of a new product. The production department, the advertising department, and the selling department cannot be each allowed to go its independent way in performing its operations. Otherwise output might pile up before sales were being made, or advertising might induce consumers to ask for the product before retailers were carrying it, or retailers might be loaded with it long before advertising created a consumer demand for it. Just as production must be "scheduled" so that all constituent elements become available at the proper times and in the quantities needed for an assembly operation, so all of the operations associated with marketing a product must be "campaigned" so that they dovetail for major effectiveness.

A "break" or "goal" date must be set when the new product goes on sale through the market area. This may be determined by some special "selling season" for the product. It may be determined by whichever of three factors will take longest—producing a sufficient quantity of the product to stock the retailers in the market area, developing and putting over the promotional campaign, or selling to the middlemen in the market area and reselling by them to the retailers. With the "break" date established, time schedules for production, promotion, and selling are calculated. As in production scheduling, or the timing of a cook who must have the component parts of a dish all ready at a predetermined moment, time schedules for all the elements that enter a marketing campaign must be calculated *backward* from the "break" date. If all elements of a campaign are properly scheduled, and if all schedules are properly adhered to, the "break" date will see the consuming market induced to purchase the new product, and a sufficient supply of it in all the outlets in which purchasers would ask for it.

MARKET EXPANSION

Grow or wither away are the alternatives for most manufacturing businesses. There is little possibility of standing pat over an extended period. The three methods of manufacturers' market growth are: (1) more intensive penetration of a given market; (2) broadening the scope of production; and (3) territorial expansion.

1. More intensive penetration of a given market is usually a matter of operational improvement rather than policy decision. This penetration is ordinarily accomplished by improved promotion, by obtaining more retail or wholesale outlets through better selling brought about by better sales force management, and by improved customer relations achieved through better traffic management, credit management, and general public relations. Sometimes policy issues may be involved, as when price is a major factor in determining the degree of market penetration, or when channel-of-distribution issues arise.

2. Market expansion through broadening the scope of production may be accomplished by "diversifying" a particular product through making it in a variety of models or sizes, by line expansion through entering upon the production of related products that belong to the same merchandise "line" as the manufacturer's original ones, or by branching out into new market "lines." The policy issues involved in each of these methods of market expansion were explored in Chapter 16. Here we need note that where line or extra-line expansion is involved, it is often accomplished these days by acquisition of or merger with another manufacturing enterprise already making and selling the related or extra-line products.

3. Territorial expansion may come about from continuing growth of a manufacturer's production facilities and financial resources, or it may be part of a large company's program of introducing a new product to the national market on an area-by-area basis. In either case, enlarging a company's market territory is a policy issue that may not be treated casually. It does much more than merely expand quantitatively marketing problems that have already been more or less solved for smaller magnitudes. On the contrary, it commonly raises a host of new market policy issues. If additional production facilities are needed, should they be located at the old production sites or should they be related to the new market territories? Should the expanding sales force be reorganized on a territorial basis?

Should there be centralized shipping, or should branch depots associated with branch sales offices be established, or should territorially-scattered general merchandise warehouses be utilized? What of the possibility of shifting advertising from local to national media? The opening of each new market area involves the planning of a coordinated marketing cam paign such as is required for the introduction of a new product.

DEALING WITH COMPETITION

Although American business is frequently described as operating in an atmosphere of quasi-monopoly and imperfect competition, few manufacturers can ever remove themselves completely from the threat and actuality of some degree of competition. Most American competition is not the economists' pure price competition, although there are some areas of manufacturing where even this form of competition must be taken into account. American competition is generally of a type once removed—between brands, and between closely comparable products. Quasi-monopolies or new or differentiated products do exist for a time and, since new and differentiated products are constantly being brought upon the market, there is constantly a substantial area of quasi-monopoly pricing in the market at any time. But if a new or differentiated product is successful, adaptations and imitations soon appear, and the original quasi-monopoly margin of pricing freedom narrows. The quasi-monopoly of an accepted brand is real, but it is constantly being challenged by aggressive promotion of other brands.

Every expanding manufacturer, unless his growth for the time being is based upon a true "innovation" product, must undertake offensive competition. All enterprises with established markets must engage in defensive competition to hold them. In the American economy, competition among manufacturers rarely takes the form of "price wars," except in periods of recession and occasionally in oligopolistic industries. The primary weapons of American competition are advertising, other forms of promotion (particularly consumer sales promotions), and selling "drives." The competitive goal of a manufacturer forcing his way into an already occupied market by these means is not to replace completely all the other brands or similar products already established there, but to win some share of the market for himself. Similarly, the goal of defensive competition in the face of an encroaching new brand or related product is not to exclude it totally but, while losing some part of the established market, to retain a worthwhile share.

ORGANIZATION FOR MARKETING MANAGEMENT

In a small company, responsibility for all elements of marketing management, operations as well as planning, often rests with one individual—the partner responsible for the sales side of the business, or a sales manager. In larger enterprises, administrative responsibility for marketing operations is divided. There is a sales force manager, a credit manager, a purchasing manager, an advertising manager, a traffic manager. In the past the sales force manager of a company, even of a large one, usually had a double managerial responsibility. He was the operations head of the company's sales force. He also shared with top management the responsibility for planning overall marketing policy. During the past quarter-century there has been a strong trend toward separating the policy planning and operations administration aspects of marketing management.

The planning staff

An early step in this direction was to provide a sales executive who had both policy and operations responsibilities with a *staff* to assist him in policy formulation. Such a staff consists of one or more subordinates or consultants who are specialists in particular fields of sales policy preparation and who serve as a "brain trust" for the sales executive. If the company employs a marketing research man, he certainly is part of the marketing staff. So also is the advertising manager, particularly if his major operational responsibility is to serve as liaison between the company and its advertising agency. An industrial designer or marketing consultant may also participate in staff activities. These men undertake research and formulate preliminary plans for the company's marketing policies. Their suggestions are submitted to the sales executive. He may adopt them as submitted. Often, when tested in the crucible of his experience and judgment, these preliminary plans may be adjudged faulty. The sales executive may reject them categorically, or he may refer them back to the staff for further consideration and development. The staff of a sales executive *proposes;* the executive alone has the responsibility and authority to *dispose.*

To provide a sales manager with a marketing staff solves part of the marketing management problem of large companies. It provides the operational executive usually best equipped by aptitude and experience for market planning—the sales manager—with assistance that makes it more practicable for him to carry the double burden of operations administration and broad range planning. It has, however, serious weaknesses. The double burden placed on the sales manager may result in his doing less than full justice to one of his responsibilities, either to general market planning or to management of the company's sales force. Furthermore, he is given no authority, and may lack advice on such company operations as product engineering, production, credit, and finance, that are closely involved in over-all market planning.

The marketing committee

A second approach to separating market policy planning and operations responsibilities is the creation of a *marketing committee*. This substitutes group decision for the individual authoritarian decision of an absolute sales executive. The members of a company's marketing committee are usually the executives of all the major operating departments of the company that are involved in any way in the marketing process. Sometimes outside consultants are included. Besides the sales force manager, a company marketing committee is likely to include the production manager, the head of the engineering or design department, perhaps an independent design consultant, the advertising manager, the marketing research director or an outside marketing research consultant, perhaps the traffic manager, and perhaps the credit manager. Each contributes his specialized knowhow and experience to the analysis of each sales issue as it comes up, and to the formulation of policy. Adoption of marketing policy decisions by such committees, after a thrashing-out of all viewpoints that may be protracted and heated, is often unanimous. Divided or unanimous, the opinion of a marketing committee must be submitted to the company's top management for acceptance.

Marketing committees unquestionably have the great advantage of bringing to the solution of market policy problems the experience and judgment of the key individuals in all operations fields related to a company's marketing policy. There are serious offsetting disadvantages, however. Committee judgments tend to be orthodox compromises, whereas effective marketing policy commonly requires aggressiveness. Furthermore, once committee judgments on marketing policy have been made, there is no single individual at the under-top-management level with the responsibility of putting them into effect. Either executive action must also be worked out through committee consultation, or top management must take over this responsibility. There is also the possibility, where making and implementing far-reaching marketing policy is involved, that committee deliberations may take so much time and attention of the operations executives of a business that they seriously interfere with operational responsibilities.

The marketing manager

The most recent development in the movement to separate market policy planning and operations administration is to confine the sales executive's

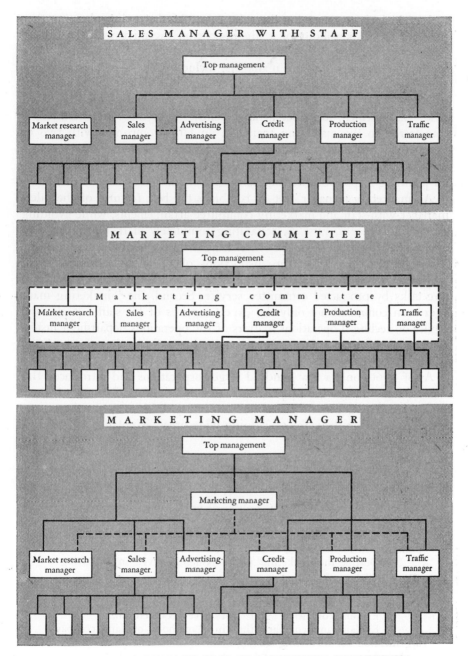

MARKETING MANAGEMENT ORGANIZATION STRUCTURES

ILLUSTRATION 27–1

task exclusively to managing the sales force. Market policy planning then becomes the responsibility of a higher-echelon executive with the title of "marketing manager" or "vice-president in charge of marketing." The various marketing operations managers, including the sales force manager, report to this marketing manager, who coordinates their operations. His major responsibility, however, is to plan the company's marketing policy. The "staff" which, in earlier arrangements, served the sales executive, is transferred to the marketing manager. In large companies with two or more major product lines, the marketing manager's staff may include a "product manager" for each product line, to whom are delegated the over-all planning responsibilities for the specific lines.

A "marketing manager" set-up combines the best features of the sales-manager-with-staff and marketing-committee arrangements, while avoiding their disadvantages. First, by separating completely market planning and operational responsibilities, the "marketing manager" can devote his efforts to policy matters without the distractions of operations administration, while the operational department heads are not diverted from their executive tasks by protracted committee service. Second, the "marketing manager" can command not only the expert services of his staff but also the advice on technical operations matters of the operations department heads. And third, he is in a favorable position to coordinate the efforts of the operational departments in putting policy decisions into effect.

As of 1960, only a few hundred large corporations had introduced the "marketing manager" concept into their organization. Reports of their experience were generally favorable, however, and this managerial arrangement appeared on the verge of gaining widespread acceptance.

REVIEW

1. Distinguish between policy planning, operations planning, and operations administration in marketing management.
2. How does the marketing management of a company arrive at decisions on its marketing issues?
3. Outline the marketing policy issues involved in launching a new product.
4. Explain "marketing campaign."
5. Explain the methods of market expansion.
6. Explain "offensive" and "defensive" competition.
7. Explain and compare the three methods of large-company organization for marketing management.

DISCUSSION TOPICS

1. "Market planning is problem solving."
2. "Market policy planning and market operations planning are interdependent."
3. "Marketing problems may originate both from within and without a business."
4. Some psychologists have suggested that there may be an inverse correlation between intelligence above a certain medium-high level and managerial ability. Could this theory have any validity as applied to marketing management?
5. "When you expand market area or a product line by acquiring a company already active in the market or the product field, you usually acquire too much irrelevant with the relevant, too much bad with the good, for the acquisition to have been worth while."
6. "Non-price competition is as natural to an Age of Plenty as price competition was to an Age of Scarcity."
7. "A 'marketing manager' is usually only a sales manager who has been given a higher-sounding title in place of a pay-increase."

PROBLEM

The research laboratories of El Dorado Soap Products Corp., manufacturer of the nationally sold El Dorado toilet soaps, laundry soaps, and detergents, have produced a chemical derivative which tests have established as the best bacteriacide for mouth bacteria so far discovered. A toothpaste or mouth wash containing it could truly be claimed to be the best mouth germ killer on the market. The chemical is patentable.

1. Should El Dorado manufacture and market a tooth paste containing the new bacteriacide, or should it license its use to one or more present tooth paste manufacturers? (Tabulate all the considerations for and against each line of action before making your decision.)
2. Should El Dorado manufacture and market a mouth wash containing the new bacteriacide or license it to present mouth wash manufacturers? (Tabulate the considerations in this case also.)
3. Assume that El Dorado has decided to make and sell its own tooth paste. List all the tactical marketing issues that must be solved to implement the basic strategic decision. For each issue, indicate actions that might be taken to arrive at the solution.
4. Describe the scheduling that would be involved in the campaign for launching the new toothpaste.

SUGGESTED READINGS

Agnew, H. E., & D. Houghton, *Marketing Policies,* McGraw-Hill Book Co., New York, 1951.

Alderson, W., *Marketing Behavior and Executive Action,* Richard D. Irwin, Homewood, Ill., 1957.

American Management Association, *Blueprint for Effective Marketing Action,* Marketing Series No. 91, 1954.

Banning, D., *Techniques for Marketing New Products,* McGraw-Hill Book Co., New York, 1957.

Corrigan, J. D., *How to Build Profit Value in Your Sales Dollars,* Ronald Press, New York, 1955.

Ewing, D. W. (ed.), *Effective Marketing Action,* Harper & Bros., New York, 1959.

Guild, W., *How to Market Your Product Successfully,* Prentice-Hall, Englewood Cliffs, N.J., 1955.

Howard, J. A., *Marketing Management: Analysis and Decision,* Richard D. Irwin, Homewood, Ill., 1957.

Johnson, L. K., *Sales and Marketing Management,* Allyn & Bacon, Boston, 1957.

Kelley, E., & W. Lazer (eds.), *Managerial Marketing: Perspectives and Viewpoints,* Richard D. Irwin, Homewood, Ill., 1958.

Larson, G. E., *Developing and Selling New Products,* 2d ed, U.S. Government Printing Office, Washington, D.C., 1955.

Lazo, H., & A. Corbin, *Management in Marketing,* McGraw-Hill Book Co., New York, 1960.

National Industrial Conference Board, *New Product Development: III. Marketing New Products,* Studies in Business Policy No. 69, NICB, New York, 1954.

Shubik, M., *Strategy and Market Structure,* John Wiley & Sons, New York, 1959.

Simmons, H., *New Techniques in Marketing Management,* Prentice-Hall, Englewood Cliffs, N.J., 1958.

PART FIVE

MISCELLANEOUS

CHAPTER 28

FOREIGN TRADE

Foreign trade operations and policies are essentially the same as those of domestic marketing. But many marketing problems of a highly distinctive nature are raised by dealing with markets where personal and business customs and commercial laws differ from those of the United States, by the peculiarities of ocean shipping, by the circumstance that one party in every foreign trade deal either pays or receives payment in a currency other than that of his own country, and by a bewildering array of government restrictions on trade and payment. Importers are involved to some extent, but the major impact of these problems is upon exporters. Exported items must be designed to meet the special tastes and standards of particular overseas markets, which are often markedly different from domestic ones. Promotion and selling must take account of unfamiliar customs and psychological reactions. Export traffic management must cope not only with a special transportation agency—the ocean freighter—whose operations, routines, and law differ in many important respects from those of domestic carriers, but with special packing requirements resulting from the nature of the transport involved and the exigencies of custom inspection. Credit and collection difficulties are magnified not only by distance but by inability to apply domestic law of creditors' rights to delinquent foreign debtors. And, finally, superimposed upon all the other risks of foreign trade, inevitably much greater than the corresponding ones attaching to domestic marketing, is the chance of loss from devaluation of foreign currencies or the blocking of foreign payments by governmental action.

Obviously a comprehensive exposition of foreign trade principles and practices is not possible within the scope of a single chapter. Our analysis will be limited to a study of special institutions that have developed for the conduct of foreign trade, and of the major respects in which export operations and policies differ from those of domestic marketing, which were analyzed in Part Four of this volume.

INSTITUTIONS

A small amount of American importing is done directly by a few large department and specialty stores. The rest is accomplished by various types of specialized middlemen. Approximately half of our exporting is likewise handled by middleman organizations.

Middlemen

Five major types of foreign trade middlemen have developed: (1) merchant exporters and importers, (2) commission houses, (3) manufacturers' export agents, (4) export and import brokers, and (5) Webb Act associations.

A *merchant exporter* or *importer* is like a merchant wholesaler in domestic marketing. He buys domestic products, and resells them abroad, on his own account; or he imports, and resells his importations in the United States. His income is derived from profits on his transactions, not from commissions or fees.

A *commission house* is a buyers' agent.* An export commission house buys in the United States on behalf of foreign principals, and exports the purchases to such principals. An import commission house does corresponding foreign buying for American principals. As the term applied to this type of middleman indicates, its income is derived from commissions paid by the buyer. The importance of this class of foreign trade middleman is currently declining.

A *manufacturers' export agent* (commonly known as a "combination export manager") acts as export selling agent for a group of manufacturers, usually noncompeting. His income is derived from the commissions paid by the manufacturers.

An *export and import broker* operates in staple goods such as grains, cotton, sugar, and coffee. On behalf of American manufacturers or middlemen, he locates suppliers of foreign staples for American purchase or foreign buyers for American products. Acting for foreign exporters or importers, he establishes contacts for them with American buyers or sellers. He is paid upon a fee basis.

A *Webb Act association* is a cooperative organization established by manufacturing concerns in some industries to control and manage the export of their products. Under the Webb-Pomerene Act of 1918, such associations are largely exempt from anti-trust law restrictions. Some 50 of these associations are currently active in the export trade.

In practice, the companies that operate as foreign trade middlemen com-

---

* Note the complete antithesis between foreign trade commission houses, and the domestic commission houses described in Chapter 10 which are *sellers'* agents.

monly overlap two or more of the first four of these categories. A single firm may perform brokerage services for some of its clients, act as an export agent or a commission house for others, and engage in some merchant exporting or importing on its own account. But considerable specialization among foreign trade middlemen has developed in other directions. Some "houses" concentrate their efforts primarily upon exporting, combining perhaps all four middleman-client export relationships, while others engage primarily in importing. There is also considerable "line" specialization. Some "houses" confine their activities almost exclusively to staples, perhaps concentrating upon a particular staple such as grains or wool. Similarly, many export houses serving primarily as manufacturers' export agencies limit themselves to related product lines. Finally, there is considerable specialization of both export and import houses by world areas or even by particular foreign countries. There are many Latin-American "houses," some Far Eastern "houses," some "houses" that operate almost exclusively in central European commerce, and some "houses" limited to the English or French trade.

Direct exporting

Foreign trade middlemen are experts in a peculiarly intricate and difficult marketing field. The ordinary small American manufacturer could not practicably duplicate, through his own organization, the skilled services which an export house or a specialized manufacturers' export agent offers him.

Like any domestic middleman, however, an export house or specialized manufacturers' export agent is not usually geared to provide each individual client exclusive, intensive promotion of that client's products. Large manufacturers, accordingly, may find it advantageous to assume the export middleman's functions, together with his costs, in order to achieve controlled development of their exporting activities. In the beginning they may endeavor to carry on their exporting through a "built-in" foreign department—by delegating the conduct of their foreign sales to their existing domestic sales or traffic department. Better results are usually obtained by setting up an independent foreign department, for which the export business is a full-time responsibility. Some large companies have established subsidiary corporations for handling their export activities.

Agencies abroad

Some direct exporters have set up complete importing and selling organizations in the countries to which they export, with warehouses and even factories for the assembling or further processing of semi-fabricated goods.

This procedure has two drawbacks. First, resentment is often engendered in the foreign country because of the engrossment of a profitable element of its domestic business by "aliens," with detrimental marketing effects. Second, the laws of many foreign countries forbid the doing of business in the country by business units of another country.* Hence the "foreign branch" of an American exporter must often be a corporation of the importing country whose stock is controlled by nationals of that country, so that it can be only nominally a "branch" of the American exporter. Consequently a large proportion of direct American exporting, and practically all exporting by American foreign trade middlemen, is to middlemen of the importing countries.

The dominance of foreign middlemen at the overseas end of the American export trade does not preclude the establishing of foreign offices or agencies by American exporters. These offices maintain direct contacts with the foreign middlemen, gather market information for their home offices or principals, help in acquiring credit information and assist collections, and in many ways perform valuable export services. Some American manufacturers, exporting direct or through middlemen, have found it profitable to send "sales representatives" to their foreign markets who function as "missionary salesmen" and undertake general promotion of the employers' export products and cooperate with the foreign middlemen in getting efficient distribution for these products.

EXPORT MARKET INFORMATION AND RESEARCH

To sell blindly in foreign markets is as provocative of disaster as to sell blindly in the domestic market. Successful export operations require a large constant flow of information on foreign market volumes, on custom and style as affecting foreign demands in product design and price ranges, on foreign reactions to various advertising and selling policies, on business conditions in importing countries as affecting import demand and the credit status of importers, and on the financial position of importing countries as affecting payments from those countries.

The principal source of information on foreign markets for most exporters is the Bureau of Foreign and Domestic Commerce of the Department of Commerce, which operates as an information bureau on foreign trade and business conditions for American exporters. The Department of Commerce publishes a valuable periodical—*Foreign Commerce Weekly*—and a series of "World Trade Information Service" reports. It also issues "trade lists" of foreign importers and individual reports on some 300,000 foreign firms. It also maintains a World Trade Directory Service which issues reports on

---

* Post-war need for American capital, and certain provisions of Marshall Plan agreements, resulted in the lifting of this ban in several countries.

foreign firms. Large banks specializing in international financing, such as Chase-Manhattan and Manufacturers Trust, collect foreign trade data through their foreign branches, and make it available to their exporter clients. Several commercial publications such as *American Exporter, International Markets, Exporters' Digest and International Trade Review,* and *Export Trade and Shipper* are valuable sources of current foreign trade information. Direct trade inquiries can be made of the American consular offices located in foreign capitals and principal port cities.

Marketing research on foreign markets to test such matters as consumer preferences in product design, reaction to advertising appeals, advertising medium coverage, and distributor efficiency, for which answers cannot be derived from available published information, is more difficult to undertake than corresponding domestic market surveys. Few exporting concerns find it practicable to set up specialized foreign marketing research units of their own. They sometimes arrange for surveys to be made by their foreign offices or agents, but the personnel of these units are not usually trained in the intricacies of scientific marketing research, and their survey reports are generally unsatisfactory. Few foreign countries until recently had marketing research agencies comparable to the American agencies. Even where they are now available, the distances involved generally preclude the close cooperation between seller and research agency that is necessary to good market survey work. Some large American advertising agencies and some marketing research agencies like A. C. Nielson and International Public Opinion Research Institute have recently established branch organizations abroad, and offer foreign survey service of high calibre.

PRODUCT PLANNING FOR FOREIGN MARKETS

Many American manufacturers in the past have looked upon their export markets merely as "dumping grounds" for surpluses unsaleable at current prices in the domestic market, or for items that did not meet American styles or tastes. While temporarily successful, such export policy has been short-sighted from a long-term view, and has cost American industry much foreign market good will. Large-scale exporters now recognize that foreign requirements and tastes in product design and packaging must be catered to as assiduously as domestic requirements and tastes, if permanent sizable foreign markets are to be established and maintained.

The prevalence of the metric system in Latin America and continental Europe compels many manufacturers of machinery to design their output intended for export to different standards than their domestic production. Unit sizes for other export items, and container dimensions and capacities, must likewise conform to metric standards. Apart from language adaptation, labels and packages intended for non-English-speaking markets must often undergo various transformations. Trademarks must be given greater prominence. Color combinations must often be made more gaudy or more somber to please particular national tastes. Symbols or colors that have prejudicial connotations in certain countries must be avoided. For example, representation of a pig or a veiled face in a trade mark for goods exported to a Mohammedan country would make them unsaleable; white, the color of death in Korea, must be avoided in goods intended for that country.

EXPORT PRICING

Export pricing involves no special pricing principles. Because of imperfect competition ordinarily resulting from nonproduction of an exported item in the importing country, or insufficient production there to meet full market demand, the American exporter has considerable control over the pricing function. The price quoted to a foreign buyer by a direct exporter is usually the domestic "factory-door" price (including normal domestic gross profit), plus all exporting costs with which the exporter is charged, including special packing costs, foreign advertising costs, foreign selling costs, and credit and collection costs plus a bad debt allowance—and in addition, some further margin to cover the special risks attached to exporting. If an exporting manufacturer utilizes agent middlemen, his direct export selling costs are likely to be low, but he must allow for commissions to his exporting agent and to various foreign importing agencies. A merchant exporter adds to the domestic purchase price of his goods a markup that covers exporting costs, overhead, and a profit margin—plus the allowance for the special exporting risks.

Quotation terms

There is no uniform rule as to whether freight charges and marine insurance premiums are to be borne by the exporter or by the consignee. In the former case, of course, the prices quoted by the exporter must include allowance for the freight charges and insurance to the point of destination; in the latter case they do not. The two most common forms of export price quotation are: (1) *F.O.B. vessel at port of shipment,* in which case the exporter assumes all costs through the loading of the cargo on the vessel designated by the consignee at the date or within the period specified, and the consignee assumes all further costs, including any resulting from delay of the designated vessel to arrive at the shipment port for loading; (2) *C.I.F. vessel at port of destination,* in which case the exporter pays the export port charges, the insurance premiums and the freight charges to the consignee's port of destination. Less commonly, terms may be quoted *F.O.B. exporter's factory, mill, or warehouse,* or *C. & F.* (whereby the exporter pays the freight charge, but not the insurance premium, to the port of destination).

Dollar vs. foreign currency pricing

Most American exports are now priced in dollars. This throws the risk of loss through devaluation of the currency of the importer's country on the importer.

Sometimes an importer whose patronage is valued may insist upon, and obtain, quotations in his own currency. Or an importer whose location is not convenient to hedging facilities and who knows that the exporter will have no dfficulty in placing a hedge, requests that the price terms of the contract be in his country's currency. Export pricing in terms of the importer's currency places the risk of that currency's devaluation on the American exporter. He can protect himself against such risk, however, by hedging through "forward selling" of the importing country's currency, as explained later in this chapter. The cost of this operation, of course, would be one of the cost elements included in the exporter's pricing quotation.

EXPORT ADVERTISING AND PROMOTION

One important distinction between domestic and export advertising is the major emphasis in the latter on advertising to importers and dealers. This is natural, since marketing effort for a considerable proportion of our exports is limited to persuading foreign importers and dealers to carry our exported products. The creation of the foreign consumer markets in these cases is the task of the importers and foreign distributors. The most important advertising media for reaching these foreign importers and distributors are the foreign editions of general American export publications such as *American Exporter* and *Universal Commerce,* and of special trade publications such as *Ingenieria Internacional* and *El Farmaceutico.* Direct mail is also a natural promotional approach to these importers and distributors.

Consumer advertising media abroad, available to American exporters, parallel those of the United States. There are newspapers, general reader magazines (including foreign editions of *Time* and *Reader's Digest* magazines), special field magazines, billboards, and radio (both local stations and short-wave from the United States). Motion picture trailers and shorts offer a special advertising opportunity not generally available in this country.

Advertising to foreign consumers involves special medium problems and pitfalls in the use of psychological appeals. Foreign advertising agencies in most countries are of little help to the American export advertiser, since they are little more than "space placers" and do not satisfy the critical standards of advertising accomplishment and service to which American business is accustomed. Some of the larger domestic advertising agencies, however, and several specialized export advertising agencies, serve American exporters effectively. Some of these organizations maintain foreign branches. Others operate through foreign advertising agencies which they have trained to American advertising standards. Whereas domestic agencies derive a major part of their income from the media in which their clients' advertising is placed, export advertising agencies, and the foreign divisions of domestic agencies, are paid on a commission basis by their clients. These commissions customarily range from 15 to 20 percent of the advertising costs involved.

TRANSPORTATION AND TRAFFIC MANAGEMENT

Transportation costs bulk much larger in export commerce than they do in domestic marketing. Packing problems are more intense. Shipping paper requirements are complicated. Traffic management, a minor marketing operation for most domestic selling units, is a major consideration for all exporters, whether direct or middlemen, and special traffic service agencies have developed in the exporting field which have no counterpart in domestic marketing.

Choice of carriers

A few large exporters and importers, like the oil companies, Bethlehem Steel Company, and United Fruit Company, operate their own shipping lines. Other exporters have a choice among three classes of ocean carriers —express liners, combination passenger and cargo ships, and tramps.

The express liners, and the combination passenger and cargo ships, operate established routes on regular schedules. They carry 85 to 90 percent of the world's shipping. The liners, designed primarily for passenger traffic, and usually serving only a few ports on their routes, offer high speed, carry only certain types of freight, and charge high rates. The combination ships, designed primarily for freight traffic, operate on slower schedules, serve larger numbers of ports, and charge lower rates than do the liners. Ordinarily there is no freight rate competition among the liners or among the combination ships of different companies. Rate schedules reflecting speeds and service variations are agreed upon periodically at "conferences" of the shipping companies. Exporters may make contracts for freight shipments on liners or combination ships, either directly with the shipping companies or through ship brokers.

Tramp ships, designed for economical operation rather than speed, operate without definite schedule. They go wherever there are cargoes to be shipped. Their rates, determined by individual bargaining, are usually lower than those of the scheduled combination ships. Often they are the only carriers available for shipments to out-of-the-way ports. Contracts with them are usually made through ship brokers.

Packing

Packing for overseas transport presents more difficult problems than packing for domestic rail or truck transport. Packing containers must be strong enough to withstand the strains of loading and unloading, sometimes with primitive equipment, and the pressures of cargo hold storing. Resistance to moisture and often to high temperatures must be incorporated. Packing must protect against pilfering, yet be susceptible of being opened for customs inspection. Since freight rates are usually charged on a basis of weight or measurement, whichever option is more favorable to the carrier, and since some foreign customs duties are based on gross weight, lightness and shape of the packing container may contribute substantially to minimizing export costs. Marine insurance premiums, and the "normal loss" which cannot be covered by insurance, also depend to some extent on the type of packing used.

Rarely do all the packing considerations with which an exporter is faced point to a single all-advantage solution. Usually he has to effect a compromise between protection and economy, and considerable technical research may be needed to establish optimum packing specifications.

Shipping papers

To meet ordinary trade requirements, and to conform to domestic and foreign legal requirements, an exporter must ordinarily prepare six types of "shipping papers."

1. *Commercial invoice.* This document, like the ordinary invoice of domestic trade, is a bill or statement for the goods sold. It must contain detailed identification and description of the items and packages covered, and must state the carrier vessel, the price terms, and the terms of payment. Some countries require that it be one of the papers submitted for customs declaration. But even without this requirement normal business practice would require its preparation.

2. *Ocean bill of lading.* Like a domestic bill of lading, this document serves as a document of title (when it is a "to order" bill), as a contract between the shipper and the carrier, and as a receipt for the shipped goods by the carrier. Customarily three copies signed by the carrier are sent by different mails to the consignee or to the shipper's foreign representative,

so that loss of any one copy will not interfere with the delivery of the goods at destination. Other unsigned copies are also made for the shipper's and carrier's files.

3. *Consular invoice* or *certificate of origin.* This document must be prepared to conform with the laws of the country of destination. It establishes that a shipment belongs to a permissible import category. Blanks are obtained from the consular office of the importer's country. After being filled out, a specified number must be presented to the consular office for visé and signature.

4. *Export declaration.* This document is required by the U.S. government, to be used as a basis for its foreign trade statistics. Declarations covering export shipment by boat must be notarized before submission.

5. *Marine insurance policy* or *certificate.* The shipper's responsibility for exported goods usually ends when the goods are loaded on a vessel at the port of shipment. Accordingly, when a shipper insures goods to destination, he acts as an agent for the consignee. He therefore sends the original insurance policy, or a certificate issued against an open policy carried by the shipper, to the consignee, so that the latter can claim upon the policy or certificate if necessary.

6. *Draft* or *bill of exchange.* This is the seller's credit instrument, through which he will obtain payment directly from the importer or from an "accepting" bank. Export drafts and bills of exchange, and bankers' acceptances, are explained in the next section of this chapter.

Foreign freight forwarders

The complexities of the paper work attached to exporting hold many costly pitfalls for small exporters who cannot afford foreign departments or skilled traffic managers. Accordingly there has developed a specialized agency—the foreign freight forwarder—that assumes complete responsibility for preparing all shipping papers needed by its exporter clients. In addition, these foreign freight forwarders are often able to consolidate shipments to particular ports, thereby obtaining freight rate reductions for their clients. They also handle the documentary procedures involved in obtaining payments.

EXPORT CREDIT AND PAYMENT

Export credit is based on the same considerations as domestic mercantile credit—the character, capacity, and financial position of the buyer. The major differences between the two classes of credit are: (1) the terms, (2) the instrumentalities employed, and (3) the sources of credit information utilized.

Terms

In the case of new foreign customers about whom little credit information can be obtained, and when orders involve production to special specifications, exporters are likely to ask for cash payment in advance—i.e., when the order is placed, or at time of shipment. Such advance payment may also be asked whenever there is strong probability that the currency of the importer's country may soon be devalued. Otherwise, advance payment has little place in export trade.

Some C.O.D. exporting is done by sight drafts which must be paid by the importer before he can obtain the bill of lading and other shipping papers that enable him to claim the shipment; this arrangement is called "D/P terms" (documents on payment of draft).

Export credit generally runs to longer terms than domestic. Ninety to 120 days, counting from the date when the draft is accepted, are most common. Agricultural produce and machinery are sold on still longer terms.

Instrumentalities

The open-book account, the predominant instrumentality of domestic mercantile credit, has little place in export credit except in the Canadian trade.

The most common export trade instrumentality is the *trade draft* or *bill of exchange,* drawn by the exporter on the foreign importer, and accepted by the latter as a condition of his obtaining the bill of lading and other shipping papers that entitle him to the shipment. In effect, this is equivalent to the trade acceptance of domestic credit. The credit period on most trade drafts begins to run from the date of acceptance by the importer. The export contract may call for acceptance on sight; since the draft and shipping papers are commonly sent by air mail, this usually involves acceptance before the shipment arrives. Some contracts provide for acceptance on arrival of the goods. The accepted draft is returned to the exporter who can hold it until maturity and then transmit it through his bank for collection, or may discount it as explained later in this chapter.

Bank drafts against letter of credit substitute the credit of a bank for that of the importer, and hence reduce the exporter's credit risk and provide him with a payment instrument which can be more readily discounted. The importer must pay a charge for the bank guaranty and the bank services involved, so this payment provision increases his costs. The steps involved in an export credit extension and payment by means of bank drafts against a dollar irrevocable letter of credit issued by the importer's bank and confirmed by a domestic bank are:

1. The importer arranges with a bank in his country for a letter of credit to the exporter. This letter of credit is in effect a promise by the importer's bank to pay drafts drawn upon it by the exporter, covering his shipments to the importer, provided all the conditions related to the shipments stated in the letter are complied with. The importer's bank undertakes this obligation on the basis of the importer's being an acceptable credit risk or his deposit of security with it, and on his agreement to repay the bank when the accepted drafts come through to it for payment.

2. The importer's bank sends notice of this letter of credit to a correspondent bank in the exporter's country (commonly in the exporter's city), which "confirms" or guarantees it on the basis of its confidence in the importer's bank and for a commission charged to that bank.

3. The confirming bank prepares the actual letter-of-credit document shown in Illustration 28–1, advises the exporter of its availability, and delivers it to him.

4. Upon loading each shipment made in conformity with the terms of the letter of credit, the exporter prepares a draft for the amount involved and submits it, together with all shipping papers involved, to the confirming bank. If the terms of the letter have been strictly complied with, the bank discounts the draft for the exporter, who obtains immediate payment, less the discount charge.

5. The confirming bank then sends the draft and accompanying shipping papers to the importer's bank, which accepts the draft (thereby making it a "bankers' acceptance" or "bank bill") and returns it to the confirming bank. This bank may either hold the acceptance until maturity, and thus earn the discount charge, or it may sell the acceptance on the open market.

6. At maturity of the acceptance, it is transmitted by whoever is holding it to the importer's bank, for payment.

7. At the time the importer's bank accepted the exporter's draft on it, it drew a domestic draft for a like amount plus charges, and for the same due date, on the importer. Payment of this second draft by the importer on the due date reimburses the bank for its payment on its banker's acceptance.

The importer's bank that arranges the letter of credit is often a branch of one of the large American banks engaged in world-wide foreign trade financing. If so, the exporter obtains acceptance of drafts drawn under the letter of credit directly from the home office of the bank. He can then hold the bankers' acceptance himself to save the discount charge, or he can discount it with the accepting bank or with his own bank, or he can sell it on the open market.

Sources of credit information

If an exporter sells on advance payment terms, or if he can arrange for payment by bankers' acceptances under letter of credit, he does not need to make any credit inquiry about the importer, since the importer's credit standing is immaterial to the exporter's probability of getting paid. But if an export sale is to be made on the basis of an accepted time draft, the importer must be established as an acceptable credit risk. Otherwise there is

Guaranty Trust Company of New York

New York Offices	Foreign Department	Foreign Offices
140 Broadway	140 Broadway	
Fifth Avenue at 44th St.	New York 15, N. Y.	London
Madison Avenue at 60th St.		Paris
40 Rockefeller Plaza	March 5, 19*	Brussels

Smith Tool Co., Inc.
29 Bleecker Street
New York, N. Y.

On all communications please refer to
NUMBER IC 152647

Gentlemen:

We are instructed to advise you of the establishment by
.Bank of South America, Puerto Cabello, Venezuela . . . .

of their IRREVOCABLE Credit No. 19845 . . . .

in your favor, for the account of John Doe, Puerto Cabello, Venezuela . . . .

for . . . . U. S. $ 3,000 (THREE THOUSAND U. S. DOLLARS) . . . .

available upon presentation to us of your drafts at sight on us, accompanied by :

Commercial invoice, in triplicate, describing the merchandise as indicated below,

Consular invoice, in triplicate, all copies signed and stamped by the Consul of
      Venezuela

Negotiable marine insurance policy and/or underwriter's certificate, including war
      risks, with loss payable to Bank of South America, Puerto Cabello

Full set of straight ocean steamer bills of lading showing consignment to Bank of
      South America, Puerto Cabello, stamped by Venezuelan Consul

evidencing shipment of UNA MAQUINA DE SELLAR LATAS consigned to Bank of South
      America, Puerto Cabello, Venezuela

The above bank engages with you that all drafts drawn under and in compliance with the terms of this advice will be duly honored if presented at this office on or before March 31, 19*

We confirm the foregoing and undertake that all drafts drawn and presented in accordance with its terms will be duly honored.

Except so far as otherwise expressly stated herein, our commitments hereunder are subject to the Uniform Customs and Practice for Commercial Documentary Credits fixed by the Thirteenth Congress of the International Chamber of Commerce. For the definitions of certain export quotations, reference is made to the general descriptions of those terms included in the "Revised American Foreign Trade Definitions, 1941."

Yours respectfully,

Authorized Signature   Authorized Signature

Immediately upon receipt, please examine this instrument and if its terms are not clear to you or if you need any assistance in respect to your availment of it, we would welcome your communicating with us. Documents should be presented promptly and not later than 3 P.M.

A CONFIRMED IRREVOCABLE EXPORT LETTER OF CREDIT.
Courtesy of Guaranty Trust Co.

ILLUSTRATION 28–1

too great a chance that the acceptance may not be paid upon maturity. Even where exporting is done on the basis of sight drafts, inquiry into the credit standing of the importer is essential, since the draft might not be honored upon presentation, in which case the exporter would be faced with the

INTERNATIONAL REPORT
DUN & BRADSTREET, INC.

| SALAZAR & CIA., FRANCISCO | GLOVE MFRS. | SANTIAGO, CHILE |
| (C 1) | (5) | 53 Ave. de Republica |

CD   JUNE 27, 19-

PARTNERS:
Francisco Salazar   Mrs. Inez Salazar
Francisco Salazar, Jr.   Miss Joanna Salazar

SUMMARY
GENERAL PARTNERSHIP REGISTERED 1945 TO SUCCEED BUSINESS FOUNDED BY THE SENIOR PARTNER IN 1908. RECORD GOOD. FINANCIAL CONDITION SOUND. NET WORTH ESC. 167,502. PAYMENTS PROMPT.

HISTORY
A general partnership registered on May 10, 1945, with a capital of Esc. 100,000, controlled by the Salazar family, above listed.

The business itself was founded as a proprietorship in 1908 by Francisco Salazar, Sr., who has since retired from active participation herein, entrusting the management to his son.

Salazar Jr., has been with the business all his life and is well acquainted with all phases of the venture. He is experienced and well regarded.

METHOD OF OPERATION
Engaged in the manufacture of high fashion womens' gloves made from a variety of materials. Has own retail sales outlet and wholesale department. The factory and shop combined are located at the above address on one of the more fashionable shopping streets of Santiago. Sells on cash and credit terms of 30-60 days. Equipment is in good repair and the shop is attractive. There are 10 employees on the payroll.

FINANCIAL INFORMATION
The following balance sheet for period ending May 31, 19- was submitted over the signature of Francisco Salazar Jr.

ASSETS	(ESCUDOS)	LIABILITIES	(ESCUDOS)
Cash	7,926	Accts. Payable	17,147
Accts. Rec.	71,847	Notes pay.	38,904
Inventory	132,673	Due Banks	20,700
CURR. ASSETS	212,446	CURR. LIABS.	76,751
Prepaid expenses	1,003	Mortgage on realty	8,500
Furn., Fix. & Equip.	19,931	Capital	100,000
Real estate, net	19,373	Surplus	67,502
TOTAL ASSETS	252,753	TOTAL LIABS.	252,753

The figures reflect a favorable condition with strong current position and satisfactory cash. Sales for the period Esc. 800,000 - Net profits Esc. 20,000. Inventory and real estate are fully insured.

CURRENCY
The Escudo is quoted at .95 in U.S. Cy.

TRADE INVESTIGATION
A checking conducted in the local market revealed the following experiences:

HC	OWE	P.DUE	TERMS	PAYMENTS
23,500	--	--	60 days S/D	Prompt
18,700	8,800	--	75 days S/D	Prompt
3,000	--	--	Net 60 days	Prompt
RR: 6/27/-				

A DUN & BRADSTREET INTERNATIONAL REPORT. *Courtesy of Dun & Bradstreet.*

ILLUSTRATION 28–2

equally unfavorable alternatives of extending credit to an account which has already established itself as an unfavorable risk, or of arranging for return of the shipment and bearing the costs of double transport.

The sources of credit information on foreign importers parallel those utilized in domestic credit. There are mercantile agency ratings and reports, interchange information, bank reports, and financial statements. The respective value of these various sources differs considerably, however, from the corresponding sources for domestic credit.

Ratings and reports. Dun & Bradstreet publishes *International Market Guide,* which rates 190,000 Latin-American importers. A second volume, started in 1961, covers 75,000 European firms. D & B, the magazine *American Exporter,* and several trade associations prepare individual reports on foreign importers. These reports on foreign buyers usually explore personal histories and family backgrounds of the principals of a foreign importing firm more thoroughly, but are weaker on financial information, than mercantile agency reports on domestic customers.

Interchange information. Exporters exchange ledger information on common accounts just as domestic sellers do. In addition, they can draw interchange reports from the Foreign Credit Interchange Bureau of the National Association of Credit Management. These resemble in some respects N.A.C.M. domestic interchange reports described in Chapter 24, but through a code system provide much fuller information on terms of sale and manner of payment.

Bank reports. Bank reports, of minor value in domestic credit inquiry, are a major reliance of most exporters, who usually keep their accounts with one of the large seaboard banks that engage in foreign trade financing and have foreign branches. Through their branch offices, these banks are able to obtain detailed information on foreign importers. Bank letters in reply to inquiries sometimes contain pertinent items or recent developments not included in the agency reports.

Financial statements. Foreign business houses are not so accustomed to submitting financial statements as are domestic buyers. In many cases, for an exporter to request a statement from a foreign buyer would risk losing the account. When statements are submitted by foreign buyers, they are often found to be woefully inadequate by American accounting standards. Hence financial statement analysis has only a rudimentary role in most export credit analysis.

The international financial situation as an export credit factor

A foreign account, or a foreign accepting bank, may be prepared to pay when the accepted draft is presented for payment, but the national government of its country may in the meantime have placed restrictions on transmitting payments to the United States. Or the account or bank may make payment in the foreign currency called for by the export contract, but the currency may have been devalued between the dates of shipment and payment, so that the payment converted into dollars results in loss instead of gain to the exporter.

These contingencies, which do not arise in domestic credit transactions, compel export credit managers to pay close attention to the international financial situation as it affects the countries of their accounts, as well as to the actual credit status of the accounts themselves. At times during the past two decades, this factor has been the crucial one in most export credit decisions.

EXPORT FINANCING

Because of the long credit terms involved in exporting, most exporters require external financing to liquidate their working capital tied up in receivables.

Exporters who obtain domestic or confirmed foreign bank acceptances can, as previously indicated, sell these on the open market, or discount them without recourse with the confirming bank (which, in effect, constitutes selling them to that bank). The discount allowance in either case is the low open-market rate on bankers' acceptances, which in recent years has ranged between 1⅛ percent and 3½ percent.

Accepted trade drafts (i.e., time drafts drawn on importers and accepted by them) may also be discounted at commercial banks at some proportion up to 80 percent of their face value. Such discounting is usually "with recourse"; if the draft is not paid at maturity, the exporter must reimburse the bank. The rate for "recourse" discounting of trade drafts is considerably higher than that for bankers' acceptances.

Some large factoring houses also discount their clients' foreign trade receivables. This method of financing has increased rapidly since World War II.

EXPORT RISK MINIMIZATION

The risks of loss in exporting are: (1) damage or pilferage of goods during transport; (2) destruction of the goods through loss of the carrier; (3) nonpayment by the importer; (4) blockage of payment by foreign government action; and (5) devaluation of foreign currencies in cases where export contracts provide for payment in the foreign currency.

In most export contracts, the exporter is responsible for loss through damage, pilferage, or destruction of goods until such time as they are loaded on the ocean carrier. From that point on the risk is the importer's. The exporter has an interest in minimizing importers' losses from damage and pilfering, however, since his trade good-will is determined in part by the condition of his shipments on arrival and by the lowness of the marine insurance rates that the importer must pay. Effective packing is the exporter's contribution to minimization of damaging and pilfering risks. It also reduces the insurance premiums that are billed to the importer, and the normal loss deduction that the importer must bear under marine insurance policies.

Marine insurance to cover movement of goods from the shipping port to the port of destination is taken out by the exporter. Since under most export contracts this part of export movement is at the responsibility of the importer, the exporter acts as agent of the importer in taking out the insurance, and charges the premium to the importer.

Export credit loss can be minimized only by sound credit and collection policy. In this matter little criticism can be made of American export credit managers, for the bad debt loss on export credits has long been much lower than that on domestic mercantile credit. Insurance of export credits was possible during the 1920's and 1930's, but was discontinued during the 1940's. Through the federal Export-Import Bank, certain types of export credit risks can now be guaranteed. Broader protection, through complementary coverage provided by insurance companies, is in prospect for the 1960's.

Constant vigilance with respect to developments in international finance is the way of avoiding loss, or delay in receipt of payments, through "blocking" actions by foreign governments. Such vigilance also provides protection against loss through foreign currency devaluation when payments for exports are to be made in such currency. In this latter case there is a second line of protection. An exporter in this situation can hedge his position, in the same way as a domestic grain dealer who acquires grain at spot prices and must hold it for several months before he can sell it, during which time grain prices may fall. An exporter who contracts to accept payment of £1,000 approximately 120 days after shipment can, upon committing himself, make a forward sale of £1,000 at the current quotation. If, by the time the importer pays the £1,000, the pound has been devalued, whatever the exporter loses in dollars on this payment he will gain when he covers his previous forward sale. The costs of this hedging transaction, of course, are taken into account in the price quoted to the English importer.

VOCATIONAL CONSIDERATIONS

The field of foreign trade needs college-trained men and women and offers them, in addition to compensation equivalent to that attached to domestic business employment, some possibility of foreign travel. Since the field embraces every business operation, there is full opportunity for every personality type and aptitude. The extrovert will find his opportunity in sales, promotion, and contact work. Introverted individuals will find theirs in the traffic, credit, and financing departments.

One special aptitude is essential, however, in all phases of foreign trade work—the ability to learn readily and become fluent in one or more foreign languages. In the past, American exporting relied too much on the capacity of educated nationals of other countries to speak and write English. Now it is realized that successful importing as well as exporting requires that correspondence and conversations be conducted as readily in the client's or customer's language as in our own.

REVIEW

1. How important are middlemen in American foreign trade? Describe the classes of foreign trade middlemen. To what extent are these foreign trade middlemen specialized?

2. Explain "built-in foreign department."

3. From what sources can an exporter obtain information on foreign markets? To what extent can he utilize marketing research on his foreign markets?

4. Why do manufacturers often design and package their products differently for foreign and domestic markets?

5. Explain export prices quoted "F.O.B. vessel" and "C.I.F."

6. Under what circumstances do American exporters specify payment in dollars? in the currency of the importer's country?

7. Through what media would an American exporter advertise to foreign importers? to foreign consumers? What types of advertising agencies would he employ? How would such agencies be compensated?

8. What type of carriers are available for export shipping? How do their services and rates differ?

9. Why are packing considerations even more important for export than for domestic shipment?

10. Describe the six shipping papers commonly involved in export shipments.

11. What is a foreign freight forwarder?

12. Explain D/P terms, trade draft, bank draft against letter of credit.

13. Compare and contrast the sources for foreign credit information with those for domestic credit information.

14. What special marketing risks does an exporter face? How can he minimize them?

DISCUSSION TOPICS

1. "American foreign trade would be better off if there were more direct exporting and importing."
2. "The American manufacturer will never be able to understand foreign consumers' buying motivations."
3. "If only American importers and exporters always insisted on dollar payment they would free themselves of all the risks of international exchange."
4. "Don't let Madison Avenue handle your foreign advertising."
5. Why add one more exporting cost by arranging for letter-of-credit financing by the importer?
6. "The only possibility of export credit insurance is through government agencies."
7. Would you be interested in a career in foreign trade?

PROBLEM

Eastern Mills Corp., is a large vertical integration in the cotton textile field including several mills which produce a wide variety of fabrics, several printing and dying plants, and a converting unit. In recent years a growing proportion of its sales has been to several export houses, and through a combination export manager, which have developed Central and South American markets for Eastern Mills fabrics.

Eastern Mills Corp. has now established Eastern Mills Export Corp., a wholly-owned subsidiary. A vigorous program to expand Latin American sales of Eastern Mills fabrics is projected.

1. Should Eastern Mills Corp. discontinue selling to the export houses and through the combination export manager?
2. Who will be the ultimate Latin American purchasers of Eastern Mills fabrics? Through what individuals or agencies will Eastern Mills fabrics reach these ultimate purchasers?
3. How will Eastern Mills Export Corporation ascertain what fabric weaves and designs are in popular demand in the various Latin American countries? How will it ascertain the market potential for Eastern Mills fabrics in each of these countries? How will it ascertain the names and addresses of potential customers?
4. To whom would Eastern Mills Export Corporation advertise? through what media?
5. The general credit period in this export line is 120 days. What payment arrangements should Eastern Mills Export Corp. provide for? To what extent should it make credit inquiries about its customers? From what sources can it obtain credit information upon them?
6. Should the export sales contracts specify payment in dollars or in the currency of the importer's country? Why?
7. Describe the papers that will have to be prepared in connection with each shipment.

SUGGESTED READINGS

Angel, J. L., *Principles of Import Procedure,* World Trade Academy, Chicago, 1952.

Heck, H. J., *Foreign Commerce,* McGraw-Hill Book Co., New York, 1953.

Horn, P. V., & J. Gomez, *International Trade: Principles and Practices,* 4th ed, Prentice-Hall, Englewood Cliffs, N.J., 1959.

An Introduction to Doing Import and Export Business, Foreign Commerce Department, Chamber of Commerce of the U.S.A., Washington, D.C., 1959.

Kramer, R. L., *International Marketing,* South-Western Publishing Co., Cincinnati, 1959.

MacDonald, P., *Practical Exporting and Importing,* 2d ed, Ronald Press, New York, 1959.

McDowell, E. E., & H. M. Gibbs, *Ocean Transportation,* McGraw-Hill Book Co., New York, 1953.

Pratt, E. E., *The Foreign Trade Handbook,* Dartnell, Chicago, 1948.

Pratt, E. E., *Modern International Commerce,* Allyn & Bacon, New York, 1956.

Reaching Foreign Markets, National Industrial Conference Board, New York, 1956.

A Review of Export and Import Procedure, Guaranty Trust Co. of New York, New York, 1957.

Sanchez, J. R., *Foreign Credits and Collections,* Prentice-Hall, Englewood Cliffs, N.J., 1947.

PERIODICALS: *American Exporter, Foreign Commerce Weekly.*

CHAPTER 29

MARKETING COSTS

The consumer's dollar spent on woolen apparel goes roughly 60 cents for production and 40 cents for marketing. Of the 20 cents paid for a loaf of bread, 9.7 cents covers the costs and profit margins of raising the wheat, milling the flour and baking the bread, and 10.3 cents covers the costs and profit margins of marketing the wheat, flour, and bread. The marketing "spread" for packaged drugs and for coal is around 80 percent. Overall, half the ultimate price of American goods represents marketing costs.

Are marketing costs too high? There are many who argue that they are, that consumers and the general economy are the victims of improper practices and of gross inefficiency on the part of our marketing agencies. Some take a radically contrary position and claim that the more advanced the civilization and culture of a country, the higher should be its marketing costs relative to costs associated with production. They argue that, if our present marketing "spread" appears high, it should be cause for self-congratulation rather than criticism, since it indicates our cultural progress is well advanced. The majority who have written upon this issue, including most of the authoritative scholars on the subject, admit the possibility of more efficient cost-saving operation at certain points of the marketing system but hold that such improvements would have only minor influence on the overall ratio of production and marketing costs, which reflects a sound balance for the American economy in its present development.

Our study of the problem will cover: (1) the issue of marketing "costs" v. "value added" by marketing; (2) the facts as to marketing costs in general; (3) some factors that contribute to these costs and the possibilities of modifying them; and (4) individual company distribution cost analysis as one factor which is currently contributing to improved marketing efficiency.

"MARKETING COSTS" VS. "VALUE ADDED BY MARKETING"

Currently there is a forceful campaign on the part of a number of Marketing writers to substitute the term "value added by marketing" for the familiar "marketing costs." Their arguments are: (1) When applied to national operational or institutional figures, the two terms have identical meaning—the difference between the selling value of goods shipped or delivered and the cost of goods, materials, supplies, and services purchased. (2) "Value added" has a favorable connotation, "costs" an unfavorable one. (3) Economists and the Bureau of the Census have long utilized the "value added" term when referring to the producers' "spreads" in manufacturing, agriculture, and mining. Custom has retained the term "costs" to denote marketing "spreads." (4) As a consequence, there is an implication that there is nothing to criticise in the "spreads" associated with manufacture, agriculture, and mining, since they are an "addition" favorable to the economy, while marketing "spreads" are to be condemned as "costs" which subtract from economic yield.

There can be no question but that a real semantic issue is involved in the application of these two terms. Whenever we think of "costs," we do so with an unfavorable feeling that somehow or other they are probably excessive and should be cut. Part of the never-ending unfavorable comparison of marketing with production activities on the basis of relative efficiency may well stem from this semantic consideration.

The solution, however, is not to substitute the term "value added" for "costs." The term "value added" has always been false as applied to manufacturing "spread," and would be equally false applied to marketing. "Spread," whether manufacturing or marketing, is increased by inefficiency. With "value added by manufacture" used to mean "manufacturers' spread," we are driven to the misleading conclusion that the greater the inefficiency in our industrial structure, or in any manufacturing line, the greater the value it contributes to the economic system! Also, excessive profits derived by manufacturers in a position to charge high monopoly or quasi-monopoly prices appear in the favorable light of additional "value added." To substitute "value added by marketing" for "marketing costs" would extend these and other fallacies to the field of distribution.

The ideal solution would be to drop the term "value added" as applied to manufacture, agriculture, and mining and return to the term "costs," which is correct in an economic sense. The next best, to free marketing from the semantic implications of the term "costs," would be to substitute the more colorless term "spread." Neither of these solutions is in immediate prospect, however, so the term "marketing costs" should be retained, for the time being at least, as being less harmful and less misleading than the proposed "value added by marketing."

THE FACTS OF MARKETING COSTS

At a superficial glance, there would appear to be ample statistics on marketing costs. The federal Department of Agriculture has made a valuable series of calculations on what the consumer pays and what the farmer receives for various agricultural commodities. But since processing and marketing costs are lumped together in most of these analyses, they do not present a clear picture on marketing costs as such. A few Federal Trade Commission reports make a true analysis of marketing costs for some individual commodities. Trade associations in various lines have published excellent data on the marketing costs of particular categories of manufacturers, or wholesalers, or retailers. Individual scholars have attempted to derive broad estimates of over-all marketing costs for scattered years by correlating various Census figures, but their conclusions are little better than loose estimates and for the most part are in wide conflict. Taken together, despite their impressive bulk, these studies provide only a fragmentary and not too reliable picture of what marketing costs are for individual commodities, by categories of marketing agencies, by marketing operations, and for the economy as a whole. Generalizations and conclusions on this subject should therefore be treated as tentative—a consideration not always allowed for by writers on the subject.

Problems of calculating

An initial problem in the calculation of marketing costs is whether the profits of the various marketing agencies should be included in the "cost" concept. Most marketing cost calculations include distributors' profit, if only because the data available do not readily permit separation of this item. In defense of the procedure, it is argued: (1) "profit" for the great numbers of unincorporated enterprises active in marketing is largely labor recompense of the proprietors or partners, and (2) a "normal" true profit is a proper social cost compensating for entrepreneurial risk, initiative, and capital. Such inclusion of profits in "costs" confuses the picture, however, as to marketing efficiency. An apparent low "cost" at some points of the marketing structure might actually reflect unduly low profits or actual loss to the operators rather than efficient operation, with the consequence that these operators were being inadequately compensated for their labor or their capital was being disinvested. Either of these would be a social cost which ought to be included in marketing costs. Contrariwise, an apparent high marketing "cost" might be caused by unusually high profits, attributable to a monopoly situation or some other special factor. Such extra profits, while added to prices paid by consumers, would not be a true social cost involving application of labor and resources, but only an incidental diversion of the national income flow.

There are three approaches to calculating marketing costs (with profit included), whether for an individual commodity or for the economy as a whole.

1. Producers' sales may be subtracted from consumer payments for an individual commodity, for a class of commodities, or for all commodities. This is the procedure on which most of the Department of Agriculture studies, such as those embodied in Illustration 29–1, are based. It has two

PERCENT OF RETAIL DOLLAR RECEIVED BY PRODUCERS AND DISTRIBUTORS FOR SELECTED COMMODITIES

COMMODITY	FARM-ERS	LONG-HAUL TRANS-PORTA-TION [1]	ASSEM-BLING MIDDLE-MEN	MANU-FAC-TURERS AND PROCES-SORS	WHOLE-SALING MIDDLE-MEN	RETAIL-ERS	TOTAL
Apples [2]	24	21	23	..	9	23	100
Potatoes [3]	26	24	21	..	11	18	100
Meat products	51	4	4	20	1	24	100
Bakery products	7	2	1	75	3	12	100
Prepared cereals	17	5	2	48	7	21	100
Canned beans	14	2	4	46	8	26	100
Fluid milk	55	4	..	39	..	6	100
Cheese	49	1	2	14	10	24	100
Cotton textiles	14	4	2	44	8	32	100
Wool textiles	14	4	2	49	2	33	100

Source: U.S. Department of Agriculture studies.
[1] Exclusive of transportation costs included in purchase or delivery costs of producers or distributors.
[2] Pacific Northwest apples sold in Pittsburgh, December 1949 through May 1950.
[3] Sold in Cleveland, February through June 1950.
[4] Included with farmers' proportion.

ILLUSTRATION 29–1

weaknesses. First, farmers, manufacturers, and other producers undertake various marketing operations when selling their output. Costs and profits attributable to these distributional operations should be counted as *marketing* costs; and only the *production* costs of these producers should be subtracted from consumer payments. Hardly any farmers and only a few manufacturers, however, have accounting systems that satisfactorily distinguish between their production and marketing costs. Practically all calculations based on this procedure, including those of the Department of Agriculture, accordingly start with payments received by producers, not with their production costs and profit attributable to production. This throws an element of marketing cost, which can be very substantial in the case of manufactured consumer goods, in with production. Secondly, in some lines, middlemen physically improve the commodities they handle—terminal grain elevators "condition" grain holdings, lumber yards "season" stock, coffee merchants roast the bean coffee, converters have their fabric printed. These are production operations and their costs—if separately ascertainable—should be excluded from marketing cost calculation.

2. Gross margins—sales less cost of goods and services purchased in the case of merchant dealers, and commissions in the case of agent middlemen —for each class of marketing agencies engaged in the distribution of a commodity, or for distribution in general, may be totalled. The periodic *Census of Business* contains comprehensive detailed figures on the expenses (but not the profits) of wholesalers and retailers, and of various classes of auxiliary marketing agencies. This approach to determining marketing costs has the advantage that the marketing cost calculations it gives can be broken down by classes of marketing agencies. It also has four disadvantages: (a) as in the case of the first procedure, producers' marketing costs are excluded, and the costs of processing done by some middlemen are included; (b) middlemen's profits, part of the economic cost of marketing, are not included; (c) accurate data on the expenses of some important classes of auxiliary marketing agencies are lacking; and (d) since many marketing agencies, particularly at retail level, handle several commodities and even commodity classes, the costs of marketing particular commodities or commodity classes cannot be calculated from available data.

3. If data were available, marketing costs might be tabulated by the various marketing operations—buying, promotion, selling, transportation, credit, marketing research, storage, financing. Data for such a calculation are fragmentary, however, and little progress has been made along this line.

Generalizations

The following generalizations upon marketing costs, highly tentative and subject possibly to substantial amendment by future studies, may be advanced.

1. Marketing costs (including profits attributable to marketing operations) account for around half of the final sale price of all goods.* In the case of consumer goods, the proportion is well over half. Various published estimates of the proportion of total marketing costs range from 30 to 60 percent. Those in the lower range, however, exclude producers' marketing costs, or exclude profits attributable to marketing activity and

---

* See Chapter 1, p. 10.

otherwise limit the cost concept, or exclude various categories of marketing agencies.

2. Retailing costs are the largest element in the total marketing cost. According to Illustration 1–2, retailers were responsible in 1959 for 33% of the total marketing bill, manufacturers for 28%, and wholesalers for 18%.

3. There is considerable variation in the proportions of marketing and production costs for classes of commodities. The proportion of marketing costs for farm products is around 50 percent. For cigars and cigarettes, it is around 35 percent. For some classes of items it is as high as 80 percent. In general, marketing costs are heavier proportionately for consumer goods than for industrial equipment and materials. Specialty products must bear a higher proportion of marketing costs than staple products, in spite of frequent direct manufacturer-to-retailer distribution of the former, because of the heavy promotional expenses and high retailer markup involved. New products coming upon the market have heavier marketing costs than corresponding established items. Items of high unit value, such as automobiles, carry a lower marketing cost, proportionately, than low-unit-value commodities.

4. There is a cyclical variation in the relative proportions of marketing and production costs. Distributors' margins are apparently more rigid, in the face of business fluctuations, than producers' margins. Hence the proportion of marketing costs in retail prices tends to rise in recessions and decline during economic upswings.

5. Historically there has been a consistent upward trend in the ratio of marketing to production costs.* Prior to the 1870's this rise can only be inferred from scattered bits of evidence. For the years since 1869 there are statistical series to confirm some elements in this rise. It has resulted from a combination of factors. The predominant group have tended to lift the ratio, but there have been some offsetting considerations.

Among the factors contributing to the rising ratio of marketing costs have been the following:

1. Territorial expansion of American settlement until the 1920's extended the distance between manufacturers and consumers, and increased marketing emphasis on transportation and systems of middlemen.

2. Territorial specialization in the production of many items, particularly agricultural products, while lowering their production costs, has increased their costs of distribution by extending their market movements.

---

* Some Marketing writers argue on the basis of recent *Census of Business* figures that this upward trend of relative marketing costs has been slowed down or even brought to a stop. This argument fails to take into account that *Census of Business* figures have a purely institutional basis, and do not allow for the relative expansion of marketing operations by manufacturers, or the shift of some marketing operations, such as packaging, backward from retailers to manufacturers.

PROPORTION OF MIDDLEMAN COSTS TO ULTIMATE COMMODITY SALES VALUE, 1869–1948

	COMMODITY OUTPUT METHOD							VALUE OF SALES METHOD		
	1869	1879	1889	1899	1909	1919	1929	1929	1939	1948
Wholesalers	9.5	9.6	9.6	9.2	8.9	8.5	8.1	8.0	7.6	7.7
Retailers	23.2	24.1	25.1	26.2	27.6	28.0	28.9	28.6	29.7	29.7
Combined	32.7	33.7	33.7	35.4	36.5	36.5	37.0	36.6	37.3	37.4
Including freight charges	37.7	39.1	39.1	39.8	40.1	39.6	41.7			

(Note: This tabulation shows only wholesalers', retailers', and transportation costs. It does not include the substantial and growing marketing costs of manufacturers and other producers.)

From H. Barger, *Distribution's Place in the American Economy since 1869*, (National Bureau of Economic Research, Princeton, 1955), pp. 57, 60.

ILLUSTRATION 29–2

3. Improvements in production techniques, which lower production costs, cause the proportion of marketing costs which have remained unchanged to rise. Even though the absolute marketing cost of a commodity may be declining because of more efficient distribution, if a proportionately greater reduction of its production costs occurs at the same time, its relative marketing cost will appear to have risen. If an item which originally cost 50¢ to produce and 50¢ to market has its production cost reduced to 30¢ and its marketing cost to 40¢, the relative marketing cost rises from 50 to 57 percent. In general, over the past century, while distribution of commodities has become definitely more efficient, progress in production techniques has been even more marked. Goods are manufactured by horsepower but are distributed by manpower, and the possibilities of technological modification are always greater for horsepowered processes than for manpowered procedures. Output per man-hour in production industries increased 6½ times between 1869 and 1948, while output per man-hour in wholesaling and retailing increased only 2½ times. This consideration would certainly exert a strong upward pressure on *relative* marketing costs.

4. Paradoxically, certain advances in marketing technology have had the effect of raising relative marketing cost. While improved storage techniques such as quick freezing of fresh foods have time-widened consumption possibilities, the products thus made available for out-of-season consumption bear additional storage costs. Improved transportation techniques such as air freight have territorially-widened consumption possibilities, but again through the addition of higher marketing costs.

Among the factors which have tended to hold down marketing costs and so check the rising trend of the marketing cost ratio have been the following.

1. There has been substantial improvement in the technical efficiency of many marketing activities. Warehouse operations have been mechanized. Electronic computing is now being applied to many forms of market records. Opportunities for improvement, however, are not as great as those in production fields, and by any comparative standard, marketing accomplishments do not measure up to those in production. But technical efficiency has been steadily stepped up in all marketing operations. The 2½-fold increase in output per man-hour in wholesaling and retailing between 1869 and 1949 is evidence of this. If there were historically comparable measures for transportation, storage, credit, and other specific marketing operations, the technological improvement would probably be even more marked.

2. The trend during the past quarter-century toward self-service and limited-service retailing, spectacularly exhibited in the supermarket and discount house, has cut costs in this area.

3. Vertical integration in American marketing, sometimes on an institutional basis as indicated in Chapter 10, sometimes operationally as in the absorption of wholesaling operations by retailing chains and retailer cooperatives or the reduction of selling costs by voluntary groups, has accomplished some cutting of operational costs.

4. Westward movement of industry, lagging after the westward movement of population, by bringing production of many items closer to their markets, has reversed the earlier trend toward ever lengthening lines of distribution.

SPECIFIC FACTORS IN MARKETING COSTS

Three factors about whose contribution to marketing cost there is considerable dispute are: (1) the relative operating efficiency of marketing agencies, (2) wastes of competition, and (3) retail customer services.

Marketing inefficiency

The charge is widely made that marketing agencies and techniques are less efficient than producers and production techniques, and that overcoming this inefficiency would substantially reduce marketing costs. There is some truth but also considerable misunderstanding in this charge.

A true element of the charge is that retailing and some categories of middleman activity draw a larger proportion of incapable individuals than do manufacturing or farming. One reason for this is that many lines of retailing and some types of middleman distribution can be entered by persons with little capital, no technical knowledge, and little or no prior experience. To establish a manufacturing enterprise or operate a farm, the second and third attributes are practically prerequisites, and a substantial capital investment is commonly involved. Over-all operational ability is more likely to be associated with the possession of these attributes than with their lack. Extreme cases of inefficiency among marketing enterprises are constantly being weeded out by failure, but are constantly being replaced by new lots of business ineffectuals. The one possibility of raising the general level of retailing efficiency in this respect is to educate those merchants who may be ignorant of effective business practice in their lines, but who can learn. The U.S. Department of Commerce is doing much to educate the small merchant in better business methods, and so are a number of wholesalers' and retailers' trade associations.

It is commonly argued that marketing agencies are backward in adopting mechanized procedures and systems of work organization that have been so effective in many lines of industrial production. This charge overlooks the tremendous technological advances that have been made by transportation agencies, which have substantially reduced the costs of moving goods. Warehouses and many large-scale middlemen have highly mechanized goods handling systems, including belt conveyors and fleets of lift trucks. Machine techniques, developed in some cases almost to the point of automation, have cut the billing, sales control, and other distribution costs of particular companies to fractions of their earlier unit costs. Between 1929 and 1957 advertising multiplied $2\frac{1}{2}$ times the "per prospect exposure" per constant dollar of advertising cost, and intensified the impact of exposure. Still, it is quite true that most distributive activities do not involve mechanized procedures and standard-practice operations to the extent that characterizes industrial production. They cannot; there are not the same opportunities. To a substantial extent, manufacturers can preplan production and formulate economical procedures for preplanned output. Distributive agencies operate in an atmosphere of fluctuating demand and sometimes of fluctuating supply. They must be highly flexible, geared to deal with variables rather than routine. This sort of flexibility is not conducive to operating economies such as result from assembly line production, but their absence is not necessarily a mark of inefficiency.

Furthermore, at retail level, where a major part of marketing costs are concentrated, mechanized large-scale operations are out of the question. Each customer has a different combination of purchasing demands, buys in small quantities, and often needs individual sales or service treatment. The supermarkets succeeded in putting the "checking out" operation on a "line" basis, but there are few other opportunities in retailing for labor-saving "volume" operations. There are wide possibilities for greater efficiency in retailing, but not through general adoption of mechanized or standard-practice procedures.

Competitive waste

At all levels of distribution, according to some critics, there is unnecessary duplication of agencies and facilities. Why have a half-dozen local dealers and agents for a particular class of farm products in a country market center when one, operating on a slightly more extensive scale and at lower unit cost, could assemble all the production of the surrounding area? Why share the business of a central market among a number of commission houses, dealers, and brokers when one or two could handle it with only a fraction of the overhead costs incurred by the group? Why not concentrate the business of three or four neighborhood center drug stores, or grocery stores, in a single establishment and save on store space, clerk hire, and all the other duplicated costs of the separate units?

There can be no question but that competition results in duplication of marketing personnel and facilities. Sometimes this competitive duplication is clearly visible—customers sufficient for one store are scattered through two or three with counters inactive and clerks idle in all the stores. More often the duplication is concealed by employment of the excess personnel and facilities in competitive activities that cancel out with no social or general economic return. Salesmen from competing wholesalers carrying practically identical lines may call upon the same group of retailer customers or prospects. All of these salesmen are fully occupied by their calls, yet the total of their sales volume or service to the retailers is no greater than any one of them could accomplish by himself. Indeed, from the retailers' viewpoint, the set of competing salesmen take up more of their time, and thereby do them a disservice, than would the representative of a single wholesaler without competitors. Whether competitive duplication of marketing personnel and facilities is overt or concealed, it exists and it represents economic waste, which adds to the marketing costs ultimately paid by consumers.

There is another side to the picture, however. Competition is an inherent element of the American tradition. It preserves the consuming public from the danger of monopoly pricing, which in many instances might impose a greater burden on consumers than do the wastes of competition. Quite as important, it places a premium on providing all fractions of the consuming public with the variety of goods those fractions want, and on making these goods available in the ways those consuming groups want it. It is a spur to improvement, for the better has a competitive advantage over the good, and the best outdistances the better. Hence by law and popular reaction, a substantial degree of competition is maintained in most parts of the American business structure. Quasi-monopolies of all sorts are widespread, as was indicated in Chapter 19, but these, while of vital importance to the manufacturing and marketing enterprises that enjoy them, are for the most part effective only within narrow price margins.

A certain degree of economic waste is the price that must be paid for the maintenance of competition. Such waste is not peculiar to the marketing structure. It is quite as prevalent in agriculture and manufacture, where it takes the form of excess productive capacity and occasional production gluts which in the short run cause loss to the producers but in the long run are paid for by the consumers. For so long as a competitive economy is deemed desirable, the wastes of competitive production and marketing will persist. It is no adverse reflection upon either the marketing or production systems that those wastes still exist and will continue.

Retail customer services

A store that offers charge account or installment credit must, upon a large or small scale, make credit inquiries, establish an order-taking routine including charge-send and charge-take as well as cash orders, establish a billing system, provide for collection correspondence that may become long-drawn-out, and take occasional bad debt losses. Here are cost and expense items that would not occur under a "cash only" policy. Delivery service, whether directly by the store or through a contracted parcel delivery service, also means extra cost. So do the modelling rooms of "name" dress shops, and the children's play rooms and husbands' lounges provided by some department stores.

The full amount of these customer service costs does not always have to be charged, either directly or indirectly, to the patrons of the stores that provide them. By attracting additional customers, these services may give a store various economies on volume business and distribution of overhead that offset, to some extent, the special costs of the services. In general, however, retail customer services provided by a store must be paid for by its customers, either those who specifically utilize the services in question, or by the entire group.

Occasionally stores makes special charges for particular services; thus many supermarkets and other cash-carry grocery stores make deliveries for a 25-cent surcharge per delivery. The costs of installment credit—sometimes plus an overcharge—are commonly passed on to the customers buying "on time" through interest and "carrying charges." The general American tradition, however, is to provide customers with "free" services, and cover their costs through higher markups of the store's merchandise, which raise its prices for nonusers of its special services as well as for the users.

At first glance, this practice might appear to be inequitable. Apparently some consumers are charged, without their consent, for services they do not want and do not use. In rural communities where there may be only a single drug store, or hardware store, or apparel store, the apparent inequity may be a real one. Except at the inconvenience of mail order buying or shopping trips to other retailing centers, consumers not using the special customer services must none the less pay, through higher prices, for such services. In larger retailing centers, however, where there are several stores for each line, customer services offered range widely from self-service cash-carry to full service. Consumers can select the stores they choose to patronize on the basis of services, or lack of services, offered. Those who prefer full-service establishments pay for the services through higher prices. Those who prefer no-service economy can obtain it. Under such circumstances, there is no inequity in incorporating the cost of various customer services in retail markup, and there should be no criticism of the cost of such services, since it represents fulfillment of a demand on the part of those who pay for it.

MARKETING COST ACCOUNTING

No one has greater interest in improving marketing efficiency, and cutting marketing costs, than the business organizations—manufacturers, wholesalers, retailers, and facilitating institutions—whose profit would be increased by reducing their marketing costs. Sometimes a cost-shaving possibility is manifest, as when a salesman for a freight forwarding company proves to a shipper, by literal figures, that it can save him on his shipping costs, or give him fuller transportation service for the same charges he has previously paid. More often, the inefficiency of some aspect of a company's marketing policy is concealed by a confusion of joint costs. A technique of marketing cost accounting is needed to unravel the intricacies of joint marketing costs and show business executives which aspects of their marketing policies are soundly conceived and which need overhauling.

Cost accounting applied to industrial production has long been a well-developed and useful management tool. Marketing cost accounting is more difficult than industrial cost accounting, and interest in it was largely dormant until the late 1930's. The Robinson-Patman Act abruptly made marketing cost accounting of vital importance to many manufacturers and wholesalers. Under that law, differential price treatments within a customer class, including certain types of quantity discounts, had to be justified, among other considerations, by differences in the costs of selling to these customers. Countless companies whose pricing policies were threatened by the law devised systems of marketing cost accounting to provide them with the data needed to sustain their claims of customer cost differentials.

Once effective systems of marketing cost accounting were developed, they proved to have other, and in the long run more valuable, uses than merely providing Robinson-Patman Act defenses. They established a foundation for marketing cost analysis—the study and evaluation of the relative profitability or costs of different marketing operations in terms of customers, marketing units, products, territories, or marketing activities. Sounder pricing became possible. Discovery and correction of uneconomic elements in companies' marketing policies—high-cost selling to low-volume customers and selling in high-cost territories, for example—were facilitated. Ways to improve sales force management were indicated. All in all, this development of marketing cost accounting systems is turning out to be one of the most valuable approaches to a general stepping up of marketing efficiency and consequent lowering of marketing costs.

Objectives

The initial objective of marketing cost accounting is to determine differences in cost of sales as related to one or more factors in a company's marketing set-up. The factor might be various customer classifications—by purchase volume, or distributive characteristics (i.e., whether they are wholesalers or retailers, or full-service or limited-service operators, or chain or independent retailers, etc.), or distance from a company warehouse, or other-cost pertinent consideration. Or the factor might be the company's individual salesmen, or sales territories, or classes of products sold, or alternative channels of distribution.

With the determination of the cost-sales ratio for each product, or customer, or customer class, or salesman, the arithmetic objective of marketing cost accounting is completed. But this is just a foundation for the constructive analysis that now begins. Variations in the cost-sales ratio among the various factor units or classes are noted. Next, the causes of these variations must be determined. Often this requires intensive research. With the weak points in a company's marketing policy thus spotted, and causes of weakness ascertained, management is in a position to seek cures. If a product analysis shows that certain items in a company's line have a disproportionate cost-sales ratio, the answer may be to reprice them, or to drop them, or to train the sales force to do a better job of selling them. A customer-class marketing cost study might lead to the conclusion that customers whose purchases fell under a certain amount were unprofitable and should be dropped or solicited by mail order instead of salesmen; or the conclusion might be that the company's schedule or trade or quantity discounts should be revised; or it might be advisable to limit selling area to a certain radius around the company's warehouses.

Calculation procedure

There is no single formula for marketing cost accounting. The individual circumstances of each company's marketing position dictate special calculation procedures which it must devise. All procedures, however, involve more or less the following steps.

1. Production and distribution costs are separated. In this connection, various overhead costs have to be allocated between the two categories.

2. A detailed schedule is prepared of all distribution costs, including allocated overhead. This often requires modification and elaboration of a company's prior system of records and accounts.

3. The detail cost items are now attributed to the units in the market factor being studied—to the individual salesmen, or to each sales territory, or to each customer or customer class, or to each class of products. Sometimes a detail cost item can be *attributed directly* to a factor unit, as where a salesman's compensation and reimbursed expense can be assigned directly to him. More often the cost items must be *allocated* by some formula or "measure" among the factor units, as in the case of dividing a salesman's salary compensation and expense among his customers. All overhead and office expenses, of course, require allocation.* Constructive intelligence of a high order is needed in devising appropriate measures of allocation, since the validity of marketing cost accounting depends substantially upon this point. Sometimes special records or research studies may be needed to provide a good allocation measure. For example, the sales force may have to be asked to make call-and-time reports on the basis of which their compensation and other selling expenses may be divided among their customers; or the sales supervisors may have to make sample observations of the salesmen's selling procedures to determine the division of selling time, and hence salesmen's compensation and other selling costs, among the various products of their line.

---

* For example, one company, undertaking a marketing cost accounting for the purpose of determining if it was sustaining a loss on its sales to small-purchase customers and if so where the breakeven point was, used the following "measures" for allocating its various distribution costs among the individual customers:

COST GROUPS	ALLOCATION MEASURES
Direct selling expense (salesmen's salaries and commissions, travel expense)	Number of salesmen's calls
Compensation of home and branch sales managers	Number of salesmen's calls
Freight	Weight of shipments
Branch office expense	Number of salesmen's calls
Home office expense	Number of invoices
Credit department	Number of invoices
Advertising	Relative media circulation (in customer's trading area)
Dealer helps	80% to customers in smaller towns and then on basis of sales volume

From C. H. Sevin, *How Manufacturers Reduce Their Distribution Costs* (U.S. Department of Commerce, 1948), p. 14.

4. The cost items thus attributed to each factor unit—each product, each customer, or each salesman—are totalled and related to the sales associated with that unit. In the case of a customer marketing cost analysis, the costs and sales attributed to the individual customers are then totalled for the subdivisions of whatever customer classification is being studied.*

Marketing cost accounting would be immensely facilitated if standard-practice cost-sales ratios, applicable to the marketing of particular commodities or commodity classes, or by particular types of distributors, were generally available. Some trade associations, particularly in the wholesaling fields, are doing pioneer work in the development of standard distribution cost ratios for their members. Generally, however, a company undertaking an analysis of its distribution costs has no external measures for checking on the efficiency of its marketing activities. Almost its only recourse is a cross-comparison of the cost-sales ratios of the items in its own commodity line, or of its customers, or of its own salesmen.

* When the company noted in the preceding footnote had completed its distribution of costs among its customers grouped by their annual purchase volume, the following results were disclosed:

CUSTOMER-VOLUME GROUP, AMOUNT OF ANNUAL PURCHASES	PERCENT OF TOTAL			PERCENT OF SALES		
	Number of accounts	Number of calls	Sales	Gross Profit	Selling Expense	Operating Profit
$20,000 and over	0.07	0.16	10.91	15.9	4.0	11.9
$10,000–$20,000	.07	.64	2.89	23.6	9.5	14.1
$5,000–$9,999	.60	3.40	11.71	19.8	10.2	9.6
$4,000–$4,999	.40	1.54	5.40	18.4	10.2	8.2
$3,000–$3,999	.40	1.25	3.99	21.8	9.6	12.2
$2,000–$2,999	1.17	3.19	8.47	22.8	10.9	11.9
$1,000–$1,999	3.29	7.21	13.24	23.9	13.4	10.5
$500–$999	7.67	13.40	15.66	25.9	16.8	9.1
$400–$499	3.79	5.09	4.96	29.0	19.3	10.3
$300–$399	5.12	6.25	5.21	31.6	21.9	9.7
$200–$299	9.83	10.75	7.11	31.2	25.3	5.9
$100–$199	16.17	15.65	6.94	30.7	34.3	−3.6
$1–$99	25.64	20.40	3.51	30.9	75.3	−44.4
No sales	25.78	11.05	—	—	∞	∞
Totals or averages	100.00	100.00	100.00	25.1	18.7	6.4

All customers buying less than $200 annually were found to be unprofitable. These were 42% of the total number of customers. To these had to be added the 26% of customers from whom no sales were obtained during the year, who represented absolute loss.

REVIEW

1. What is the general proportion of marketing cost to final price for American goods in general? for consumer goods? What is the largest single element in marketing costs? What classes of commodities involve the highest relative marketing costs?

2. Are relative marketing costs higher or lower in recessions? Why?

3. What would be the explanations for the long-term upward trend in relative marketing costs indicated by some studies?

4. What is meant by "individual company distribution cost analysis"? Of what value is it? What is the general procedure?

DISCUSSION TOPICS

1. "With continued rise of the American standard of living, the proportion of marketing costs will rise still higher."

2. "Marketing agencies and techniques are less efficient than producers and production techniques. Overcoming this relative distributive inefficiency would substantially reduce marketing costs and lower prices."

3. "Economic waste in marketing is the price that must be paid to maintain competition."

4. "Stores should cover the costs of customer services by special charges to the customers who use these services."

PROBLEM

The P.Q.R. Corporation manufactures men's and boys' underwear and men's dress shirts and pyjamas. Its mills are located in North Carolina. It sells throughout the United States direct to retailers. It insists on resale price maintenance and sells on F.O.B. destination terms. It establishes the retail prices for its items by multiplying direct production costs by five. Retailers are allowed a $33\frac{1}{3}$ percent trade discount, and quantity and cash discounts.

The company makes moderate profits each year. Management suspects that this overall profit may conceal losses on certain items, on certain territorial areas, on some of its smaller customers, on some of its salesmen. It decides to make a distribution cost analysis.

1. As a preliminary to this analysis, what classes of internal statistical information should it start collecting which it would not previously have bothered about, and what new classifications should it start making of previously available figures?

2. Assume that the classes of information that you have indicated in the answer to (1) have been collected for a reasonable period. Set up schedules for all marketing costs, showing whether each cost would be attributed directly or allocated, and if allocated what the measure of allocation would be, for determining (a) unprofitable customers, (b) unprofitable salesmen.

SUGGESTED READINGS

Clark, C. M., *Cost of Distribution Services,* Domestic Distribution Department, U.S. Chamber of Commerce, Washington, D.C., 1950.

Crisp, R. C., *How to Reduce Distribution Costs,* Funk & Wagnalls, New York, 1948.

Culiton, J. W., *The Management of Marketing Costs,* Division of Research, Harvard Business School, Boston, 1948.

Eisner, F. M., *Profit Analysis, Distribution Costs and Working Papers,* F. M. Eisner, White Plains, N.Y., 1954.

Heckert, J. F., & R. B. Miner, *Distribution Costs,* 2d ed, Ronald Press, New York, 1953.

Longman, D. R., *Practical Distribution Cost Analysis,* Richard D. Irwin, Homewood, Ill., 1955.

National Industrial Conference Board, *Cutting Costs in Industry: III. Distribution Costs,* Studies in Business Policy No. 41 (1950); *Keys to Efficient Selling and Lower Marketing Costs,* Studies in Business Policy No. 71 (1954), NICB, New York.

Packard, V., *The Waste Makers,* David McKay Co., New York, 1960.

Sevin, C. H., *How Manufacturers Reduce Their Distribution Costs,* Economic Series No. 72, U.S. Department of Commerce, Washington, D.C., 1948.

CHAPTER 30

GOVERNMENT, MARKETING, AND THE CONSUMER MOVEMENT

The relation of Government to Marketing activities is commonly thought to be exclusively one of control. Federal and state laws, and federal and state administrative regulations are looked upon as a straitjacket to confine business and prevent its untrammeled distributional operations from injuring the public interest. True, during the past thirty-five years governmental control of marketing activity, originally instituted on a small and ineffective scale, has grown to substantial proportions and now influences, in one way or another, almost every producer and distributor. But it should not be overlooked that Government, by establishing basic patterns of commercial law and by assuring civil security, provides the very foundations for the structure of American marketing activity. Moreover, certain of the expenditures and activities of Government are undertaken expressly to assist business in its marketing efforts.

The degree to which Government intervenes at any time in marketing activities, as well as in other phases of business operation, is determined largely by the relative dominance of one of three political theories—individualism or *laissez faire*, "statism" (to use a recently coined term), and socialism.

The *"individualistic"* doctrine, in its extreme form, is that Government should confine itself, in its domestic role, to the role of a "passive policeman." It should, through the evolution of common law or by legislation, provide society with a foundation of civil and criminal law that protects the personal and business rights of each individual with a minimum of limitation on the personal and business rights of other individuals. Government should engage in no activities that can be effectively undertaken by individual enterprise. It should not expend the public revenue in any activity intended to promote the interest of any social or business group or class. It should place no restrictions, other than those necessary to preserve basic law and order, upon business or personal actions.

Statism would preserve individual ownership and operation of business, but would substitute governmental planning, guidance, and control for individual and managerial initiative whenever such planning, guidance, and control would seem to yield a general social or economic benefit.

Socialism would go a long step further than statism, and substitute government ownership and operation of business for private ownership and operation whenever a balance of social or economic benefit would seem to result from the substitution. The goal of the older school of moderate socialists was government ownership and operation of public utilities and such basic industries as steel production and coal mining. For the more radical communists, the goal is expropriation and operation of all industry and business, down to and including the retail level.

Statism, under the name of "Mercantilism," was the dominant political philosophy during the Seventeenth and Eighteenth Centuries. The American Revolution, and a legislative evolution in England during the early Nineteenth Century, resulted in the triumph of individualistic political doctrine throughout most of the Nineteenth Century in those countries. For a long time, the only important trace of statism left in the United States was the protective tariff. A revival of statist policy occurred in the 1870's and 1880's with the inauguration of state control of public utilities. The Interstate Commerce Act of 1887 and the Sherman Anti-Trust Act of 1890 mark the spread of such policy to the federal field. These were limited applications of statist policy, however, and affected only specific areas of business activity. Substantial expansion of statist regulation of business, including a broad range of marketing activity, began with the Wilson Administration in 1913. The Republican administrations of the 1920's not only did not undo the previous federal regulatory legislation, but added to it a federal program of statist promotion of marketing activities. A new wave of regulatory legislation, on a state as well as a federal basis, began in the 1930's with Roosevelt's "New Deal." While the initial legislative momentum of this wave has subsided, its tide is still evident at the administrative level.

Our analysis of how Government influences American marketing practices will begin with a summary of the legal foundation established for marketing activities by state and federal law, proceed to a brief presentation of administrative activities of the federal and state governments that assist marketing activities, and conclude with a more extended analysis of the regulation of marketing operations by the federal and state governments. The chapter will be closed with an explanation of the so-called "Consumer Movement" which operates in part through governmental agencies, in part through other organizations.

LEGAL FOUNDATIONS OF MARKETING

The state and federal governments have established a basic body of civil and criminal law necessary to, or contributory to, effective marketing. Legislative enactment and judicial development of such a body of mercantile law is consonant with both individualist and statist political philosophy. The major fields of law that create the pattern for present American marketing practices are: (1) state mercantile law, (2) federal bankruptcy law, and (3) federal patent and trade-mark law.

State mercantile law

The major state contributions to establishing a legal foundation for marketing activities are the civil law of contracts and negotiable instruments, and such bodies of mercantile criminal law as that punishing the issue of false financial statements.

Marketing of any product or service is accomplished through a series of purchase-and-sale contracts between a chain of sellers and buyers. A clear, comprehensible law of sales, in conformity with general trade practices, is essential to the development of smooth mercantile relationships. Originally, sales contracts in each state were governed by the general common law of contracts as evolved by the state courts and as modified in divergent ways by state legislation. In many states it was needlessly complex. Differences between state laws of sales were a hazard in interstate market relations. A Uniform Sales Law, prepared by the Committee on Uniform Laws, was first adopted by Arizona, Connecticut, and New Jersey in 1907, and is now on the statute books of thirty-two states. Most of the other eighteen states, although they have not adopted all details of the Uniform Law, have brought their variant sales laws into fairly close agreement with it. This nation's wide development of a law of sales suitable to the complex needs of business, yet simple enough in its statement that a layman can understand the essentials, and uniform in its application in the major commercial states, has been a boon to American marketing.

Enactment of state laws to cover other marketing relationships, and a trend toward simplification and interstate uniformity, in such laws, have also been of great importance to the development of American marketing. Most states have enacted legislation to cover the special type of sales relationship involved in conditional sales (the usual legal basis of installment buying), and ten have adopted a Uniform Conditional Sales Act. The legal aspects of checks, promissory notes, trade acceptances, and similar instruments are governed by a Uniform Negotiable Instruments Law which has been adopted by every state. The relations of storer and warehouseman are governed by a Uniform Warehouse Receipts Act in every state.

These elements of state mercantile law are applied and enforced in a tiny minority of cases through the state and federal courts. Their major influence on marketing results from their application, without any dispute to be litigated, to the millions of day-to-day business transactions. It is this commonplace anticipatory application of the provisions of state mercantile law that makes this body of law the legal foundation of practically all of our marketing procedures.

Federal bankruptcy law

Because of its limited delegated sovereignty under the Constitution, the federal government's contribution to the underlying legal structure of marketing is not in the basic field of contractual mercantile relationships, but in certain supplementary fields.

Protection of the rights of trade creditors when a customer becomes insolvent reduces certain of the risks of selling, and thereby encourages a certain amount of selling that might otherwise not take place. Such protection to creditors' rights is given by the federal bankruptcy law. The primary objective of this law is not to protect creditors, but to release insolvent debtors from obligations impossible for them to meet, so that they can once again take their place in economic society with a clean financial slate. But protection of the creditors' rights, subject to the primary objective, has been an important secondary accomplishment of the bankruptcy law.

Both the states and the federal government have the power to enact bankruptcy or insolvency laws. Prior enacted state laws become inoperative, with respect to discharge of the bankrupt, however, whenever a federal law is in effect. Four federal bankruptcy laws have been enacted—in 1800, in 1841, in 1867, and in 1898. The first three of these acts were repealed within one to three years after enactment. The Act of 1898, frequently amended (the last major amendment was the Chandler Act of 1938), is still in effect and constitutes the American law on bankruptcy.

Under federal bankruptcy law, an insolvent business can file a *voluntary* petition in bankruptcy, or some of its creditors can file an *involuntary* petition. If upon a hearing before a federal court, the business is adjudicated bankrupt, the court transfers the case to a *referee*—an officer of the court responsible to the judge. A *trustee* is appointed to liquidate the bankrupt debtor's assets and distribute them fairly among the creditors who have filed and proven claims against the debtor. Upon completion of this liquidation, if no fraud by the debtor has been established, he is discharged of all further liability for the debts covered by the bankruptcy proceeding.

Since 1938, federal bankruptcy law has provided protection of trade creditors' rights in business reorganizations (as distinguished from business liquidations). If an insolvent business can be salvaged instead of liquidated by legally authorized procedures that allow it an extension of time on its payments or some reduction of its obligations, creditors can have such "arrangements" or "reorganizations" supervised by the federal courts, thus ensuring themselves against fraud.

Federal patent law

As indicated in Chapter 16, new products and product designs are developed largely because patent rights protect the developers of these products and designs from competition of identical items manufactured and sold by other producers. This incentive to marketing is provided by the federal patent law. A *general* patent is a right granted by federal law to the inventor or discoverer of a new and useful art, machine, method of manufacture, or composition of matter, or any new and useful improvements * of such items, to exclude others from making, using, or selling such items for a period of 17 years. A *design* patent is a similar right, running for $3\frac{1}{2}$, 7, or 14 years, according to the fee paid, based upon the development of a new, original, and ornamental design for some article of manufacture, provided such design has not previously been known or used. The recipient of a general or design patent in effect obtains a legal monopoly on the production and sale of his product or design. The monopoly profit he may expect to derive from its marketing, or from licensing his patent or design to other producers, is the incentive for his inventive effort. Holders of patents on complementary features of a product may pool their respective patent monopolies by cross-licensing their patents to each other, though not in such a way as to create a price-fixing group or suppress competition. A patentor at present has full freedom to suppress his patented product or process by not making or applying it himself and refusing to license it to other producers.

Federal trade-mark law

Trade-mark laws have been enacted by the states as well as by the federal government. The importance of the federal law so overshadows

---

* In a number of recent decisions, the U.S. Supreme Court has emphasized that a modification or improvement of an existing product or process must, to be patentable, display a "flash of genius," rather than mere technical skill in accomplishing the variation. Under this rule, many important patents issued in recent years are probably invalid.

that of state statutes, however, that most advertising and marketing executives are unaware that there are state laws on the subject. Advertising and other forms of promotion, as was established in Chapter 21, would be impossible if manufacturers and distributors could not have exclusive rights to the brand names, symbols, and slogans around which their advertising is framed. The first federal law to provide such rights was passed in 1870. It has been many times amended; the latest important revision, the Lanham Act, occurred in 1947. A manufacturer or distributor may register a product or service brand name or symbol provided it is not confusingly similar to some prior registered brand name or symbol used for a competing product or related line of business, and provided it does not contravene a number of other limitations such as being immoral, deceptive, or scandalous, or merely descriptive of the goods, or merely a geographical name, or merely a surname. The manufacturer or distributor then has exclusive use of the registered brand name or symbol, now established as a *trade mark,* for 20 years, with the possibility of renewal for additional 20-year periods. Non-use of a trade mark forfeits the registration.

GOVERNMENTAL ADMINISTRATIVE MARKETING ASSISTANCE

Statist political philosophy advocates the creation of governmental administrative agencies to undertake activities helpful to private production and marketing. The state governments to a moderate degree, and the federal government substantially, have been influenced by this philosophy to develop various forms of marketing aid. Several of these have been studied in earlier chapters.* Here we may note a recent addition to the list of federal marketing aids. The Small Business Administration was created in 1953 to assist small businesses in their management and financing problems. One of its most valuable contributions has been the publication of a series of marketing management studies for retailers, small wholesalers, and small manufacturers. The Office of Distribution publishes Bulletins on such Marketing subjects as laws affecting distribution, and marketing research uses and techniques.

FEDERAL CONTROL OF MARKETING PRACTICES

An outstanding tenet of statist political philosophy is that private business enterprise, if given free rein in its marketing procedures, would indulge in "tooth and claw" practices that would in the long run be harmful to the competitive business system, to consumers, and to the American economic system in general. In a series of laws beginning with the

---

* Federal standardization and grading activity in Chapter 15, federal and state contributions to marketing information in Chapter 23, the parcel post system in Chapter 25, and federal assistance to agricultural marketing cooperatives in Chapter 12.

Sherman Anti-Trust Act of 1890, Congress has forbidden three classes of marketing practices involving interstate commerce: * (1) those, including discriminatory pricing, which would "restrain trade"; (2) those which would constitute "unfair competition"; and (3) "unfair" and "deceptive" marketing practices which would injure consumers.

Prohibition of discriminatory pricing and other "restraint of trade" practices

The Sherman Anti-Trust Act declared illegal "every contract, combination in the form of trust or otherwise, or conspiracy, in restraint of trade or commerce among the several states." The Clayton Anti-Trust Act of 1914 specified as illegal certain corporate and financial practices and three specific marketing practices—exclusive dealing agreements,** "tying contracts," *** and discriminatory pricing to like customers—whenever they tend to lessen competition or create monopoly.

Most of the applications of the Sherman and Clayton Acts have been to corporate combinations and financial practices that fall outside the scope of "marketing policy" as analyzed in this book. Except for the price discrimination prohibition discussed below, federal restraint of trade legislation has resulted in little limitation of normal marketing practices. Trade association efforts, however, to eliminate price competition—for example, by agreement upon common "basing points" for the quotation of F.O.B. prices—or territorial competition among their members, or to blacklist delinquent customers, have been held violations of federal anti-trust law. So, too, have been agreements among individual manufacturers or distributors upon uniform prices and mutually exclusive territories, credit terms, advertising allowances, trade-in allowances, container-returns allowances, and guarantees against price declines.

One element of pricing policy that would otherwise be illegal under the Sherman and Clayton Acts has been specifically authorized by an amendment to those laws. The Miller-Tydings Act of 1937, as amended by the McGuire Act of 1952, exempts from the provisions of the federal anti-trust laws resale price maintenance provisions in manufacturers' and wholesalers' sales contracts in the case of brand-named or trade-marked commodities. This law is the foundation of "fair trade" resale price maintenance of goods involved in interstate commerce, explained in Chapter 20.

Judicial construction seriously weakened the discriminatory price pro-

---

* In sustaining specific exercises of federal control over marketing practices, the federal courts have made very broad interpretations of the interstate commerce concept.

** An *exclusive dealing agreement* is one requiring a seller or lessor to agree not to deal in the goods of another supplier.

*** A *tying contract* is one whereunder a supplier sells or leases certain of its products only in conjunction with certain other of the products it sells or leases.

hibition of the Clayton Anti-Trust Act, and the restriction was practically a dead letter during the 1920's and early 1930's. Meanwhile, associations of wholesalers and independent store owners instituted a powerful lobbying movement for legislation to check the growing power of chain store systems. Most of the legislation sought was at the state level, as explained later in this chapter. From Congress the independent store owners asked a revitalization of the discriminatory price prohibition of the Clayton Act. This would prevent the chains from employing their massed purchasing power to obtain lower prices from suppliers than the smaller independents had to pay. The Robinson-Patman Act of 1936, passed as an amendment to the Clayton Act, gave the independent store owners their desire.

The Robinson-Patman Act has played a vital role in shaping certain important elements of pricing policy. Its provisions accordingly deserve careful consideration by students of Marketing. The significant provisions of the Act are:

1. Sellers in interstate commerce must not sell "commodities of like grade and quality" at different prices;

2. if such discrimination would "substantially lessen competition" or "injure, destroy or prevent competition" among sellers, buyers, or the customers of buyers;

3. except for price differentials (a) that make "only due allowances" for savings in production, sale, or distribution costs of the seller resulting from differences in quantities purchased or methods of delivery (subject to the proviso that the Federal Trade Commission may set maximum quantity limits for quantity discounts where further discounts for larger quantities, though reflecting cost savings, would promote monopoly among the purchasers); or (b) which are due to changing conditions affecting the market for, or the marketability of, the goods, such as deterioration of perishable goods, obsolescence of seasonal goods, etc.; or (c) which are made in good faith to meet the equally low prices of competition.

4. Price discriminations embodied in a form other than selling price, such as special allowances, special discounts, or brokerage fees, where no corresponding service is performed by the buyer, are specifically forbidden.

5. Buyers who *knowingly* receive a discriminatory price are guilty of a breach of law, and are subject not only to Federal Trade Commission proceedings, but also to civil suits by injured parties who, under the provisions of the Sherman Act, of which the Robinson-Patman Act is an amendment (since it amended the Clayton Act which itself was an amendment of the Sherman Act), may receive triple damages.

Interpretation of the Robinson-Patman Act by the FTC and the federal courts has extended its application to fields far removed from the discriminatory pricing favoring chain stores that motivated the act. It has been used by the FTC as a potent weapon in its attack on basing-point pricing and territorially uniform prices.* Cumulative quantity discounts and restricted use by manufacturers of store demonstrators and other dealer aids have been held violations of the law. The FTC has not always been consistent in the pricing restrictions it has developed under the authority of the Robinson-Patman Act, and currently many business men are more bewildered than guided in their pricing policy by this law. Recent court decisions have tended to hold the Commission's application of the law to more of an "economic rule of reason" than in the past.

Prohibition of practices constituting "unfair competition"

The Federal Trade Commission Act of 1914 declared "unfair methods of competition in commerce" illegal, and established the FTC to administer this prohibition and certain of the "restraint of trade" prohibitions of the Clayton Act. The statute itself does not specify any marketing practices forbidden under this general prohibition. Instead, the rulings of the FTC and court decisions reviewing them have built up a lengthy list of practices deemed illegal. Among marketing practices and policies held by the FTC to constitute "unfair competition" are the following:

> False or misleading advertising that gives the advertiser an unfair competitive advantage.
>
> Bribing or giving substantial presents to employees of customers to gain or retain the customers' patronage.
>
> Inducing customers of competitors to break contracts with such competitors by making misrepresentations about them, or generally making false statements as to the quality of the competitors' products, their financial standing, business integrity, etc.
>
> Threatening competitors' customers with patent infringement suits, to intimidate such customers, when there is no intent actually to carry out such threats.
>
> Tampering with machines or equipment sold by competitors to discredit such products.
>
> Preventing competitors from procuring advertising space by misrepresenting their standing, or otherwise prejudicing advertising media against them.
>
> Giving premiums, bonuses, or presents to jobbers' salesmen or retailers' clerks, to induce them to push particular lines of goods, without the employers' knowledge.
>
> Giving away goods, or selling goods below cost, for the purpose of injuring small competitors or driving competition out of the territory.

---

* See Chapter 20.

Critique

In its interpretation of the federal laws that control marketing practices, the FTC has not followed a consistent line. Some of its rulings appear definitely self-contradictory. Only by checking through all currently applicable FTC rulings by means of a trade regulation report service (an excerpt from the Commerce Clearing House service is shown in Illustration 30–1) could a business man, or his legal counsel, be certain that some projected marketing practice is not already specifically forbidden—and there are literally thousands of such rulings. Even then he would have no assurance that the projected practice will not be outlawed by the FTC later. If the business belongs to an industry whose trade association has adopted an FTC-approved "voluntary fair-trade practice code," as described in Chapter

---

Number 107—189   Under Clayton Act, Sec. 2(f)   **5291**
8-18-58   ➠ *See the Cumulative Index (last pages of this division) for new matters.*

KNOWINGLY INDUCING OR RECEIVING DISCRIMINATION

Under Clayton Act, Section 2 (f)

[¶ 3526]

[Editorial Comment:] Any person who knowingly induces or receives a discrimination in price does so unlawfully under Section 2(f) of the Clayton Act. The text of the law is found at ¶ 186, in this volume.

Trade practices involving discrimination in price are discussed at ¶ 3508 and following, in this volume. CCH.

Annotations to ¶ 3526 Appear Topically Below, as Follows:

Analysis (Congressional) .... .100	Inducing or Receiving Price Discrimina-
Complaints—Sufficiency of Allegations	tion .... .400
FTC proceedings .... .200	"Knowingly" Inducing or Receiving Price
Private proceedings .... .220	Discrimination .... .500
Defenses or Justifications Under Sections	Price Induced or Received—Legality.:... .600
2(a) and 2(b), Clayton Act	
Cost justification .... .300.	
Market conditions and meeting com-	
petition ......: .... .320	

Analysis (Congressional)	Complaints—Sufficiency of Allegations
.100 "The closing paragraph of the Clayton Act amendment, for which section 1 of this bill provides, makes equally liable the person who knowingly induces or receives a discrimination in price prohibited by the amendment. This affords a valuable support to the manufacturer in his efforts to abide by the intent and purpose of the bill. It makes it easier for him to resist the	.200 **FTC proceedings.**—The Commission refused to dismiss two complaints charging jobbers of automotive products with knowingly inducing and receiving price discriminations in violation of Section 2(f) of the Clayton Act. The jobbers, relying on *Automatic Canteen Co. of America v. FTC*, 1953 Trade Cases ¶ 67,503, 346 U. S. 61, had contended that the allegations of

EXCERPT FROM CCH *TRADE REGULATION REPORTS.* Reprinted by permission from *Trade Regulation Reports, published by and copyright, Commerce Clearing House, Inc., Chicago 46, Ill.*

ILLUSTRATION 30–1

22, he is on fairly safe ground so long as it stays strictly within the scope of the practices approved by the code. Even with these codes, however, the whole field of marketing practice regulations as developed by the FTC is sadly in need of clarification.

Prohibition of "unfair" and "deceptive" practices injurious to consumers

Federal protection of consumers against deceptive marketing practices was initiated by the Pure Food and Drug Act of 1906, which prohibited shipments of adulterated or mislabelled foods or drugs in interstate commerce. The Meat Inspection Act of the same year established standards for meat, and provided for federal inspection and stamping of slaughtered animals at the packing houses. The FTC from the outset gave a broad interpretation to the prohibition of "unfair methods of competition" by the Federal Trade Commission Act, and issued cease and desist orders in cases involving misbranding, misrepresentation of quality, condition or value of merchandise, false packaging, false claims to endorsement, misrepresentation of trade status, and misrepresentation of origin, where the primary injury was to customers and any injury to competitors could be established only by indirection.

Two laws passed in 1938 and one in 1939 enlarged and strengthened federal control of marketing practices in the interest of consumers. A 1938 amendment to the Pure Food and Drug Act brought cosmetics and therapeutic and medical devices within the scope of the act, broadened the definitions of adulteration and mislabelling of the controlled items, authorized the Food and Drug Administration (subsequently the Federal Security Administration) to establish standards for these items, and gave the Administration power to act by injunction. The Wheeler-Lea Act of 1938 amended the Federal Trade Commission Act by specifically outlawing (1) "unfair or deceptive acts or practices in commerce," and (2) "materially misleading *advertising* of food, drugs or cosmetics." The Wool Products Labelling Act of 1939 required manufacturers of wool products to state, on a label attached to the product, the proportion and kind of wool contained in the cloth. A 1951 law forbade deceptive labelling of furs. A Textile Fiber Products Identification Act that went into effect in 1960 required apparel items and other textile products to carry labels or tags that identify the textiles from which they are made.

The Wheeler-Lea Act, under fairly liberal interpretation by the courts, has given the FTC broad powers to protect consumers from "deceptive" trade practices, and it has applied these powers aggressively. It has directed a persistent and effective campaign against unwarranted claims in advertising, and has worked a revolution—conceded by most advertising men to be fundamentally beneficial—in the writing of advertising copy. "Free offers" that are in effect only premiums or combination sales can no longer be called "free." "Special sales" that involve nothing special as to goods offered, price reductions, or time limits, cannot be so named. Canvassers have been forbidden to use the pretext of making a "consumer survey" as a means of introducing themselves to prospects. Slack filling of packages, so that they seem to contain greater quantities than they actually do, is outlawed.

Full protection of consumers from malpractices of advertisers and sellers, however, has not yet been achieved. Minimum standards for consumer goods have been established only for foods, drugs, and cosmetics. Exaggerated and flamboyant advertising claims are still permitted by the courts, which have overruled the FTC in this matter, on the ground that they are mere "puffing" which does not mislead even the more gullible elements of the buying public. "Pressure" methods of selling to consumers that fall short of being outright "deceptive" cannot be checked unless they can be construed as "unfair to competitors." As far as federal protection is concerned, "caveat emptor" still applies to many important aspects of consumer buying.

Enforcement of federal marketing regulation

Four agencies—the federal Department of Justice, the Federal Trade Commission, the Federal Security Administration, and the Post Office—are charged with the enforcement of most of the federal controls over marketing practices.*

The *Department of Justice* acts upon violations of the "restraint of trade" provisions of the Sherman and Clayton Anti-Trust Acts. It investigates complaints to determine whether violations of the law—as previously construed by the courts and in accordance with the Department's own interpretation of the law on points upon which the courts have not yet ruled —have occurred. If it is persuaded that the law has been violated—and political considerations as well as the shifts of current economic and social doctrine sometimes seem to influence the Department's decisions on this matter—it has the choice of three courses of action:

1. In many instances Department of Justice attorneys confer with representatives of a business charged with alleged violations, win their agreement to abstain from repetition of the marketing practices at issue, and submit the agreement to a federal court for approval. When so approved, this agreement is known as a "consent decree." It saves the Depart-

---

* Many other federal agencies are responsible for enforcement of federal marketing controls in special fields. Thus 21 agencies share in the control of advertising, including the SEC, the Post Office Department, the Alcohol and Tobacco Tax Division of the Internal Revenue Service, and the Federal Communications Commission.

ment of Justice the costs and uncertainties of a trial, and the business unit involved avoids not only trial costs but the possibility of criminal penalties in the event of an unfavorable decision.

2. Where the representatives of a business charged with a violation refuse to agree to a consent decree, and in some instances where the Department of Justice prefers to make no attempt to obtain a consent decree, the Department may sue in the federal courts for an injunction forbidding continuation of the practices under complaint.

3. Where the Department of Justice considers the violation a wilful one, it may institute criminal prosecution in a federal court against the alleged violator. Conviction is usually punishable by fines imposed on the offending company, very rarely by imprisonment of its officers or principals.

The *Federal Trade Commission* has jurisdiction over violations of the Federal Trade Commission Law (including the Wheeler-Lea amendment), and over violations of certain provisions of the Clayton Anti-Trust Act and its amendments such as the price discriminations forbidden by the Robinson-Patman Act. Its procedure on violations is markedly different from that of the Department of Justice, and involves the following actions:

1. It investigates complaints of violations of the laws it administers, and it may initiate investigations into business practices on its own account.

2. If it believes that a violation may exist, it serves a complaint upon the alleged offending business, and appoints a date for the hearing.

3. At the hearing all interested parties may have their say.

4. If, as a result of the hearing, the Commission concludes that a violation has occurred, but not a serious one, the matter may be settled by an informal promise or a stipulation by the offender to discontinue the practice. If the violation is deemed serious, the Commission issues a "cease and desist" order. Unless appealed, this order becomes final in sixty days. Each violation of such an order, upon its becoming final, makes the offender liable to a $5,000 fine.

5. A company subject to a cease and desist order may appeal it to the federal courts within a sixty-day period, and obtain judicial review of the Commission's jurisdiction and its interpretation of the law.*

A little-known aspect of FTC activity is its preventive work on unfair trade practices. It has a Bureau of Consultation to which any marketing executive may write for an opinion on the legality of any aspect of his company's pricing, advertising, or selling practices. Currently the Bureau receives some 600 such inquiries a year.

---

* Effective policing of improper marketing practices by the FTC is weakened by the circumstance that offenders may continue such practices without penalty during the period of investigation (often protracted) and hearing, during the 60-day period after issue of the cease and desist order, and during the appeal of such an order unless the court issues an injunction against the practice.

The *Federal Security Administration* acts much more as an advisory and corrective agency than as a punitive one. It has conducted nation-wide campaigns to induce the public to study the labels of foods, drugs, and cosmetics. It warns manufacturers when their products violate the law, and suggests changes to avoid the violation. But when wilful violations are involved, it has the power, and exercises it, to seize substandard or mislabelled products. It also initiates prosecutions of the offenders.

The *Post Office Department* has the power to exclude fraudulent direct-mail advertisement from the mails, and to issue "fraud orders" under which mailed responses to fraudulent advertisements are stamped "fraudulent" and returned to the senders. Fraudulent misuse of the mails may also be made the basis for criminal prosecution.

STATE CONTROL OF MARKETING PRACTICES

Federal control of marketing practices is limited to those affecting interstate commerce. A parallel control of intrastate marketing practices is effected by state law.

Most of the states have *anti-monopoly laws,* some antedating the Sherman Act. The substance of these state acts is surprisingly uniform, generally condemning actions which would suppress trade with a view to increasing prices or reducing production. Just as the federal Miller-Tydings Act excepts retail price maintenance contracts from the federal anti-trust law, so such contracts have been specifically excepted from most of the state anti-monopoly laws by so-called state *fair-trade acts.*

The states do not have "unfair competitive practice" laws similar to the Federal Trade Commission Act. Specific state legislation to this effect has not been necessary, since under common law malicious interference with competitors, the "palming off" of a product as that of a competitor, the misappropriation of trade secrets, and any other business procedures that might be construed as "unfair competitive practice" have long been actionable. With legal redress already available to an injured competitor, there has been no pressure for general regulatory legislation at the state level.

Nineteen states have laws similar to the Robinson-Patman Act, prohibiting discriminatory pricing in intrastate transactions.

In one detail, however, recent state legislation has limited retail pricing practices in a way not covered by federal law. Thirty states now have *unfair-trade-practice laws* which forbid sales below "cost"—variously defined—plus a specified markup percentage, usually 6 percent. Exceptions are provided to cover the meeting of competition, clearing perishable goods and "overstocks," and other special circumstances. Seven of these states, and an additional six without general unfair-trade-practice acts, have special laws prohibiting sales of cigarettes below cost. The unfair-trade-practice laws, intended to complement the state fair-trade laws (which permit resale price maintenance for brand-name goods) and protect independent retailers against certain aspects of chain competition, are generally enforced through the trade associations of the independent retailers. Violations of the laws are reported to them. They warn the offenders. If the warning is unheeded, they report the offender to the state prosecuting authorities. Enforcement has not generally been effective.

The state fair-trade and unfair-trade-practice laws, although they have come to have a wider application than first planned, were originally passed as anti-chain-store measures at the behest of pressure groups of wholesalers and independent retailers. These two types of laws were intended as curbs on the buying and selling practices of the chains. A direct attack on the chains as a marketing institution was made through *anti-chain-store taxes,* enacted and sustained in twenty-nine states and several cities during the 1930's and early 1940's, and currently in effect in twelve states. These taxes are generally imposed as a lump-sum levy per store, with the amount determined by the number of the chain's units in the state or in the country. The highest levy is found in Texas, where the amount is $825 per store when there are more than fifty units in the chain. The purpose of these taxes is not to produce revenue, but to discourage large chains from operation in the state.

Common law provides purchasers with little protection against unfair or deceptive acts of sellers, and state laws contain no blanket prohibition of such acts, as does the federal Wheeler-Lea Act. Most of the states, however, have enacted *pure food and drug laws,* modeled on the federal law of 1906, which forbid the intrastate sale of adulterated or misbranded foods and drugs. The marketing of milk is closely regulated and controlled in most states. Forty-three states have also enacted *"truth in advertising"* *laws,* many of them based upon the *Printers' Ink* Model Law,* which provide for criminal prosecution of, or the issue of injunctions against, advertisers who indulge in "untrue, deceptive, or misleading" advertising. Application of these "truth in advertising" laws has been, in general, very weak.

FEDERAL PRICE CONTROL

Statist political philosophy accords the federal government an important role in checking excessive economic depression or inflation. Federal price control—either directly through specific administrative determination, or in various indirect ways—is an important tool, though not an exclusive one, in this economic regulation. Beginning in 1917, the federal government

---

* So-called because it was prepared at the behest of, and advocated by *Printers' Ink,* the magazine of the advertising profession.

has engaged in price control on six occasions. In three cases the objective was to check general depression, or depression in specific fields, through establishing minimum prices: (1) the National Recovery Administration episode of 1933–1935; (2) the federal farm maintenance program, culminating in the parity price system; and (3) the federal coal price maintenance program. The objective of federal price control on the other three occasions—during World War I, during World War II, and again briefly during the Korean War—was the checking of inflation through establishing maximum prices. Of these six essays in federal pricing control we shall study the only currently operative one, the farm price maintenance program.

Farm price maintenance

Through the 1920's, while the rest of the country prospered, American farmers suffered a continued depression. Their volume of production balanced against existing domestic and foreign demand resulted in prices so low in relation to their costs of production that a large proportion of them were producing at a loss. Because concerted action among the millions of individuals involved was impossible, they could not bring their over-all production into such alignment with demand that resulting prices would fairly compensate them. Governmental action for their relief was both socially and economically desirable, and politically expedient. Among the various efforts at such relief was a federal program for raising and sustaining the prices of farm products.

Upon the theory that the low farm prices of 1930 were only temporary, a Federal Farm Board was established in that year with a fund of $500,-000,000 to be used for the purchase and storage of crop excesses. The agricultural impact of the 1929–1933 recession, and the failure of the farmers to meet the problem of excess crops by reducing production, resulted in failure of this effort at farm price maintenance.

The second effort was the Agricultural Adjustment Act of 1933. This law provided for predetermination of the quantities of important crops to be produced each year, the break-down of these quantities into "allotments" for individual farms, and the payment of a subsidy to farmers who reduced their cultivated acreages to conform with their allotments. Funds for the subsidy were derived from "processing" taxes levied upon processors of the products in question, which were added to the prices of the processed products. For the period of the operation of this act, prices of products derived from farming were thus raised by two factors—the limitation of the supply of these products at the farm level, and the tax imposed at the processing level.

The subsidy provisions of the Agricultural Adjustment Act were declared unconstitutional in 1936. Two years later its place was taken by the

Agricultural Act of 1938, still in effect. As modified through 1960, this law provides, with respect to farm prices:

1. If, upon referendum conducted by the Department of Agriculture, two-thirds or more of the producers of a crop specified by the law approve, such crop is then "covered" by the program.

2. "Parity prices" are established each year for "covered" crops by multiplying the unit cost of producing each crop (as determined by Department of Agriculture statisticians) by the ratio that existed between average cost of production of the crop and its average price for the preceding ten years.

3. Production allotments for individual producers of the "covered" crops (except corn) are established annually by the Department of Agriculture.

4. Farmers who abide by their allotments may borrow on their harvests from the federal-financed Commodity Credit Corporation, on the basis of the current "support price" of the crop. The "support prices" are set by the Secretary of Agriculture within 87½ to 90 percent of "parity prices" for the various crops. The "support price" for corn is 90 percent of the average market price for the three preceding years, but not less than 65 percent of "parity price." These loans are "without recourse," so that a farmer who fails to repay simply forfeits the crop pledged as security for the loan.

The pricing effect of this legislation is two-fold. First, the production allotment program reduces the supplies of the covered crops and so tends to maintain their prices. Second, if at any time the market price of a crop falls below its "support price," farmers simply pledge their crops with the Commodity Credit Corporation as security for loans at this ratio, default on their loans, and forfeit the pledged crops. The Commodity Credit Corporation is obligated to dispose of crop holdings it so acquires in ways that will not bring these products into competition with crops already on the market. Thus this crop loan system operates to remove elements of the current crop from the market, thereby reducing supply, whenever the market price for the crop falls under the "support price." The effect is obviously to sustain the market price close to the "support price."

This farm price support program has sustained farm prices, and has been a boon to farmers, but it has not succeeded in adjusting farm production to the demand for farm products. Technological improvements in agriculture during the past two decades have more than offset reduction of the acreage allotments for covered crops, so that the country has continued to be plagued by surpluses throughout the post-war years. Dissatisfaction with the program is widespread, but political issues involved preclude any solution based on purely economic or marketing considerations.

THE CONSUMER MOVEMENT

Most consumers are unskilled buyers. They are usually unable to judge soundly the relative utility of items with which they are not intimately familiar. They are lured by selling design. Most are unwittingly manipulated by advertising. Many are submissive to adroit selling techniques.

Many manufacturers and some retailers have taken advantage of consumer ignorance and innocence, and have induced consumers to buy in ways contrary to their best interests. This widespread abuse of the consumer—which still exists, though not in gross forms and less extensively than in the past—has produced a reaction, a broad movement for consumer education and protection, operating on several fronts and through a large number of agencies, generally referred to as "The Consumer Movement." It has three broad objectives: (1) supplying consumers with product, producer, and distributor information which will enable them to buy more intelligently; (2) educating consumers to buy more intelligently; and (3) obtaining the passage and enforcement of legislation that will protect consumers against the consequences of their ignorance and indifference.

Consumer information

Intelligent buying by consumers is impossible without adequate information about the products they purchase, so that they can make sound comparisons of products offered under various brand names. Three agencies— manufacturers and distributors themselves, governmental units, and product rating organizations—supply product information to consumers.

Through labelling, advertising, specialty salesmen, and sales clerks, manufacturers and distributors flood consumers with information about products they have to sell. The FTC and the state truth-in-advertising laws bar the making of wilfully deceptive claims. Unfortunately for consumers, however, while labelling, advertising, and selling disseminate some truth about the products they promote, they do not disclose *all* the truth. Emphasis is naturally given to a product's advantages, with little said about its possible inferiority to other products yielding comparable utilities. Information imparted by labels is not always conveyed in language comprehensible to the average housewife.* Moreover, advertising and selling do not confine themselves to providing product information. A great part of advertising and selling effort is devoted to emotional appeals, deliberately

---

* A major part of the effort of National Consumer-Retailer Council, a Consumer Movement organization, is devoted to educating manufacturers to the marketing advantages of providing their products, particularly those sold on a quality appeal, with labels that will be truly informative to consumers.

intended to sidetrack any rational approach by the consumer to his buying problem.

Several federal governmental units, particularly the Clothing and Housing, Household Economics, and Human Nutrition Research divisions of the Department of Agriculture, perform yeoman service by issuing informational pamphlets on foods and other agricultural products. Unfortunately, these reach only a minute fraction of the buying population.

The first consumers' *rating agency,* Consumers' Research, Inc., was organized in 1929. Several more, including Consumers Union, Consumers' Guild of America, and Intermountain Consumers' Service, were subsequently established. Only Consumers Union and the original Consumers' Research have survived. These two rating agencies are organized on a nonprofit membership basis. They maintain laboratories to test consumer items of all descriptions. On the basis of these tests, and of the prices charged,

---

Check before you buy

Because of sample-to-sample variations, you should—before you put your money down, if possible—inspect the particular skillet you plan to buy.

for even fit all the way around the pan. Check cover and pan for freedom from sharp edges. Reject a pan whose cooking area is not smooth or which has deep scratches or scars. Check the handle for metal screw-heads that are not sufficiently recessed or shielded from accidental touch.

RATINGS OF ELECTRIC FRYING PANS

Listed in order of estimated overall quality within type. Check-rated (✔) brands merit first consideration. All samples tested operated on a-c only and had a cooking-temperature guide printed on the handle. Prices are list. With the exception of mail-order brands, discounts are generally available.

TOTALLY IMMERSIBLE MODELS

❡ *The following pans had a detachable heat-control unit (containing thermostat, control knob, signal light, and electric plug) which plugs into the side of the pan and, unless otherwise noted, can also be used with certain other electric cooking appliances made by the same manufacturer. With control removed, all of these models can be totally immersed in water for cleaning. Price includes heat control, but not cover, unless otherwise noted. In most cases, the heat control (about $5 to $8 on the models tested) must be ordered separately.*

ACCEPTABLE

(S. W.) Farber Inc., NYC), $31.45. Matching metal cover, *Model 311,* $4.50 extra. Stainless-steel pan with aluminum-clad bottom exterior. Along with the essentially similar *Sears* model, below, judged easiest to clean of all pans tested. Medium weight; cool auxiliary handle. Fast warm-up. Good recovery and fairly good overshoot characteristics.

(Sears, Roebuck), $25.40 plus shipping. Matching metal cover, *Cat. No. 34H6524,* $4 extra plus shipping. Similar to *Farberware 310,* above, except for trim details. All comments apply.

(National Presto Industries, Inc., Eau Claire, Wis.), $19.90. Matching metal cover, $3.25 extra; glass cover, $2.25 extra. Aluminum pan. Relatively light weight; no auxiliary handle. Relatively slow warm-up. Fairly good recovery and overshoot characteristics.

(Sears, Roebuck), $14.90 plus shipping. Matching metal cover, *Cat. No. 34H6506,* $2.50 extra plus shipping. Essentially similar to *Presto SS-32A,* above. All comments apply.

❡ *The following pans scored relatively low in overall quality. Listed alphabetically.*

(Mirro Aluminum Co., Manitowoc, Wis.), $19.95, including matching vented metal cover. Aluminum pan. Lightweight; no auxiliary handle. Relatively large temperature variation across cooking surface of pan may cause uneven cooking. Fairly good warm-up and recovery. Fair overshoot characteristics. Three samples tested.

(Landers, Frary & Clark, New Britain, Conn.), $25.90 including matching vented metal cover (manufacturer designates pan plus cover as *Model 8243).* Cover with glass window, $1 extra. Aluminum pan. Medium weight; no auxiliary handle. Relatively slow warm-up. Slow recovery time after relatively large temperature fall-off under load. Fairly good overshoot characteristics.

NOT ACCEPTABLE

EXCERPT FROM A *CONSUMER REPORTS* RATING (Specific Brand Names Deleted). *Courtesy of Consumers Union.*

ILLUSTRATION 30–2

they rate products on a quality basis, and publish these ratings in monthly bulletins and annual booklets.

There are a number of inherent limitations to testing and rating consumer goods: (1) general utility standards for many consumer goods can not be established, because scattered market groups value the various qualities and attributes of any product differently; (2) only branded items may be rated, since there would be no way for purchasers to identify rated but unbranded items; (3) quality variation of many branded items has wide range, and the tested items may not fairly reflect the quality of the bulk of a product on the market; (4) relative durability of many "durable" appliances may be difficult to establish in short-time tests. The consensus of competent judges has been that, taking these limitations into account, the two consumers' rating agencies that survived the 1930's—Consumers Union and Consumers' Research—have done a competent job in their testing and rating. Until the late 1940's, however, these two organizations had such small memberships and limited incomes that their testing and rating services were sharply restricted. Moreover, part of their limited resources was dissipated in a doctrinaire fight against advertising *per se*.

Following World War II, both Consumers Union and Consumers' Research experienced phenomenal growth. Circulation of *Consumer Reports,* published by Consumers Union, increased from 55,000 in 1945 to 865,000 in 1960, with readership in the latter year estimated at over 4 million. With increased resources and widening influence, the testing and rating services of these two organizations are beginning to exercise considerable effect, beneficial from the consumer point of view, on the consumer goods field.

Grade labelling is a special phase of the movement to inform consumers about the products they buy. The Agricultural Marketing Service of the U.S. Department of Agriculture has established four quality standards for each canned fruit and vegetable—A (fancy), B (extra standard), C (standard), and Offgrade or Substandard. There are seven official grades for meat, four for eggs. Since 1941 the Agricultural Marketing Service has made available to food packers an official inspection service. Foods packed subject to this inspection may be labelled with the official grades.

Many small food packers and several large retail grocery chains utilize this inspection service, and their canned products are grade labelled. Large food packers that have invested heavily in advertising to persuade consumers of the real or imaginary quality standards of their branded products are bitterly opposed to grade labelling. What advantage would it be to them to have their products inspected by the Agricultural Marketing Service and have them labelled A or B, only to have consumers see competing, nonadvertised, lower-price brands also labelled A or B, which would indicate that they were equal in quality? The opponents of grade labelling argue that (1) the official grades are arbitrary, (2) they do not take into account flavor and other significant food factors, (3) consumers are unaware that each official grade embraces a wide quality range, and are misled into assuming that two items with the same grade label are necessarily identical in quality, and (4) grade labelling induces food packers to just barely meet minimum requirements for each grade. Each of these arguments has some merit. The purchasing guidance that grade labelling gives consumers, however, would seem to outweigh all the criticisms that have been directed against it.

Consumer education

Availability of product information alone will not turn consumers into skilled purchasers. They must be taught the importance of intelligent buying, where they may obtain product information, and how to appraise and utilize that information.

A major effort at consumer education is being made through the home economics classes that are part of the high school curriculum in most states, and through evening classes for housewives offered by many school systems. Discussion groups and lectures sponsored by women's clubs and such organizations as the National League of Women Voters and the League of Women Shoppers contribute to the spread of consumer education. Publications of the federal Bureau of Home Economics, Agricultural Marketing Administration, and Federal Security Administration, besides providing consumers with product information, also contain educational guidance on the application of such information.

Consumer pressure group activity

Leaders of the Consumer Movement are generally agreed that, besides being provided with product information and educated in its effective use, consumers should be afforded statutory protection against deceptive labelling, advertising and selling practices. Accordingly one important phase of the Consumer Movement is pressure group activity for the passage and enforcement of protective legislation. The organizations most active in this endeavor are the General Federation of Women's Clubs, the National League of Women Voters, the League of Women Shoppers, and the National Consumers' League. Upon occasion they receive the support of such professional organizations as the American Medical Association and the American Dental Association. The Better Business Bureaus, whose support is mainly from large advertisers and advertising agencies, are often a welcome ally in obtaining enforcement of the laws against deceptive advertising and marketing practices.

The Wheeler-Lea and the Pure Food, Drugs and Cosmetics Acts of 1938 were passed largely at the urging of Consumer Movement groups. These pieces of legislation fell short of the wishes of the groups agitating for greater consumer protection, but even in their limited scope would probably not have been enacted without strong Consumer Movement pressure.

REVIEW

1. In what ways does the federal bankruptcy law aid American marketing?

2. State the provisions of the federal patent and trademark laws. How do they aid American marketing?

3. State five classes of federal and state administrative assistance to marketing.

4. In what respects are marketing practices constrained by the Sherman and Clayton Anti-Trust Acts?

5. State the provisions of the Robinson-Patman Act. How is it enforced?

6. What federal law makes "unfair methods of competition" illegal? What agency determines what marketing practices are "unfair competition"?

7. What federal laws protect consumers from unfair and deceptive marketing practices?

8. What fields of marketing control are enforced by the federal Department of Justice? What are its methods of enforcement?

9. What fields of marketing control are enforced by the FTC? What are its methods of enforcement?

10. What fields of marketing control are enforced by the Federal Security Administration? What are its methods of enforcement?

11. Through what forms of legislation do the states control and limit marketing practices?

12. Describe federal farm price support procedure.

13. What are Consumers' Research and Consumers Union?

14. What efforts are being made, and by whom, to educate consumers to better buying?

DISCUSSION TOPICS

1. Should there be more, or less, government control of marketing activities?

2. "State mercantile law provides the legal foundation for American marketing institutions and procedures."

3. Is the federal government spending too much, or too little, on administrative assistance to marketing activities?

4. Has the Robinson-Patman Act been essentially helpful or harmful to American business?

5. Is more federal legislation needed for consumer protection? If so, what?

6. Is the FTC in general doing a good or a poor job?

7. Should the states exercise more control over marketing practices than they do?

8. Would you depend upon Consumers Union or Consumers' Research guidance if you were equipping and furnishing a newly purchased home?

9. "Grade labelling should be made compulsory for all canned fruits, vegetables, and meats."

SUGGESTED READINGS: I

Anderson, R. A., *Government Regulation of Business,* South-Western Publishing Co., Cincinnati, 1950.

Bernstein, M. H., *Regulating Business by Independent Commission,* Princeton University Press, Princeton, 1955.

Cole, A. H., *Business Enterprise in its Social Setting,* Harvard University Press, Cambridge, 1959.

Dimock, M. E., *Business and Government,* 3rd ed, Henry Holt, New York, 1957.

Dirlam, J. B., & A. E. Kahn, *Fair Competition,* Cornell University Press, Ithaca, 1954.

Edwards, C. D., *Big Business and the Policy of Competition,* Western Reserve University Press, Cleveland, 1956.

Fleming, H., *Ten Thousand Commandments: a Story of the Antitrust Laws,* Prentice-Hall, Englewood Cliffs, N.J., 1951.

Hall, F. P., *Government and Business,* 3rd ed, McGraw-Hill Book Co., New York, 1949.

Koontz, H., & R. W. Gable, *Public Control of Economic Enterprise,* McGraw-Hill Book Co., New York, 1956.

Lane, R. E., *The Regulation of Business Men: Social Conditions of Government Control,* Yale University Press, New Haven, 1954.

Mund, V. A., *Government and Business,* 3rd ed, Harper & Bros., New York, 1960.

Palamountain, J. C., *The Politics of Distribution,* Harvard University Press, Cambridge, 1955.

Smith, H. R., *Government and Business: a Study in Economic Evaluation,* Ronald Press, New York, 1958.

Steiner, G. A., *Government's Role in Economic Life,* McGraw-Hill Book Co., New York, 1953.

Stocking, G. W., & M. W. Watkins, *Monopoly and Free Enterprise,* Twentieth Century Fund, New York, 1951.

Wilcox, C., *Public Policies Toward Business,* Richard D. Irwin, Homewood, Ill., 1955.

SUGGESTED READINGS: II

Campbell, P., *The Consumer Interest,* Harper & Bros., New York 1949.

Casselman, P. H., *The Cooperative Movement and Some of its Problems,* Philosophical Library, New York, 1952.

Coles, J. V., *Standards and Labels for Consumers' Goods,* Ronald Press, New York, 1949.

Kelley, P. C., *Consumer Economics,* Richard D. Irwin, Homewood, Ill., 1953.

Troelstrup, A. W., *Consumer Problems,* McGraw-Hill Book Co., 1952.

Waite, W. C., & R. Cassady, *The Consumer and the Economic Order,* 2d ed, McGraw-Hill Book Co., New York, 1949.

PERIODICALS: *Consumer Reports, Consumers' Research Bulletin.*

APPENDIX

GLOSSARY OF MARKETING TERMS

This glossary is based upon the tentative definitions formulated by the Definitions Committee of the American Marketing Association in May, 1960. The author has added his own definitions of a few marketing terms not included in the Definitions Committee's list. These added definitions are indicated by asterisks.

ADVERTISING. Any form of nonpersonal presentation and promotion of ideas, goods, or services by an identified sponsor through direct mail or a paid medium.

AGENT MIDDLEMAN (AGENT). A business unit that negotiates purchases or sales, or both, but that does not take title to the goods in which it deals.

ASSEMBLING. The activities involved in concentrating supplies or assortments of goods or services to facilitate sale or purchase.

AUCTION (commercial). An organization, acting in agent capacity that effects the sale of goods through an auctioneer who, under specified rules, solicits bids or offers from buyers and has power to accept the highest bids of responsible bidders and thereby consummates the sale.

AUTOMATIC SELLING. The retail sale of goods or services through currency-operated machines activated by the ultimate-consumer buyer.

BRANCH HOUSE (manufacturer's). An establishment maintained by a manufacturer, detached from the headquarters establishment, and used primarily for the purpose of carrying stocks of, selling, delivering, and servicing his product.

BRANCH OFFICE (manufacturer's). An establishment maintained by a manufacturer, detached from the headquarters establishment and used primarily for the purpose of selling his product or providing service.

BRAND. A name, term, sign, symbol, or design, or a combination of these, which is intended to identify the goods or services of one seller or group of sellers and to differentiate them from those of competitors.

635

BRAND NAME. A brand or part of a brand consisting of a word, letter, group of words, or letters comprising a name, which is intended to identify the goods or services of a seller or group of sellers and to differentiate them from those of competitors.

BROKER. An agent middleman who does not have direct physical control of the goods in which he deals but represents either buyer or seller in negotiating purchases and sales for his principal.

CHAIN STORE SYSTEM. A group of retail stores of essentially the same type, centrally owned and with some degree of centralized control of operation.

CHANNEL OF DISTRIBUTION. The structure of intra-company organization units and extra-company agents and dealers, wholesale and retail, through which a commodity, product, or service is marketed.

COMMISSION HOUSE (sometimes called COMMISSION MERCHANT). An agent middleman who usually exercises physical control over, and negotiates the sale of, the goods he handles.

COMMODITY EXCHANGE. An organization, usually owned by the member-traders, that provides facilities for bringing together buyers and sellers of specified commodities, or their agents, for promoting trades, either spot or futures or both, in these commodities.

CONSUMERS' COOPERATIVE. A retail business owned and operated by ultimate consumers to purchase and distribute goods and services primarily to the membership.

CONSUMERS' GOODS. Goods destined for use by ultimate consumers or households, and in such form that they can be used without commercial processing.

CONVENIENCE GOODS. Those consumers' goods that the customer usually purchases frequently, immediately, and with the minimum of effort in comparison and buying.

COOPERATIVE MARKETING. The process by which independent producers, wholesalers, retailers, consumers, or combinations of them, act collectively in buying or selling or both.

DEALER. A firm that buys and resells merchandise at either retail or wholesale. (Should not be used except with qualifying "retail" or "wholesale.")

DEPARTMENT STORE. A large retailing business unit that handles a wide variety of shopping and specialty goods, including women's ready-to-wear and accessories, men's and boys' wear, piece goods, small wares, and home furnishings, and which is organized into separate departments for purposes of promotion, service, and control.

DIRECT SELLING. The process whereby the establishment responsible for production sells to the user, ultimate consumer, or retailer without intervening middlemen.

* DISCOUNT. A percentage reduction from list price allowed to business purchasers for buying in quantity, paying in advance of due date, or performing operations or services that stimulate sales of the seller's goods or reduce his marketing costs.

DISCOUNT HOUSE. A retailing business unit featuring consumer durable items, competing on a basis of price appeal, and operating on relatively low markup and with a minimum of customer services.

* DISPLAY. Nonpersonal stimulation of demand for a product, service, or selling organization to prospective buyers by direct appeal to vision or the other senses.

DISTRIBUTION. A synonym for MARKETING. Also refers to the extent of market coverage.

DISTRIBUTOR. Generally synonymous with WHOLESALER, particularly where a manufacturer has an exclusive outlet policy, or where a wholesaler gives preference to a manufacturer.

* DROP SHIPPER (DESK JOBBER). A limited-service wholesaler who usually sells and buys on arrangements whereby his suppliers ship the goods involved directly to his customers.

EQUIPMENT. Those industrial goods that do not become part of the physical product and are exhausted only after repeated use, such as machinery, installed equipment, accessories, or auxiliary equipment.

EXCLUSIVE OUTLET SELLING. That form of selective selling whereby sales of an article, service, or brand of an article to any one type of buyer are confined to one retailer or wholesaler in each area, usually on a contractual basis.

FACILITATING MARKETING AGENCIES. Those agencies that perform or assist in the performance of one or a number of the marketing functions but that neither take title to goods nor negotiate purchases or sales.

FACTOR. (1) A specialized financial institution engaged in factoring and lending on the security of inventories. (2) A type of commission house that often advances funds to the consignor, identified chiefly with the raw cotton and naval stores trades.

FACTORING. A specialized financial function whereby producers, wholesalers, and retailers sell their accounts receivable to financial institutions including factors or banks, often on a nonrecourse basis.

FAIR TRADE. Retail resale price maintenance imposed by suppliers of branded goods under authorization of state and federal laws.

* FASHION. A design or design element involving a characteristic or distinctive conception, expression, or presentation, given by manufacturers to their products, which succeeds in appealing to immediate mass criteria of social acceptability and/or beauty.

* FINANCE COMPANY (see SALES FINANCE COMPANY).

GENERAL STORE. A small retailing business unit, not departmentalized, usually located in rural communities and primarily engaged in selling a general assortment of merchandise of which the most important line is food, and the more important subsidiary lines are notions, apparel, farm supplies, and gasoline. (These stores are often known as "country general stores.")

GRADING. Assigning predetermined standard quality classifications to individual units or lots of a commodity.

HOUSE-TO-HOUSE SALESMAN (CANVASSER). A salesman who is primarily engaged in making sales direct to ultimate consumers in their homes.

INDEPENDENT STORE. A retailing business unit controlled by its own individual ownership or management rather than from without, except insofar as its management is limited by voluntary or co-operative group arrangements.

INDUSTRIAL GOODS. Goods which are destined to be sold primarily for use in producing other goods or rendering services, as contrasted with goods destined primarily to be sold to the ultimate consumer.

INDUSTRIAL STORE. A retail store owned and operated by a company or governmental unit to sell primarily to its employees.

JOBBER. This term is now widely used as a synonym of WHOLESALER or DISTRIBUTOR.

LOSS LEADER. A popular established product priced at a loss or no profit for the purpose of attracting patronage to a store.

MAIL ORDER HOUSE (retail). A retail business unit that makes its sales primarily from a catalog or other printed material, and receives most of its orders by mail or phone.

MANUFACTURERS' AGENT. An agent middleman that generally operates on an extended contractual basis, sells within an exclusive territory, handles noncompeting but related lines of goods, and possesses limited authority with regard to prices and terms of sale.

MARKET. (1) The aggregate of forces or conditions within which buyers and sellers make decisions that result in the transfer of goods and services. (2) The aggregate demand of the potential buyers of a commodity or service.

MARKET ANALYSIS. A subdivision of marketing research that involves the measurement of the extent of a market and the determination of its characteristics.

MARKET POTENTIAL. A calculation of the maximum possible sales opportunity for all sellers of a good or service during a stated period.

MARKET SHARE. The ratio of a company's sales to total industry sales on either an actual or a potential basis.

MARKETING. The performance of business activities that direct the flow of goods and services from producer to consumer or user (including such facilitating activities as marketing research, credit, transportation, and certain aspects of product and package planing).

MARKETING BUDGET. A statement of the planned dollar sales and planned marketing costs for a specified future period.

MARKETING COOPERATIVE. An organization of independent producers, wholesalers, retailers, or consumers, or combination of them, to act collectively in buying, or selling, or both, with distribution of profit primarily to the membership.

MARKETING COST ACCOUNTING. That branch of cost accounting which involves the allocation of marketing costs according to customers, products, territories, or marketing activities.

MARKETING COST ANALYSIS. The study and evaluation of the relative profitability or costs of different marketing operations in terms of customers, marketing units, products, territories, or marketing activities.

MARKETING FUNCTION. A major specialized activity or group of related activities performed in marketing.

MARKETING MANAGEMENT. The planning, direction, and control of the entire marketing activity of a firm or division of a firm, including the formulation of marketing objectives, programs, policies, and strategies, and commonly embracing product development, organizing and staffing to carry out marketing policy, supervising marketing operations, and controlling marketing performance.

MARKETING PLANNING. The work of setting up objectives for marketing activity and of determining and scheduling the steps necessary to achieve such objectives.

MARKETING POLICY. A course of action established to obtain consistency in marketing decisions and operations under recurring and essentially similar circumstances.

MARKETING RESEARCH. The systematic gathering, recording, and analyzing of data about problems relating to the marketing of goods and services.

* MARKUP. The percentage ratio of the margin between cost of purchase of an item or product line by a wholesaler or retailer and its selling price, divided by the selling price.

* MERCANTILE AGENCY. A facilitating marketing institution that collects and issues credit information about its members' or subscribers' business customers.

MERCHANDISING. The planning and supervision involved in marketing particular merchandise or services at the places, times, and prices and in the quantities that will best serve to realize the marketing objectives of the business.

MERCHANT. A business unit that buys, takes title to, and resells merchandise.

MIDDLEMAN. A business concern that specializes in performing operations or rendering services directly involved in the purchase and/or sale of goods in the process of their flow from producer to consumer.

MOTIVATION RESEARCH. A group of techniques developed by the behavioral scientists and used by marketing researchers to discover factors influencing marketing behavior.

NATIONAL BRAND. A manufacturer's or producer's brand, usually enjoying wide territorial distribution.

PERSONAL SELLING. Oral presentation in a conversation with one or more prospective purchasers for the purpose of making sales.

PRICE CUTTING. Offering merchandise or a service for sale at a price below that recognized as usual or appropriate by its buyers and sellers.

PRICE LEADER. A business unit whose pricing behavior is followed by other companies in the same industry.

PRIVATE BRAND. A wholesaler's, agent's or retailer's brand, as distinguished from a manufacturer's or producer's brand.

PRODUCERS' COOPERATIVE MARKETING. That type of cooperative marketing which primarily involves the sale of goods or services of the associated producing membership.

PRODUCT LINE. A group of products that are closely related because they satisfy a class of need, are used together, are sold to the same customer groups, are marketed through the same class of outlets, or fall within given price ranges.

PRODUCT MANAGEMENT. The planning, direction, and control of all phases of the life cycle of products, including the creation or discovery of ideas for new products, the screening of such ideas, the coordination of the work of research and physical development of products, their packaging and branding, their introduction on the market, their market development, their modification, the discovery of new uses for them, their repair and servicing, and their deletion.

PRODUCT MIX. The composite of products offered for sale by a business unit.

* PROMOTION. All forms of nonpersonal stimulation of purchasing demand for a product, service, or selling organization, including advertising, display, price promotion, publicity, and sales promotion.

PUBLICITY. Nonpersonal stimulation of demand for a product, service, or business unit by planting commercially significant news about it in a published medium, or obtaining favorable presentation of it upon radio, TV, or stage, that is not paid for by the sponsor.

RACK JOBBER. A wholesaling business unit that markets specialized lines of merchandise to certain types of retail stores, and provides special services of selective brand and item merchandising, and arrangement, maintenance, and stocking of display racks.

RESALE PRICE MAINTENANCE. Control by a supplier of the selling prices of his branded goods at subsequent stages of distribution by means of contractual agreement under fair trade laws or other devices.

RESIDENT BUYER (RESIDENT BUYING OFFICE). An agent middleman that specializes in buying, chiefly in apparel and furnishing lines, on a fee or commission basis, chiefly for retailers.

RETAILER. A merchant whose main business is selling directly to ultimate consumers.

RETAILER COOPERATIVE. A group of independent retailers organized to buy cooperatively either through a jointly owned warehouse or through a buying club.

RETAILING. The activities involved in selling directly to ultimate consumers.

SALES ANALYSIS (SALES RESEARCH). A subdivision of Marketing Research that involves the systematic study and comparison of sales data.

SALES BUDGET. The part of the marketing budget which is concerned with planned dollar sales and planned personal selling costs for a specified future period.

* SALES FINANCE COMPANY (FINANCE COMPANY). A specialized financial institution engaged in purchasing and discounting notes and accounts receivable, including consumer installment finance notes.

SALES FORECAST. An estimate of sales in dollars or physical units, for a specified future period, under a proposed marketing plan or program, and under an assumed set of economic and other forces outside the unit for which the forecast is made.

SALES MANAGEMENT. The planning, direction, and control of the personal selling activities of a business unit, including recruiting, selecting, training, equipping, assigning, routing, supervising, paying, and motivating, as these tasks apply to the personal sales force.

SALES MANAGER. The executive who plans, directs, and controls the activities of salesmen.

SALES PROMOTION. (1) In a specific sense, activities other than personal selling, advertising, and publicity that stimulate consumer purchasing and dealer effectiveness. (2) In retailing, all methods of stimulating customer purchasing, including personal selling, advertising, and publicity.

SALES QUOTA. A projected volume of sales assigned to a marketing unit for use in the management of sales efforts.

SELF-SELECTION. The method used in retailing by which the customer may choose the desired merchandise without direct assistance of store personnel.

SELF-SERVICE. The method used in retailing whereby the customer selects his own merchandise, removes it from the shelves or bulk containers, carries it to a check-out stand to complete the transaction, and transports it to the point of use.

SELLING. The personal or impersonal process of assisting and/or persuading a prospective customer to buy a commodity or a service, or to act favorably upon an idea that has commercial significance to the seller.

SELLING AGENT. An agent middleman that operates on an extended contractual basis, sells all of a specified line of merchandise or the entire output of its principal, and usually has full authority with regard to prices, terms, and other conditions of sale.

SERVICES. Activities, benefits, or satisfactions which are offered for sale, or are provided in connection with the sale of goods.

SHOPPING CENTER. A geographical cluster of retail stores, collectively handling an assortment of goods varied enough to satisfy most of the merchandise wants of consumers within convenient travelling time and thereby attracting a general shopping trade.

SHOPPING GOODS. Those consumers' goods which the customer in the process of selection and purchase characteristically compares on such bases as suitability, quality, price, and style.

SPECIALTY GOODS. Those consumers' goods with unique characteristics and/or brand identification for which a significant group of buyers are habitually willing to make a special purchasing effort.

STANDARDIZATION. The determination of basic limits or grade ranges in the form of uniform specifications to which particular manufactured goods may conform, and uniform quality classes into which the products of agriculture and the extractive industries may or must be sorted or assigned.

STOCK CONTROL (INVENTORY CONTROL). The use of a system or mechanism to maintain stocks of goods at desired levels.

STORAGE. The marketing function that involves holding goods between the time of their production and their final sale.

* STORE. A business establishment (in the physical sense), or a physically distinct section of a business establishment, used primarily for retail selling.

* STYLE. A characteristic or distinctive mode or method of conception, expression, or presentation in any field involving aesthetic elements.

SUPERMARKET. A large retailing business unit, usually departmentalized, selling mainly food and grocery items on the basis of a low markup, wide variety of assortments, self-service, and the use of extensive merchandise appeal.

TRADE MARK. A brand that is given legal protection because it is capable of exclusive appropriation; because it is used in a manner sufficiently fanciful, distinctive, and arbitrary; because it is affixed to the product when sold; or because it otherwise satisfies the requirements set up by law.

TRADING AREA. A district whose size is usually determined by the boundaries within which it is economical in terms of volume and cost for a marketing unit to sell and/or deliver a good or service.

TRAFFIC MANAGEMENT. The planning, selecting, and directing of all means and methods of transportation involved in the movement of goods in the marketing process.

* TRUCK JOBBER (formerly called WAGON JOBBER). A limited-service wholesaler without storage facilities, who transports the goods or commodities he purchases directly from his suppliers to his customers.

ULTIMATE CONSUMER. One who buys and/or uses goods or services to satisfy personal or household wants rather than for resale or use in business, institutional, or industrial operations.

VARIETY STORE. A retailing business unit that handles a wide assortment of goods, usually in a low or popular price segment of the price range.

VOLUNTARY GROUP. A group of retailers, each of whom owns and operates his own store, which is associated with a wholesale organization or manufacturer to carry on joint merchandising activities, and which may be characterized by some degree of group identity and uniformity of operation.

WHOLESALER. A business unit that buys and resells merchandise to retailers and other merchants and/or to industrial, institutional, and commercial users, but that does not sell in significant amounts to ultimate consumers.

* WHOLESALING. The activities involved in selling to other than ultimate consumers.

* WHOLESALING MIDDLEMAN. A business unit whose major activity is wholesaling, on either a merchant or agent basis.

INDEX

Page numbers for major treatment of a topic are printed in **boldface** type. Page numbers for incidental reference to a topic are printed in lightface type.

A

A & P, 129, 130, 131, 422
Acceptances:
  bankers':
    domestic, **541-542**
    export, **583-585**, 588
    trade, **499-500**, 537, 538, 583
Accounts receivable discounting, **538-541**
Advertising, 8, 28, 35, 67-68, **117-118**, 119, 123, 136, 138, 140, 144, 180, 200, 248, 257, 260, 273, 281, 293, 318, 319, 329, 330, 341, 354, 389, 405, **419-441**, **447-451**, 473, 474, 543, **561-562**, 563, 614-615, 635
  agencies, 177, 292, **431**, 474, 483, 577, 579-580
  control, **431-433**, 618, 620, 624
  export, **579-580**
  media, 22, 38, 117-118, 293, 294, **427-429**, 483, 564
  purposes, **424-427**
Advertising Federation of America, 432
Agent middlemen:
  domestic, 177, **181**, 183, **192-201**, 201-207, 261, **267-268**, **291**, 292, 527, 635
  foreign trade, **574-575**, 578
  see also *Commission houses, Manufacturers' agents, Merchandise brokers, Purchasing agents, Resident buying offices,* and *Selling agents*
Agricultural marketing, 5, 6, **72**, 179, 182, 183, 187, 193-196, **231-254**, **307-310**, 335, 360-364, 373, 382, 472, 515
  see also *Farmers' marketing cooperatives* and under particular crops

Agricultural Marketing Acts, 245, 596, **625-626**
Agriculture, U.S. Department of, 15, 223, 252, 309, 310, 469, **472**, 595, 596, 626, 628-630
Air freight, 7, **515-516**, 518, 525, 528
American Association of Advertising Agencies, 432
American Dental Association, 630
American Exporter, 577, 579, 587
American Express Co., 491-492
American Marketing Association, **15**, 635
American Medical Association, 630
American Standards Association, 306, 318
American Warehousemen's Association, 370
Anti-chain-store movement, 129, **136-137**, 141, 402, 624
Apparel:
  brokers, 194
  marketing, 193-194, 197, 260, 269-270, 328, 341, 347, 545
  stores, 67, 68, 71, 91, 92, 94, 122, 132, 135, 143-144, 159, 200, 402
Aristotle, 13
Assembling:
  line, 265, 267, 290, 300, **335**, 635
  quantity, 12, 180, 233, 242, 244, 246, 247, 300, **335**, 635
Associated Merchandising Corporation, 131
Association of National Advertisers, 432
Associations:
  credit, 17, 227
  manufacturers', **224-225**, 306-307,

645